JOHN STUART MILL

John Stuart Mill (1806–1873) was the most influential British philosopher of the nineteenth century. More than just a writer, he was a public figure. His technical work in philosophy and economics was always in the service of controversial issues of public policy. In many ways he was the quintessential Victorian intellectual, bringing his critical faculties to bear on all the major issues of the day in a manner that was accessible to the average intelligent layperson. Only Bertrand Russell in the twentieth century has come close to achieving the kind of general public recognition accorded to Mill in the nineteenth.

Nicholas Capaldi's biography (no competitor is currently in print) traces the ways in which Mill's many endeavors are related and explores the significance of Mill's contributions to metaphysics, epistemology, ethics, social and political philosophy, the philosophy of religion, and the philosophy of education. He shows how Mill was groomed for his role in life by both his father, James Mill, and Jeremy Bentham, the two most prominent philosophical radicals of the early nineteenth century. Yet Mill revolted against this education and developed friendships with Thomas Carlyle and Samuel Taylor Coleridge, who introduced him to Romanticism and political conservatism.

A special feature of this biography is the attention devoted to the relationship with Harriet Taylor. No one exerted a greater influence on Mill than the woman he was eventually to marry. Nicholas Capaldi reveals just how deep her impact was on Mill's thinking about the emancipation of women. Clarifying this relationship helps to explain why Mill was concerned not only with such issues as the franchise and representation, but also with a fundamental concept of personal autonomy that became pivotal to his thought.

There has never been a serious attempt to set out the interconnections of Mill's thought in this manner. Moreover, this biography presents the private life as both a reflection and an instantiation of ideas and values – a life so constructed as to be a Romantic work of art.

Nicholas Capaldi is Legendre-Soulé Distinguished Chair in Business Ethics at the College of Business Administration at Loyola University, New Orleans.

John Stuart Mill
A Biography

Nicholas Capaldi
Loyola University, New Orleans

CAMBRIDGE
UNIVERSITY PRESS

PUBLISHED BY THE PRESS SYNDICATE OF THE UNIVERSITY OF CAMBRIDGE
The Pitt Building, Trumpington Street, Cambridge, United Kingdom

CAMBRIDGE UNIVERSITY PRESS
The Edinburgh Building, Cambridge CB2 2RU, UK
40 West 20th Street, New York, NY 10011-4211, USA
477 Williamstown Road, Port Melbourne, VIC 3207, Australia
Ruiz de Alarcón 13, 28014 Madrid, Spain
Dock House, The Waterfront, Cape Town 8001, South Africa

http://www.cambridge.org

First published 2004

Printed in the United States of America

Typeface Ehrhardt 10.5/13 pt.   *System* $\text{\LaTeX}\,2_\varepsilon$ [TB]

A catalog record for this book is available from the British Library.

Library of Congress Cataloging in Publication data
Capaldi, Nicholas.
John Stuart Mill : a biography / Nicholas Capaldi.
p.   cm.
Includes bibliographical references and index.
ISBN 0-521-62024-4
1. Mill, John Stuart, 1806–1873.   2. Philosophers – England – Biography.   I. Title.
B1606.C36   2003
192–dc21
[B]   2003051546

ISBN 0 521 62024 4 hardback

This book is dedicated to the memory of
Jack Robson

Contents

Preface

John Stuart Mill (1806–1873) was the most influential British philosopher of the nineteenth century, making significant contributions to all of the major areas of philosophy, including metaphysics, epistemology, ethics, social and political philosophy, the philosophy of religion, and the philosophy of education. The *System of Logic* (1843) achieved the status of a canonical textbook. In addition, Mill achieved fame as an economist in 1848 with the publication of the *Principles of Political Economy*, a work that went through seven editions in his own lifetime. Difficulties aside, Mill was the last major British philosopher to present an integrated view of the whole of philosophy and to relate the theoretical and normative dimensions of his thought in a direct fashion.

More than just a writer, Mill was a public figure. His technical work in philosophy and economics was always in the service of the discussion of controversial issues of public policy. In many ways, he was the quintessential Victorian intellectual, bringing his critical faculties to bear on all of the major issues of the day in a manner that was accessible to the average intelligent layperson. Early in his life, Mill conceived the role of being the conscience of his society as a function of journalism, but toward the end of his life he increasingly associated that function with the university. In the twentieth century, only Bertrand Russell has come close to achieving the kind of general public recognition accorded to Mill in the nineteenth.

Mill's active involvement with the affairs of the day, including a term as a member of Parliament, was hardly fortuitous. He was, in fact, groomed for this role by both his father, James Mill, and Jeremy Bentham, the two most prominent philosophical radicals of the early part of the nineteenth century. From them, he imbibed the methods and goals of the Enlightenment Project, the attempt to use empirical science as the model for a social science that would serve as the foundation for social analysis, social critique, and a social technology. It was they who introduced him to the classics of British empirical philosophy and to French writers such as Condillac and Helvétius, writers who had been instrumental in formulating the intellectual and practical dimensions of the Enlightenment Project.

Mill was expected to be not only the articulate messenger but also the fullest embodiment of what the Enlightenment Project could achieve in an individual life. More remarkable than this design was Mill's revolt against it. The revolt, originally occasioned by a mental crisis between 1826 and 1830, began to take an intellectual shape as Mill searched for and was exposed to intellectual traditions different from those he had inherited. Specifically, Mill initiated friendships with Thomas Carlyle and Samuel Taylor Coleridge, who introduced him to the Romantic and conservative movements. Mill's crisis and revolt reflect in microcosm the massive nineteenth-century reaction against the Enlightenment.

Contemporaneous with Mill's recovery from his mental crisis was the beginning of his relationship with Harriet Taylor. Aside from his father, no one exerted a greater influence on Mill's life. Although the nature of Mill's relationship with the woman whom he was ultimately to marry is a matter of some speculation, and the true extent of her influence a matter of some dispute, there is one area where her influence was undeniable. That area was the emancipation of women, an issue of enormous importance for Mill and for our understanding of Mill. Given his role as the conscience of his culture, Mill used the role of women and the relationship between the sexes as a focus for bringing together all of the problematic issues of liberal culture. Specifically, Mill was concerned not only with issues of the franchise, representation, "gender," sex, and the way the subordinate role of women contributed to poverty, but also with how the equality of the sexes contributed to fulfillment in the personal lives of autonomous individuals in the liberal culture he so prized.

Today, it is as a social and political philosopher that J. S. Mill's reputation endures. It would be fair to say that, in retrospect, he was the most significant British political philosopher of the nineteenth century. His restatement of liberalism, including his identification of its most salient features and problems, continues to be the starting point for all subsequent discussion within the liberal tradition.

There are five reasons why an intellectual biography of Mill is especially useful. First, an intellectual biography helps to make clear all the ways in which his various endeavors are related. Although there is a vast secondary literature on Mill, there has never been a serious attempt to work out the interconnections in his thought. Precisely because Mill encompassed so many of what now constitute different academic disciplines, his corpus is typically read in piecemeal fashion. Philosophical treatments usually focus on isolated aspects of his work. The exceptions, such as the fine book by Skorupski, do try to tie together the epistemology with the ethics and the social philosophy. However, Skorupski's book focuses on only four of Mill's works (*System of Logic, Examination of Sir William Hamilton's Philosophy, Utilitarianism*, and *On Liberty*), thereby excluding from consideration some of the political works, such as *Considerations on Representative Government*, as well as both the economic and the religious writings. Sir John Hicks regards Mill as "the most undervalued economist of the nineteenth-century."[1] It would thus be a shame to ignore this dimension of his thought. While philosophy – specifically, metaphysics, epistemology, and ethics – is in a very special sense foundational to all thinking, it is not at all clear that we comprehend Mill's philosophy if we read his technical philosophical works in abstraction from his works on politics and economics. As Mill himself said in his 1865 *Examination of Sir William Hamilton's Philosophy*, one can evaluate a writer only if one has read all of his or her work and has tried to see each idea in the context created by the corpus as a whole.

Political theorists focus on *On Liberty* and sometimes *Utilitarianism*, but they do not connect these with either the epistemological or the metaphysical doctrines. Both philosophers and political theorists almost always (C. L. Ten is the exception) read *On Liberty* in the light of *Utilitarianism*, even though the former was written before the latter. Economists seem to be the exception, taking a much broader view of Mill. In his authoritative and comprehensive discussion of Mill's economics, Samuel Hollander does look into Mill's epistemology and his conception of methodology and also examines his larger social and political philosophy with regard to issues of the role of government in the economy. But Hollander does not really discuss either the metaphysics or the evolution of Mill's thinking. Pedro Schwartz, on the other hand, discusses the evolution of Mill's economic thinking – specifically, the influence of Mill's father and of Harriet. But Schwartz does not provide the methodological dimension that Hollander does. One thing that an intellectual biography can do is to combine the virtues of Hollander and Schwartz. In short, there is a great deal of valuable secondary literature, but it has not yet crystallized into a comprehensive vision.

The second reason why an intellectual biography is useful is because it leads to a greater appreciation of the complexity of Mill's sources. Most scholars take for granted the vast knowledge that Mill accumulated in his youth, and it is duly noted that Mill was a synthetic thinker who tried to combine the insights of different traditions. What is not always appreciated is the extent to which he incorporates and transforms his sources. There are many instances, but two stand out. One example is the incorporation of Kantian moral insights from the reading of Humboldt; only recently have scholars (e.g., Bernard Semmel, Charles Taylor, and John Skorupski) begun to take seriously exactly how *On Liberty* is structured by Humboldt and Tocqueville. The second example is Mill's relation to Comte. Comte certainly broadened Mill's understanding of the historical dynamic of social structure, and Mill's rejection of Comte's positivism is well documented. Yet Mill's transformation of what he accepted from Comte brings Mill remarkably close to Hegel.

The third reason is that the evolution of Mill's thinking is part of the very subject matter of his thought, hence the aptness of the allusion to Hegel. In explaining why he wrote his autobiography, Mill acknowledged that "in an age of transition in opinions, there may be somewhat both of interest and benefit in noting the successive phases of any mind which was always pressing forward, equally ready to learn and to unlearn either from his own thoughts or from those of others."[2] Specifically, when Mill rejected the Enlightenment Project of his father and of Bentham, he did not reject the goal of relating social understanding to social reform. Instead, he reformulated not only his theoretical and practical enterprise but also the relationship between the two. Mill came to believe that genuine social reform originated in self-reformed actors, individuals whose self-consciousness became the prototype for society as a whole. This is also why the arguments against censorship in *On Liberty* ultimately hinge on the moral transformation of individuals who reconstruct the arguments on all sides of a controversy. All lasting political reform is not accomplished directly, through partisan activity, but indirectly, through the reform of culture.

The fourth reason is, paradoxically, that the very existence of the *Autobiography* has been an obstacle to writing an intellectual biography.

In his Preface to Packe's *Life of John Stuart Mill*, F. A. Hayek comments:

There are few other eminent figures in the intellectual life of the nineteenth century about whom some unusual facts are so widely known, and yet of whose whole character and personality we know so little, as John Stuart Mill. Perhaps in no other instance can we see how misleading an impression even the most honest of autobiographies can give. Mill's account of his own life is of course a document of such psychological interest that its very popularity was bound to discourage others from attempting to draw a fuller picture. This alone, however, does not adequately explain why, for eighty years after his death, no satisfactory biography of Mill has been available. In many ways the unique value of his own description of his intellectual development has increased rather than diminished the need for a more comprehensive account of the setting against which it ought to be seen.[3]

Mill's own *Autobiography* in many ways is the greatest obstacle to writing an intellectual biography of Mill. The *Autobiography* is in large part an intellectual autobiography and is itself a classic worth reading in its own right; it will undoubtedly outlive any secondary source. But by the beginning of the twenty-first century we have been taught by literary critics and others not to take any author at face value. I do not wish to contend that Mill suppressed or distorted significant features of his life. What I want to call attention to is the "spin" he gives to his life and intellectual development in the *Autobiography*. As Collini has stressed, Mill wrote in order to achieve certain effects. Justifying his relationship with Harriet Taylor Mill to Victorian society, memorializing her to a largely incredulous audience, and explaining how much she meant to him are just a few of the various items on his agenda. These items have to be taken into account if we are to be aware of the impression he tries to create in the *Autobiography*. In short, Mill's interests, stated and unstated, in writing the *Autobiography* are not necessarily the interests of a reader or biographer who is trying to see Mill against the backdrop of nineteenth-century social, moral, economic, religious, economic, cultural, and philosophical intellectual developments. On the other hand, Mill's *Autobiography* is what the Germans call a *bildungsroman*, a deliberate attempt to re-create oneself through one's ongoing self-understanding. This conception of autobiography is not a misleading self-editing, but rather a view of the human person that reflects important currents of nineteenth-century thought.

The fifth and final reason for an intellectual biography is one that Mill himself would have appreciated. As he said in an 1846 article, "What shapes the character is not what is purposely taught, so much as the unintentional teaching of institutions and social relations." Mill was very much a figure of his time, both shaped by it and helping to shape it. He was, in the best sense, the quintessential Victorian liberal. Recent scholarship has begun to make a more balanced assessment of Victorian Britain, both its influence upon and its continuing relevance to our own world. An intellectual biography of Mill constitutes a contribution to that larger enterprise and benefits from that larger contextualization.

I have taken seriously Mill's claims about Harriet and attempted to see what light they throw on Mill's life and thought. I have concluded not only that Harriet exerted a great influence but also that her influence was by and large a positive one. Clarifying their relationship does a great deal to explain the evolution of Mill's thought. It also exhibits in important respects the larger cultural background of his thought, sometimes in unexpected ways. To the extent that there is a fundamental concept in Mill's life and thought, it is the concept of personal autonomy, and it was Harriet who helped to make that concept pivotal in Mill's writings.

I have been fortunate in having available to me the biographies of Bain and Packe, both of which will long continue to be prime sources of information for Mill scholars. The limitations of Bain's approach are reflected in his dismissal of the importance of Harriet, his failure to recognize the Romantic influence on Mill (Coleridge, for example, is never mentioned), and Bain's own philosophical agenda, which was not identical to Mill's. Packe's book is a gold mine of information, but the stress is more on the life than on the thought. Although Packe recognizes the influence of Harriet, that influence is not cast in a systematic or wholly positive light.

An enormous amount of scholarship has been produced since Packe's biography, and while very few new or significant details about Mill's life have been uncovered, the interpretation of those facts is very different when seen in the light of that scholarship. I have had the good fortune to be given a chronology of Mill's life prepared by John Robson, and this has helped to clarify the sometimes puzzling chronology that appears in Packe. The collected works of Mill edited by Robson is a scholar's dream, but the challenge of mastering it has been somewhat daunting. In any case, the splendid scholarly work done on Mill since the publication of Packe's biography certainly calls for a fresh look at Mill's life, his work, and their relationship. I would reiterate that it is not so much the presence of new information as the sheer weight of information that should, and will, inspire fresh looks at Mill's life and thought.

The real problem is the sheer volume of material that has been available for some time. The claim that I put forward is that no one has yet wrestled with the whole of Mill and put it into a coherent form. This "volume problem" is present in two dimensions. The first dimension is that Mill wrote in so many fields that few commentators either know or care about the areas with which they are not familiar. Textbook caricatures of Mill as a "utilitarian" or a "socialist" abound, with little awareness of what those terms meant to Mill or in his historical context.

In contrast with the first, the second dimension does bear directly on the biography. Enormous amounts of material have been available for some time but are ignored. For example, Mill was greatly influenced by the Romantic movement in an enormous number of ways (Austin spent time in Germany and came back with many of those ideas; Sarah Austin taught Mill to read German, etc.). You would never know about this from Bain's biography; Packe dwells on the influence of Carlyle but scarcely understands the depth of Coleridge's influence on Mill. The word "Romanticism" does not appear in Packe's index, and Humboldt is mentioned only once. Packe, in general, provides a wealth of detail, but there is no real principle of relative importance at work. His knowledge of philosophy and intellectual history, especially of the nineteenth century, is sketchy at best. All this limits the extent to which his biography can illuminate Mill's intellectual dimension and development. Here and there one finds serious scholars who recognize the Romantic influence, but they do not apply it specifically to Mill's intellectual development.

Aside from seeing the relationship between Mill and Harriet from a new and positive perspective, the other important emphasis in this intellectual biography is the recognition of the influence of Romanticism on Mill's thought. Rarely acknowledged, it has certainly never been considered at length. I argue that it is crucial. A number of commentators have mentioned the extent to which Mill tries to combine ideas or systems of thought that do not seem to fit comfortably with each other. I shall explain this as the consequence not of fuzzy thinking but of trying to maintain loyalty to his father's practical program of liberal reform and, at the same time, to defend and explicate that program by appeal to nineteenth-century Romantic philosophical ideas that his father did not really understand (and probably would have rejected if he had). Can these systems be coherently combined? I think they can, but it would initially require an extraordinary effort for readers to read the texts in this fashion, an effort they are not likely to make if they are ignorant of Mill's personal struggles and of the alternative Romantic system and its influence upon Mill. Would it have been better for the readers, at any rate, if Mill had not attempted such a compromise and had simply abandoned the philosophical framework he inherited from his father? Undoubtedly this would make reading the published works easier and their integrity more visible. But it would not have resolved Mill's internal psychological struggle, and that underscores why an intellectual biography can be useful.

My aim is to try to provide the big picture – a coherent vision of Mill – and an explication of how his thought evolved. Where I think I am breaking new ground is in presenting an in-depth discussion of how Mill was in fact a Romantic; moreover, during the period from 1830 to 1840, Mill sought to preserve the radical program he had inherited from his father but within a Romantic and conservative framework. By a "conservative" I do not mean a Tory or a defender of the status quo, but one who appreciates the historical and evolving nature of institutions and how they shape us (Coleridge, e.g., but also Macaulay). It would be quite impossible to read the *Logic* without understanding this; perhaps this is why philosophers simply ignore the discussion of the relation between science and art in Book VI.

Another obstacle to understanding Mill is the clarity of his style. Mill's writings seem so accessible that his strengths and weaknesses seem to float clearly on the surface. We are lulled into looking no further. But the ease of expression masks both the enormous capacity for intellectual synthesis – he makes it look so easy – and the painful psychological drama going on in the background. Finally, tracking the evolution of his thinking shows its greater continuity and integrity. In this respect, an intellectual biography, more than anything else, helps us to see the architectonic and wholeness of an author's work.

Perhaps the greatest challenge is trying to see Mill the person, as opposed to focusing on Mill the author and intellectual icon. Mill is such an imposing figure that discovering he even had a private life is analogous to a schoolchild discovering a teacher shopping in a supermarket. Mill was himself quite reticent about such things. However, this reticence is itself an important feature of his life that sheds light on his thought. Most important, Mill's private life was itself in large part a reflection of, and an instantiation of, the ideas and values that appear in his published works. This integration of life and thought was not only what he espoused but also a reflection of the world in which he found himself, as he understood it. In short, he constructed a life that strove to be a Romantic work of art.

Acknowledgments

In dedicating this book to Jack Robson, I am not only acknowledging a personal debt but also calling attention to how much Mill scholars everywhere are forever in his debt for his splendid editing of the *Collected Works of John Stuart Mill*. His wife, Ann Robson, kindly made unpublished material available to me.

I should begin by acknowledging my teacher Ernest Nagel, who first introduced me to Mill's writings. The scholar whose work on Mill first attracted my attention, and who has continued to inspire me, is Alan Ryan. Three other scholars who have significantly influenced my reading of Mill are C. L. Ten, Bernard Semmel, and John Gray. A special debt is owed to the Liberty Fund for inviting me to participate in and direct a number of colloquia on Mill; specifically, I wish to thank Emilio Pacheco and Douglas Den Uyl. Among those who participated in these colloquia, special thanks goes to Stuart Warner, Timothy Fuller, Ray Frey, David Levy, Aurelian Craiutu, Nicholas Rescher, Geoff Smith, Janice Carlisle, Geoffrey Brennan, Chandran Kukathas, Gordon Lloyd, Dwight Lee, Stephen Davies, Norman Barry, Joseph Hamburger, Shirley Letwin, Maurice Cowling, Michael Laine, and John Lachs. Three individuals with whom I have discussed Mill's "socialism" are my former student Eric McDaniel, Dale E. Miller, and Jonathan Riley. I also wish to acknowledge the librarians at Somerville College, Oxford, who kindly permitted me to work with their collection of books from Mill's personal library. The Earhart Foundation provided generous support for this project.

Three individuals deserve special thanks. My former colleague and a great Mill scholar in his own right, Eldon Eisenach, read and commented on the entire first draft of the manuscript. Alan Kahan, a friend and an intellectual historian whose knowledge of the nineteenth century never fails to amaze me, read and commented on the second draft. I thank Russell Hahn for his extraordinary work as copy editor.

Finally, two individuals who have been especially helpful and patient with me during the writing of this book are Terence Moore of Cambridge University Press and my wife, Nadia Nedzel.

Childhood and Early Education: The Great Experiment (1806–1820)

THE TWO most important facts about the life of John Stuart Mill were that he was the son of James Mill and that he fell in love with Harriet Hardy Taylor. We shall begin our story with John Stuart Mill's (hereinafter referred to as "Mill") relation to his father (hereinafter referred to as "James Mill").

James Mill was the leader of a group of thinkers, known as the Philosophic Radicals,[1] who were intent upon a vast campaign of social reform. The other key figures included Jeremy Bentham and David Ricardo. What prompted their interest in social reform? During the last half of the eighteenth century, Britain had experienced the extraordinary economic transformation of the Industrial Revolution. The revolution succeeded not only in spurring economic growth but also in creating or uncovering an unprecedented number of political, economic, social, moral, and religious problems. The human and moral center of gravity had shifted. Just about every fundamental belief had to be rethought, and most institutions reformed.[2] The story of Mill's life is intimately tied to that reform and to the rethinking of liberal culture.

James Mill had been born in Scotland on April 6, 1773.[3] His father had been a shoemaker. His mother had changed the original family name of Milne. His mother had great ambitions for him, and from the very first James was made to feel that he was superior and the center of attention. His intellectual prowess was recognized at an early age, and as a result he acquired as patrons Sir John and Lady Jane Stuart. They arranged for him to attend the University of Edinburgh so that he could prepare for the Scottish Presbyterian ministry, and they also arranged for him to tutor their daughter.

James Mill was seventeen at the time he served as the tutor of Wilhelmina Stuart. A special friendship developed with the daughter of his patron, Sir John Stuart, a relationship that could never be consummated, given the social structure of the time. From this point on, James Mill was the implacable enemy of the class system in Britain. James Mill wrote of her that "besides being a beautiful woman, [she] was in point of intellect and disposition one of the most perfect human beings I have ever known." Even Sir Walter Scott had fallen in love with her. James would later name one of his daughters Wilhelmina. This throws a great deal of light both on why Mill would later cherish his relationship with Harriet and on why he wrote of her with such lavish praise, in a manner not unlike his father's. It also tells us something more about James Mill.[4]

Among James Mill's university friendships could be counted Jeffrey Thomson, later editor of the Whig *Edinburgh Review*, and Henry Brougham, a brilliant political leader who would be allied with James Mill in the Great Reform Bill of 1832. James Mill was influenced by the lectures of Dugald Stewart, the reigning philosopher of the Scottish school of common sense, but he also read, in addition to theology, Plato, Rousseau, David Hume, Voltaire, and the works of Condillac and Hartley on the functioning of the mind. These were among the authors who formed James Mill's mind, and they would do likewise for Mill.

James Mill was licensed by the Presbytery to preach. The parishioners considered his sermons to be a bit too learned. Unfortunately, the scripts of the sermons were eventually destroyed when the Mill family moved to Kensington. However, James Mill could not accept the doctrines of any church and abandoned his career in the ministry. In the early years of his marriage he continued to attend church and had all of his children baptized. By 1810, under the influence of Bentham and another friend, the Spanish general Miranda, he had given up all religious attachments. The other members of his family, including his son John, continued to attend. The young son was even heard to say to his aunt that "the two most important books in the world were Homer and the Bible."

After briefly considering the possibility of a career in law, James Mill moved to London to pursue a career as a journalist. While in London, he met and married Harriet Burrow (on June 5, 1805) when she was twenty-three and he almost thirty-two. Harriet's mother had taken over the management and ownership of a residence for "lunatics" from her late husband; she was an attractive woman whose daughter had inherited her beauty; there was a dowry of £400, and the couple was given a house by Harriet's mother – 12 Rodney Terrace, Pentonville. During 1810 the family lived briefly in the poet John Milton's former house. Until his appointment at India House, James Mill was under constant financial pressure, not the least of which was the pressure of paying his own father's debts. These debts had resulted from the bankruptcy of his father's shoe repair business following the loss of James Mill's mother and brother to consumption and his father's subsequent paralysis.

Despite fathering nine children with her – four boys and five girls – at regular two-year intervals over a twenty-year period,[5] James Mill became contemptuous of his wife's lack of intellect and her weakness of character.

The one really disagreeable trait in [James] Mill's character, and the thing that has left the most painful memories, was the [contemptuous] way that he allowed himself to speak and behave to his wife and children before visitors. When we read his letters to friends, we see him acting the family man with the utmost propriety, putting his wife and children into their due place; but he seemed unable to observe this part in daily intercourse.[6]

In commenting on James Mill's book *The Analysis of the Human Mind*, Bain noted that "the section on the Family affections is replete with the ideal of perfect domestic happiness: and, if the author did not act up to it, as he did to his ideal of public virtue, the explanation is to be sought in human weakness and inconsistency."[7]

It was there at Rodney Terrace that Mill was born on May 20, 1806, and christened John Stuart in honor of James Mill's former patron. Although James Mill might have been bitter about the class barrier that had prevented him from courting Wilhelmina, he was ever mindful of the importance of patronage for social mobility. An expanding family – they ultimately had nine children – and general economic difficulties plagued the Mills until the success of James Mill's *History of British India* in 1818. Despite burdens and obstacles that would have crushed a lesser man, including his unorthodox political views, James Mill achieved both financial security and a significant place in the employment of India House in 1819. Along with Edward Strachey[8] and Thomas Love Peacock, James Mill was one of three outsiders brought in to deal with the escalating demands of the correspondence between the directors in the home office and Indian officials.

James Mill had started writing an essay on India in 1806 in order to prove a specific point, namely, that the East India Company had mishandled and monopolized foreign trade. He did not realize at the time that the essay would take twelve years to complete and become a work of ten volumes.[9] The East India Company ("John" Company, in common parlance) was a quasi-autonomous commercial enterprise that would rule India in conjunction with the crown until 1857. In 1818, the possibility arose of gaining the chair of Greek at Glasgow University, but being unwilling to sign the confession of faith, James Mill could not pursue an academic career. At the same time, James Mill established a personal relationship with several members of the board of governors of India House in the hope of obtaining employment. It was his friends Joseph Hume and David Ricardo who called to the attention of George Canning, then president of the India Board, the publication of the history. This was enough to offset the opposition of the Tory members of the board. James Mill's expertise on India, his organizational skills, and his industriousness would eventually permit him to rise to the position of chief examiner in 1830.

In addition to his career at India House, James Mill became one of the leaders of the reform movement known as Philosophic Radicalism, and among his political friends were Bentham, Ricardo, Grote, and Francis Place. Grote described James Mill at their first meeting as follows:

He is a very profound thinking man, and seems well disposed to communicate, as well as clear and intelligible in his manner. His mind has, in deed, all that cynicism and asperity which belong to the Benthamian school, and what I chiefly dislike in him is the readiness and seeming preference with which he dwells on the *faults and defects* of others – even of the greatest men! But it is so very rarely that a man of any depth comes across my path, that I shall most assuredly cultivate his acquaintance a good deal farther.[10]

One of the most remarkable aspects of the final published version of Mill's *Autobiography* is that he talks about his mother only indirectly. One might suggest that this is not surprising, as the *Autobiography* is primarily about Mill's intellectual and moral development. Even if this is so, it points to the fact that his mother played no major role in his intellectual and moral development. From what little evidence we have, it appears as if she conformed to the eighteenth-century notion of women as genteel and useless. Mill's indirect comment about his mother is his pointing out what a mistake it was for his father to have married early and had a large family before being capable of supporting them. Mill attempted to draw a moral lesson from this, noting that such behavior on his father's part was later to be criticized by James Mill himself, not only as imprudent but also as inconsistent with the kind of advice that the Philosophic Radicals were to give members of the working class.

Although Mill never directly mentions his mother in his published *Autobiography*, he does give us an account of her in an unpublished draft, an unflattering reference that Harriet Taylor Mill had him remove for the published version.

That rarity in England, a really warm-hearted mother would in the first place have made my father a totally different being and in the second would have made the children grow up loving and being loved. But my mother with the very best intentions only knew how to pass her life in drudging for them. Whatever she could do for them she did, & they liked her, because she was kind to them, but to make herself loved, looked up to, or even obeyed, required qualities which she unfortunately did not possess. . . . I thus grew up in the absence of love and in the presence of fear: and many and indelible are the effects of this bringing up in the stunting of my moral growth.[11]

This sounds very much like a plea for a mother of character who would have stood up for him against his father's harshness and at the same time would have introduced an element of affection based upon strength. For the rest of his life, and despite the fact that his mother always doted on him, Mill would remain as contemptuous of his mother as his father had been.[12]

What we do know about his mother, Harriet Barrow Mill, is that when she married James Mill at the age of twenty-three she was very pretty, and that Mill inherited her acquiline appearance. She was described by one of her husband's professional associates as "good-natured and good-tempered, two capital qualities in a woman," but also as "not a little vain of her person, and would be thought to be still a girl."[13] One of Mill's sisters, also named Harriet, describes her mother as follows:

Here was an instance of two persons, as husband and wife, living as far apart, under the same roof, as the north pole from the south; from no 'fault' of my poor mother most certainly; but how was a woman with a growing family and very small means (as in the early years of the marriage) to be anything but a German Hausfrau? How could she 'intellectually' become a companion for such a mind as my father?[14]

A later acquaintance, Mrs. Grote, described the relationship as follows: "He [James Mill] married a stupid woman, 'a housemaid of a woman', and left off caring for her and treated her as his squah but was always faithful to her."[15] Another visitor described her as "a tall, handsome lady, sweet-tempered, with pleasant manners, fond of her children: but I think not much interested in what the elder ones and their father talked about."[16]

Mill offered the following reflection on his father's relationship with his mother:

Personally I believe my father to have had much greater capacities of feeling than were ever developed in him. He resembled almost all Englishmen in being ashamed of the signs of feeling, and by the absence of demonstration, starving the feelings themselves. In an atmosphere of tenderness and affection he would have been tender and affectionate; but his ill-assorted marriage and his asperities of temper disabled him from making such an atmosphere. It was one of the most unfavourable of the moral agencies which acted on me in my boyhood, that mine was not an education of love but of fear.[17]

The importance of affection and the inability of James Mill to express affection is a repeated theme in Mill's' *Autobiography*:

The element which was chiefly deficient in his moral relation to his children was that of tenderness. . . . If we consider further that he was in the trying position of sole teacher, and add to this that his temper was constitutionally irritable, it is impossible not to feel true pity for a father who did, and strove to do, so much for his children, who would have valued their affection, yet who must have been constantly feeling that fear of him was drying it up at its source. This was no longer the case later in life, and with his younger children. They loved him tenderly: and if I cannot say so much of myself, I was always loyally devoted to him.[18]

Early Education

James Mill spent a considerable period of time almost every day in educating his own children. As an example of his father's commitment to education, the largest part of the first chapter of Mill's *Autobiography* focuses on what has become the most famous early childhood reading list of all time. Mill was taught Greek at the age of three. At the age of five, Mill accompanied George Bentham on a visit to Lady Spencer, the wife of the head of the admiralty, whereupon Mill discoursed on "the comparative merits of Marlborough and Wellington."[19] Mill read Plato in Greek by the age of seven; he read the histories by Robertson, Hume, and Gibbon at the same time; at the age of eight, he studied Latin; Newton's *Principia Mathematica* was mastered by the age of eleven, the classics of logic by twelve, and the rigors of higher mathematics, Adam Smith's *The Wealth of Nations*, and David Ricardo's *Principles of Political Economy and Taxation* by fourteen. At the age of fifteen, Mill was introduced to the writings of Jeremy Bentham, and this was soon followed, at age sixteen, by the philosophical works of Locke, Berkeley, Helvétius, and Condillac. Among the many authors Mill cites are Plutarch, Virgil, Ovid, Lucretius, Cicero, Homer, Sophocles, Euripides, Aristophanes, Thucydides, Tacitus, Juvenal, Polybius, Aristotle, Shakespeare, Milton, Spencer, and Dryden.

Some indication of the extent and rigor of this regimen can be gathered from the following summary. In 1814, at the age of eight, Mill was reading Thucydides, Sophocles' *Electra*, Euripides' *Phoenisae*, Aristophanes' *Plutus* and the *Clouds*, and the *Philippics* of Demosthenes in Greek; in Latin, he was reading the *Oration for Archias* of Cicero, as well as the *Anti-Verres*. In mathematics, he was studying Euclid and Euler's *Algebra*, as well as Bonnycastle's *Algebra* and West's *Geometry*. In 1814, he also began reading Ferguson's *Roman History*, Mitford's *Grecian History*, and Livy (in English). At the same age of eight he was himself writing a history of the united provinces from the revolt from Spain, in the reign of Phillip II, to the accession of the *Stadtholder*, William III, to the throne of England. He also wrote a history of Roman government to the Licinian Laws. The latter were significant in Roman history for promoting democratic reforms, such as mandating that at least one consul had to be a plebeian.

The 1815 reading list included (in Greek) the *Odyssey*, Theocritis, two orations of Aeschines, and Demosthenes' *On the Crown*. The Latin reading list included the first six books of Ovid's *Metamorphoses*, the first six books of Livy's *Bucolics*, the first six books of the *Aeneid*, and Cicero's *Orations*. To the works in mathematics were added Simpson's *Conic Sections*, West's *Conic Sections* and *Spherics*, Kersey's *Algebra*, and Newton's *Universal Arithmetic*. In 1816, he was reading (in Greek), Xenophon's *Hellenica*, Sophocles' *Ajax* and *Philoctetes*, Euripedes' *Medea*, and Aristophanes' *Frogs*; in Latin, he read Horace's *Epodes* and Polybius. In mathematics, he studied Stewart's *Propositions Geometricae*, Playfair's *Trigonometry*, and Simpson's *Algebra*. By 1817, Mill was reading Thucydides in Greek for the second time, Demosthenes' *Orations*, and Aristotle's *Rhetoric* (for which he made a synoptic table). In Latin, he read Lucretius, Cicero's *Letter to Atticus, Topica*, and *De Partitone Oratoria*. In mathematics, he began an article on conic sections in the *Encyclopaedia Britannica*, Euler's *Analysis of Infinities*, Simpson's *Fluxions*, Keill's *Astronomy*, and Robinson's

Mechanical Philosophy. At an age when most adolescents today are just beginning to think about higher education, Mill had already completed what would today be considered the most rigorous honors program in existence.

What is curious about this extensive reading list are the omissions. Much of the Scottish Enlightenment is omitted, except for Robertson's history and Smith's *Wealth of Nations* (doubtless misread). There is no work by David Hume other than the *History*. There is almost no moral philosophy; even the works of Cicero chosen avoid his moral pieces. There is no theology.

Mill did have a number of good things to say about his early education. Among the important analytical skills he acquired from his father was the ability to dissect arguments in order to discover their strengths and, especially, their weaknesses. In later life, Mill was to become a formidable advocate and polemicist. The practice of the Socratic method – not only upon others but also, by internalization, upon himself – enabled him to critique his own position before submitting it to others. This capacity for self-criticism and self-analysis could have a destructive impact upon the practitioner, but it could also have a liberating and ennobling effect. Many years later, in the essay *On Liberty*, Mill would emphasize the morally transforming effect on character of the willingness to examine every side of every argument. Perhaps the most positive lesson of Mill's early education was his coming to learn, in true Socratic fashion, the importance of discovering the truth for oneself. As he put it in the *Autobiography*, "a pupil from whom nothing is ever demanded which he cannot do, never does all he can."

There was one cardinal point in this training, of which I have already given some indication, and which, more than anything else, was the cause of whatever good it effected. Most boys or youths who have had much knowledge drilled into them, have their mental capacities not strengthened, but overlaid by it. They are crammed with mere facts, and with the opinions or phrases of other people, and these are accepted as a substitute for the power to form opinions of their own: and thus the sons of eminent fathers, who have spared no pains in their education, so often grow up mere parroters of what they have learnt, incapable of using their minds except in the furrows traced for them. Mine, however, was not an education of cram. My father never permitted anything which I learnt to degenerate into a mere exercise in memory. He strove to make the understanding not only go along with every step of the teaching, but, if possible, preceded it. Anything which could be found out by thinking I never was told, until I had exhausted my efforts to find it out for myself.[20]

Given the content and rigor of Mill's education, no reader could possibly confuse this with those contemporary critiques of memorization that suggest a strict dichotomy between the acquisition of content and the development of critical skills. Mill is here advocating not an either/or but a both/and. Some indication of this can be gathered from a later (1835) critique of the "system of cram." Mill specifically attacks the French mathematician Joseph Jacotot for a method that "surpasses all former specimens of the cram method in this, that former cram-doctors crammed an unfortunate child's memory with abstract propositions [without] meaning; but Jacotot . . . actually makes the unfortunate creature get by rote not only the propositions, but the reasons too."[21] In opposition to this, Mill suggests instead a method of "cultivating mental power." Throughout his life, and most significantly in *On Liberty*, Mill advocated the liberating effects and the moral transformation that accompanies the self-critical examination of all ideas.

In addition to his required reading, Mill was required to render a *compte rendu*, a daily written summary of what he had discussed that day with his father. Later, he helped his father correct the proofs of the *History of British India*, thereby gaining additional valuable editorial and writing skills. It was in the editorial process that Mill thought that his father almost treated him as an equal. Despite all this, Mill insisted that his father never allowed him to become conceited.

In the midst of this pedagogical regimen, Mill found the time and had the interest to read other things on his own, such as history. He referred to this as his "private reading." This private reading was also accompanied by "private" writing, that is, writing without "the chilling sensation of being under a critical eye."[22] The ominous nature of this remark is borne out by the critical comments that Mill later makes about his father's educational program.

His education was for the most part academic and cerebral. Mill faulted his father for being too abstract and not giving enough concrete examples of the principles he espoused. Mill had little contact with his peers in play situations and remained deficient all his life in things requiring manual dexterity. But beyond this is revealed the harshness and impatience of a too-demanding parent. James Mill, as his son tells us, "was often, and much beyond reason, provoked by my failures in cases where success could not have been expected." "I was constantly meriting reproof by inattention, inobservance, and general slackness of mind in matters of daily life."[23] This impression is borne out by another witness, who described James Mill's teaching method as "by far the best I have ever witnessed, and is infinitely precise; but he is excessively severe. No fault, however trivial, escapes his notice; none goes without reprehension or punishment of some sort."[24] The same witness goes on to describe a particular situation.

Lessons have not been well said this morning by Willie and Clara [Mill's younger sisters]; there they are now, three o'clock, plodding over their books, their dinner, which they knew went up at one, brought down again; and John, who dines with them, has his books also, for having permitted them to pass when they could not say, and no dinner will any of them get until six o'clock. This has happened once before since I came. The fault today is a mistake in one word.[25]

James Mill, according to Bain, did make one attempt to give his son something more than an academic upbringing.

Having been in his youth, a full-trained volunteer, he had a due appreciation of army discipline, in giving bodily carriage. He, accordingly, engaged a sergeant from the adjoining barracks, to put them [his male children] through a course of marching drill; while John was practiced in sword exercise. Very little came of this, as far as John in particular was concerned; he was, to the end, backward in all that regarded bodily accomplishments, saving the one point of persistence as a walker. The fact, no doubt, was, that his nervous energy was so completely absorbed in his unremitted intellectual application, as to be unavailable for establishing the co-ordinations of muscular dexterity.[26]

One of the more interesting criticisms Mill makes of his father's system is that Mill was forced to teach his younger siblings, a responsibility that lasted into his early thirties. Among other things, Mill was forced to turn down social invitations, such as one to accompany the Grotes on a vacation, because, as his father said, John was needed to teach the younger children. Mill notes here, somewhat cryptically, that the "relation between teacher and taught is not a good moral discipline to either."[27] We are left wondering what he meant by that. Mill "often acted the part of mediator between his father and his elder sister."[28] The household, in addition to the parents and Mill, himself consisted of Mill's five sisters – Wilhelmina Forbes, Clara, Harriet, Jane, and Mary – as well as his three brothers – Henry, James Bentham Mill, and George. Despite this demanding role, Mill always had the capacity to make his siblings laugh by mimicking adults. "John Mill, from pride and assumption was freer than most, yet the deference paid him by his brothers and sisters was profound. When unable to determine any matter for themselves the suggestion came from one or other of them as a matter of course, 'Ask John: he knows.' "[29]

Keeping in mind that Mill was drafting his *Autobiography* in the 1850s, we can reasonably speculate that the relation between the teacher and the pupil is analogous, at least at this point in his life, to the relationship between the master and the slave, the superior and the inferior. The master-slave metaphor is one that will appear in Mill's later writings in discussing the relationship between husbands and wives in Victorian England. Such a relationship is to the obvious detriment of the inferior, because it tends to perpetuate a sense of inferiority reinforced by deference. It is also detrimental to the superior, who comes to find his identity tied up in the subordination of others. The autonomy of the inferior is postponed indefinitely, and the autonomy of the superior is undermined. The intended benevolence is not enough to counterbalance the pathologically incestuous nature of the relationship. Mill experienced the benevolence, but he also experienced the demeaning and stultifying dimensions of a relationship with an extraordinary father. Mill would not achieve his full autonomy until the death of his father.

What is the self-image that Mill acquired from his extraordinary early education? One of the evils most liable to attend on any sort of early proficiency, and which often fatally blights its promise, my father most anxiously guarded against. This was self-conceit. He kept me, with extreme vigilance out of the way of hearing myself praised, or of being led to make self-flattering comparisons between myself and others. From his own intercourse with me I could derive none but a very humble opinion of myself; and the standard of comparison he always held up to me, was not what other people did, but what a man could and ought to do. He completely succeeded in preserving me from the sort of influences he so much dreaded. I was not at all aware that my attainments were anything unusual at my age. . . . My state of mind was not humility, but neither was it arrogance. . . . I did not estimate myself at all. If I thought anything about myself, it was that I was rather backward in my studies, since I always found myself so in comparison with what my father expected from me. . . . I was always too much in awe of him to be otherwise than extremely subdued and quiet in his presence. Yet with all this I had no notion of any superiority in myself; and well was it for me that I had not.[30]

Even after he achieved fame as the author of the *System of Logic* and the *Principles of Political Economy*, Mill could look back on his life and make the following, seemingly incredible claim:

... [h]ad [I] been by nature extremely quick of apprehension, or had possessed a very accurate and retentive memory, or were of a remarkably active and energetic character . . . in all these natural gifts I am rather below than above par; what I could do, could assuredly be done by any boy or girl of average capacity and healthy physical constitution: and if I have accomplished anything, I owe it, among other fortunate circumstances, to the fact that through the early training bestowed on me by my father, I started, I may fairly say, with an advantage of a quarter of a century over my contemporaries.[31]

This is a tricky point. Even before he wrote his *Autobiography*, Mill had no doubt that he was a superior person. "I had always a humble opinion of my own powers as an original thinker, except in abstract science (logic, metaphysics, and the theoretic principles of political economy and politics), but thought myself much superior to most of my contemporaries in willingness and ability to learn from everybody."[32] However, he attributed this superiority not to native endowment but to two other sources: his father's rigorous educational program and a particular moral virtue, his openness to learning from others. It has been pointed out that Mill was perhaps overly optimistic about the extent to which education could affect the mind, but there is no doubt that education is both a crucial and an underutilized resource.

Among the things Mill did not know was that when he was twelve years old (1818) some Oxford and Cambridge notables had already expressed to James Mill their interest in the younger Mill. James Mill's former patron, Sir John Stuart, gave him a gift of £500 intended to make it possible for John to attend Cambridge. As late as 1823, another Cambridge don, Professor Townsend, urged James Mill to allow his son to become better acquainted with his "Patrician contemporaries" by attending Cambridge. "Whatever you may wish his eventual destiny to be, his prosperity in life cannot be retarded, but must, on the contrary, be increased by making an acquaintance at an English University with his Patrician contemporaries."[33]

As we shall see, Mill did not attend the universities of his day.[34] He was always educated at home and not in any school. From one point of view there was hardly any reason for him to attend school, given what he had mastered intellectually. There were other reasons. The major universities were still in James Mill's time controlled by the Anglican Church; they insisted upon doctrinal orthodoxy and largely focused on preparing students for the ministry. This had been James Mill's own experience. Bentham, who had attended the university, always regretted his lapse of integrity in agreeing to the religious oath required of students. Other forms of pre-professional training were still done through apprenticeship. Nor had the sciences yet achieved a dominant position in higher education.[35] All of this was to change during the last half of Mill's life, and the reform of the universities would in part be influenced by his mature views. During his own lifetime, two of Mill's works, the *Logic* and the *Principles of Political Economy*, would become standard university textbooks.

An Initiation in Retrospect

Mill's account of his childhood and early education up to the age of twelve is a retrospective glance at the formative influences of his life. There are three important points that he stressed about this early phase. First, he tells us that "from about the age of twelve, I entered into another and more advanced stage in my course of instruction; in which the main object was no longer the aids and appliances of thought [i.e., information and the thoughts of others], but the thoughts themselves."[36] That is, Mill thought that at the age of twelve he was able to engage in the self-conscious critique of ideas, and not merely in their acquisition. He couples this with the fact that it was at this age that he was allowed to participate with his father in the editing of James Mill's *History of British India*. This editorial exercise also allowed Mill to acquire knowledge of India that would qualify him for a future post as his father's successor in India House. In this sense, Mill is being true to one of his stated purposes in writing his *Autobiography* – that is, to chart his own intellectual development.

Mill also couples his new stage of thought with his study in 1819, at the age of thirteen, of David Ricardo's *The Principles of Political Economy and Taxation* (1817). David Ricardo, whose parents were Sephardic Jews, married a Quaker but later became a Unitarian. He represents the important social community formed by the interaction of Unitarians with utilitarians. Ricardo was a highly successful investor in the stock market as well as a "loved and intimate friend" of James Mill. It had been James Mill who prevailed upon Ricardo to write and publish an abstract treatise on political economy and subsequently to enter Parliament, where his friend could be a voice both for his own and James Mill's "opinions both on political economy and on other subjects."[37]

This is connected with the second important element in Mill's life, an initiation into a leadership role in the economic, political, social, and moral transformation of Great Britain as it moved from feudalism to industrialism. It is not merely that Mill read Ricardo but also that it was "one of my father's main objects to make me apply to [Adam] Smith's more superficial view of political economy, the superior lights of Ricardo, and detect what was fallacious in Smith's arguments, or erroneous in any of his conclusions."[38]

In what way was Smith's analysis perceived to be deficient? According to Smith, there were three factors crucial to the production of wealth: natural resources (land), capital, and labor. Corresponding to these three factors there were three kinds of income: rent, interest, and wages. A consequence of these three sources of income was three social classes: landlords, capitalists, and laborers. Wealth is maximized to the extent that all parties in the process engage in postponed gratification: Landlords should charge minimal rents, capitalists reinvest their profits, and laborers accept subsistence wages and only modest increases. Anything beyond subsistence wages leads to a decrease in the amount of capital and a subsequent decrease in the amount of potential wealth. Ultimately, equilibrium will be attained among a stationary population, wages, and profits. This equilibrium is the idea of a *stationary economic state*. On the whole, Smith had presented a harmonious growth model.

What Ricardo added to this analysis was an antagonistic distribution model – specifically, a critique of landlords. For Ricardo, the landlords were always identified with Tory aristocratic landowners who had acquired their land not through labor but originally through conquest and later through inheritance. The landlords tended to think in feudal terms, rather than in industrial terms, and seemed more interested in maintaining their position of social preeminence and political control than in increasing national or international wealth. Landlords tended to favor mercantilist policies, including monopolistic privileges and tariffs. Tariffs on the importation of grain (corn) lead to a corresponding increase in the cost of subsistence. This in turn leads to an increase in wages. The increase in wages leads to a decrease in profits. This will be followed by less incentive to save and form capital, and so growth will come to an end more quickly. The weak link in this chain is the rapacious and profligate landlords bent on conspicuous consumption.

Henceforth, Mill was to understand himself as a leader in the class warfare between those who favored industrial and commercial growth and those who favored the retention of feudal privilege. To this end, his father prepared a simple introduction to Ricardo's thesis for students by lecturing to Mill and having him prepare written summaries of the lectures, which where repeatedly edited and revised. The result was James Mill's *Elements of Political Economy*, and although he does not claim it, Mill participated in a major way in its being written. For the rest of his life, Mill would remain an enemy of Tory rentiers, but his views on growth would undergo an evolution.

The third important element in Mill's initiation was his career in India House. Both James Mill and later Mill himself thought of themselves as leaders of the emerging elite who possessed the intellectual and moral gifts necessary to lead Britain out of feudalism and into the modern liberal world. The natural place in Victorian Britain for the exercise of such leadership was in Parliament. Members of Parliament were unpaid, and this, along with other reasons, left a career in Parliament available primarily to members of the aristocracy and the wealthy few. At the time of the Industrial Revolution, the aristocracy controlled most of the wealth (land), most of the political power, and most of the leadership positions in the society as a whole, including the Anglican Church. But economic considerations do not tell the whole story. Men no more wealthy than James Mill did serve in Parliament, through the favor of patrons. Before 1832, in many cases a patron would simply appoint a protégé to a seat he controlled. Bentham could have bought a seat for James Mill had he chosen to do so – it was easy enough to do this even after 1832, and very easy before then. While it is true that aristocracy and wealth controlled most of the seats in the unreformed House of Commons, there were always a few districts with almost universal male suffrage, which is why there were always a few radicals in the House, even before 1832. It is most likely that religious reasons stood in the way of a Parliamentary career for James Mill. He would have had to be willing to swear an oath or affirm "on the true faith of a Christian." James Mill chose not to serve in Parliament. His leadership had to be exercised indirectly, through his writings, through acquaintances, through his career as a quasi–civil servant in India House, and through the shaping of his son's career.

In words that were prophetic of his own subsequent career in India House, Mill described his father's career as follows:

He was appointed one of the Assistants of the Examiner of India Correspondence; officers whose duty it was to prepare drafts of despatches to India, for consideration by the Directors, in the principal departments of administration. In this office, and in that of Examiner, which he subsequently attained, the influence which his talents, his reputation, and his decision of character gave him, with superiors who really desired the good government of India, enabled him to a great extent to throw into his drafts of despatches, and to carry through the ordeal of the Court of Directors and Board of Control, without having their force much weakened, his real opinions on Indian subjects. In his History he had set forth, for the first time, many of the true principles of Indian administration: and his despatches, following his History, did more than had ever been done before to promote the improvement of India, and teach Indian officials to understand their business. If a selection of them were published, they would, I am convinced, place his character as a practical statesman fully on a level with his eminence as a speculative writer.[39]

Mill would spend the rest of life reconciling his intellectual role with the political role that he also relished but was unable to realize until his retirement from India House. As he put it in the *Autobiography*, "I was not indifferent to exclusion from Parliament, and public life."[40] This, as we shall see, had an enormous impact on both the substance and the style of his writing.

There was something lacking in Mill's early education, and it was a lack that would eventually undermine his initiation into Philosophic Radicalism. Years later, in writing his *Autobiography*, and with the advantage of perspective and hindsight, Mill was able to offer a cooler assessment of his relationship with his father and the significance of distancing himself from his father's shortcomings. Among the significant items, he identified James Mill's inability to hear the voice of poetry. Although his father required him to write in English verse, the reasons given reflected James Mill's views: "[S]ome things could be expressed better and more forcibly in verse than in prose: this, he said was the real advantage. The other was that people in general attached more value to verse than it deserved. . . . Shakespeare my father had put into my hands, chiefly for the sake of the historical plays. . . . My father never was a great admirer of Shakespeare, the English idolatry of whom he used to attack with some severity. He cared little for any English poetry except Milton (for whom he had the highest admiration). . . . The poetry of the present [nineteenth] century he saw scarcely any merit in. . . ."⁴¹

The Shaping of a Prodigy

The other formative influence in Mill's life was James Mill's friendship with Jeremy Bentham. The elder Mill had met Bentham (1748–1832), already the eccentric and famous philosopher and noted social reformer, in 1808, and together they formed a lasting personal friendship and professional partnership. It was at Bentham's house in 1811 that James Mill met and befriended David Ricardo. Mill was introduced to Bentham at the age of three (1809). In July of 1809, Bentham rented Barrow Green House in Surrey. Thereafter, the Mills visited every summer from 1809 to 1813.

Until meeting Bentham, James Mill had carefully suppressed his resentment toward the system of aristocratic patronage that allowed lesser men than he to achieve eminence, even though he himself had been a recipient of patronage. By 1809, James Mill was writing to Bentham and describing himself as "your zealous pupil" and later as "your affectionate pupil." These acknowledgments of a kind of discipleship would be repeated in Mill's own later relationships with Carlyle and Comte, but with a very different outcome. I mention this issue of "discipleship" because some readers have inferred from Mill's correspondence that he always needed to be directed by someone else. No one would ever think that about James Mill, and since James Mill could call himself someone's disciple, it is clear that this was an expression of respect and deference, not of submission.

In 1794, Bentham had submitted to Parliament a plan for a model prison called the Panopticon, so named because its architectural structure permitted all of the prisoners to be seen at once. When this project was finally rejected in 1811, Bentham turned to political reform. In this he was guided by his new friendship with James Mill. In 1814, the British government paid Bentham £23,000 for the abandoned project of the Panopticon. This payment was successfully invested in the social reformer Robert Owen's venture at New Lanark, and Bentham achieved financial independence. He made the then-impecunious Mills his neighbors at 1 Queens Square, in Westminster. The Mills were to live at Queen's Square until 1830.

As a result of his new riches, Bentham was able to rent Ford Abbey, near the town of Chard in Somerset. The abbey was palatial, with an eclectic mixture of Gothic, Tudor, and Inigo Jones architecture. The interior was adorned with tapestries of Raphael cartoons. It had several lakes and a deer park. The Mill family spent almost six months a year with Bentham in the country at Ford Abbey until 1818. It was there that Mill was introduced to a lifestyle far beyond the confines of the middle class, one that could almost be called aristocratic.

This sojourn was, I think, an important circumstance in my education. Nothing contributes more to nourish the elevation of sentiments in a people, than the large and free character of their habitations. The middle-age architecture, the baronial hall, and the spacious and lofty rooms, of this fine old place, so unlike the mean and cramped externals of English middle class life, gave the sentiment of a large and freer existence, and were to me a sort of poetic cultivation, aided also by the character of the grounds in which the abbey stood; which were riant and secluded, umbrageous, and full of the sound of falling waters.[42]

Bentham played the organ, and often he would play privately for Mill. Later in life, Mill would play the piano only privately for Harriet. It was also at Ford Abbey that Bentham gave Mill a copy of Daniel Defoe's *Robinson Crusoe*. Later, Mill was to have the full run of Bentham's library. Although Mill could not have so understood it at such an early age, Defoe's work was not merely the great epic of Protestant individualism that we all know; it was also a nostalgic look at the loss of Christian unity and paved the way for thinking about a new form of philosophical unity for Western culture. This is prophetic of Mill's later life.

Daily life at Ford Abbey also gives us a glimpse of the world in which Mill was raised.

[James] Mill is up between five and six. He and John compare his proofs. Willie and Clara [Mill's younger sisters] are in the saloon before seven, and as soon as the proofs are done with, John goes to the farther end of the room to teach his sisters. Then he turns to geometry till breakfast, at nine. Mr. Bentham rises soon after seven and gets to work about eight. After breakfast, [James] Mill hears Willie and Clara and John at their lessons, under a broad balcony. All the lessons and reading are performed aloud, and occupy full three hours, say till one o'clock. From nine to twelve Mr. Bentham continues working: from twelve to one he performs upon an organ in the saloon. At one we all three [Francis Place, Bentham, and James Mill] walk in the lanes and fields for an hour. At two all go to work again until dinner at six, when Mrs. Mill, [James] Mill, Bentham, I [Francis Place] and Colls [assistant to Bentham] dine together. We have soup or fish, or both, meat, pudding, generally fruit, viz: melons, strawberries, gooseberries, currants, grapes; no wine. The first day I came, wine was put upon the table; but as I took none, none has since made its appearance. After dinner . . . Mrs. Mill marches in great style round the green in front of the house . . . with all the children, till their bedtime. . . . [James] Mill and I take a sharp walk for two hours, say, till a quarter past eight, then one of us alternately walks with Mr. Bentham for an hour; then comes tea, at which we read the periodical publications, and eleven o'clock comes but too soon and we all go to bed.[43]

Bentham had been a child prodigy. He had mastered Latin and Greek by the age of six. His father had been a Francophile, so the Bentham family spent a great deal of time in France. If these facts sound vaguely familiar, it is because they will be echoed in the life of Mill. It was Bentham who was among the first to advocate the educational importance of controlling the psychological environment of the pupil – a view known as association-ism – and who later prompted James Mill to formulate the younger Mill's rigorous educational program.

In 1811, James Mill suffered a severe attack of gout, and having inti-mations of mortality, began to worry about the future of his son. It was at this time that James Mill asked Bentham to become John's guardian in case of mishap. Bentham responded with enthusiasm.

If you will appoint me guardian to Mr. Mill, I will, in the event of his father's being disposed of elsewhere, take him to Q.S.P. [Queens Square Place] and there or elsewhere, by whipping or otherwise, do whatsoever may seem most necessary and proper, for teaching him to make all proper distinctions, such as between the Devil and the Holy Ghost, and how to make Codes and Encyclopedias, and whatsoever else may be proper to be made, so long as I remain an inhabitant of this vale of tears.[44]

James Mill's response reflects both a humorous dimension and a deeply earnest commitment to make Mill the spokesperson for their joint efforts at social and political reform:

I am not going to die, notwithstanding your zeal to come in for a legacy. However, if I were to die any time before this poor boy is a man, one of the things that would pinch me most sorely, would be the being obliged to leave his mind unmade to the degree of excellence, of which I hope to make it. But another thing is, that the only prospect which would lessen that pain, would be the leaving him in your hands.

I therefore take your offer quite seriously, and stipulate, merely, that it shall be
made as good as possible; and then we may perhaps leave him a successor worthy
of both of us.[45]

Bentham became Mill's guardian, taking a keen interest in the young-
ster's education. In 1813, Mill accompanied his father and Bentham on
a summer trip to Oxford, Bath, Bristol, and Portsmouth and soon developed a love for natural scenery. So Mill was tied at an early age to Britain's
most famous late eighteenth- and early nineteenth-century philosopher,
and before the end of his life Mill was to become the godfather of one of
Britain's most famous twentieth-century philosophers, Bertrand Russell.
Mill would also spend a year in France with the family of Jeremy's brother,
Samuel, and out of this grew Mill's fascination with French life and
politics.

As previously noted, James Mill had had a difficult time supporting
his family. By 1814, James Mill was earning about £150 per year but
could not keep out of debt. James Mill also referred disparagingly in a
letter about his "incumbrances, mastery of a wife, and five brats, and a
maid." The radical tailor and sometime leader of the workers Francis
Place paid some of the debts. James Mill did later repay that debt. When,
in 1814, the Mill family moved to Queens Square, in part to be closer to
Bentham, Jeremy Bentham paid half the cost of the rent, about £50. The
close proximity of two independent minds such as those of Bentham and
James Mill, as well as James Mill's dependency on Bentham's generosity,
occasionally led to disagreements between them. However, on May 12,
1819, something like financial independence became possible when James
Mill was appointed second assistant to the examiner at India House and
given an annual salary of £800. All of this helps to explain the preoccupation
with financial security reflected in some of the future decisions that James
Mill would make on behalf of his son.

Mention should be made here of Francis Place and the importance of
his presence beyond that of generosity. Place was a member of the working
class, a self-educated and successful tailor with a thriving shop at Charing
Cross. He became a leader and spokesperson for laborers and provided a
free library at the rear of his shop for all those interested in reform. Place
also organized worker's cooperatives, a key policy that Mill was to advocate
in his economic writings. James Mill's friendship with Place and the belief
that through education workers could rise to the status of autonomous

and responsible citizens became a model for Mill's own later relationship with leaders of the working class.

James Mill had a highly developed theory of education. He published his views in 1818 in the supplement to the fifth edition of the *Encyclopaedia Britannica*. His theory of education is based upon the epistemology he had acquired from his reading of Locke and Hartley. The mind at birth is a blank tablet upon which experience writes. All ideas thus originate from external stimuli. Knowledge consists of ideas and the sequence of ideas. The sequence of ideas is the result of the association of ideas (Hartley's view). Once the teacher knows the sequence, he can use this information to condition the pupil in such a way that beneficial sequences occur. A sequence is beneficial if it contributes, first, to the happiness of the individual, and then to the happiness of society. The ultimate goal of education is to render "the human mind to the greatest possible degree the cause of human happiness."[46] What this meant to James Mill was that the "keystone of the arch" of the system was political education, that is, education for social reform.[47] This is all the more reason why James Mill thought it important that the educator protect the pupil from "the influence of a vicious and ignorant society."[48] He believed that this process should commence as early as possible and that it should be reinforced constantly through the vigilance of the educator. Finally, he advocated that education became more economical to the extent that students taught each other. James Mill tried to institutionalize some of these ideas in various educational projects undertaken along with Bentham, Francis Place, and Joseph Lancaster.[49] One such project was a secular for-profit system of elementary education. None of these ambitions flourished, and all were soon abandoned.

One element in James Mill's views on education deserves special mention – the view that control of the student's environment is crucial for avoiding the corruption of the world. This is not a reflection of Hartlean associationism but shows instead two other influences, one classic and one modern. The classic influence goes back to James Mill's reading of the great Romans, some of whom, such as Cato, had educated their own sons. The modern influence was Rousseau's *Emile*, a work with which James Mill was familiar. To this end, James Mill carefully controlled Mill's environment in order to avoid contamination. He was not permitted to have playmates of his own age, or to have playmates at all from outside his family. He worked always in the same room under the watchful eye of his father.

All of these views were put into practice in Mill's case, including requiring John to educate his younger siblings. What deserves special mention about this process is the title of the third section of James Mill's article: "Happiness, the End to which Education is devoted. – Wherein it consists, not yet determined."[50] These were to prove to be prophetic words in the education of Mill.

Mill's precociousness aside, there are a number of remarkable features about his education. First, although James Mill had become an agnostic, he never abandoned his puritan conscience. Mill was certainly inculcated with the gospel of work and self-reliance. Deprived of much acquaintance with religious practice or with religion in any sense except as a set of intellectual positions, Mill inherited from his father a contempt for natural theology, an abhorrence of the Calvinist notion of an avenging God, and the belief that traditional religion's reliance upon such a God perverted morals. Mill presented an elaborate summary of his father's religious beliefs, worth noting because they are also part of Mill's beliefs as well as the basis for his religious speculation at the end of his life. James Mill, following the rigorous empiricism of the French Enlightenment, denied the intelligibility both of miracles and of revelation and concluded that nothing could be known "concerning the origin of things."[51] Hence, natural theology was as useless as revelation. But precisely because nothing could be known intelligibly concerning origins, dogmatic atheism was as unjustified as theism. More interestingly, the Calvinistic notion of an avenging God to whom obeisance was due was considered to be inconsistent with true virtue and the fundamental dignity of a moral agent, an example of the incoherence at the heart of Christianity. A further incoherence, for James Mill, was the existence of evil on the part of an allegedly omnipotent God. The irony of these apparent inconsistencies is that they did not seem to have much effect on morality. Christianity remained a set of irrelevant and meaningless doctrines and practices with no ennobling effect on moral life. The only religious position to which James Mill gave any credence was Manicheanism, in which good and evil are "struggling against each other for the government of the universe."[52]

Mill described James Mill's character as stoical, but it could just as easily be described as Calvinist without theology.

My father's moral convictions, wholly dissevered from religion, were very much of the character of the Greek philosophers. . . . he had . . . scarcely any belief in pleasure. . . . He was not insensible to pleasures; but he deemed very few of them worth the price which, at least in the present state of society, must be paid for them. The greater number of miscarriages in life, he considered to be attributable to the overvaluing of pleasures. . . . He thought human life a poor thing at best, after the freshness of youth and of unsatisfied curiosity had gone by. . . . He never varied in rating intellectual enjoyments above all others. . . . For passionate emotions of all sorts, and for everything which had been said or written in exaltation of them, he professed the greatest contempt. He regarded them as a form of madness.[53]

In addition, Mill was exposed at an early age to Bentham's work *Not Paul but Jesus*, a book in which Bentham argued that Paul had perverted the teachings of Jesus as represented in the Gospels and institutionalized them in a clerical manner at odds with the original teachings. The Kantian argument that God is a necessary presupposition of morality never received consideration or mention. Along with the absence of a religious consciousness,[54] came the absence of the notion that there were substantive truths in literature or that literature was a source of insight into the human condition. Any truth about the human condition was the domain of a social science modeled after physical science. Bentham is infamous for having asserted that "the game of pushpin is of equal value with the arts and sciences of music and poetry";[55] he also maintained, somewhat in jest, that "*Prose* is where all the lines but the last go on to the margin – poetry is where some of them fall short of it."[56] All of Mill's readings among the modern authors constituted a textbook presentation of the views leading up to and expressing the Enlightenment Project of the French *philosophes*. That project assumed that physical science told us the ultimate truths about the universe, that there could be a social science modeled after physical science, that it was possible to define and explain the human predicament solely through science, and, finally, that we could achieve mastery over the human predicament through social technology. No contemporary critic of those views appears on the list. Mill's reading of Roman history and the French Revolution encouraged the conception of himself as a champion of "democracy," or at least of eliminating class differences. Finally, the classical authors were read either to enhance appreciation of the Socratic dialectic or to inculcate the Stoic notion of a duty to support the common good.

We are left with the question of what sort of person Mill was at the age of thirteen. His protégé and biographer Bain, who also knew and wrote about the father, believed that in the case of Mill's education,

the application was excessive. . . . This health suffered, we have ample evidence.
. . . his mental progress might have been as great with a smaller strain on his
powers. . . . I cannot help thinking that the rapid and unbroken transitions from
one study to another must have been unfavourable to a due impression on the
memory. . . . What his reading of Thucydides could be at eight, we may dimly
imagine; it could be nothing but an exercise in the Greek language. . . . It is apparent enough that his vast early reading was too rapid, and, as a consequence
superficial.[57]

Even in later life, "There was one thing he never would allow, which was
that work could be pushed to the point of being injurious to either body
or mind."[58]

His claim that his natural intellectual gifts were no more than average cannot be taken literally, although Mill does not mention his gift for
analysis on that list. It is clear that his father recognized his extraordinary intellectual promise and chose to lavish his attention and his dreams
on him among all of the children. Place recognized that "John is truly a
prodigy, a most wonderful fellow."[59] To some extent, Mill's remark may
indicate a rhetorical modesty; to some extent, it reflects a commitment to
the importance of early education; but it also reflects, in part, the world in
which Mill was raised. Bentham had been a child prodigy. Some of Mill's
near-contemporaries had also been prodigies – figures such as Macaulay,
who had written an historical work before the age of eight, and Tennyson,
who had written an epic poem at twelve. More than anything, it reflects
being raised in an almost exclusively adult world of towering intellects.

Mill did not believe himself to have an overpowering intellect. He could
not, as his father did, bully and browbeat others into accepting his views.
What Mill did possess and develop was a consummate skill in presenting,
dissecting, advocating, and critiquing any position. However, this ability
did not lead to automatic acceptance of the positions that Mill advocated.
Quite the contrary, Mill encountered the resentment of those whose positions he attacked. Mill was not a creative genius in either of the two
conventionally recognized forms – namely, in the arts or in the sciences
and mathematics. His technical contributions in philosophy, in logic, and
in economics were noteworthy but not groundbreaking. He was not a
great scholar in the sense that Grote and Austin and Macaulay were. His
prodigious reading made him realize how much had been said before, and

his honesty made him acknowledge how much he had borrowed from contemporaries such as Coleridge, Carlyle, Comte, Harriet Taylor, and Tocqueville. As Mill put it, "the greatest part of mental growth consisted in the assimilation of those truths, and the most valuable part of my intellectual work was in building the bridges and clearing the paths which connected them with my general system of thought."[60] One is left wondering to what extent originality is overrated.

Mill was extraordinary in two special ways. First, he recognized as his special skill the ability to identify and restate issues and arguments with exemplary clarity, simplicity, and rhetorical force. Bain puts it this way:

If I were to compare him in his fifteenth year with the most intellectual youth that I have ever known, or heard or read of, I should say that his attainments on the whole are not unparalleled, although, I admit, very rare.... Where Mill was most markedly in advance of his years, was Logic. It was not merely that he had read treatises on the Formal Logic ... but that he was able to chop Logic with his father in regard to the foundations and demonstrations of Geometry. I have never known a similar case of precocity.... his father ... could and did teach effectually ... Logic; the others [subjects] were Political Economy, Historical Philosophy and Politics. ... On these, John was a truly precocious youth; his innate aptitudes, which must have been great, received the utmost stimulation that it was possible to apply.[61]

Second, Mill possessed a kind of genius that had no analogue prior to the development of historical imagination in the late eighteenth and early nineteenth centuries, and that therefore was only dimly recognized by himself and his contemporaries. What Mill, like Hegel and even to some extent Marx, could do was to synthesize all of the major intellectual and cultural factors of his time into a coherent narrative. The great philosophers have always achieved a comprehensive view; what the great nineteenth-century philosophers had to achieve was a comprehensive view that recognized the historical and dynamic dimensions of such a view. Mill's *Autobiography* is in large part the story of his constructing such a comprehensive view.

There are, however, issues of character that go beyond the state of one's intellect. James Mill had a strict policy on whom he would invite to be a guest in his home. He refused to invite those "whom he could not, as he said, make as comfortable as they were at home."[62] This reflected in part the limitations of James Mill's income. It also reflected his desire to entertain those who shared his unorthodox views. Mill listened in on these conversations, and later interacted with these adults.

[Some of these adults] as I have since found thought me greatly and disagreeably self-conceited; probably because I was disputatious, and did not scruple to give direct contradictions to things which I heard said. I suppose I acquired this bad habit from having been encouraged in an unusual degree to talk on matters beyond my age, and with grown persons, while I never had inculcated in me the usual respect for them. My father did not correct this ill-breeding and impertinence, probably from not being aware of it, for I was always too much in awe of him to be otherwise than extremely subdued and quiet in his presence.[63]

Mill may have been browbeaten into obsequiousness where his father was concerned, but this obviously did not extend to other adults.

What does emerge is the picture of a precocious adolescent and young man wholly dependent emotionally, intellectually, and morally upon his father. In one respect this was fortuitous, in the sense that James Mill was a powerful intellect, a man of prodigious energy, incorruptible character, and dedication to a great cause. Mill was clearly a beneficiary of all this. On the other hand, James Mill's view of the world seems to have been dominated by the left hemisphere of his brain, by which we mean that he seems not to have recognized the more imaginative and poetic dimensions of life. In her memoir on her husband entitled *Personal Life of Grote*, Mrs. Grote described James Mill as regarding "the cultivation of individual affections and sympathies as destructive of lofty aims, and indubitably hurtful to the mental character."[64] To be sure, he was dedicated, but he was dedicated to the point of being overbearing. "James Mill . . . is the prototype of the Utilitarian character, almost to the point of caricature: self-made, manly, independent, rationally controlled (especially in the areas of sex and work), not giving way to feelings of any kind (especially of love). . . . "[65] Even Bentham had some critical remarks about James Mill's character, describing him as someone who "expects to subdue everybody by his positiveness. His manner of speaking is oppressive and overbearing."[66]

Mill was aware of this dimension of his father's character, but he chose to put it in a positive light:

[H]e [James Mill], in a degree once common, but now very unusual, threw his feelings into his opinions. . . . None but those who do not care about opinions will confound it with intolerance. Those, who having opinions which they hold to be immensely important, and their contraries to be prodigiously hurtful, have any deep regard for the general good, will necessarily dislike, as a class and in the abstract, those who they think wrong what they think right, and right what they think wrong: though they need not therefore be, nor was my father, insensible to the good qualities in an opponent, nor governed in their estimation of individuals by one general presumption, instead of by the whole of their character. I grant that an earnest person, being no more infallible than other men, is liable to dislike people on account of opinions which do not merit dislike; but if he neither himself does them any ill office, nor connives at its being done by others, he is not intolerant; and the forbearance which flows from a conscientious sense of the importance to mankind of the equal freedom of all opinions, is the only tolerance which is commendable, or, to the highest moral order of minds, possible.[67]

What concerned Mill at the time he wrote this – in the 1850s, while he was planning *On Liberty* – was the lack of deep and informed moral conviction, as opposed to sentiment, and the failure to appreciate the moral as well as the intellectual need for freedom of thought and discussion. In the end, what Mill, following his father, stood for was the forthright presentation of deeply held and considered opinions. What he opposed was indoctrination, intimidation, and indifference.

Mill was subjected to constant correction on the part of his father, inculcated with the constant necessity for self-criticism. James Mill was a committed believer in the power of the environment, and, as a consequence, Mill himself attributed all of his positive achievements to that influence. As Mill sadly put it in the part of his *Autobiography* that he suppressed:

[There was] another evil I shared with many of the sons of energetic fathers. To have been through childhood, under the constant rule of a strong will, certainly is not favourable to strength of will. I was so much accustomed to expect to be told what to do, either in the form of a direct command or of rebuke for not doing it, that I acquired a habit of leaving my responsibility as a moral agent to rest on my father, my conscience never speaking to me except by his voice. The things I ought *not* to do were mostly provided for by his precepts, rigorously enforced whenever violated, but the things which I *ought* to do I hardly ever did of my own mere motion, but waited till he told me to do them; and if he forbore or forgot to tell me, they were generally left undone. I thus acquired a habit of backwardness, of waiting to follow the lead of others, an absence of moral spontaneity, an inactivity of the moral sense and even to a large extent of the intellect, unless roused by the appeal of someone else, – for which a large abatement must be made from the benefits, either moral or intellectual, which flowed from any other part of my education.[68]

One qualification is worth noting. Recalling the extent to which his father's scheme of education was more theory than practice, we note the effort on the part of James Mill to build a strong character in Mill. "He was fond of putting into my hands books which exhibited men of energy and resource in unusual circumstances, struggling against difficulties and overcoming them...."[69]

Love Affair with the Continent

Mill was originally invited in 1820 to spend six months with the family of Sir Samuel Bentham, brother of Jeremy, in their chateau near Toulouse, France. James Mill was somewhat reluctant to send him, but his responsibilities at India House made it difficult for him to spend much time on his son's education. The invitation was accepted, and the visit eventually lasted a full year. On the journey there, Mill stopped in Paris and met, through his father's introduction, the eminent French laissez-faire economist and follower of Ricardo, Jean Baptiste Say. Mill stayed for over a week with the Say family, visiting the Palais Royal, which he described in his diary as an "immense building belonging to the profligate Duc d'Orleans, who, having ruined himself with debauchery, resolved to let the arcades of his palace to various tradesmen." While in Paris, he even claims to have spotted Saint-Simon, someone who would influence, both directly and indirectly, a great deal of his later thinking. A planned visit with the eminent French mathematician and scientist Laplace did not materialize.

While with the Benthams, Mill felt like a member of the family, and he was especially impressed by Mrs. Samuel Bentham, the daughter of the eminent chemist Dr. Fordyce. Mill describes her as "a woman of strong will and decided character, much general knowledge, and great practical good sense.... she was the ruling spirit of the household, as she deserved, and was well qualified, to be."[70] This was a very different image of a wife and mother from the one with which he was familiar. It was an image not incompatible with Sir Samuel Bentham's personal achievements. It was this sort of image that left a lasting impression on Mill and foreshadowed the kind of woman for whom he would search, someone to be the ruling spirit of his household.

The Benthams had an older son who later became a famous botanist. The Benthams also took Mill on a tour of the Pyrennees Mountains. From that day forward, hiking in the mountains became Mill's favorite form of relaxation and amateur botany his hobby.[71] Even the choice of botany as a hobby reflects certain features of Mill's personality. It was a hobby in which one collected and classified plants, so in the end it was a sort of "working" hobby, in which Mill learned something about science, engaged in an activity that was systematic, and was allowed to exercise his analytical bent. Like many adolescents, Mill found that natural beauty awakened his dormant aesthetic sense. "This first introduction to the highest order of mountain scenery made the deepest impression on me, and gave a colour to my tastes through life."[72]

The Benthams tried their best to drag John away from his books and to make him a facile man of the world. Writing to James Mill, Lady Bentham remarks that "we trust that you will have satisfaction from that part of his education we are giving him to fit him for commerce with the world at large."[73] He was required to take lessons not only in French but also in singing, the piano, fencing, riding, and even dancing. The lessons in all but French and the piano were to no avail. For the rest of his life, Mill was fluent in French, although he spoke it with an English accent. In a journal that John kept for his father, he recorded the following on July 21, 1820:

My time is now divided as follows – I rise at 5, to the river till 8 [swimming], French lesson till 9½, breakfast till 10, solfeges till 10½, from 10½ till 2 my French exercises, Greek Latin mathematics, logic and political economy, i.e. as many of the latter as possible, from 2 till 4 music lesson and practice at Mme. Boulet's, from 4 till 5 dinner, riding till 6, fencing till 7, dancing till 8 ½, tea till 9. . . . wrote parts of a dialogue on benefit of large estates to commerce (assigned by Lady B).

Lady Bentham also had Mill read the Code Napoleon. What is clear from this period is that Mill delighted in reading and writing above all else, that these were not simply tasks imposed upon him by his father. For the rest of his life, these were the activities that gratified him, that made him feel secure and successful, that served as a refuge from the world when he needed it. What Mill did not express in any of his letters to his father was any loneliness or any thought that he missed being home. This trip was also the occasion of Mill's first real friendship with someone his own age (Antoine Ballard, who later became a chemist and who discovered bromine). As he later described it to Comte, "It was also there that for the first time I found a friend, that is to say a friend of my own choice, as opposed to those given me by family ties."[74]

Mill singles out two important elements of his experience: the importance of expressing feelings and the deleterious effect on morals of the habitual English coldness and reserve. In England, he said, society had a "low moral tone" for "conduct is of course always directed towards low and petty objects." There is a "general abstinence . . . from professing any high principles of action at all." The result is an English culture in which there is "the habit of not speaking to others, nor much even to themselves, about the things in which they do feel interest, [and this] causes both their feelings and their intellectual faculties to remain undeveloped, or to develop themselves only in some single and very limited direction; reducing them, considered as spiritual beings, to a kind of negative existence." Mill then contrasts the English to the French,

among whom sentiments, which by comparison at least may be called elevated, are the current coin of human intercourse, both in books and in private life; and though often evaporating in profession, are yet kept alive in the nation at large by constant exercise, and stimulated by sympathy, so as to form a living and active part of the existence of great numbers of persons, and to be recognized and understood by all. Neither could I then appreciate the general culture of the understanding which results from the habitual exercise of the feelings. . . . I even then felt, though without stating it clearly to myself, the contrast between the frank amiability of French personal intercourse, and the English mode of existence in which everybody acts as if everybody else (with few, or no exceptions) was either an enemy or a bore.[75]

Mill does mention taking some courses at the university at Montpellier, but the intellectual growth he experienced during this period had a different source.

But the greatest, perhaps, of the many advantages which I owed to this episode in my education, was that of having breathed for a whole year, the free and genial atmosphere of Continental life. . . . The chief fruit which I carried away from the society I saw, was a strong and permanent interest in Continental liberalism . . . keeping me free from the error always prevalent in England, and from which even my father with all his superiority to prejudice was not exempt, of judging universal questions by a merely English standard.[76]

On one level, Mill is making an oft-repeated observation about the insularity of the English. As late as the 1870s, a headline appeared in the *Times* of London informing its readers that a fog had descended on the Channel and as a result the continent was cut off!

In a more traditional vein, Mill is engaged in a practice that goes as far back as Herodotus and is famously exemplified in Montesquieu's *Persian Letters* and in the works of many later writers – that is, he is using his exposure to a different culture to engage in a constructive critique of his native culture. By the time he was writing his *Autobiography* in the 1850s, Mill had become the conscience of Victorian England. Mill's critique of the moral core of Victorian England is best expressed in the essays he wrote during the 1830s, which we shall discuss in a later chapter. It seems that from an early age he had adopted a Socratic pose with regard to his relationship with his own countrymen. Very much like his younger contemporary Matthew Arnold (1822–1888), Mill would call attention to the cultural impoverishment of Protestant England. Mill's later critique of the British class system is echoed in Arnold's criticisms of the aristocracy ("Barbarians" with correct manners but an obtuseness with regard to ideas), the middle class especially ("Philistines," who were religious nonconformists and hard workers), and the working class (the "Populace," who were blind to the great issues).[77]

On a more significant intellectual level, Mill is calling attention to the two main traditions of thought that had developed since the end of the eighteenth century. With some notable exceptions, the Enlightenment emphasis on science and reductive materialism had prevailed in English-speaking countries; the Romantic movement, with its humanistic emphasis, has prevailed upon the continent. In his later essays on Bentham and Coleridge, whom Mill will identify as the great seminal minds of the age, Mill will remind us that Coleridge is the English bearer of the continental tradition, and especially of German Romanticism. Mill will set for himself the task of synthesizing these two great traditions of thought, attempting to bridge an intellectual gap that many think prevails to this very day. More specifically, Mill will argue that modern liberal culture, as best exemplified in England, cannot be adequately explained and defended except with the resources of Romantic continental thought.

A more specific interest lies in the evolution of French politics. The French Revolution of 1789 had momentous symbolic significance for liberals everywhere. It became the symbol of the overthrow of feudalism and the dawn of a new day of freedom. Liberals as well as conservatives in Britain were later horrified by the excesses of the revolution, but the destruction of feudal privilege was looked upon as a necessary prerequisite for the development of a truly free and responsible society. This was especially important in Britain, where aristocratic privilege and dominance lasted through the whole of the nineteenth century. Liberals, including Mill, continued to look at France as the great experiment in democracy. Mill himself did not permanently change his focus from France to the United States until after 1849, and in this a French thinker, Tocqueville, had already paved the way.

Mill gained a fluency in French that made him a leading British authority on French life and politics. He always felt comfortable in France and spent a good deal of vacation time there. As he would express it in a letter to Harriet in 1854, "any place in France if it be ever so far off seems so much a home to us."[78] He and Harriet had hoped to retire to France, and both of them are buried in Avignon.

Father and Son

Despite the extraordinary amount of speculation to which Mill's early life naturally gives rise, I am inclined to think that he is his own best storyteller. Mill was obviously precocious. If he appears overly modest about his quick-wittedness, memory, and energy level, this can be attributed, as he himself pointed out, to his judging himself by unrealistically high standards. That he is perhaps overoptimistic about the potential of the average student does not invalidate his claim that such students could accomplish a good deal more if more were legitimately demanded of them. Bear in mind that the first stated purpose of Mill's *Autobiography* was to make available "some record of an education which was unusual and remarkable, and which, whatever else it may have done, has proved how much more than is commonly supposed may be taught, and well taught, in those early years which, in the common modes of what is called instruction, are little better than wasted."[79]

Mill's relationship to his father must be assessed in two dimensions, intellectually and personally. The parallels between the careers and writing projects of the two are remarkable, and Mill spent a great deal of time revising his father's views. Psychoanalysis aside, the relationship between fathers and sons remained an especially important issue in the nineteenth century. The locus of conflict can be understood in a broader cultural context. It became clear by the mid nineteenth century that within liberal culture the function of parents was to promote autonomous individuality in their children, an autonomy that encouraged the child eventually to choose his or her own career, spouse, and place of abode. In important respects, James Mill did encourage some elements of this state of mind. At the same time, James Mill's drive to control all of those around him, his somewhat old-fashioned desire to produce an heir who would be an extension of his own life, and his eighteenth-century conception of education as a form of conditioning were at odds with the cultivation of autonomy in one's children. Mill lived through this painful transition on his way to becoming the chief exponent of the autonomy and sense of personal responsibility inherent in liberal culture. Mill's *Autobiography* is a witness to the struggle between these opposed conceptions of the relationship between parents and children.

What would have been the fate of this precocious young man if he had not had the guidance of James Mill and had gone to the university? At best, he would most likely have become an outstanding scholar – perhaps of ancient Greece, like his acquaintance Grote, or perhaps of the law, like another of his teachers and friends, John Austin. But, alas, he couldn't have gone to the university and become a scholar at Oxford or Cambridge University, since he would not have taken Anglican orders. And like his father, he probably would have refused a Scottish university post. He could not have pursued a life of public service, for again he would have had to take the religious oath. What he could not have received was an introduction to the fundamental philosophical, moral, social, economic, and religious issues of his day. Most of those subjects, such as classical economics, simply did not exist as recognized academic disciplines and certainly were not taught. Nor, more importantly, was any synthesis, grand narrative, or coherent cultural narrative provided, other than that of Anglican orthodoxy. Despite the extraordinary achievements of all of the great British intellectuals of the nineteenth century, none of them, with the exception of the Philosophic Radicals, offered an alternative grand new synthesis. Neither could Mill have been initiated into the world of Philosophic Radicalism and come to the realization that the transformation of Britain from feudal agrarianism to modern industrial capitalism required a serious rethinking of all the major institutions if he had not grown up in the world of Bentham, James Mill, Place, and Ricardo. Even if, in the end, Mill realized the deficiencies of the Philosophic Radicals' grand narrative and saw the need to create a new one using resources unavailable to them, it is highly unlikely that he could have done so if he had not been the son of James Mill and had not experienced, in the most intense and personal manner, the strengths and weaknesses of that narrative. After all, it was a cardinal point in his father's theory of education never to permit "anything which I learnt to degenerate into a mere exercise of memory."[80] Despite the serious deficiencies of James Mill's vision, deficiencies of which Mill was both aware and records for us in the most authoritative manner – and which he strove mightily, as we shall see, to overcome – it is still the case that Mill could not be seen in retrospect as arguably the greatest British mind of the nineteenth century if he had not been the son of James Mill. In the most literal sense, Mill did owe it all to his father.

Company Man and Youthful Propagandist (1821–1826)

Career Path: India House[1]

URING THE WINTER of 1821–22, some consideration was given to possible career choices. Mill describes the scene as follows: "My father, notwithstanding his abhorrence of the chaos and barbarism called English Law, had turned his thoughts towards the bar as on the whole less ineligible for me than any other profession."[2] What is clear from this description is that it was James Mill who was to decide on Mill's career. What is also clear is that the choice was a problematic one. The desirable career, from the point of view of both father and son, was a career in Parliament, but religious principles eliminated that possibility. An academic career would also involve a public commitment to religious principles that neither father nor son held. As late as 1839, Mill would decline offers of academic positions. A career in journalism was a natural choice, but it was rejected for two reasons: first, the Mills had already had enough experience with the financial strain of living by one's pen; second, financial pressures forced most journalists to sacrifice their integrity. A professional career of some kind seemed the most likely prospect. Given Mill's lack of manual dexterity, medicine would not have been a fortunate choice. That left the study of law as the least of the evils.

What reconciled the Mills for a time was a new neighbor at Queens Square, John Austin. During 1821, Mill read Blackstone and Roman law with Austin for several hours a day.[3] John Austin (1790–1859) was a barrister and later professor of jurisprudence at London University until 1832, when he published *The Province of Jurisprudence Determined*. Based on Bentham's views, the book became the most authoritative exposition of legal positivism, that is, the attempt to describe law and legal systems from a purely social scientific perspective. Austin, unlike Bentham, combined utilitarianism with a belief in a Unitarian deity. For Austin, divine law was the ultimate test of the merit of positive law.[4] Mill described this as having "made Bentham's best ideas his own."[5]

Austin married Sarah Taylor, a member of a prominent Unitarian family related to the Martineaus. Sarah Austin tried all of her life, but without success, to help John Austin overcome his debilitating perfectionism. Sarah supported the family by teaching and translating German, and ran a salon in order to give her husband's ideas greater exposure. Beginning in 1826, the Austin's were to spend a great deal of time on the continent, specifically in Germany and France, where they became acquainted with and transmitted Romanticism to Mill. Sarah later was to teach German to Mill. The relationship developed into a special fondness, with Mill referring to her as "Mutterlein." Sarah was another source for Mill's advocacy of women's equality.[6]

Over the next decade, John Austin exercised an enormous influence on Mill, who was deeply impressed by his high-mindedness and saddened by the fact that "the strength of will of which his manner seemed to give such strong assurance, expended itself principally in manner. . . . he hardly ever completed any intellectual task of magnitude."[7]

In the autumn of 1822, Mill visited the Austins in Norwich. It was there that Mill lost a watch given to him by his father. In a manner typical of their relationship, Mill wrote the following letter to his father:

I must inform you that I have lost my watch. It was lost while I was out of doors, but it is impossible that it should have been stolen from my pocket. It must therefore be my own fault. The loss itself (though I am conscious that I must remain without a watch till I can buy one for myself) is to me not great and much less so than my carelessness deserves. It must, however, vex you, and deservedly, from the bad sign which it affords of me.[8]

For anyone else, this would be a typical and trivial childhood experience. But on Mill it had a lasting effect. When his father died fourteen years later, Mill was bequeathed the watch his father had been given by Ricardo. Mill promptly insisted that the watch be given to his brother Henry, for whom it could not possibly have had the kind of association with Ricardo that it would have had for Mill.

In 1822, Mill visited Charles Austin, the younger brother of John Austin, at Cambridge. Through the auspices of Charles Austin, Mill was introduced to the Union Debating Society at Cambridge. That this sixteen-year-old with a thin voice could hold his own in conversation duly impressed the undergraduates.

The year 1823 was to be a decisive one in Mill's life. David Ricardo died in September of that year, and the flirtation with a legal career came to an abrupt end on May 21, 1823, when James Mill obtained for his son an appointment to the East India Company one day after Mill's seventeenth birthday. At the time, James Mill was still receiving letters from a professor at Cambridge encouraging him to enroll Mill there. But it was not to be. As Mill described it, his professional occupation and status for the next thirty-five years of his life were decided by his father, under whose direct supervision Mill was to work for thirteen of those years in the office of the examiner of India correspondence. At the time of his appointment, it was understood that he would receive a gratuity of £30 for the first three years; after that, he was to receive a salary of £100 with increments of £10 a year, and was to be in line for the first available senior vacancy.[9]

According to the ordinary course of things in those days, the newly appointed junior would have nothing to do, except a little abstracting, indexing, and searching, or pretending to search, into records; but young Mill was almost immediately set to indite dispatches to the governments of the three Indian Presidencies . . . [on] "political" subjects – subjects, that is, for the most part growing out of the relations of the said governments with "native" states or foreign potentates. This continued to be his business to the last.[10]

It is worth noting that the company had lost its monopoly of trade with India in 1813 and that by the Charter Act of 1833 it would be relieved of its commercial activity. Its principal responsibility became administrative, the governance of India. In 1828, it took six months for a letter to travel from Bombay to London; by 1852, the travel time would be cut to two months. One remarkable fact worth noting is that neither Mill nor his father ever set foot in India!

For Mill, the disappointing aspect of this decision was reconciling himself to not having a career in Parliament and having to live in London. Mill solved the latter problem by taking long walks in the country on Sunday and holidays. The hoped-for parliamentary career would have to be surrendered, or at least postponed. Frankly, a career in Parliament was not feasible in any case, but accepting a position with the East India Company gave this a kind of finality.

It was not simply political ambition that drove Mill. What he wanted was to be an expositor of the fundamental values of his culture and to occupy a position of intellectual leadership. In nineteenth-century Britain, there were but two ways of doing this – a career in Parliament or a career in journalism. The Anglican clergy no longer occupied this position, and, in any case, Mill's religious convictions made such a career path impossible. Largely owing to its ecclesiastical orientation, the university had not yet emerged as a repository of social critique. Mill had also learned from his father's experience the difficulty of surviving financially as a journalist with unorthodox views.

Writing for the press, cannot be recommended as a permanent resource to any one qualified to accomplish anything in the higher departments of literature or thought: not only on account of the uncertainty of this means of livelihood, especially if the writer has a conscience, and will not consent to serve any opinions except his own; but also because the writings by which one can live, are not the writings which themselves live, and are never those in which the writer does his best. Books destined to form future thinkers take too much time to write, and when written come, in general, too slowly into notice and repute, to be relied on for subsistence. Those who have to support themselves by their pen must depend on literary drudgery....[11]

The positive side of the chosen career track was the amount of time it left free for the higher journalism and for the exercise of Mill's aspiration for intellectual leadership. As he expressed it in a passage that Harriet had him omit from the *Autobiography*, employment at India House "precluded all uneasiness about the means of subsistence, they occupied fewer hours of the day than almost any business or profession, they had nothing in them to produce anxiety, or to keep the mind intent on them at any time but when directly engaged in them."[12] Mill was able to divide his day between serving the East India Company and focusing on his writing. At times, he even found his office work a welcome relief from his writing that allowed him to return to the latter refreshed. Mill's office at India House, situated on Leadenhall Street in the City, was on the third floor. Its three windows faced a brick courtyard. He arrived at his office at ten in the morning, wearing a black suit with necktie, later substituting a more comfortable coat known as a surtout. It was in his office that he ate a breakfast consisting of a boiled egg, bread and butter, and tea. He did not eat or drink again until dinner at six in the evening. He read dispatches while eating his breakfast. The remainder of the morning was spent reading and writing at a high desk, where he either stood or sat on a tall stool. He was able to complete his responsibilities for India House by one or two in the afternoon at the latest. The rest of the day was spent either conversing with colleagues and visitors or attending to his own voluminous writings and correspondence. From 1824 until 1858, the dispatches written in his hand constitute a quarto volume of close to four hundred pages.[13]

The man who was to become his editorial assistant and protégé after their meeting in 1842, Alexander Bain, called on Mill at least twice a week at four in the afternoon and often accompanied him on his walk back to Mill's mother's house, where Mill later resided in Kensington Square. Bain described how Mill greeted him some years later:

His tall slim figure, his youthful face and bald head, fair hair and ruddy complexion, and the twitching of his eyebrow when he spoke, first arrested the attention: then the vivacity of his manner, his thin voice approaching to sharpness, but with nothing shrill or painful about it, his comely features and sweet expression – would have remained in my memory though I had never seen him again.[14]

Later in life, Mill came to realize that working for the East India Company had provided an unexpected benefit. As other nineteenth-century writers were beginning to realize, the Industrial Revolution meant an increasingly bureaucratized world, in both the public and private sectors. Mill was to become an acute observer and critic of that bureaucratization. "It gave me opportunities of perceiving when public measures, and other political facts, did not produce the effects which had been expected of them, and from what causes; above all, it was valuable to me by making me, in this portion of my activity, merely one wheel in a machine, the whole of which had to work together."[15] Mill's writings on public policy were never the product of ivory tower speculation. They were always informed by years of work within a quasi-public corporation.

Proselytizer for Radicalism

When Mill began his studies with Austin in 1821, his father also had him read Dumont's edition of Bentham's *Traité de Législation*. In combination

with Austin's tutoring in jurisprudence, this work proved to be a revelation
to Mill.

My previous education had been, in a certain sense, already a course in
Benthamism. . . . Yet in the first pages of Bentham it burst upon me with all
the force of novelty. . . . The feeling rushed upon me, that all previous moralists
were superseded, and that here indeed was the commencement of a new era in
thought. . . . there seemed to be added to this intellectual clearness, the most inspir-
ing prospects of practical improvements in human affairs. . . . When I laid down the
last volume of the Traité, I had become a different being. The 'principle of utility'
understood as Bentham understood it . . . fell exactly into its place as the keystone which held together the detached and fragmentary component parts of my
knowledge and beliefs. It gave unity to my conception of things. *I now had opinions;
a creed, a doctrine, a philosophy: in one among the best senses of the word, a religion*: the
inculcation and diffusion of which could be made the principle outward purpose
of a life. And I had a grand conception laid before me of changes to be effected
in the condition of mankind through that doctrine. . . . the vista of improvement
which he did open was sufficiently large and brilliant to light up my life, as well
as to give a definite shape to my aspirations.[16] [italics added]

What was it in Bentham that Mill found so convincing? Bentham was
a psychological egoist, maintaining that all human beings were driven
by the twin desires of maximizing pleasure and minimizing pain. These
desires were guided by beliefs about what caused pleasure and pain. At
the most primitive level, the connection between an external cause and
the internal pleasure or pain was direct and immediate, as in touching
something hot and feeling pain. As a consequence, most individuals tended
to respond only to immediate and short-term stimuli. Truly enlightened
self-interest required knowledge of long-term stimuli. Building upon the
work of Locke, Condillac, Helvétius, and Hartley as amended by James
Mill, one could construct an educational system in which the principles
of association would induce consideration of long-term stimuli. Among
the long-term stimuli, the most important was recognition of the need
for social cooperation in order to achieve a lasting and enlightened self-
interest. "Let every individual be so educated as to know his own interest.
Thus by the simultaneous action of a vast number of agents, everyone
drawing in the direction of his own happiness, the happiness of the whole
will be attained."[17]

To be a utilitarian was (1) to be a psychological egoist, that is, to
hold a specific view of basic human motivation; (2) to subscribe to the

principle that public policy should seek to achieve the greatest good for the greatest number, understood as the consistency and continuity of the individual good with the common good; and (3) to believe that the psychological theory of association accounted for how individuals could come to identify their interest with the common good. At this time, Mill, following Bentham, subscribed to all three. In later life, he would reject the first belief, subscribe only to the second, and modify the third.

What traditional Christianity had identified as human sinfulness in the form of self-assertion could now be overcome with education in true self-interest rather than by priestly craft. Rather than a repression of our basic drives, what we needed was an informed expansion of those drives. Mill was persuaded by the views of Thomas Malthus that the problems of industrialization were due to overpopulation. According to Malthus, the growth of the food supply could never keep up with the unchecked growth of population. The workers would produce more children and put them to work in order to maximize income; but more children would lead in time to an increase in the number of workers. This increase would put pressure on the total cost of subsistence wages and lead willy-nilly to either stagnation or tragedy. Such social consequences could be avoided through knowledge and foresight.

An incident occurred in 1823 that exemplifies Mill's conversion to this view. While on his way to work at India House, Mill routinely passed through St. James' Park. There he discovered one morning the body of a strangled newborn child. Thereafter, the horrified Mill and a friend were led to distribute a pamphlet written by Francis Place, entitled "To Married Working People." In it, Place had not only advocated contraception but explained the use of the "sponge" by French women. Human tragedy could seemingly be avoided through education.

As a consequence, Mill and his friend were arrested. Appearing before the lord mayor, they were sentenced to two weeks' imprisonment for distributing obscene literature. They were, however, released after two days when the lord mayor came to understand that their motive had been to prevent infanticide. Mill's family hoped that the incident would be forgotten. However, the lampoonist Thomas Moore soon satirized Mill:

> There are two Mr. M . . ls, whom those who like reading
> What's vastly unreadable, call very clever;
> And whereas M . . l senior makes war on *good* breeding,
> M . . l junior makes war on all *breeding* whatever.

This was an issue that his critics would never let him forget, and the verses would be reprinted in the *Times* obituary of Mill in 1873.

Imbued with these beliefs and in imitation of his father, who had recently founded the Political Economy Club, Mill organized a discussion group under the Benthamite aegis called the Utilitarian Society (1822–25). Bentham's influence remained strong through 1825, when Mill edited for publication Bentham's *Rationale of Judicial Evidence*. In explaining his use of the term "utilitarian,"[18] Mill specifically contrasts it with traditional Christianity. "I did not invent the word, but found it in one of John Galt's novels, the 'Annals of the Parish,' [1821] in which the Scotch clergyman, of whom the book is a supposed autobiography, is represented as warning his parishioners not to leave the Gospel and become utilitarians."[19]

One of the members of the society was Mill's new friend Charles Austin. It was through Charles Austin that Mill met the Whig historian Thomas Babington Macaulay and the diplomat Henry Bulwer Lytton and his brother, the novelist Edward Bulwer Lytton, among others. Mill later became estranged from Charles Austin, whom he blamed for bringing disrepute upon utilitarianism.

[H]e, on the contrary, presented the Benthamic doctrines in the most startling form of which they were susceptible, exaggerating everything in them which tended to consequences offensive to anyone's preconceived feelings. . . . much of the notion popularly entertained of the tenets and sentiments of what are called Benthamites or Utilitarians had its origin in paradoxes thrown out by Charles Austin.[20]

This critique of Charles Austin needs to be put into context. In anticipation of a point we shall later make at greater length, Mill's own relationship to utilitarianism evolved. Mill was in the beginning as enthusiastic a proselytizer as Charles Austin. In the next decade, he was himself to write the most devastating critique of Bentham, in an essay of that name. It was only much later, after Mill had redefined and qualified Bentham's utilitarianism, that he could look back at Austin and identify him as an extremist. Mill is here taking on the mantle of the true defender and keeper of the utilitarian faith as he had redefined it, but others, including Grote, would have demurred. Why Mill found it necessary to do this is something we shall have to discuss later.

In 1824, Mill met and befriended John Arthur Roebuck. Roebuck, who had come from Canada to read for the bar, was to become the leading radical voice in Parliament. Roebuck was introduced to Mill by his relative Thomas Love Peacock, who also held a position under James Mill at India House. Peacock described Mill to Roebuck as a "young friend of mine in this house, who belongs to a disquisitive set of young men."[21] Roebuck's impression of Mill at this time is quite interesting.

> Although possessed of much learning, and thoroughly acquainted with the state of the political world, [it was clear that Mill] was, as might have been expected, the mere exponent of other men's ideas, these men being his father and Bentham; and that he was utterly ignorant of what is called society; that of the world, as it worked around him, he knew nothing; and above all, of *woman* he was a child. He had never played with boys; in his life he had never known any, and we, in fact, who were now his associates, were the first companions he had ever mixed with.[22]

Mill, for his part, immediately recruited Roebuck for the Utilitarian Society.

Mill also met George Grote, the son of a Tory banker and an evangelical mother who was nevertheless attracted to the circle surrounding James Mill. Grote was to become a lifelong friend of Mill's, someone Mill admired because, although born into wealth, he combined a career in banking with serious scholarly writing and devotion to radical reform. In 1825, a new group began to meet in George Grote's house, where they discussed the central ideas behind the Philosophic Radical movement: James Mill's and Ricardo's economics, Hartley, and James Mill's *Analysis of the Human Mind*, as well as Hobbes and Whately on logic. Mrs. Grote encouraged the group as she had aspirations for being the center of a salon. The members, calling themselves the "Society of Students of Mental Philosophy," included Grote, Mill, Roebuck, William Ellice, William Henry Prescott, two Whitmore brothers, and George John Graham.[23] Each work was read and discussed carefully. In fact, the group proceeded by reading each paragraph aloud and then having each member comment on it, followed by general discussion. They did not move on until each point had been thoroughly exhausted.

Among the central ideas discussed was associationism, a concept suggested by Hume in his *Treatise of Human Nature* (1739). The doctrine of associationism was the view that elementary sensations, originating either from the physical environment or the body itself, were combined in the mind according to mechanical laws analogous to the law of gravity. But associationism did not become an all-encompassing doctrine until articulated by David Hartley in his *Observations on Man* (1749). What gives special significance to associationism is the additional thesis of intellectual hedonism, namely, that the sole basis of human response to environmental stimuli is the desire to maximize pleasure and minimize pain. The alleged basic truth about human psychology is that every individual is by nature governed by rational self-interest. This thesis is to be found in Helvétius, but it is more immediately to be found in Bentham's utilitarianism and in James Mill's *Analysis of the Human Mind* (1829), and it is a mainstay of classical political economy. Since human nature partakes of the natural harmony of the universe, *enlightened* self-interest implies that human beings can manage their own affairs without government interference. As the intellectual historian Randall put it:

[S]ensationalism, associationism, hedonism, and intellectualism were ostensibly the outcome of a mechanical analysis of human nature. Actually, they were dictated by the demands of the middle class for social change. They became the philosophic justification of nineteenth-century British Liberalism, its method of criticizing traditional institutions, by their consequences in individual pleasures and pains. They provided a "rational" basis for a society of laissez-faire and free competition, the trust in the reason of the common man.[24]

Mill's close friendship with John Arthur Roebuck and with another young man, George John Graham, did not go unnoticed by his father. Mill spent a great deal of both his social time and his intellectual life with these contemporaries. The three Johns became inseparable and were referred to affectionately as the "Trijackia." Fearing the influence they might have upon Mill, his father warned him about becoming too tied to them.

In the midst oft his busy professional and intellectual life, what did Mill do for relaxation? He, along with his father and other of his friends, used to ramble over the beautiful country near Croyden. Domestically, the Mills were still living together at Queen's Square, although by now they also had a weekend and summer cottage at Mickleham. Sometime during the summer of 1824, while Roebuck and Graham were weekend guests at Mickleham, Mill and his father quarreled over the friendships. Mill's mother was even heard to exclaim that "John was going to leave the house, all on account of Graham and Roebuck"; but the upshot was that Mill showed his independence by continuing the close friendships, although neither Roebuck nor Graham was ever invited to Mickleham again. Mill was beginning to exercise more personal autonomy.

In 1825, Mill and Roebuck found themselves debating the Owenites, espousers of an early utopian form of socialism. One of the important points that Mill makes about these debates is that the Owenites had the same objective as he, namely, improving the lot of the worker with an eye on the population problem.

It was a *lutte corps-à-corps* between Owenites and political economists, whom the Owenites regarded as their most inveterate opponents: but it was a perfectly friendly dispute. We who represented political economy, had the same objects in view as they had, and took pains to show it; and the principal champion on their side was a very estimable man, with whom I was well acquainted, Mr. William Thompson, of Cork, author of a book on the Distribution of Wealth, and of an "Appeal" in behalf of women against the passage relating to them in my father's Essay on Government.[25]

Out of this debate grew the idea of establishing the London Debating Society, designed to be the center of liberal intellectual debate in Britain, with Mill as its guiding spirit. Part of the inspiration for the emphasis on debate had been Mill's exposure to the Union Debating Society at Cambridge, through the auspices of Charles Austin. Mill's father approved greatly of this attempt to influence the leading lords of the next generation. It was initially attractive to the most liberal members of the Oxford and the Cambridge Unions, as well as to Macaulay, Samuel Wilberforce, the Bulwers, and many others. In the meantime, Mill participated in its debates a number of times, specifically attacking a (by now) customary litany of villains: the aristocracy, primogeniture, the universities, the British Constitution, and Irish landlords.

In all of this, it is clear that both Mills, despite being unable to participate directly, were seeking to influence Parliament. They soon turned their attention to that other avenue for the promotion of radicalism, journalism. At this time, there were two major political periodicals: *The Quarterly Review* (begun in 1809), which articulated Tory orthodoxy, and *The Edinburgh Review* (begun in 1802), which was the organ of Whig aristocratic entrepreneurs. A secondary Whig publication was the *Morning Chronicle*. In 1823, Mill began publishing articles in the *Chronicle*, whose new editor, John Black, was a disciple of his father's who had turned this traditional Whig publication into an organ of utilitarian radicalism.

James Mill founded a new political party, the Philosophic Radicals, and with Bentham's financial support launched the *Westminster Review* in 1823 as its organ in opposition to the Whig *Edinburgh Review* (although publication did not begin until January 1824). The Philosophic Radicals were clearly to the left of the Whigs. James Mill wrote the inaugural article for the *Westminster Review*, and in it he analyzed the English Constitution as defining representation only by reference to the landed aristocracy. James Mill specifically went after the Whigs. Mill, whose father had him read and scour all of the previous issues of the *Edinburgh Review*, carried out most of the research for this article. The question is, why? James Mill saw the future as resting with the middle class. The Whigs claimed to represent the middle class. But from his point of view, Whigs and Tories were merely rival aristocratic elites. He accused the Whigs of "coquetting with popular principles for the sake of popular support."

James Mill's most important publication, and one vital to understanding the evolution of the younger Mill's thinking, was the previously published "Essay on Government" (1820).[26] In this article, it is argued that the role of government is to provide the conditions for maximizing pleasure and minimizing pain.[27] Scarcity mandates that we must labor in order to maximize pleasure. Government, therefore, must be redesigned in order to achieve the equitable distribution of the "scanty materials of happiness."[28] The practical problem generated by this view is the potential abuse of governmental power. According to James Mill, hereditary monarchies are not an adequate solution, because they "are deprived of the strongest motives to labor" and are thereby less intelligent because our "intellectual powers are the offspring of labor."[29] He also goes on to reject the notion of checks and balances.[30] His reason is that two of the three powers (i.e., interest groups), monarchy and aristocracy, will combine against the third. Furthermore, since there will always be disparities of achievement and unequal bargaining power, misperception of interest is inevitable.

The way to prevent the abuse of government power is to create "an identity of interest with the community."[31] Extending the suffrage to adult males over forty who possess a modest amount of property can do this, he thinks. He was opposed to the representation of special vested interests. James Mill equated this defense of democracy with the religious Reformation. The individual interpretation of the Bible without priestly guidance "has totally altered the condition of human nature and exalted

man to what may be called a different stage of existence."[32] The primary
political virtue is prudence, and it is lodged in the middle class.

There can be no doubt that the middle rank, which gives to science, to art, and to
legislation itself their most distinguished ornaments, and is the chief source of all
that has exalted, and refined human nature, is that portion of the community of
which, if the basis of representation were ever so far extended, the opinion would
ultimately decide. Of the people beneath them a vast majority would be sure to
be guided by their advice and example.[33]

What James Mill did not entertain were the following questions: Could
there be a tyranny of the majority (Tocqueville's concern)? Can the identity
of interest be achieved simply by relying upon laws of human nature
without moral principles? Will the lower classes always accept the guidance
of the middle classes? Would the process degenerate into the brokering of
interests? Is there a potential conflict between scientific guidance of the
intellectual elite and the need for individuals to assume more control over
their own lives? These are exactly the questions that Mill will raise and
that will lead to a different set of answers.

The inauguration of the *Westminster Review* reflected the political fer-
ment of the third decade of the nineteenth century. Mill described it as
follows:

It was a time, as is known . . . of rapidly rising Liberalism.[34] When the fears and
animosities accompanying the War with France had been brought to an end . . . the
tide began to set towards reform. . . . The enormous weight of the national debt
and taxation occasioned by so long and costly a war, rendered the government
and parliament very unpopular. . . . At this period, when Liberalism seemed to be
becoming the tone of the time, when improvement of institutions was preached
from the highest places, and a complete change of the constitution of Parliament
was loudly demanded in the lowest, it is not strange that attention should have
been roused by the regular appearance in controversy of what seemed a new
school of writers, claiming to be the legislators and theorists of this new tendency.
The air of strong conviction with which they wrote, when scarcely any one else
seemed to have an equally strong faith in as definite a creed; the boldness with
which they tilted against the very front of both the existing political parties;
their uncompromising profession of opposition to many of the generally received
opinions, and the suspicion they lay under of holding others still more heterodox
than they professed; the talent and verve of at least my father's articles, and the
appearance of a corps behind him sufficient to carry on a review; and finally, the
fact that the review was bought and read, made the so called Bentham school in

philosophy and politics fill a greater place in the public mind than it had held
before, or has ever again held since. . . .[35]

The only thing to mar the initial enthusiasm surrounding the founding
of the *Westminster Review* was the role of Sir John Bowring. Bowring was an
ardent radical and disciple of Bentham's, as well as his biographer and later
the editor of his collected works. Among his other accomplishments, he
was a composer of Unitarian hymns and later governor of Hong Kong.
Bowring sought to make himself Bentham's Boswell and to exclude or minimize any other influence upon or access to the aged Bentham. Bowring,
in a manner of speaking, was attempting to gain complete control over
Bentham and his endeavors and to promote himself as the official voice of
radicalism. This brought him into conflict with both Mills. Later, Bowring
went out of his way to denigrate James Mill in his biography of Bentham
in order to glorify his hero. Although there were some substantive disagreements, a large part of the conflict between Bowring and the Mills
concerned a competition for the leadership of philosophic radicalism.

There was during the last few years of Bentham's life (he died in 1832) less frequency and cordiality of intercourse than in former years, chiefly because Bentham
had acquired newer, and to him more agreeable intimacies; but Mr. [James] Mill's
feeling never altered toward him, nor did he ever fail, publicly or privately, in
giving due honor to Bentham's name and acknowledgement of the intellectual
debt he owed to him.[36]

The conflict came into the open when James Mill refused the editorship
of the *Westminster Review*. Bentham then entrusted the job to Bowring.
Despite its popular success, the *Review* almost immediately fell into financial difficulties. Bowring saved his position as editor by slyly arranging for
the wealthy political economist Perronet Thompson to assume ownership.
For a while, the Mills as well as some of the other younger radicals were
disinclined to publish in the *Review*.

During this period, the last essay that Mill published in the *Review*,
on the French Revolution, appeared in April of 1826. Mill defended the
"early French revolutionists against the Tory misrepresentations of Sir
Walter Scott in the introduction to his Life of Napoleon."[37] Here Mill
partly followed Bentham's lead. Like most radicals, Bentham was initially
sympathetic to the French Revolution, since he saw in it the overthrow
of the aristocratic regime and its replacement with what he hoped would

be a middle-class democracy. He even designed a plan for the reform of the French judicial system and was as a consequence made an honorary citizen of France. Horrified by the later excesses, Bentham attributed the Revolution's descent into tyranny to the use of misleading abstractions such as "natural rights." He was to say that whereas natural rights were "simple nonsense," "natural and imprescriptible rights" were "nonsense upon stilts."[38] The overthrow of the old regime was seen as the overthrow of the dead hand of unreflective custom and tradition. This is why it was so important for Mill to stress the defense of the early revolutionists and to blunt the Tory argument that all radical change led inevitably to terror. At the same time, Mill shared the romantic notion that true freedom existed only when individuals adopted social practices in a self-conscious and responsible fashion.

One of the consequences of Mill's prodigious research on this project, in addition to his love of France and growing knowledge of French culture, is that he became a recognized expert on French affairs. Many of his journalistic publications over the next decade were devoted to commentaries on contemporary affairs in France. Mill managed to accumulate quite a library on the French Revolution and even contemplated writing a history of it. He never carried out the project, but his library became an important resource for Carlyle's work on the French Revolution.

Radicalism

What was radicalism? Philosophic radicalism did not possess the cohesiveness that is often attributed to it. The radicals comprised a disparate group with overlapping but not identical views. The initial success of the *Review* reflected the times rather than the strength or size of radicalism. Insofar as anything held the radicals together, it was in small part the reputation of Bentham's writings, and in much larger part the intellectual and personal charisma and integrity of James Mill.

To the extent that philosophic radicalism had a core of beliefs, those beliefs were the opinions of James Mill, "though none of us, probably, agreed in every respect with" him.[39] What were those beliefs? Mill enumerates eight. To begin with, radicals subscribed to Hartley's metaphysics – namely, the view that the contents of our consciousness originate in experiences caused by external objects (empiricism) and associated in the mind by quasi-mechanical laws of the mind (associationism). Second, radicals asserted that our response to these external stimuli is guided by the desire to maximize pleasure and to minimize pain (Bentham's psychological hedonism). To these philosophical assumptions, the radicals added two others of a social scientific nature: the belief that national economies grow faster and better under conditions of competition and minimal government interference (Ricardo's political economy), and the Malthusian belief that population growth was outstripping the food supply. Malthus's views on population were interpreted to mean "securing full employment at high wages to the whole labouring population through a voluntary restriction of the increase of their number" (i.e., birth control).[40] The radicals advocated as well greater freedom in relationships between men and women, accompanied by a lessening of sexual obsession. The most important political assumption was that representative government and freedom of discussion led to a clearer conception of the public interest and to the maximization of social welfare. At the same time, radicals favored utopian social engineering based upon the presupposition of environmental determinism. (James Mill's "fundamental doctrine was the formation of all human character by circumstances through the universal Principle of Association, and the consequent unlimited possibility of improving the moral and intellectual condition of mankind by education.")[41] Finally, radicals opposed "asceticism and priestcraft," both for being in conflict with the doctrine of psychological hedonism and for undercutting the possibility of utopian social engineering. What these beliefs amount to, of course, is the Enlightenment Project,[42] the attempt to provide a completely scientific account of both the natural and social worlds along with a social technology for the solution of human problems. "The French *philosophes* of the eighteenth century were the example we sought to imitate, and we hoped to accomplish no less results."[43]

The real center of radicalism was James Mill, not Bentham. "It was my father's opinions which gave the distinguishing character to the Benthamic or utilitarian propagandism of that time." In maintaining this, Mill was not merely expressing loyalty or paying homage to his father. It was James Mill who provided the intellectual cement and coherence for radicalism by bringing together Bentham's utilitarianism and psychological associationism, and it was James Mill who applied these theoretical positions to public policy by connecting them to the Malthusian population doctrine and Ricardian economics. It was also the character of James Mill that created a radical movement and held it together.

The influence which Bentham exercised was by his writings. Through them he has produced . . . effects on the condition of mankind, wider and deeper, no doubt, than any which can be attributed to my father. He is a much greater name in history. But my father exercised a far greater personal ascendancy. He *was* sought for the vigour and instructiveness of his conversation, and did use it largely as an instrument for the diffusion of his opinions. I have never known any man who could do such ample justice to his best thoughts in colloquial discussion. His perfect command over his great mental resources, the terseness and expressiveness of his language and the moral earnestness of as well as intellectual force of his delivery, made him one of the most striking of all argumentative conversers: and he was full of anecdote, a hearty laughter, and, when with people whom he liked, a most lively and amusing companion. It was not solely, or even chiefly, in diffusing his merely intellectual convictions that his power showed itself: it was still more through the influence of a quality, of which I have only since learnt to appreciate the extreme rarity: that exalted public spirit, and regard above all things to the good of the whole, which warmed into life and activity every germ of similar virtue that existed in the minds he came in contact with . . . the encouragement he afforded to the fainthearted or desponding among them, by the firm confidence which . . . he always felt in the power of reason, the general progress of improvement, and the good which individuals could do by judicious effort.[44]

In his reading during this period, Mill called attention to and praised Condorcet's *Life of Turgot*. Foreshadowing his own movement away from radicalism, he points out that "this book cured me of my sectarian follies. . . . Turgot always kept himself perfectly distinct from the Encyclopedists. . . . I left off designating myself and others as Utilitarians, and by the pronoun 'we' or any other collective designation, I ceased to *afficher* sectarianism. My real inward sectarianism I did not get rid of till later, and much more gradually."[45]

The Writer's Vocation

Mill learned two things about himself during this period. First, although he was a good public speaker and debater, he had a high shrill voice and lacked the dominating skill his father possessed. "I never, indeed, acquired real fluency, and had always a bad and ungraceful delivery: but I could make myself listened to."[46] Participation in the debating societies, however rewarding, did not offer him the possibility to be the intellectual leader of social reform in Britain. Second, he discovered his literary gift. Curiously, this came about as a result of his being asked to edit Bentham's *Rationale of Judicial Evidence*. Bentham had written three different drafts, and it was part of Mill's job to synthesize those drafts into a harmonious whole. As Mill put it, this "gave a great start to my powers of composition. Everything which I wrote subsequently to this editorial employment, was markedly superior to anything I had written before."[47] For the rest of his life, Mill would make two separate drafts of his major compositions and then engage in extensive editing of his own work. He learned that there was no good writing, only good rewriting.

From 1822 until his death in 1873, Mill kept a meticulous list of all of his publications. He first began publishing in the *Traveller* newspaper in 1822. In 1824, he began publishing in the *Westminster Review*;[48] his articles included a scathing attack on David Hume's *History of England* by way of a review of George Brodie's history. Hume was critiqued for presenting an allegedly Tory view and for defending Charles I. "Hume possessed powers of a very high order; but regard for truth formed no part of his character. . . . it would be a vain attempt to describe the systematic suppression of the truth which is exemplified in this portion of his history."[49] This critique of Britain's greatest philosopher and one of the country's most noted historians does not say much for Mill, but it does reveal something of the partisan spectacles he wore when reading and evaluating the work of others at this early point in his life.

Mill noted how ponderous and convoluted Bentham's later style had become, as opposed to the earlier *Fragment on Government*, which was "a model of liveliness and ease combined with fullness of matter."[50] Having resolved to preserve the virtues of readability and liveliness, he went on to study the styles of English and French writers such as Goldsmith, Fielding, Pascal, and Voltaire. "I greatly increased my power of effective writing; acquiring not only an ear for smoothness and rhythm, but a practical sense for telling sentences, and an immediate criterion of their telling property, by their effect on a mixed audience"[51] Bentham had become through his writings more famous than James Mill, so Mill resolved to combine the depth and breadth of his father's views and thereby, he hoped, to attain the same influence as Bentham's writings. One of the most famous examples of this kind of rhetoric comes from his critique of Hamilton (1865): "I will call no being good who is not what I mean when I apply that epithet to my fellow creatures; and if such a creature can sentence me to Hell for not so calling him, to Hell I will go."[52]

Another of Bentham's followers, a Mr. Marshall of Leeds, who represented Yorkshire in Parliament, hit upon the idea in 1825 of using Bentham's work on *Fallacies* to comment on Parliamentary debates.

[T]he thought had occurred to him that it would be useful to publish annually the Parliamentary debates, not in the chronological order of Hansard, but classified according to subjects, and accompanied by commentary pointing out the fallacies of the speakers. . . . The work was called "Parliamentary History and Review." Its sale was not sufficient to keep it in existence and it lasted only three years. It excited, however, some attention among parliamentary and political people. The best strength of the party was put forth in it; and its execution did them much more credit than that of the Westminster Review had ever done.[53]

Among the contributors were Edward Strutt and John Romilly (both of whom later served as radical members of Parliament), John and Charles Austin, James Mill, and Mill himself. This endeavor was an indirect way for both Mills to participate in the parliamentary debate, which they were unable to do directly because of their relationship with India House. Mill also describes his writing in the review as "no longer mere reproductions and applications of the doctrines I had been taught; they were original thinking, as far as that name can be applied to old ideas in new forms and connexions . . . there was a maturity, and a well digested character about them which there had not been in any of my previous performances."[54]

Participating in these various debating and journalistic activities marked an important turning point in Mill's life. He felt that he had become an independent thinker:

I have always dated from these conversations my own real inauguration as an original and independent thinker. It was also through them that I acquired, or very much strengthened, a mental habit to which I attribute all that I have ever done, or ever shall do, in speculation; that of never accepting half-solutions of difficulties as complete; never abandoning a puzzle, but again and again returning to it until it was cleared up; never allowing obscure corners of a subject to remain unexplored, because they did not appear important; never thinking that I perfectly understood any part of a subject until I understood the whole.[55]

These are prophetic words. They perfectly capture Mill's grappling with important theoretical and public policy issues throughout the rest of his life. They exemplify an intellectual integrity that is reflected in Mill's persistent attempt to see the logic of his critics and adversaries. They are immortalized in his opposition to censorship and his defense of the

importance of free speech. Unlike his father, whose persona was that of
the individual who had grasped and articulated the final and definitive
truth with complete confidence, Mill presented himself as an individual
for whom growth and openness were the ultimate intellectual virtues. This
reflected not only the history of his life but, he would argue, the evolution
of civilization. In his eyes, it was not merely an intellectual virtue but a
reflection of a more fundamental and objective truth about the world. It
is this kind of openness that frustrates and gives the lie to many scholarly
attempts to give a static view of Mill's beliefs. Finally, it is precisely this
unwillingness to accept half-truths that precipitated the great crisis in his
intellectual development.

As Packe put it so well in his biography of Mill,

[I]n the single year 1825 when he was nineteen, John Mill set out to edit Bentham,
founded the Debating Society, discussed Political Economy three hours a week
at Grote's house in Threadneedle Street, wound up the Utilitarian Society, contributed major articles to the *Westminster Review*, went for long country walks
with Graham and Roebuck, carried out his mounting duties at the India House
with conspicuous success [he had been given a raise to 100 pounds yearly], and
continued to be solely responsible for the education of his brothers and sisters. He
also found time to write an article to lead off the first number of the *Parliamentary History and Review*, a periodical sponsored by Mr. Marshall, a worthy Leeds
manufacturer and friend of his father. To fill up the remaining cracks of leisure he
decided to learn German: languages never bothered him, and he took a course of
lessons with Sarah Austin. . . . The intellectual activities in this fantastic list were
none of them of a transitory nature and all of them continued unabated into 1826.
Retribution inevitably followed.[56]

3

Crisis (1826–1830)

IN 1826, Mill experienced the great crisis of his life. This crisis had two interrelated dimensions, a personal-psychological one and an intellectual one. The personal crisis was the need to become independent of his father; the intellectual crisis was the growing awareness of the inadequacies of philosophic radicalism even in its most coherent form, namely that of his father. Needless to say, Mill does not in his *Autobiography* directly confront the psychological crisis; rather, he discusses at great length his intellectual disenchantment with radicalism. There are two important reasons for this. First, the intellectual crisis, although real enough, became the surrogate forum in which he asserted and achieved independence from his father's thought. Second, the psychological crisis, as we shall see, was never honestly and directly resolved during James Mill's lifetime. Mill chose to live a double life. In all outward respects he was loyal to his father's wishes and views, but he harbored a secret intellectual life in which he asserted his independence. Mill genuinely admired and respected his father more than any other man, appreciated and shared what James Mill was trying to do in the larger cultural arena, and remained grateful for the independence of intellect that his father had cultivated in him. But he inevitably resented the paternal demand that personal loyalty required him to pay lip service to views that he did not really share. Perhaps Mill was ashamed that during his father's lifetime he lacked the courage to confront directly their differences. Again and again, this resentment will be reflected both in Mill's actions and in his publications, but it was always a resentment inextricably bound up with awe at his father's integrity and accomplishments. As a young adult, Mill learned how difficult it is to declare one's intellectual independence.

The Psychological Crisis

Mill's depiction of himself at the age of twenty is worth noting.

From the winter of 1821, when I first read Bentham, and especially from the commencement of the Westminster Review, I had what might truly be called an object in life; to be a reformer of the world. My conception of my own happiness was entirely identified with this object. The personal sympathies I wished for were those of fellow labourers in this enterprise. . . . But the time came when I was awakened from this as from a dream. It was in the autumn of 1826.[1]

Introspectively, Mill described his crisis as follows:

I was in a dull state of nerves, such as everybody is occasionally liable to; unsusceptible to enjoyment or pleasurable excitement; one of those moods when what is pleasure at other times, becomes insipid or indifferent; the state, I should think, in which converts to Methodism usually are, when smitten by their first 'conviction of sin.' In this frame of mind it occurred to me to put the question directly to myself: 'Suppose that all your objects in life were realized; that all the changes in institutions and opinions which you are looking forward to, could be completely effected at this very instant: would this be a great joy and happiness to you?' And an irrepressible self-consciousness distinctly answered, 'No!' At this my heart sank within me: *the whole foundation on which my life was constructed fell down.* All my happiness was to have been found in the continual pursuit of this end. The end had ceased to charm, and how could there ever again be any interest in the means? I seemed to have nothing left to live for.[2] [Italics added]

Although he had not yet met Carlyle, Mill's description of the crisis, written many years later, incorporated features from Carlyle's *Sartor Resartus* (1833). The protagonist of Carlyle's work, Herr Professor Teufelsdruckh, is driven to contemplate suicide in the face of the conception of a mechanistic universe devoid of God and purpose. The professor overcomes his despair by an act of will and a commitment to the program of "Know what thou canst work at."[3] Mill also noted how Coleridge's "Dejection," although he was not acquainted with it at the time, captured his mood:

A grief without a pang, void, dark and drear
A drowsy, stifled, unimpassioned grief,
Which finds no natural outlet or relief
In word, or sigh, or tear.

It is significant that when Mill writes about these events in his *Auto-biography*, he quotes Romantic writers whom he had not yet read at the time in order to identify his state of mind and his problem. Philosophic Radicalism was inadequate as a way of conceptualizing his problem. It was through Romanticism that he would work his way through his mental crisis and finally resolve his problems.

Mill found some solace in listening to music – specifically, Weber's *Oberon* – but, as a sign of his state of mind at the time, he was "seriously tormented by the thought of the exhaustibility of musical combinations."

The octave consists only of five tones and two semi-tones, which can be put together in only a limited number of ways, of which but a small proportion are beautiful: most of these, it seemed to me, must have been already discovered, and there could not be room for a long succession of Mozarts and Webers, to strike out as they had done, entirely new and surpassingly rich veins of musical beauty.[4]

The psychological root of Mill's crisis was his need to express his in-dependence of his father. The closest he comes to acknowledging this in the *Autobiography* is the following statement:

My father, to whom it would have been natural to me to have recourse in any practical difficulties, was the last person to whom, in such a case as this, I looked for help. Everything convinced me that he had no knowledge of any such mental state as I was suffering from, and that even if he could be made to understand it, he was not the physician who could heal it. My education, which was wholly his work, had been conducted without any regard to the possibility of its ending in this result; and I saw no use in giving him the pain of thinking that his plans had failed, when the failure was probably irremediable, and at all events, beyond the power of *his* remedies.[5]

There is a peculiarly double-edged character to the crisis that Mill was about to undergo. On the one hand, the crisis was a reflection of an important new development within liberal culture. Carlyle, Coleridge, Wordsworth, and Matthew Arnold, just to name a few, had all experi-enced similar periods of tension within their lives at about the same age. During the late eighteenth and early nineteenth centuries, the child be-came an object of cultivation, the purpose of which was to make the child into an autonomous human being. "The purpose of the exercise was [paradoxically] not subservience of the child to the father but rather to the values (notably responsibility, discipline, and industriousness) that the father embodied."[6] Mill's crisis and subsequent emancipation (partial and whole) reflected the logic of autonomy.[7] Mill, as we shall see, overcame his crisis by growing beyond his father's Benthamism and incorporating it into a larger synthesis.

At the intellectual heart of Mill's crisis was the disenchantment with radicalism. The form taken by Mill's march toward autonomy reflected his recognition of the theoretical and practical inadequacies of his father's program. Mill's early education had made him into the complete embodiment of the Enlightenment Project. But he came to see the self of that process to be as distorted as Mary Shelly's monster in *Frankenstein*. "[T]he description so often given of a Benthamite, as a mere reasoning machine . . . was during two or three years of my life not altogether untrue of me."[8]

Instead of facing the challenge of independence directly, Mill chose to sublimate his problem by focusing on how he had become disenchanted with his father's program. The disenchantment took three forms.[9] First, there was the recognition of the impoverished conception of emotional life to be found in Benthamism. Mill's reading of Wordsworth for the first time in 1828 introduced him to the Romantic poetry that his father disliked, and his stormy friendship with Carlyle exposed him to the German Romantic philosophical movement that was ultimately to provide the basis of his philosophical liberation. Second, Mill struggled with the dilemma of trying to make sense of human freedom and responsibility within the deterministic framework of Benthamism. He resolved this problem, at least temporarily, and later expounded his solution in the *Logic*. It is a problem to which he would return frequently in his writings. It was during the five-year period when he was working with his father on the latter's *Analysis of the Phenomena of the Human Mind* that Mill saw the weaknesses of associationism. Third, Mill was moved by Macaulay's critique of his father's essay on government to change his views on the conception of the relation between individual self-interest and the social interest or common good. Finally, 1826, marks the year that Mill terminated the Utilitarian Society.

The Philosophic Radicals believed themselves to be offering a scientifically accurate account of human nature as well as a prescription for solving humanity's problems that was consistent with scientific fact. They were untroubled by the commitment of science to determinism, or the view that everything in the universe, including human beings, was governed by inexorable laws. We may well ask how the existence of inexorable laws can be compatible with the idea of change inherent in the notion of improvement. To begin with, the radicals believed that the inexorable laws that governed us on the psychological level were the laws they identified as the universal desires to maximize pleasure and minimize pain. They also believed that these laws played themselves out in contexts in which the desires were influenced by knowledge of means-ends relationships. A social world in which everyone cooperated was a world in which it was further presumed that pleasure was maximized and pain minimized, both on the aggregate level and on the individual level. Educating people on the means-ends relationships through the process of association – itself an example of determinism – ensured that the best of all possible worlds would be the likely outcome.

Nevertheless, nagging questions and doubts remained. While aggregate pleasure might be maximized through cooperation, might not individual pleasure be maximized by cunning and ruthless manipulation? There is no way to rule out this possibility, perhaps a manifestation of the operation of original sin. From Hobbes and Mandeville to Hume and Smith, among many others, no one could guarantee philosophically the desired outcome. Hume and Smith had resorted in analogous ways to postulating some kind of benevolent concern for others, but this denied the fundamentally lawlike character of the desire to maximize pleasure and minimize pain. Radicals such as Bentham would have none of this. Finally, as a way out, James Mill's doctrine of association was formulated as a mechanical way of generating a concern for the social or common good. Bain summarized James Mill's position as follows:

He accounts for the Virtues, by showing them to be means to the more primary ends of securing pleasures and warding off pains; Prudence operating in this way, as regards ourselves, and Justice and Benevolence, as regards others. The grand difficulty here is to account for seeking other men's pleasures, or to trace to self-seeking causes, our Disinterested Benevolence. Reciprocity goes a good way, and is adduced accordingly.[10]

Two questions were raised by this use of the doctrine of association. First, could associationism mechanically induce an irreversible desire for the common good? Second, how are we to understand the initial benevolent impulse on the part of the radical reformers to bring about

this state of affairs? Was this impulse an historical accident? What was
its ontological status? Was it consistent with the alleged basic self-seeking
laws of psychology?

In his own eyes, Mill appeared in retrospect as a kind of ideologue. He
wanted to improve mankind but the motive was

> ... little else ... than zeal for speculative opinions. It had not its roots in genuine
> benevolence, or sympathy with mankind. ... Nor was it connected with any high
> enthusiasm for ideal nobleness. ... While fully recognizing the superior excellence
> of unselfish benevolence and love of justice, we did not expect the regeneration
> of mankind from any direct action on those sentiments, but from the effect of
> educated intellect, enlightening the selfish feelings ... a means of improvement in
> the hands of those who are themselves impelled by nobler principles of action.[11]

What worried Mill here was whether he had a real affection for the common
good or whether it had been induced in him by association. Moreover, if
this realization, arrived at through analysis, could discredit the effect of
the association, then it could eventually undermine the whole project in
everyone else as well.

Two things are clear from this self-description. First, there is either an
inherent conflict or a lack of clear connection between the selfishness that
is considered basic to human nature and the benevolence that seemingly
and necessarily prompts the desire for reform. Second, there is a growing
recognition of the inadequacy of this view of human nature, especially its
"neglect both in theory and in practice of the cultivation of feeling."[12]
Mill also describes this period as one from which he dated his "own real
inauguration as an original and independent thinker."[13] How long would
it be before Mill came to terms with the tensions in the views he had
inherited from his father?

The second dimension of Mill's disenchantment with his father's
views had to do with the issue of free will. James Mill was committed by
the Enlightenment Project to a form of determinism – specifically, to the
views (a) that internally we are physiologically determined to seek the
maximization of pleasure and the minimization of pain, (b) that we are
in addition guided by our beliefs about what caused pleasure and pain,
(c) that these beliefs are organized by the mind according to the fundamental laws of associationism, and (d) that an educator familiar with the laws of
association could arrange the environment so that pleasure accompanied
ideas of virtue or duty.

Several aspects of his father's views made, on reflection, no sense to Mill. To begin with, there was no guaranteed connection between the pursuit of individual happiness and working for the ideal betterment of mankind. That is, how can we objectively ascertain that it is always in the individual's best interest to pursue the ideal (or some version of the common good)? The answer is that we cannot. Mill's solution to this problem, which is reflected in his final reconceptualization of utilitarianism, is as follows. He holds onto his father's contention that our ultimate objective is happiness, but he adds to this the claim that it is only in the pursuit of the ideal that we achieve happiness. Mill thinks it is not possible for individuals to pursue their happiness directly. This resolution, or compromise, was suggested to Mill by Carlyle's doctrine of anti-self-consciousness, that is, the deliberate effort not to focus upon oneself or to engage in introspection. Mill's doctrine differs from Carlyle's in that whereas Carlyle sought to subordinate himself to the ideal, Mill argues, in the manner of Hegel, that it is only in the pursuit of the ideal that we achieve a deeper level of self-awareness.

The experiences of this period . . . led me to adopt a theory of life, very unlike that on which I had before acted, and having much in common with what at the time I certainly had never heard of, the anti-self-consciousness theory of Carlyle. I never, indeed, wavered in the conviction that happiness is the test of all rules of conduct, and the end of life. But I now thought that this end was only to be attained by not making it the direct end. Those only are happy (I thought) who have their minds fixed on some object other than their own happiness; on the happiness of others, on the improvement of mankind, even on some art or pursuit, followed not as a means, but as itself an ideal end. Aiming thus at something else, they find happiness by the way. . . . This theory now became the basis of my philosophy of life.[14]

By itself, this resolution of the happiness issue only solves the problem of how and why individuals come to pursue some ideal. What needs still to be resolved is the problem of how the pursuit of one's individual ideal can be made compatible with the common good or the pursuit of someone else's ideal. This resolution was still a few years away for Mill, but we can anticipate its form. The problem of the individual good and the common good can be resolved only if my ultimate ideal is compatible with everyone else's ultimate ideal. When Mill came to identify the ultimate ideal as autonomy and insisted that personal autonomy requires both a common set of conditions and the transcending of any kind of paternalism, then it became clear that one individual's autonomy is not only compatible with, but also both permits and ultimately requires, everyone else's autonomy. It is this conception of autonomy ("freedom"), ultimately religious in origin,[15] that explains Mill's peculiar conception of and passion for equality, his abhorrence of philanthropy, his defense of liberty, and his sense of public responsibility, both local and international.

The resolution of the free will issue is based upon Mill's understanding of associationism. The notion of solving public policy issues by a vast Benthamite program of externally and publicly induced conditioning is inconsistent with the individualism of the Philosophic Radicals and an affront to the dignity of the individual. What Mill will contend is that individual human beings can "deprogram" and "reprogram" themselves. Nevertheless, the capacity for doing this implies the existence of an agent or agency that lies beyond conditioning. Those familiar with Freudian psychoanalysis will recognize an analogue here that is no mere coincidence, for Sigmund Freud had read and translated some of Mill's works during the early part of his own career.

[D]uring the later returns of my dejection, the doctrine of what is called Philosophical necessity weighed on my existence like an incubus. I felt as if I was scientifically proved to be the helpless slave of antecedent circumstances; as if my character and that of all others had been formed for us by agencies beyond our control, and was wholly out of our own power. . . . I pondered painfully on the subject, till gradually I saw light through it. . . . I saw that though our character is formed by circumstances, our own desires can do much to shape those circumstances. . . . our will, by influencing some of our circumstances, can modify our future habits or capabilities of willing. All this was entirely consistent with the doctrine of circumstances, or rather, was the doctrine itself, properly understood. . . . [This] [n]ow forms the chapter on Liberty and Necessity in the concluding Book of my *System of Logic*.[16]

A lot more needs to be said about the issue of free will, and it is an issue that shall be addressed in a later chapter. Two things are worth noting here. First, Mill himself recognized this as a kind of temporary psychological solution rather than as a full-blown philosophical solution.[17] The final resolution came late in life, in his *An Examination of the Philosophy of Sir William Hamilton*.

Another event that contributed to Mill's psychological crisis was a loss of confidence in some of his father's views. James Mill's highly influential essay entitled "Government" had been written for the *Encyclopaedia Britannica* in 1820. Bain claims that this article was the intellectual origin of what eventually became the Reform Bill of 1832. James Mill maintained there that the interests of children and women were included within the interests of their fathers or husbands and therefore did not require representation.

[I]f one man has power over others placed in his hands, he will make use of it for an evil purpose – for the purpose of rendering those other men the abject instruments of his will. . . . It is very evident that, if the community itself were the choosing body, the interest of the community and that of the choosing body [representative body] would be the same. . . . One thing is pretty clear, that all those individuals whose interests are indisputably included in those of other individuals may be struck off without inconvenience. In this light may be viewed all children, up to a certain age, whose interests are involved in those of their parents. In this light, also, women may be regarded, the interest of almost all of whom is involved either in that of their fathers or in that of their husbands.[18]

There is an evident inconsistency here, as Macaulay pointed out in his critique of James Mill's essay. Macaulay asks James Mill why, if a monarch cannot always share the interests of his subjects, we should assume that a father or husband always shares the interests of his wife or daughter. "Without adducing one fact, without taking the trouble to perplex the question by one sophism, he [James Mill] placidly dogmatizes away the interests of one half of the human race."[19] It was precisely Macaulay's critique of his father that Mill cited in his *Autobiography* as leading him to question his father's position. Macaulay (1800–1859) had been raised among Evangelicals and was the son of the leader of the movement against slavery. He was the leading contributor to the *Edinburgh Review*. His fame is as an historian, the author of the *History of England* (1848–61). He first came to prominence by attacking James Mill's essay on government in the March 1829 issue of the *Edinburgh Review*. What Macaulay attacked was the theoretical and deductive character of James Mill's approach, arguing instead for a more empirical and historical or Burkean conception of political theory. Macaulay also excoriated James Mill for his inconsistency in not advocating the extension of the franchise to women,[20] something about which we shall have more to say shortly.

Despite the disagreement, Macaulay and the Mills remained on good terms. Macaulay acknowledged the stature of the author of "a *History of*

India, which, though certainly not free from fault it, I think, on the whole, the greatest historical work which has appeared in our language since that of Gibbon...."[21] James Mill was a friend of the elder Macaulay, Zachary Macaulay. When Macaulay was mentioned as a possible candidate for the Supreme Council in Calcutta, James Mill supported him. In Macaulay's own words about his "old enemy James Mill": "The late Chairman consulted him about me, hoping, I suppose, to have his support against me. [James] Mill said, very handsomely, that he would advise the Company to take me; for as public men went, I was much above the average, and, if they rejected me, he thought it very unlikely that they would get anybody so fit."[22]

Macaulay's attack led Mill eventually to reformulate his conception of social science, and we shall address those issues in a subsequent chapter. What is important here is to note how Macaulay's telling critique impacted Mill's crisis of confidence.

[T]here was truth in several of his [Macaulay's] strictures on my father's treatment of the subject; that my father's premises were really too narrow, and included but a small number of the general truths, on which, in politics, the important consequences depend. Identity of interest between the governing body and the community at large is not, in any practical sense which can be attached to it, the only thing on which good government depends; neither can this identity of interest be secured by the mere conditions of election. I was not at all satisfied with the mode in which my father met the criticisms of Macaulay.... This made me think that there was really something more fundamentally erroneous in my father's conception of philosophical method, as applicable to politics, than I had hitherto supposed.[23]

With regard to feminist issues, Mill asserted the following:

It was my father's opinions which gave the distinguishing character to the Benthamic or utilitarian propagandism of that time.... But indeed there was by no means complete unanimity among any portion of us, nor had any of us adopted implicitly all my father's opinions. For example, although his Essay on Government was regarded probably by all of us as a masterpiece of political wisdom, our adhesion by no means extended to the paragraph of it, in which he maintains that women may consistently with good government, be excluded from the suffrage, because their interest is the same with that of men. From this doctrine, I, and all of those who formed my chosen associates, most positively dissented. It is due to my father to say that he denied having intended to affirm that women *should* be excluded, any more than men under the age of forty, concerning whom he maintained, in the very next paragraph, an exactly similar thesis. He was, as he truly said, not discussing whether the suffrage had better be restricted, but only (assuming that it is to be restricted) what is the utmost limit of restriction, which does not necessarily involve a sacrifice of the securities of good government. But I thought then, as I have always thought since, that the opinion which he acknowledged, no less than that which he disclaimed, is as great an error as any of those against which the Essay was directed; that the interest of women is included in that of men exactly as much and no more, as the interest of subjects is included in that of kings; and that every reason which exists for giving the suffrage to anybody, demands that it should not be withheld from women. This was also the general opinion of the younger proselytes; and it is pleasant to be able to say that Mr. Bentham, on this important point, was wholly on our side.[24]

A temporary resolution of Mill's predicament was achieved in the following way. Mill decided to save his father's views by reinterpretating them in the light of a number of new and philosophically Romantic perspectives. This kind of resolution helps to explain the following remark in the *Autobiography*:[25]

[A] small ray of light broke in upon my gloom. I was reading, accidentally, Marmontel's *Memoirs*, and came to the passage which relates his father's death, the distressed position of the family, and the sudden inspiration by which he, then a mere boy, felt and made them feel that he would be everything to them – would supply the place of all that they had lost.[26]

While much has been made of this reference to Marmontel, the one thing it did show to Mill was that he still had feelings! What this tells us, with a great deal of plausibility, is that Mill was determined to be a loyal and dutiful son committed to extolling the virtues of his father's work while at the same time augmenting and supplementing that work by placing it on what he took to be a more profound philosophical basis.

This temporary resolution took two forms. During his father's lifetime, Mill presented a common front and either suppressed or hid his disagreement. After his father's death, Mill paid lip service to the letter of his father's doctrines – for example, he still called himself a utilitarian – but he so redefined and reconceptualized those doctrines that they no longer retained his father's spirit or meant on the deepest philosophical level what his father had meant by them. To this day, the psychological sublimation of Mill's intellectual disagreements with his father continues to play havoc with scholarly attempts to reconstruct the logic of Mill's thought.

In later chapters we shall see examples of both Mill's successes and his failures at this psychological sublimation. And even if many contemporary readers remain pleased with the extent to which Mill transcended his father's views, some of Mill's own contemporaries, such as his friend Grote and his rival Jevons, saw through the thinly disguised transformation.

Wordsworth[27]

What Mill discovered in the poetry of Wordsworth was an expression of the affective dimension of human life. It is not surprising, on a superficial level, that Mill would have turned originally to the works of Wordsworth. During his sojourn in France, Mill had developed a lifelong passion for botany and for hiking in mountain scenery, the rudimentary awakening of the aesthetic sense. At a deeper level, Wordsworth provided the deeper moral significance in poetry, something that appealed to Mill's moral sense, namely, the internal culture of the individual.

I, for the first time, gave its proper place, among the prime necessities of human well-being, to the internal culture of the individual. I ceased to attach almost exclusive importance to the ordering of outward circumstances, and the training of the human mind for speculation and action. . . . The cultivation of the feelings became one of the cardinal points in my ethical and philosophical creed.[28]

It is this internal culture that Mill will see as leading to the discovery of personal autonomy. According to Robson,[29] it was Mill's way of connecting altruism with personal cultivation, relating autonomy to the common good. As Mazlish put it, "in seeking to emancipate himself from his father's 'mechanical' making of him, [Mill] also sought to emancipate liberalism. He envisioned it more as representing an ongoing 'organic process', responsive to emotional as well as rational needs, and aiming at the fullest individual self-development."[30] Wordsworth was a perfect vehicle for making this transition, for his poetry showed how sensitivity to natural beauty, something that everyone could share, makes us more conscious of the pettiness of individual interest.

A second reason for Wordsworth's appeal is that he was familiar with and had used the language of association. In the Preface to the *Lyrical Ballads*, Wordsworth employed the language of association to define the role of the poet as illustrating "the manner in which our feelings and ideas are associated." James Mill, in his *Analysis of the Phenomena of the Human Mind* (1829), had reduced all of aesthetic experience to the laws of association. According to James Mill, there was nothing real or important about aesthetic experience; it represented neither a truth about the external world nor a truth about the internal human world; rather, it was induced by external stimuli operating through the laws of association. On the one hand, Wordsworth recognized that our feelings could be "modified and directed by our thoughts," thereby suggesting to Mill that some version of association was compatible with self-governing autonomy. On the other hand, Wordsworth suggested to Mill that there was an autonomous realm of feeling that was not the simple by-product of association. As Wordsworth put it, "the knowledge both of the Poet and the Man of Science is pleasure; but the knowledge of the one cleaves to us as a necessary part of our existence, our natural and inalienable inheritance; the other is *a personal and individual acquisition*, slow to come to us, *and by no habitual and direct sympathy connecting us with our fellow beings.*"[31] Many years later, when Mill reissued his father's work, he noted his disagreement with his father: "The examples . . . do not prove that there is no original beauty in colours."[32]

Wordsworth's understanding of association had an enormous influence on Mill. The aspect of his father's theory of association that troubled Mill involved the connection between virtue and happiness, which was rendered artificial by association. A connection that was established merely by association could be undone just as easily. When we analyze things in the external physical world, we discover "things which are always joined together in Nature." But "the habit of analysis has a tendency to wear away the feelings." Why is this so?

Analytic habits may thus even strengthen the associations between causes and effects, means and ends, but tend altogether to weaken those which are, to speak familiarly, a *mere* matter of feeling. . . . A perpetual worm at the root both of the passions and of the virtues; and above all, fearfully undermines all desires, and all pleasures, which are the effects of association. . . . to know that a feeling would make me happy if I had it, did not give me the feeling. My education, I thought, had failed to create these feelings in sufficient strength to resist the dissolving influence of analysis, while the whole course of my intellectual cultivation had made precocious and premature analysis the inveterate habit of mind.[33]

The point about analysis is a subtle one. To analyze something is to break it down into parts. What radicalism needed was an argument or doctrine that would connect the good of separate individuals with the common good or the good of the whole. To see unity is to see a whole. Analysis has the opposite effect. This is precisely where imagination can come into play. It is not possible for reason to provide a comprehensive account of the whole; that is what is meant, in part, by saying that the pre-conceptual, around which reason constantly circles, cannot itself be conceptualized. The world is not such that a comprehensive view of the whole can be achieved. It is only in the imaginative act, in poetical vision, that we intimate a totality when only the parts are perceived. Imagination properly understood is not sheer autonomous creativity; imagination is the source of the discovery of objective reality. This insight had been obscured if not obfuscated by the classical insistence that all structure is external.

Mill worried that his critics might be right to regard his intellectual inheritance as "cold calculation; political economy as hard-hearted; anti-population doctrines as repulsive to the natural feelings of mankind."[34] In a letter written to his new friend Sterling, Mill expressed his sense of alienation:

By loneliness I mean the absence of that feeling which has accompanied me through the greater part of my life, that which one fellow-traveler, or one fellow-soldier has towards another – the feeling of being engaged in the pursuit of a common object, and of mutually cheering one another on, and helping one another in an arduous undertaking. This, which after all is one of the strongest ties of individual sympathy, is at present, so far as I am concerned, suspended at least, if not entirely broken off. There is now no human being (with whom I can associate on terms of equality) who acknowledges a common object with me, or with whom I can cooperate even in any practical undertaking, without feeling that I am only using a man, whose purposes are different, as an instrument for the furtherance of my own.[35]

A fourth reason for the attraction of Wordsworth has to do with Mill's conception of the role of art within social science. What Wordsworth's view contends is that there is no conflict between the truths of science and the emotional truths made manifest in poetry. This had been Shelley's position, and indeed the position of most Romantic writers. Mill not only agreed with this view, thereby underscoring the contention that there were truths about humanity that were different from truths about the world but still consistent with those truths, but was led by it to develop a unique conception of poetry. Emotions can be aroused by or associated with ideas in such a way that those emotions or feelings and subsequent actions became important facts in themselves. As Hegelians would put it, we are in ourselves what we are for ourselves, that is, we are who we think and feel we are.

A crucial element in Mill's rethinking was the recognition of the vital role of imagination as opposed to reason. Reason was identified with analysis, the reduction of things to their parts, where the parts are understood to have causal relations that are themselves reducible to sequences of space and time. Analysis enables us to discover structure, but what it cannot give us is meaning. During the eighteenth century, both Hume and Kant had recast the imagination, hitherto viewed only pejoratively as a distorting force, into a positive force. Like animals, we observe sequences of regularity in our experience. But unlike animals, we are free to choose how to interpret the significance or meaning of a great part of that experience. One of the most important ways in which we utilize our imagination is in reconstructing the thoughts of other persons. Again unlike animals, we learn to engage the world through our inherited culture and not merely through instinct. But our culture is not merely something we inherit; it is something we have to appropriate. It is the ordering of our experience in imagination that makes us unique individuals. It is taking responsibility for our ordering that makes us free.

The stress on imagination, as opposed to intellect, is a familiar Romantic theme. It reflects the nineteenth-century rejection of the eighteenth century's narrow rationalism, although we have noted how Hume and Kant had anticipated much of it. It expresses an underlying philosophical dispute that plays an important part in Mill's thinking. The dispute is over whether it is how we understand the physical world or how we understand ourselves that is fundamental. We understand ourselves through the appropriation of our whole cultural inheritance. Intellect can teach us about sequences in the physical world, but only imagination and sympathy can teach us about the significance of the human world. It is clear on which side of the dispute Mill will find himself, and why this will bring him into conflict with the views of his father. The dispute is still a critical point of contemporary debate among those who have seemingly identified two conflicting cultures, the culture of analysis, instrumental reason, and technocracy versus the culture of imagination.

The first consequence of this view of the primacy of imagination is the recognition that ultimate values are apprehended through imagination.

This is why Mill will contend, in the *System of Logic*, that science needs to be supplemented by art, intellect supplemented by imagination. In a letter to Carlyle, Mill asserted that "most of the highest truths, are, to persons endowed by nature in certain ways which I think I could state, intuitive."[36] The second consequence will be Mill's embrace of the German Romantic concept of *Bildung*, the idea that our freedom consists in the continuous creation and re-creation of ourselves. The third consequence is the role of external liberty in cultivating the enactment of our internal freedom. One of the reasons Mill will be so adamant about opposing censorship and encouraging debate is that it is only in the imaginative re-creation, the rehashing, of the arguments that we come to understand truly the meaning of ultimate values and to make that meaning a vital part of who we are. It is liberty in the service of freedom, freedom understood as self-definition, and self-definition conceived as an imaginative process that underscore the transformation of Mill's thought as a result of his engagement with the Romantic poets.

Another way of putting this point is that analytic reason is concerned with the identification of structure, whereas imagination is the faculty that enables us to identify meaning or the whole as opposed to the parts that make it up. The meaning of an individual life or the meaning of our relationship to a larger social whole is an imaginative construct, and sustaining that construct requires cultivation of the inner person, or what Mill came to call the "internal culture of the individual." In a letter to Carlyle, Mill defined his task as making "those who are not poets, understand that poetry is higher than Logic, and that the union of the two is Philosophy."[37]

There is an intimate tie between Mill's discovery of imagination and the vindication of human freedom. If everything were subject to analysis, then everything could be conceptualized. If everything could be conceptualized, then, as Mill understood it, everything could be reduced ultimately to unalterable sequences in nature. Our feelings and values would not so much be "ours" as they would be the consequences of impersonal forces over which we had, in the end, no control. To be one's own person is to take responsibility for one's deepest feelings; this can only be done if individuals are ultimately free in some real sense. If individuals were not free, then among other things Mill could never be anything but the product of his father's will.

A final reason for Wordsworth's appeal is that he spoke directly to Mill's emancipation from his father. The poem that impressed Mill the most was

"Intimations of Immortality from Recollections of Early Childhood."[38]
Wordsworth began the poem by quoting

> *The child is father of the man;*
> *And I could wish my days to be*
> *Bound each to each by natural piety.*

He spoke to Mill's disillusionment in saying that

> The things which I have seen I now can see no more
> . . .
> But yet I know, wher'er I go,
> That there hath past away a glory from the earth.

He recognized that it was time to

> Forget the glories he hath known,
> And that imperial palace whence he came.

But he also understood the new attitude that

> Though nothing can bring back the hour
> Of splendor in the grass, of glory in the flower;
> We will grieve not, rather find
> Strength in what remains behind.

What transpires is a situation in which we

> Behold the child among his new-born blisses
> . . .
> With light upon him from his father's eyes!
> See, at his feet, some little plan or chart,
> Some fragment from his dream of human life,
> Shaped by himself with newly-learned art;
> . . .
> We will grieve not, rather find
> Strength in what remains behind;
> . . .
> In the faith that looks through death,
> In years that bring the philosophic mind.
> . . .
> I only have relinquished one delight
> To live beneath your more habitual sway.

Mill first met Wordsworth at one of Henry Taylor's London breakfasts.[39] In 1831, Mill visited Wordsworth in the lake country. He found him not only to be a great conversationalist but someone interested in public policy issues. Wordsworth was a Tory, but a philosophic one. Mill found his political differences with Wordsworth to be matters of factual detail, while that his own differences with the Philosophic Radicals he found to be matters of principle.[40] No doubt this suggested to Mill a new philosophical synthesis and new possibilities for forming a political constituency.

Mill's emphasis on the poetical dimension of human life connects with other themes in his writing. Mill's dislike of certain features of English cultural life and his dislike of the more austere dimension of Protestantism reflect recognition of the perceived impoverishment of a Calvinist-Protestant culture that had failed to assimilate the humanist dimension of traditional Christianity.[41] This was a critique that Matthew Arnold shared, and it would later be reflected in Arnold's praise, on becoming rector of St. Andrews, for Mill's *On Liberty* and Mill's educational philosophy. Mill would make a similar criticism of Americans in the early editions of his *Principles of Political Economy*, where he said that American men are devoted to dollar hunting and American women to breeding dollar hunters. Despite Mill's critique of organized religion in general and of Catholicism in particular, Mill was known to attend mass when he later traveled to Rome,[42] perhaps to share in the appreciation of the aesthetic dimension of religious life.

Disenchantment with Radicalism

We have now completed our survey of the three dimensions of Mill's disenchantment with his father's view. The three dimensions are (a) an impoverished conception of human fulfillment, (b) a denial of freedom of the will, and (c) the inability to deal with the issue of how the individual good is related to the common good. These three issues are intrinsically related, and Mill's resolution of them forms part of a larger synthesis in his work. Although we shall be discussing each of these issues in greater detail as they emerge in later works, some indication of their interrelationship can be given here.

If one denies the freedom of the will – as Benthamites, including James Mill, did – then liberty can be understood only as the absence of external constraints. If one has a simplistic, hedonistic account of human nature, then one can construe human motivation only as the attempt to maximize pleasure and to minimize pain. If one holds both of these beliefs, as James Mill did, then the issue of how the maximization-minimization of one individual is related to the maximization-minimization of other individuals has to be understood in terms of the common good as a set of general conditions within which each is at liberty to pursue his or her self-interest. James Mill believed and asserted that democracy was the means to sustain those general conditions. James Mill's argument will not work. The critique of democracy is as old as Plato and Aristotle. Macaulay's critique recalled the wisdom of the ancients and was reinforced by Tocqueville's reconceptualization of democracy as the tyranny of the majority. Given the impoverished conception of human nature and the lack of free will, there can be no appeal to other or higher motives to maintain the common good.

What Mill needs to replace his father's position is the notion of the higher motives that can sustain the common good. These higher motives require a richer conception of human fulfillment. These higher motives require that individuals possess the internal freedom (i.e., free will) as well as the external liberty to develop them. If we come to the view, as Mill does in time, that human beings possess internal freedom; and if the exercise of that freedom in ourselves and in others becomes our higher motive; and if we understand the exercise of that freedom as personal autonomy, so that no autonomous person can sustain his or her personal autonomy when treating others paternalistically (Hegel's master-slave relationship argument), then true maximization of personal welfare becomes identical with the maximization of the welfare of others. Everything turns on making sense of human freedom. Can this be done in a way consistent with some notion of social science? It is this question that Mill tries to resolve in the *System of Logic*.

Before we turn to that work, we must do two things. First, we must explore Mill's continuing recognition of the need for a richer conception of human fulfillment, and this we shall do in the discussion of his relationship with Harriet Taylor. Second, we must see the extent to which that richer conception can be understood in a deeper philosophical way, and it is the influence of the Romantic movement which made that possible for Mill.

How, then, does Mill come in time to differ from his father and from Bentham? What Mill admired in the Philosophic Radicals was the defense of liberal culture and the attempt to free it from the remaining shackles of feudalism. What he disliked was their philosophic rationale. What Mill disliked about the Romantic movement, at least in its English manifestation (e.g., Coleridge), was its defense of the status quo against liberal culture. What he admired about the Romantic movement was its historicism and its philosophic rationale. What he will go on to construct is a Romantic rationale for liberal culture. Mill's utilitarianism adds a moral psychology that rejects hedonism in favor of higher moral ideals. It is Benthamite only in retaining the language of hedonism and in maintaining universality or social utility as the ultimate standard; Mill will combine Kant's conception of duty with Bentham's conception of individual self-interest by making the pursuit of autonomy the ultimate end. He will embrace Alexander Bain's improved version of his father's associationism as a way of explaining how higher sentiments are properties that emerge from simpler feelings of pleasure and pain. Mill will also ultimately accept the existence of free will. Mill recognized the danger of democracy (from Tocqueville) – specifically, its egalitarianism, homogenization, and denial of individuality – and advocated intermediate institutions that promote both internal culture and social cooperation. He came to see that Benthamism led to liberticide, the tyranny of public opinion.[43]

Mill managed to resolve the personal crisis in his life. His resolution is noted in a letter to Carlyle:

None however of them all ["the old narrow school of Utilitarians"] has become so unlike what he once was as I myself, who originally was the narrowest of them all, having been brought up more exclusively under the influence of a peculiar kind of impressions than any other person ever was. Fortunately however I was not *crammed*; my own thinking faculties were called into strong though but partial play; & by their means I have been enabled to *remake* all my opinions.[44]

New Friendships

Mill's discovery of the imagination was reflected in his activity at the London Debating Society that he had helped to establish. In 1827, he spoke on Byron, in a talk entitled "On the Present State of Literature;" in 1828, on "Perfectibility;" in January of 1829, he spoke on Wordsworth; and again in January of 1829, Mill championed the poetry of Wordsworth against that of Byron (who was defended by the *Westminster Review* crowd, including Roebuck, who particularly liked the fact that Byron was an aristocrat who died fighting for freedom in a foreign land). This was an early indication of the distance between Mill and his friends among the Philosophic Radicals. In fact, the whole issue of the status of art and the role of the poet was a frequent topic of debate in the *Westminster Review*. On April 15, 1829, Mill resigned from the London Debating Society, a move that reflects his total disenchantment with radicalism and his recognition that he could not achieve what he wanted through live debate. He would debate no more, except in print.

The whole notion of debating now struck Mill as reflecting that part of the worldview of Philosophic Radicalism that he had come to reject. The logic of debate presupposes a world in which all practice is based on self-conscious theory, that theories are composed of timeless first principles, and that victory in debate and subsequent influence on public policy comes about when one has established the superiority of one's own set of first principles. The influence of Macaulay and the subsequent influence of Saint-Simon had made Mill too conscious of the importance of history and context, and of the far more complex relationship between practice and theory, to embrace this logic.

Something happened to Mill during the debate with Roebuck. Although they had been close friends, and although Mill would continue to admire Roebuck's political courage in the decades to come, Mill saw how he had grown apart from Roebuck. Further, what Mill saw in Roebuck was a general failing he attributed to English national character.

Roebuck, all whose instincts were those of action and struggle, had, on the contrary, a strong relish and great admiration for Byron . . . while Wordsworth's [writing], according to him, was that of flowers and butterflies. . . . The schism between us widened from this time more and more, though we continued for some years longer to be companions. In the beginning, our chief divergence related to the cultivation of the feelings. Roebuck was in many respects very different from the vulgar notion of a Benthamite or Utilitarian. He was a lover of poetry and most of the fine arts. . . . But he never could be made to see that these things have any value as aids in the formation of character. . . . Like most Englishmen who have feelings, he found his feelings stand very much in his way. . . . Roebuck [who had been born in Canada] was, or appeared to be, this kind of Englishman. He saw little good in any cultivation of the feelings, and none at all in cultivating them through the imagination, which he thought was only cultivating illusions. It was in vain I urged on him that the imaginative emotion which an idea, when vividly conceived, excites in us, is not an illusion but a fact as real as any of the other qualities of objects. . . .

Something else had happened at the Society. It was at a debate during February of 1828 on the role of the church that Mill met John Sterling (who had belonged to the Apostles at Cambridge). It was to be Sterling and Frederick Denison Maurice who introduced Mill to Coleridge. Sterling, the son of the influential Edward Sterling of *The Times*, had studied the works of the German Romantic philosopher Friedrich von Schelling. Mill described their presence as follows: "[T]he Coleridgians, in the persons of Maurice and Sterling, made their appearance in the Society as a second Liberal and even Radical party, on totally different grounds from Benthamism and vehemently opposed to it; bringing into those discussions the general doctrines and modes of thought of the European reaction against the philosophy of the eighteenth century. . . ."[45] Mill went on to delineate their characters and their influence upon him:

Maurice was the thinker, Sterling the orator, and impassioned expositor of thoughts which, at this period, were almost entirely formed for him by Maurice. With Maurice . . . though my discussions with him were almost always disputes, I had carried away from them much that helped to build up my new fabric of thought, in the same way as I was deriving much from Coleridge, and from the writings of Goethe and other German authors which I read during those years. . . . He [Maurice] might be described as a disciple of Coleridge, and Sterling as a disciple of him.[46]

By his own admission, Mill was more attached to Sterling than to any other man in his life. With the exception of Sterling and, later, Harriet Taylor, all of Mill's friendships were professional and intellectual, focusing on common causes and projects. Only Sterling and Harriet allowed him to feel comfortable with expressing his emotions, let alone having them.

With Sterling I soon became very intimate, and was more attached to him than I have ever been to any other man. . . . An equal devotion to Liberty and Duty, formed a combination of qualities as attractive to me, as to all others who knew him as well as I did. . . . He told me how he and others had looked upon me (from hearsay information) as a "made" or manufactured man . . . and what a change took place in his feelings when he found, in the discussion of Wordsworth and Byron, that Wordsworth, and all which that name implies, 'belonged' to me as much as to him and his friends.[47]

Sterling's description of Mill is also worth noting. He described Mill as "uniting a warm, upright and really lofty soul with a still and even cold appearance, and with a head that reasons as a great Steam Engine works."[48] Sterling and Mill saw a good deal of each other from 1828 until 1831, when Sterling left for the West Indies. Letters aside, their close association resumed in 1838 and continued until Sterling's death in 1844.

Mill never really got along with Maurice, but he considered Maurice to have had one of the really great minds, superior even to Coleridge's. What disturbed Mill about Maurice was the latter's insistence upon making his views seem consistent with the thirty-nine articles of the Anglican Church. He thought Maurice typical of those who displayed "timidity of conscience, combined with original sensitiveness of temperament," which drives these "highly gifted men into Romanism from the need of a firmer support than they can find in the independent conclusions of their own judgment."[49] What Mill did like about Maurice was his advocacy of Christian Socialism in 1848, by which was understood opposition to Benthamite individualism and support of worker's cooperatives.

The Saint-Simonians

Another lifelong friendship had also emerged from the London Debating Society. In May of 1828, Mill had met Gustave d'Eichthal, a follower of Saint-Simon. D'Eichthal had been impressed when he heard Mill in debate. "M. Mill, who spoke last . . . and took up one after the other all the points touched on in the discussion, even those furthest from the subject, giving his opinion on each in a few words with a measure, a good sense and a grasp of the matter altogether astonishing."[50] D'Eichthal worked hard to recruit both Mill and Mill's friend William Eyton Tooke for the Saint-Simonian cause and had even hoped to have Mill edit a journal for the Saint-Simonians. Tooke was a fellow clerk whom Mill had met and befriended at India House.

Claude-Henri de Rouvroy, comte de Saint-Simon (1760–1825), was, among other things, an aristocrat, someone who had fought with Lafayette in America, had been imprisoned at the time of the Terror, and at one point had formulated a plan for a Panama Canal. Saint-Simon became famous for formulating a quasi-Newtonian deterministic account of historical progress. Every society was allegedly based on a set of beliefs, of which the most important were the nexus between metaphysical-theoretical knowledge and practical economic activity. Once those beliefs become dysfunctional, the social order erected upon them either collapses or transforms itself into another system. For example, according to Saint-Simon, the Enlightenment attack on religious belief had led to the collapse of feudalism. Modern or postfeudal society would be based upon science, technology, and industry. It would witness the end of the domination of the old ruling class of aristocracy and clergy and their replacement by a kind of new technocracy composed of the rising middle class of entrepreneurs and technicians. Although among the first to recognize the existence of (economic) class conflict, Saint-Simon did not foresee either a classless society or inevitable class conflict. Conflict would be avoided and a new harmony established, as he argued in his 1825 work *Nouveau Christianisme*, through the leadership of the new technocracy of intellectuals and industrialists. Although Saint-Simon's own views were hospitable to private property, after his death some of his followers transformed his movement into a kind of religious collectivism. One of his more influential followers was to be Auguste Comte, whose relationship to Mill we shall explore later.

What was especially important in the works of Saint-Simon was his view of history. Mill was still reeling from Macaulay's critique of his father's ahistorical account of government. Mill accepted Macaulay's point, but he was uncomfortable with Macaulay's essentially classical conservative view of history as a repetitive process from which one could draw lessons. Macaulay's view seemed to support some (Whig) version of the status quo, whereas what Mill sought was a view of history that promised reform. The Saint-Simonians, including Comte, saw history as a teleological process developing toward a final phase. At the time, this was a much more attractive view to Mill. Nevertheless, Macaulay's critique had paved the way for recognizing the significance of Saint-Simon. Saint-Simon dealt with all of the issues central to Mill's concerns at this time, and he did so by using a philosophy of history. In addition to providing some kind of philosophy of history, Saint-Simon advocated a special leadership role for the intellectual class in overcoming aristocratic feudalism and leading the workers into harmony with the new economic order. In addition, the Saint-Simonians advocated the equality of women.

At first, the Saint-Simonians seemed to be traveling on the same road, and what impressed Mill the most about them was the notion that historical conditions introduced an element of variability and progress, that the conditions of one's own time might not be universal. Moreover, institutions that played a positive role at one point in history could become counterproductive at another, as witness the Catholic Church, which in the Saint-Simonian scheme of things was a constructive force during the Middle Ages but a reactionary one during the rise of the new industrialism. Another element of their thinking to which Mill was particularly susceptible at this time was their emphasis on the new intellectual elite.

The Saint-Simonians led Mill to rethink his economic theory. The virtues of the new entrepreneurial class – the idea that merit accrues to one from thrift, postponed gratification, ingenuity, and hard work – and most especially its autonomy left no room for a traditional philanthropic relationship with workers. At the same time, workers emerging out of a feudal context were not always ready to adopt the habits of responsible and autonomous individuals. Two things were needed: (a) an economic theory that recognized historical context and proposed transitional policies for turning workers with feudal thought patterns into autonomous individuals, and (b) a new kind of leadership that was neither hierarchical-feudal nor indifferent to, or ignorant of, the nature of the potential new class conflict.

It was shortly after this time that Mill published a series of seven anonymous articles[51] in the *Examiner*, entitled "Spirit of the Age." Mill's own assessment of the importance of these articles, or extended essay, was that they reflected the Saint-Simonian insight that "in the character of the present age," there were "anomalies and evils characteristic of the transition from a system of opinions which had worn out, to another only in process of being formed."[52] It has been suggested by Gertrude Himmelfarb that this piece, along with "Civilization," marks a more conservative pre–Harriet Taylor phase in his life.[53] While there is some truth to this, this claim does not get at the heart of what Mill was doing.

Mill's flirtation with conservatism is something we shall discuss in the next chapter. For the moment, it is important to note that Mill's conservatism was never a defense of the status quo; that it was, as we shall show, intimately tied to his embrace of Romanticism;[54] that it remained embedded in his conception of history and in other features of his thinking; and that these aspects of conservatism were never challenged by Harriet Taylor. To exemplify the complexity of the issue, we note Mill's letter to Sterling in which he casually says: "I should not care though a revolution were to exterminate every person in Great Britain and Ireland who has [an

income of] £500 a year."[55] What we must not lose sight of is that Mill never
wavered in his commitment to liberal culture. What he sought was both a
more satisfactory philosophical basis for it, some device by which he could
convince the elite of his own time to prepare the workers for meaningful
reform and participation in liberal culture, and an institutional locus from
which the Socratic voice of liberal culture could be heard. For a time, the
Saint-Simonians seemed to offer some of this.

Their criticisms on the common doctrines of Liberalism seemed to me full of
important truth; and it was partly by their writings that my eyes were opened to
the very limited and temporary value of the old political economy, which assumes
private property and inheritance as indefeasible facts, and freedom of production
and exchange as the dernier mot of social improvement. The scheme gradually
unfolded by the St.-Simonians, under which the labour and capital of society
would be managed for the general account of the community, every individual being required to take a share of labour, either as thinker, teacher, artist, or producer,
all being classed according to their capacity, and remunerated according to their
works, appeared to me a far superior description of Socialism to Owen's. Their aim
seemed to me desirable and rational, however their means might be inefficacious;
and though I neither believed in the practicability, nor in the beneficial operation
of their social machinery, I felt that the proclamation of such an ideal of human
society could not but tend to give a beneficial direction to the efforts of others to
bring society, as at present constituted, nearer to some ideal standard.[56]

What had attracted Mill to the Saint-Simonians was their concern for
poverty, their recognition of meritocracy, their support of the emancipation of women, and the importance they attributed to cultural leadership.
As he expressed it in a letter to d'Eichthal,

You were very naturally struck with the superiority of the English to the French
in all those qualities by which a nation is enabled to turn its productive and
commercial resources to the best account. But this superiority is closely connected
with the very worst part in our national character, the disposition to sacrifice
everything to accumulation, and that exclusive and engrossing selfishness which
accompanies it.[57]

In time, Mill became disenchanted with the Saint-Simonians, as he would
with their most influential successor, Comte. It is easy to anticipate the lines
of disenchantment. Mill disapproved of their rejection of private property,
the focus on social as opposed to individual moral reform, the stereotypical
view of women as spiritual, and of their authoritarianism. Moreover, any

mechanistic theory of progress such as one finds in Saint-Simon leaves no
room for individual initiative. Any conception of a technocracy or even
a meritocracy is ultimately incompatible with personal autonomy. As he
wrote to d'Eichthal, he objected to Comte's view that government exists
for just one end. Instead, Mill urged that

the highest and most important of these purposes is the improvement of man
himself as a moral and intelligent being, which is an end not included in M.
Comte's category at all. The untied forces of society never were, nor can be,
directed to one single end.... Men do not come into the world to fulfil one single
end, and there is no single end which if fulfilled even in the most complete manner
would make them happy.[58]

What Mill did conclude from all this was the centrality of a philosophy
of history:

[T]he human mind has a certain order of possible progress, in which some things
must precede others, an order which governments and public instructors can
modify to some, but not to an unlimited extent: That all questions of political
institutions are relative, not absolute, and that different stages of human progress
not only *will* have, but *ought* to have, different institutions: That government is
always either in the hands, or passing into the hands, of whatever is the strongest
power in society, and that what this power is, does not depend on institutions,
but institutions on it: That any general theory or philosophy of politics supposes
a previous theory of human progress, and that this is the same thing with a
philosophy of history.[59]

This view of history, and especially the Saint-Simonian distinction between "organic" and "critical" periods, enabled Mill to transcend Philosophic Radicalism. On the psychological level, at least, Mill could accept
the critique that the Philosophic Radicals advanced against entrenched
interests without having to embrace their positive solution. The radicals
could be seen as a reflection of a critical period but as offering an inadequate
organic resolution.

   Although greatly influenced by their thinking in many areas, Mill disso-
ciated himself from the Saint-Simonians as a movement, especially under
the leadership of Enfantin. By 1832, the organization would be splintered,
with Comte and d'Eichthal refusing to follow Enfantin – who moved to
Constantinople in hopes of finding the female Messiah! Mill wrote to
Carlyle that "there was much in the conduct of them all [Saint-Simonians],

which really one cannot help suspecting of quackery."[60] On the other hand, Mill continued until the end of his life to correspond with d'Eichthal.

ક્ષ

One of Mill's friends and allies at this time was William Eyton Tooke, whose father had founded the Political Economy Club and whom Mill had recruited for the now defunct Utilitarian Society. Tooke was at this time deeply in love, and feeling this love unrequited committed suicide in January of 1830. Sadly, it turns out that Tooke had been mistaken about his love not being returned. This is an important incident in Mill's life, not only because it marks an early tragedy but also because it reflects the deeply romantic nature of some of Mill's closest friends.

It was in 1830 that Mill commenced what he called the most valuable friendship of his life. He met the woman who was to become his wife, except that at the time she was already married. Mill met Harriet Taylor in the summer of 1830 at a dinner party given by her husband, John Taylor, a druggist and successful City businessman, at their home in Finsbury Circus, the City; also in attendance were Graham and Roebuck; William Fox, the minister of South Place Chapel; and Harriet Martineau. At the time, Harriet (née Hardy) was twenty-three and Mill almost twenty-five. She had married John Taylor when she was eighteen and already was the mother of two sons. John Taylor was eleven years her senior.[61] Harriet's first son, Herbert, was born on September 24, 1827; a second son, Algernon (called Haji), was born on February 2, 1830; a daughter, Helen (called Lily) was to be born on July 27, 1831. Harriet had asked Fox for guidance on philosophical issues, and Fox had suggested that she meet Mill. There is some evidence that John Taylor was not a suitable intellectual companion for Harriet. Carlyle characterized Taylor as "an innocent dull good man."[62] But there may have been more to this planned meeting than meets the eye, as we shall see later.

This meeting had been arranged by the charismatic Fox, a Unitarian clergyman who was soon to be the editor of the *Monthly Repository*. Fox had been one of the original contributors to the *Westminster Review* when it was founded in 1824. His circle had included, at one time or another, the feminist author Harriet Martineau and the poet Robert Browning. The circle gathered around Fox reflected not only his personal charisma but the large extent to which among Protestant dissenters an individual congregation in England at this time was the defining cultural unit.

The connection between Unitarianism and utilitarianism had an important basis. The earliest example of a convergence of Unitarians and utilitarians can be seen in the works of Joseph Priestley.[63] Both Harriet and John Taylor were Unitarians and utilitarians, and Harriet was as well a forthright Romantic. She had written reviews, poems, and articles for the *Monthly Review*. A contemporary description of Harriet pictures her as follows:

> Mrs. Taylor . . . was possessed of a beauty and grace quite unique of their kind. Tall and slight, with a slightly drooping figure, the movements of undulating grace. A small head, a swan-like throat, and a complexion like a pearl. Large dark eyes, not soft or sleepy, but with a look of quiet command in them. A low sweet voice with very distinct utterance emphasized the effect of her engrossing personality. Her children idolized her.[64]

Given what we know, it would seem quite remarkable if Mill had not fallen in love with her. Aside from her beauty and vivaciousness, she shared a similar social background, had internalized the same general set of values, reflected the distaste of dissenters for the landed aristocracy, had married someone who reflected entrepreneurial ideals, was ardently in favor of social reform, possessed the intellectual depth to perceive the incongruity between holding to determinism and expecting individuals to improve themselves (a theme widely discussed among Unitarians), had a poetic soul as well as an intellect, belonged to a group of Fox's followers who espoused greater freedom and equality for women,[65] shared Mill's concern for the paralyzing conformity and mediocrity of the middle class, and understood at this early date the need for universal autonomy. As she put it in an early (1832) essay:

> What is called the opinion of Society is a phantom power. . . . It is a combination of the many weak, against the few strong; an association of the mentally listless to punish any manifestation of mental independence. The *remedy is to make all strong enough to stand alone*; and whoever has once known the pleasure of self-dependence, will be in no danger of relapsing into subserviency.[66] [Italics added]

The poetic dimension of Harriet's character appealed to something very deep in Mill's character and concerns at the time. Recall that he had just emerged from the Philosophic Radical denigration of poetry into something like a recognition of its intrinsic value. In an early draft of the

Autobiography, Mill referred to this poetic dimension:

The first years of my friendship with her were, in respect of my own development, mainly years of poetic culture. It is hardly necessary to say that I am not now speaking of *written* poetry, either metrical or otherwise; though I did cultivate this taste as well as a taste for paintings and sculptures & did read with enthusiasm her favorite poets, especially the one whom she placed far above all others, Shelley. But this was merely accessory. The real poetic culture was, that my faculties such as they were, became more & more attuned to the beautiful & elevated, in all kinds, & especially in human feeling & character & more capable of vibrating in unison with it.[67]

At precisely the time that Mill had discovered that the truths of feeling were as important as the truths of fact, he found someone who seemed to embody a great passion for both.

Shortly after meeting Harriet for the first time, Mill went over to Paris in July 1830 with Roebuck and some others, ostensibly to witness the Revolution of 1830 and the fall of Charles X firsthand. He was disillusioned by the failure of the middle class to embrace democratic reform and became less hopeful about the possibility of radical change. The failure of the middle class in the Revolution of 1830 led Mill to become more sympathetic to Saint Simonian elitism as a vehicle for reform.[68] He even met with some of their leaders in August, including Enfantin. This was around the same time that he was becoming imbued with Coleridge's notion of a "clerisy."

In 1830, the building for the Athenaeum Club was completed. James Mill had been one of the original members in 1824, and he was now one of the members of a committee to elect 100 new members. Among others, the committee selected Mill. Mill later was to tell Bain that he would not have been admitted except through his father's influence, as he had aroused personal dislike.[69] By 1831, Mill had come to reject large parts of radicalism; had been introduced to Romanticism by a series of new friends and acquaintances; had come to recognize the virtues of conservatism; had met his future wife, whose subsequent influence would be as great as his father's had been; had seemingly resolved his personal crisis; and was earning £600 a year at India House, where he was now sixth in rank of seniority. He summed up his position as follows:

[T]hough I no longer accepted the doctrine of the Essay on Government [James Mill's work] as a scientific theory; though I ceased to consider representative democracy as an absolute principle, and regarded it as a question of time, place, and circumstance; though I now looked upon the choice of political institutions as a moral and educational question more than one of material interests, thinking that it ought to be decided mainly by the consideration, what great improvement in life and culture stands next in order for the people concerned, as the condition of their further progress, and what institutions are most likely to promote that; nevertheless this change in the premises of my political philosophy did not alter my practical political creed as to the requirements of my own time and country. I was as much as ever a radical and a democrat for Europe, and especially for England. I thought the predominance of the aristocratic classes, the noble and the rich, in the English Constitution an evil worth any struggle to get rid of . . . as the great demoralizing agency of the country. Demoralizing, first, because it made the conduct of government an example of gross public immorality, through the predominance of private over public interests in the State, and the abuse of the powers of legislation for the advantage of classes. Secondly . . . because . . . riches and the signs of riches, were almost the only things really respected, and the life of the people was mainly devoted to the pursuit of them. I thought, that while the higher and richer classes held the power of government, and the instruction and improvement of the mass of the people were contrary to the self-interest of those classes, because tending to render the people more powerful for throwing off the yoke; but if the democracy obtained a large, and perhaps the principal, share in the governing power, it would become the interest of the opulent classes to promote their education, in order to ward off really mischievous errors, and especially those which would lead to unjust violations of property. On these grounds I was not only as ardent as ever for democratic institutions, but earnestly hoped that Owenite, St. Simonian, and all those other anti-property doctrines might spread widely among the poorer classes; not that I thought those doctrines true, or desired that they should be acted on, but in order that the higher classes might be made to see that they had more to fear from the poor when uneducated, than when educated.[70]

In reading Mill's *Autobiography*, it becomes clear that he presented the crisis as a positive event in his life. It marks the transition from Mill the radical proselytizer of Benthamism to Mill the Romantic synthesizer. It marks the discovery of his soul and of the woman who would become the great influence in his life when his father's influence waned. But behind this literary transcendence was a compromise with his father's views, a compromise that would continue to haunt his published work for years to come.

4

The Discovery of Romance
and Romanticism
(1830–1840)

THE PERIOD of Mill's life following his great crisis was defined nega-
tively by the death of the two great intellectual influences of his early
life, Bentham in 1832 and James Mill, his father, in 1836. These deaths,
coming so quickly after his crisis, created a vacuum that was shortly to be
filled by the influential movements of Romanticism and conservatism. It
was also defined positively by the growth of his relationship with the great
love of his life, Harriet Taylor.

In 1830, Henry Taylor (not to be confused with John Taylor) described
Mill as follows:

His manners were plain, neither graceful nor awkward; his features refined and
regular; the eyes small relatively to the scale of the face, the jaw large, the nose
straight and finely shaped, the lips thin and compressed, the forehead and head
capacious; and both face and body seemed to represent outwardly the inflexibility
of the inner man. He shook hands with you from the shoulder. Though for the
most part plainly grave, he was as sensible as anybody to Charles Austin's or
Charles Villier's sallies of wit, and his strong and well-knit body would heave for
a few moments with half-uttered laughter.[1]

Mill was now part of the larger social scene, attending the salons organized by Sarah Austin, Mrs. Grote, and Mrs. Charles Buller. Mill also
frequented the salon of Lady Harriet Baring. For a while Mill was quite
infatuated with her (this was even after he had first met Harriet Taylor),
but Lady Baring was unresponsive, so he abruptly stopped attending. No
doubt much speculation will result from the observation that Mill persistently seemed attracted to women who bore his mother's name. The other
point worth noting is Mill's attraction to married women. It is worth keeping in mind that outside his immediate family Mill had always moved in
a world of adults, including adult married women. From adolescence on,

he had always contrasted, in his own mind, the difference between his own mother's lack of both strength of character and seeming affection for him and the warmth, strength, and organizational skills of Mrs. Samuel Bentham, whom he had described in his *Autobiography* as the "ruling spirit of her household." One exception to the foregoing is the attraction Mill felt toward Eliza Flower when he joined Fox's circle.[2]

In 1831, James Mill, who was now chief examiner of India House, moved to a larger house at Vicarage Place, Church Street, Kensington. Mill continued to live there with his mother and family even after his father died; he did not leave until he himself married in 1851. The family continued to spend their summer holidays at the house in Mickleham that James Mill had purchased in 1828. Carlyle, who visited there as Mill's guest, described it as "a pleasant summer mansion connected by shed-roof passages, the little drawing-room door of glass looking out into a rose lawn."[3] Mill spent weekends and six weeks during the summer at Mickleham.

Having survived his crisis, Mill took stock of where he was:

If I am asked what system of political philosophy I substituted for that which, as a philosophy, I had abandoned, I answer, no system: only a conviction, that the true system was something much more complex, and many sided than I had previously had any idea of, and that its office was to supply, not a set of model institutions, but principles from which the institutions suitable to any given circumstances might be deduced. The influences of European, that is to say, Continental, thought, and especially those of the reaction of the nineteenth century against the eighteenth, were now streaming in upon me.[4]

Following on his new concern for the relation between individuals and the social whole, he read Saint-Simon and Comte for the first time in 1830 and traveled to Paris after the July Revolution. He was also to meet Thomas Carlyle in 1831. What St. Simon, Comte, and Carlyle had in common for Mill was the fact that they introduced him to the voice of Continental Romanticism.

Mill had first heard that voice through John Austin. John Austin, with whom Mill had studied law, had himself spent time in Germany from 1826 to 1828. It was Carlyle who described Austin as one who "set forth Utilitarianism *steeped* in German metaphysics not dissolved therein. . . ."[5] It was Austin's wife, Sarah, who taught Mill to read German[6] and who introduced Mill to Carlyle. (In the 1820s there were only two academics

at Oxford who knew German!) Sarah Austin would also go on to publish, in 1833, *The Characteristics of Goethe*, and the writings of Goethe[7]
to which Mill was thus introduced had a tremendous impact on his
thinking.

> Among the persons of intellect whom I had known of old, the one with whom I
> had now [1830] most points of agreement was the elder Austin. I have mentioned
> that he always set himself in opposition to our early sectarianism; and latterly he
> had, like myself, come under new influences. . . . he had lived for some time at
> Bonn to study for his Lectures; and the influences of German literature and of
> the German character and state of society had made a very perceptible change in
> his views of life. . . . His tastes had begun to turn themselves towards the poetic
> and contemplative. He attached much less importance than formerly to outward
> changes; unless accompanied by a better cultivation of the inward nature. . . . Like
> me, he never ceased to be an utilitarian, and with all his love of the Germans,
> and enjoyment of their literature, never became in the smallest degree recon-
> ciled to the innate-principle metaphysics. He cultivated more and more a kind of
> German religion, a religion of poetry and feeling with little, if anything, of positive
> dogma. . . . he rejoiced in . . . Socialism, as the most effectual means of compelling
> the powerful classes to educate the people, and to impress on them the only real
> means of permanently improving their material condition, a limitation of their
> numbers.[8]

All of this is by way of reinforcing the claim of the enormous number
and diversity of sources from which Mill imbibed Romanticism.

Romanticism[9]

It is now generally conceded that Mill was influenced by the Romantic
movement in general and by specific representatives of that movement.
Francis Place[10] and Dicey both tell us that Mill tried to reconcile the
eighteenth- and nineteenth-century elements in his thinking.

> In plain fact Mill was between 1838 and 1840 deeply moved by the changing
> sentiment of the age. He conceived that the dogmas in which he had been educated
> represented but half the truth. He would willingly have taken to himself Goethe's
> device of many-sidedness – a motto which, whatever its worth, was not applicable
> either to Bentham or to his followers. . . . Yet the true peculiarity of John Mill's
> position is that while to his dying day he defended principles derived from his
> father and from Bentham, he had to a great extent imbibed the sentiment, the
> sympathies, and the ideals of the later nineteenth century. The labour of his life

was the reconciliation of inherited beliefs, from which he never departed, with moral and intellectual ideas and sympathies which, belonging to himself and to his time, were foreign, if not opposed, to the doctrines of his school. This double aspect of Mill's work can be discerned in his writings.[11]

This notion of the reconciliation of opposites will be articulated in Mill's reconciliation of poetry and science; within poetry, in his reconciliation of Wordsworth and Shelley; and in philosophy, in his reconciliation of Bentham and Coleridge.[12] It will be cited in the *Autobiography*, and it will be immortalized in Mill's critique of censorship in the essay *On Liberty*.

What is not generally recognized is how pervasive that influence was. Nor has it been recognized that the very idea of reconciling the eighteenth-century Enlightenment Project and the Romantic reaction of the nineteenth century is itself both a reflection of Romanticism and an indication that the nature of that reconciliation must itself be Romantic.

Mill's personal crisis from 1826 to 1830 was a response to the perceived inadequacy of the Enlightenment Project, its mechanized conception of the world and humanity and its attempt to conceptualize the world in geometric or spatial terms, without reference to temporality. It was the friendship with Carlyle that first made Mill aware of the Romantic alternative in historical terms. This was soon followed by the influence of the Saint-Simonians. It was his reading of Wordsworth that made Mill aware of the Romantic conception of the world in aesthetic terms and of the role of the artist. It was from Coleridge that Mill learned the importance of imagination and made his first acquaintance with German philosophic idealism. By the mid-1830s, Mill had formulated the project of reconciling Bentham and Coleridge. Mill's lifelong obsession with overcoming dualisms and harmonizing antagonistic modes of thought was neither a quirk nor an expression of insecurity but rather an instantiation of the methodology of Romanticism.[13]

Romanticism had two dimensions, literary and philosophical. In Romanticism as a literary movement, as represented in the works of Goethe, Schiller, Coleridge, and Wordsworth, imagination was thought to be more important that reason or ratiocination. Imagination, which from the time of the ancients had been viewed as a distorting force that clouded our vision of the external objective structure, became for the Romantics a positive force. Standards and guidance came from an inward source, and literary Romanticism fastened upon imagination as the fundamental source. Our inner emotional life became the source or medium of universal truths. Wordsworth, in "The Tables Turned," put it this way:

> One impulse from a vernal wood
> May teach you more of man,
> Of moral evil and of good,
> Than all the sages can.

Mill's first expression of these Romantic themes appeared in two articles in the *Monthly Repository*, "What Is Poetry?" (January 1833) and "The Two Kinds of Poetry" (October 1833).[14] Here Mill argued that there were two kinds of truth and that poets accessed an inner and more fundamental realm, a realm of truths about ourselves as opposed to truths about the world.

Great poets are often proverbially ignorant of life. What they know has come by observation of themselves; they have found *there* one highly delicate, and sensitive, and refined specimen of human nature, on which the laws of human emotion are written in large characters, such as can be read off without much study; and other knowledge of mankind, such as comes to men of the world by outward experience, is not indispensable to them as poets.[15]

Moreover, these emotional truths have a logic or structure of their own. That is, they are not simply the result of external conditioning (as in James Mill's theory of association).

Where, therefore, nature has given strong feelings, and education has not created factitious tendencies stronger than the natural ones, the prevailing associations will be those which connect objects and ideas with emotions, and with each other through the intervention of emotions. . . . All the combinations which the mind puts together . . . will be indebted to some dominant feeling, not as in other natures to a dominant thought.[16]

To be a poet is to be someone whose succession of thoughts is "subordinate to the course of his emotions."[17] At the time he wrote this, Mill ranked Wordsworth and Shelley highest on this scale, but later he would come to recognize Shelley as the supreme example – and ultimately the poet would be best exemplified by Harriet Taylor!

Although recognizing these two sources of truth, Mill insisted that poetic sensibility and intellectual analysis are not incompatible. Nevertheless, the poet is superior in possessing both a greater desire to know and a greater depth of motivation. "The greater the individual's capability of happiness and of misery, the stronger interest has that individual in arriving at truth; and when once that interest is felt, an impassioned nature is sure to pursue this, as to pursue any other object, with greater ardour; for energy of character is always the offspring of strong feelings."[18]

As a philosophical movement, Romanticism, as represented in the works of Humboldt, Fichte, Schelling, and Hegel, still proclaimed reason as the source or medium of universal truths. But reason could no longer be understood as a mirror held up to a contextless independent structure. Epistemologically, Romanticism exemplified modernity and Kant's Copernican revolution in philosophy. Rather than being the result of grasping an external structure, our understanding of the world reflected the imposition upon it of an internally generated frame of reference. The internal framework was not just intellectual but imaginative and affective as well. It is in this sense that art was construed as the expression of feeling and not as the mere representation of external structure. The internal sources of the framework were not subjective but again reflected both universal truths about humanity and the larger cultural context. In discovering the meaning of something, we discover our own meaning, for we are the givers of meaning. This is the view one finds in writers as varied as Herder, Novalis, Goethe, Wordsworth, Shelley, Keats, and Byron.

Reason originated within the human frame of reference. The basic form of human awareness in our mental life is time. Reason has to be understood as having a temporal or historical dimension. Although Kant had recognized moral progress, he still postulated a rigid set of categories. The Romantic philosophers, on the other hand, went further and saw even transcendental truths as evolving through time. The temporal and historical transformations of a concept or category become part of the very meaning of that concept or category. Internal standards are dynamic, not static, for they evolve over time. Purely inductive or empirical explanations (general causal laws of succession among particulars) are inadequate. Good thinking relates individuals to larger wholes. Consequently the static analysis needs a larger dynamic framework. Understanding social institutions, for example, requires not atomistic analysis but recognition of the larger historical context; the utility of an institution cannot be measured independent of its history.

Although Romanticism shared with the Enlightenment a belief in the importance of freedom, it nevertheless quarreled over the formulation of the meaning of freedom and about how it was to be cultivated. Processes were to be understood in terms of their function or goal. This organicism opposed the atomistic reductivism of the Enlightenment in favor of holistic analysis. The parts, whatever they were, could not be understood, or even identified, apart from some larger functioning whole. As Wordsworth was to put it, "We murder to dissect." Applied to humanity, this meant that we could not understand ourselves apart from culture and history.

How was it possible for the internal framework to be both universal and culturally specific? In appropriating our cultural inheritance, we come to realize (a) that there is no such thing as human nature – in the fixed, classical, Aristotelian sense – but only what we can call the human condition; (b) that we create and define ourselves; (c) that what distinguishes us from animals is that we are free to choose how we interpret our experience; (d) that our initial framework is the result of a cultural inheritance; and (e) that in accepting responsibility for our freedom and in developing the inheritance, we enact ourselves. This is what permitted Kant to maintain that ethical conduct presupposes freedom, that to be free is to prescribe moral standards for oneself, and that our only consistent self-imposed obligation is to will the good for everyone. As opposed to the Enlightenment notion of environmental redesign, Romanticism advocated internal self-cultivation, what the Germans came to call *Bildung*.

One other element was central to Romantic philosophy – nostalgia for Greek institutions. Mill shared in the nostalgia for classical Greece. It is reflected in his friendship with the historian Grote, in his articles on classical philosophy and philosophers, in his address at St. Andrew's on becoming rector, in his praise of Pericles in *On Liberty*, and in the concern in his social writings to close the gap between individual self-development and civic responsibility. This Romantic view of the world and of the place of humanity within it is not unproblematic, as later developments were to show. But figures as diverse as Goethe, Hegel, and Mill[19] all thought that some conception of wholeness, an integrated view of humanity and nature, a new science, was still possible. As Mill expressed it in a later letter to Comte:

... I have myself read neither Kant nor Hegel, nor any of the other leaders of that school; I know them only through their English and French interpreters. This philosophy has been extremely useful to me. It has corrected the excessively analytic disposition of my thought, nourished by Bentham and the French philosophers of the eighteenth century. Add to that its critique of the negative school, and above all a real, if incomplete, appreciation of the laws of historical development and of the filiation of the different states of man and society – a sense of all this, I believe, most developed in Hegel.[20]

It is difficult to see how Mill could have avoided being a Romantic. He was driven to it by the logic of his basic philosophical position and by the nineteenth-century critique of the Enlightenment Project. None of this should be surprising, given the cultural and intellectual currents of the nineteenth century. He was driven to it by the emotional dimension of his personality, as reflected in his personal crisis, in his discovery of poetry, and of Wordsworth, and in his meeting Harriet Taylor. Among other things, this Romantic resolution solves the riddle of modernity – namely, how to synthesize the individual good and the common good. This resolution is not identical to Hegel's, but Hegel is a natural analogue, given the breadth, depth, and commitment to the explication of liberal culture. Finally, we should not be surprised that British Idealism is the natural heir to Mill's philosophical endeavor.

Carlyle[21]

A key influence in Mill's movement away from radicalism was Thomas Carlyle (1795–1881). The main theme of Carlyle's work is the sense that mankind's most important convictions no longer found adequate expression. In part, this reflected Carlyle's deeply Calvinistic sense of life and his disengagement from any church. He found in German Romantic philosophy a medium for his religious convictions. He came to see history as the providential embodiment of divine justice, where the providence was reflected in social moral consensus. The "hero" – who could be a prophet, a poet, a man of letters, or a political leader – expressed the consensus. When the consensus was violated, revolution against a corrupt leadership, as in the French Revolution, was justified. In place of the Enlightenment's mechanistic and atomistic view of the universe, Carlyle saw the world in organic terms, as the material expression of divine purpose. This larger metaphysical view permitted Carlyle to imagine a mystical state uniting all to a higher end. Serious differences aside, this was precisely the kind of new framework for which Mill was looking.

Carlyle was very critical of the Philosophic Radicals. In "Signs of the Times" (1829), he had berated them for thinking that good government would emerge from enlightened self-interest instead of virtue. He pointed out how the doctrines of Hartley lead to fatalism, how the radicals denied the existence of the inner person, how they believed that events resulted from impersonal forces and not human responsibility and that people were ruled not by virtue but by public opinion. In opposition to all of this, Carlyle asserted that social reform must begin with self-reform. The important lesson that Mill learned from both Wordsworth and Carlyle is that real change comes through changes in human self-consciousness and not by engineering new types of government.

Carlyle read and was impressed by Mill's essay *The Spirit of the Age* (1831). Sarah Austin then arranged for Mill to be introduced to Carlyle. On first meeting Mill, Carlyle described him as follows: " . . . a slender, rather tall and elegant youth, with a small Roman-nose face, two small earnestly-smiling eyes; modest, remarkably gifted with precision of utterance, enthusiastic, yet lucid, calm; not a great, yet a distinctly gifted and amiable youth."[22] Mill had first read *Sartor Resartus* in manuscript form in 1831 and found it an "insane rhapsody." Later, he recognized that

What truths they [the works of Carlyle] contained, though of the very kind which I was already receiving from other quarters, were presented in a form and vesture less suited than any other to give them access to a mind trained as mine had been. They seemed a haze of poetry and German metaphysics, in which almost the only clear thing was a strong animosity to most of the opinions which were the basis of my mode of thought.[23]

Mill's later description of Carlyle to Sterling is equally interesting:

Another acquaintance which I have recently made is that of Mr. Carlyle. . . . I have long had a very keen relish for his articles in the *Edinburgh* and *Foreign Reviews*. Which I formerly thought to be such consummate nonsense; and I think he improves upon a nearer acquaintance. He does not seem to me so entirely the reflection or shadow of the great German writers as I was inclined to consider him; although undoubtedly his mind has derived from their inspiration whatever breath of life there is in it. He seems to me as a man who has had his eyes unsealed. . . . [24]

Mill realized that he had found a great new source of inspiration. As he wrote to Carlyle: "You I look upon as an artist, and perhaps the only genuine one now living in this country."[25] "And if I have any *vocation*,

I think it is exactly this, to translate the mysticism of others into the language of Argument."[26] Later, Mill became disenchanted with Carlyle and came to see Harriet as one of the best embodiments of the true poet and philosopher. This progression in Mill's thought is often viewed as a sign of his needing a spiritual director to run his life, but in truth it is a reflection of his Romantic philosophical mission.

Mill immediately set about helping Carlyle, by introducing him first to Henry Taylor and then to Wordsworth and Southey.[27] At the time, Mill was the reigning English authority on France; he helped Carlyle to write on the French Revolution and was among the first, in a highly influential review, to endorse Carlyle's views. The general tendency among both radicals (including Bentham) and Romantics (including Kant) was initially to be enthusiastic about the French Revolution but then to turn against its excesses. In his 1833 review of Alison's *History of Europe*, Mill had described the French Revolution as part of a progressive transformation of the whole human race that originated as a "moral revolution."[28] Historically, the French Revolution was an important and necessary milestone in overcoming the vestiges of feudalism, but it had failed. In Carlyle's terms, the aftermath of the Revolution was God's vengeance on the *philosophes*.

Carlyle remained a severe critic of Philosophic Radicalism. In *Sartor Resartus* (The tailor retailored), published in 1836,[29] Carlyle critiqued the Mills as follows: "Shall your Science proceed in the small chink-lighted, or even oil-lighted, underground workshop of Logic alone; and man's mind become an Arithmetical Mill, whereof Memory is the Hopper, and mere tables of Sines and Tangents, Codification, and Treatises of what you call Political Economy, are the Meal?"[30] It was also in this work that Carlyle advocated heroic self-assertion against middle-class complacency, another theme that resonated with Mill. These political themes were restated in *Chartism* (1840), and Carlyle's ongoing critique of democracy was expressed in both *Heroes and Hero-Worship* (1840) and *Past and Present* (1843), published at about the same time that Mill was digesting Tocqueville. Mill shared with Carlyle the view that changing the franchise without changing people's hearts and minds would produce little positive good.[31]

It was Thomas Carlyle who initially helped Mill both to see the shallowness of his father's views and to discover Romanticism. Carlyle was uniquely positioned to play this role in Mill's life. Like James Mill, Carlyle was a Scotsman, raised as a pious Calvinist and prepared for the ministry but eventually abandoning that career to pursue the life of higher journalism. Unlike James Mill, Carlyle found inspiration in the German Romantic writers, most especially Goethe.

There were, however, significant differences between Carlyle and Mill. Mill never really shared Carlyle's version of anti-self-consciousness. Carlyle denied self-centeredness in the interest of submission to extrapersonal moral purposes, known to the individual through intuition; Mill denied self-centeredness but in the interest of a deeper awareness of self. Mill rejected Carlyle's assumption that self-discipline meant self-repression. Mill rejected duty as an end in itself. We are reminded of Mill's assertion in *On Liberty* that we have a need for pagan self-assertion, that Pericles is a better model than John Knox.

The tendency among scholars since the nineteenth century has been to see a sharp contrast between Mill, seen as the representative of utilitarianism and scientific materialism, and Carlyle, who is seen as the voice of Romanticism.[32] This view has been effectively challenged by Semmel, who asserts that "Mill was, like the Scotsman [Carlyle], a proponent of virtue and free will, of individual autonomy and responsibility."[33] The difference between the two is that Mill thought it was possible to combine the Stoic and Christian inheritance with the modern commitment to self-cultivation. In many ways, Mill and Carlyle were odd bedfellows, and eventually their friendship, as we shall see, came to a bitter end. However, during the 1830s and early 1840s, Mill felt very close to Carlyle. Part of the explanation was the critique of radicalism and the introduction to Romanticism, but another dimension was Mill's feeling that he could share confidences with Carlyle. This feeling would be further strengthened by Carlyle's initial support of Mill during the early scandal surrounding Mill's relationship with Harriet Taylor.

Coleridge[34]

The most influential source of Mill's Romanticism was Samuel Taylor Coleridge. Coleridge (1772–1834) was not only a great poet but also the most important English conservative thinker of the nineteenth century. Foreshadowing Mill's own journey, Coleridge had begun as a supporter of the Enlightenment Project, accepting Hartley on association and determinism, William Godwin's notion of a utopian social world as expressed in his *Inquiry Concerning Political Justice* (1793), and Godwin's view that social dysfunction was produced by environmental and institutional factors. But by 1796, his journal *The Watchman* showed how his thoughts had evolved into the view that social dysfunction could be overcome only by moral and religious education. He had also been a radical who sympathized with the French Revolution, but his "France: An Ode" (1798) marked the end of his support. Coleridge almost became a Unitarian minister; Josiah Wedgwood gave him a small annual pension so that he could devote his time instead to writing poetry.

In 1801, Coleridge looked elsewhere for inspiration and found it in the English philosophy of Berkeley and in the German philosophies of Kant and Schelling, a good deal of which he may be said to have plagiarized. Kant had argued that God was the presuppositonal source of the moral law, freedom, and immortality. What Coleridge added was the claim that we could come to know God and to receive his revelation. In his embrace of Romantic idealism he denied any dualism of nature and mind. Moreover, dialectical conflict and the resolution or synthesis of opposites is a fundamental feature of life and the source of creativity. Unification is achieved through art and philosophy. Any symbolization or conceptualization is an inherent part of the process it represents; the artist or creative thinker becomes symbolic of God himself. It should be clear by now that Mill's *Autobiography* exemplifies the belief that the intellectual development of a truly representative individual mirrors the intellectual development of his time.

Coleridge was also a notorious drug addict. In 1816, he moved to Highgate into a home run by James Gillam for treating drug addicts (although Coleridge continued to feed his habit). He gathered around himself a group of disciples who would listen endlessly to his monologues. Carlyle, in his *Life of Sterling*, describes the famous Thursday evening events as follows: "[H]e sat on the brow of Highgate Hill, in those years, looking down on London and its smoke-tumult, like a sage escaped from the inanity of life's battle. . . . To the rising spirits of the younger generation he had this dusky sublime character; and he sat there as a kind of Magus, girt in mystery and enigma."[35]

Among Coleridge's important and influential political works are two *Lay Sermons* (1816 and 1817) and *On the Constitution of Church and State according to the Idea of Each* (1830). In the latter work, he maintained that institutions embody inherent norms and that such norms constitute both the origin and the end of the institution. These works show how he was greatly influenced by the German idealist philosophers Kant, Fichte, and Schelling. He adopted the idealist distinction between reason and understanding, with reason considered to be the faculty by which we discover ultimate truths. Among these ultimate truths are the norms embodied in institutions. Coleridge also maintained that the British political system embodied two dynamically contending forces, which he called "permanence" and "progression." Though opposed, these two forces supported a moral consensus articulated by the "clerisy," the new intellectual class. The role of the clerisy is to initiate subjects into the cultural inheritance through an explication of its fundamental values, "to develop . . . those faculties, and to provide for every native that knowledge and those attainments, which are necessary to qualify him for a member of the state, the free subject of a civilized realm."[36] Coleridge also saw the church as the repository of all national wealth not personally owned.

Like T. H. Green later, Coleridge combined a Burkean conception of history with Kantian and Hegelian idealism. Specifically, he sought to reconcile the forces of permanence (landed aristocracy) and progression (rising commercial interests). He distinguished, for the first time, between civilization (which he equated with material progress) and cultivation (which he understood to be the "harmonious development of these qualities and faculties that characterize our humanity"). This was a philosophical and social expression of the solitary interior drama of individual moral development that is to be found in the "Ancient Mariner" and in the *Prelude*. Culture is not the same as material progress. Moreover, cultivation requires a clerisy. The clerisy – all professionals, not just the clergy – were to be the cultural guardians.[37]

Among Coleridge's former and present friends were to be found Wordsworth, Southey, and Carlyle – all of whom were Tories! It was Wordsworth who led Mill to "the higher flights of Coleridge."[38] It had been Sterling and Maurice who had first introduced Mill to the prose work of Coleridge. Sterling had even gone to Bonn to study the work of Schelling (especially) and of other German philosophers who had inspired Coleridge. Mill's relationship to Coleridge dates from the period 1829–30. Mill had been learning to read German since 1825. In April of 1829, Mill had written a favorable review of Thomas Wirgman's treatise on Kant. Subsequently, Mill attended several of the famous Thursday evening sessions to hear Coleridge.

In a letter to J. P. Nichol in 1834, Mill acknowledged Coleridge's influence:

Few persons have exercised more influence over my thoughts and character than Coleridge has; not much by personal knowledge of him, though I have seen and conversed with him several times, but by his works, and by the fact that several persons with whom I have been very intimate [Sterling and Maurice] were completely trained in his school. Through them, too, I have had opportunities of reading various unpublished manuscripts of his; and, on the whole, I can trace through what I know of his works, pieced together by what I have otherwise learned of his opinions, a most distinct thread of connection. I consider him the most systematic thinker of our time, without excepting even Bentham, whose edifice is as well bound together, but is constructed on so much simpler a plan, and covers so much less ground. On the whole, there is more food for thought – and the best kind of thought – in Coleridge than in all other contemporary writers.[39]

It was Coleridge who represented the conservative strain in Mill's thinking. It was Coleridge who suggested to Mill that the coalescence of individual interest and communal good was to be achieved through custom and tradition. Coleridge's defense of historic culture was also a defense of a view of human nature that celebrated its reflexive capacity to alter itself through self-education. When, in 1831, Mill wrote *The Spirit of the Age*, he questioned whether the lack of an authoritative center in liberal culture was a good thing. In 1835, he reviewed Tocqueville's *Democracy in America* for the first time and began to entertain serious doubts about the efficacy of democracy. His 1836 essay *Civilization* was to indict contemporary society for giving power to the masses without raising their level of intelligence or morality. His essay "Reorganization of the Reform Party" questioned both the narrow sectarian basis of the Radical Party and its emphasis on universal suffrage as a panacea.

The problem for Mill was a complex one. He saw liberal culture (individual rights, the rule of law, a market economy, representative government, and toleration) as the culmination of a long (inevitable, but not final) historical process and as a good thing. The Philosophic Radicals of the Enlightenment Project had supported liberal culture with bad arguments. In 1830, Mill began writing *Essays on Some Unsettled Questions in Political Economy*, thereby signaling his ongoing methodological concern for coming up with better arguments in support of liberal culture. The conservatives, on the other hand, were hostile to liberal culture but seemed to provide a much better understanding of social institutions. What Mill was seeking was some kind of synthesis in which conservative insights and arguments would support liberal culture.

What did Mill get from Coleridge? We shall have a great deal to say on this issue when we compare and contrast the essays on Bentham and Coleridge. In the meantime, we may note the broad outline of Coleridge's influence. Mill accepted the Romantic critique of the Enlightenment Project, especially the critique of the latter's reductive and atomistic conception of human nature. Individuals cannot be fully understood abstractly but must be seen in cultural and historical context. What this entails is a deeper understanding of cultural context. On the grand methodological plane, Mill adopted Coleridge's Romantic idealism; he adopted the view of the intimate relationship between art and philosophy; and he forever after saw himself as the synthesizer of half-truths.

Instead of doing what the Benthamite radicals were inclined to do – that is, judge social institutions by reference to an abstract model of human nature – Romantic social analysis attempts to understand social institutions both in their own right and with regard to their ongoing interaction with individuals within those institutions. As Mill was to put it, we must get beyond the reductivism and institution bashing of Bentham, for

an enlightened Radical or Liberal . . . must know, that *the Constitution and Church of England* [italics mine, to call attention to the echo of Coleridge] . . . are not mere frauds, or sheer nonsense – have not been got up originally, and all along maintained, for the sole purpose of picking people's pockets; without aiming at, or being found conducive to, any honest end during the whole process.[40]

Institutions, moreover, are not abstract and timeless structures. Rather, the meaning of institutions can be understood organically in the way they evolve and respond to changing circumstances.

Mill rejected the conceptions of history of both Macaulay and the Saint-Simonians; neither left space for individual initiative. Coleridge was the happy medium, and Tocqueville would be the great example. Traditions were a fertile source of adaptation. The recognition of this feature of social institutions led to the perceived need for two things: (1) a criterion for significant events [which will be, it turns out, the growth of freedom] and (2) a recognition of the value of social experimentation for adaptation.

Mill's essay "Corporation and Church Property," which appeared in the *Jurist* (February 1833), reflected, at least temporarily, a further Coleridgean influence, the need for a clerisy. What we need from government, more than protection, is the recognition that "the primary and perennial sources of all social evil, are ignorance and want of culture."[41] This lack can be fulfilled by the "unremitting exertions of the more instructed and cultivated [clerisy]." Echoing Coleridge, Mill maintained, both here and a quarter of a century later in the essay *On Liberty*, that the "[c]ulture of the inward man – his moral and intellectual well-being, as distinguished from the mere supply of his bodily wants"[42] – should be the focus of our concern. Mill suggested that after an initial period, the state should take over the assets of philanthropic bequests and use them to fulfill the spirit of the bequest. Mill suggested something similar for India as well, namely, the cultivation of a special learned class.[43]

This view of the clerisy was echoed in an 1835 article on Sedgwick that appeared in the *London and Westminster Review*. In the introduction to that article, Mill contended that endowed universities have as their purpose "to keep alive philosophy." As Bain tells us, "In his [Mill's] mind, philosophy seemed to mean chiefly advanced views in politics and ethics; which, of course, came into collision with religious orthodoxy and the received commonplaces of society."[44]

What Mill could not completely share with Coleridge, at this point in his life, were Coleridge's religious beliefs. For Coleridge, humanity's alienation from God and the need to overcome it were basic. Mill did not reject this out of hand, but wondered whether this signaled some lack in him. In a letter to Carlyle at this time, Mill wrote that "there is wanting something positive in me."[45] What Mill was able to share was a belief in something like immortality. This was also expressed to Carlyle:

[W]ith respect to the immortality of the soul I see no reason to believe that it perishes; nor sufficient ground for complete assurance that it survives; but if it does, there is every reason to think that it continues in another state such as it has made itself here. . . . Consequently in all we do here we are working for our 'hereafter' as well as our 'now.'[46]

Finally, Mill was not sympathetic to Coleridge's Burkean idea of a divine plan in history. [47]

The Beginning of the "Affair"

In his private life, Mill was spending more and more time with William Fox's Unitarian circle. In one respect, this is not surprising. Unitarians were comprised of members of the intellectual, professional, and rising commercial classes. Their eighteenth-century founder and leader was the famous chemist Joseph Priestley, who combined a commitment to Unitarianism with the espousal of the Enlightenment Project and utilitarianism. Fox's circle[48] had all of the elements that might initially appeal to Mill. Among its members was Harriet Martineau, sister of the famous Unitarian James Martineau and an early feminist. Deaf from the age of twelve, she was the first female journalist to earn a living from writing under her own name. She was an exponent of political economy and an early enthusiast and translator of Comte – all things that would have appealed to Mill. Another member was the rising poet Robert Browning, about whom we shall have more to say later. For the moment, we note that Mill entered the circle at a time when he was beginning to feel comfortable with his own aesthetic feelings. Among the other female members were the talented Flower sisters,[49] Sarah[50] (remembered as the composer of the hymn "Nearer, My God, to Thee") and Eliza, and of course Harriet Taylor. This was the only group in which Mill could feel comfortable talking about his feelings. For the rest of his life, with the exception of Sterling and Harriet, all of Mill's friendships were professional.

Fox had introduced Mill to Harriet, supposedly in order to help Harriet find intellectual stimulation that she could not find at home. "He told her that John Mill was the man among the human race to relieve in a competent manner her dubieties and difficulties."[51] We do know from Roebuck, who was present, that "Mrs. Taylor was much taken with Mill."[52] But there was more to this meeting. Before his meeting with Harriet, Mill had been attracted to Eliza Flower, who was three years older than he. They shared a common passion for music. Mill proposed to Eliza but was refused, allegedly because "[s]he was the spouse of her art, consecrated to its ideal."[53] What we do know is that Eliza was in love with the married Fox. It is plausible to suggest that Fox may have arranged the meeting between Mill and Harriet Taylor not only to help Mrs. Taylor but also to distract Mill with another highly attractive person.

Fox was also interested in drawing Mill into becoming a contributor to his publication the *Monthly Repository*, thereby upgrading it from a mere sectarian organ into a prominent literary and political organ. For his part, Mill was clearly infatuated with this beautiful woman who was well educated, who spoke Italian, who had grown up in a family where passionate argumentation was something highly valued, who shared his views and values, and who defended them with passion, wit, and feminine charm. They shared a common dislike of Byron and a passion for Shelley, especially his poem "Hymn to Intellectual Beauty."

Mill describes Harriet as follows in his *Autobiography*:

Although it was years after my introduction to Mrs. Taylor before my acquaintance with her became at all intimate or confidential, I very soon felt her to be the most admirable person I had ever known. It is not to be supposed that she was, or that any one, at the age at which I first saw her, could be, all that she afterwards became. . . . Up to the time when I first saw her, her rich and powerful nature had chiefly unfolded itself according to the received type of feminine genius. To her outer circle she was a beauty and a wit, with an air of natural distinction, felt by all who approached her: to the inner, a woman of deep and strong feeling, of penetrating intuitive intelligence, and of an eminently meditative and poetic nature. . . . shut out by the social disabilities of women from any adequate exercise of her highest faculties in action on the world without; her life was one of inward meditation, varied by familiar intercourse with a small circle of friends. . . . I have often compared her, as she was at this time, to Shelley: but in thought and intellect, Shelley, so far as his powers were developed in his short life, was but a child compared with what she actually became.[54]

It was Harriet who introduced Mill to Shelley's poetry, and it was to Shelley, therefore, that he compared her at their first acquaintance. Percy Bysshe Shelley (1792–1822), son-in-law to William Godwin, is now known primarily as a poet, but in his own lifetime he expressed many of the beliefs of the radical English intelligentsia. In 1811, Shelley had been expelled from Oxford for writing a piece in which he argued that there were no convincing arguments for the existence of God. He went on to argue that God was an allegorical expression of humanity's most precious values: tolerance and equality. Religion appeared to him as analogous to poetry in providing a comprehensive view of the world and humanity's place within it. Influenced by Berkeley and Kant, Shelley embraced philosophical idealism, holding the view that only minds existed and that there was one infinite universal mind, in which individual minds participated. Politically, Shelley advocated an expansion of the suffrage and a tax on unearned wealth. One of Harriet's favorite works was Shelley's *Prometheus Unbound*

(1820), in which he had expressed the view that oppressors as well as the oppressed were victims of dysfunctional social institutions. This is a major theme (master-slave) that Harriet transmitted to Mill. The Amberleys would recall an evening in 1870, long after Harriet's death and toward the end of Mill's life, in which he read out loud Shelley's *Ode to Liberty*. "He got quite excited and moved over it rocking backwards and forwards and nearly choking with emotion; he said himself: 'it is almost too much for one.'"[55]

Eventually, Mill was inspired by Harriet to write an essay entitled "On Genius," which appeared in October 1832 signed "Antiquus." In this essay, Mill tried to combine the commitment to the rationalism of the Enlightenment Project he had inherited from Bentham and his father with the importance attributed to the imagination in the Romantic movement. To be a "genius" in the rational sense, it turns out, is to think for oneself. It has nothing to do with discovering new truths or originality. What is crucial is the moral transformation that occurs during the process. Analogously, to be a Romantic is not to write poetry in a novel form but to embrace *Bildung*, understood in the German sense of the self-transformation of character. This essay bears comparison to the 1831 series *The Spirit of the Age*, in which Mill advocated the need for cultural elitism. "Genius" advocates originality in an age intent on "supplying our deficiency of giants by the united efforts of a constantly increasing multitude of dwarfs."[56]

This conceptualization of "genius" permitted Mill to solve or to overcome two important problems he faced at the time. On the personal level, it allowed him to believe that one could have a poetic soul without being a creative artist – to have a poetic or artistic soul was to be able to reproduce, not to originate, the creative process and thereby to share in something that one could not originate. Mill here articulates the notion that high art requires a degree of participation and re-creation on the part of the audience. On the political level, it helped him to transcend his incipient elitism. His great concern was that modern liberal culture could not survive unless those who participated in it understood and cherished its fundamental norms and grasped how to relate those norms to newly emerging contexts. His recent and ongoing despair was that in an increasingly democratic context, the average laborer and would-be voter was totally unprepared to exercise this kind of judgment. But if Mill's understanding of "genius" was correct, then almost anyone could become autonomous. Originality and brilliance were not necessary; what was necessary was the willingness and opportunity to rethink the insights of those who saw the truths first. The rethinking was inevitably accompanied by an internal transformation, what today we would call a paradigm shift.

Mill was also among the first to recognize Alfred Tennyson's genius, writing a review of Tennyson's second volume of poems for the *Monthly Repository* in November of 1833. At the time, Tennyson was viewed as a political radical, and Mill was in part responding to a negative review of Tennyson's work that had appeared in the Tory publication the *Quarterly Review*. Another poet to whom Mill was introduced was Robert Browning. Browning's first major poem, "Pauline," was published in 1833. It is said that Eliza Flower had inspired it. The Flower sisters had in fact introduced Browning, their former neighbor in Hackney, to Fox. Fox gave the poem a special review in the *Monthly Repository*, and Mill wrote some kind words about it. However, for a variety of circumstantial reasons, Mill could not get his positive review published in any of his usual outlets. At the same time, Mill had expressed his real, and somewhat negative, opinion to Fox by writing a few comments on the flyleaf of his copy. Mill applied his ultimate negative epithet to Browning's work by describing the heroine as "Byronic." The copy was given to Fox along with the request that it not be shown to Browning. Unfortunately, Fox ignored Mill's request, and Browning later saw the comments. Worse yet for Browning, not a single copy of the poem was sold. Browning was so embarrassed that he did not reprint the poem until his collected works appeared thirty-five years later, and then only reluctantly. It seems as if Browning came to share Mill's evaluation of the early work. Browning "had exposed his callow soul in his first poem, and the shrewd Mill had seen it."[57]

As Mill's infatuation turned into love, something else was happening. The Flower sisters had been left in Fox's care by a deceased father. The relation between Fox and Eliza Flower soon went beyond that of a guardian to his charge as she assumed more and more the role of his chief helper. They too were in love. But Fox was already a married man with children. Soon, William Fox, Eliza Flower, Mill, and Harriet Taylor were an inseparable foursome, each couple serving as a camouflage for the forbidden relationship of the other. Unitarians held advanced views about the relationship between men and women and looked forward to greater liberation in those relationships; the relationships in question, at least in the eyes of those involved, had not yet gone beyond the bounds of propriety.

Being the people they were, Mill and Harriet began exchanging notes on marriage and divorce, ostensibly with the purpose of writing on the subject for the *Monthly Repository*. Mill's views express a contrast between what marriage had been and what it could be.

If all, or even most persons, in the choice of a companion of the other sex, were led by any real aspiration towards, or sense of, the happiness which such companionship in its best shape is capable of giving to the best natures, there would never have been any reason why law or opinion should have set any limits to the most unbounded freedom of uniting and separating: nor is it probable that popular morality would ever, in a civilized and refined people, have imposed any restraint upon that freedom. But ... the law of marriage as it now exists, has been made by *sensualists*,[58] and for *sensualists* and to bind *sensualists*. ... There can be no doubt that for a long time the indissolubility of marriage acted powerfully to elevate the social position of women.

The more important issue, claimed Mill, was

whether marriage [in the future] is to be a relation between two equal beings, or between a superior & an inferior, between a protector and a dependent. ... But in this question there is surely no difficulty. There is no natural inequality between the sexes. ... The first and indispensable step, therefore, towards the enfranchisement of woman, is that she be educated, as not to be dependent either on her father or her husband for subsistence. ... women will never be what they should be ... until women, as universally as men, have the power of gaining their own livelihood.[59]

Inevitably, these notes turned into revelations of their affection for each other. Harriet wrote to Mill in 1832, saying: "If I could be Providence for the world for a time, for the express purpose of raising the condition of women, I should come to *you* to know the *means* – the *purpose* would be to remove all interference with affection, or with anything which is ... demonstrative of affection."[60] Here was an open invitation for Mill to declare himself. And declare himself he did. Harriet acknowledged that declaration:

I am glad that you have said it – I am *happy* that you have. ... I have always yearned to have your confidence. ... the only being who has ever called forth all my faculties of affection is the only one in whose presence I ever felt constraint. At times when that has been strongly felt I too have doubted whether there was not possibility of disappointment – that doubt will never return.[61]

Harriet confided to her husband, John Taylor, the existence of this state of affection. Taylor gave Harriet an ultimatum: she must terminate her relationship with Mill before it became a scandal. In August of 1832, she acquiesced, and subsequently Mill did so as well. Mill was devastated, but he conveyed his resignation gallantly by a note through Eliza Flower: "She will not refuse, I trust, the offering of these little flowers, which I have brought for her from the depths of the New Forest. Give them to her, if necessary, as if they came from you."[62]

But before long, Harriet and Mill had reestablished their liaison. Harriet had worked out a compromise and rationalization for what was to become one of the most talked-about affairs of the nineteenth century. Mill needed her, she was sure, in order to make his great contribution to the world. Serving him in that endeavor would fulfill Harriet. At the same time, she would remain loyal and faithful to John Taylor and thereby avoid scandal. This double loyalty was to be achieved by abjuring sexual contact with both men!

At the time, neither Mill nor Taylor took this to be anything but a temporary compromise that merely postponed the inevitable hard choice. Taylor proposed a six-month separation, during which time Harriet was to take the children to Paris in order to reconsider her situation. Taylor was confident that she would realize the error of her ways. During this six-month sojourn, Mill visited her in Paris and stayed six weeks, everything being carried out with the utmost propriety, such as having Mill accompanied by his younger brothers, who were introduced to Harriet's children. Mill fully expected Harriet to ask for a divorce and to embrace a new life with him. After all, they had talked about running off together to Australia, a thought that had occurred to Mill as a result of his work with Wakefield's plans for colonization.

All of this was very difficult to handle emotionally for Mill. Once more he was tempted to give way to despair, but, writing to Carlyle, he was able to express his capacity to overcome it. Recalling his earlier insight into the paralyzing effects of excessive self-analysis, an abhorrence he had come to share with Carlyle, he repeated his fear that excessive self-analysis was debilitating. "I will and must . . . master it, or it will surely master me."[63]

Much to the surprise and chagrin of both men, Harriet got her way. Both Taylor and Mill finally acquiesced and found themselves caught up in this new triangular relationship. In order to avoid scandal and to minimize association with Fox and Eliza Flower, Taylor moved his family to 17 Kent

Terrace, along Regent's Park. Mill was permitted to visit Harriet almost every day, and twice a week, on evenings when Taylor chose to dine at his club, he had dinner with her. Mill was allowed to accompany Harriet in public to attend concerts or lectures. Harriet was also given a country place in Kent for weekends and holidays. Even there, Mill was welcome. Mill and Taylor were coldly polite to each other. Finally, Harriet continued to run the Taylor household and to be a faithful wife in every respect except the sharing of John Taylor's bed. From this point onward, Harriet's daughter Helen accompanied her everywhere to perform a number of practical tasks and even slept in the same room. Harriet, Mill, and Helen, from a very early age, formed a different kind of triangular relationship.

Some will perhaps judge Harriet harshly for putting two men in very awkward and uncomfortable circumstances seemingly in order to create the appearance of propriety and for the benefit of the children. As she had expressed herself earlier to Mill, "Yes – these circumstances *do* require greater strength than any other – the greatest – that which you have, & which if you had not I should never have loved you, I should not love you now."[64] Mill suffered from all this, as noted by his then-friend Carlyle, who remarked that "he [Mill] was a most luckless man, seeming to himself all the way to be a very lucky one."[65] But after all, Harriet also surrendered a form of intimacy as well. In addition, it is well to remember the fate of married women with children who ran off with lovers in the nineteenth century, a common and tragic theme of the literature of that time. It is also important to remember in this context the reputation of another feminist, Mary Wollstonecraft. Wollstonecraft had married the political writer William Godwin in 1797 and then died in childbirth five months later. The child, a daughter, later became Mary Shelley. More important is the *Memoirs* Godwin then published in 1798, describing in intimate detail the love relationships in the life of his former wife. The *Memoirs* created a scandal that still reverberated in the 1830s.

The only grounds for judicial separation, to say nothing of divorce, recognized by the ecclesiastical court were adultery and brutality; the children would remain under the control of the father, whose property they were under the law; remarriage required a special act of Parliament. I think it is fair to say that Harriet and Mill did the honorable thing. They not only preserved appearances but also avoided compromising anyone involved, and they did so at great personal sacrifice.

In the meantime, Fox, who had been living apart from his wife, although occupying the same house, since 1832, suddenly found his wife lodging a formal letter of complaint with the congregation in 1834. This was precipitated by the close relationship that had developed between Fox and Eliza Flower. This led to a scandal, with parishioners taking sides, but with the help of Mill and even John Taylor, Fox survived the scandal and was able to retain his professional position. As Mill urged Fox, "We all think it of great importance that every public mention of the charge [of adultery] should be accompanied by mention of your denying it."[66] In 1835, Fox went even further by leaving his wife and began living openly with Eliza and two of his three children in a new house in Bayswater. Having survived the scandal and managed to retain his professional position, Fox turned on Mill. Fox disapproved of the relationship Harriet had worked out with Mill. He would have preferred that she make a more open and honest break, as he had done himself. The advanced views on marriage and divorce that had emerged in the Unitarian circle were best exemplified, Fox thought, in his own case. Although he remained one of Harriet's greatest admirers, he regretted that she had not lived up to the standard of the woman his group had all admired, George Sand. What Harriet and Mill had done was, to his mind, a knuckling under to hypocritical social pressure. Although the four remained on friendly terms, their differing situations led to less frequent contact. Eliza would eventually succumb to tuberculosis in 1846.

Carlyle's evaluation of the larger context is interesting. He wrote the following to his brother, John:

Mill and one or two of his set are on the whole the reasonablest people we have.... Mill himself, who would be far the best of them all, is greatly occupied of late times with a set of quite opposite character, which the Austins and other friends mourn much and fear much over. It is the fairest Mrs. Taylor you have heard of: with whom, under her husband's very eyes, he is (Platonically) over head and ears in love. Round her came Fox the Socinian and a flight of really wretched-looking 'friends of the species', who (in writing and deed) struggle not in favour of duty being *done*, but against duty of any kind being required.... Jane and I often say 'Before all mortals beware a friend of the species!' Most of these people are very indignant at marriage and the like, and frequently, indeed are obliged to divorce their own wives, or be divorced; for though this world is already blooming (or is one day to do it) in everlasting 'happiness of the greatest number', these people's own *houses* (I always find) are little hells of improvidence, discord, and unreason. Mill is far above all that, and I think will not sink into it.... he is one of the best people I ever saw and – surprisingly attached to *me*, which is another merit.[67]

Harriet had come to terms with her situation and could feel noble about what she was doing.

I do not hesitate about the certainty of happiness, but I do hesitate about the rightfulness of, for my own pleasure, giving up *my* only earthly opportunity of 'usefulness'. *You* hesitate about your usefulness and that however greater in amount it may be, is certainly not like mine *marked out* as duty. . . . I think any systematic middle plan between this and all is impracticable.[68]

Not only was her relationship with Mill fulfilling to her, she had reason to presume that she was providing irreplaceable sustenance to one of the great voices of the nineteenth century:

It is for you – the most worthy to be the apostle of all the highest virtues to teach such as may be taught, that the higher the kind of enjoyment, the greater the degree, perhaps there is but one class to whom this can be taught – the poetic nature struggling with superstition: you are fitted to be the saviour of such.[69]

In response to some hesitation on Mill's part, Harriet reprimanded him:

Good heaven have you at last arrived at fearing to be 'obscure and insignificant'. What can I say to that but 'by all means pursue your brilliant and important career'. Am I one to choose to be the cause that the person I love feels himself reduced to 'obscure and insignificant'! Good God what has the love of two equals to do with making obscure and insignificant. If ever you could be obscure and insignificant you are so whatever happens and certainly . . . not one to brave the world. I never before (for years) knew you to have a mesquin feeling. . . . There seems to be a touch of Common Place vanity in that dreads of being obscure and insignificant – *you never will be that* [italics added] – still more surely I am not a person who in any event could give you cause to feel that I have made you so.[70]

Three important things are worth noting about these comments. First, they reveal a deep-seated desire on Mill's part to achieve prominence (and his insecurity about achieving it). Second, they reveal the extent to which Harriet was able to provide Mill with the reassurance he needed. Finally, they reflect the concern that Mill was to articulate in *On Liberty* about the devastating effect of social pressure on individuals who dared to be different.

Mill, on the other hand, was not quite sure what face to present to the world. All of the members of his family and all of his friends were aware of the awkward relationship and disapproved of it. Among his family and friends, it was less an issue of propriety and more a matter of his future welfare. Those who felt it was their duty to advise and remonstrate with him soon discovered that their relationship with Mill had been terminated by him. In one striking example, Mill and Harriet appeared in public together at a reception given by Mrs. Charles Buller in 1833. Roebuck, who considered himself Mill's closest friend, felt called upon to advise Mill to end the "affair." As Roebuck described it, he saw

Mill enter the room with Mrs. Taylor hanging on his arm. The manner of the lady, the evident devotion of the gentleman, soon attracted universal attention, and a suppressed titter went round the room. My affection for Mill was so warm and sincere that I was hurt by anything which brought ridicule upon him. I saw, or thought I saw, how mischievous might be this affair, and as we had become in all things like brothers, I determined, most unwisely, to speak to him on the subject.[71]

He did so. When Roebuck went to Mill's office at India House the next day, as was his custom and "not with any intention of renewing the subject.... The moment I entered the room I saw that, as far as he was concerned, our friendship was at an end." Mill and Roebuck never spoke again, even when both were in Parliament many years later.[72] Their friendship had become the first casualty of the "affair."

When Mill described his relationship with Roebuck, a man whom he otherwise admired, in the *Autobiography*, he did not mention this episode but attributed their falling out to differences of temperament regarding poetry. This is a telling remark. Roebuck did not have a poetic soul in the way that Sterling and Harriet did. Roebuck had disagreed with Mill in a debate over the relative merits of various British poets. Roebuck, who considered himself a man of the world with regard to his knowledge of women, did not share Mill's philosophic Romanticism and therefore could not appreciate the importance in Mill's eyes of the relationship with Harriet. There was something at the most profound depth of Mill's personality that Roebuck could never grasp, and therefore he had no idea of how deeply disappointed and hurt Mill was by his proffered advice. It was precisely because Mill had thought of Roebuck as a close friend that he was most hurt by the lack of support. It might be easy to dismiss Mill's feelings as the infatuation of an inexperienced lover, but it is probably closer to the truth to recognize that Mill found something in Harriet that resonated with his whole being – physical, spiritual, and otherwise.

When Mrs. Grote came to Mill's office at India House to urge him to break off the relationship, Mill responded by never again appearing at the Grote house, although he continued to remain friendly with Mr. Grote. Harriet was not permitted to visit Mill's family in Kensington, and Mill did not permit her name to be mentioned in his presence by any family member. As James Mill expressed it in a letter to his son James, "John is still in a rather pining way, tho as he does not choose to tell the cause of his pining, he leaves other people to their conjectures."[73]

According to Bain,

the connexion soon became known to his father, who taxed him with being in love with another man's wife. He [Mill] replied, he had no other feeling toward her, than he would have towards an equally able man. The answer was unsatisfactory, but final. His father could do no more, but he expressed to several of his friends, his strong disapproval of the affair.[74]

It is worth recalling in this context, Mill's autobiographical comment about his early family life:

I grew up with an instinct of closeness. I had no one to whom I desired to express everything which I felt and the only person I was in communication with to whom I looked up [James Mill], I had too much fear of to make the communication to him of any act or feeling ever a matter of frank impulse or spontaneous inclination.[75]

One can imagine the early embarrassment of all concerned, covered over by the hope that things would soon come to a head. Months passed, and then years, to the point where a temporary solution had hardened into a routine that it was now too late to alter. Mill made every effort to protect the woman he loved from scandal, and part of that effort was the pretense that they were just friends – hence there was no need to discuss the relationship at all. Mill took on an increasingly defensive posture with regard to the rest of the world. In order to obtain some privacy, Mill and Harriet would meet in the London Zoo, just a short walk from the Taylor residence at Kent Terrace, within sight of the rhinoceros, whom they referred to as their "old friend Rhino." Hereafter they corresponded with each other only by *Poste Restante* in order to ensure privacy. Those who saw through this charade and challenged him failed, in Mill's mind, to be sensitive to the extraordinary virtues of Harriet and thereby were suggesting that he deny himself the kind of fulfilling relationship of which others were either totally ignorant or could only dream about.

We also know something about Mill's preceding emotional state, at this time of his intellectual and emotional crisis. He had described it as follows (1829) to Sterling: "There is now no human being (with whom I can associate on terms of equality) who acknowledges a common object with me, or with whom I can cooperate even in any practical undertaking, without feeling that I am only using a man, whose purposes are different, as an instrument for the furtherance of my own."[76] Harriet Taylor seems, in retrospect, almost perfectly designed for the part. She could offer Mill precisely the kind of friendship for which he was looking and, moreover, being the woman she was, share the poetic cultivation of the internal life in a way that it would have been difficult at the time for Mill to do with most other men. At precisely the time in his life when Mill had recognized his father's limitations and had come to recognize the emotional poverty of the relationship between his mother and father, Harriet Taylor appeared as the woman who could do for him what his mother had not been able to do for his father.

What was the opinion of the time about the relationship, sexual and otherwise, between heterosexual men and women? In the 1790s, William Godwin and his son-in-law Shelley had advocated the morality of free love. Among the Saint-Simonians, Enfantin had advocated a version of free love, while Amand Bazard had differed from Enfantin and advocated the importance of marriage for both men and women as a way of achieving personal growth and genuine freedom. Saint Simon had striven "to afford all members of the society the greatest possible opportunity for the development of their faculties"[77] Mill acknowledged their influence, but he advocated marriage based on equality – not promiscuity – and he credited his father with a similar view. There was also a religious context for these issues in Unitarianism, where women's emancipation was a dominant theme. (Mary Wollstonecraft had been a Unitarian.)

On the surface, the serious obstacle to the relationship was the obvious fact that Harriet Taylor was already married to John Taylor. Even here, further insight into Mill's character helps to explain why this was an advantage rather than an obstacle. Mill's psyche was Calvinist, almost puritanical. He experienced life as a contest between spiritual impulses and base material impulses (Augustinian-Manichean). He analogized the conflict between these personal impulses to the social tension between the individual good and the common good. The conflicts or tensions can only be resolved by transcending them in a higher synthesis.[78] This he attempted to do in every aspect of his life and thought. Autonomy or self-rule was the key. Mill's relationship to Harriet Taylor was a symbol and microcosm of these larger macrocosmic tensions. Aside from the attraction of her obvious charms and their shared philosophical interests, the challenge she represented for Mill was whether he could achieve the higher synthesis with and through her. The story of their relationship as he experienced it is the story of that achievement.

He shared the Romantic[79] critique of conventional marriage relationships as involving the subordination of one partner to the other in something like a Hegelian master-slave relationship. Unlike some other Romantics, such as William Godwin and Shelley, who advocated free love, Mill reached for a higher romantic plateau.[80] It is important to remember that unconsummated love, such as one finds in the story of Tristan and Isolde, is as much a legitimate romantic motif as is so-called free love. Mill's relationship to Harriet was an example to him of all the good that flowed from a higher synthesis. "[G]ratification of this [sexual] passion in its highest form" required "restraining it in its lowest."[81] Nor was the notion of unconsummated love merely an artistic theme. Sarah Austin had translated a book from the German entitled *Tour of a German Prince*, written by Prince Puckler Muskau. The translation led to a love affair between Sarah Austin and the prince carried on only through correspondence, which lasted for years. The same can be said, in a manner of speaking, of Fox and Eliza Flower. Although Fox and Eliza Flower had set up an independent household, they and their friends steadfastly maintained that adultery had not been committed. According to Fox's biographer, Eliza would not have accepted "an ambiguous relation. She would have assumed his name, and declared herself his wife. . . . Her omission to do so ought to have convinced all who knew her" that this involved "no blemish of personal purity."[82] The poet Robert Browning was apparently prepared to endure the same kind of relationship with Elizabeth Barrett. Even Comte, whose views about women were very different from those of Mill, had a relationship with Mme. Clothilde de Vaux that could only be described as platonic love. Finally, we should recall what Mill said in writing about poetry: ". . . the old romances, whether of chivalry or faery, which, if they did not give a true picture of actual life, did not give a false one, since they did not profess to give any, but (what was much better) filled the youthful imagination with pictures of heroic men, and of what are at least as much wanted, - heroic women."[83]

For a while the only one of his friends who seemed supportive of Mill was Carlyle. Carlyle observed that Mill was suffering: "Poor Mill is in a bad way. Alas, tho' he speaks not, perhaps his tragedy is more tragical than that of any of us: this very item that he does not speak, that he never could speak, but was to sit imprisoned as in the thick ribbed ice, voiceless, uncommunicating, is it not the most tragical circumstance of all?"[84] At the same time, Carlyle was convinced of their innocence: "His *Platonica* and he are constant as ever: innocent I do believe as suckling doves, and yet suffering the clack of tongues, worst penalty of guilt."[85] In fact, it was probably this early support that helped to preserve an intellectual relationship that eventually could not endure the kind of broad differences that emerged between Mill and Carlyle. As Carlyle related to his brother,

Our most interesting new friend is a Mrs. Taylor, who came here for the first time yesterday, and stayed long. She is a living romance heroine, of the clearest insight, of the royalest volition, very interesting, of questionable destiny, not above twenty-five. Jane is to go and pass a day with her soon, being greatly taken with her.[86]

But even here there were clouds on the horizon.[87] On March 6, 1835, shortly after Mill had borrowed the manuscript of the first volume of Carlyle's *French Revolution*, the manuscript was burned. Mill never recorded the details of the incident, but there was some later speculation that the manuscript had been accidentally burned while in Harriet's possession.[88] However, there is reason to believe that the manuscript had been burned by a servant of the Mills, because Mill later suggested to Carlyle that the new manuscript could be given to a responsible third party – namely, Harriet. Harriet accompanied the distraught Mill as he went to tell the Carlyles of the mishap at their home at No. 5 Great Cheyne Row in Chelsea. Carlyle was on this occasion very gracious and forgiving, although there seems to have been a later falling out between Jane Carlyle and Harriet. Carlyle did not work from notes but wrote straight from his head after voluminous reading, so he had no trouble in reconstructing and rewriting the volume, and Mill lavished praise on it after its publication, thereby permanently establishing Carlyle's reputation.

Much speculation has been given to how and why the manuscript had been destroyed. This speculation was fueled by the fact that the Carlyles, at a much later date, became convinced that Harriet had deliberately and spitefully been responsible for destroying the manuscript, and this charge was aired by them after Mill's death. What would provoke such a hypothesis? Carlyle never did understand, or would not understand, the differences between himself and Mill. Moreover, Carlyle became convinced that Mill ceased being one of his "disciples" because of Harriet. That they were capable of bringing such a charge after Mill's death does reveal, if anything, something about the character of the Carlyles.

One hypothesis that has emerged in later scholarly speculation is that since Mill had at one time intended to write a book on the French Revolution, Harriet thought she was somehow protecting Mill. In any case, Mill subsequently suggested leaving the newer version of the manuscript with Harriet, if that made Carlyle feel more comfortable, something he would hardly have suggested if it were thought that Harriet had destroyed the original manuscript. Another speculation is that this was an unconscious act perpetrated by Mill himself! The problem with such speculation is that there is no evidence for it; that it is totally out of character, on both Mill's part and Harriet's; and that for several years thereafter Harriet trusted Carlyle, to the point of asking him to be an executor of her inheritance. It is also worth noting that Mill had so many projects in mind that even he could not possibly have had the time to carry them all out, most especially a book of this kind. There is also reason to believe that during the period from 1830 to 1833 Mill had become at least temporarily disenchanted with France and the French because of the failure of the middle-class victors in the Revolution of 1830 to extend the franchise. As Mill expressed it in the *Examiner*, the "bourgeois oligarchy, who have enthroned themselves in the yet warm seats of the feudal aristocracy, have that very common taste which makes men desire to level down to themselves, but not an inch lower."[89]

Many questions have been raised about Mill's sexuality and his conception of sexuality.[90] Four things should be kept in mind. First, we have come to understand that different people have different complexes of needs and that there is no one ideal way of responding to them. Second, Mill shared the view that most public discussions of sexuality were inevitably degrading; in short, he was – by our contemporary standards, not his – somewhat prudish with regard to public disclosure. This makes it difficult to draw many conclusions from what he does say. Third, Mill did recognize the physical dimension of emotional life.

What any persons may freely do with respect to sexual relations should be deemed to be an unimportant and purely private matter, which concerns no one but themselves. If children are the result, then indeed commences a set of important duties towards the children. . . . But to have held any human being responsible to other people and to the world for the fact itself, apart from this consequence, will one day be thought one of the superstitions and barbarisms of the infancy of the human race.[91]

Finally, in a letter to Harriet, Mill related a dream in which he finds himself asserting that "the best would be to find both ["a sincere friend and a sincere Magdalen"] in one."[92] There is more here than meets the eye.

Flirtation with Conservatism

As Mill moved further away from Philosophic Radicalism, he began to investigate conservatism. This is reflected in Mill's attitude toward Bentham. Jeremy Bentham had died in 1832. His was the first corpse to be donated voluntarily to a medical school for dissection. His skeleton was dressed in his usual outfit and outfitted with a wax head supplied by the famous Madame Tussaud. His disciples met twice a year after his death at dinners held in his honor and at which the skeleton presided. The dressed skeleton is now to be found in the library of University College, London. Following Bentham's death, Mill published an anonymous and scathing piece entitled "Remarks on Bentham's Philosophy" as an appendix to Edward Bulwer Lytton's *England and the English* (1833).[93] This piece in many ways signaled Mill's break with Philosophic Radicalism and his movement toward some sort of accommodation with conservatism. Mill never was or became a conservative, but he was influenced by conservative thinkers.

The term "conservatism," like the term "liberalism," can have many and sometimes conflicting meanings. In the nineteenth century, "conservatism" could be identified either as a disposition, or as a political movement, or as a political and social philosophy. As a perennial disposition, it is the defense of the achievements of the past against the encroachments of the present. As a political movement, conservatism in the nineteenth century meant a defense of the status quo: an attachment to traditional economic forms of production and distribution, including agriculture; the identification of honorable labor only with the farmer, merchant, and artisan; paternalism in dealings between superior and inferior; and the identification of leadership with an entrenched and experienced class coupled with a distrust of all other elites, whether entrepreneurial, intellectual, or bureaucratic. In 1818, the French writer Chateaubriand gave the term "conservative" its modern political meaning by writing in *Le Observateur* that the conservative is "one who is a partisan of the maintenance of the established social and political order." It was Wellington who in 1827 identified the Tories as the conservative party, but it was Peel and later Disraeli who developed the notion of conservatism as the willingness to engage in needed reform by gradual means. In neither of these first two senses was Mill a conservative – quite the contrary.

As a political philosophy, conservatism argues that an understanding of traditional institutions requires the recognition of norms that cannot be captured by abstract political theories, and consequently that progress can come only from a gradual development out of existing institutions. The first and most important expression of conservatism as a political philosophy is to be found in Edmund Burke's *Reflections on the Revolution in France* (1790). There is some analogy here to the practice of reform by Disraeli, but differences remain.

What is interesting with regard to Mill is the fact that all of those writers from whom he imbibed his Romanticism (Austin, Sterling, Wordsworth, the Saint-Simonians, Carlyle, and Coleridge) were also conservatives of one kind or another. As he once expressed it, he and Wordsworth were "like two travelers pursuing the same course on the opposite banks of a river."[94] Curiously, Romanticism in Germany was often allied to conservatism, as in the thought of Novalis, another writer whom Mill admired and quoted. Just as Romantics did not want to separate man from nature, so they opposed the separation of nature and history. Historical change could not be understood or brought about, so they claimed, through merely mechanical means. History had to be understood as an evolutionary process.[95]

Conservatism is not about opposing change, it is about the manner in which change is to be understood. Conservatism is opposition not to change but to "radical" change. In the nineteenth century, there were Tories who opposed all change, but there were also Tories who supported change. The kind of change that Mill envisaged seemed "radical" in the nineteenth century, but it was only "radical" in the sense of going much further than others, especially Mill's Tory critics, wanted to go. Nor did Mill think of change as a grudging concession, in the manner of the more flexible Tories. The more flexible Tories, in the end, were willing to be philanthropic and to exercise noblesse oblige, but philanthropy in Mill's eyes merely exacerbated the problems of the working class and made the achievement of universal autonomy more difficult.

The kinds of changes that Mill foresaw and advocated were changes that he understood to be necessitated by the facts of economic and political life, such as the Industrial Revolution and the evolution of democracy, as noted by Tocqueville. Instead of simply opposing or bemoaning what he took to be a dangerous egalitarianism, he sought to ameliorate it by what he took to be modest proposals for containing and minimizing it. As such, these changes had nothing to do with any utopian scheme but instead reflected new circumstances. To ignore these new circumstances was, in Mill's view, to risk plunging Britain into something like the French Revolution.

Among the things that Mill will object to in the Saint-Simonians and in Comte is their utopian scheming. Among the theoretical constructs he opposed, following Bentham, were appeals to abstract rights, to a social contract, and to religious fanaticism. In the realm of economics, he rejected as chimerical the notion of central planning. Nor was Mill an ideological capitalist (another form of utopianism, namely, the ideology of endless growth) – that is, he never identified consumer values with the more important moral, social, and political values. Moreover, every policy change advocated by Mill always reflected a gradual evolution out of existing social arrangements. Wherever possible, Mill sought vehicles of change outside the use of state power. If anything, Mill was deeply concerned about changes introduced under the auspices of the state and about the potential tyranny of the majority.

Mill was not by disposition a conservative. Moreover, he was unalterably opposed to a defense of the economic and political status quo and to the presumed hereditary leadership of Tories. He could never be a member of the Tory Party. What he most objected to in conservatives was the paternalism inherent in a feudal society and those who wished to return to the Middle Ages.[96]

They [Wordsworth and Coleridge] are duly sensible that it is good for a man to be ruled; to submit both his body and mind to the guidance of a higher intelligence & virtue. It is therefore the direct antithesis of liberalism, which is for making every man his own guide and sovereign master, & letting him think for himself & do exactly as he judges best for himself, giving other men leave to persuade him if they can by evidence, but forbidding him to give way to authority. . . . It is difficult to conceive [in Toryism] a more thorough ignorance of man's nature.[97]

But in the sphere of political philosophy, he was deeply attracted to conservative thought. Always anxious to defend the need for a revolution in France, Mill – along with many others, such as Bentham – had to admit the legitimacy of Burke's critique of the excesses of the revolutionaries. In the end, what Mill praised about Carlyle's book on the French Revolution was Carlyle's critique of its misguided leadership. It was, however, Carlyle's defense of the British status quo that Mill could never share.

One of the deep affinities between Coleridge and Mill was Coleridge's evolutionary conception of historical change and his championing of a clerisy. The clerisy comprised the intellectual elite, with which Mill always identified and within which he always sought a leadership role. The clerisy comprised those who were supposed to oversee the identification, articulation, and guidance of necessary social and economic change. It was the idea of a clerisy that separated Coleridge as well as Mill from the Tory Party, for whom leadership belonged to a hereditary elite. It would be quite accurate to say that Mill was a political conservative in the theoretical sense: He shared with the radicals the prescient perception of the needed economic and political changes necessitated by the Industrial Revolution, but he did not share their radical adherence to abstract theories, either political or economic, of the functioning of the social world, and he certainly abhorred the suggested mechanical remedy of democratization. Thus, Mill's flirtation with conservatism during the first half of the decade of the 1830s reflected both his disenchantment with Philosophic Radicalism and his fascination with the elitism of Saint-Simonianism, Carlyle, and Coleridge. Except in the case of Carlyle, Mill was intrigued by intellectuals who recognized the need for change directed by an intellectual elite rather than guided by the ineffective hand of democracy. It should be added that Mill's flirtation lasted several years and coincided with the period during which he was working out his relationship with Harriet. If Harriet had any influence at all, it probably was in reinforcing Mill's abhorrence of authoritarianism and their joint commitment to promoting universal autonomy, features that would move Mill away from his flirtation.

It was also during the period 1830–33 that Mill wrote five *Essays on Some Unsettled Questions of Political Economy*. These essays, which were not published until 1844,[98] reflect a specific rejection of the timeless and abstract quality of classical political economy and the insistence that what was defensible in the classical political economy of which radicals were enamored were some highly qualified truths about a particular historical period.[99] This will set the stage for the writing of the *Principles of Political Economy* during the last half of the following decade.

Death of James Mill

The year 1836 was a difficult one for Mill. Consumed as he was with defining and defending his relationship with Harriet Taylor, he had also been recently promoted at India House, with new duties and responsibilities. He continued to engage in editorial work, turned out articles as a journalist, and still had responsibility for teaching the youngest of his eight brothers and sisters. When his father became ill, Mill took on the further burden of the elder Mill's tasks at India House. Having had some trouble with his eyes as early as 1833,[100] Mill now developed a permanent twitch of his right eye. In addition, he suffered from weakened lungs and stomach disorders. The stress was extraordinary. It became necessary for Mill himself to go on medical leave, a leave spent at Brighton.

Mill's relationship with his father during the two years prior to his father's death was an ambivalent one. On the one hand, his father was still very much in charge. In fact, his article attacking the Church of England in the second issue of the *Review* was so angrily received that it seriously damaged circulation. On the other hand, Mill was able to insinuate his new views.

I could not exercise editorial control over his articles, and I was sometimes obliged to sacrifice to him portions of my own. The old Westminster Review doctrines, but little modified, thus formed the staple of the review; but I hoped by the side of these, to introduce other ideas and another tone, and to obtain for my own shade of opinion a fair representation. . . . [101]

At the same time, there had been a softening in the elder Mill.

[M]y father was not so much opposed as he seemed to the modes of thought in which I believed myself to differ from him. . . . he did injustice to his own opinions by the unconscious exaggerations and intellect emphatically polemical; and that when thinking without an adversary in view, he was willing to make room for a great portion of the truths he seemed to deny. . . . [102]

Mill goes on to note the favorable reception his father gave to both Tocqueville's *Democracy in America* and Mill's essay *Civilization*.

It was while Mill was on leave that his father died. Although he had been ill for some time, James Mill's death from tuberculosis (consumption) on June 23, 1836, came as a surprise. At the time of James Mill's death, tuberculosis was not understood as a contagious viral disease. Numerous people suffered and died from it, and it is quite likely that the elder Mill had unknowingly transmitted this disease to other members of his family. Owing to his own convalescence, and still not anticipating the worst, Mill was not one of the members of the family at the elder Mill's bedside. Everyone was so used to his strength and domination that it was hard to accept his demise. James Mill was buried in Kensington Church. When Carlyle visited the bereaved family at Mickleham, he noted that "[t]here was little sorrow visible in their house, or rather none, nor any human feeling at all; but the strangest unheimlich kind of composure and acquiescence, as if all human spontaneity had taken refuge in invisible corners."[103]

Following his father's death, Mill took an additional three-month leave of absence, from July through September. He spent the first two months in France and Switzerland, accompanied by his two brothers, George and Henry. Harriet and her three children soon joined them. In September, Mill and Harriet went on alone to Nice. The October issue of the *Review* contained his piece on the "Definition and Method of Political Economy," a contribution he had had lying around for some time.

In looking back, it is easy to discern how two such strong-minded individuals as Bentham and James Mill could be competitors for the claim to preeminence while remaining friends. Bentham always thought of James Mill as a disciple. In 1828, Bentham wrote a letter expressing just such a view. "With Mr. Mill's work on British India you can scarcely fail to be more or less acquainted. For these three or four-and-twenty years he has numbered himself among my disciples; for upwards of twenty years he has been receiving my instructions; for about the half of each of five years, he and his family have been my guests."[104] After Bentham's death, his assistant, Bowring, attempted to claim Bentham's mantle by reporting disparaging remarks made about James Mill by Bentham.[105] Mill addressed the issue in an "obituary" of his father in the *Autobiography*:

His principal satisfaction, after he knew that his end was near, seemed to be the thought of what he had done to make the world better than he found it; and his chief regret in not living longer, that he had not had time to do more.... His place is an eminent one in the literary, and even in the political history of his country; and it is far from honourable to the generation which has benefited by his worth, that he is seldom mentioned, and, compared with men far his inferiors, so little remembered. This is probably to be ascribed mainly to two causes. In the first place, the thought of him merges too much in the deservedly superior fame of Bentham. Yet he was anything but Bentham's mere follower or disciple. . . . he will be known to posterity as one of the greatest names in that most important branch of speculation [analytic psychology], on which all the moral and political sciences ultimately rest. . . . The other reason which has made his fame less than he deserved . . . [was that] there was . . . a marked opposition between his spirit and that of the present time. As Brutus was called the last of the Romans, so was he the last of the eighteenth century . . . partaking neither in the good nor in the bad influences of the reaction against the eighteenth century, which was the great characteristic of the first half of the nineteenth. . . . By his writings and his personal influence he was a great center of light to his generation. During his later years he was quite as much the head and leader of the intellectual radicals in England, as Voltaire was of the *philosophes* of France. It is only one of his minor merits, that he was the originator of all sound statesmanship in regard to the subject of his largest work, India.[106]

As Bain, the biographer of both Mills, added, "[I]t will be said of James Mill that his greatest contribution to human progress was his son, whom he educated to be his fellow-worker and successor."[107] In an ironic way, it can be said that James Mill would undoubtedly rank higher in the history of thought if his son had not been so successful. That is, Mill's own success eventually overshadowed that of his domineering father.

Mill was quite conscious of the fact that the event that made possible his final liberation was the death of his father. In a letter to Edward Bulwer Lytton, Mill noted: "[The death of James Mill] has deprived the world of the man of greatest philosophical genius it possessed," but it "has made it far easier to do that, in the hope of which alone I allowed myself to become connected with the review – namely to soften the harder & sterner features of its radicalism and utilitarianism, both which in the form in which they originally appeared in the *Westminster*, were part of the inheritance of the 18th century."[108]

Despite his meteoric rise at India House before that time, Mill was to remain first assistant to Peacock for the next twenty years, from 1836 to 1856. At times, he thought of his relationship with India House as that of "a thorough mechanical drudge."[109]Nevertheless, he continued to enjoy

a workday that permitted him time to write, to engage in personal correspondence, and to use his office as a locus for a social life now complicated
by his relationship with Harriet Taylor.

Forging a New Synthesis

The Reform Bill of 1832 had marked the apex of political achievement
for the Philosophic Radicals. Although the Philosophic Radicals had been
successful in getting themselves elected to Parliament (Roebuck, Grote,
Buller, Sir William Molesworth, and John and Edward Romilly, among
others), they lacked any clear-cut programmatic sense of what to do once
there. As early as 1833, Mill described them as follows: "Some of them are
full of crotchets, others fastidious and overloaded with petty scrupulosity;
none have energy, except Roebuck and Buller; Roebuck has no judgment,
Buller no persevering industry."[110] In his retrospective *Autobiography*,
Mill described them as follows:

[T]hey left the lead of the radical portion of the House to the old hands, to
Hume and O'Connell [leader of the Irish delegation]. . . . It would have required
a great political leader, which no one is to be blamed for not being, to have effected really great things by parliamentary discussion when the nation was in
this mood. . . . [They] could have used the House of Commons as a rostra or a
teacher's chair for instructing and impelling the public mind; and would either
have forced the Whigs to receive their measures from him, or have taken the lead
of the Reform party out of their hands. Such a leader there would have been, if
my father had been in Parliament. For want of such a man, the instructed radicals
sank into a mere coté gauche of the Whig party.[111]

What was needed to fill the gap was an authoritative periodical. The
Examiner, the *Morning Chronicle*, and the *Monthly Repository* were deemed
inadequate. The distrusted Bowring was still editing the older *Westminster
Review*. With the help of Charles Molesworth – a young, wealthy, and
eccentric radical – the Mills had decided that a new publication was needed
in which they could once again assert their leadership. It was called the
London Review, with Mill as its "real" but not "ostensible" editor. The
Review would be unabashedly partisan, directly discussing issues instead
of insinuating policy behind book reviews, and all articles would be signed.
    In 1834, Molesworth purchased the *Westminster Review* from Thomp-
son, and the two publications were merged as the *London and Westminster*.

Among Molesworth's other achievements was the establishment of the Reform Club, from which he initially excluded the Whigs. Mill, in his attempt to create a broader political coalition, persuaded Molesworth to change his mind. The coalition that Mill sought to create would have included everyone except reactionary Tory aristocrats. By 1837, Mill had even had Molesworth write an article for the *Review* entitled "The Terms of the Alliance between Radicals and Whigs."

From 1834 to 1840, Mill concentrated all of his effort not devoted to India House to managing the *Review*. Those invited to contribute included his father, Grote, John Austin, James Martineau, Roebuck, Charles Buller, Bulwer Lytton, Tocqueville, and John Pringle Nichol. Nichol was a professor of astronomy at the University of Glasgow who had become known to Mill through his contributions on political economy in *Tait's Magazine*. This initiated a correspondence between Mill and Nichol that stretched over many years.

Following his father's death, Mill tried to synthesize the radical perception of the need for change with the conservative philosophical conception of how best to achieve it. He described this as his project for "conciliation between the old and the new 'philosophic radicalism'."[112] He scandalized his more radical friends[113] both by having Carlyle and Sterling contribute to the *Review* and by writing in 1837 a positive review of Carlyle's *History of the French Revolution*. Mill asserted:

This is not so much a history as an epic poem: and notwithstanding, or even in consequence of this, the truest of histories. It is the history of the French Revolution, and the poetry of it, both in one; and on the whole no work of greater genius, either historical or poetical, has been produced in this country for many years.[114]

Carlyle's rejection of the impersonal and material categories of Enlightenment rationalism and his Romantic espousal of the importance of the individual and the heightened examination of human personality appealed to Mill. The other important aspect of Carlyle's treatment that particularly impressed Mill reflected the engagement with Romanticism. Carlyle, according to Mill, combined the gifts of the historian with the gifts of the poet and dramatist, thus capturing a truth about events that could not be reduced to mere facts. This became a fundamental theme of Mill's philosophy. At the same time, Mill did criticize Carlyle's treatment for its lack of a larger intellectual organizing theory. Mill's endorsement of

Carlyle's conception of history was a stage in Mill's development toward a more full-blown philosophy of history, which he found exemplified in Guizot and Tocqueville and which he would later articulate in Book VI of the *Logic*.

It was also at this time that Tocqueville exercised an enormous and lasting influence upon Mill's thought. Alexis de Tocqueville (1805–1859) had been born into an aristocratic French family, but he understood the irreversible factors that had led to the French Revolution. He had traveled to America with his friend Gustave de Beaumont in order, as he said, to see the future. The result was a remarkably insightful and prescient account of American culture, *Democracy in America*, still revered as a classic. He distinguished between political democracy and social democracy. Social democracy espoused equality as its primary virtue. Curiously, the enthronement of equality reflected a pervasive egoism that expressed itself not only in an unimaginative materialism but also in disdain for any form of superiority, including intellectual and cultural superiority, and a resulting growth in a public opinion that despised significant difference. Egoistic concern for private welfare led, according to Tocqueville, to an apathy toward public responsibility and eventually to a new form of despotism in which individuals gradually acquiesced in the illusion of security provided by centralized control.

Mill reviewed *Democracy in America* twice. This reflected the fact that Tocqueville published the work in two parts, the first in 1835 and the second in 1840. Tocqueville visited Great Britain in 1837 and was lionized. He also met Mill, with whom he had already been in correspondence, and thanked him for the first review.

> Of all my reviewers you are perhaps the only one who has thoroughly understood me; who has taken a general bird's-eye view of my ideas; who sees their ulterior aim, and yet has perceived a clear conception of the details. . . . I wanted this testimony to console me for all the false conclusions that are drawn from my book. I am constantly meeting people who want to persuade me of opinions that I proclaim, or who pretend to share with me opinions that I do not hold.[115]

After the second review, Tocqueville wrote to Mill telling him that he had bound together his personal copy of *Democracy in America* along with the review. "The two ought to go together, and I wish to be able to turn from the one to the other."[116]

One of the things Mill learned from Tocqueville was the extent to which political philosophy was determined by social philosophy, and therefore the importance of understanding the social forces behind political movements. As Mill expressed it in his essay "Armand Carrel" (1837), social philosophy is "a study of agencies lying deeper than forms of government, which, working through forms of government, produce in the long run most of what these seem to produce, and which sap and destroy all forms of government that lie across their paths."[117] Political philosophy, henceforth, was the practice of identifying transitions and making the best of what was coming. It was also Tocqueville who helped Mill to see that there were at least two forms of despotism: despotism from the top, as in Comte, and the potential despotism of democracy. Mill followed Tocqueville in arguing that civil liberty could only be protected by greater political participation (i.e., self-government), and that this was all the more reason to hasten the awareness and growth of an autonomous citizenry. An important parallel to the support for intermediate political institutions would be Mill's espousal in economics of workers' cooperatives as the intermediate institution between the individual and the large industrial enterprise.

On the whole, 1837 was a bad year for the radicals. It marked the advent of Queen Victoria's reign and the electoral triumph of the Tories. The Whigs suffered losses, and many of the radicals, including Roebuck, were defeated. Even among the radicals there was disagreement. Some of these differences were exacerbated when Mill took on John Robertson in 1837 as his assistant at the *Review*. On the one hand, Roebuck was critical of Mill's inclusion of Carlyle. Writing to Roebuck in April of 1837, Mrs. Grote complained that she was "persuaded the Review will cease to be the engine of propagating sound and sane doctrines on Ethics and Politics under J. M."[118] At the same time, Albany Fonblanque, editor of the *Examiner*, was critical of the influence of the radical Grotes on the *Review*. Mill had to fire back in all directions at once. Responding to Fonblanque, Mill replied:

What is the meaning of *your* insisting upon identifying me with Grote or Roebuck or the rest? . . . Have you forgotten . . . that my Radicalism is of a school the most remote from theirs, at all points, which exists? *They* knew this as long ago as 1829, since which time the variance has been growing wider & wider. I never consented to have anything to do with the London Review but for the sake of getting together a body of writers who would represent radicalism more worthily

than they did . . . but in proportion as I did find such persons I have been divesting
the review of its sectarian character. . . . [119]

There was also an unpleasant episode in which Mill declined to publish something written by Harriet Martineau,[120] whom he disliked and
thought to be a spiteful gossip about his relationship with Harriet Taylor.
He noted that "[s]he has . . . the faculty of making herself personally disliked, by . . . inattention to Christ's precept 'judge not, that ye be not
judged'. . . . "[121] Mill's assistant, Robertson, with whom he was having
increasing difficulties, had accepted a piece from Martineau on the new
queen that Mill thought inappropriate for the *Review*. Despite their many
similarities, Mill always thought of Harriet Martineau as an ideologue.
Commenting to Carlyle on her discussion of political economy, Mill observed that she had managed to reduce the "*laissez-faire* system to absurdity as far as the principle goes, by merely carrying it out to all its
consequences."[122]

In 1838, Mill took over ownership and sole control of the *Review*.
Sterling was permitted to write an article on Carlyle. Carlyle had been
introduced to Sterling's novel *Arthur Coningsby* by Mill and to Sterling
himself in 1835. Sterling, in the meantime, had already converted to
Anglicanism in 1832. All of this further widened the gap between Mill
and the orthodox radicals. It became the fashion to attribute anything
one disliked about Mill to Harriet's influence. Godefroy Cavaignac, the
president of the Revolutionary French Society of the Rights of Man, described Harriet as the "Armida of the *London and Westminster Review*" –
Armida[123] being a character in the popular Rossini opera (1817), a siren
luring sailors to their doom. Although it is true that Mill trusted Harriet's
judgment and deeply resented any slur against her, real or imagined, the
fact remains that his distance from the Philosophic Radicals reflected both
his decade-long recognition of their shortcomings and the attractions of
both Romanticism and conservatism.[124]

The one attempt to move beyond journalism and to engage the political
world involved the earl of Durham ("Radical Jack"), an independent Tory.
Durham was known to some of the radicals because of their association
with the ideas of colonization and the formation of a commonwealth. This
group included Mill, Molesworth, Buller, and Edward Gibbon Wakefield,
the womanizing head of the National Colonization Society. These men saw
colonization as a way of easing the economic pressure on, and improving

the prospects of, the working class. Durham was seen by Mill and other radicals – except for Roebuck, who hated all "lords" – as a potential leader who could cut across the old political spectrum. Durham had been made governor of Canada and head of a government mission to determine the future status of the dominion. Durham favored extremely liberal policies, including dominion self-government. Mill, who exerted some influence on Durham through Charles Buller, Durham's secretary, endorsed Durham in 1838, and one of the consequences was that the *Review* lost one-third of its subscribers. Durham was recalled by the government and forced to resign, but he returned to London and a triumphal popular reception. Mill even hoped that Durham would assume financial responsibility for the *Review*. But Durham chose to become a Whig instead.

At the time, Mill was on a six-month sick leave from India House and had chosen to spend it, somewhat surreptitiously, in Naples and Sorrento with an ailing Harriet. Commenting on his physical condition, Mill says, "I shall have no great reason to complain, as hardly anybody continues after my age [thirty-three] to have the same vigorous health they had in early youth."[125] Later he would look back on this period as the happiest in his life. But, for the moment, on hearing the news about Durham, Mill expressed his disappointment:

[I]t cannot lead to the organization of a radical party, or the placing of radicals at the head of the movement, – it leaves them as they are already, a mere appendage of the Whigs: and if there is to be no radical party there need be no *Westminster Review*, for there is no position for it to take, distinguishing it from the *Edinburgh*. . . . For my own part, I feel that if the time is come when a radical review should support the Whigs, the time is come when I should withdraw from politics. . . . In short, it is one thing to support Lord Durham in *forming* a party; another to follow him when he is only joining one, and that one which I have so long been crying out against. . . . As for the Review, even if he would bear the whole expense, and leave me the entire control, I doubt *now* whether I should accept it. . . . I do not feel clear about publishing even another number.[126]

In any case, it all came to naught. Durham soon became ill and died suddenly. This marked the demise of radicalism as a political movement. Buller and his allies became Whigs; Grote left politics altogether; the Austins became Tories; and Francis Place became disillusioned with the idea of uniting the workingmen and the rising middle classes. Disgusted, Place wrote to Mill about his loss of confidence. Mill remarked to

Fonblanque that he would save Place's letter as a "memorial of the spiritless heartless imbecility of the English Radicals."[127] All of this foreshadows the splintering of Mill's lifelong ambition to unite the middle and working classes in support of liberal culture. Hereafter, Mill himself started contributing to periodicals with a wider audience, including the Whig *Edinburgh Review*. In 1839, Nichol invited Mill to become the holder of the chair in moral philosophy at Glasgow, but he declined. Carlyle and Sterling also declined.

Recognizing at last that there was no Philosophic Radical constituency, Mill terminated the *Review* in 1840,[128] and the final issue contained his response to the radicals, an essay on Coleridge. Looking back at the *Review*, Mill thought that his greatest achievements were the defense of Lord Durham, the publicity given to Carlyle's book on the French Revolution, and calling attention to the importance of the French Historian Guizot. From a much later perspective, we might cite the importance of the essays on Bentham, Coleridge, and Tocqueville, all of which continue to be reprinted and anthologized long after the others have fallen into neglect. Retrospectively, Mill summarized this period as follows:

In the conduct of the Review I had two principal objects. One was to free philosophic radicalism from the reproach of sectarian Benthamism . . . to show that there was a Radical philosophy, better and more complete than Bentham's which is permanently valuable. In this first object I, to a certain extent, succeeded. The other thing I attempted, was to stir up the educated Radicals, in and out of Parliament, to . . . induce them to make themselves . . . a powerful party. . . . This attempt was from the first chimerical . . . because as Austin so truly said, "the country did not contain the men . . . none capable of forming and leading such a party."[129]

We note in passing that Mill did not see himself in that role, although he could imagine his father occupying it.[130] As much as he wanted to have an impact on politics and even to pursue a career in politics (had it not been for his employment at India House), he did not see himself as a parliamentary leader. What he thought he was best at becoming was the intellectual leader of a newly synthesized radicalism. This self-conception foreshadows his later parliamentary career. Mill knew that his leadership could be exercised only through the pen and not, as in the case of his father, by force of personality.

In early 1840, Henry Mill, Mill's favorite brother, became noticeably ill with tuberculosis. He was sent to Falmouth to recuperate, and Mill visited him as much as possible, as well as seeing Sterling, who was also staying there. On April 4, Henry died. Again Mill suffered the loss of one of the few people with whom he could share intimacies. Mill confided to Caroline Fox, with whom he had stayed during Henry's illness, that he too expected to die of consumption. Trying to come to grips with this tragedy, Mill established the pattern by which he always responded to tragedies in his life: work. Quoting Carlyle, he wrote to Caroline Fox, "Work while it is called today; the night cometh in which no man can work." He went on to elaborate: "[T]here is only one plain rule of life eternally binding ... embracing equally the greatest moralities and the smallest; it is this – try thyself unweariedly till thou findest the highest thing thou art capable of doing, faculties and outward circumstances being both duly considered and then DO IT."[131]

Amid this tragedy but in the company of Sterling, Mill was able to explore Pendennis Cavern and to picnic at Penjerrick. Mill expressed "the elation of spirits he always experienced in the country, and illustrated it, with an apology, by jumping." Later, "Mill joined us at dinner, and Sterling came to tea." The evening was filled with "a glorious discourse on Reason, Self Government. ... Sterling was the chief speaker, and John Mill would occasionally throw in an idea to clarify an involved theory or shed light on a profound abysmal one."[132]

This was also a period of growing disillusionment with the prospect of a coalition with the conservatives. Many things contributed to this, including the events surrounding Durham. But something else happened that led Mill to see the unbridgeable gap between himself and the apologists of conservatism, such as Carlyle. Carlyle, now a celebrity as a consequence of his book on the French Revolution, gave a series of lectures based on his forthcoming book on *Heroes and Hero Worship and the Heroic in History* (1841) at the Hall in Portman Square. Mill and Harriet dutifully attended. At the second lecture, "The Hero as Prophet," Carlyle launched a vicious attack on the radicals. Unable to contain himself, Mill rose to his feet and shouted "No."[133] Thereafter, they did not attend.

The great personal and intellectual dilemma of Mill's life was the discovery of the conflict between his father's views and the Romanticism of such figures as Carlyle and Coleridge. In addition to the sense of loyalty, what Mill owed to his father was the vision of reform necessitated by the

Industrial Revolution. While he wholeheartedly embraced the need for reform, what Mill could not accept was the Philosophical Radical conceptualization of the issues involved. The intellectual and cultural resources that appealed to him were in the writings of the Romantics, but they eschewed the needed reforms. This conflict was expressed in Mill's handling of the *London and Westminster Review* and in the now-classic essays on Bentham and Coleridge. It was also represented in his unsuccessful attempt to build a new political coalition. The personal and intellectual resolution of the dilemma was to restate his father's views within the context of Romanticism. What this amounted to was a celebration of reason but the ultimate transcendence of reason by poetry. We have already had some examples of this, and it will become increasingly clear when we discuss the *Logic* in a later chapter. What made the resolution of the synthesis psychologically and intellectually bearable was meeting and falling in love with Harriet Taylor. She shared Mill's agenda and infused it with a passionately poetical soul. She embodied what Mill wanted to become. And if his homage to her seems at times excessive, it is because the homage is to an ideal that she represented. He met her precisely at the time that he was working through the great crisis and defining his personal, public, and intellectual self. Whereas it was his father who had defined Mill's world, it was Harriet Taylor who helped him to come to terms with and transcend that world.

5

The Transitional Essays

T HE TRANSITIONAL ESSAYS reflect Mill's attempt to understand and to restate the Philosophic Radical agenda in the light of the new continental, conservative, and especially Romantic influences on his thinking. They also lay the groundwork for his explication of liberal culture that we have come to identify as his major (later) works.

The Spirit of the Age[1]

Mill announced two general themes in this essay. The first is that the age he lived in reflected a remarkable historical development that needed to be addressed – namely, that it was an age of transition. "Mankind have outgrown old institutions and old doctrines and have not yet acquired new ones."[2] The transition to which Mill is alluding is the transition from feudalism to an industrial and commercial society accompanied by the growth of liberal culture (individual rights, the rule of law, free markets, etc.). The old institutions, including Parliament and the Church of England, were no longer able to understand, articulate, or guide the transition. The second general theme, in somewhat embryonic form, is that a philosophy of history had now become an important parameter for understanding ourselves.

With regard to the theme that his age is an age of transition, Mill makes four important points. First, the members of the landed aristocracy had exercised positive leadership of society during the feudal period. Their experience had promoted the kind of virtues that made positive leadership possible. However, this was no longer the case. To begin with, we have moved economically into an age of industry and commerce. The aristocracy, as a whole, no longer have the kind of experience that promotes the requisite virtues. In addition, they have become enervated and undermined by their inherited wealth. They continue to exercise enormous political and social power, but it is a political power that is at odds with the economic transformation of Britain and Europe, a kind of anachronisms; they no longer possess the skills or inclination for virtuous leadership.

Second, the Church of England had become the same kind of anachronism. It continued to reflect the values of a feudal age. It was no secret or accident that the leading men of business belonged to the dissenting sects. Mill finds this religious anachronism all the more deplorable in the light of the historical role of the clergy. Here Mill makes reference to the intellectual and moral leadership that the Catholic Church had exercised during the Middle Ages, in cooperation with the aristocracy. Mill looked back with regret to the loss of the "natural" state in which "worldly power, and moral influence, are habitually and undisputedly exercised by the fittest persons whom the existing state of society affords."[3] What the Catholic Middle Ages possessed was a clear locus of authority for the articulation of the fundamental values of the culture. Mill believed that it was necessary for there to be something like "received doctrines."[4]

To have erroneous convictions is one evil; but to have no strong or deep-rooted convictions at all, is an enormous one. Before I compliment either a man or a generation upon having got rid of their prejudices, I require to know what they have substituted in lieu of them.[5]

There is a difference, of course, between a received doctrine, which implies acceptance of some authority, and a strong conviction based not on outside authority but on a critical process. It is the latter that Mill had in mind.

Mill never abandoned the notion that there had to be received doctrines. In the essay on Coleridge, he will enumerate those doctrines; he will throughout his lifetime enumerate the same doctrines, often quoting himself. What he will worry about is the locus of authority for those doctrines and the best manner of sustaining them.

The third point is the need for authority.

It is, therefore, one of the necessary conditions of humanity, that the majority must either have wrong opinions, or no fixed opinions, or must place the degree of reliance warranted by reason, in the authority of those who have made moral and social philosophy their peculiar study. It is right that every man should attempt to understand his interest and his duty. It is right that he should follow his reason as far as his reason will carry him, and cultivate the faculty as highly as possible. But reason itself will teach most men that they must, in the last resort, fall back upon the authority of still more cultivated minds, as the ultimate sanction of the convictions of their reason itself.[6]

Mill never abandoned his belief in the vast intellectual differences among human beings, a belief perfectly compatible with the recognition that the environment and historical accident play a significant role in whether people reach their potential. It is a point he will repeat in *Utilitarianism* in distinguishing between quantitative and qualitative differences in pleasure. The practical and moral problem is to reconcile this with the egalitarian impulses in a democracy. This is precisely the problem he will attempt to solve in *On Liberty* and in *Representative Government*.

Fourth, despite the fact that the men of commerce and industry are the real power in society at the moment, they have created an industrial proletariat that would soon surpass them in power and influence. These entrepreneurs also lack the kind of wisdom needed for exercising positive leadership in a modern liberal culture. What is needed, apparently, is a new authoritative locus for articulating the fundamental values. Without saying so in an outright fashion, what Mill seems to suggest is that the new intellectuals, as represented by himself and some of the other Philosophic Radicals, were the proper vehicle for performing this function. Some hint of this new meritocracy that Mill seemed to have had in mind can be gleaned from the following comment:

[T]here must be a change in the whole framework of society, as at present constituted. Worldly power must pass from the hands of the stationary part of mankind into those of the progressive part. There must be a moral and social revolution, which shall, indeed, take away no men's lives or property, but which shall leave to no man one fraction of unearned distinction or unearned influence.[7]

It is only after this has been achieved that a new natural condition will obtain.

They [the landed aristocracy] must, therefore, be divested of the monopoly of worldly power, ere the most virtuous and best-instructed of the nation will acquire the ascendancy over the opinions and feelings of the rest, by which alone England can emerge from this crisis of transition, and enter once again into a natural state of society.[8]

The suggestion seems to be that giving power to a coalition of middle-class and lower-class forces will be good, since they will be more amenable than the aristocrats to guidance by the intellectuals.[9]

The second general theme in this essay is a nascent philosophy of history. There are two elements in Mill's philosophy of history, a universal element and a contextual element. We should not be surprised that someone like Mill, who believed in the existence of "received doctrines," also believed in universal truths, some of which repose in his beloved classical literature. "The speeches of the great orators, and those in Thucydides, are monuments of long-sighted policy, and keen and sagacious observation of life and human nature, which will be prized as long as the world shall endure, or as wisdom shall be understood and appreciated in it."[10] At the same time, Mill had absorbed from the Saint-Simonians the Hegelian belief that there was an evolution in both the material and spiritual dimensions of civilization such that universal truths are always contextualized differently.

To find fault with our ancestors for not having annual parliaments, universal suffrage, and vote by ballot, would be like quarrelling with the Greeks and Romans for not using steam navigation . . . finding fault with the third century before Christ for not being the eighteenth century after. It was necessary that many other things should be thought and done, before, according to the laws of human affairs, it was possible that steam navigation should be thought of. Human nature must proceed step by step, in politics as well as in physics. . . .

From these remarks it will be seen how greatly I differ, at once from those, who seeing the institutions of our ancestors to be bad for us, imagine that they were bad for those for whom they were made [e.g., the Philosophic Radicals] and from those who ridiculously invoke the wisdom of our ancestors as authority for institutions which in substance are now totally different, howsoever they may be the same in form [e.g., the classical conservatives].[11]

It is clear from these remarks that seven years before he wrote the essay on Coleridge Mill had come to a new understanding of both social institutions and social reform that was more sympathetic to conservatism. It was a view that always guided his public policy analysis, much to the consternation of both radicals and classical conservatives. It was a view according to which he always qualified his recommendations, a view that made him comfortable when he changed his mind, a view that traps the unwary scholar who attempts to attribute to Mill a rigid public policy position.

Invoking the dual notions of universal truths and inevitable contextualization raises a serious philosophical problem. By what criterion do we determine whether a current or proposed institutional structure instantiates a universal truth or truths? In the *Logic*, Mill will try to provide a criterion in the form of the proposed science of ethology. Mill ultimately will abandon ethology and recognize that holding the dual positions requires an act of faith, a faith that Mill expresses in *Theism*. In the end, Mill's philosophy of history is supplemented by theology.[12]

Civilization[13]

The essay is an indictment of nineteenth-century Britain for giving to the masses the means and the will to exercise a formidable collective power, without giving them a corresponding accession of intelligence or morality. It also indicts utilitarianism for assuming that material progress is necessarily beneficent. What is most important about this essay, however, is that it constitutes the earliest formulation of Mill's project to explicate, defend, and preserve liberal culture.

Mill begins the essay with a definition of "civilization" that owes much to Scottish Enlightenment thinkers such as Hume, Smith, and Ferguson. By "civilization" he means a modern industrial and commercial society with a liberal culture, such as Great Britain.

[A] country rich in the fruits of agriculture, commerce, and manufactures, we call civilized. . . . Wherever, therefore, we find human beings acting together for common purposes in large bodies, and enjoying the fruits of social intercourse, we term them civilized. . . . We accordingly call a people civilized, where the arrangements of society, for protecting the persons and property of its members, are sufficiently perfect to maintain peace among them.[14]

The rise and development of civilization is dependent upon "the natural laws of the progress of wealth, upon the diffusion of reading, and the increase of the facilities of human intercourse."[15] Mill sees examples of these combined features in military operations, commerce and manufacturing, the rise of joint stock companies, benefit societies, and even "the more questionable Trades Unions."[16]

For Mill, the consequences of the rise of civilization are economic, political, social, and moral. Economically, there has been a vast increase in wealth in which the masses and the middle class have been the greater beneficiary, as opposed to the landed aristocracy.[17] Politically, power is shifting from a few individuals to the masses. This leads Mill to formulate a thesis whose origin he notes in Tocqueville.

[B]y the natural growth of civilization, power passes from individuals to masses, and the weight and importance of an individual, as compared with the mass, sink into greater and greater insignificance.[18]

Socially, the most serious consequence has been the decline of both conspicuous vice and heroic virtue.

[T]here is in the more opulent classes of modern civilized communities much more of the amiable and humane, and much less of the heroic. . . . There has crept over the refined classes . . . a moral effeminacy. . . . One of the effects of a high state of civilization upon character, is a relaxation of individual energy: or rather, the concentration of it within the narrow sphere of the individual's money-getting pursuits. . . . There remain, as inducements to call forth energy of character, the desire of wealth or of personal aggrandizement, the passion for philanthropy, and the love of active virtue. . . . The energies of the middle-classes are almost confined to money-getting, and those of the higher classes are nearly extinct.[19]

In words that anticipate *On Liberty*, Mill worries about the fact that "[t]he individual becomes so lost in the crowd [that] an established character becomes at once more difficult to gain."[20]

The future of civilization depends upon the masses' exercising their power in such a responsible way that we shall continue to enjoy the benefits of civilization. Mill did not believe that this would happen on its own. Civilization would not endure unless the masses came to understand and appreciate the moral foundations of liberal culture. Unlike both classical liberals, such as the Philosophic Radicals, and orthodox Marxists, Mill was not an economic determinist. The moral world was not a mere product of material forces. The very functioning of the economy presupposed certain virtues. Mill states the problem as follows:

With regard to the advance of democracy, there are two different positions which it is possible for a rational person to take up, according as he thinks the masses prepared, or unprepared, to exercise control which they are acquiring over their destiny, in a manner which would be an improvement upon what now exists. If he thinks them prepared, he will aid the democratic movement; or if he deem it to be proceeding fast enough without him, he will at all events refrain from resisting it. If, on the contrary, he thinks the masses unprepared for complete control over their government – seeing at the same time that, prepared or not, they cannot long be prevented from acquiring it – he will exert his utmost efforts in contributing to prepare them; using all means, on the one hand, for making the masses themselves wiser and better; on the other, for so rousing the slumbering energy of the opulent and lettered classes, so storing the youth of those classes with the profoundest and most valuable knowledge, so calling forth whatever of individual greatness exists or can be raised up in the country, as to create a power which might partially rival the mere power of the masses, and might exercise the most salutary influence over them for their own good.[21]

Herein is the explanation of Mill's economic position in the later *Principles of Political Economy*; herein lies the germ of the recommendations of *Representative Government*; and here is the project that *On Liberty* will address.

We ought not to lose sight of one important point. Mill was an advocate of liberal culture. He was a friend of market economies, saying of the rise of joint stock companies that he is "not among those who believe that this progress is tending to the complete extinction of competition";[22] he was a champion of representative government.[23] It is not an inevitable consequence of civilization that it will destroy itself.

[T]he question has been seriously propounded, whether civilization is on the whole a good or an evil? Assuredly, we entertain no doubt on this point; *we hold civilization is a good, that it is the cause of much good, and not incompatible with any* [italics added]; but we think there is other good, much even of the highest good, which civilization in this sense does not provide for, and some which it has a tendency (though that tendency may be counteracted) to impede.[24]

We note that among the many things that both Mill and his father had objected to most vehemently about the new industrial economy was the spoiling of the countryside by all of the new, and in many cases unnecessarily duplicative, railway lines. As inveterate hikers, the two were especially sensitive to the destruction of natural beauty and the disappearance of solitude.

Bentham[25]

Following his father's death, and emboldened to formulate the case against extreme radicalism, Mill reshaped his earlier and anonymously published critique of Bentham. The idea of contrasting two thinkers as the seminal minds of their age was first suggested to Mill by Carlyle's review in 1831 of Croker's edition of Boswell's *Life of Johnson*. Carlyle identified Johnson as the progenitor of the Tories and Hume as the progenitor of the Whigs. He then went on to suggest that whoever synthesized the two would become

the "whole man of a new time."[26] Mill identified Jeremy Bentham and
Samuel Taylor Coleridge as "the two great seminal minds of England in
their age."[27] Mill clearly intended in this essay to present himself as the
positive synthesis of these two perspectives, the best of the Enlightenment
Project and the best of the Romantic movement. What is remarkable about
this essay is how little of the Enlightenment Project actually remains to
be praised. Mill comments positively only on Bentham's articulation of
the need to get beyond feudalism if liberal culture is to flourish and the
need for the law to be clarified and reformed. Beyond that, the essay in
one long, almost unrelieved – and, we might add, devastating – critique
of Bentham.

Mill represents Bentham as the "great subversive" of his age, denying
the legitimacy of everything that did not conform to his scheme – an
exemplar of what Carlyle called "the completeness of limited men." But
Bentham's error as a reformer was his ignorance both of human nature and
of social institutions. Bentham failed to derive light from other minds.[28]
In his work the *Deontology*, Bentham had accused Socrates and Plato of
talking nonsense under the pretense of discussing morality.

Bentham's contempt, then, of all other schools of thinkers; his determination to
create a philosophy wholly out of the materials furnished by his own mind, and
by minds like his own; was his first disqualification as a philosopher. His second,
was the incompleteness of his own mind as a representative of universal human
nature . . . [h]is deficiency of imagination.[29]

[N]o one, probably, who, in a highly instructed age, ever attempted to give a rule to
all human conduct, set out with a more limited conception either of the agencies
by which human conduct *is*, or of those by which it *should* be, influenced.[30]

Mill details three important respects in which Bentham failed. First,
Bentham failed to understand the fundamental truth about human nature.

Man is never recognized by him as a being capable of pursuing spiritual perfection
as an end; of desiring, for its own sake, the conformity of his own character to his
standard of excellence, without hope of good or fear of evil from other source than
his own inward consciousness.[31]

This passage is crucial. What Mill is suggesting is nothing less than the
Kantian position, namely, that the ultimate value is freedom understood
as personal autonomy, as the imposing of rules upon oneself in the interest of a higher ideal. This is a point, as we shall see, that he repeats

even more eloquently in the *Logic*, and it is the basis of his reinterpretation of utility in *Utilitarianism*. What Mill is also telling us is that liberal culture cannot survive the loss of conscience and duty as motives, and any reductive hedonistic view will lead to the decline of moral sensibility.[32]

Second, the human faculty least understood by Bentham was imagination. "Self-consciousness, that daemon of the men of genius of our time, from Wordsworth to Byron, from Goethe to Chateaubriand ... never was awakened in" Bentham.[33] Mill's understanding of the human condition was by now extraordinarily different from Bentham's. There is no such thing as human nature, only the human condition. We do not find in human experience that the world makes sense of itself. The bewildering variety of stimuli we receive from the external world has to be interpreted. The laws of association supply part of the interpretation; part of the interpretation is supplied by the larger cultural context in which we operate. But in the end, the human predicament is reflected most accurately in the "ordeal of consciousness,"[34] the need to accept responsibility for continually and imaginatively creating and recreating ourselves and our understanding of the world based on our experience of it.

To be human is to be free, and our freedom is employed in our imagination and intelligence; these faculties are used in defining ourselves as individuals and in giving meaning to our experience of the world we inhabit; this engagement is what it means to learn and is the source of our humanity, itself an adventure in self-definition. An individual freely chooses meaningful ways of understanding him- or herself and the surrounding world. This is what Mill means by self-culture.

There is no need to expatiate on the deficiencies of a system of ethics [Bentham's] which does not pretend to aid individuals in the formation of their own character; which recognizes no such wish as that of self-culture, we may even say no such power, as existing in human nature; and if it did recognize, could furnish little assistance to that great duty. . . .[35]

[T]here was needed a greater knowledge of the formation of character, and of the consequences of actions upon the agent's own frame of mind, than Bentham possessed.[36]

We must use our imagination in order to learn. It is the unique ordering of our experience in imagination that makes us unique individuals. "Without it nobody knows even his own nature."[37]

One of the most important ways in which we utilize our imagination is in reconstructing the thought of another person, or of another age, or even our own cultural inheritance.

This is the power by which one human being enters into the mind and circumstances of another. This power constitutes the poet. . . . It constitutes the dramatist entirely. It is one of the constituents of the historian; by it we understand other times; by it Guizot interprets to us the middle ages. . . .[38]

Our cultural inheritance is a set of achievements and practices, not a doctrine to be learned. The content of an inheritance can be conveyed only in the form of meanings, most especially artistic ones. The inheritance is re-created through its imaginative appropriation by outstanding individuals.

Two important conclusions follow from this discussion of the imagination. First, Mill is reinforcing the case he made earlier in *The Spirit of the Age* for a space to be created within which individuals can engage in the ongoing explication of the cultural inheritance. Second, Mill anticipates here the very technical sense in which he will use the term "poet" in the *Logic* – that is, someone with the special capacity to explicate the meaning or inherent norms of a culture. This is a function that cannot be reduced to a science.

The third important thing that Bentham failed to understand was the need for an account of national character. What does Mill mean by this, and why is it important? Meaningful social reform must proceed upon the basis of a sound account of the cultural context within which individuals exist – that is, an account of both the social and historical dimensions of human existence. A contextless – or, even worse, a misinformed – account of humanity in the abstract is not sufficient. Social reform presupposes an accurate and "poetically" derived understanding of the inherent norms that guide human beings, what Mill calls the "spiritual interests of society."

That which alone causes any material interests to exist, which alone enables any body of human beings to exist as a society, is national character: *that* it is, which causes one nation to succeed in what it attempts, another to fail; one nation to understand and aspire to elevated things, another to grovel in mean ones; which makes the greatness of one nation lasting, and dooms another to early and rapid decay. The true teacher of the fitting social arrangements for England, France, or America, is the one who can point out how the English, French, or American character can be improved, and how it has been made what it is. A philosophy of law and institutions, not founded on a philosophy of national character, is an absurdity.[39]

Even Bentham's philosophy of law was limited by the fact that he "was precluded from considering, except to a very limited extent, the laws of a country as an instrument of national culture."[40]

No one could read the essay on Bentham and fail to realize the extent to which Mill had gone far beyond Philosophic Radicalism, the extent to which it is highly misleading to continue to link him, in textbook-like fashion, with Bentham. This essay and the subsequent one on Coleridge demand a reexamination of the cardboard figure that appears under the heading "Mill" in the history of thought. The culmination of this period was twofold: Mill's rejection of the radical version of the Enlightenment Project, as exemplified by Bentham and James Mill, and his attempt to synthesize radical and conservative thought. The essay on Bentham (1838) reflects the rejection, and the essay on Coleridge (1840) marks the synthesis and culmination of this period.[41]

Coleridge[42]

Early in the essay, Mill gives one of the clearest statements of his problematic, namely, how to maintain the benefits of liberal culture (i.e., civilization) and how to overcome its limitations.

Take for instance the question of how far mankind have gained by civilization. One observer is struck by the multiplication of physical comforts; the advancement and diffusion of knowledge ... the decline of war and personal conflict; the progressive limitation of the tyranny of the strong over the weak. ... Another fixes his attention ... upon the high price which is paid for them[:] the relaxation of individual energy and courage; the loss of proud and self-relying independence; the slavery of so large a portion of mankind to artificial wants ... absence of any marked individuality, in their characters ... the demoralizing effect of great inequalities in wealth and social rank. ...[43]

Mill's position is clear and unequivocal. He does not wish to accept the premises of Rousseau – that "the work of civilization should as far as possible be undone" – because "they lead to the practical conclusions of Rousseau's disciple, Robespierre."[44] He wants instead to have liberal culture preserve its benefits and overcome its limitations.

This can be done, according to Mill, by combining the strengths of the philosophy of the Enlightenment and the philosophy of the German Romantics, as reflected in Coleridge. The fundamental department of philosophy is the philosophy of mind, in which Mill seems to include metaphysics and epistemology. It is on the basis of the philosophy of mind that we will arrive at the correct axiology, or theory of value. He goes on to give a remarkably clear and concise summary of the differences between Lockean empiricism and the Kantian conception of the synthetic a priori.[45] Rather than argue the case, he contents himself "with a bare statement of . . . opinion. It is, that the truth . . . lies with the school of Locke and Bentham."[46]

It is his choice of empiricism (Locke and Bentham) over Kant's epistemology that has led to much misunderstanding about Mill's position. Although accepting Coleridge's conception of the imagination, as well as the recognition of the two different kinds of truth and the priority of internal truths, Mill rejected one aspect of what he took to be continental epistemology ("innate-principle metaphysics"). Mill rejected the notion that the imagination was a source of absolute and timeless a priori transcendent truths. At the same time, he accepted the idea that the imagination was the source of internal truths about human emotion. Nevertheless, Mill insisted, in Hegelian fashion, on the temporality of the internally accessed truths. It is their temporality that allowed for growth and change.

The parallels with Hegel are remarkable. Even Mill's critique of Kant is a Hegelian critique. Although Mill did read some Hegel, mostly the *Logic*, he did not read much else, including the *Philosophy of Right*. In fact, Mill detested reading Hegel, claiming once in a letter to Bain that

conversancy with him [Hegel] tends to deprave one's intellect. The attempt to unwind an apparently infinite series of self-contradictions not disguised but openly faced, really, if persisted in, impairs the acquired delicacy of perception of false reasoning and false thinking which has been gained by years of careful mental discipline with terms of real meaning. For some time after I finished the book all such words as reflection, development, evolution, &c., gave me a sort of sickening feeling which I have not yet entirely got rid of.[47]

The similarity between Mill and Hegel was the result of the indirect influence of their reading the same sources in German and French Romanticism (e.g., Victor Cousin) and also the influence on Mill of friends like Sterling.[48] Mill worked his way to the same conclusions. The congruence is not so remarkable once we realize that both men were attempting to make sense of the same new world of liberal culture, that both had begun with a rejection of the Enlightenment Project, that both had seen the importance of coming to terms with Kant,[49] and that both had recognized the need for a more historicized position.

On a more positive note, Mill maintained in this essay that it was possible to see the continuity between Kant's categorical imperative, as expressed in Coleridge's essay "The Friend," and the doctrine of utility, as expressed in Coleridge's "Aids to Reflection." This further exemplifies the claim we made in our discussion of the essay on Bentham that Mill's *Utilitarianism* is meant to show the congruity of utility (teleology) and duty (Kantian deontology). This will have important implications for the essay *On Liberty*.

Where the philosophy of the Enlightenment Project went wrong was in its limited understanding of experience. The Philosophic Radicals could not make sense of the social world because they lacked a social epistemology. That is, they did not understand "the binding forces which hold society together."[50] That social epistemology, moreover, has an historical dimension. Therefore, an adequate "philosophy of society" or a "philosophy of human culture" depends upon a philosophy of history.[51] It was this essay on Coleridge that led the radical Francis Place to complain that Mill was becoming a German metaphysician.[52]

What would an adequate philosophy of history encompass? In Coleridge, Mill identifies the task as discerning or intuiting the inherent norms reflected in institutional practice, what Coleridge calls "the Idea of it."[53] Once one has identified those norms, one is in a position to see the "agencies which have produced and still maintain the Present."[54] Armed with this information, one can both predict and guide the future.[55] To *explicate* is to try to clarify that which is routinely taken for granted – namely, our ordinary understanding of our practices – in the hope of extracting from our previous practice a set of norms that can be used reflectively to guide future practice. Meaningful social reform is both an act of retrieval and a projection that expands to incorporate things that might from an earlier perspective even seem alien. The act of retrieval through explication inevitably involves a reformulation. To encompass the past is to make it our own in some fashion. That is why Mill could say the following about Coleridge as a way to chide the Philosophic Radicals:

[A] Tory philosopher cannot be wholly a Tory, but must often be a better Liberal than Liberals themselves; while he is the natural means of rescuing from oblivion truths which Tories have forgotten, and which the prevailing schools of Liberalism never knew.[56]

That is why Mill could suggest that instead of trying to convert conservatives into liberals, social reform must get conservatives "to adopt one liberal opinion after another, as a part of Conservatism itself."[57]

A social epistemology could have saved the Philosophic Radicals from another error. In their simplistic model of human beings, reform becomes a simple matter of transmitting information and removing external barriers. But Mill rejects the notion that the removal of barriers is sufficient. It is not enough to root out the noxious weeds; one must also till the soil. Mill went on to specify three classic ways in which the social soil needed to be tilled – "essential requisites of civil society the French philosophers of the eighteenth century unfortunately overlooked."[58]

First, there must be a system of education. Education cannot mean the simple imparting of information. Education is an exercise in "restraining discipline."[59] Self-discipline is not merely a restraining force but a progressive force, calling forth and invigorating "the active faculties."[60] Mill identified the chief issue in education as "the culture of the inward man."[61] For Mill, the culture of the inward man included the notion of personal autonomy or self-discipline in the traditional Christian[62] sense of self-rule, as well as Goethe's Romantic conception of self-development.[63]

This combination, which is the core of his idea of individuality in *On Liberty*, has confused and baffled many a reader. It is not the classical notion of submission to a higher authority or a collective good. It is not the Aristotelian notion of bringing one's will into conformity with one's objectively given and discoverable telos. Mill denied that we have such a telos. It is the notion of a freely chosen ideal along with the understanding that each individual has to find for him- or herself what ideal can be the most meaningful focus in his or her life.[64] By its very nature, the notion of a freely chosen "ideal" precludes the choice of a self-indulgent lifestyle. It never amounted, either logically or inherently, to the unbridled libertinism that critics see in Mill's espousal of liberty. Nor did it have the ominous consequences attributed to it by other critics.[65]

Second, there must be *loyalty* to some substantive norm. Mill was quite specific about what that substantive norm had to be in the future of liberal culture. The substantive norm is the universal promotion of personal autonomy.

[T]his is the only shape in which the feeling is likely to exist hereafter. . . . it [must] . . . attach itself to the principles of individual freedom and political and social equality, as realized in institutions that exist nowhere, or exist only in a rudimentary state.[66]

We are to be equal in being free. It is precisely the promotion of personal autonomy that will not only capture the positive dynamism of liberal culture but also overcome its serious internal threats: "the relaxation of individual energy and courage; the loss of proud and self-relying independence; the slavery of so large a portion of mankind to artificial wants . . . absence of any marked individuality, in their characters . . . the demoralizing effect of great inequalities in wealth and social rank."[67] The essay *On Liberty* will make this case, specifically in the discussion of individuality. The *Principles of Political Economy* and Mill's other economic writings all have one goal, the encouragement and promotion of an entrepreneurial attitude among the working class, on the understanding that being entrepreneurial allows a space for the development of human excellence in other than monetary forms.

Third, the social soil must be tilled so as to promote the common good – or, more specifically, the recognition of the continuity between the individual good and the common good.

The third essential condition of stability in political society, is a strong and active principle of cohesion among the members of the same community or state. We . . . do not mean nationality in the vulgar sense of the term. . . . We mean a principle of sympathy, not of hostility; of union, not of separation. We mean a feeling of common interest . . . that they set a value on their connexion . . . that evil to any of their fellow-countrymen is evil to themselves; and do not desire selfishly to free themselves from their share of any common inconvenience. . . .[68]

It is with regard to the promotion of the common good that Mill articulates the role of government, making the case in a manner that never varied throughout the rest of his life.

[G]overnment ought not to interdict men from publishing their opinions, pursuing their employments, or buying or selling their goods, in whatsoever place or manner they deem the most advantageous. Beyond suppressing force and fraud, governments can seldom, without doing more harm than good, attempt to chain up the free agency of individuals. But does it follow from this that government cannot exercise a free agency of its own? - that it cannot beneficially employ its powers, its means of information, and its pecuniary resources . . . in promoting the public welfare by a thousand means which individuals would never think of, would have no sufficient motive to attempt, or no sufficient power to accomplish? . . . a State ought to be considered as a great benefit society, or mutual insurance company, for helping (under the necessary regulations for preventing abuse) that large proportion of its members who cannot help themselves.[69]

Where exactly this places Mill on the political spectrum is a matter of some scholarly debate, and we shall discuss this issue at length in the chapter on Mill's economic philosophy. However, it is fair to say that (a) Mill's ideal of a good society is based on personal autonomy – that is, it is one in which individuals are as free and independent and self-sufficient as possible; (b) government intervention is needed and justified only where individuals "cannot help themselves" (including cases where individuals might be capable of helping themselves but only by means "which individuals would never think of" or "have no sufficient motive to attempt"); and (c) even where (b) is the case, we must be cognizant of the ever-present possibility of the cure being worse than the disease (unintended consequences). What is clear is that Mill was no ideologue. What is also clear is that (b) and (c) are context-specific and historically variable and therefore have to be determined on a case-by-case basis by reference to facts and not by reference to ideology. What Mill contributed was not another position on the political spectrum but a framework for asking the relevant public policy questions.

Tocqueville and *Democracy in America*[70]

Mill reviewed Tocqueville twice, in 1835 and again in 1840, after the publication of each of the two volumes of *Democracy in America*. The second review reflected Mill's own deeper understanding[71] as a result of having read the second part. Mill's second review summarized the first part as well, sometimes borrowing sentences from the first review but also signaling an attempt to reach a deeper synthesis. In Volume I, Tocqueville described the federal virtues of an agrarian republic while warning about the tyranny of the majority. In Volume II, Tocqueville analyzed the sociology of the masses in an egalitarian society. It is instructive to contrast Mill's review of Volume I, where he tries to defend democracy against Tocqueville's critique in institutional terms, and his review of Volume II, where he comes to appreciate fully the dangers of democracy without the virtues of a moral culture.

What attracted Mill's attention in Tocqueville was the issue of democracy. Tocqueville's understanding of the spirit of the age was that we were living through the triumph of the democratic spirit. In Mill's eyes, Tocqueville was an aristocratic conservative who recognized democracy as the wave of the future. This fit perfectly with Mill's recognition, expressed in the essay on Coleridge, of the need to move conservatism in a more liberal direction.

There is a tendency for democracy to encourage the omnipotence of the majority and for the majority to become tyrannical. Mill recognized that this kind of tyranny is a threat to the notion of limited government, the key political institution connecting the technological project with the culture of personal autonomy. Mill further acknowledged that Tocqueville's thesis was not merely the recognition of the danger but a diagnosis of it and a normative response. Tocqueville was not making a prediction but calling attention to a tendency. However, although "this irresistible current [democratization]... cannot be stemmed, [it] may be guided, and guided to a happy termination."[72] Tocqueville's recommendation was to promote the value of intermediate institutions (local government, economic institutions, religion, the family, voluntary organizations, etc.) as a buffer to defend individual liberty from the increasing power of a centralized democratic government. Mill quoted with approval Tocqueville's view that "the first duty... imposed upon those who direct our affairs is to educate the democracy; to reanimate its faith... to purify its morals; to regulate its energies; to substitute for its inexperience a knowledge of business, and for its blind instincts an acquaintance with its true interests."[73] What Tocqueville saw and what he suggested clearly reflected how Mill had come to understand his own role.

Tocqueville had also intimated in Part I of *Democracy in America* that a democratic culture leads to a loss of the heroic aristocratic virtues. This is a point that Mill himself had made in his essay *Civilization*. However, in the first review, Mill distanced himself to a slight degree from Tocqueville.

The good which mankind have lost, is coloured, we think, rather too darkly; and we think, also, that more than our author seems to believe, of what was good in the influences of aristocracy, is compatible, if we really wish to find it so, with a well-regulated democracy. But though we would soften the colours of the picture, we would not alter them; M. de Tocqueville's is, in our eyes, the true view of the position in which mankind now stand.[74]

Part of the reason for Mill's confidence is his belief that an intellectual-leisured class (clerisy) stands ready to perform the task of educating the rising democracy. Note that this makes Mill sanguine about England, but not about the United States, where, according to Tocqueville, there is no leisure class, and none will develop.

In the existence of a leisured class, we see the great and salutary corrective of all the inconveniences to which democracy is liable. We cannot, under any modifi-cation of the laws of England, look forward to a period when this grand security for the progressiveness of the human species will not exist. . . . we see nothing in any of those tendencies, from which any serious evil need be apprehended, if the superior spirits would but join with each other in considering the instruc-tion of the democracy, and not the patching of the old worn-out machinery of aristocracy.[75]

By the time he wrote the second review, Mill's position had shifted. We think this shift accounts for the fact that he chose to publish the sec-ond review in the Whig publication *The Edinburgh Review* instead of in the radical publication the *London Review*. Mill began by noting that "democ-racy," for Tocqueville, means "equality of conditions; the absence of all aristocracy, whether constituted by political privileges, or by superiority in individual importance and social power."[76] Moreover, what Tocqueville attributed to equality, Mill found to rest ultimately with the development of commercial society. It is the market economy that promotes democ-racy! In fact, Mill even quoted with approval and at length Tocqueville's historical account detailing the economic changes driving the process.[77] The Millian argument is now clear. If the economic forces that lead to egalitarianism are the same in England as they have been in America, then England in time will be democratically indistinguishable from America. If that is the case, then no clerisy or special class can be relied upon to avert the danger.

Mill abandoned his notion of a clerisy as inadequate to a modern democ-racy. Apparently, in a democracy no one institution can be authoritative.

The preservation of liberty requires that it be supported by all institutions, but in different ways. Failure to articulate and rearticulate the norms leads to a quiet customary despotism. Any authoritarian articulation leads to tyranny. For liberty to remain a living truth instead of a dead dogma, it must be widely discussed. Mill, in short, abandoned the quest for an authoritative locus of received opinion and for the preservation and promotion of the fundamental norms. If liberty is to be preserved, then a major reconceptualization of social, economic, and political institutions is required. *The Principles of Political Economy*, the essay *On Liberty, Considerations on Representative Government*, and *The Subjection of Women* all address the need for a major reconceptualization. Later in life, Mill would exclude his essay on *The Spirit of the Age* from his collected works, published during his lifetime as *Dissertations and Discussions* (1859). Democracy, Tocqueville had taught him, is inevitable; there was a need to instruct the average person; the clerisy was valuable only insofar as it instructs, not leads.

Mill's discussion of commercial society in this essay is important because it spells out in detail exactly what Mill approved of and what he disapproved of in such societies. It also makes clear the larger context in which his economic philosophy is to be understood. Taking notice of that larger context will, we contend, show that Mill had fully worked out his economic philosophy by 1840 and that what may look like shifts in his political economy actually reflect a consistent vision responding to different sets of circumstances. To begin with, Mill, as an advocate of liberal culture, saw the central role of a free market economy within liberal culture and tirelessly expressed our indebtedness to it for many, if not all, of the good things we enjoy.

The spirit of commerce and industry is one of the greatest instruments not only of civilization in the narrowest, but of improvement and culture in the widest sense: to it, or to its consequences, we owe nearly all that advantageously distinguishes the present period from the middle ages. So long as other coordinate elements of improvement existed beside it, doing what it left undone, and keeping its exclusive tendencies in equipoise by an opposite order of sentiments, principles of action, and modes of thought – so long the benefits which it conferred on humanity were unqualified.[78]

What is also clear from this statement is that liberal culture depends upon more than a free market economy. Mill was not an economic determinist, and this will explain why his writings continue to exasperate both doctrinaire libertarians and doctrinaire socialists.

[H]uman affairs are not entirely governed by mechanical laws, nor men's characters wholly and irrevocably formed by their situation in life. Economical and social changes, though among the greatest, are not the only forces which shape the course of our species; ideas are not always the mere signs and effects of social circumstances, they are themselves a power in history.[79]

Insisting upon this point will help to explain where and how Mill thinks he has improved upon Tocqueville's analysis. Mill specifically corrects Tocqueville for not seeing that the ultimate source of the problem is neither democracy nor equality but the unqualified spirit of commerce.

M. de Tocqueville, then, has, at least apparently, confounded the effects of Democracy with the effects of Civilization [what we have called the technological project expressed though a market economy]. He has bound up in one abstract idea the whole of the tendencies of modern commercial society, and given them one name – Democracy; thereby letting it be supposed that he ascribes to equality of conditions, several of the effects naturally arising from the mere progress of national prosperity, in the form in which that progress manifests itself in modern times.[80]

Neither democracy nor equality of condition is objectionable in principle to Mill. The real source of our problem is the unqualified commercial spirit. "[T]he most serious danger to the future prospects of mankind is in the unbalanced influence of the commercial spirit."[81]

Why is this the case? Mill believes that the "unbalanced influence of the commercial spirit" produces a race of humans whose only value is creature comfort and who will sacrifice everything to that. In the end, they will lose everything, including the creature comforts. What we shall have is Nietzsche's "last man." There are other, more immediate consequences. The pursuit of wealth has become an end in itself, sacrificing quality to quantity, or to the appearance of quantity.

[B]y the intense competition which necessarily exists where an entire population are the competitors, arises the restlessness so characteristic of American life.[82]

... that entire unfixedness in the social position of individuals – that treading upon the heels of one another – the habitual dissatisfaction of each with the position he occupies, and eager desire to push himself into the next above it. . . . As if everybody had but one wish – to improve his condition, never to enjoy it. . . . 'The hypocrisy of luxury,' as M. de Tocqueville calls the maintaining an appearance beyond one's real expenditure, he considers as a democratic peculiarity. It is surely an English one.[83]

[T]here are fewer who devote themselves to thought for its own sake, and pursue in retirement those profounder researches, the results of which can only be appreciated by a few. Literary productions are seldom highly finished – they are got up to be read by many, and to be read but once. If the work sells for a day, the author's time and pains will be better laid out in writing a second, than in improving the first.[84]

It is easy to miss the point of these criticisms. Mill is not decrying producer pride but consumer pride. Wealth is enormously important in providing the means for achievement. But achievement does not consist in lavish consumption and display but in the exercise of personal autonomy, of self-discipline in the cause of some ideal. The purpose of wealth is to provide the means for accomplishment, not display. A successful market economy has made it possible for more and more people to become consumers, but has it made it possible for them to become producers of anything significant? Or even consumers of the significant, which would be a first step?

The culprit is not the spirit of commerce. The culprit is the unbalanced spirit of commerce. Balancing the spirit of commerce is not the responsibility of commerce. More importantly, it is not within the capacity of commerce. The issue is, whose responsibility is it? Some, I suspect, will answer religion. Of course, for many the spirit of commerce was the antidote to religious warfare. Mill, eventually, will answer that it is the responsibility of intellectuals – back to the clerisy, but not as an authority, merely as a voice. Mill joined Tocqueville in recognizing that progress in the equalization of conditions needs to be accompanied by progress in "the spirit of liberty" and in "public spirit" in general.[85] The reality is clear enough.

The ascendancy of the commercial class in modern society and politics is inevitable, and, under due limitations, ought not to be regarded as an evil. . . . Any counterbalancing power can henceforth exist only by the sufferance of the commercial class; but that it should tolerate some such limitation, we deem as important as that it should not itself be held in vassalage.[86]

Mill had surrendered the idea of an authoritative institution or clerisy as a possible solution in a democratic society. The problem of problems for him had become the institutional structure for the promotion of personal autonomy.

[For] the formation of the best public opinion, there should exist somewhere a great social support for opinions and sentiments different from those of the mass. The shape which that support may best assume is a question of time, place, and circumstance; but (in a commercial country, and an age, when, happily for mankind, the military spirit is gone by) there can be no doubt about the elements which must compose it: they are an agricultural class, a leisured class, and a learned class.[87]

It is worth recalling that, despairing of the future of a purely philosophic radical party, Mill had tried during the period 1838–39 to forge a new union of radicals with Whigs under the leadership of Lord Durham. Identifying the learned class with the agricultural class and the leisured class reflected that abortive union.[88]

In addition to the peculiar character of a commercial society, what Tocqueville and Mill were concerned about was the negative consequence of the homogenization of modern society. Homogenization in a democratic society takes the form of "the rejection of authority, and the assertion of the right of private judgment."[89]

From such habits and ways of thinking, the consequence which would be apprehended by some would be a most licentious abuse of individual independence of thought. The fact is the reverse.... 'Faith in public opinion,' says M. de Tocqueville, 'becomes in such countries a species of religion, and the majority its prophet.'[90]

What was Mill's concern with public opinion? In order to understand his concern, we must first recognize that Mill believed that there were universal truths about the human predicament and that these truths embodied fundamental norms. One such fundamental norm was personal autonomy. We cannot understand, retrieve, invigorate, and apply our norms to novel circumstances without intellectual conflict and debate. As long as there exists more than one center of power in the social world – for example, different social classes – the interaction of these classes provides a potential context for the dialectical process. If the world were to become homogenized, there was a danger that the process of debate would come to an end. It did not matter which set of values triumphed, because the disappearance of the debate process meant that even the meaning of those values would itself be lost. For example, the triumph of the middle class in a commercial world (e.g., the triumph of the bourgeois) meant that people would pursue the acquisition of wealth but forget what the wealth was itself a means to achieve. This is a problem not just for commercial society but for any society in which one view dominates.[91]

Finally, note should be made of Mill's praise for Tocqueville's method. There are two aspects to what Tocqueville did. He was concerned with both the "art and science of government."[92] With regard to the notion of a social science, Tocqueville exemplifies what Mill would later call in the *Logic* the inverse deductive or historical method. It is in this essay that Mill gives the clearest statement of that method.

His method is, as that of a philosopher on such a subject must be – a combination of deduction with induction: his evidences are, laws of human nature, on the one hand; the example of America, and France, and other modern nations, as far as applicable, on the other. His conclusions never rest on either species of evidence alone; whatever he classes as an effect of Democracy, he has both ascertained to exist in those countries in which the state of society is democratic, and has also succeeded in connecting Democracy by deductions a priori, tending to show that such would naturally be its influences upon beings constituted as mankind are, and placed in a world such as we know ours to be. . . . this [is] . . . the true Baconian and Newtonian method applied to society and government.[93]

What is the "art" of government? Earlier, we noted that in Mill's critique of Bentham the "poet" is someone with the special capacity to explicate the meaning or inherent norms of a culture. This is a function that cannot be reduced to a science. One of the things that Bentham failed to understand was the need for an account of national character.[94] Social critique and reform presuppose a "poetically" derived understanding of the inherent norms that guide human functioning, what Mill called the "spiritual interests of society." This is what Mill found in Tocqueville.

That part of *Democracy in America* which was first published, professes to treat of the political effects of Democracy: the second is devoted to its influence on society in the widest sense; on the relations of private life, on intellect, morals, and the habits and modes of feeling which constitute national character. The last is both a newer and more difficult subject of inquiry than the first; there are fewer who are competent, or who will even think themselves competent, to judge M. de Tocqueville's conclusions.[95]

Mill never wavered in his commitment to explicate liberal culture. Throughout his life, he continued to share the view of the Philosophic

Radicals that we were all working for the happiness of mankind and that there was no ultimate conflict between that pursuit on the part of the individual and on the part of mankind as a whole. Achieving human happiness in a postfeudal world required serious social reform. However, the Philosophic Radicals had failed to understand the complexity of social life. Specifically, they had failed to comprehend the complexity of human psychology and the important part played by history in the very meaning of beliefs and their impact upon human beings.

Mill employed the distinction between "organic" (or "natural") periods, when there is a received opinion and a naturally authoritative elite, and "transitional" (or "critical") periods, when these features are absent. Not realizing that they lived in a "transitional" age,[96] and not understanding at a deep level either human nature in general or conservatism in particular, the Philosophic Radicals had mistakenly attempted to reform society by trying to persuade the social and economic elite of the truths of the new political economy. By calling attention to the importance of imagination and poetry, after having witnessed their profound transformation in his own character, Mill hoped to show the Radicals how they could come to understand, appreciate, and eventually overcome the limitations of the conservative mind, thereby transforming it into a positive power for reform.

His new strategy for achieving radical reform based upon new Romantic and conservative insights also suggested another change to Mill. Reform could not be achieved simply by bombarding people with information. One had to change their way of thinking if the information was to have any effect. What this suggested to Mill was the idea of improving the way in which public policy issues were considered. Specifically, since everyone was still agreed about what good reasoning meant in the physical sciences, perhaps it was possible to use the physical sciences as a springboard for developing the social sciences. A full-scale treatment of the social sciences would, he hoped, clarify both the discussion of public policy and, ultimately, public policy itself.

6

Intellectual Success (1840–1845)

B Y THE EARLY 1840s, a balding Mill was still taking long walks on Sunday, which he claimed was the time that he did his best thinking. He also characterized the period from 1830 to 1840 as the final stage in the maturation of his thought. Writing in his *Autobiography*, he said that

from this time [1840], what is worth relating of my life will come into a very small compass; for I have no further mental changes to tell of, but only, I hope, a continued mental progress; which does not admit of a consecutive history, and the results of which, if real, will be best found in my writings. I shall, therefore, greatly abridge the chronicle of my subsequent years.[1]

The decade from 1840 to 1850 is the period during which Mill made his mark and achieved an eminence that transcended the fact that he was James Mill's son. Two important publications marked his emergence as a major independent thinker: *A System of Logic* (1843) and the *Principles of Political Economy* (1848). The first work established the authoritative methodological basis from which he could express his public policy positions, and the second reflected his most profound thoughts on the major social issues of his time.

Logic

Having put the *Review* behind him in 1838, Mill turned his attention to a project about which he had been thinking for some time. As far back as 1829, Mill had conceived the idea of writing a book on logic. During the 1820s, among the many activities in which Mill had been engaged was a reading group devoted to the study of logic. What he had read up until that time were the relatively technical treatises of Bacon, Hobbes, and Whately. More important was what he intended to do with logic.

The great dream in which Bentham and his father had shared was the idea of constructing a science of human nature that could be used to guide public policy. Mill sought to hold onto part of that dream, but in a manner compatible with and qualified by the insights he had garnered from Romanticism. It is important to keep in mind that Mill had worked on the *Logic* intermittently throughout the 1830s, that his discussion of the use of social science as a guide to public policy was deeply imbued with the philosophy of history of the Romantics, and that the technical aspects he needed to resolve were prolegomena to the solution of practical problems.

In order to accomplish his goal, Mill had to do a number of things. First, he had to address some technical issues in logic in order to ascertain the origin of knowledge. This he accomplished by rehashing, throughout the 1830s, views he had inherited from his father or acquired in his early reading. Second, in order to get from technical issues in logic to public policy, Mill needed a better grasp of the role of logical principles in physical science, and, third, he needed a clearer conception of how these principles applied to the social sciences. The former need was met by reading Whewell and Herschel. William Whewell (1794–1866) was a professor of moral philosophy at Cambridge and later became master of Trinity College in 1841. In 1837, he had published one of the first general histories of the natural sciences, a *History of the Inductive Sciences from the Earliest to the Present Time*, and in 1840 he had followed it with *The Philosophy of the Inductive Sciences Founded upon Their History*. In fact, Whewell had coined the term "scientist." Mill disagreed with Whewell but found his book both a stimulus and a target for his thought. Mill had also hoped that Whewell's eminence and character – for Whewell had published on an extraordinary range of topics, from science to philosophy to ethics to poetry – would lead to an exchange that would publicize the controversy. Ironically, that exchange did not take place until Whewell's 1850 review, which appeared almost a decade after Mill's *Logic* had already become a success on its own.

Whewell's philosophy of science was ahead of its time, and it is only in the light of twentieth-century developments in the philosophy of science[2] that we are beginning to appreciate his insights. It is doubtful that any figure of the nineteenth century, including Herschel and Mill, really appreciated the depth of Whewell's understanding of the development of science. Whewell was a critic of Bacon's conception of the process of induction and wanted to redefine induction as the process by which scientific hypotheses are formulated. He understood this process as a creative act rooted in history but not amenable to strict rules. In this, he was close to the Kantian view that the most general principles of our knowledge are not based upon experience but are instead presuppositions. A successful hypothesis starts out as a happy guess and evolves over time into a larger structure of thought, incorporating both empirical and nonempirical elements. Whewell also insisted on the historically evolving nature of scientific hypotheses and laws. In this respect, Whewell's views are prescient of contemporary views in the philosophy of science. Mill objected on the grounds that Whewell was conflating induction with hypothesis formation and that what mattered was not the original happy guess but the subsequent inductive process by which we prove or confirm the guess. Confirmation was a matter of empirical observation. At this level, Mill's dispute with Whewell was merely semantic.

However, there was a deeper disagreement. Whewell added to his philosophy of science the metaphysical and theological contention that these structures of thought are located in the divine understanding and gradually discovered over time by scientists. That is, the happy or successful guess revealed a deeper metaphysical and religious truth. The structures in God's mind were permanent, and it was only our knowledge that evolved. Because of this claim, Whewell's views lent, in a way unacceptable to Mill, credence politically and socially to the intuitionists and the defenders of the status quo. That is, the defenders of the status quo used Whewell's views to claim that the present social arrangements had evolved to their final stage, wherein they fully exemplified the permanent structures in God's mind, and therefore that no further evolution or change was justified. This is precisely the kind of argument that Mill would oppose in later life in his critique of Hamilton.

Although Mill's technical views on epistemology, metaphysics, and religion are interesting and important in their own right, they are important for two other special and complementary reasons. First, Mill always conceived of his work in the technical areas of philosophy as a foundation for his social and political philosophy. From childhood, his father had inculcated in him the view that metaphysics and epistemology are the foundations of ethics and politics – that is, that metaphysical and epistemological positions have either political presuppositions or political consequences. In one sense, this is a traditional view of the relation of the divisions of philosophy. What this meant in practice, both for James Mill and for Mill himself, is that their handling of technical issues was not only motivated by the practical implications but also guided by the practical implications.[3] Readers have often been exasperated by Mill's reluctance to continue or follow the argument past a certain point, but in Mill's mind the technical dimension of thought was not of intrinsic interest. Once he had established what he needed, Mill leapt from technical considerations to their practical implications. In short, Mill's views on metaphysics, epistemology, and religion were always another expression of his moral and political agenda. Second, it is also an Enlightenment Project theme that all metaphysical and epistemological views, as well as all religious views, have been and continue to be used to rationalize various political stances. Mill never lost sight of the political dimension of technical philosophy. In addition to grounding his own public policy positions, he was self-consciously engaged in discrediting the intellectual foundations of the positions with which he disagreed.

The whole point of the discussion of the origins of knowledge in the *System of Logic* is to prepare the ground for the social sciences, and, of course, the point of the discussion of the social sciences is to prepare the ground for Mill's moral, political, and economic views. Mill's purpose in the first five books of the *Logic* is largely polemical. He wants to undermine the philosophical position known as intuitionism, because in the nineteenth century intuitionism had served as the epistemology of political conservatism. Intuitionism covered both the views of Kant on the existence of a priori knowledge and the views of the Scottish realists such as Thomas Reid.

The German or *a priori* view of human knowledge, and of the knowing faculties, is likely for some time longer . . . to predominate among those who occupy themselves with such enquiries, both here and on the Continent. But the *System of Logic* supplies what was much wanted, a text-book of the opposite doctrine – that which derives all knowledge from experience and all moral and intellectual qualities principally from the direction given to the associations. I make as humble an estimate as anybody of what either an analysis of logical processes, or any possible canons of evidence, can do by themselves, towards guiding or rectifying the operations of the understanding. Combined with other requisites, I certainly do think them of great use; but whatever may be the practical values of a true philosophy of these matters, it is hardly possible to exaggerate the mischiefs of a false one. The notion that truths external to the human mind may be known by intuition or consciousness, independently of observation and experience, is, I am persuaded, in these times, the great intellectual support of false doctrines and bad institutions. By the aid of this theory, every inveterate belief and every intense feeling, of which the origin is not remembered, is enabled to dispense with the obligation of justifying itself by reason, and is erected into its own all-sufficient voucher and justification. There never was such an instrument devised for consecrating all deep seated prejudices. And the chief strength of this false philosophy in morals, politics, and religion, lies in the appeal which it is accustomed to make to the evidence of mathematics and of the cognate branches of physical science. To expel it from these, is to drive it from its stronghold: and because this had never been effectually done, the intuitive school, even after what my father had written in his *Analysis of the Mind*, had in appearance, and as far as published writings were concerned, on the whole the best of the argument. In attempting to clear up the real nature of the evidence of mathematical and physical truths, the System of Logic met the intuition philosophers on ground on which they had previously been deemed unassailable; and gave its own explanation from experience and association, of that peculiar character of what are called necessary truths. . . . prejudice can only be successfully combated by philosophy, no way can really be made against it permanently until it has been shewn not to have philosophy on its side.[4]

Intuitionism in this context takes the view that there are innate truths, among them moral truths. Innate truths are truths known independent of experience, or, to use the technical vocabulary of Kant, known to be true a priori. What Mill wanted initially to refute was the notion that there are any a priori truths. Mill's concern throughout this discussion was not really technical – that is, it is not the case that he had some cherished epistemological view that he wanted to advance or that he claimed to introduce a technical methodological innovation, although many readers in philosophy interpret this discussion in that way. Mill's concern was ideological. Nor is it the case that when Kant formalized the use of the concept of the a priori that he had intended to provide a rationale for the status quo. The notion of the a priori was a strictly epistemological doctrine for Kant. However, others had invoked Kant in this way. Specifically, whatever had been the customary understanding or traditional conception of a social practice was now elevated to the status of an a priori truth, that is, a timeless truth impervious to empirical refutation. On the contrary, Mill wanted to argue that customary practice is often no more than an historical accident or a practice that, while it may have been justified under past social circumstances, had outlived its usefulness, and that all practice should be subject to revision in the light of changing circumstances. The status of women would be an example. Through over eight hundred torturous pages of the discussion of technical issues, Mill established to his satisfaction that all thinking begins with experience and proceeds by means of the association of ideas based upon those experiences.

Even Mill's defense of induction over deduction as primary reflects his political agenda. Let us examine this point. In a deductive argument, we go from a general principle to its application in a more specific case. For example:

> All X is Y. (general principle)
> This is an X.
> Therefore, this is a Y. (conclusion)

The most famous textbook example of a deductive argument is the following:

> All men are mortal.
> Socrates is a man.
> Therefore, Socrates is mortal.

The intuitionists had held that such general principles were known intuitively and independent of experience. Such principles were impervious to change or challenge. Mill, on the contrary, was prepared to argue that almost every general principle, no matter in what domain, was itself the result of an inductive process that began with individual experiences. We know or are justified in believing that men are mortal based upon the fact that no one has lived past a certain age. Mill did concede that there were a few exceptions. For example, the general principle that nature is uniform seems to be an assumption that we bring to our experience. Despite the fact that there are many things we do not understand as examples of uniformity or of which we have no experience, we nevertheless continue to subscribe to this belief, no matter what.[5] There are diseases for which we do not know the cause or cure, yet we presume, despite the failure of past research, that we shall someday discover the hidden uniformity behind them. Mill insisted that these few exceptions had no moral or political implications.

The issue of induction took on a special additional meaning in the social sciences – specifically, in Macaulay's critique of James Mill's methodology.

According to Macaulay,

Mr. [James] Mill is an Aristotelian of the fifteenth century, born out of due season. We have here an elaborate treatise on government, from which, but for two or three passing allusions, it would not appear that the author was aware that any governments actually existed among men. Certain propensities of human nature are assumed; and from these premises the whole science of politics is synthetically deduced! We can scarcely persuade ourselves that we are not reading a book written before the time of Bacon and Galileo.[6]

Macaulay's attack had led Mill to reformulate his conception of social science.

[T]here was truth in several of his [Macaulay's] strictures on my father's treatment of the subject; that my father's premises were really too narrow, and included but a small number of the general truths, on which, in politics, the important consequences depend. Identity of interest between the governing body and the community at large, is not, in any practical sense which can be attached to it, the only thing on which good government depends; neither can this identity of interest be secured by the mere conditions of election [i.e., democracy]. I was not at all satisfied with the mode in which my father met the criticisms of Macaulay. . . . This made me think that there was really something more fundamentally erroneous in my father's conception of philosophical method, as applicable to politics, than I had hitherto supposed.[7]

This problem was solved through the reading of Comte and Tocqueville. In addition to all this was the special contribution of Romanticism to his understanding of the human sciences. We shall turn to Comte's influence shortly.

Working intermittently, Mill had finished the first draft of the *Logic* by 1840. In April of 1841, he engaged in a complete rewriting of the book. As was his custom, Mill wrote everything at least twice as independent drafts. Afterward, his editing consisted of merging the two drafts.

From April . . . to the end of 1841, my spare time was devoted to a complete rewriting of the book from its commencement. It is in this way that all my books have been composed. They were always written at least twice over; a first draft of the entire work was completed to the very end of the subject, then the whole begun again *de novo*; but incorporating, in the second writing, all sentences and parts of sentences of the old draft which appeared as suitable to my purpose as anything which I could write in lieu of them. I have found great advantages in this system of double redaction. It combines . . . the freshness and vigour of the first conception, with the superior precision and completeness resulting from prolonged thought. . . . The only thing which I am careful, in the first draft, to make as perfect as I am able, is the arrangement.[8]

At this point, a fortuitous delay in the publication process occurred. Alexander Bain (1818–1903), a student at Aberdeen, was introduced to Mill by John Robertson, Mill's former assistant at the *Review*. Bain's analytical skills impressed Mill enough for Bain to be allowed to read the proofs and make additions and corrections. This was the beginning of a long period of discipleship, by the end of which Bain had established himself as an expert in the intersection of philosophy and psychology, had written biographies of both Mills, and had become the founder and first editor of Britain's most prestigious philosophical journal, *Mind*. With the benefit of Bain's assistance, the *Logic* was finally published in March of 1843.

Comte and Mill

Auguste Comte played a crucial role in Mill's intellectual evolution. Gustave d'Eichthal, a disciple of Saint-Simon and later of Comte, had sent Mill a copy of Comte's *Système de politique positive* in 1828. Initially, this did not make much of an impression on Mill. However, Mill was impressed by the *Cours de philosophie positive* (a major multivolume work of Comte published between 1832 and 1840).[9] Mill had read the first two volumes in 1837, and he described this work as "one of the most profound books ever written on the philosophy of the sciences."[10]

Comte was engaged in precisely the same enterprise as the Philosophic Radicals – that is, he was attempting to rationalize the economic and social transformation of European feudalism by the Industrial Revolution, and he was attempting to do so by means of the Enlightenment Project. Like Mill, he had come to see the weaknesses of the doctrinaire versions of the Enlightenment Project and the importance of a philosophy of history. Mill had already absorbed Saint-Simon by the time he read Comte. Like Mill, Comte was concerned to formulate a more adequate conception of the human sciences, one that could serve as a basis for social reform. What Mill sought was to be the intellectual leader of Britain's transition from feudalism to liberal culture. As such, he wanted his explication of social institutions, including his recommendations on how their future evolution should be guided, to be authoritative. He inherited this self-conception from his father, and it was reinforced by familiarity with Coleridge's conception of the clerisy. Initially, Comte seemed to fit perfectly into this scheme.

Auguste Comte (1798–1857)[11] was committed to the view that there was a cosmic order but that it was accessed through science and not religion. Religion and now science were themselves understood as part of a larger historical process. As a disciple of and secretary to Saint-Simon, and following the example of Turgot and Condorcet, Comte believed that history was a progressive process. The history of the intellect moved through three stages – a theological stage, a metaphysical stage, and a scientific or positive stage. In the theological stage, explanation appealed to supernatural agencies; in the metaphysical stage, explanation appealed to abstractions; but now in the final scientific stage, explanation appeals to uniform laws of succession among phenomena. According to Comte, a scientific explanation is expressed in terms of empirically identifiable underlying causes, as opposed to speculative causes such as "God." A scientific explanation is thus not "speculative" but "positive," that is, an explicitly identifiable and empirically confirmable explanation. Hence, Comte and his followers identified themselves as "positivists."

Comte denied that science could be explained simply as an extension of commonsense epistemology. Rather, the logic of science is revealed only in the historical development of that science. Moreover, science yields positive knowledge – laws as relations of succession and resemblance – but not absolute knowledge. Comte's understanding was then essentially historicist. To explain is to identify the temporal regularities as far as we can know them and not to give speculatively ultimate meanings about God's purpose. It is this version of historicism that appeared to Mill to be superior to Whewell's.

Comte advocated that social science be based upon physical science, now understood historically, and that such social science be the basis for social reform. The fundamental social science for Comte was "sociology" (a term he invented) – the study of sui generis regularities at the macro or social level. The social world in itself contained a structure of regularities. Comte specifically denied that there was an additional autonomous and more basic discipline of psychology. Comte favored phrenology (another "discipline" he invented). Advocates of phrenology maintain that all mental functions can be explained exclusively in physiological terms by reference to specific locations within the brain. There are, according to Comte, no specifically psychological laws to be discovered by introspection. Introspection was an inadequate holdover from the naïve empiricism of the older Enlightenment. As a consequence, Comte rejected James Mill's view that emphasized reduction to the micro level of individual motivation. This would become a bone of contention with Mill. Moreover, intelligence, according to Comte, was correlated with the size of the brain, and men had bigger brains than women! This, as we shall see, will become a source of much irritation to Mill and Harriet.

Since Comte's conception of social science was historicist, we need to look at his account of history in order to understand both his conception of social science and the derivative conceptualization of social reform. There is a general historical development of the mind that is replicated in the individual sciences. Corresponding to each stage there is a corresponding social structure. Societies, like the mind, are characterized by alternating periods of order and critique. The study of societies in order to understand their order is called "social statics," whereas the study of social transition is called "social dynamics." The relation of statics to dynamics is Hegelian – that is, it involves the dynamic dialectic of practice and theory, which Comte referred to respectively as material and spiritual forces. History is a dynamic conflict of spiritual and material forces. When these two forces are united, we have a positive epoch. The Middle Ages represented such an epoch for him. When the forces are antagonistic to each other, we have a negative epoch. Comte thought that he was living during a negative epoch and that his calling was to lead the world to a new positive epoch. Huxley would later describe this Comtean view as "Catholicism minus Christianity."

In his role as historian, Comte specifically emphasized that the great transition was from feudalism to industry. He viewed his own epoch (i.e., the nineteenth century) as critical and negative – specifically, as a conflict between industrialists and the proletariat. He foresaw a future positive epoch in which there would be a harmony of the ruling class (consisting of capitalists, who attended to production, and intellectuals, who exercised spiritual authority in order to maintain the common good) with the proletariat. There would be a corresponding move from selfish interests to the interests of humanity as a whole. The entire system would be based upon "altruism," another word coined by Comte.[12] At this point, history would come to an end.

For Comte, social reform has to be understood as based upon this historicist conception of social science. Social reform cannot be deduced simply from more fundamental sciences, such as physics or the law of gravitation, as Saint-Simon himself had held. Comte's grand vision was to recapture the unity and integrity of the ancien régime in the aftermath of the French Revolution (here he had been influenced by de Maistre) but in the light of the newly emerging industrial society (he had read Hume, Smith, J. B. Say, and Condorcet). The unity was to be achieved through positive science. In society's present form, which Comte believed to be its final form, the reforms would be carried out under the direction of the scientific-industrial-managerial elite[13] in the light of the science of sociology. After all, Comte was a graduate of and professor at the École Polytechnique! Sociology would show us how to abolish class conflict, provide a moral dimension to capitalism, and allow us to preserve private property.

To sum up, Comte combined social science with a philosophy of history in which there were laws of historical progression. Comte differed from Bentham and James Mill in advocating that the basic laws of human nature existed only on the sociological level and not on the psychological level. Comte also recognized the importance of history, but he differed from Macaulay in advocating a progressive historicism. Comte's view also had practical implications. In addition to the laws of human nature, there are historical laws, such that within each given historical period we can specify what institutional arrangements are dictated by the combined action of both sets of laws. This was a view that Comte had inherited from Saint-Simon, and it was a view reflected in the later work of Karl Marx.

Comte's views played an important role in the evolution of Mill's thinking. Mill saw Comte as combining social science with the recognition of the importance of a philosophy of history. Up to this point, Mill was in complete agreement with Comte. Beyond this, Mill attempted to supplement Comte by stressing the importance of the psychological level. In his endeavor to do this, Mill formulated the notion of a science of "ethology" that combined sociology with the associationist psychology he had inherited from his father and Hartley. Ethology was supposed to explain just exactly how cultural context affected the psychological mechanism of associationism.

The specific methodological innovation of Comte that impressed Mill the most was what Mill called the "inverse deductive or historical" method.

What Comte had argued was that the study of history revealed sociological uniformities that could serve as the foundation for social reform. By contrast, Bentham and James Mill had tried to deduce their reforms directly from psychological generalizations, a procedure for which Macaulay had taken them to task. Macaulay, in turn, had relied upon history simply as a source of inductive analogies. Mill, in opposition to both the Philosophic Radicals and Macaulay, agreed with Comte that history was the source or suggestive fountain of carefully qualified generalizations from which we could deduce social policy. More important, these carefully qualified generalizations were themselves the result of an inductive process. What Mill proposed to add to Comte's method was the attempt to explain those historically qualified sociological generalizations by further reduction to the psychological laws of association, via the alleged ethological laws. That is, Mill would combine his father's notion of basic generalizations with Macaulay's insistence that these generalizations must have inductive support from history, tying them together via Comte's notion that the generalizations not only reflect historic specifics but also are derivable from more basic general principles of human nature. Comte, in short, enabled Mill to combine his father's views and Macaulay's views.

In a merely logical point of view, the only leading conception for which I am indebted to him [Comte] is that of the Inverse Deductive Method, as the one chiefly applicable to the complicated subjects of History and Statistics: a process differing from the more common form of the Deductive Method in this – that instead of arriving at its conclusions by general reasoning, and verifying them by specific experience (as is the natural order in the deductive branches of physical science), it obtains its generalizations by a collation of specific experience, and verifies them by ascertaining whether they are such as would follow from known general principles. This was an idea entirely new to me when I found it in Comte: and but for him I might not soon (if ever) have arrived at it.[14]

What constitutes the "inverse deductive or historical" method? It was "historical" in taking history as its starting point; it was "deductive" in beginning with generalizations; it was "inverse" because those historical generalizations were themselves based upon inductive experience and were themselves, in principle at least, deducible from more fundamental laws of ethology and psychology. The theorist had to identify significant generalizable experiences that reflected both the more fundamental laws and the particular historical context.

Why was the inverse deductive (historical) method so important to Mill? It was important for two reasons. First, it is essential for his conception of logic that all general principles be themselves the result of an inductive process derived from experience. We are reminded that Mill rejects the notion of a general principle that has any other source, and he does so because the epistemological view that there are innate general principles had been used as a rationalization for the status quo. This was the respect in which he felt he was being loyal to the methodological views he had inherited from his father. Second, Mill insisted that the general principles on which social reform were to be based had to be more or less progressive historical principles. This was the respect in which he had gone beyond his father's narrow psychological base and contextualized psychology within a broader historical and specifically Romantic framework. The long and the short of it is that Mill supplemented and qualified his father's views of human psychology with historical context. This will have important consequences for Mill's discussion of economics, especially for his important reconceptualization of the relationship between production and distribution as it relates to labor.

One other noteworthy aspect of the similarity between Comte's and Mill's respective methodologies was the Comtean division between the social science of statics and the social science of dynamics. This distinction had already appeared – and been noted by Mill – in the works of Saint-Simon, as the distinction between "organic" and "critical" periods. In addition, Mill was receptive to this idea because it mirrored the Coleridgean distinction between the forces of permanence and the forces of progression. Comte and Mill shared the goal of reintroducing harmony into the world in the aftermath of the Industrial and French Revolutions. Both conceptualized this process as the reconciliation or synthesis of order and progress in the form of a Hegelian dialectic.

Intrinsic to this methodology is the notion that reform is to be carried out under the aegis of those who possess an understanding of the larger historical and social processes. Comte, like the Philosophic Radicals in general and Mill in particular, was one of those nineteenth-century intellectuals who belonged neither to the landed aristocracy nor to the working class, but who thought he and others like him had a special role to play in mediating the relationship of social science and social reform. The notion of statics (order) and dynamics (progress) in alternating stages required something like a new clerisy to unify society. Comte, in short, aspired, like

Mill, to the role of cultural leadership. In opposition to the radicals, both Comte and Mill accepted the Hegelian insight that institutions mirror the ideas of their time, and hence that there could not be a timeless deduction of remedies from a priori premises about the human condition.

From both Coleridge and Comte, Mill absorbed the notion of a new clerisy. The spiritual allusion is not an accident, for the clergy had provided the intellectual leadership of the medieval and feudal world. Seemingly tied to an outmoded and historically dated form of thought, and seemingly tied thereby to reactionary elements in society, the clergy were no longer able to provide that leadership. Implicit in all of this is the assumption that there must now be a separation of the spiritual and temporal powers, along with the recognition that, as in the Middle Ages, the former must accept and work with the latter. The intellectual community (that is, the "spiritual power") needs the help and support of the industrial class (that is, the "temporal power"). A further assumption is that the articulation of a new social unity would lead to the formulation of a new spiritual unity. The "Religion of Humanity" was another aspect of Comte's thought that resonated with Mill, although with some qualification. "[T]he *culte de l'humanité* is capable of fully supplying the place of religion, or rather (to say the truth) of *being* a religion . . . notwithstanding the ridiculousness which everybody must feel in his [Comte's] premature attempts to define in detail the *practices* of this *culte*."[15]

The concrete deductive method associated with Auguste Comte is in the end misguided. Advocates of this method attempt to deduce the explanation of all social phenomena from the so-called laws of sociology alone. Mill has three objections to this approach. First, it ignores the role that (autonomous) individuals play in the social process. That is, it violated Mill's inherent belief in the ultimate dignity of the individual. Second, the most it can ever discover are qualified generalizations in the form of tendencies rather than anything that can be called a social law. Third, social phenomena are organic, in the sense that everything interacts with everything else. What this means is that we must learn to disentangle the various strands and not mistakenly fasten upon one of them. The most influential example of the misguided concrete deductive method, claimed Mill, was political economy. It reflects both the value and the limitations of the concrete deductive method. The most important application of Mill's conception of logic would appear in his *Principles of Political Economy*, to be discussed later.

Political Economy considers mankind as occupied solely in acquiring and consuming wealth, and aims at showing what is the course of action into which mankind, living in a state of society, would be impelled if that motive . . . were absolute ruler of all their actions. . . . Not that any political economist was ever so absurd as to suppose that mankind are really thus constituted, but because this is the mode in which science must necessarily proceed.[16]

Mill began a correspondence with Comte[17] – whom he was never to meet despite many subsequent trips to France – in November of 1841. In addition to lavish praise of Comte's ideas and inspiration as well as frequent mention in the *Logic* itself, what Mill proposed was the joint production of a new philosophic system. From the beginning, Comte assumed that Mill was offering to become a disciple. Comte's response to the correspondence was patronizing. Comte even

did Mill a great honour. When his complimentary copy of the *Logic* came, he was in the midst of a course of Cerebral Hygiene; a periodic treatment whereby, in order to preserve the purity and clarity of his own genius, he refrained from reading a single word that anyone else had ever written. He interrupted the process against his habitual rule especially to read Mill's book, and was greatly pleased by its praises of himself.[18]

A further sign of Comte's self-absorbed and intransigent attitude was his refusal to respond to a question about mathematical method that Herschel had raised against him and for which Mill sought some clarification.[19]

   The first sign of trouble in the relationship appeared over the issue of women. As the founder of phrenology, Comte held that intelligence was correlated with brain size, and since women had smaller brains than men, it followed that women were less intelligent than men. At first, Mill politely disagreed; subsequently, he felt it necessary to offer counterarguments. Mill had even gone to the trouble of reading Franz Joseph Gall's six-volume work on phrenology.[20] At last, Mill showed the correspondence to Harriet, who responded as follows:

These [letters] have greatly surprised and disappointed me: and also they have pleased me. All this regarding only *your* part in them – Comte's is what I expected – the usual partial and prejudiced view of a subject which he has little considered. . . . Comte is essentially *French*, in the sense in which we think [the] French mind less admirable than [the] English – Anti-Catholic, Anti-Cosmopolite.
   I am surprised in your letters to find your opinion undetermined where I had thought it made up – I am disappointed at a tone more than half apologetic with

which you state your opinions – and I am charmed with the exceeding nicety elegance and finesse of your last letter.

Do not think I wish you had said *more* on the subject, I only wish that what was said was in the tone of conviction, not of suggestion.

This dry root of a man is not a worthy coadjutor scarcely a worthy opponent. With your gifts of intellect of conscience and of impartiality it is probable, or is there any ground for supposing, that there exists any man more competent to judge that question than you are?

You are in advance of your age in culture of the intellectual faculties; you would be the most remarkable man of your age if you had no other claim to be so than your perfect impartiality and your fixed love of justice. These are the two qualities of different orders which I believe to be the rarest and the most difficult to human nature.[21]

This letter reveals something, as well, about the relationship between Harriet and Mill. Among other things, it reveals the extent to which she served as his sternest critic, editor, and conscience, without substantially challenging his basic positions. It also reveals the extent to which she admired Mill and, apparently, how much he needed to hear that admiration expressed in a private context.

On the other hand, the correspondence between Mill and Comte also permits us to see something of the character of Harriet's mind. It was Harriet who pointed out to Mill that if Comte was right about women, then the argument applied to men as well.[22] That is, the argument implied a biological determinism fatalistically applied to men such that their eventual order in the hierarchy would be objectively determined independent of their efforts to improve themselves. This was as unsatisfactory to Mill as it was to Harriet.

This dispute between Mill and Comte has three levels. On one level, it is a dispute between a biological determinist (Comte) and someone who believes that the environment is a significant factor (Mill). On a second level, it is a dispute between someone who believes that biology is all-important (Comte) and someone who believes that information and education play a significant factor in social reform (Mill). The former will tend toward a kind of authoritarian social order, while the latter will emphasize education and persuasion. On a third level, it is a dispute between someone who denies the fundamental freedom of human beings in the name of social science and social technology (Comte) and someone who believes at some level in human freedom and therefore needs to limit severely the pretensions of social science (Mill). Finally, if Comte is right, then there could come a time when all relevant knowledge was available, such that there would be no need for further intellectual endeavor and no need for further social development and experimentation. Mill eventually recognized this as a social philosophy that "would make everybody's way of life (or at all events after one choice) . . . inexorably closed against all change of destination or purpose."[23] As Mueller put it,

Comte could never discuss 'opinions' with Mill because Comte had none, in the sense that Mill used the term. . . . He [Comte] had a completely systematized doctrine founded on a relatively few observations which, once established, required that 'opinion' be proved compatible with it or be discarded as demonstrably in error. After the system was established there was little more observation of fact required, and, since Comte could not bring himself to doubt the validity of his original observations, he did not even bother to reobserve them. Mill, on the other hand, had a body of opinions rather than a system of ideas. . . . he was always willing to grant the possible error in his opinions and willing to re-examine the scientific evidence.[24]

The year 1844 marked the beginning of Comte's financial problems.[25] All of his life he had been obsessed with finances and financial pressures. In 1826, he had suffered a nervous breakdown over them. When he married, he had married a former prostitute (in a somewhat unusual religious ceremony) who had subsequently gone back to prostitution to earn income. In 1842, exasperated with his views on women, his wife had left him. He gave her a generous financial settlement. However, in 1844 Comte did not gain reelection to his academic position at the École Polytechnique, largely because of the hostility of fellow academics who objected to his unorthodox views. Comte appealed to Mill for help.

At Mill's suggestion, John Austin approached Guizot, who was then serving as French prime minister, but to no avail. Mill then raised money from Grote and Molesworth. Comte – who looked upon these efforts as his entitlements, given his presumption that he was somehow the head of positivism and that he was dealing with his dutiful English disciples – continued to press for more help. When more financial assistance was not forthcoming, Comte became indignant, warning the English that he was one of the few intellectuals who could protect the propertied class from the masses. By 1847,[26] the correspondence came to an end on this unpleasant note.

A decade latter, Comte would be dead, and his followers in England would include Frederick Harrison, George Eliot, her lover G. H. Lewes, Harriet Martineau, and Richard Congreves. They established a Church of Humanity in Lamb's Conduit Street honoring the saints that Comte had designated, including such disparate figures as Frederick the Great and Adam Smith. They had established a periodical appropriately called the *Beehive* – an apt symbol of the kind of utopian society envisaged by Comte.

The fundamental disagreement in methodology between Comte and Mill centers on individual autonomy. Mill expressed this by emphasizing the autonomy of psychology from sociology. Human beings cannot simply be the products of larger social forces.

Men, however, in a state of society are still men; their actions and passions are obedient to the laws of individual human nature. Men are not, when brought together, converted into another kind of substance, with different properties. . . . Human beings in society have no properties but those which are derived from, and may be resolved into, the laws of the nature of individual man. In social phenomena the Composition of Causes is the universal law.[27]

It follows from this that Mill would reject the Comtean notion that there is or can be a collective good over and above the good of the individuals who make up society. Mill strenuously disagreed and insisted upon the importance of freedom and autonomy. Writing to d'Eichthal in 1829, Mill had said that government does not exist for "one end," but "for all the purposes whatever that are for man's good: and the highest & most important of these purposes is the improvement of man himself as a moral and intelligent being, which is an end not included in M. Comte's category at all."[28] While agreeing that reform cannot simply be political but must be moral (a reflection of Mill's disenchantment with radicalism and the influence of Carlyle), and while agreeing that the ultimate end cannot be selfish individual affluence but must be a new kind of unity, and while assenting to the view that the aim is a new moral order, Mill rejected Comte's altruism for autonomy. Finally, although agreeing that women and workers would be the focus of social reform, Mill had a different conception of women and the nature of the working class, a disagreement rooted in Mill's insistence upon autonomy. "There is also a positive doctrine, without any pretension to being absolute, which claims the direct participation of the governed in their own government, not as a natural right, but as a means to important ends, under the conditions and with the limitations which those ends impose."[29] There could be no spiritual and moral regeneration unless all human beings engaged in self-governance.

Mill agreed with the need for an elite, but he did not share Comte's conception of its precise role. This disagreement is rooted in a profound difference of methodology. Although Mill and Comte both saw the dynamic of social evolution as a dialectical process, Mill denied that one could conceptualize the preconceptual, that is, give a theory about the relation of theory and practice. A larger metatheoretical account of how practice and theory interact leads to three things: (1) a denial of the reality of human autonomy, (2) a potential fatalism about the course of human events, and (3) the presumption that if one possessed that metatheory then one was entitled to dictate all future reformulations of practice.

This is precisely the kind of knowledge that Mill denied anyone could have, in addition to insisting that it is the art of practical reason that makes this kind of determination, as it is not within the province of any science. From Mill's point of view, Comte had betrayed his own metaphysical insight about the nature of the dialectic of historical change. In metaphysics and epistemology, there can be no absolute knowledge, only the study of laws as "relations of succession and resemblance" – an essentially historical mode of understanding. Mill was much too Burkean for this. This is why, in the end, Mill critiqued Comte for remaining an authoritarian.[30] Mill rejected Comte's system, then, for the same reasons that he had rejected Bentham's system.

What Mill did not recognize at the time was that this argument against the possibility of a larger theory of how theory and practice themselves are related would be fatal to his own proposed science of ethology. A radically free dialectic is incompatible with any notion of complete explanation. It was to be some time before even Mill despaired of producing the proposed science of ethology. If he had recognized this immediately, then he would also have recognized that there would be no way of salvaging his father's associationist psychology and ultimately no point in talking about a social "science" as opposed to social studies.[31]

What Mill thought he saw at this point was that there can be a science or sciences of human nature – that is, a human science – and that its basic laws are the psychological laws of association. Moreover, whatever basic truths there are about human affairs (including questions of ends) are not part of the content of the psychological laws of association. "[T]hey are not the principles of human nature, but results of those principles under the circumstances in which mankind have happened to be placed."[32] Hence, in order to explain the basic truths of human action we must supplement the psychological laws of association with information about the circumstances in which the laws operate. Human action, unlike physical interaction, cannot be explained simply in terms of the present circumstances. Actions of human beings are not solely the result of their present circumstances, but the joint result of those circumstances and the characters of the individuals; and the agencies that determine human character are numerous and diverse.

Can we give a systematic account of the circumstances, past as well as present? Mill, at one time, thought that we could.[33]

Human beings do not all feel and act alike in the same circumstances; but it is possible to determine what makes one person, in a given position, feel or act in one way, another in another. . . . In other words, mankind have not one universal character, but there exist universal laws of the Formation of Character. And since it is by these laws, combined with the facts of each particular case, that the whole of the phenomena of human action and feeling are produced, it is on these that every rational attempt to construct the science of human nature in the concrete and for practical purposes must proceed.[34]

He called the science that was to discover and formulate the hypothetical laws of the formation of character the science of *ethology*.[35]

The laws of the formation of character are, in short, derivative laws, resulting from the general laws of mind, and are to be obtained by deducing them from those general laws by supposing any given set of circumstances, and then considering what, according to the laws of mind, will be the influence of those circumstances on the formation of character.[36]

Whereas the psychological laws of association are discovered through introspection, the laws of ethology are discovered by hypothetical deduction. "In other words, Ethology, the deductive science, is a system of corollaries from Psychology, the experimental science."[37] Mill insisted that even if we had a comprehensive science of ethology, it was not possible to predict the future unerringly. Even so, such knowledge was practically useful.

There is, indeed, no hope that these laws, though our knowledge of them were as certain and as complete as it is in astronomy, would enable us to predict the history of society, like that of the celestial appearances, for thousands of years

to come. . . . The multitude of the causes is so great as to defy our limited powers of calculation. . . . But, as before, remarked, an amount of knowledge quite
insufficient for prediction may be most valuable for guidance.[38]

What judgment can we make so far about Mill's conception of the
human sciences? Book VI of the *Logic* remains to this day the classic
statement[39] of what human science, modeled after physical science, might
be at its best, what limitations and qualifications it has to accept, and the
extent to which it may or may not be useful. As a statement of the aims and
obstacles to the creation of the human sciences, it is unsurpassed. Neither
in Mill's time nor to this day has there been a reason to retract its statement
of aims and obstacles. In addition, Mill went out of his way to make clear
that this conception of human science does not presuppose determinism,
is compatible with human beings being able to shape their own characters,
and does not, as we shall see, entitle social scientists to set the ultimate
aims of society. It is, in short, a carefully qualified and modest program.

In keeping with the modesty of the program, nowhere does Mill claim
to have established the laws of ethology. What must be pointed out is that
nothing in the program dictates that there must be such laws or reliable
generalizations at any specific level. As Alexander Bain pointed out, Mill
"despaired, for the present [1840s] time at least" of formulating such
laws, and decided instead to write the *Principles of Political Economy*.[40]
Mill never even began constructing the ethology. What does this tell us
about Mill, about human science, and about Mill's subsequent explication
of liberal culture?

What this tells us about Mill is the following. Mill makes a case for
how there might be ethological laws serving as bridge principles between
the psychological laws of association and the reliable generalizations of the
various human sciences. He does not show that there must be such laws. He
never produces or claims to produce such laws, and he eventually abandons
the enterprise. The explanation for his initial insistence or hope that such
laws exist can only be explained, in part, biographically. If there were such
laws, then despite his sharp criticism of his father's political philosophy,
he would at least have vindicated the importance of the psychological laws
of association.

The implications of the later abandonment of ethology for human science are even more drastic. If there are no ethological laws to serve as
bridge principles between psychology and the rest of the so-called human

sciences, then there may not be anything like a coherent hierarchy within the science of human nature. If all empirical generalizations about human action must remain forever heavily qualified, as Mill always insisted, and are unsupported by a coherent hierarchical structure, then the so-called human sciences might never be anything more than a collection of qualified generalizations. They might not, in short, be anything like true sciences. The systematic study of human action and culture might produce a great deal of valuable and useful information, but there could never be an authoritative appeal to such information. Without an authoritative appeal, there can be no consensual expert opinion with which to counter either aristocratic conservatism or working-class prejudice. Mill, unlike Marx and Comte, never articulated a grand historical narrative.

What are the implications for Mill's future work? There are two. First, Mill will need a more refined conception of the explication of the cultural world. This he found in Tocqueville. Arguably, Tocqueville in *Democracy in America*, especially in Volume 2, is an ethologist, which is why Mill liked him. Second, after coming to recognize the qualified use of generalizations about the human condition, Mill will have to formulate carefully the conditions that distinguish the responsible from the irresponsible use of such generalizations. This is precisely what he articulated in the essay *On Liberty* in his critique of censorship. Tying these two things together with the other aspects of his various endeavors is something that he eventually does in his Romantic theology.[41]

Still, one may wonder if the abandonment of ethology makes a significant difference in either Mill's explanation of social phenomena or his public policy positions. There are three things that do not change in Mill's philosophy of the human sciences. First, he always insisted upon human autonomy. Second, from the 1830s on he recognized the need for a larger philosophy of history, a macronarrative within which human autonomy is played out. Third, he always recognized the existence and importance of qualified and carefully delimited social generalizations such as one finds in political economy. Those are the constants in his understanding of human and social phenomena. What he was never able to do was to provide a hierarchical, lawlike arrangement of these elements in the form of a system of human sciences, such that his total understanding of the social world would achieve a quasi-scientific authority.

This is not a personal failing. No one has ever been able to achieve this sort of scientific, authoritative understanding of the social world. It has not been achieved in the strong Comtean sense of a total conceptualization that dictates policy, and it has not been achieved even in the modest sense in which Mill aimed for it. More to the point, even if Mill had constructed such a chain of sciences, that system would not dictate policy. At most, it could only provide an impressive rationale for specific public policy recommendations. The reason for this is quite important. Mill did not believe that he lived in the kind of universe in which it was possible to achieve total conceptualization. If total conceptualization is out of the question, then it will always be possible for alternative narratives to be fashioned such that alternative policies can contest the field. Isn't this, in fact, what we still find to be the case today – and isn't this precisely the way Mill wanted it to be?

This is how Mill was to put it in *On Liberty*:

[O]n every subject on which difference of opinion is possible, the truth depends on a balance to be struck between two sets of conflicting reasons. Even in natural philosophy, there is always some other explanation possible of the same facts. . . . But when we turn to subjects infinitely more complicated, to morals, religion, politics, social relations, and the business of life, three-fourths of the arguments for every disputed opinion consist in dispelling the appearances which favour some opinion different from it.[42]

There is no reason to believe that Mill offered a different account of the social world or that he suggested different public policies as the result of the abandonment of his social scientific ambitions. If anything, one could argue that he gained a deeper insight into the dialectical nature of the social world.

Mill believed that intellectuals had an important role to play in the modern world. Armed with a proper understanding of scientific method, history, and the relevant qualified social scientific generalizations, intellectuals could contribute both to the transition from feudalism to industrialism and to the harmonious operation of a modern industrial society by helping to conceptualize our predicament. But Mill was opposed to any kind of intellectual dictatorship or social technocracy. He was opposed to it because among the generalizations he thought to be true was that personal autonomy and individual self-government were vital to a free society. Free peoples needed persuasion, not coercion, and no society would pull itself out of the depths of despotism unless it recognized the freedom of all. In the end, Mill's rejection of Comte paralleled his rejection of both

Bentham's and his own father's narrow conception of human nature, one that left no place for human autonomy.

Beyond the technical discussion designed to discredit the reactionary use of intuitionism, and beyond the Comtean methodological innovation adopted in order to overcome the limitations of James Mill's and Bentham's conception of the correct method in social science and social reform, two issues stand out in the *Logic*: the defense of individual freedom against determinism, and the Romantic conception of the role of imagination in discerning the inherent norms of evolving social institutions.

The problem of determinism was central to religious life in the nineteenth century, especially among dissenting Protestant sects of Calvinist origin. Vaguely expressed forms of social determinism allowed some to hold the view that God had ordained the present hierarchical class structure or the present division of wealth and power. This was not a view that sat well with a rising commercial middle class, most of whom were dissenters. John Wesley, the founder of Methodism, formulated a version of Arminianism (belief in free will) in which he claimed that people can perfect themselves through their own efforts. William Johnson Fox, the editor of the Unitarian publication *Monthly Repository*, published two articles in 1828 trying to harmonize Hartley and free will (the author, identified only as W.T., supplemented Hartley by an appeal to German philosophy). James Martineau, the leading Unitarian theologian, was an early enthusiast for Hartley, Priestley, and Bentham, but he came in time to discard his belief in determinism under the influence of Carlyle and Coleridge.

There was similar concern among more secular thinkers. James Mill had started out as a supporter of the Scottish intuitionist school of Francis Hutcheson, Thomas, Reid, and Stewart and had originally criticized Hartley's determinism. However, James Mill was converted, becoming a supporter of Hartley after adopting Benthamism. It is not difficult to see why. Benthamites generally saw determinism as a positive basis for the employment of social technology. On this basis, James Mill came to be a critic of the Scottish school.[43] Carlyle, on the other hand, in his "Sign of the Times," saw Hartley's determinism as leading to fatalism, a position that aggravated Mill's crisis. Coleridge started out as an admirer of Hartley's views but later came to reject them because they led to the doctrine of "necessity" (determinism). It is easy to surmise from all this that Mill inherited from his father and Bentham a belief in the doctrine of determinism, that his personal crisis was accentuated by this belief, that this aspect of his crisis was deepened by association with Carlyle and Coleridge, and that concern over this issue was prevalent in the Unitarian circles in which Mill traveled and where he had met Harriet Taylor. It was also among these Unitarians that some sort of compatibilism was popular – that is, some way of trying to harmonize the belief in determinism and the belief in freedom.

Mill's earliest attempt at harmonizing the belief in determinism with freedom came in the *Logic*. In Book VI,[44] Mill distinguished between fatalism and the doctrine of causality as applied to human beings. First, he softened the opposition by defining causality as constant succession among mental phenomena. To say that x causes y is to say that y is always preceded by x. This way of describing constant succession rhetorically disarms the fear that physical forces beyond our control are controlling us. Second, he tried to overcome the fear of fatalism, understood as the doctrine that the universe is a chain of causes and effects in which we cannot intervene. He stressed the extent to which constant succession does not imply that all desires are irresistible. Our experience of being able to choose is itself a real experience and a true event. Our beliefs and desires are themselves elements in the causal chain. By having certain thoughts, we can cause our desires to change. What Mill achieved was a form of compatibilism that seemingly enabled him to eat his cake and have it too. Mill thought that his idea, like a similar argument made by Hume, preserved the kind of causality that makes social science and its relevance to public policy possible and that he had preserved our feeling of moral freedom.

Mill prided himself on this resolution. He thought the two chapters on freedom were the best chapters in the *Logic*.[45] It was this discussion of freedom that most impressed Tocqueville. In the 1840 review of Tocqueville, Mill had reiterated that economic and social forces are not entirely responsible for making us who we are; it depends upon how we choose to respond. Ideas are not mere epiphenomena but "a power in history."[46]

It was clear to some of Mill's critics at the time, including the Owenites, that Mill had not really provided an argument in favor of human freedom. To be sure, the critics said, we can mold our characters and even change aspects of ourselves, but only if we choose to do so. The problem is that the choice to do this is itself the result of prior causes. Mill seemed content to concede this point, because it did not in principle deny our ability to form our own characters. It is a perfect example of his not thinking all the way through a technical philosophical issue when he thinks he has enough to justify a favored political or social position. People do have the ability to change their characters, and that, at the time, was enough for Mill. However, as later philosophically sophisticated critics have persisted in pointing out, what does this ability that we do not ultimately control really amount to?[47] In order for autonomy to be the basis of individuality in any meaningful sense, Mill needed a stronger case for, or version of, freedom of the will. This is an issue to which he will return in the 1860s in *Hamilton*.

It is at this point that the Romantic movement makes its greatest impact on Mill's conception of the relationship between social science and social reform. It does so by providing Mill with an innovative conception of the role of the artist and the importance of a philosophy of history. This Romantic resolution of the *Logic* had already been foreshadowed. In April of 1838, Mill had published in the *Review* an essay on Alfred de Vigny in which the crucial role of the poet was noted. "Genius, whether in poetry or in philosophy, is the gift of seeing truths at a greater depth than the world can penetrate."[48] Moreover, at Sterling's suggestion, Mill had read Hegel's *Logic*.

If there is to be a "useful" human science, there cannot be a complete and comprehensive deductive social science. A complete and comprehensive social science would be able to explain and predict all future human and social permutations. If there were or could be that kind of knowledge, then the notion of using social scientific information would make no more sense than the notion of manipulating the physical world in the absence of some form of human freedom. Hence, any useful social scientific information must be in the form of limited and qualified generalizations. Those generalizations must be capable of being plugged into hypothetical statements of the form, "if X, then Y," where X states what we are trying to achieve and Y constitutes the limited and qualified social generalization that can serve as a means to achieve X. X cannot itself be part of the domain of human science.[49] As Mill put it, it forms the domain of *art*.

It is the artist (poet) who imaginatively explicates the inherent norms within evolving social practice.

The relation in which rules of art stand to doctrines of science may be thus characterized. The art proposes to itself an end to be attained, defines the end, and hands it over to the science. The science receives it, considers it as a phenomenon or effect to be studied, and having investigated its causes and conditions, sends it back to art with a theorem of the combinations of circumstances by which it could be produced. Art then examines these combinations of circumstances, and according as any of them are or are not in human power, pronounces the end attainable or not. The only one of the premises, therefore, which Art supplies is the original major premise, which asserts that the attainment of the given end is desirable.[50]

Where do we start? Mill had ruled out starting with the psychological laws of association; he had not formulated, and eventually abandoned the project of ever formulating, ethological laws; he had rejected the notion that past history by itself is a sufficient foundation. That left qualified generalizations on the social level. The explanatory social generalizations are, of necessity, limited and qualified. Specifically, what is generally true in one historical epoch will not necessarily be true in another historical epoch. It is at this point that Mill borrowed from Comte the distinction between explanatory social generalizations within one social context, called the science of social statics, and explanatory social generalizations of the development from one such context to another, called the science of social dynamics.

If, then, we are going to commence the project of social explanation in the service of some useful project, we will have to provide the following: an explication of the present state of society as given by the artist, and an historical account of how the present has emerged from the past. This historical account constitutes a philosophy of history. A philosophy of history cannot itself be a social science, for a social science consists of generalizations or laws of uniformity. A rigid law of historical development would render human beings powerless to change the course of events. Hence, what Mill needs is (a) some notion of how to explicate the present state of society and (b) a philosophy of history.

What is called a state of society is the simultaneous state of all the greater social facts or phenomena. Such are the degree of knowledge, and of intellectual and moral culture, existing in the community, and of every class of it; the state of industry, of wealth and its distribution; the habitual occupations of the community; their division into classes, and the relations of those classes to one another; the common beliefs which they entertain on all the subjects most important to mankind, and the degree of assurance with which those beliefs are held; their tastes, and the character and degree of their aesthetic development; their form of government, and the more important of their laws and customs. The condition of all these things . . . constitute the state of society or the state of civilization at any given time.

. . . [I]t is implied that there exists a natural correlation among these different elements; that not every variety of combination of these general social facts is possible, but only certain combinations; that, in short, there exist Uniformities of Co-existence between the states of the various social phenomena. And such . . . is indeed a necessary consequence of the influence exercised by every one of these phenomena over every other. It is a fact implied in the *consensus* of the various parts of the social body.

. . . But the uniformities of co-existence . . . must . . . be . . . a derivative law, resulting from the laws which regulate the succession between one state of society and another; for the proximate cause of every state of society is the state of society immediately preceding it. The fundamental problem, therefore, of the social science, is to find the laws according to which any state of society produces the state which succeeds it and takes its place. This opens the great and vexed question of the progressiveness of man and society. . . .[51]

What sort of philosophy of history could he provide? Keeping in mind that Mill always insists upon the reality of individual choice, any qualified generalization must be such that it is compatible with the reality of choice. Mill thinks that we can find useful statistical generalizations on the macro level that are compatible with human choice. He also believes that social institutions and practices interact in organic fashion. Hence, once we form an account of how social practices interact, we can come to see how one social whole leads to another social whole. In providing this latter account, we must keep in mind that it too must be compatible with human freedom.

In the end, Mill did not and could not provide a philosophy of history. He could provide a narrative of how things had evolved, how that evolution was to some extent shaped by human choices, and, within those choices, how regularities could be discerned. He could even make room for those who advocated pursuit of what was intimated in the narrative. But there could not, in principle, be a supernarrative that was compatible with human freedom. The only legitimating narrative would be a personal one, within which any interpretation of the whole human drama depends on an intimately personal decision concerning the part we mean to play within it. It is for this reason that Mill needed the artist or the role of the artist, that of discerning the norms of practice and the intimations of how to develop them further.[52] What, then, has happened to Mill's dream of a proper social science upon which to base public policy and reform? The answer is that it has been replaced by the idea of a narrative of possible reform at both the individual and social levels. Despite its technical pretension and modesty, and despite its refusal to appeal to further contentious metaphysical or religious positions, Mill's narrative makes room for individuals' personally holding some of those metaphysical and religious positions,[53] a metanarrative that in the end forces us to accept responsibility for our freedom.

Success

The *Logic* was published in 1843, the same year as Macaulay's *Essays*, Carlyle's *Past and Present*, Ruskin's *Modern Painters*, and works by Dickens, Thackeray, Tennyson, and Browning. Mill, being Mill, saw in his work on the *Logic* only the victory over intuitionism, the establishment of a modest and highly qualified sense in which there might be a social science, and the need for the intimations of the "social" artists. He was therefore amazed at the instant success of the work. The success reflected the fact that Mill's *Logic* appealed to two different and conflicting constituencies. On the one hand, the *Logic* seemed to be a vindication of the possibility of social science, all the more admirable because it recognized its limitations and did not actually deliver the goods, merely proposed how it might be done. Those who remained committed to this project – and this included the rising technocracy in Britain, as reflected in Bain – were impressed with the programmatic nature of the book. Bain prepared a highly laudatory account for the *Westminster Review*, but Mill insisted upon editing out some of the effusive praise. Others in the science community expressed praise, including Sir John Herschel at the meeting of the British Association.

On the other hand, those who were imbued with the historicism of the Romantic movement saw in it their vindication. Sterling wrote to Emerson on its publication:

His [Mill's] big book on Logic is, I suppose, the highest piece of Aristotelianism that England has brought forth, at all events in our time. How the sweet, ingenuous nature of the man has lived and thriven out of his father's cold and stringent atheism is wonderful to think, and most so to me, who during fifteen years have seen his gradual growth and ripening.[54]

The *Logic* stood as an example of the proposed synthesis of Bentham and Coleridge. It was for this reason that it was a great success. The *Logic* was immediately adopted by Oxford and then by Cambridge, and it remained canonical for over half a century. It became an important part of the curriculum and examination system, quickly displacing more theologically oriented texts in moral philosophy. It was this text that both attracted passionately loyal, energetic, and talented followers to Mill and served to anchor his reputation in higher intellectual culture. It was, however, read as Coleridgean and not as Benthamite, as incorporating and extending extant ideas and values in the university curriculum. It replicated from a new perspective the liberal evangelical ways of perceiving both history and the role of ideas in history and was therefore directly opposed to Anglican orthodoxy. The challenge to orthodoxy can be gauged by noting a hundred-page attack on the book in the *British Critic* by the Newman-Puseyites.[55] Their attack amounted to the charge that if Mill's "principles be adopted as a full statement of the truth, the whole fabric of Christian theology must totter and fall."[56]

In a manner of speaking, it was precisely because Mill had failed to see and state the ultimate conflict between Bentham and Coleridge – and why there could be no reconciliation of them without a capitulation to Romanticism – that his book was a success. It was not the case that the book had solved an important problem, but rather that Mill had allowed both adversaries to believe that they had prevailed. It also enabled Mill to believe that he was still carrying on his father's work, but in a better version.

Although the truth had been obscured both for Mill and for the rest of the world, the success of the *Logic* nevertheless enabled Mill to find his authentic voice and to discover his true place as an intellectual leader. Intellectual leadership consisted in vision – the combination of the artistic or imaginative discernment of the inherent norms, a store of reliable but qualified social generalizations, an understanding of their historical context and ongoing development, and a logical sense of how they held together. This was neither the program of the Benthamites, nor the alleged science of "ethology" as articulated in the *Logic*, nor the rigid historicism of continental historicists such as Comte. This was uniquely Mill! The role of intellectual leadership was not to be sullied by political activism or confused with journalism. Secure in this self-conception, Mill felt released from any attempt to compromise with the upper classes and reverted to a more Socratic stance with regard to society as a whole.

Being now released from active concern in temporary politics, and from any literary occupation involving personal communication with contributors and others, I was enabled to indulge the inclination, natural to thinking persons when the age of boyish vanity is once past, for limiting my own society to a very few persons. General society, as now carried on in England, is so insipid an affair, even to the persons who make it what it is, that it is kept up for any reason rather than the pleasure it affords. All serious discussion on matters on which opinions differ, being considered ill-bred, and [given] the national deficiency in liveliness and sociability . . . the sole attraction of what is called society to those who are not at the top of the tree, is the hope of being aided to climb a little higher in it. . . . such society . . . must be supremely unattractive: and most people in the present day, of any really high class intellect, make their contact with it so slight, and at such long intervals, as to be almost considered as retiring from it altogether. Those persons of any mental superiority who do otherwise, are almost without exception, greatly deteriorated by it. . . . A person of high intellect should never go into unintellectual society unless he can enter it as an apostle; yet he is the only person with high objects who can safely enter it at all. . . . All these circumstances united, made the number very small of those whose society, and still more whose intimacy, I now voluntarily sought.[57]

Granted that Mill was writing this a decade later and describing a new mood and confidence about his abilities and his role that he had never previously experienced. Part of this was attributable to the success of the *Logic*. But a large part of it was the result of his relationship with Harriet and to their social ostracism, imposed from both within and without.

Harriet and Complete Companionship

What was Harriet's influence upon Mill during this period? What Mill says about it in his *Autobiography* is most instructive. What makes these remarks doubly significant is that they were written with Harriet's approval:

To be admitted into any degree of mental intercourse with a being of these qualities, could not but have a most beneficial influence on my development; though the effect was only gradual, and many years elapsed before her mental progress and mine went forward in the complete companionship they at last attained. The benefit I received was far greater than any which I could hope to give; though to her, who had at first reached her opinions by the moral intuition of a character of strong feeling, there was doubtless help as well as encouragement to be derived from one who had arrived at many the same results by study and reasoning: and in the rapidity of her intellectual growth, her mental activity, which converted everything into knowledge, doubtless drew from me, as it did from other sources, many of its materials. What I owe to her [was in] . . . two main regions of thought. One is the region of ultimate aims; the constituent elements of the highest realizable ideal of human life. The other is that of the immediately useful and practically attainable. . . . My own strength lay wholly in the uncertain and slippery intermediate region, that of theory, or moral and political science . . . whether as political economy, analytic psychology, logic, philosophy of history. . . . I have derived from her a wise skepticism, which, while it has not hindered me from following out the honest exercise of my thinking faculties to what ever conclusions might result from it, has put me on guard against holding or announcing these conclusions with a degree of confidence which the nature of such speculations does not warrant, and has kept my mind . . . open. . . .[58]

Although much has been written about the alleged influence of Harriet on Mill's thought, nothing comes as close as this comment to telling the truth. To begin with, Mill makes clear that he had well-formed and thought-out views before he met Harriet; and even after they met, it was a long time before their intellectual growth moved in unison. Certainly the problematic Mill inherited from his father – the explication, defense, and advance of liberal culture – had been instilled in him in his youth. The Romantic and conservative dimensions of his thought were added during the 1830s, from the other sources we have documented and long before Harriet exerted any deep influence. What attracted Mill to Harriet intellectually was not her well-worked-out system – for she had none – but her instinctive sharing of similar values and the general attributes of her mind and character. What Mill specifically claims to have derived from her intellectual influence was a clearer perception of the ultimate and ideal social vision that they shared, as well as the benefit of her practical judgment about what was feasible at present. In both these respects, the influence is well documented. There is good evidence that she reinforced his belief that he was right and encouraged him in doing what was practically feasible. Given what he said in the *Logic*, it is easy to understand what Mill has in mind here. Mill knew that he had great analytical ability, but he did not believe that he possessed to any great degree the kind of imaginative insight into where society was, or where it was going or could go, that is the province of the artist. For example, the deep appreciation of the future direction of democracy and its potential threat was an insight he derived from and attributed to Tocqueville. Mill could analyze that insight, express it cogently in *On Liberty*, and surround it with a host of powerful and now-classic arguments. But it was an insight that was originally neither his nor Harriet's.[59]

In modestly subordinating his systematic thinking to these other dimensions of the ideal and the practical, nowhere does Mill indicate that his systematic thought either originated in or was significantly altered by Harriet. The clearest statement is in Book VI of the *Autobiography*, where he states explicitly that the relationship "did not alter the path" of his thinking, and the first statement of Book VII, where he makes clear that no great changes in his thought took place after 1840. Inspired, he was; guided, he was not. Harriet made significant contributions to Mill's works, as we shall see, but Mill saw these as consistent with and improvements of his own fundamental system of thinking. During that period when Mill claims that their thought went hand in hand, during the last decade of their life together (1847–58), Mill was busy writing and publishing on themes in which his thought had already been completed. After Harriet's death, Mill's thought continued to evolve, but in retrospect, as we shall see, the evolution was along lines that had been set long before.

With regard to Mill's ideas, Harriet influenced their future evolution and articulation but not their fundamental nature. Her greatest contribution was in the clarification of the centrality of autonomy, the main idea in Mill. Indeed, this was a microcosm of her influence: a clarification and deeper appreciation of what he already believed. She provided Mill with the emotional support and sustenance he needed; she reinforced his need to believe that his was a major voice of the time, and in so doing she helped him to become just that voice. Fanny Sterling, an actress who was later to befriend Harriet's daughter Helen, described Harriet as follows: "[T]he more I read or see or hear of anything or anyone of beauty or mind the more strongly I am reminded of her who to my poor narrow way of seeing things had more of strength, and beauty and poetry, generosity and goodness than I've ever yet met with in a woman."[60]

A commonplace criticism of Mill is his overly effusive praise of Harriet. Even if Mill exaggerated, it is not unreasonable to believe that she possessed all of the virtues he cites: intelligence, sensitivity, great presence – especially for him. The evidence against this claim is the lack of great written work on her part; but we all know some extraordinary people whose intellectual and moral virtue is not evident in their written work. There are also the negative comments by her contemporaries, such as Carlyle, Mrs. Grote, and Harriet Martineau; but these can easily be dismissed as reflecting resentment, jealousy, or envy on their part. Finally, there is the great wealth of correspondence (much of it focused on editorial matters, household details, and illnesses). But these letters, mostly of Mill to Harriet, are hardly an adequate basis for evaluating what took place either in intimate moments or within the personalities of the individuals involved.[61] When contemporary critics lambaste Harriet's alleged influence, either she is a surrogate target for what they dislike in Mill, or think they have found to dislike in Mill; or it smacks of misogyny.

Some readers have been led to believe that as a result of his early upbringing Mill needed for the rest of his life to be subordinated by a stronger personality. First, it is alleged, it was James Mill, then Carlyle, then Comte, and finally Harriet. There is something quite misleading about this analysis of Mill's relationship with Harriet. To begin with, Mill broke with all of the above-mentioned individuals, but he remained devoted to Harriet even after her death. More important, his father had instilled in him and continued to reinforce a sense of failure. Even when it was well intentioned and designed to spur Mill to greater achievement, criticism from his father always left Mill with a sense of his own inadequacy. Harriet, on the other hand, was completely different. Despite all of her criticism, nagging, and sudden and unexpected reproaches, or maybe because of them, Mill was always left with a sense of his greatness. His public expressions about his own intellectual prowess were always tempered by a calculated sense of extreme modesty, but the private correspondence between Mill and Harriet reflects an almost embarrassing sense of elitism, mission, and superiority in both of them. Even the visitor Gomperz noted what he thought was a kind of self-righteousness in them. Harriet's constructive criticism reminded Mill of his superiority and importance. As Mill expressed it in his diary (1854):

[N]early all the writers, even the good ones [are] . . . but commentators. . . . Among those of the present time I can think only of two (now that Carlyle has written himself out . . .) who seem to draw what they say from a source within themselves . . . Comte, on the continent; in England (ourselves excepted) I can think only of Ruskin.[62]

There were two individuals with whom Mill had successful close relationships. One, of course, was Harriet. The other was John Sterling. What Harriet and Sterling had in common were poetic souls, a personal warmth within which Mill felt comfortable about his feelings, a sense of high-mindedness, and a genuine admiration for Mill's moral and intellectual integrity.

Mill's intellectual success was marred by a number of incidents. In June of 1841, Harriet (at the age of thirty-four) experienced a serious decline in her health. For the rest of her life she would have rheumatic pains, periodic paralysis, neuralgia, chronic toothache, and indigestion. She medicated herself for the rest of her life with laudanum (an opium derivative). In 1842, Mill suffered some severe financial reverses as a result of the American repudiation of public debt. The government was unable to refund capital on demand, and this led to bank failures as well as a credit crunch. Given the large amount of speculative investment in America by Europeans, Europeans suffered as well. Mill lost £1000 of his own money as well as several thousand pounds left in trust for the family by James Mill. Needless to say, Mill eventually repaid the trust from his own resources. The debt repudiation had another effect. It reinforced in Mill's mind one of the dangers of democracy – namely, the capacity of the majority to respond to immediate needs by overlooking the long-term consequences of financial irresponsibility.

7

Worldly Success (1846–1850)

FOLLOWING on the heels of the success of the *Logic*, the publication in 1848 of the *Principles of Political Economy* established Mill as "the" leading British intellectual and as a major voice in public policy debate. What he addressed in that monumental work were the social implications of the Industrial Revolution.

Mill's understanding of the history and evolution of the Industrial Revolution was influenced by his early reading. Mill had read Adam Smith in 1819, when he was thirteen, as well as Ricardo. He had read the histories of Hume, Robertson, Millar, and Ferguson, and, eventually, Hume's *Essays*. From these he derived the typical Scottish Enlightenment historical thesis that economic and social progress is marked by three stages: savagery, barbarism, and civilization. The economy of the savages is based upon war. However, there is no large-scale organization, so in the end "a savage tribe consists of a handful of individuals, wandering or thinly scattered over a vast tract of country."[1] It is, moreover, characterized by its lack of agriculture, commerce, industry, or the rule of law. What passes for the administration of justice is the fiat of rulers. The savage has virtues, such as energy and courage, but his main vice is a lack of discipline and a consequent inability to cooperate in any large common venture. The "savage cannot bear to sacrifice, for any purpose, the satisfaction of the individual will."[2] The only meaningful form of government or social organization (the two are synonymous at this stage) is despotism, designed to impose discipline.[3] What you do not find is self-imposed discipline.

Barbarism is the second stage. Based on his reading of Guizot, Mill identified barbarism in Europe with the feudalism that commenced with Charlemagne. The economy of feudalism is agricultural, but its social structure is local and tied to the land. The political structure is hierarchical and based upon personal loyalty. Liberty emerged within the feudal structure both because of the need to given local authority some space for initiative and because of the absence of a strong central authority. On the whole, the system was unstable, subject to sudden shifting alliances. When a strong enough central authority emerged – "French history, from Hugh Capet to Richelieu and Louis XIV . . . is a continued example of this course of things"[4] – two possibilities arose. Either there appeared a benevolent despot – a rarity – or stagnation ensured what came to be called "Chinese stationariness."

The third stage is *civilization*, described in Mill's essay of that title, and marked economically by industry, politically by limited government and the rule of law, and socially by liberty. In short, Mill identifies civilization with what we have been calling liberal culture. But there were problems on the horizon. Whereas Adam Smith and David Hume had detailed the influence of changes in economic structure with the promotion of ideals specific to it, Mill was concerned to stress how commercial society might undermine both the traditional values needed for stability and the values needed for progress.

Mill's own understanding of, and response to, the economic concerns raised by the Industrial Revolution began with Ricardo. The importance of Ricardo is recognized in a letter to Austin: "I doubt if there will be a single opinion (on pure political economy) . . . which may not be exhibited as a corollary from his [Ricardo's] doctrines."[5] Mill presented Ricardian doctrine as a positive and helpful system. In an 1825 statement, he pointed to three discoveries: the principle of population, the theory of rent, and Ricardo's theory of foreign commerce.

Nevertheless, Mill was not enamored of the economic ideals held by his father and Bentham. Mill's notion of avoiding class warfare went far beyond simply providing for democracy, redistributing resources, and encouraging entrepreneurship. Recall that Mill was extremely critical of the bourgeois culture of his day, something we have already seen in the essays of the 1830s.[6] What Mill objected to was a morally stultifying life based wholly on the pursuit of materialism. In this, Mill joined a host of other critics of the nineteenth century, including Constant, Tocqueville, Burckhardt, Marx, and Nietzsche. Such a life was without any redeeming moral dimension. In an 1829 letter to d'Eichthal, Mill observed that the "very worst point in our national character [is] . . . the disposition to sacrifice every thing to accumulation, & that exclusive & engrossing selfishness which accompanies it"; this leads to "moral insensibility."[7] Mill had been disappointed by the middle class in France after the Revolution of 1830.[8] In his historical account in *The Spirit of the Age*, he had seen the need for ending the monopoly on public opinion exercised by the landed aristocracy and the monied class. In *Civilization* (1836), he identified as the negative effects of commercial society the cultivation of "mortal effeminacy, and inaptitude for every kind of struggle."[9] In *Coleridge*, he noted the demoralization that results from the "great inequalities in wealth and social rank."[10] In *Tocqueville* (1840), he saw the "yoke of bourgeois opinion" (conformity and mediocrity) as resulting from commercial society, not from democratization. The triumph of the middle class in commercial society, even under democracy, leads to servility and not to anarchy.[11] In a democracy, people are virtuous only out of self-interest.[12] In an 1847 letter to Austin, Mill claimed that even the aristocracy "bend with a willing submission to the yoke of bourgeois opinion."[13]

It is partly his concern for the corruption of the bourgeoisie that explains why Mill was not so appalled by the idea of a stationary or no-growth state of the economy. In an early letter to d'Eichthal, Mill had objected that "conquest & production . . . [are not] the only two conceivable purposes that human beings can combine for. . . . the highest & most important of these purposes is the improvement of man himself as a moral and intelligent being. . . ."[14] The stationary state could be good; the progressive state could be bad:

> I confess I am not charmed with the ideal of life held out by those who think that the normal state of human beings is that of struggling to get on; that the trampling, crushing, elbowing, and treading on each other's heels, which form the existing type of social life, are the most desirable lot of human kind, or anything but the disagreeable symptoms of one of the phases of industrial progress.[15]

What sometimes leads readers to draw the wrong conclusion is the positive face that Mill gives to the possibility of the stationary state. The stationary state is an economy that no longer grows. Mill did not think that we had arrived at that state, that more growth in the foreseeable future was probable. However, he did not believe that a stationary state was necessarily bad. In his famous discussion of the stationary state, Mill wanted to do two things: (a) to defend a more optimistic view of wealth creation and (b) to make the case that wealth is not an end in itself but a means to human fulfillment and individual liberty. Even if there were a stationary state of zero growth (a concern for classical economists, but not for neoclassical economists), freedom would not necessarily be lost or diminished. Economic growth creates resources. But income is not merely a means to consumer satisfaction, nor merely an incentive. Rather, income is a means to accomplishment. Participation in a market economy informed by an individualist moral culture actually promotes a variety of forms of virtuous behavior. Nevertheless, he insisted that there had to be a moral purpose to the technological project. The desire to engross the whole surface of the earth in the mere production of the greatest possible quantity of food and manufactured goods, Mill believed, was founded on a mischievously narrow conception of the requirements of human nature.

It should be clear that what Mill objected to was the assumption of the universal truth of psychological egoism, an idea he had inherited from Bentham and that seemed to permeate so much of classical political economy. He was concerned that an economic abstraction like *homo economicus* would be used to reinforce vulgar materialism and create a new form of bourgeois psychological bondage that would be conveyed to the working class. It should also be clear that what he objected to was not only the old agrarian feudalism but also the neofeudalism of nineteenth-century Tory philanthropy. None of this is a critique of the technological project, or a critique of market economies, or a critique of limited government or private property or the rule of law or individual autonomy – it is the underlining of the moral dimension of autonomy. Once again, it is the concept of autonomy that is the key to understanding Mill.

Carlyle and Coleridge were further influences in this direction. Carlyle's critique of the materialism and the ethical egoism of classical political economy made Mill question both the truth of those views and the long-term social consequences of accepting them. From Coleridge, he absorbed the notion of a safety net as well as the idea that the larger social community has some responsibility for promoting autonomy.

[A] State ought to be considered as a great benefit society, or mutual insurance company, for helping (under the necessary regulations for preventing abuse) that large proportion of its members who cannot help themselves. 'Let us suppose (says Coleridge) the negative ends of a State already attained, namely, its own safety by means of its own strength, and the protection of persons and property for all its members; there will then remain its positive ends [positive freedom]: 1. To make the means of subsistence more easy to each individual: 2. To secure to each of its members the hope of bettering his own condition or that of his children: 3. The development of those faculties which are essential to his humanity, that is

to his rational and moral being.' [*Second Lay Sermon*, 1839, pp. 14–15] In regard
to the two former ends, he of course does not mean that they can be accomplished
merely by making laws to that effect; or that, according to the wild doctrines now
afloat, it is the fault of the government if every one has not enough to eat and
drink. But he means that government can do something directly, and very much
indirectly, to promote even the physical comfort of the people; and that if, besides
making a proper use of its own powers, it would exert itself to teach the people
what is in theirs, indigence would soon disappear from the face of the earth.[16]

But Mill's original views on economics were modified, as was everything
else, by his reading of continental thinkers. Specifically, in this case, both
Comte and Saint-Simon contributed. To begin with, Comte led Mill to
question whether economic generalizations were sui generis and therefore
unqualifiable or whether they were instead parasitic on more fundamental truths. If the latter was the case, then the economic scenario painted
by the classical political economists had to be qualified and reexamined.
The Saint-Simonian evolutionary view of history had its influence as well.
Mill came to recognize the very limited and temporary value of the old
political economy that assumed private property and inheritance as indefeasible facts, and freedom of production and exchange as the *dernier
mot* of social improvement. This reconsideration was reflected in an 1833
letter to Carlyle[17] and in two essays, the *Essay on Some Unsettled Questions
in Political Economy*, written in 1830 but not published until 1844, and
the review of Harriet Martineau's *Summary of Political Economy* (1834).
In the latter work, he chided Martineau for trying to make a "permanent
fabric out of transitory material," for taking "for granted the immutability
of arrangements of society." He charged her with reducing

the principle of laissez faire to logical absurdity as far as the principle goes, by
merely carrying it out to all its consequences. In the meantime that principle like
other negative ones has work to do yet, work, namely of a destroying kind, & I am
glad to think it has strength left to finish that, after which it must soon expire. . . .[18]

Specifically, what Mill rejected was Martineau's presumption of the in-
evitability of a class-structured society. It is important that the reader
not interpret Mill's objection to a class-structured society as an objection
to differences in income. What is at issue is not differences in income –
although that may be relevant – but differences in the opportunity to become autonomous. The positive power of laissez-faire is the destruction
of feudal and aristocratic obstacles to a free market economy. The negative

power of laissez-faire is its use to perpetuate a class society, that is, a permanent division between employers and employees. The dissatisfaction with classical political economists was epitomized in Mill's complaint that they "revolve in their eternal circle of landlords, capitalists, and labourers, until they seem to think of the distinction of society into those three classes, as if it were one of God's ordinances, not man's, and as little under human control as the division of day and night"[19]

Mill's economic odyssey was, thus, an interesting one. In the 1820s, he advocated the amelioration of the current system primarily by improving the conditions of the laboring poor and by encouraging voluntary restraint on population. "I was a democrat, but not the least of a Socialist."[20] However, given the new influences in his life, his views began to diverge from those of his father. Specifically, Mill rejected his father's analogy between domestic economy and political economy, for this smacked too much of paternalism. Instead of believing in a smoothly functioning economy, Mill accepted the existence of a trade cycle and the possibility of a glut. He came in time to reject a rigid interpretation of the wages fund doctrine. Most especially, he thought that socialist critics deserved a hearing. He was especially intrigued by the ideas of Owen and the Saint-Simonians. As he put it in his *Autobiography*, "their aim seemed to me desirable and rational"; but he did not think that their systems were either "true" or workable or that "they should be acted on."[21] He also wanted to dramatize for the upper classes the need for reform, so that they "might be made to see that they had more to fear from the poor when uneducated than when educated."[22]

By the 1840s, under the influence of the Saint-Simonians, Carlyle, Coleridge, and Harriet Taylor, Mill could say:

Our [Mill's and Harriet's] ideal of ultimate improvement went far beyond Democracy, and would class us decidedly under the general designation of Socialists. While we repudiated with the greatest energy that tyranny of society over the individual which most Socialistic systems are supposed to involve, we yet looked forward to a time when society will no longer be divided into the idle and industrious; when the rule that they who do not work shall not eat, will be applied not to paupers, only, but impartially to all; when the division of the produce of labour, instead of depending, as in so great a degree it now does, on the accident of birth, will be made by concert, on an acknowledged principle of justice; and when it will no longer either be, or thought to be, impossible for human beings to exert themselves strenuously in procuring benefits which are not to be exclusively their own, but to be shared with the society they belong to.... [This] did not make us overlook the folly of premature attempts to dispense with the inducements of private interest in social affairs, while no substitute for them has been or can be provided: but we regarded all existing institutions and social arrangements as being (in a phrase I once learned from Austin) 'merely provisional,' and we welcomed with the greatest pleasure and interest all socialistic experiments by select individuals (such as the Co-operative Societies), which, whether they succeeded or failed, could not but operate as a most useful education of those who took part in them, by cultivating their capacity of acting upon motives pointing directly to the general good, or making them aware of the defects which render them and others incapable of doing so.[23]

Although this statement raises all sorts of questions that we shall have to address about the meaning of "socialism," the following should be clear. From about the mid-1840s onward, Mill did not alter his fundamental position in economics any more than he did in other areas of his thought. There will be some tinkering at the margins and adjustments of specific public policy recommendations as the context changed, but the overall position remained the same. What should also be clear is Mill's economic agenda when seen as part of his overall position. Mill accepted the idea that the modern world was dominated by the technological project. He accepted the view that a free market economy was the most efficient means for achieving the productive benefits of the technological project. He maintained that a free market economy required private property. He recognized that a free market economy and private property could be maintained only if there were limited government, individual rights, the rule of law, and toleration. Mill's specific contribution to the foregoing list are the following claims. The extrinsic value of the technological project is the production of the material conditions that make possible the institutionalization of individual autonomy, and individual autonomy is the intrinsic goal of that project, the moral quest of modernity. Limited government, individual rights, the rule of law, and toleration can be justified and preserved only as expressions of and protections for individual autonomy. Unless autonomy is recognized as the intrinsic goal, a free market economy will undermine the very moral foundations that it requires for its own functioning. A market economy is not just about making money. Unless as many individuals as possible are encouraged to obtain private property and participate as entrepreneurs within the market economy, liberal culture will breed its own self-destructive Frankenstein.

Mill's self-designation as a socialist, his critique of capitalism, his critique of "socialism," and his specific policy recommendations all make sense when seen against the background of this larger view. Mill was always a critic of status quo capitalism; he maintained an open mind with respect to voluntary association "socialism"; he was always unalterably opposed to centralization; his two major concerns with "socialism" were its potential threats to liberty and to efficiency (because of its opposition to competition); and he was always a reformer of the free market economy, aiming to render it consistent with its own inherent principles, especially individual autonomy. "In the end, it was his overriding concern for the fate of individual freedom and development which guided all his social and political proposals."[24]

The concept of "autonomy" is the key to understanding Mill. We shall have more to say about it in a later chapter, but for now it is important to note that there is no ultimate conflict between the pursuit of autonomy on the part of one person and that same pursuit on the part of others. When autonomy is the ultimate goal and when wealth is seen as a means to autonomy, then the pursuit of wealth properly understood is not an inevitable source of conflict. In order for one autonomous person to preserve his or her autonomy, it is necessary for him or her to interact with other autonomous persons. *What this means is that the pursuit and preservation of autonomy obligates us to promote autonomy in others.* This is what altruism means for Mill and Harriet Taylor. It is not putting the interests of others before our own; it is the recognition that our ultimate objective must be the pursuit of universal autonomy. This is why Mill became a critic of Bentham's psychological egoism and ethical egoism in *Utilitarianism*, and why Mill insisted in his *Essay on Some Unsettled Questions in Political Economy* that *homo economicus* was a useful economic abstraction but not a literal truth. This is why the discussion in the sixth book of the *Logic* of provisional generalizations in the social sciences must be related to more fundamental truths about human beings and ultimately to the norms explicated by the artist.

Mill insisted that it was Harriet who should get credit for articulating this ideal.[25] It was she – as we saw earlier, in her 1832 essay[26] – who first made Mill realize the true significance of universal autonomy. What he took upon himself was the troubling task of trying to see how this ideal could be institutionalized. He readily admitted that there was no currently foreseeable institutionalization.[27] They both recognized that the great obstacle was the conflict between an erroneously narrow and unimaginatively conceived self-interest and an interest in the common good. Harriet was, in Mill's view, overly optimistic about correcting this myopic vision. In the meantime, Mill suggested social experiments on a small scale with worker cooperatives, experiments that could discredit the assumptions on which they were based. They both favored the present "provisional" arrangement until something better could be exemplified. They both insisted that the ultimate goal is the "greatest liberty of action."

Mill got a chance to address the practical embodiment of these issues in the so-called Irish Question. The dominant public policy issue of his time was the plight of Ireland. In 1846 and 1847, Mill wrote some forty-three articles in the *Morning Chronicle* on the Irish potato famine. He opposed outdoor relief (instead of the workhouse) because he feared that everyone would be induced to become a beggar. Mill was passionately opposed to what he considered misguided philanthropy, the effect of which was to undermine autonomy.[28]

All you hear of today is giving the poor not just money, but . . . all one considers useful for them. For instance: their working hours are being shortened, sanitary conditions are being improved, as is education, especially of the Christian Protestant kind. . . . In short, it is a matter of governing [the poor] in paternal fashion. The court, nobility and the wealthy calmly set about the task without ever suspecting that anything other than good will was required . . . that is to say . . . by completely disregarding the self-respect of the poor.

That is quite natural since they have no idea what it means in their own lives, for they have lost the self-respect they manifested in the past and have not yet acquired that of the future. . . . they never knew, that well-being is attained not just by being passive; that generally what one does for people serves them only if it supports what they do for themselves. . . . [the] attempt to substitute social action for individual virtues . . . will inevitably do more harm than good.[29]

What Mill advocated was state-subsidized waste cultivation and peasant proprietorships (a policy that had worked in India). Instead of following Mill's suggestions, the Tory-controlled government allowed the landlords to get the new land with state subsidies. Whenever Mill advocated that the state might engage in "takings" or the redistribution of resources, he insisted that there be compensation to the original owners.[30] In his own time, when the state saw fit to use public money to enrich landlords, Mill's suggestions led him to be denounced as "the most recent and thorough-going apostle of communism."[31]

Principles of Political Economy

Mill began working on his economic treatise in the autumn of 1845 and had completed it by 1847. This short span of time reflects both the fact that he had thought and written about these issues for over a decade and that it was during 1846 and 1847 that he was addressing the Irish famine in the *Morning Chronicle*. The *Principles of Political Economy* was published in 1848. It was an immediate success and, along with the *Logic*, established Mill's reputation as an expert. The book was republished in numerous editions (thirty-two editions before the end of the century) as well as being translated into several foreign languages, and Mill's restatement of Ricardo was "the" textbook in economics until replaced in 1890 by Alfred Marshall's more mathematical restatement, the *Principles of Economics*. Harriet contributed substantially to the book in several ways, as we shall discuss. She also negotiated a better royalty arrangement for Mill with the publishers.

The first of my books in which her [Harriet's] share was conspicuous was the "Principles of Political Economy." The "System of Logic" owed little to her except in the minute matters of composition, in which respect my writings, both great and small, have largely benefited by her accurate and clear-sighted criticism. The chapter of the Political Economy which has had a greater influence on opinion than all the rest, that on 'the Probable Future of the Labouring Classes', is entirely due to her: in the first draft of the book that chapter did not exist. She pointed out the need of such a chapter, and the extreme imperfection of the book without it: she was the cause of my writing it; and the more general parts of the chapter, the statement and discussion of the two opposite theories respecting the proper condition of the labouring classes, was wholly an exposition of her thoughts, often in words taken from her lips. The purely scientific part of the Political Economy I did not learn from her; but it was chiefly her influence that gave to the book that general tone by which it is distinguished from all previous expositions of Political Economy that had any pretensions to being scientific, and which has made it so useful in conciliating minds which those previous expositions had repelled. . . . What was abstract and purely scientific was generally mine; the properly human element came from her: in all that concerned the application of philosophy to the exigencies of human society and progress, I was her pupil, alike in boldness of speculation and cautiousness of practical judgment. . . . she was much more courageous and far-sighted than without her I should have been, in anticipations of an order of things to come, in which many of the limited generalizations now so often confounded with universal principles will cease to be applicable.[32]

In recognition of her contribution, Mill proposed to dedicate the book to her. Harriet was deeply moved and flattered and subsequently mentioned this proposal to her husband, John Taylor. Mr. Taylor, fearing scandal, disapproved:

My dear Harriet, I was so much surprised . . . when I received your note and found you to be inclined to have the Book dedicated to you. . . . [It evinces] on the author's part, as well as the lady to whom the book is to be dedicated, a want of taste and tact. . . . It is not only 'a few common people' who will make vulgar remarks, but all who know any of us – the dedication will revive recollections now forgotten and will create observations and talk that cannot but be extremely unpleasant to me. . . . It is never pleasant to differ with you – most of all upon questions such as this.[33]

A compromise was reached in which a limited number of "gift copies" bore the following added inscription:

TO

MRS. JOHN TAYLOR

AS THE MOST EMINENTLY QUALIFIED

OF ALL PERSONS KNOWN TO THE AUTHOR

EITHER TO ORIGINATE OR TO APPRECIATE

SPECULATIONS ON SOCIAL IMPROVEMENT,

THIS ATTEMPT TO EXPLAIN AND DIFFUSE IDEAS

MANY OF WHICH WERE FIRST LEARNED FROM HERSELF,

IS

WITH THE HIGHEST RESPECT AND REGARD

DEDICATED

The work has both a methodological and an ideological dimension. Methodologically, it is an example of the *Logic* applied to a specific domain. That is why Mill stated in the Preface that "there are perhaps no practical questions . . . which admit of being decided on economical premises alone."[34] Policy decisions, according to the *Logic*, depend upon an "artistic" explication of fundamental values, followed by scientific consideration of means and consequences. Political economy comprises an interrelated set of economic policies based upon a unifying normative principle. That principle, for Mill, is autonomy. The production, distribution, and consumption of wealth are necessary but not sufficient conditions for autonomy. Mill evaluates policies along two axes: (1) efficiency and (2) the promotion of autonomy. The following topics are considered: competition, private property (capitalism vs. socialism), production versus distribution, growth versus a stationary state, redistribution, population, liberty (limited government), government intervention, the theory of value, population, trade unions, socialism, money and crises, international trade, colonization, and the poor laws. As he said in one of his letters, the *Principles of Political Economy* was written to "rescue from the hands of such people the truths they misapply, and by combining these with other truths to which they are strangers, to deduce conclusions capable of being of some use to the progress of mankind."[35]

The social crisis created by the Industrial Revolution was class conflict. This crisis was exacerbated, in Mill's mind, by the perceived coming of an increasingly democratic society. Mill identified four possible responses.

The Tory response (i.e., the response of those who spoke for the landed aristocracy) was a defense of the status quo and an attitude of paternalism toward the working class. Mill was vehemently critical of this response. In the famous chapter of the *Principles of Political Economy* inspired by Harriet, he begins by contrasting the feudal-paternalistic view of Disraeli and Carlyle with autonomy.

According to the former theory, the lot of the poor, in all things which affect them collectively, should be regulated for them, not by them. They should not be required or encouraged to think for themselves, or give to their own reflection or forecast an influential voice in the determination of their destiny. It is supposed to be the duty of the higher classes to think for them, and to take the responsibility of their lot, as the commanders and officers of an army take that of the soldiers composing it. This function, it is contended, the higher classes should prepare themselves to perform conscientiously, and their whole demeanour should impress the poor with a reliance on it, in order that, while yielding passive and active obedience to the rules prescribed for them they may resign themselves in all other respects to a trustful *insouciance*, and repose under the shadow of their protectors. The relation between rich and poor, according to this theory (a theory also applied to the relation between men and women) should be only partly authoritative; it should be amiable, moral, and sentimental: affectionate tutelage on the one side, respectful and grateful deference on the other. The rich should be *in loco parentis* to the poor, guiding and restraining them like children.[36]

In an earlier letter to McVey Napier, editor of the *Edinburgh Review* (November 9, 1844), Mill had attacked the presumption that it was necessary "to rivet firmly in the minds of the labouring people the persuasion that it is the business of others to take care of their condition, without any self-control on their own part; – & that whatever is possessed by other people, more than they possess, is a wrong to them, or at least a kind of stewardship, of which an account is to be rendered to them."[37] It was his opposition to feudalism that explains Mill's opposition to the wage system: It perpetuated the master-servant relationship; it created class conflict; and it demoralized the working class.

Mill's critique of philanthropy[38] was rooted in his rejection of the notion that the rich should take care of the poor. One of Mill's specific targets was the embrace of Tory philanthropy to be found in Carlyle's *Past and Present*, published in 1843. Clearly, what he sought was a situation in which universal autonomy no longer made it necessary for anyone to take care of anyone else. The real problem of the working poor was not the problem of a lack of resources however real this might be; for that was what he called "superficial philanthropy," concerned with such things as housing and sanitation. The real problem was the need to develop self-control and foresight.[39] As Mill pointed out to Comte in his correspondence, "our would-be philanthropists have not the slightest idea" about autonomy.[40] For Mill, "the future well-being of the labouring classes is principally dependent on their own mental cultivation."[41] Later, in *The Subjection of Women*, Mill would assert that the emancipation of women could further contribute to the end of misguided charity.

The landowning aristocracy was an anachronism in an industrial age. The Tories, moreover, exercised political power in a reactionary direction. Given the classical economists' fears about the choking off of economic progress by landlords, and given his own fears during the 1840s and thereafter about the rising threat of democracy, Mill believed that the only way to maintain the benefits of the Industrial Revolution and to preserve freedom was to reduce the power of the aristocracy. To this end, he advocated breaking up the old estates by ending entail and primogeniture and by limiting how much could be inherited (an inheritance tax is not to be confused with an estate tax)[42] by one individual. Mill even advocated government ownership of the landed resources, as long as this governmental "taking" was not an expropriation but a policy for which compensation was provided. He was also quick to add that moveable wealth, as opposed

James Mill (Photo: akg–images, London)

Jeremy Bentham (National Portrait Gallery, London)

John Sterling (National Portrait Gallery, London)

Samuel Taylor Coleridge
(National Portrait
Gallery, London)

William Wordsworth
(National Portrait
Gallery, London)

Thomas Carlyle (National Portrait Gallery, London)

Harriet Taylor Mill (National Portrait Gallery, London)

Auguste Comte (Bibliothèque Nationale, Paris)

William Gladstone
(National Portrait
Gallery, London)

Herbert Spencer
(National Portrait
Gallery, London)

to landed wealth, should not be government-owned, nor should large and successful enterprises in moveable wealth be broken up.[43] Finally, he did not want to penalize through taxation the inclination to save that is the basis of capital formation on which economic progress depends. In short, what Mill tried to achieve was a balancing act in which wealth was maximized in such a way as to increase the possibilities of entrepreneurship and autonomy.

What is most interesting is Mill's critique of the second response, namely, classical political economy's response, as represented by his father. Mill faulted that response, in the first place, because it blithely ignored a potentially serious conflict between the entrepreneurial middle class and the workers, a conflict that would be exacerbated by the growth of democracy. Sooner or later there would be some public policy concerning the production and distribution of wealth, but Mill worried that it would be a coercive oligarchy. Moreover, classical political economists never questioned their own personal presumption of Puritanism and hence ignored the extent to which the single-minded pursuit of wealth in production led inexorably to a hypocritically disguised and corrosive materialism. Finally, the inadequacy of the methodology of classical political economy – specifically, its presumption of *homo economicus* – would eventually undermine the ideals of social cooperation and the notion of a common good. The inevitable result would be class conflict and the destruction of the whole structure of liberal culture. Given the fundamental nature of this critique of his father's economic position, it is no wonder that Mill suppressed the publication of his essay on economic methodology until after his father's death!

It was Mill's intention to recast Ricardian and Malthusian economics in a positive and optimistic way. Specifically, Mill held out the possibility that workers could better their lives both by improving their incomes and by controlling the size of their families. "We cannot . . . foresee to what extent the modes of production may be altered, or the productiveness of labour increased, by future extensions of our knowledge of the laws of nature, suggesting new processes of industry of which we have at present no conception."[44]

Toward this end, Mill introduced a strategic distinction between production and distribution. Mill defined political economy as "the science which traces the laws of such of the phenomena of society as arise from the combined operations of mankind for the production of wealth, in so far as those phenomena are not modified by the pursuit of any other object." It was generally agreed that Mill wanted to emphasize the element of production in the definition of political economy and to eliminate both consumption and distribution. There are two reasons for this. First, to the extent that political economy is a science, it can make true generalizations about the production of wealth. However, the current patterns of distribution reflect historical accident. This was an idea that Mill had acquired from the Saint-Simonians.[45]

Political economy should not be seen as an apology for the status quo (Mill's judgment about Newman). J. E. Cairnes pointed out that Mill's greatest novelty as a political economist was his suggestion that scientific generalizations alone do not dictate normative conclusions – a point that Mill had already expressed in his *Logic*, where he insisted that the basic norms were to be supplied by art. It is no accident that this insight is emphasized in the chapter of the *Principles* inspired by Harriet, for it is there that Mill stressed the extent to which income expectations, as Cairnes put it, "in the case of a progressive community, [are,] in point of fact, constantly rising, as moral and intellectual influences are brought to bear on the masses of the people."[46]

Mill was not ignorant of the interrelationship of production and distribution. Mill never suggested or thought that distribution or redistribution did not itself have consequences for productivity. Mill was not a fool: "Society can subject the distribution of wealth to whatever rules it thinks best: but what practical results shall flow from the operation of those rules, society cannot choose, but must be content to learn."[47] What Mill was articulating was the insight that changes in the way production was organized could alter patterns of distribution. Hence we could contemplate alternative schemes designed both to increase productivity and to increase the number of people who engaged in entrepreneurial activity and benefited therefrom.

The second reason for limiting political economy's scientific definition to production is that the production of wealth is not the only or the highest human objective. Mill stressed that while political economy usefully employs the notion of the pursuit of self-interest (*homo economicus*) as a construct, this construct does not exhaustively characterize human nature. Mill's priorities are quite clear. Autonomy is the highest good. Economic efficiency is a means to autonomy. The Industrial Revolution and a free market economy are infinitely superior to feudalism precisely because they liberate the human potential for autonomy. On the other hand, if we lived in a world where we were forced to choose between autonomy and more material benefits, there is no question that Mill would favor autonomy. However, Mill also believed that autonomous laborers were more productive, so that autonomy was itself a means to efficiency.

Mill had a unique understanding of the predicament of labor. Mill was concerned to argue that the medieval feudal economy was agrarian, limited, and hierarchical in its economic, social, and political organization. This led to a class distinction whereby some were forever paternalistic and others forever dependent. The growth of a commercial and industrial economy with a free market created the possibility for a world where all could be equally free and responsible. It was the purpose of political economy to help all of us to realize the potential of the new order. Mill understood the class structure of his society to be a remnant of feudalism. He recognized that in an agrarian economy, feudal relationships give "power over other human beings."[48] Feudalism was marked by a hierarchical and paternalistic class structure. Not only was paternalism bad in itself and incompatible with autonomy, but paternalism of that kind would not survive the coming of democracy. The capitalist was in danger of replicating the feudal Tory world. What Mill objected to was a capitalist as chief and workers without a voice in the management.

[T]o work at the bidding and for the profit of another, without any interest in the work – the price of their labour being adjusted in hostile competition, one side demanding as much and the other paying as little as possible – is not, even when wages are high, a satisfactory state to human beings of educated intelligence, who have ceased to think of themselves naturally inferior to those whom they serve.[49]

Nor would the situation change or be helped by raising wages, both because of the revolution of rising expectations and because feudal relationships were always demeaning. Mill rejected the idea that a liberal culture with a free market economy must always be marked by class conflict.

This was precisely where Harriet had her greatest influence. At her suggestion, Mill added the chapter entitled "On the Probable Futurity of the Labouring Classes." Many of the ideas expressed in that chapter originated with her. Mill acknowledged this influence in his *Autobiography*: "In this third period (as it may be termed) of my mental progress, which now went hand in hand with hers, my opinions gained equally in breadth and depth, I understood more things, and those which I had understood before, I now understood more thoroughly."[50] Specifically, what Harriet underlined for Mill was the importance of achieving autonomy for the members of the working class.

The third response to the problem of class conflict was that of communism. The communist response to the class problem was to close the gap by endorsing collective ownership and state control of the whole economy. Mill's response to this is telling.

If, therefore the choice were to be made between Communism with all its chances, and the present state of society with all its sufferings and injustices; if the institution of private property necessarily carried with it as a consequence, that the produce of labour should be apportioned as we now see it, almost in an inverse ratio to the labour – the largest portions to those who have never worked at all, the next largest to those whose work is almost nominal, and so on in a descending scale, the remuneration dwindling as the work grows harder and more disagreeable, until the most fatiguing and exhausting bodily labour cannot count with certainty on being able to earn even the necessaries of life; if this or Communism were the alternative, all the difficulties, great or small, of Communism would be but as dust in the balance. But to make the comparison applicable, we must compare Communism at its best, with the régime of individual[51] property, not as it is, but as it might be made. The principal of private property has never yet had a fair trial in any country; and less so, perhaps, in this country than in some others. The social arrangements of modern Europe commenced from a distribution of property which was the result, not of just partition, or acquisition by industry, but of conquest and violence: and not withstanding what industry has been doing for many centuries to modify the work of force, the system still retains many and large traces of its origin. The laws of property have never yet conformed to the principles on which the justification of private property rests[52]. They have made property of things which never ought to be property, and absolute property where only a qualified property ought to exist. They have not held the balance fairly between human beings, but have heaped impediments upon some, to give advantages to others; they have purposefully fostered inequalities, and prevented all from starting fair in the race. That all should indeed start on perfectly equal terms, is inconsistent with any law of private property;[53] but if as much pains as has been taken to aggravate the inequality of chances arising from the natural working of the principle, had been taken to temper that inequality by every means not subversive of the principle itself;[54] if the tendency of legislation had been to favor the diffusion, instead of the concentration of wealth – to encourage the subdivision of the large masses, instead of striving to keep them together; the principle of individual property would have been found to have no necessary connexion with the physical and social evils which almost all Socialist writers assume to be inseparable from it.

Private property, in every defense made of it, is supposed to mean, the guarantee to individuals of the fruits of their own labour and abstinence. The guarantee to them of the fruits of the labour and abstinence of others, transmitted to them without any merit or exertion of their own, is not of the essence of the institution, but a mere incidental consequence, which, when it reaches a certain height, does not promote, but conflicts with, the ends which render private property legitimate. To judge of the final destination of the institution of property, we must suppose everything rectified, which causes the institution to work in a manner opposed to that equitable principle, of proportion between remuneration and exertion, on which in every vindication of it that will bear the light, it is assumed to be grounded. We must also suppose two conditions realized, without which neither Communism nor any other laws or institutions could make the condition of the mass of mankind other than degraded and miserable. One of these conditions is, universal education; the other, a due limitation of the numbers of the community. With these, there could be no poverty, even under the present social institutions: and these being supposed, the question of Socialism is not, as generally stated by Socialists, a question of flying to the sole refuge against the evils which now bear down humanity; but a mere question of comparative advantages, which futurity must determine. We are too ignorant either of what individual agency in its best form, or Socialism in its best form, can accomplish, to be qualified to decide which of the two will be the ultimate form of human society.

If a conjecture may be hazarded, the decision will probably depend mainly on one consideration, viz. Which of the two systems is consistent with the greatest amount of human liberty and spontaneity. . . .[55]

The fourth response to the problem of class conflict was that of socialism. The term "socialism" came into use around 1830. From 1830 to about the time of the 1864 meeting of the First International (again, the period from 1830 to 1870 emerges as a distinctly important one, for the nineteenth century and for Mill), the term was applied to three movements deriving from the writings of Saint-Simon (1760–1825) and Fourier (1772–1837) in France and Robert Owen (1771–1858) in England. Together, this trio is often referred to as advocating "utopian socialism." Each of the movements emerged out of the utopian literature of the Enlightenment, and each proposed a comprehensive program for the reformation of the social world. These three writers are the ones whom Mill discussed most thoroughly and whom he almost always had in mind.

In this context, Mill defined socialism as follows: "any system, which requires that the land and instruments of production should be the property, not of individuals, but of communities or associations, or of the government."[56] This is an accurate definition in Mill's historical context, but a potential source of confusion in ours. We use the term "socialism" to designate government ownership or control. Associations of individuals who own property – for example, modern corporations – are "socialistic" in Mill's sense, but hardly socialistic in the contemporary political and economic sense. The source of the confusion is not in Mill but in the historical context: Until 1855, Parliament had proscribed all but a few limited liability joint stock companies. The world in which Mill lived was a world in which property was largely owned by individuals and families. For example, a small start-up software company in Silicon Valley where all of the employees are involved in a limited partnership or jointly own the stock would be an example of what Mill meant by "socialism"; it would be ludicrous to call this "socialism" in our present context.

Saint-Simon was among the first to describe the social dislocation caused by the Industrial Revolution and to see the emergence of individualism as a consequence of the breakdown of feudal hierarchy. Saint-Simon himself (and later Auguste Comte) proposed reaping the benefits of industrialism without incurring its vices by having the entire social world organized and run by a technical elite. The society would still be marked by inequality, but it would also be a thoroughgoing meritocracy. Some of Saint-Simon's followers departed from him by arguing that private property was incompatible with the rule of the technical elite. Fourier, who agreed with Saint-Simon's diagnosis, imagined a series of utopian model communities in which all human beings could fulfill themselves, but without the rule of experts.

Robert Owen was a successful British entrepreneur who recognized the evils of industrialism. He advocated eliminating these evils by eliminating competition and substituting cooperation. Cooperation involved both centralized control of industry on the national level and the creation of what he called Villages of Unity, within which there would be cooperation and equality of ownership. One other important feature of Owen's plan was its emphasis on education as a transforming and enlightening influence in promoting cooperation. What Mill objected to in Owen's scheme was the belief in complete environmental determinism. Owen believed that the source of the workers' problems lay in conditions completely beyond their control, and that the solution to their problems lay in a communal arrangement that deemphasized individuality. This is why it was so important for Mill to argue in favor of autonomy, the ability of individuals to transform their own lives.

In England, Mill was also familiar with the Christian socialist movement inaugurated by Frederick Denison Maurice (1805–1872) and Charles Kingsley (1819–1875). Originating in Anglican anti-industrial paternalism, the Christian socialist movement tried to combine cooperative economics with political conservatism.

Three other French figures with whom Mill was familiar are worth mentioning in connection with early versions of socialism. Louis Blanc (1811–1882), the author of *L'Organisation du travail* (1840), proposed the formation of worker cooperatives in the form of national workshops; the funding of such workshops was to be provided initially by the government. Thereafter, the workshops would be independent of government control. It was Blanc who had first proclaimed the slogan "From each according to his abilities, to each according to his needs." Blanc was obsessed with the view that competition was a great evil. Blanc is now viewed as the transitional figure from utopian to scientific socialism. Pierre-Joseph Proudhon (1809–1865), an anarchist and critic of the evils of private property, advocated a federation of producers' cooperatives without centralized control. The third figure, the one with whom Mill was most sympathetic,[57] was Charles Fourier (1772–1837). Fourier was a proponent of something like a workers' cooperative in what he called a "phalanx," an economic and communal unit of 1,620 people. The organization of the unit remained consistent with capitalism. Fourier's utopian socialism received continuous advocacy through his disciple Victor Prosper Considérant.[58]

Mill considered himself to be an "ideal" socialist, which is why he always qualified his use of the expression "socialism" by such words as "ideal," "general," and "qualified." What this meant, first of all, is that he, like the utopian socialists of the 1830s and 1840s, rejected psychological hedonism and egoism. Fourier was the great exponent of the idea that the natural passions properly directed (self-interest properly understood) resulted in social harmony. Mill argued with Harriet only over the time it would take to turn people from selfishness to other forms of motivation. Unlike many other socialists, Mill rejected the notion of a collective good. Hence, "altruism" for Mill (recall his dispute with Comte on this term) did not mean the surrendering or subsuming of the private good. According to

Mill, what we pursue both for ourselves and for others is autonomy. Since universal autonomy is the ultimate common good, Mill wanted to replace the class distinction between employers and employees, but his envisaged solution was a liberal culture in which everyone was entrepreneurial and autonomous.

It was precisely this ideal kind of socialism of which Marx and Engels were most critical. In explaining the title of the "Communist Manifesto" – and why it could not be the "socialist manifesto" – Engels says the following:

> By socialists, in 1847, were understood, on the one hand, the adherents of the various utopian systems: Owenites in England, Fourierists in France, both of them already reduced to the position of mere sects, and gradually dying out; on the other hand, the most multifarious social quacks, who, by all manners of tinkering, professed to redress, without any danger to capital and profit, all sorts of social grievances, in both cases men outside the working-class movement and looking rather to the 'educated' classes for support. . . . Thus socialism was, in 1847, a middle-class movement, communism a working class movement.[59]

Mill favored workers' and even consumers' cooperatives,[60] "the association of the labourers themselves on terms of equality, collectively owning the capital with which they carry on their operations, and working under managers elected and removable by themselves."[61] His reasons were to promote autonomy, to promote the cooperation that flows from autonomy, and to turn workers into entrepreneurs. The class distinction between employers and employees would disappear and be replaced not by a nationalized economy but by a completely entrepreneurial one. He favored the Rochdale system, in which the workers pooled their own resources and were co-owners as opposed to merely sharing in the profits, and in which the workers received both a minimum guarantee but incentives and bonuses as well – but, of course, no maternity benefits! Mill even advocated government loans to responsible groups of workers with a reasonable expectation of forming a successfully competitive cooperative. The loans, he insisted, would have to be paid back. This differs from market socialism in that there is no central allocation of resources.[62] The cooperatives would have to compete with existing private enterprises. The cooperatives were never to be immunized from competition – rescued from the prospect of failure – and they were to recognize individual merit and excellence within. Mill always recognized the importance of pride of

ownership; specifically, he quoted the following view: "Give a man the secure possession of a bleak rock, and he will turn it into a garden; give him
a nine years' lease of a garden, and he will convert it into a desert."[63] He
insisted that peasant proprietorships foster efficiency, self-respect, and respect for the institution of private property. He supported the Poor Laws
of 1834 (orchestrated by Nassau Senior), insisting that the standard of
living of the pauper should be less than that of the lowest wage earner
and that relief should be given in a workhouse with limited amenities, the
separation of men from women, and menial tasks to perform. Welfare was
not to be an attractive alternative to hard work, the work that helped to
promote a sense of autonomy. Where and when Mill did consider public
intervention, the general rule was always focused on restricting to the narrowest compass the intervention of a public authority in the business of the
community. George Holyoake, the founder of Rochdale, was so heartened
by these remarks that he republished parts of Mill's work in his weekly
publication, *The Reasoner*. However, both Mill and Harriet were deeply
offended by his adding a preface in which he welcomed the support of a
"militant atheist" like Mill.

Mill's advocacy of cooperatives went back as far as 1834. In the 1848
edition of the *Principles*, he advocated partnership because the law at
that time did not permit suits against corrupt managers of cooperative
ventures. During the 1850s, there was much interest in cooperatives among
the middle class as a result of the experiments in France. In the 1852
edition, Mill added the following:

> The form of association . . . which, if mankind [continued] to improve, must be
> expected in the end to predominate, is not that which can exist between a capitalist
> as chief, and workpeople without a voice in the management, but the association
> of the labourers themselves on terms of equality, collectively owning the capital
> under which they carry on their operations, and working under managers elected
> and removable by themselves.[64]

In his review of Help's *Claims of Labour* (1845), he had identified workers
who were trying "to make themselves capitalists."[65] It was always Mill's
belief that the establishment of cooperatives might enable democracy to
avoid tyranny. Does this mean that Mill favored industrial democracy?
This can hardly be the case, given Mill's critique of democracy. What he
was suggesting was an economic enterprise in which all the participants
had an entrepreneurial interest. In a letter to Harriet (February 7, 1854),

Mill criticized the *Examiner* for dismissing profit sharing because allegedly it would "retard society in its natural growth."

Besides production and distribution, another functional pair of economic concepts that Mill considered was competition and cooperation and their relationship to alienation. Alienation is a special problem in the modern world because, unlike the classical and medieval worlds, modernity rejects the conception of a collective good in favor of the notion of an individual good. The loss of the sense of a greater whole constitutes alienation. Mill, like Hegel and T. H. Green, among others, sought to formulate some conception of a common good (not a collective good) that cohered with the notion of an individual good. For Mill, the common good was the cultivation of personal autonomy in ourselves and in others. That is why Mill could raise the possibility of public (specifically governmental) efforts to promote autonomy in everyone. Toward this end, Mill believed that competition (something he always defended) was compatible with cooperation, and in fact was itself a form of cooperation. Competition, both economic and otherwise, promoted personal autonomy and created the wealth that served as a resource that others could use to pursue their autonomy.

Unlike the Christian socialists, who rejected competition and tried to restore feudal paternalism, Mill wanted competition both inside and outside the cooperative:

I utterly dissent from the most conspicuous part of their teaching, their declamations against competition. . . . They forget that wherever competition is not, monopoly is; and that monopoly, in all its forms, is the taxation of the industrious for the support of indolence, if not rapacity. They forget too, that with the exception of competition among labourers, all other competition is for the benefit of the labourers, by cheapening the articles they consume; that competition even in the labour market is a source not of low but of high wages, wherever the competition *for* labour exceeds the competition *of* labor, as in America.[66]

He also maintained that "no one can foresee the time when it [competition] will not be indispensable to progress."[67] Although Mill and Harriet agreed with the socialists on the value of cooperatives, neither accepted their critique of competition.[68]

This brings us to the question of how Mill understood the role of government with regard to the economy. In his essay *On Liberty*, Mill would maintain that liberty in the marketplace differs from personal liberty. The latter is more generic, because autonomy is more basic than efficiency. In the *Principles*, he takes up the question of the grounds and limits of laissez-faire. Mill was generally favorable to laissez-faire but, at the same time, allowed for a potentially limited role for government. Mill advocated freedom (understood as autonomy or self-government) as the only intrinsic end, with laissez-faire justified as a means to it. Deviations from laissez-faire could be justified only if they led to increases in individual freedom and personal responsibility. Mill, following Tocqueville, had as his greatest fear the rise of rampant democracy. If the adversarial relation between employers and employees continued, and if the employees (labor) achieved the right to vote, then private property might disappear altogether. Mill sought to obviate that possibility by making labor more hospitable to a regime of private property. To the extent that he contemplated government action, he saw it as a means to this end. With regard to the role of the government, it is generally conceded that at no time was Mill an advocate of central planning. He even articulated the Hayekian principle that central planning was rationally impossible. Consistent with his later position in *On Liberty*, it is clear that the onus is always "on those who recommend government interference. *Laissez-faire*, in short, should be the general practice: every departure from it unless required by some great good, is a certain evil"[69]

Believing with M. Comte that there are no absolute truths in the political art, nor indeed in any art whatever, we agree with him that the *laissez-faire* doctrine, stated without large qualifications, is both unpractical and unscientific; but it does not follow that those who assert it are not, nineteen times out of twenty, practically nearer the truth than those who deny it.[70]

He distinguished, first, between necessary and optional intervention. Necessary (legislative) intervention includes taxes for government activity itself – enforcing contracts, maintaining order, national defense, protecting against force and fraud; the precise limits of this kind of intervention cannot be determined by any universal rule except "the simple and vague one, that it should never be admitted but when the case of expediency is strong."[71] Optional (executive or administrative) intervention can be either coercive ("authoritative") or a form of public service ("nonauthoritative"). Because optional intervention can be coercive, even if it is expedient, we need to be wary of violations of liberty. In short, the cure could be worse than the disease. Efficient authoritative intervention is a "much more limited sphere of legitimate action than the other."[72] Authoritative intervention is permissible only in cases where individuals cannot know their interests and the means to attain them better than the government or some other public agency. He advocated, for example, government financing of public schools if there were no other way to provide such schooling. He permitted government regulation in certain areas, such as labeling, where the consumer is an incompetent judge.

Freedom always overrides efficiency. Where a natural monopoly has to be established – for example, the municipal water supply – Mill thought that government regulation of private agency was better than government operation of the enterprise, even when less efficient. He was opposed in principle to centralization (all arguments in *On Liberty*), even if it was more efficient. In a letter to Pasquale Villari, he wrote: "[T]he little tract [Land Tenure Reform Association] has been reviewed in the Deux Mondes by a person so ignorant of my opinions as to call me a partisan of extreme centralization. It is about the last reproach I should have expected."[73] The test of any policy was whether it rendered individuals independent of all assistance and promoted self-help.[74] For Mill, the ultimate question was always liberty, not efficiency. He always favored "leaving to voluntary associations all such things as they are competent to perform . . . [even] if it were certain that the work itself would be as well or better done by public officers."[75] Mill did not support any form of intervention in an a priori or timeless fashion. There is no policy position that he would not retract if circumstances changed. This should be kept in mind when discussing specific examples.

Among the economic policies that Mill favored were piecework, not daily wages; no tax on capital; free trade; no government interference with either strikes or lockouts; death duties only on *landed* estates; and a flat tax – otherwise we penalize thrift.[76] He preferred a rate tax (real estate tax) to an income tax, an inheritance tax to compel all to work,[77] and no breakup of viable large industrial enterprises.[78] Public ownership, where necessary, did not imply state management.[79] He believed that the current system of property was unjust and inefficient and needed to be reformed. He preferred "to restrict, not what any one might bequeath, but what any one should be permitted to acquire, by bequest or inheritance."[80] He did not think it consistent to have property in natural resources; he advocated proportional taxation on income and investment but a graduated tax on gifts, inheritances, resource rents, and windfalls.

How then shall we label Mill's position? It is not the label, of course, but the meaning we attach to it that is crucial. The difficulty contemporary readers have is that we tend to read back into the labels a meaning that they simply did not have for Mill. What Mill is defending is the modern liberal state or modern liberal culture, with its commitment to the technological project, a more or less free market economy, limited government, the rule of law, individual rights, and a culture of autonomy. It would be highly misleading to call Mill an economic libertarian, if by a libertarian we mean someone who limits the role of government to that of the night watch-man. Mill believes in limited government, but *what* limits depend upon context and circumstance. It would be misleading to call him a defender of capitalism, if by capitalism we mean what Marx meant by the term. On the other hand, Mill is a kind of capitalist in advocating a world in which the gap between employers and employees is eliminated by having all be-come entrepreneurs. It would be misleading to call him a socialist in the contemporary sense, if by socialism we mean centralized governmental control of the economy. He is a "utopian socialist" in the mid-nineteenth-century sense of making everyone a member of the entrepreneurial class.

Mill was somewhat surprised by the reaction to the first edition of the *Principles of Political Economy*. Many of his readers seemed to have missed the point. It is no wonder that this was the case, given the fact that Mill was critiquing and trying to transcend all of the extant positions. In a strange sort of way, the *Principles* was a success in part because it appealed, like the *Logic*, to different and conflicting constituencies – to those who saw it as a defense of capitalism and to those who, like the Kingsleys, saw it as an endorsement of Christian socialism. Mill claimed in his *Autobiography* that his attitude toward socialism was expressed "less clearly and fully in the first edition [1848], rather more so in the second [1849], and quite unequivocally in the third [1852]."[81] In the second edition (1849), he introduces the discussion of Fourier, noting that Fourierism is not usually recognized as a form of socialism because it "does not contemplate the abolition of private property."[82] In the posthumously published *Chapters on Socialism*, Mill would identify the Fourier scheme as precisely the kind of limited experiment worth trying. Mill felt that he had given the wrong impression in previous editions. The Preface to the third edition (1852) makes clear to his readers that what Mill was trying to achieve was an even-handed critique of all forms of economic organization, and that he retained an open mind with regard to socialistic experiments. Two letters bring this out:

The *North Atlantic Review* gives a totally false idea of the book and of its author when he makes me a participant in the derision with which he speaks of Socialists of all kinds and degrees. I have expressed temperately and argumentatively my objections to the particular plans proposed by Socialists for dispensing with private property; but on many other important points I agree with them. (November 1848)[83]

To his German translator, he wrote:

I observe in your preface you recommend the book to your readers as a refutation of Socialism: I certainly was far from intending that the statement it contained of the objections to the best known Socialist schemes should be understood as a condemnation of Socialism regarded as the ultimate result of human improvement, & further consideration has led me to attach much less weight than I did even to those objections, with one single exception – the unprepared state of the labouring classes & their extreme moral unfitness at present for the rights which Socialism would confer & the duties it would impose. (March 18, 1852)[84]

Hayek suggested a thesis later developed by Gertrude Himmelfarb about the influence of Harriet on Mill with regard to economic matters. The thesis is that Mill was initially more favorably inclined toward a free market economy but that Harriet bullied him into toning down his objections to socialism and eventually into embracing socialism. The later critique of socialism in the *Chapters on Socialism* was supposedly evidence of Mill's return to a free market position after Harriet's death. The evidence for this thesis lies in a series of letters written about the revisions to the *Principles of Political Economy*.[85]

There are three main objections to this thesis. First, there is a serious misunderstanding of what the term "socialism" meant for Mill. Hayek presupposes that what Harriet and Mill meant by "socialism" was incompatible with a free market economy. There is no reason to believe this. Mill was, as we have pointed out, a "utopian socialist." Second, what was debated in those letters was the likelihood of achieving near-universal autonomy in the foreseeable future. The question was whether most workers were now ready to participate even in a cooperative! In order for a cooperative to function, the co-owner workers must learn to cooperate in a joint venture without external coercion. Feudal organizational principles were inefficient. This was recognized even by capitalists. As Mill put it, "capitalists are almost as much interested as labourers in placing the operations of industry on such a footing, that those who labour may feel the same interest in the work they perform, which is felt by those who labour for themselves."[86] While Mill did tone down his objections to "socialism," he did not eliminate them. A careful reading of the letters shows Mill arguing with Harriet about whether the inclusion or exclusion of certain arguments would obscure or obfuscate these distinctions. Moreover, Mill pointed out in a letter to Harriet how difficult it is to overcome selfishness. "I cannot persuade myself that you do not greatly overrate the ease of making people unselfish."[87] Finally, in the *Autobiography* (the part of the draft that Harriet did edit), the following was left standing: Universal autonomy can be achieved "only by slow degrees, and a system of culture prolonged through successive generations"[88] Writing in another context during this period, Mill reiterated his concern for the autonomy of the working class:

[T]he commonest self-control for one's own benefit – that power of sacrificing a present desire to a distant object or a general purpose which is indispensable for making the actions of the individual accord with his own notions of his individual good; even this is most unnatural to the undisciplined human being; as may be seen by the long apprenticeship which children serve to it ... and the marked absence of the quality in ... a somewhat less degree in nearly the whole of the poorer classes in this and many other countries. ... [Although it] requires a course of teaching, it is more susceptible of being self-taught. ... Nature does not of herself bestow this, anymore than other virtues; but nature often administers the rewards and punishments which cultivate it, and which in other cases have to be created artificially for the express purpose.[89]

The third reason for resisting Hayek's hypothesis is that it does not explain why the changes were not introduced until the second and third editions. If Harriet had such a great influence, if she was intimately involved in the composition of the *Principles* – especially in the chapter on the future of the working class – why would the alleged promotion of socialism arise only after the publication of the first edition?

Himmelfarb,[90] repeating Hayek's error, has made much of Harriet's influence (via correspondence) on Mill's allegedly changing his mind, the assumption being that Harriet made Mill far more radical. It is difficult to see that. It would be ridiculous to maintain that Mill suddenly started supporting "socialism" in the later editions. The only form of socialism that Mill ever seriously considered endorsing was a form of workers' cooperative. He had always done so. Under Harriet's influence, Mill softened the tone of criticism. He retracted some of his objections – for example, considering the possibility that in a cooperative community there might be more pressure to prevent people from reproducing needlessly – but he still expressed concern about freedom. He added a section on Fourier, but the Fourier version of socialism retained private property. He admitted that some of the obstacles to the success of the cooperatives might be removed, but he did not say that all would be so, and he still insisted that the goal should be improvement of the present system. In all of the editions, he indicates how the present capitalist system might accommodate the problems at issue: "*The object to be principally aimed at in the present stage of human improvement, is not the subversion of the system of individual property, but the improvement of it, and the full participation of every member of the community in its benefits.*"[91] [italics mine] Mill pointed out how incentives can be improved under capitalism – for example, by using profit-sharing – and how middlemen can be eliminated through consumer cooperatives. He noted that cooperatives might not be able to compete in international markets and that even if there can be equality of reward, there cannot be equality of input without a price system: "The produce might be divided equally, but how could the labour? There are many kinds of work, and by what standard are they to be measured one against the other?"[92]

What is overlooked in this debate about Mill's revisions are the events of 1848. Up until the late 1830s, Mill still had thought that government leadership was crucial. He had been sympathetic to the calls of elitism; he had agreed with Tocqueville that one of the dangers of democracy was that it led to the leadership of mediocre men, for great men came only from a leisured class. By 1847, Mill had changed his mind. Writing to Austin, he said, "I have even ceased to think that a leisured class, in the ordinary sense of the term, is an essential constituent of the best form of society. What does seem to me essential is that society at large should not be overworked, nor over-anxious about the means of subsistence."[93]

The most overlooked fact about Mill's revisions is that they were prompted by the French Revolution of 1848. Once more, just as he had in 1830, Mill became overly enthusiastic about the prospects of social and political change in France.[94] He wrote on those events not only in his essay

"The French Revolution of 1848" but in numerous articles and letters.[95] Writing to Henry Samuel Chapman, a former associate at the *Westminster Review* then living in New Zealand, Mill asserted that "the whole problem of modern society will be worked out, as I have long thought it would, in France and nowhere else."[96] Moreover, Mill believed that the role of labor was the crucial element in the Revolution. In 1847, Tocqueville had already proclaimed that the coming struggle would be between the "haves" and the "have nots," that "property will form the great field of battle; and the principal political questions will turn upon the more or less important modifications to be introduced into the right of property."[97] In a letter to Sarah Austin, Mill reiterated not only that "the most striking thing in these memorable events is the evidence afforded of the . . . unanimous acquiescence of all France in a Republic," but also that "[t]here will be a good deal of experimental legislation, some of it not very prudent, but there cannot be a better place to try such experiments in than France. I suppose that regulation of industry in behalf of labourers must go through its various phases of abortive experiment . . . before it is abandoned, or its proper limits ascertained."[98]

The Revolution of 1848 had a strong socialist dimension. The socialist writer Louis Blanc was a member of the provisional government. Mill saw two sides forming in France, the "friends of 'order' and the Socialists." He conceded that the socialists had "generally very wild and silly notions and little one can sympathize with except the spirit and feelings which actuate them." But what was needed were "rational principles on which to construct an order of society which, retaining the institution of private property" nevertheless facilitated "all possible experiments for dispensing with it by means of association" and eventually would "hurl all inequalities out necessarily inherent in that institution."[99] His great fear was that the socialist cause would not get a fair hearing,[100] that the typical English response to French socialism would be "in crushing it down, and preventing it from being mooted at all."[101] The underlying economic issues would not be addressed or resolved, and the end result would be universal disaster.

It was in the second edition of the *Principles of Political Economy* (1849) that Mill mentioned Fourier for the first time, claiming that "the most skillfully combined, and with the greatest foresight of objection, of all the forms of Socialism, is that commonly known as Fourierism."[102] It was also in this edition that he specifically mentioned the French

Revolution of 1848.[103] In 1850, Mill testified before a committee in Parliament that experiments were important "in the way of education to the working classes, both intellectually and morally."[104] This reinforces Mill's concern, expressed to Harriet, about whether the workers were ready for the challenges of a cooperative. Mill would continue to stress the importance of socialist experimentation in his review of Newman's *Political Economy* in 1851.[105] This was a theme he repeated in the third edition (1852) of the *Principles*: "The thing to be desired, and to which they have a just claim, is opportunity of trial."[106] It is clear, then, that the revisions to the second and third editions were not prompted by the pernicious presence of Harriet's whimsical and sudden lurch to the left but rather by events in France.

In the minds of Mill and Harriet, the revolutions on the continent in 1848 made it all the more imperative that Britain respond to the serious problems of the Industrial Revolution. Mill never changed his mind on the potential threat to liberty.[107] Mill always remained concerned about whether most people could operate with higher motives, concerns he would repeat in the *Chapters on Socialism*. We would have to conclude, with Hollander, that he made no substantive modification to the *Principles of Political Economy* between 1849 and 1852.[108] Lord Robbins is right in calling this "a plea for an open mind."[109] Against the interpretation that Mill moved gradually from nonintervention to intervention, Schwartz has maintained instead that Mill

started with an inclination in favor of State interference, let it wax stronger under Continental influence, then in the forties reacted against interventionism, helped by his contacts with Tocqueville; and finally, by 'incessantly weaving anew the fabric of his old and taught opinions' was able to combine the claims of an active State with those of liberty into a single edifice of thought.[110]

We would concur with Schwartz's view about the evolution of Mill's economic thought. In the beginning, Mill accepted his father's views on economics and politics. He began politically as a radical, favoring democracy as the cure for political and economic problems. During the 1830s, under the influence of Carlyle, Saint-Simon, and conservatives such as Coleridge, he adopted a more authoritarian and elitist stance. The subsequent reading of Tocqueville led Mill to understand that democracy was inevitable and that it was itself fueled by the growth of a market economy. Authoritarian and elitist responses had become irrelevant. Inspired by Harriet in the 1840s, Mill came to believe more than ever that both economic and political institutions were subordinate to a great moral end – namely, autonomy. Political and economic institutions were to be evaluated based upon their contribution to, and if possible structured to promote, autonomy. Economically, this meant expanding market opportunities for workers; to the extent that politics intervened in economic processes, its raison d'être was the promotion of more entrepreneurship and thereby of more autonomy.

We may summarize Mill's economic views as follows. Wealth is a means to personal autonomy (a necessary but not sufficient condition); all other explications of a free market economy will doom that economy. Wealth is best promoted by private property; central planning is impossible and inefficient; autonomy limits state action; redistribution is justified only to the extent that it promotes autonomy (usually through increasing productivity) and not equality. It is never wrong to contemplate redistribution as long as it is viewed as an open question (e.g., schooling for children of poor workers; redistributing land in Ireland, with compensation). He was opposed to militant unionism as inimical to autonomy, and he was opposed to a workers' party. What he wanted was a society in which all were entrepreneurs (i.e., one in which there was no owner-vs.-worker distinction).

Given Mill's contention that a commercial and industrial market economy made liberty available to the masses for the first time in history, and given Mill's continued concern that a liberal culture could not survive unless the moral underpinnings of liberty were grasped by the masses, it becomes clear why he suggested some sort of public role to bring those values to the attention of the masses. Here we should emphasize the importance of intermediate institutions and the fact that government programs often not only fail but actually undermine these institutions. Given Mill's conception of political economy as a policy science that seeks to explicate the workings of the market in a given historical context, it became clear why he does not and could not offer timeless solutions to social problems. Nevertheless, what remains clear is his identification of the major policy problems confronting political economy for those who embrace the importance of liberty.

Mill's response to the issues of his day, his suggested public policies, always reflected his fundamental commitment to the principle of autonomy. He was never opposed to the production of wealth. He did, however, see it from a moral point of view. As Collini points out,

the individual is not primarily regarded as a member of a political community, but
as an already private (though not thereby selfish) moral agent whose mastering
of his circumstances is indirectly a contribution to the vitality and prosperity of
his society. Here the getting of wealth, even in quite substantial quantities, is a
salutary experience, provided the emphasis is placed on the getting.[111]

The origin of the problems of the working class was their relatively recent
emergence from feudalism. As a remnant of feudalism, they had failed to
develop a sense of individuality. The remedies proposed by Mill included
(a) private, voluntary promotion of the ideal of individuality; (b) carefully
circumscribed intervention (e.g., loans to cooperatives); (c) rhetoric, that
is, public speech designed to promote autonomy; and (d) defense and
cultivation of institutions that promote autonomy (e.g., the family), and
especially full equality, and autonomy for women.

Death of John Taylor

The decade from 1840 to 1850 is the time during which Mill achieved the
worldly success he craved. Specifically, it was the decade of the publication of the *System of Logic* (1843) and the *Principles of Political Economy*
(1848). The success of the first work established Mill as the preeminent
philosopher in Great Britain, one who had achieved an integrated view
of the physical sciences and the application of its methods to the social
sciences and public policy. The success of the second work established
Mill and his book as the intellectual authority in economics and political
economy for the next half-century.

In the midst of great success, life was also filled with major annoyances,
and unexpected surprises, even of a tragic nature. In 1848, while entering
Hyde Park, Mill tripped over a loose paving brick and injured his back.
The doctor applied a belladonna plaster to the injury. Uncomfortable
with the plaster, Mill removed it but inadvertently touched his eyes. As a
result, he suffered a temporary impairment of his vision, and he needed
the assistance of others for some time to help with his correspondence and
duties at India House.

During the spring of 1849, both Mill and John Taylor began to experience health problems. Mill took an extended health leave from India
House, and Harriet joined him in the Pyrenees for a leisurely journey back

to Paris. Harriet advised Mr. Taylor, known for his frequent overindulgence in food and wine, to go to Brighton for a change of air. By the time Harriet returned to the Taylor residence at Kent Terrace in May, it was only to discover that Mr. Taylor was dying of cancer. John Taylor died on July 18, 1849. Always concerned with propriety, Harriet and Mill agonized over whether Mill should attend the funeral. In the end, it was decided that he should not. Harriet's feelings toward her former husband are best summed up in her own words: "Alas, poor thing, what a mocking life has been to him! Ending in this fierce contest in which death gains inch by inch! The sadness and horror of Nature's daily doings exceed a million fold all the attempts of Poets! There is nothing on earth I would not do for him & there is nothing on earth which *can* be done."[112]

Carlyle and Racism

That same year, in December of 1849, Carlyle published his "Occasional Discourse on the Negro Question" in *Fraser's Magazine*. Having become more than ever an apologist for the status quo, Carlyle accused black people in Jamaica of being lazy, and he derided those who were appalled at their harsh treatment. Britain had ended slavery in 1835. In this article, Carlyle used the expression "the dismal science" to characterize political economy.[113] By that he meant "black science"! What Carlyle espoused was the doctrine that black people were natural slaves in the old Aristotelian sense, namely, that they were constitutionally unable to govern themselves and therefore needed to be directed by others. This view was consistent with Carlyle's defense of a feudal hierarchical society. What Carlyle resented was the role that classical political economists had played in the abolition of slavery. The antislavery movement in Britain had always been a movement among middle-class dissenters, both those dissenting in the religious sense and those who argued for independence. The economists had added to the moral argument the technical case that free labor was more productive than slave labor. A prominent member of both the religious dissenting community and the community of economists was Harriet Martineau. In 1853, Carlyle would expand the essay and publish it separately with a change in title, calling it this time *Occasional Discourse on the Nigger Question*.

Carlyle was one of a group of several literary figures who espoused a belief in racial differences. The others included Kingsley and Anthony

Trollope. Their views were supported by the anthropologist James Hunt. Kingsley was also the author of the novel *Alton Locke*, which served not only as a classic critique of the rising commercial society but expressed the latent anti-Semitism often to be found in this critique. Recall that in the background the seminal figure in the defense of the rising commercial classes and an ardent critic of the feudal landed aristocracy was the Jewish-born banker and writer David Ricardo.

Mill was outraged! Not only did he vehemently disagree with Carlyle's views, but he took the essay as a personal affront and as an expression of resentment at the success of his *Principles of Political Economy*. In that work, Mill had defended the Irish against a similar charge that they were inferior human beings. Mill fired back in the very next issue of *Fraser's*. He excoriated Carlyle for subscribing to the doctrine that "one kind of human beings are born servants to another kind." Mill also put forward the following Afrocentric hypothesis:

[T]he earliest known civilization was, we have the strongest reason to believe, a negro civilization. The original Egyptians are inferred, from the evidence of their sculptures, to have been a negro race: it was from negroes, therefore, that the Greeks learnt their first lessons in civilization; and to the records and traditions of these negroes did the Greek philosophers to the very end of their career resort (I do not say with much fruit) as a treasury of mysterious wisdom.[114]

Mill concluded by noting that Carlyle's essay would likely have a deleterious effect on the antislavery movement in the United States: "The words of English writers of celebrity are words of power on the other side of the ocean; and the owners of human flesh . . . will welcome such an auxiliary. . . . I hardly know of an act by which one person could have done so much mischief. . . . by thus acting, he [Carlyle] has made himself an instrument of. . . . 'a true work of the devil'."[115]

By 1850, both Mill and Harriet were preoccupied with health problems. Nevertheless, the world for them was completely different from the one they had encountered at the beginning of the decade. Mill had achieved the intellectual and political stature he craved, and he now had the undivided attention of the great love of his life.

8

Private Years (1850–1859)

Marriage

MILL AND HARRIET had carried on an "affair" of extraordinary intimacy, heroic sexual abstinence, and scrupulous concern for both privacy and the appearance of propriety for twenty years. Now that John Taylor had died, it would seem that Mill and Harriet could simply marry and leave the past behind them. On the contrary, nothing would prove more difficult.

To begin with, the mere fact of getting married would serve to confirm all of the old rumors that malicious gossips had been spreading about them for years. In an ironic way, legalizing and consummating their relationship would give credence to those who had sought in one way or another to delegitimate their earlier relationship. Second, both Mill and Harriet had been very critical of marriage relationships, so that taking the step of getting married would require both acquiescence in an institution of which they had been critical in print and symbolic gestures to indicate the extent to which their marriage was not to be a merely conventional one. Finally, the redefinition of relationships with others, especially for Mill, was extremely complicated. Emotionally, they had been dependent solely on each other for some time. His best and closest friend, Sterling, had died, and the same was true for Harriet – Eliza had passed away. Mill and Harriet had wrapped themselves in a cocoon of seeming propriety in isolation from others, and they now found that making a public declaration was the hardest thing to do.

Some time earlier, Harriet had written an essay entitled "Enfranchisement of Women," in which she had argued for complete equality between men and women. Mill approached W. E. Hickson, the man to whom he had sold the *Westminster Review*, and presented the essay to him unsigned.

That is, Mill deliberately obfuscated the fact that the essay was Harriet's. Hickson published it in July of 1851. When the subsequent editor, John Chapman, and his assistant, the famous George Eliot, wanted to reprint it, Mill and Harriet refused to grant permission. When Holyoake reprinted it without permission, for distribution among the working classes, Mill and Harriet were outraged. On the surface, their claim was that the essay was not "the best we could do, or the real expression of our mind on the subject."[1] One surmises that *The Subjection of Women* was the promised sequel. After Harriet's death, Mill acknowledged the essay as hers alone and reprinted it as such in his *Dissertations and Discussions*. Was Mill embarrassed by the deliberate obfuscation of the authorship? Was Mill protecting Harriet from public exposure, something she dreaded as she fought her own internal battles to reconcile the appearance of propriety with the desire to hold and advocate radical views? Is Harriet the very model of the person Mill later came to describe in *On Liberty* as the person of enlightened views who is dissuaded from pronouncing them publicly for fear of public pressure? Is this event a significant illustration of how much Harriet needed and admired Mill because of his fearless integrity in espousing unpopular public opinions? We think all of these things are true.

Much to his consternation, Mill was reminded that marriage meant legally that he was entitled to control the financial assets that Harriet had inherited from John Taylor. Appalled at this prospect, he wrote the following on March 6, 1851:

Being about, if I am so happy to obtain her consent, to enter into the marriage relation with the only woman I have ever known, with whom I would have entered into that state; & the whole character of the marriage relation as constituted by law being such as both she and I entirely & conscientiously disapprove, for this amongst other reasons, that it confers upon one of the parties to the contract, legal power & control over the person, property, & freedom of action of the other party, independent of her own wishes and will; I, having no means of legally divesting myself of these odious powers (as I most assuredly would do if an engagement to that effect could be made legally binding on me) feel it my duty to put on record a formal protest against the existing law of marriage, in so far as conferring such powers; and a solemn promise never in any case or under any circumstances to use them. And in the event of marriage between Mrs. Taylor and me I declare it to be my will and intention, & the condition of the engagement between us, that she retains in all respects whatever the same absolute freedom of action, & freedom of disposal of herself and of all that does or may at any time belong to her, as if no such marriage had taken place; and I absolutely disclaim & repudiate all pretension to have acquired any rights whatever by virtue of such marriage.[2]

The time had come for Mill to inform his family, with whom he was still living, that he intended to marry Harriet. What complicated the making public of this seemingly happy event was that up until then they (his mother and sisters) had not been allowed either to meet with Harriet or even to mention her name. The presumption is that at an earlier date, probably while James Mill was still alive, they had tried as a family to dissuade Mill from maintaining his relationship with Harriet. A polite silence was the truce at which they had arrived, and it was a silence they had honored for many years. Mill had introduced Harriet's two sons, Herbert and Algernon (known as Haji), to his family, but only as friends of his own brother George.

Mill abruptly and without explanation announced his impending marriage. The stunned family did not know how to react. Mill took offense at this response and at the fact that they did not go immediately to Kent Terrace to congratulate and warmly embrace Harriet. All of the pent-up resentment that Mill had harbored against the female members of his family, a resentment rooted in his early tutorial relationship with his sisters, his resentment against his mother's inability to make his father happy, perhaps his resentment at having to take care of them after his father's death, all of this erupted in an uncharacteristic expression of emotion and led to a fatal break with his family. Mill wanted what he thought that his father and most men had never had, a meaningful relationship with a woman. He had paid a heavy price in self-denial to achieve this goal, and when it appeared in sight, he felt betrayed by his family. Beneath the forbidding exterior that Mill had cultivated as a defense mechanism against the world was a deeply sensitive soul in search of a fulfilling romantic relationship.

Harriet tried to come to Mill's rescue. She persuaded him to go with her to visit his family in Kensington in order to patch things up. Unfortunately, his sister Clara refused to leave her room to greet Harriet. Several days later, when Clara had regained her composure and finally decided to visit Harriet at Kent Terrace, Mill turned her away at the door! When his mother appeared at his office at India House to plead with him to repair the break, she was rebuffed.

As if to make matters worse, Mill's brother George, who had always looked up to Mill and approved of his relationship with Harriet as a challenge to social humbug, disapproved of the marriage, but for very different reasons. Writing to Harriet's son Algernon, with whom he had become friendly as a result of earlier travels together with Mill and Harriet, George Mill expressed disappointment that Mill and Harriet had betrayed their principled objections to social convention! With their emotions already seriously frayed, Mill and Harriet were displeased when they discovered the letter and so informed George, with whom they thereafter cut off all future contact. Mill was especially hurt by what he perceived as George's lack of loyalty. Mill had in fact previously sponsored George's employment at India House in 1844. George's own bout with consumption had led to his retirement in 1850. He was to die in Madeira in 1853.

Mill and Harriet were married on Easter Monday of 1851 by the registrar of Melcombe Regis near Weymouth. The only witnesses were Harriet's two children, Helen and Algernon. Finally, Mill and Harriet were able to consummate their relationship. Much speculation has been given over to whether in fact they had a sex life in any sense of that term. The gossips of their own time have not hesitated to suggest that they had always been sexually intimate. Others have suggested just the opposite – namely, that Mill and Harriet never had a sex life either before or after their marriage, the latter being the result of their health problems. Not a scrap of evidence exists for either one of these extreme speculations. There is no reason to believe that the truth is other than what Mill reports in his *Autobiography*, which was thereby subscribed to by Harriet as well. Complete intimacy or "union," what Mill called a "partnership of our entire existence," did occur after their marriage. Mill speaks in the *Autobiography* of

my marriage, [i]n April 1851, to the lady whose incomparable worth had made her friendship the greatest source to me both of happiness and of improvement, during many years in which we never expected to be in any closer relation to one another. Ardently as I should have aspired to this complete union of our lives at any time in the course of my existence at which it had been practicable, I, as much as my wife, would far rather have foregone that privilege for ever, than have owed it to the premature death of one [John Taylor] for whom I had the sincerest respect, and she the strongest affection. . . . it was granted to me to derive from that evil my own greatest good, by adding to the partnership of thought, feeling, and writing which had long existed, a partnership of our entire existence.[3]

Mill was fond of Harriet's two sons, who had become friends of his own brother George. He introduced them to the works of all the great British philosophers, from Hobbes and Locke to Hume, and even to the works of James Mill. Mill even tried to obtain a position for Algernon with the East India Company, but without success. It was with Harriet's daughter Helen that a special relationship would later develop.

Feeling more than ever isolated from the world, Mill and Harriet withdrew from society. They leased a house in Blackheath Park, some seven miles from London, and – except for the presence of Helen and, in the first five years, of Harriet's son Algernon – lived a secluded life behind a wall of shrubbery. They hired a cook and had as pets some tame song birds and a Persian cat. Aside from his work at India House, Mill attended only the meetings of the Political Economy Club. He would allow Bain and Grote to walk with him to Charing Cross, from which he took the train to Blackheath. For seven years until Harriet's death, the only guests welcome at Blackheath were Fox and the foreigners Gomperz, Villari (an Italian philosopher), and the famous Mazzini. In his only act of domestic responsibility, Mill made tea on returning from work. Mill played the piano for Harriet, but only when they were alone. She was the only person before whom he felt he could express his emotions. Perhaps in this he recaptured the moments of intimacy he had felt as a child when Bentham had played the organ just for him. Sundays were given over to his hobby of botany, collecting specimens on long walks in the country. Looking back at this period, Algernon Taylor would recall that he "never knew him [Mill] to utter a cross word or show impatience in her [Harriet's] regard, nor to demur to any expressed wish on her part; and, it must be added, she no less considered his wishes in all things."[4]

Theodor Gomperz was an Austrian who, as well as being an accomplished classical scholar in his own right, had translated Mill's *Logic* into German and would later be responsible for the first collected edition of Mill's works. Gomperz described the atmosphere at Blackheath Park as one in which "complete spiritual freedom encompassed this tranquil family whose moral rectitude and spiritual pride seemed almost puritanical."[5]

Mill's letters to his mother during the ensuing few years were bitter in tone. In an attempt to heal the wound, Mill's sister Mary wrote to him on April 3, 1854:

My dear John,
My Mother is very unhappy because she thinks that she has not behaved well to your wife: She is constantly urging me to go to Blackheath and call on her, saying that it would please her very much, and nothing will divert her mind from this one point. She is still very weak, unable to stand, and thinks evidently that you are very angry with her and do not come to see her on that account. . . . We cannot of course intrude upon Mrs. John Mill unless she would wish to receive us. . . . Will you therefore either let me know what you think we had better do, or, for my mother's sake, write her a *few* lines . . . or in some way set her mind at ease.[6]

Mill wrote the following peeved letter to his mother in response:

My dear Mother,
I received . . . another of Mary's vulgar and insolent letters. The impertinence appears the only motive for writing them and I cannot waste my time in answering any more of them. In this she affects to think that I wish to see her. Will you tell her that neither I nor my wife will keep up any acquaintance with her whatever. I hope you are gaining strength and will soon be quite well again. When you are able to write will you let me know how you are. I need not say that we shall always be glad to see you. yrs. affy. J.S.M.[7]

He paid a perfunctory visit only once before her death in 1854. He was not at her bedside but away in Brittany when she died. He received the news of her death with detachment. In her will, his mother bequeathed to him some silver plate and the sum of £500. Mill offered the plate to his sisters but was rebuffed. The breach could not be healed.

Joint Productions

At about this time, both Mill and Harriet began to have serious health problems. Harriet had already experienced periodic bouts of paralysis for the past decade. The great health scourge of the nineteenth century was tuberculosis, also known as consumption. It was not known then that tuberculosis was an infectious disease caused by the tubercle bacillus. Instead, people mistakenly believed that it was a hereditary disease. Mill's circle was especially hard hit by it; it took the lives of his father, two brothers, Harriet's brother, John Sterling, and Eliza and Sarah Flower.

Tuberculosis bacteria affect not only people but also cattle, swine, and fowl. The bacteria can be spread through the respiratory system by close contact with an infected person, or gastrointestinally through the consumption of infected (nonpasteurized) milk. In the latter case, the disease spreads to the bones and joints. Given her symptoms, Harriet had quite possibly contracted the disease in this fashion. Nowadays there are a variety of drugs to treat tuberculosis. Until recently, however, bed rest was an important part of the cure. The frequent trips or medical leaves to the continent taken by both Mill and Harriet undoubtedly helped. Sometimes children contract the disease but do not show symptoms of it; sometimes they not only recover but also develop a subsequent immunity. As the disease progresses among the unfortunate, lung capacity decreases and the patient dies from failure of ventilation and exhaustion.

Mill began to have all of the symptoms of tuberculosis: a persistent cough, blood in his expectorant, and feverish night sweats. In 1854, he consulted Dr. Sir James Clark, physician in ordinary to Queen Victoria, who advised him that he had incurable consumption. Shortly thereafter, Mill read a book that had been published twenty years earlier by Dr. Francis Hopkins Ramadge entitled *Consumption Curable*. Mill then consulted Dr. Ramadge himself, who prescribed breathing through a metal trumpet three times a day in order to increase lung capacity. Although it was not understood at the time, increasing lung capacity also inhibited the growth of tubercules. Mill experienced a great improvement in the symptoms, but he remained convinced that he was in declining health and doomed to die of consumption. There is an entry in his diary in which he says that "the most disagreeable thing about dying is the intolerable ennui of it. There ought to be no slow deaths." [8] He would, of course, live for another nineteen years, but the shadow of death was never to leave him. Hereafter his letters to Harriet are filled with an obsessive concern for illness and symptoms.

In January of 1854, Mill began to keep a diary, ostensibly as an experiment in order to record one thought worth recording each day. But it is clear that the diary, whose last entry is April 15, was a record of his concern about the imminence of death. A large part reflects Mill's sense that he had not lived up to his own expectations. "I seem to have frittered away the working years of life in mere preparatory trifles, and now 'the night when no one can work' [John 9:4] has surprised me with the real duty of my life undone."[9] He was also worried about his posthumous reputation, noting that "there is hardly a more striking example of the worthlessness of posthumous reputation than the oblivion into which my father has fallen among the world at large."[10] Mill seemed to believe at the time that an enormous amount of intellectual talent had been wasted by humankind on "German metaphysics, the whole of Christian theology, and the whole of the Roman and English systems of technical jurisprudence."[11] The only consolation he found is the thought of "communion with those who are already what all well-organized human beings will one day be, and by the consciousness of oneself doing something, not altogether without value, toward helping on the slow but quickening progress towards that ultimate consummation."[12]

Aside from his responsibilities at India House, Mill did not take an active part in the great public issues of this decade. For example, he had little to say about the Crimean War, which lasted from 1853 to 1856 and in which Britain joined France and Turkey in opposing Russia. Mill detested the French leader Napoleon III for his usurpation of power in the coup d état of 1851. He also saw in Louis Napoleon a demagogue who had succeeded in being democratically elected, thereby exhibiting the dangers to which democracy was prone. It was an example not lost on Mill when he wrote the essay *On Liberty*. It was of course during this war that Florence Nightingale rose to prominence, someone whom Mill would later meet.

Mill and Harriet spent the winter of 1853–54 convalescing in France. Convinced that time was short, Mill and Harriet were persuaded that now was the time to commit everything they possibly could to writing. A great deal of time was spent in planning and drafting outlines of proposed works.

We must finish the best we have got to say, & not only that, but publish it while we are alive. I do not see what living depository there is likely to be of our thoughts, or who in this weak generation that is growing up will even be capable of thoroughly mastering & assimilating your ideas, much less of re-originating them – so we must write them & print them, & then they can wait until there are again thinkers. But I shall never be satisfied unless you allow our best book the book which is to come, to have our *two* names on the title page. It ought to be so with everything I publish, for the better half of it all is yours, but the book which will contain our best thoughts, if it has only one name to it, that should be yours. I should like everyone to know that I am the Dumont & you the originating mind, the Bentham, bless her.[13]

The "best book" to which Mill refers is his *Autobiography*. Preoccupied with this task of organization and writing, Mill published nothing major from *The Principles of Political Economy* (1848 and revised during the early 1850s) until the essay *On Liberty* in 1859, a year after Harriet's death.

Mill outlined his plans to Harriet in a letter dated February 7, 1854.

I finished the 'Nature' on Sunday as I expected. ["Nature" and "Utility of Religion" appeared in *Three Essays on Religion*, 1874; the third essay, "Theism," was written in 1869, long after Harriet's death, and reflects an important development in Mill's thought.] I am quite puzzled what to attempt next – I will just copy the list of subjects we made out in the confused order in which we put them down. Differences of Character (nation, race, age, sex, temperament) [*Representative Government*, 1861]. Love. Education of tastes. Réligion de l'Avenir [*Auguste Comte and Positivism*, 1865]. Plato ["Plato," *Edinburgh Review*, April 1866]. Slander. Foundation of Morals [*Utilitarianism*, 1861]. Utility of Religion. Socialism [*Chapters on Socialism*, 1891]. Liberty [*On Liberty*, 1859]. Doctrine that Causation Is Will [*Examination of Sir William Hamilton's Philosophy*, 1865]. To these I have now added from your letter, Family, and Conventional [*The Subjection of Women*, 1869].[14]

Under Harriet's watchful eye, Mill completed the first draft of the *Autobiography* in 1856. *Dissertations and Discussions* (also published in 1859, a year after Harriet's death) was a selected and revised version of the articles previously published in the *Westminster* and *Edinburgh Reviews*. Chapman, then serving as editor of the *Westminster*, encouraged Mill to write on Comte, whose *Système de philosophie positive* had recently been translated into English by Harriet Martineau. Harriet Mill discouraged Mill from taking on this project because she felt that he would be bound to say some favorable things about the translation written by the hated gossip Martineau.

Having acknowledged all of this frenetic activity, I am persuaded that, with two exceptions,[15] Mill had established the main problems he would work on for the remainder of his life. By that I mean that all of his subsequent publications, despite being his best-written (from a literary point of view), his most famous, and his most enduring works (*On Liberty*, *Utilitarianism*, *The Subjection of Women*) were either rewritten versions of earlier works or extensions and applications of ideas that he had developed during the two previous decades. One example will suffice to underscore this point. The central idea of *On Liberty* had already been expressed in the *Principles of Political Economy*:

Whatever theory we adopt respecting the foundation of the social union, and under whatever political institutions we live, there is a circle around every individual being, which no government, be it that of one, of a few, or of the many, ought to be permitted to overstep: there is a part of the life of every person who has come to years of discretion, within which the individuality of that person ought to reign uncontrolled either by any other individual or by the public collectively. That there is, or ought to be, some space in human existence thus entrenched around, and sacred from authoritative intrusion, no one who professes the smallest regard to human freedom or dignity will call in question: the point to be determined is, where the limit should be placed; how large a province of human life this reserved territory should include. I apprehend that it ought to include all that part which concerns only the life, whether inward or outward, of the individual, and does not affect the interests of others, or affects them only through the moral influence of example. With respect to the domain of the inward consciousness, the thoughts and feelings, and as much of external conduct as is personal only, involving no consequences, none at least of a painful or injurious kind, to other people; I hold that it is allowable in all, and in the more thoughtful and cultivated often a duty, to assert and promulgate, with all the force they are capable of, their opinion of what is good or bad, admirable or contemptible, but not to compel others to conform to that opinion; whether the force used is that of extra-legal coercion, or exerts itself by means of the law.

Even in those portions of conduct which do affect the interests of others, the onus of making out a case always lies on the defenders of legal prohibitions.[16]

The exception, the area in which Mill's thought would continue to progress, is in metaphysics and religion. Here he will struggle to bring his technical philosophy, especially in *Hamilton* (1865) and in the posthumously published religious essays, in line with his practical philosophy. And what this means, as we shall see in a subsequent chapter, is that the recognition of human freedom or autonomy in the highest sense required Mill to embrace the full Romantic implications of his philosophy and brought him much closer to the British Idealists who succeeded him.

Spurred on by the impending sense of the termination of life, Mill and Harriet lived an almost reclusive existence and worked together feverishly to plan and execute the remainder of what they took to be their intellectual legacy to the world. Although from the point of view of works actually published this was the least productive period in Mill's life, it was during this period that he drafted *On Liberty*, *The Subjection of Women*, *Representative Government*, the *Autobiography*, and *Utilitarianism*.

Of the *Autobiography*, the first six chapters were drafted by 1854 and edited in the early draft by Harriet; the final chapter would be written in 1869. Harriet and Mill were both intent upon vindicating the propriety of their relationship. It was always intended that the *Autobiography* be published posthumously as a way of defending Mill – especially his religious views – against his critics.

Having said all this about the motives behind the publication, we do not want to forget that the *Autobiography* is also intended as a *Bildungsroman*.[17] Some critics have argued that, in one way or another, the *Autobiography* is contrived and misleading.[18] These concerns raise several important issues. First, there is a question of fact. Are there facts about Mill's life that are misreported? There are, of course, different kinds of facts. There are dates that are fairly objective. This is not what the critics have in mind. There are other kinds of facts that are not mentioned in the *Autobiography*, such as Mill's relationship to his mother. That is, there are facts of omission. There are also facts that require interpretation, such as the report of Mill's crisis. It goes without saying that in writing an autobiography, as opposed to a biography, the author is interpreting and reinterpreting his life, something that we all do, regardless of whether we construct a formal narrative of our lives. Is there a real story to one's life, or do later events alter the meaning of earlier events? Isn't the interpretation we give to our lives itself a factor that influences our subsequent action and self-conception?

The term "autobiography" was first used by Southey in 1809. This is itself significant, as significant as the fact that the novel makes its appearance as a genre during the late eighteenth century. There were, in an important sense, no autobiographies prior to the nineteenth century. There were no autobiographies because to write an autobiography, as opposed to a biography written by the subject, is to interpret "the life of one's mind by imposing on past ideas an order derived from present ideas."[19] In order to write an autobiography in this sense, one has to believe that history (as opposed to nature, reason, or revelation) is the meaningful framework for understanding oneself. Clearly, this is a view that emerged only in the late eighteenth and nineteenth centuries, and it was a view to which Mill subscribed.[20] This underscores all the more the sense in which Mill was a Romantic who had moved away from the Enlightenment Project.

Nor is it history in some generic sense. Previous histories had understood the world and humanity either as a decline in the biblical sense or as an organic cycle in the classical Greek sense. This new conception of history sees the world and the story of mankind as an evolution in which later stages can give us a deeper understanding. Ideally, at least, in an autobiography we do not change our ordinary understanding of our lives but rather come to know it in a new and better way. There are those who would reject historical understanding in this sense as a meaningful category, and for them all autobiographies are therefore suspect. There are those who interpret human nature in terms of hidden structures – economic conditions (e.g., Marx), early and suppressed sexual experiences (e.g., Freud), or other social structures of which the agent is not necessarily aware. For them, all autobiographies are suspect. Unlike these detractors, Mill insisted in all of his writings that consciously held ideas are among the main forces that direct our lives. His writings are a forceful example of the influence of that belief and in that sense constitute confirmation of his contention. The most a critic, constructive or otherwise, can offer is an alternative analysis accompanied by the claim that the alternative analysis gives us access to a substructure of which Mill was either unaware or chose to suppress.

Whatever the merits of such alternative accounts, in themselves they fail to capture the essence of Mill's intellect. Mill conceived of the world and of humanity in terms of the Romantic conceptions of organism and history. Organic and human forms of order exhibit a temporal dimension; they are qualitatively transformed through time. It is not possible to deduce temporal transformations from spatial organization alone. The qualitative changes produced in an organic system by interaction with the surrounding environment become part of the organic system. The same is true of human historical systems, except that in historical systems, there must be a conscious or deliberate incorporation. In his essay "On Genius," Mill identified the genius not as someone who discovers new ideas but as someone who is able to incorporate old ideas and in so doing to transform himself or herself. "The most important phenomena of human nature cannot even be conceived, except by a mind which has actively studied itself. Believed they may be, but as a blind man believes the existence and properties of colour. To *know* these truths is also to *discover* them."[21]

The writing of the early essays on Bentham and Coleridge was presented as a deliberate exercise in the history of ideas and as a conscious attempt to achieve a new synthesis. Mill's *Logic* began with the insistence that logic is ultimately rooted in psychology, Mill's so-called psychologism. In 1859, Mill republished some of his earlier works in their original form in *Dissertations and Discussions*, "as memorials to the states of mind in which they were written, in the hope that they may possibly be useful to such readers as are in a corresponding stage of their own mental progress."[22] He chose to leave some out, but gave an account in the *Autobiography* of his principles of selection.

Mill's general views on history bear this out. Mill always had a love-hate relationship with the historian Macaulay, going back to Macaulay's critique of James Mill's essay *On Government*. In a letter to Harriet,[23] Mill described Macaulay as "an intellectual dwarf, rounded off and stunted, full grown broad & short, without a germ or principle of further growth in his whole being." Personalities aside, the important point is the lack in Macaulay, from Mill's point of view, of an evolutionary sense. In differentiating the stages of writing history, Mill identified three. First, there is the projecting of the present into the past (eighteenth-century Whigs); second, there is an attempt to see the past in its own terms (Carlyle, Michelet, Grote); finally, there is the science of history (Guizot), in which one sees the inherent norms calling out not only for identification but also for appropriation.

The imaginative identification of norms is a capacity that John Stuart Mill much admired, and it is a feature that explains his admiration for Harriet. Mill always saw the need to integrate art and reason.[24] It is in the "imagination" that one finds the integration. Harriet supplied more of this; Mill expressed his views in rational prose instead of in poetry, but this does not mean that he had not integrated the two. His own life is a synthesis of Enlightenment reason and Romantic imagination. Harriet, he thought, embodied that synthesis better than anyone else and helped him to achieve it.

Preoccupied with a sense of impending doom, Harriet and Mill pondered his possible retirement. They calculated that they would need an income of £500 annually in order to live comfortably in retirement, but they were not yet at that point. Among the places they considered living in retirement, of course, was France. In any case, all this talk of retirement coaxed India House to raise Mill's salary.

During the winter and spring of 1854–55, Mill returned to the continent while Harriet convalesced at Torquay. Mill revisited Montpellier, where he had spent one of the happiest years of his life with the family of Sir Samuel Bentham. He visited Avignon and fell in love with the place.

In January of 1855 he was in Rome; he visited the graves of Keats and
Shelley and attended mass at St. Peter's, where he caught sight of Pope
Pius IX, whom he and many others considered the great reactionary of
the nineteenth century. It was while climbing the steps of the capitol in
Rome that he was suddenly inspired to write the essay *On Liberty*.

On my way here cogitating thereon I came back to an idea we have talked about, &
thought that the very best thing to write & publish at present would be a volume
on Liberty. So many things might be brought into it & nothing seems more to
be needed – it is a growing need too, for opinion tends to encroach more & more
on liberty, & almost all the projects of social reformers of these days are really
liberticide – Comte's particularly so.[25]

Two days later, writing from Naples, Mill added:

We have got a power of which we must try to make a good use during the few years
of life we have left. The more I think of the plan of a volume on Liberty, the more
likely it seems to me that it will be read & will make a sensation. The title itself
with any known name to it would sell an edition. We must cram into it as much as
possible of what we wish not to leave unsaid.[26]

Mill continued his travels into Sicily and from there to the Greek island
of Corfu. He was much attracted to the island, where he discovered that the
colonial secretary, Bowen, had been a fellow at Brasenose and had read and
admired the *Logic*. Mill even entertained for a while the suggestion that
he could serve there as the British consul. He visited Greece and took in
all of the historic sights about which he had read, including Thermopylae,
Delphi, Parnassus, Athens, and Sparta, climbed mountains and collected
botanical specimens along the way. He returned to Italy and Florence,
where he spent some time with the Italian philosopher Pasquale Villari,
with whom he subsequently carried on a personal correspondence for
many years. He finally returned to Harriet in June of 1855.

Mill was greeted with new domestic concerns. Harriet's sister Caroline
was married to Arthur Ley, who served as trustee of the estate left to
Harriet and her children by John Taylor. Ley, however, was a drunkard
and abused his spouse in a brutal way. Caroline, however, continued to
defend her husband. The situation became unbearable to Harriet, who
broke with both her mother and sister over the matter.

At about this time, Harriet's daughter Helen Taylor, who had been
privy in a special way to the relationship between Harriet and Mill, took

an interest in acting. Being an actress was still a scandalous profession. Harriet reconciled herself to this career interest when Helen agreed to use the stage name "Miss Trevor." Helen had almost never left her mother's side. Her education consisted of a wide reading of the classics, including works by Madame de Staël, Jane Austen, and Maria Edgeworth. In a sense, she had always been groomed to be her mother's successor, and that is the role she would eventually play in a special way for Mill. Once more we note Harriet's excessive concern for the appearance of propriety. At the same time, this incident reinforces the perception of both Mill and Harriet that they lived in a society in which the choice of some occupations could lead to social ostracism or worse. All of his life Mill had felt the claustrophobic grip of British social life.

End of the East India Company

Mill had been employed by the East India Company since 1826. In 1856, Mill's superiors at the company, Hill and Peacock, retired. Mill was finally promoted to chief examiner, the position his father had held, a position equivalent to being a secretary of state. Thornton became Mill's assistant. However, Thornton soon became ill, and for an entire year Mill did Thornton's work as well as his own in order to protect Thornton from the threat of forcible retirement. He held that position until his retirement in 1858. For twenty-three years, Mill wrote the political dispatches of the company, producing annually "two huge volumes, five or six inches thick."[27] One of the great advantages of the position, in Mill's view, was that it left him with time to write! The other advantage was that it enabled him to combine knowledge and experience of the practical conduct of public affairs with his theoretical concerns.

Theodor Gomperz describes Mill at this time as follows:

> Mill was always the same – in his office at India House, buried under maps and files, at dinner with his friends, on top of a mountain, at the Political Economy Club, or in the wilds with his botanical box – his mind effortlessly drawn to the highest flight of ideas. At all times willing to enter in an interchange of question and answer, he yet was modest, and as unselfish as he was unaffected.[28]

In 1857, the famous Indian Mutiny occurred. Resentment against British control of India had been building for some time. The opposition came from two sources. As British influence and control were extended, the bureaucracy of the East India Company came more and more to increase its influence at the expense of the traditional Indian aristocracy of Brahmans. At the same time, both Hindus and Moslems felt threatened by the introduction of Western culture, especially through Christian missionaries. As part of a series of humanitarian reforms, Lord Dalhousie had tried to emancipate women by permitting Hindu widows to remarry.

The underlying resentment found an outlet in the revolt of Sepoy troops in the service of the British East India Company. In 1857, the new Enfield rifle was introduced. In order to load the lubricated cartridges, the end of each cartridge had to be bitten off. The cartridges, it seems – or at least it was alleged – were lubricated with lard from both pigs and cattle, thereby enraging both Moslems and Hindus. Moslems are forbidden to eat pork, and Hindus consider cattle to be sacred. The revolt was bloody, and it shook British rule on the subcontinent.

The British East India Company was embarrassed by the revolt, and its enemies at home took the occasion to challenge its role in the administration of India. The upshot of this controversy would be the termination of the East India Company, with the crown taking direct control of the governance of India. A few Indians would be allowed to serve on the Legislative Council, and the westernization of India would move even faster.

The East India Company had been faulted for its inefficiency and for its allegedly unimaginative commercialism. However, by 1857 the company no longer had any commercial monopolies in India; rather, it had become a largely bureaucratic structure responsible for the operation of a civil service, as well as for the Indian army and navy. Just as his father had been called upon many years before to defend the company, so Mill was now called upon to do likewise. He was paid an additional and remarkable sum of £10,000 for producing a defense that Lord Grey, who had met Mill in the debating society of their youth, described as the ablest state paper he had ever read.

Mill provided an eloquent defense of the role of the company in the governance of India. He opened his defense with the following remark:

Your petitioners, at their own expense, and by the agency of their own civil and military servants, originally acquired for this country its magnificent empire in the East. The foundations of this empire were laid by your petitioners, at that time neither aided nor controlled by Parliament, at the same period at which a succession of administrations under the control of Parliament were losing, by their incapacity and rashness, another great empire on the opposite side of the Atlantic.[29]

He went on to deny that the company was to blame for the mutiny, pointing instead to government interference and regulation. He expressed concern for the future of India if a newly appointed secretary of state for India were not limited or checked by an advisory council that was wholly independent. The company, he claimed, had served as just such a check. Mill was convinced that the East India Company was "the protector of the natives of India against the avarice & domineering spirit of rapacious European adventurers."[30] He had disapproved of the manner in which the mutiny was repressed[31] and believed that the move to abolish the company was caused by the unwillingness of the company to favor white residents over natives.[32] During his tenure, Mill had supported the move to involve native Indians in the administration in order to give them the experience of self-government.[33]

Mill's views on colonialism are important for three reasons. First, they reflect his experience of several decades with the East India Company's administration of what was, in effect, the largest colony of the largest colonial empire in the history of the world. Second, they reflect his understanding of and commitment to autonomy. Third, they are in marked contrast to Lenin's theory of imperialism. Mill recognized that the traditional practice of colonialism reflected what came to be know as Lenin's theory of imperialism, namely, that colonies existed (a) to provide raw materials for the home country and (b) to absorb the manufactured products of the home country, all of this understood as intended to work primarily to the advantage of the home country. At the same time, Mill maintained that this was not effective as an economic policy.

... the vicious theory of colonial policy – once common to all Europe, and not yet completely relinquished by any other people [besides Great Britain] – which regarded colonies as valuable by affording markets for our commodities that could be kept entirely to ourselves ..., allowing to the colonies the same monopoly of our market for their own productions. ... This notable plan of enriching them and ourselves by making each pay enormous sums to the other, dropping the greatest part by the way, has been for some time abandoned.[34]

Mill maintained that Britain would be better off without a colonial empire.

England is sufficient for her own protection without the colonies, and would be in a much stronger, as well as more dignified position, if separated from them. ... Over and above the commerce which she might equally enjoy after separation, England derives little advantage, except in prestige, from her dependencies, and the little she does derive is quite outweighed by the expense they cost her. . . .[35]

Mill's position with regard to maintaining colonies is a direct corollary of his conception of autonomy. Autonomous peoples ought to govern themselves. This is especially obvious in the case of those colonies settled and populated predominantly by Europeans. Here Mill recalls the late, lamented Lord Durham's report, which had urged such a course for Britain's remaining North American colonies (i.e., Canada). Durham had been the aristocrat around whom Mill and other liberals had hoped to form a new constituency with the Whigs during the early 1840s. With regard to peoples who are not yet ready for autonomy, the only justification for maintaining a colonial administration is to prepare them for autonomy and independence. The application of this policy to specific circumstances would involve judgment, but there should be no doubt about the overall intention.[36]

Four years later, in his essay *Considerations on Representative Government* (1861), Mill summed up his case as follows:

A new era in the colonial policy of nations began with Lord Durham's Report [on Canada]; the imperishable memorial of that nobleman's courage, patriotism, and enlightened liberality, and of the intellect and practical sagacity of its joint authors, Mr. Wakefield and the lamented Charles Buller. . . . the honor of having been its earliest champion belongs unquestionably to Mr. Roebuck. . . .

There are, as we have already seen, conditions of society in which a vigorous despotism is in itself the best mode of government for training the people in what is specifically wanting to render them capable of a higher civilization. . . . Such is the ideal rule of a free people over a barbarous or semi-barbarous one. We need not expect to see that ideal realized; but, unless some approach to it is, the rulers are guilty of a dereliction of the highest moral trust which can devolve upon a nation. . . . in this age of the world [there are] few more important problems than how to organize this rule, so as to make it a good instead of an evil to the subject people. . . . But the mode of fitting the government for this purpose is by no means so well understood as the conditions of good government in a people capable of governing themselves. We may even say that it is not understood at all. Their danger is of despising the natives; that of the natives is, of disbelieving that any thing the strangers do can be intended for their good. . . .

The government of a people by itself has a meaning and a reality; but such a thing as government of one people by another does not and cannot exist. . . . when a country holds another in subjection, the individuals of the ruling people who resort to the foreign country to make their fortunes are of all others those who most need to be held under powerful restraint. . . . they have the feelings inspired by absolute power without its sense of responsibility. . . . in the subject community also there are oppressors and oppressed – powerful individuals or classes, and slaves prostrate before them; and it is the former, not the latter, who have means of access to the English public.

. . . A free country which attempts to govern a distant dependency, inhabited by a dissimilar people, by means of a branch of its own executive, will almost invariably fail. The only mode which has any chance of tolerable success is to govern through a delegated body of a comparatively permanent character, allowing only a right of inspection and a negative voice to the changeable administration of the state. Such a body did exist in the case of India; and I fear that both India and England will pay a severe penalty for the shortsighted policy by which this intermediate instrument of government was done away with. . . . The institutions of the Great Britain, and those of the United States, have had the distinction of suggesting most of the theories of government which, through good and evil fortune, are now, in the course of generations, reawakening political life in the nations of Europe. It has been the destiny of the government of the East India Company to suggest the true theory of the government of a semi-barbarous dependency by a civilized country, and after having done this, to perish.[37]

When the new secretary of state for India invited Mill to become a member of the advisory council, he declined. Instead, Mill retired in 1857, on an annual pension of £1,500. His assistant, Thornton, canvassed the examiner's office and was unanimously delegated to arrange a gift for Mill, a silver inkstand. Thornton tells the following story about this retirement gift.

Mill had got wind of our proceeding, and, coming to me in consequence, began almost to upbraid me as its originator. He hated all such demonstrations, he said, and was quite resolved not to be made the subject of them. He was sure they were never altogether genuine or spontaneous . . . he would have none of it. . . . There was nothing left, therefore, but resort to a species of force. I arranged . . . that our little testimonial should be taken down to Mrs. Mill's house at Blackheath. . . .[38]

Death of Harriet Mill

Mill and Harriet were at last free to spend the rest of their lives as they wished. They planned to spend the winter of 1858 in the south of France and then to move on to Italy and perhaps to Greece. Everything went splendidly until they arrived in Lyon, whereupon Harriet developed the telltale cough. She had congestion in her lungs, ran a high fever, and was unable to sleep. They pressed on in uncomfortable circumstances to Avignon, with Harriet in a weakened and almost delirious state. Mill became increasingly alarmed and summoned a Dr. Gurney from Nice, who had helped on a previous occasion in 1853.

Dear Dr. Gurney,
My wife is lying at the Hotel de l'Europe here so very ill that neither she nor I have any hope but in you to save her. It is a quite sudden attack which came on at Lyons, of incessant coughing which prevents sleeping, and by the exhaustion it produces has brought her to death's door. I implore you to come immediately. I need hardly say that any expense whatever will not count for a feather in the balance.
I am dear Dr. Gurney
Very truly yours
J. S. Mill[39]

He even offered Dr. Gurney £1,000 if he would come immediately. But it was to no avail. Before the doctor could arrive, Harriet died on November 3. Mill summed up his agony when he wrote to Thornton with the information needed for the *Times* obituary: "It is doubtful if I shall ever be fit for anything public or private again. . . . the spring of my life is broken."[40] Helen arrived and wrote to Algernon that Mill "cannot write he suffers so dreadfully – he was twenty-four hours all alone – I must try to take care of him now."[41] So she would for the rest of Mill's life. Mill and Harriet didn't get to savor for long the life for which they had sacrificed so much.

For the next fifteen years, Helen Taylor, to whom Mill referred as his daughter, took over the running of Mill's practical life, just as her mother had done. She always referred to him as "Mr. Mill." Mill says of her in his *Autobiography* the following:

Though the inspirer of my best thoughts was no longer with me, I was not alone: she had left a daughter, my stepdaughter, Miss Helen Taylor, the inheritor of much of her wisdom, and of all her nobleness of character, whose ever growing and ripening talents from that day to this have been devoted to the same great purposes, and have already made better and more widely known than was that of her mother, though far less so than I predict, that if she lives it is destined to become. Of the value of her direct co-operation with me, something will be said hereafter, of what I owe in the way of instruction to her great powers of original thought and soundness of practical judgment, it would be vain to give an adequate idea. Surely no one ever before was so fortunate, as, after such a loss as mine, to draw another prize in the lottery of life – another companion, stimulator, adviser, and instructor of the rarest quality. Whoever, either now or hereafter, may think of me and of the work I have done, must never forget that it is the product not of one intellect and conscience but of three, the least considerable of whom, and above all the least original, is the one whose name is attached to it.[42]

Harriet was buried in the Avignon cemetery at St. Veran. Wishing to be at her side as much as possible, Mill purchased a house overlooking the cemetery and spent part of every year there. He visited the Grave several times a day (always spelling it with a capital 'G'). The five-room house, the Hérmitage de Monloisier, had originally belonged to the nuns of Sainte-Praxède before the French Revolution. It had two stories: on the first floor, a living room, dining room, and study; on the second floor, three bedrooms. It was a whitewashed house with a tiled roof and green blinds. Mill purchased the furniture from the room in which Harriet had died at the Hôtel de l'Europe, a hotel that had been one of their favorites. While there, he would breakfast at eight, work until one, have lunch, and then walk in the cemetery. He would work again until dinner, take another walk in the cemetery, and then turn to lighter reading and correspondence. Mill even went so far as to provide a pistol and cartridges for Helen for those occasions that he was away from Avignon.

Mill erected a monument made of Carrara marble, on which the following inscription was engraved:

To the Beloved Memory
Of
Harriet Mill
The deeply Beloved and Deeply Regretted
Wife of John Stuart Mill.
Her Great and Loving Heart
Her Noble Soul
Her Clear Powerful and Original
Comprehensive Intellect
Made Her the Guide and Support
The Instructor in Wisdom
And the Example in Goodness

As She was the Sole Earthly Delight
Of Those who had the Happiness to Belong to Her
As Earnest for the Public Good
As She was Generous and Devoted
To All who Surrounded Her
Her Influence has been Felt
In Many of the Greatest
Improvements of the Age
And will be in Those still to Come
Were There but a few Hearts and Intellects
Like Hers
The Earth would Already Become
The Hoped-For Heaven
She Died
To the Irreparable Loss of Those who Survive her.
At Avignon
Nov. 3, 1858

George Eliot and G. H. Lewes visited the grave on their way to Italy in 1861. From that point on, the grave site became a fixture of the Victorian travel circuit. Mill arranged for the town of Avignon to provide perpetual care for the site.

9

The Memorial Essays

Autonomy

The real memorial that Mill erected to Harriet was the dedication of the rest of his life to writings that embodied the ideal that he had realized through her. "I feel how little I have yet done as the interpreter of the wisdom of one whose intellect is as much profounder than mine as her heart is nobler. If I ever recover my health, this shall be amended."[1] What was this ideal? As we have already indicated, the ideal was autonomy. Let us explain what this means.

The word "autonomy" comes from the Greek and means self-rule. The further explication of this concept requires that we make a distinction that is often obscured in the English language, namely, a distinction between freedom and liberty. By "liberty" we understand an external condition, the absence of arbitrary external constraints. "Liberty" refers to external conditions over which individuals do not always have control. By "freedom" we understand an internal condition, one in which we always have the power to control ourselves or to control our responses, an internal condition for which individuals are responsible. Individuals may be ignorant of their freedom, they may choose to abdicate their freedom, but freedom as an internal state is something that they always have, should they choose to exercise it. Freedom is not something that can be controlled from the outside. This is what is meant by saying that individuals have "free" will,[2] and it is maintained as a fundamental truth about the human condition, a truth that defies any naturalistic-scientist explanation or reduction. If asked to account for this freedom, our only recourse is to appeal to introspection, to point out that it is a fundamental presupposition of all meaningful human action, and that no meaningful human activity has ever been, or can ever be, explained without appeal to it at some level.[3] The existence of such freedom is incompatible with the view that human beings can be explained either mechanically or organically, that human beings have a telos, or that human desires form a homeostatic system about which it makes sense to talk in terms of maximizing its welfare. Finally, it is not possible to exercise this freedom in a manner that is deleterious to others. The reason for this is that any action that requires the unwilling subordination of another human being is an act in which we define ourselves in terms of something other than ourselves. It is therefore not a free or autonomous act. We can never be free if we are defining ourselves in terms of others,[4] either in order to subordinate ourselves to them or in order to subordinate them to ourselves. Kant's notion of the categorical imperative is one expression of the concept of autonomy. When we define ourselves in terms of others, our action is said to be heteronomous.

To be autonomous is to recognize one's freedom, to make the fundamental choice of what kind of person one wants to be, to acknowledge that a free being does not and cannot act inconsistently with that freedom – specifically, that one cannot abdicate responsibility or define oneself in terms of others – and to accept responsibility for the consequences of one's actions. There is nothing in this concept that forbids two or more autonomous persons to be involved in a joint project, as long as participation is voluntary and the autonomy of each is respected throughout the pursuit of the project. What Harriet and Mill believed that marriage should be is an example of such a joint project. To be autonomous is to accept self-consciously the fulfillment and the burden of being free. For Mill the Romantic, the only sense of fulfillment comes from the performance of a creative act that is an expression of our freedom. For Mill the secular Protestant, the ever-present burden is to help others to become autonomous.

So understood, the strongest and most fundamental argument for liberty is the existence of freedom or autonomy. All meaningful human action is to be justified as an expression of human freedom or autonomy or as contributing to the conditions that allow the exercise of such freedom and the responsibility for it.[5] Liberty is a good thing insofar as it permits individuals to realize and exercise their freedom. Any attempt to manage the lives of responsible adults from the outside is a violation of, and a denial of, their freedom. It is not possible for others to impose upon a responsible adult what is good for that adult, for by definition what is good for an individual in the ultimate sense is that the individual has freely chosen it. Freedom is thus the basis for liberty.

The dignity that human beings demand is the recognition of their autonomy. Precisely because my autonomy requires recognition, I am obliged to promote yours as well. Hegel's discussion of the master-slave relationship is the most famous example of this point, but the metaphor of the master and the slave was a popular one during the nineteenth century, and it found expression in Mill's comments about slavery. Being a master is not satisfying because one's status as a master requires recognition, by way of acquiescence, on the part of one's inferiors. It is only recognition from one's equals – equal in being responsible for themselves – that gives satisfaction. That is why playing the role of master, either domestically or in public, is self-destructive. The more people who are autonomous, the more recognition my own autonomy receives. "It is only the high-minded to whom equality is really agreeable . . . they are the only persons who are capable of strong and durable attachments to their equals; while strong and durable attachments to superiors and inferiors are far more common and are possible to the vulgarest natures."[6] Being autonomous is not a finite resource but the infinite capacity of all human beings. Autonomy, therefore, is not involved in a zero-sum game.

The concept of autonomy presupposes that human beings are in some nontrivial sense possessed of free will; the possession of free will is not an obvious fact but something we come to discover about ourselves. This discovery is only possible for those who learn to control their impulses and who reject the idea that standards are external. Autonomy is the key moral concept.[7] Two important features of autonomy are worth noting. First, to govern oneself is not to be confused simply with defining oneself. Autonomy is often misrepresented by its critics (usually advocates of teleology) as a form of self-indulgence. Second, recognizing, pursuing, and sustaining autonomy is the spiritual quest of modernity.[8]

We have so far treated autonomy in a purely formal way. We do not believe this to be a wholly adequate treatment, any more than Kant's categorical imperative is satisfactory when left without content. Autonomy, we would argue, has to be seen within the context of a life narrative. That is one of the reasons Mill wrote an *Autobiography*, to chart the history of his recognition of his own autonomy, his struggle to realize it in himself first by distancing himself from his father, then by his liaison with Harriet, and finally by his dedication to a particular form of life, namely that of the public intellectual. It is why Harriet looms so large in his life and in his *Autobiography*.

The idea of autonomy was neither invented nor first recognized by Harriet Taylor.[9] Autonomy came to Mill from two sources, religious and secular. The religious source is, of course, the Puritan strain that he inherited and internalized from his father, albeit without conscious recognition of its theological origin. The secular source and the theoretical sense of autonomy is something that Mill absorbed from Romantic sources, specifically from the German notion of *Bildung*. Mill read and was influenced by thinkers who were pivotal in the Romantic movement:[10] precursors of Hegel, contemporaries of Hegel, followers of Hegel, or themselves influenced directly by Hegel: Fichte, Kant, Humboldt, Novalis, Goethe, Coleridge, the Saint-Simonians, Cousin, Lessing, and Mansel, to name a few. Gustave d'Eichthal, for example, attended Hegel's lectures in Berlin in 1824 and noted the similarities of Hegel's views to those of Saint-Simon.[11] Romanticism has been recognized as the secularization of the Protestant ethic.[12] This is precisely what Mill's background prepared him for. It is no surprise that he subscribed to the view that personal life is the endless struggle for perfection. It is no accident that he quotes Humboldt on this very point at the beginning of *On Liberty*.

The grand, leading principle, towards which every argument unfolded in these pages directly converges, is the absolute and essential importance of human development in its richest diversity. *Wilhelm von Humboldt, *Sphere and Duties of Government*[13]

The Romantic concept of *Bildung*[14] informs Mill's conception of the individual. J. W. Burrow's description of *Bildung* is highly illuminating in this context. I quote it in full.

Bildung could be represented as a quasi-organic and a dialectical process, consisting of an endless acceptance and innumerable provisional reconciliations of the creative tension between the individual and his environment and between the various contending aspects of his own nature. . . . An organism develops in time, and its form is not imposed on it from without; it is self-determining. It is neither passive in relation to its environment nor disconnected from it; it assimilates what it needs, converting it into its own tissues. . . . Above all, though it is part of nature and cannot exist without its environment, it makes itself, developing as it does out of an inner necessity.[15]

This is extremely helpful, as far as it goes. But it needs an additional dimension. Unlike purely organic entities, human beings have an historical dimension as well. It may be true that we make ourselves, but not solely out of inner necessity. We make ourselves out of the materials that history has furnished us.[16]

What does this imply for ethics? Mill is formally committed to being a utilitarian.[17] To be a utilitarian is to be a consequentialist, that is, someone who judges an action by its consequences. What kind of consequences are we considering? The relevant consequences are those that affect human well-being or happiness. Happiness, as we shall see, has two components, Romantic *Bildung* and Kantian autonomy. Mill's utilitarianism incorporated Kantian deontological idealism. The question this raises is how these two components – the consequentialist and the deontological components – go together. It appears as if Mill has to create a synthesis between the individual striving for *Bildung* and the need to impose order or form on oneself.[18] That is, Mill brings together *Bildung* and Kantian autonomy in a Hegelian synthesis. As Dicey noted, "Mill was so convinced of the value to be attached to individual spontaneity that he, in fact, treated the promotion of freedom as the test of utility."[19]

Self-expression, or self-definition, and self-rule are not identical. Mill's answer will be that self-expression, or self-definition, occurs in an historical context, not ex nihilo. Moreover, the historical context does not determine the choices; rather, it presents the possibilities in the form of an inheritance. It is through an imaginative act that the individual discerns the inherent norms and how to reexpress them in emerging contexts. The individual assimilates the past and then incorporates it into something even greater. What Mill does with his utilitarian ethics is to move in Hegelian fashion from right to duty to ethical life.

Instead of using the word "freedom" or the word "autonomy," Mill speaks about "individuality," the subject of Chapter 3 of *On Liberty*. Individuality is understood to mean self-development, what we have identified as the Romantic concept of *Bildung*. *Bildung*, as Mill understood it, is equivalent to autonomy. In short, "individuality" for Mill connotes both freedom, as autonomy, and self-development.[20] That is why *Utilitarianism* has to be read in the light of the essay *On Liberty*. "I forego any advantage which could be derived to my argument from the idea of abstract right, as a thing independent of utility. I regard utility as the ultimate appeal on all ethical questions; but it must be utility in the largest sense, grounded on the permanent interests of man as a progressive being."[21]

The relationship of the individual to society has to be understood within this broader framework. Mill rejected, over and over, the selfish hypothesis, the view that the basic truth about individuals is that they are selfish. That is why he rejected social philosophies based upon rights or contracts. He was always moved to promote concern for others. On the other hand, he rejected the view that we should be exclusively concerned about others, specifically rejecting Comtean altruism. We cannot promote the interests of others if their only interest is itself to promote the interests of others, ad infinitum. The resolution is analogous to Hegel's resolution of right and duty in ethical life. Specifically, if autonomy is our ultimate good and if the only way I can pursue by autonomy is to interact with other autonomous beings, then the promotion of my real interest is made possible only by promoting that identical interest in others.[22] This, again, illuminates why Harriet's influence was so important in getting Mill to realize how such an idea was instantiated within the family.

This triad can be carried to an even higher level. There is a need in Mill's philosophy for something like Hegel's conception of the state. The difficulty with grasping this is the prejudice that leads readers to attribute something like a collective good (totalitarian society) to Hegel. But it can be put in a Millian way. Mill recognizes the value of something like the night watchman view of the government. There are constant exhortations about the inefficiency of the government and the danger of its growing power. But Mill is also attracted, as was Hegel, to the classical Aristotelian idea that the function of the polis is to help make citizens virtuous. Therefore, the foundation of the state must be ethical and not merely prudential. What Mill wants, ideally, is a series of institutions that promote *Bildung* as the human ideal. The state is one such institution – or, perhaps more clearly, the integration of these institutions in order to serve this ideal. Mill is reluctant to specify specific functions for the state; rather, he urges that whatever arrangements or rules are needed to carry out this larger function be determined in context. By making individuality (*Bildung* and autonomy) the ultimate goal, he provides for the necessary safeguards against authoritarian and totalitarian societies. This satisfies neither libertarians, who cannot recognize ethical ideals; nor conservative critics, who either miss or do not share Mill's endorsement of *Bildung* as autonomy; nor those who simply see both sorts of passages as

hopelessly contradictory, without seeing the "Hegelian" synthesis at which
Mill is aiming. Philosophically, the combination of Aristotle and Romantic
Kantianism (something he absorbed from Humboldt) is what animates
Mill's utilitarian ethics and reflects once again the crucial synthesis in
Mill's thought.

What Burrow says of Humboldt applies equally to Mill.

> He has an Aristotelian sense of the ways in which human beings enrich each
> other's lives in society, together with a quite un-Aristotelian sense that one can
> neither predict nor set limits to human moral and cultural experimentation . . .
> a kind of informal adumbration of the status given to the greatest possible compre-
> hensiveness of consciousness in Idealist political theory. One is inclined to regard
> the Romantic notion of self-enrichment through a communion of souls as one of
> the cultural sources of the Idealist notion of Absolute Consciousness, together
> with its more strictly philosophical sources in Hegelian ontology and the theory
> of universals.[23]

In the light of this conception of the social world, we can understand
a further triad. It is the family that prepares autonomous individuals to
participate in civil society. Hence, the market economy cannot be expected
to function independent of a reform in family life that promotes equality
and autonomy, both of which will encourage more responsible procreation
as well as provide civil society with the talents of women, who are currently
excluded. Reform in family life has to be accompanied by political changes,
such as allowing women to own property in their own right and to have the
franchise. These are the kinds of things that the state can do to promote
autonomy. It is ludicrous to view this function of the state as a form of
collective authoritarianism. Autonomy entails devotion to the welfare of
others, especially to their achievement of autonomy. This is not only a
Romantic and Hegelian theme but a very Victorian conception of high-
mindedness.

When applied to Mill's political economy, the triad is even more illuminating. The market economy of the Industrial Revolution in Britain
is historically contextualized in a "capitalist" system that creates a class
conflict between employers and employees. "Socialists" critique the de-
humanizing aspects of capitalism and seek to overcome them, but only
at the risk of undermining other liberating practices, such as competition. Rather than be an apologist and defender of the status quo, rather
than merely blaming others and assuming that the destruction of the old

automatically produces utopia, Mill opts for a synthesis that preserves the virtues of a market economy without the class struggle and without surrendering competition and liberty. His vision of liberal culture is the synthesis.

Although it was Mill's problematic to explicate and preserve liberal culture, he always recognized the dark side of industrialization, its potential for dehumanization and overdevelopment, its worship of growth for growth's sake, and the danger of fragmentation inherent in the division of labor.[24] Such fragmentation was a threat to the ideal of humanity's harmonious self-development. We have already observed that delight in unspoiled scenery was for Mill a way of getting back in touch with the spiritual dimension of life. Mill's favorite form of relaxation throughout his life was to take long walks in the countryside and to engage in modest mountain climbing, an interest he shared with Leslie Stephen.

Mill already had, in a highly theoretical sense, the concept of autonomy before he met Harriet. What Harriet helped Mill to realize and to feel was the supreme importance of that concept. After her death, everything he wrote has autonomy, both its recognition and its preservation, as its object. "My objects in life are solely those which were hers; my pursuits and occupations those in which she shared, or sympathized, and which are indissolubly associated with her. Her memory is to me a religion, and her approbation the standard by which, summing up as it does all worthiness, I endeavour to regulate my life."[25]

As early as 1842, Mill recognized that social reform could not be carried out prior to moral reform. "[I]t is becoming more and more clearly evident to me that the mental regeneration of Europe must precede its social regeneration & also that none of the ways in which that mental regeneration is sought, Bible Societies, Tract Societies, Puseyism, Socialism, Chartism, Benthamism &c. will *do*."[26] We should not be surprised by this remark. The whole point of Mill's discovery of Romanticism was his coming to see that people were not simply the products of universal impulses and environmental conditioning. Human beings were capable of being free (i.e., autonomous) and responsible. This meant four things: (a) support for public policies that allowed the expression of autonomy, (b) support for public policies that promoted the conditions under which autonomy could be developed, (c) support for public policies that protected existing autonomy, and (d) finding intellectual and institutional means of promoting the moral regeneration of Europe. We shall return to the first three in a subsequent chapter. In the remainder of this chapter, we shall be concerned with the project of moral regeneration.

Utilitarianism

Although Mill discussed his ethical and moral views in many places and throughout his life, the formal presentation of his views is to be found in *Utilitarianism*.[27] Mill had begun writing this work in 1854 and finished it in 1859, but it was originally published in *Fraser's Magazine* in three numbers during October, November, and December of 1861. It was deliberately aimed at and written for a popular audience. It reflects Mill's attempt to synthesize the Enlightenment Project views of Bentham and his father and the deeper view of human nature he had absorbed from the Romantics, as well as the attempt to capture in that synthesis the everyday moral convictions that would serve as the basis for the moral regeneration.

Mill began the work by taking credit for the term *utilitarian*.

The author of this essay has reason for believing himself to be the first person who brought the word utilitarian into use. He did not invent it, but adopted it from a passing expression in Mr. Galt's *Annals of the Parish* [1821]. After using it as a designation for several years, he and others abandoned it from a growing dislike to anything resembling a badge or watchword of sectarian distinction.[28]

He then goes on to define what he takes to be the generic sense of the term: ". . . a name for one single opinion, not a set of opinions – to denote the recognition of utility as the standard, not any particular way of applying it – the term supplies a want in the language. . . ."[29]

It may at first glance seem out of character for him to make this sort of claim. What is important to notice is the suppressed background dispute. Mill is engaged in a wholesale reformulation and correction of Bentham's position.[30] He wanted to present his version of utilitarianism as the correct understanding, both against defenders of the old view, such as Grote, – who questioned Mill's "persistence in the true faith"[31] – and against the conservative defenders of a feudal society and critics of the Industrial Revolution.[32] Mill was still striving to elucidate the moral underpinnings of liberal culture.

Mill was a generic utilitarian. Beyond that, the battle lines had been drawn. Mill had already distanced himself from Bentham[33] as early as 1833 in his "Remarks on Bentham's Philosophy." There, Mill pointed out that the emphasis on expediency at the expense of virtue was incompatible with "all rational hope of good for the human species."[34] Writing in the first blush of his exposure to the German Romantic writers, Mill argued that what was needed was a change in the inner person.

The critique of Bentham insisted that Bentham had not answered "the ethical doctrines either of the Reid and Stewart school, or of the German metaphysicians" and did not understand the importance of the moral sense as a motive "for virtuous action."[35] The distancing continued in 1834 in a critique of Sedgwick in the *London and Westminster Review*. In the *Autobiography*, Mill tells us that he defended utilitarian ethics against the unjust criticisms of Sedgwick, but that the defense contained "a number of opinions which constituted my views on those subjects, as distinguished from my old associates. In this I partly succeeded, though my relation to my father would have made it painful to me in any case, and impossible in a review for which he wrote, to speak out my whole mind on the subject at this time."[36] In 1852, in "Whewell on Moral Philosophy," Mill defended utility as just as compatible with traditional virtues as the a priori view of ethics, while admitting that Bentham had failed to make this clear.[37]

Mill's differences with his father's views were more subtle. Mill noted that his father had inculcated in him all of the traditional Socratic virtues.

... justice, temperance (to which he gave a very extended application), veracity, perseverance, readiness to encounter pain and especially labour; regard for the public good; estimation of persons according to their merits, and of things according to their intrinsic usefulness; a life of exertion, in contradiction to one of self-indulgent sloth. These and other moralities he conveyed in brief sentences, uttered as occasion arose, of grave exhortation, or stern reprobation and contempt.[38]

James Mill believed in and adhered to these virtues, but he thought they could be theoretically reduced to utility and inculcated by association. Mill saw these virtues as related to utility but in a different way. More importantly, he thought they were not acquired by mere association.

Having moved away from Bentham, Mill still wanted to make clear that he was opposed to the position of moral intuitionism or the moral sense school. This is the same dichotomy we saw in his discussion of metaphysics and epistemology. The notion that timeless moral truths can be accessed independent of experience is, in Mill's eyes, the theoretical basis for a defense of the status quo. It is not that Mill believes in change for the sake of change. The status quo in his context referred to feudalism and the preliberal world. The status quo could also easily mean the entrenchment of democratic prejudice and mindless egalitarianism. More importantly, the doctrine of moral intuitionism made no room for the internal struggle and the self-formation of character that are central to autonomy.

The next part of Mill's argument in favor of utility as the standard is the need for a first principle in ethics. There are many moral rules of thumb; there are many obligations; and this means that conflicts will inevitably arise. In order to resolve those conflicts, there must be some way of prioritizing obligations, some principle in terms of which we resolve the conflicts. This is what the principle of utility is designed to do. In comparison to Hegel, we note that there are both conflicting rights and conflicting obligations, and that the domain of ethical life is the domain in terms of which those conflicts are resolved. This is the way in which Hegel overcame the perceived limitations of Kantian obligation, and Mill makes a similar point in his critique of Kant's *Groundwork of the Metaphysics of Morals.*[39]

Having critiqued Kant, Mill hastened to show the sense in which he was in agreement with Kant. Before discussing that in more detail, it will be useful to introduce some technical philosophical terminology. It has been customary to distinguish between teleology and deontology, between consequentialist and deontological ethics, between ethics and morals, between the good and the right. There are many ways of making these distinctions, but we shall use the following distinctions.

Classical ethical teleology: Human beings have a built-in end or *good* such that fulfillment is possible only in the achievement of that end. The relation of the individual good to the social good is secured by means of the presumed existence of a larger and collective social good and in the subordination of the individual good to, and its subsumption by, the social good, properly understood.

Modern ethical teleology: The end or ultimate goal of human life is not to achieve some specific telos but to maximize pleasure and minimize pain in some sort of homeostasis. The relation of the individual good to the social good (i.e., the good of others) is secured through education in enlightened self-interest.

Deontology (modern): Human beings do not have, in either their individual or collective capacity, a classical teleology, and in that sense there is no substance to ethics. Instead of *ethics*, we have *morals*. Morality tells us what is right or what our duties are. Universal and timeless moral principles are designed specifically to restrain individuals in their pursuit of private ends. At the same time, deontology does not guarantee any convergence between the pursuits of the individual and a collective social good, something it tends to deny. We are ultimately answerable to a higher power and not to our social world.

Romantic deontology: Although human beings do not have built-in ends, they all share an important truth about themselves, namely, their capacity for autonomy. Moral principles are ultimately prioritized by reference to autonomy. Promoting this universal autonomy is what ultimately overcomes any potential conflict among individuals. Instead of Bentham's ideal of universal happiness, Mill advocated universal autonomy.

Romantic deontology can also be expressed as a form of teleology. Our ultimate end is to achieve the recognition and realization of autonomy in ourselves and others. Clearly, this is part of Kant's theory, something often missed by those who ignore his insistence that there is another formulation of the categorical imperative, namely, that people should be treated as ends and never as means. This insight is expressed awkwardly in Kant. It is expressed much better in Hegel, although presented somewhat unfairly as a criticism or correction of Kantian formalism.

Classical ethical teleology is the position of Aristotle, and, with stress on the collective and subsumptive good, it is also the position of medieval Christendom. Modern ethical teleology is the position of the Philosophic Radicals. Deontology, which is inherently a modern view, is usually identified with the textbook version of Kant. The real Kant is, as we have argued, a Romantic deontologist. This is the position, as we shall see, of Mill as well. It is also easy to construe this as a teleological position, in the following way. The good has the right as part of its constitutive nature; specifically, to be autonomous or self-governing (the right) is part of what we are aiming at in order to achieve fulfillment.[40]

Mill begins to formulate this synthesis of teleology and deontology that we have called Romantic deontology in the following way.

When Kant (as before remarked) propounds as the fundamental principle of morals, 'So act, that thy rule of conduct might be adopted as a law by all rational beings,' he virtually acknowledges that the interest of mankind collectively, or at least mankind indiscriminately, must be in the mind of the agent when conscientiously deciding on the morality of the act.[41]

So, initially, when defining utilitarianism, Mill is insisting that what is right has to be defined in terms of what is good, understood in the universalizable sense.

The creed which accepts as the foundation of morals, Utility, or the Greatest Happiness Principle, holds that actions are right in proportion as they tend to promote happiness, wrong as they tend to produce the reverse of happiness. By happiness is intended pleasure, and the absence of pain; by unhappiness, pain, and the privation of pleasure.[42]

Right is defined in terms of good; good is understood as happiness; and happiness is identified by reference to pleasure and pain. So far, this looks identical to the position of Bentham. The notion that persons always act from a desire for their own personal pleasure (*psychological egoism*) is rejected by Bentham, James Mill, and J. S. Mill.

Where are the differences? To begin with, the notion that persons always act from a desire for pleasure (*psychological hedonism*) is something that Bentham accepted but that Mill rejected. There are, says, Mill differences between higher and lower pleasures, differences of quality as well as quantity. More significantly, the good is not pleasure but happiness. Pleasure is a property of happiness, the empirical confirmation of its existence.

The important transition comes when Mill goes on to reconceptualize happiness. Happiness is not contentment. Real happiness consists of dignity.

A being of higher faculties requires more to make him happy. . . . we may refer it to the love of liberty and personal independence, an appeal to which was with the Stoics one of the most effective means for the inculcation of it . . . but *its most appropriate appellation is a sense of dignity*, which all human beings possess in one form or other, and in some, though by no means in exact, proportion to their higher faculties, and which is *so essential a part of the happiness of those in whom it is strong*, that nothing which conflicts with it could be, otherwise than momentarily, an object of desire to them. . . . It is better to be a human being dissatisfied than a pig satisfied; *better to be Socrates dissatisfied than a fool satisfied*.[43] [italics added]

Happiness is further characterized as nobleness of character: "Utilitarianism, therefore, could only attain its end by the general cultivation of nobleness of character."[44] Finally, happiness is defined as a state in which virtue becomes constitutive of it.

[T]he mind is not in a right state, not in a state conformable to Utility, not in the state most conducive to the general happiness, unless it does love virtue in this manner – as a thing desirable in itself. The ingredients of happiness are very various, and each of them is desirable in itself, and not merely when considered as swelling an aggregate. . . . Happiness is not an abstract idea, but a concrete whole; and these are some of its parts.[45]

What has Mill accomplished with this reconceptualization? He has made the "right" part of the meaning of the "good." He has synthesized teleology and deontology. He has also characterized the chief ingredient of happiness as dignity, and dignity, as defined by Mill, is synonymous with autonomy. He has made autonomy our ultimate end. As Alan Ryan has put it, "Mill's concern with self-development and moral progress is a strand in his philosophy to which almost everything else is subordinate."[46] Traditional Utilitarians such as Jevons were furious with Mill's transformation. "The view which he [Mill] professes to uphold [utilitarianism] is the direct opposite of what he really upholds."[47] Mill has also made good on his claim that utilitarianism, so conceived, is neither atheistic nor a reduction of morality to expediency.

Mill's utilitarianism presupposes a nonutilitarian doctrine that specifies some content to the human good. "Utilitarianism" as a movement has usually been identified not only with the formal criterion of utility but also with a specific doctrine about the content of what is useful, namely, pleasure and pain. Although Mill subscribes to the view that utility is the formal criterion, he also subscribes to the view that the content of what is useful is happiness. Moreover, although happiness is experienced as pleasure, there are higher and lower pleasures, or higher and lower forms of happiness, that are qualitatively different. This latter contention is not consistent with – indeed, is in conflict with – Bentham's utilitarianism, but it is a contention that is consistent within Mill's moral psychology. What is important is not whether Mill is consistent with Bentham but whether Mill's own position is internally consistent. In addition, although happiness is our guide, we cannot pursue happiness directly (Aristotle's contention). Happiness is the consequence of pursuing another ideal. In the end, *it is this other ideal that is the ultimate reference of any account of Mill's moral psychology.*

I do not mean to assert that the promotion of all happiness should be itself the end of all actions or even the rule of actions. . . . *the cultivation of an ideal of nobleness of will* [italics mine] and conduct should be to individual human beings an end, to which the specific pursuit . . . of happiness . . . should give way. But I hold that the very question what constitutes this elevation of character, is itself to be decided by a reference to happiness as the standard . . . because the existence of this ideal, or a near approach to it, . . . would go further than all things else towards making human life happy, both in the comparatively humble sense of pleasure and freedom from pain, and in the higher meaning of rendering life . . . such as human beings with highly developed faculties can care to have.[48]

Grote was another longtime associate who expressed misgivings about Mill's position. Mill was able to reply to Grote in a review entitled "Grote's Plato."[49] Mill referred to Seneca's "Apologue of the Choice of Hercules," one of his father's favorite works, as being "one of the most impressive exhortations in ancient literature to a life of labour and self-denial in preference to one of ease and pleasure." Mill went on to cite Plato's *Gorgias* as an example of "the cultivation of a disinterested preference of duty for its own sake" rather than of "sacrificing self-preferences to a more distant self-interest," and he concluded with praise of the Stoics for grounding "the obligation of morals on the brotherhood . . . of the whole human race."

Mill added some important additional information about the growth of moral self-awareness. We may begin our lives by acting virtuously because it serves our narrow self-interest – pleasing our parents, say, or our teachers. In time, what was desired as a means to an end becomes an end in itself.

In these cases the means have become a part of the end, and a more important part of it than any of the things which they are means to.[50]

In further elaboration of his moral psychology, Mill noted that the will becomes independent of desire.

Will, the active phenomenon, is a different thing from desire, the state of passive sensibility, and though originally an offshoot from it, may in time take root and detach itself from the parent stock; so much so, that in the case of an habitual purpose, instead of willing the thing because we desire it, we often desire it only because we will it.[51]

This is a point of which Mill will make further use in his later address at St. Andrews – the importance of free will for virtue. The problem with the middle class is that they pursue virtue as a duty and not as an end in itself. What Mill urged college students to recognize was their capacity to let virtue become an end in itself.

The genetic (i.e., historical) account of the development of our moral conscience has the advantage of being inductive, or proceeding from individual experience; of denying the validity of the claim that the sense of virtue is innate or intuitive; and of showing how we come in time to discover the importance of autonomy. It is not a matter of association or conditioning, it is a matter of self-discovery, of irreversible emancipatory knowledge, of character formation, and of *Bildung*.

The final confirmation of this Romantic deontology is Mill's insistence that there is no ultimate conflict between one individual's autonomy and that of every other individual. With autonomy as the ultimate end, the potential conflict, with which other versions of utilitarianism are always in tension, between the good of the individual and the social or common good is overcome. In words reminiscent of Hegel, Mill spelled it out.

[I]f there were not, in short, a natural basis of sentiment for utilitarian morality, it might well happen that this association [moral faculty] also, even after it had been implanted by education, might be analyzed away. [Recall Mill's concern about this during his crisis.]

But there *is* this basis of powerful natural sentiment . . . the social feelings of mankind; the desire to be in unity with our fellow creatures, which is already a powerful principle in human nature. . . . Now, society between human beings, except in the relation of master and slave, is manifestly impossible on any other footing than that the interests of all are to be consulted. Society between equals can only exist on the understanding that the interests of all are to be regarded equally. . . . And in every age some advance is made towards a state in which it will be impossible to live permanently on other terms with anybody.[52]

One final qualification must be kept in mind. Neither Hegel nor Mill ever proposed a collective good or whole that subsumed the individual good. As Mill repeatedly insisted, "the great majority of good actions are intended, not for the benefit of the world, but for that of individuals, of which the good of the world is made up."[53] In a parting shot at Comte, Mill reiterates that concern for others should never be purchased at the cost of one's own autonomy, should never "interfere unduly with human freedom and individuality."[54]

Given the assumption that the goal of recognizing and realizing autonomy is a universal truth about human nature, and given the assumption that autonomy per se in one person can never conflict with autonomy in another person, and given the argument that autonomy can be achieved and sustained only in a society in which it is recognized that autonomy must be had by all, what can we make of Mill's proof of the principle of utility?[55] The proof runs as follows:

> ... happiness is a good: that each person's happiness is a good to that person, and the general happiness, therefore, a good to the aggregate of all persons.[56]

Just substitute autonomy for happiness and the proof becomes an obvious consequence of the preceding argument.

One final hurdle for Mill to clear in his discussion and defense of his version of utilitarianism has to do with justice. Is justice a matter of utility, or is it a matter of right? Having come this far, we must ask ourselves what is meant by utility. Utilitarianism in Mill has become a form of Romantic deontology, with autonomy as the ultimate end. So the question is, can justice be understood in terms of autonomy? Mill thinks that it can.

> Justice is a name for certain classes of moral rule, which concern the essentials of human well-being more nearly, and are therefore of more absolute obligation, than any other rules for the guidance of life. . . .
>
> The moral rules which forbid mankind to hurt one another (in which we must never forget to include wrongful interference with each other's freedom) are more vital to human well-being than any maxims, however important, which only point out the best mode of managing some department of human affairs. . . . Thus the moralities which protect every individual from being harmed by others, either directly or by being hindered in his freedom of pursuing his own good, are at once those which he himself has most at heart, and those which he has the strongest interest in publishing and enforcing by word and deed.[57]

Not only does autonomy serve as the basis of justice and of so-called rights, but "harm" has been defined as interfering with autonomy. This explains or obviates the kind of objections to Mill's *On Liberty* that cite its alleged ambiguity about harm. It also explains why in that earlier work Mill insisted that, rather than making any appeal to abstract rights, he preferred to use the concept of utility.

On Liberty

The essay *On Liberty* deserves special treatment. It does so for a number of reasons. Mill thought it was his best and most important work.

None of my writings has been either so carefully composed, or so sedulously corrected as this. After it had been written as usual twice over, we kept it by us, bringing it out from time to time, and going through it *de novo*, reading, weighing, and criticizing every sentence. . . . The *On Liberty* was more directly and literally our joint production than anything else which bears my name, for there was not a sentence of it which was not several times gone through by us together, turned over in many ways, and carefully weeded of any faults, that we detected in it. . . . The *On Liberty* is likely to survive longer than anything else that I have written.[58]

It continues to be his most widely read and controversial work. It has, finally, come to symbolize the problems and prospects of liberalism. How one understands Mill's *On Liberty* reflects not just one's interpretation of a particular philosophical work but one's engagement with modern liberal culture.

What Mill did in this essay was to begin with Harriet's own earlier essay entitled "Toleration" and restate all of the themes that had been most important to both of them, especially in the light of Humboldt's work. He began with a splendid dedication:

To the beloved and deplored memory of her who was the inspirer, and in part author, of all that is best in my writings – the friend and wife whose exalted sense of truth and right was my strongest incitement, and whose approbation was my chief reward – I dedicate this volume. Like all that I have written for many years, it belongs as much to her as to me; but the work as it stands has had, in a very insufficient degree, the inestimable advantage of her revision; some of the most important portions having been reserved for a more careful re-examination, which they are now never destined to receive. Were I but capable of interpreting to the world one half the great thoughts and noble feelings which are buried in her grave, I should be the medium of a greater benefit to it, than is ever likely to arise from anything that I can write, unprompted and unassisted by her all but unrivalled wisdom.

Mrs. Gaskell, the author of the *Life of Charlotte Brontë*, had once referred to Harriet's essay "The Emancipation of Women" as authored by someone priggish. Immediately after reading this dedication, she apologized to Mill.

"Liberalism" as a descriptive term has been applied to a wide variety of historical, social, moral, political, economic, religious, and cultural phenomena. It has been applied as a theoretical term to a whole spectrum of philosophical interpretations and defenses of some subset of those phenomena. In order to minimize confusion, we shall introduce the expression "liberal culture." By "liberal culture," we shall mean the culture that emerged in Western Europe during the post-Renaissance and post-Reformation period and eventually spread to the Western Hemisphere and beyond. The most distinctive institutions of liberal culture are the technological project (the transformation of the physical world to serve human interests), a free market economy (private property without central allocation of resources, which is thought to be the best means for carrying out the technological project because it encourages innovation through competition), limited government (whose main function is to ensure the operation of the market economy by protecting private property and sustaining competition), a set of political and social institutions – such as individual rights, the rule of law, and toleration – designed to maintain limited government, and finally, a culture that sustains these institutions by promoting individual autonomy.

Although the model of liberal culture has achieved hegemonic status, most of the world's practice, most of the people in the world, and probably most of the people who write about it are hostile to liberal culture. Not only is liberal culture opposed by many outside of the "West" (e.g., the Islamic world, China), it is also opposed by those within the "West" who either want to see a return to some version of classical culture or medieval culture or who, like socialists and Marxists, want to see liberal culture evolve into or be replaced by another set of institutions (e.g., a command economy, participatory democracy, dictatorship, etc.). It is also opposed by countercultures that disdain the moral practices necessary to sustain it, and by those who see the tensions within liberal culture and want something without those tensions but are not clear about what that could be.

There are thus two sets of disputes that must be carefully separated: (a) What is the correct understanding of liberal culture? and (b) Is liberal culture a good thing? It is part of our purpose in this chapter to show that Mill is a defender of the intrinsic worth of liberal culture, that his defense of liberal culture is significant because it is the only one that is both consistent and coherent, that his defense continues to be of the utmost relevance to liberal culture precisely because it has not been fully absorbed, and, finally, that we do not have to embrace liberal culture in order to understand and to appreciate Mill's place in liberalism.

The major institutions of liberal culture (namely, individual rights, the rule of law, limited government, and a market economy) are not self-certifying. These institutions are valid because they are the institutions most compatible with the fundamental truth about human nature. The fundamental truth about human nature, according to Mill, is that human beings can live fulfilling lives only to the extent that each individual takes responsibility for his own life. It was to remind us of the authoritative grounding of liberal culture in individual autonomy that Mill wrote *On Liberty*. What evidence is there for this? In the first place, Mill told us exactly that. In a letter written to Emile Acollas, a French law professor, Mill asserted that the central theme of *On Liberty* is autonomy, "celui de l'autonomie de l'individu."[59]

Second, there is an important relation between liberty and freedom, understood as autonomy. In the English language we tend to use the words interchangeably, but whereas liberty refers to external constraints, freedom refers to an internal condition that we have identified as autonomy. Liberty is not an end in itself, and that is why Mill stresses that it is not always appropriate to grant liberty. Freedom as autonomy is, however, an end in itself. Liberty is justified only to the extent that it promotes freedom as autonomy.

On Liberty was "a tract whose major purpose was to advocate the positive freedom of self-development – and of self-control and self-dependence – of the German philosophers, and that this constituted an important part of Mill's conception of virtue."[60] We have already had occasion to note and to trace the influence of German Romantic philosophy on Mill's thought more generally.[61] As Mill himself noted, the three most recent and important periods of European intellectual history were the Reformation, the Enlightenment ("the speculative movement of the latter half of the eighteenth century"), and German Romanticism ("the intellectual fermentation of Germany during the Goethian and Fichtean period"):

[D]uring all three, the yoke of authority was broken. In each, an old mental despotism had been thrown off, and no new one had yet taken its place. The impulse given at these three periods had made Europe what it now is. Every single improvement which has taken place either in the human mind or in institutions, may be traced distinctly to one or other of them.

But the influence of these movements "are well nigh spent." Mill's task was to attain a "fresh start" by again asserting "our mental freedom."[62]

It is important to see fully the extent to which Mill relied upon Humboldt's *The Limits of State Action*. Although it would have to be documented in much greater detail than I can provide in this context, I would strongly suggest that *On Liberty* be interpreted as a restatement of Humboldt prompted by Mill's recognition of the additional problem of the masses (Tocqueville). Humboldt was concerned with defining the limits of the state; Mill was concerned as well with defining the limits of society as a whole, a concern prompted by the rise of the masses. In his Introduction, Humboldt poses the ethical problem as one of reconciling Kant with Aristotle. Humboldt's first chapter, like Mill's, raises the question of the relation of the individual to the state and of the extent to which the state should provide for the positive welfare of its citizens. Humboldt does so against the historical backdrop of the difference between ancient and modern states. Humboldt's answer, given in his second chapter, is that the state should not be so involved because our ultimate good is autonomy. Humboldt goes on to argue, in his Chapter 7, that the state cannot provide for the positive welfare because the state has no access to the real channels of influence on morality, namely, *internal acceptance.* Humboldt then derives the policy that the only ground on which restrictions can be justified is infringement on the rights of others or on their "personal freedom."[63] He further concludes, in Chapter 11, that individuals are not free to give up their freedom. In his concluding chapter, Humboldt warns against social technology, specifically criticizing utility and advocating instead that in every reform the new condition of things be interwoven with that which precedes it. This is done most effectively when the reform proceeds from men's minds. Humboldt concludes from all this that

the State must wholly refrain from every attempt to operate directly or indirectly on the morals and character of the nation except in so far as such a policy may become inevitable as a natural consequence of its other absolutely necessary measures; and everything calculated to promote such a design and particularly all special supervision of education, religion, sumptuary laws, etc., lies wholly outside the limits of its legitimate activity.[64]

We even discover the warning in Humboldt that Mill appropriated for his own conclusion – that a paternalistic state creates "a multitude of well-cared-for slaves, rather than a nation of free and independent men. . . ."[65] Finally, the last chapter in Humboldt's work, like the last chapter in *On Liberty*, contains a plea for a government-supported system of national education to promote the conditions for autonomy.

Mill reiterated the importance of Humboldt's influence in his *Autobiography*:

... [t]he leading thought of the book [*On Liberty*]. ... The unqualified championship of it by William von Humboldt is referred to in the book; but he by no means stood alone in his own country. During the early part of the present century the doctrine of the rights of individuality, and the claim of the moral nature to develop itself in its own way, was pushed by a whole school of German authors even to exaggeration; and the writings of Goethe ... seeking whatever defense they admit of in the theory of the right and duty of self-development.[66]

It was because Mill believed liberal culture to be in danger that he thought it important to offer the reminder. In the very first paragraph of *On Liberty*, Mill not only defines his problem as establishing a principled basis for determining "the nature and limits of the power which can be legitimately exercised by society over the individual" but also calls attention to the existence of "new conditions" that "require a different and more fundamental treatment." What are these new conditions? In paragraph three, he identifies the new conditions as the substitution of democracy for a limited form of government. Instead of limiting government, we now seek to capture government and make it an agent of the national will. In paragraph four, Mill alerts us to the danger to which this gives rise, the potential "tyranny of the majority." In his *Autobiography*, Mill cites Tocqueville's *Democracy in America* (which Mill reviewed several times)[67] as the source of this insight. Mill goes on to claim that the transition from the advocacy of pure democracy to the advocacy of representative government was "the only actual revolution which has ever taken place in my modes of thinking."[68] At the end of the first chapter of *On Liberty*, he begins to identify why the rise of mass democracy is dangerous, claiming that to resist it we shall need "a strong barrier of moral conviction."[69]

Liberal culture is endangered for two reasons, one general and one specific. In general, our failure to understand the inherent norms of liberal culture leads to a situation in which "one side is at present as often wrong as the other; the interference of government is with about equal frequency, improperly invoked and improperly condemned."[70] This sentence alone, which appears early in the work, should dispel the illusion that the purpose of the book is to engage in the wholesale liberation of individuals from all authority. The general failure of liberal culture is the lack of a clear conception of its authoritative grounding. The specific threat to liberal culture, and the occasion for writing *On Liberty*, is the rise of the masses to social and political power. According to the historical thesis Mill had outlined as early as his reviews of Tocqueville, the market economy in liberal culture gives rise to democracy, but democracy threatens to undermine the conditions that give rise to liberal culture. To the extent that society becomes more homogeneous, there is less reason to set limits to government intervention in its dealings with either individuals or groups.

However different limited government might be from democracy, within a liberal culture it is the understanding that the "majority" has of representative government that decides whether the representatives act in the interests of the whole or as the agents of their respective constituencies. What Mill saw in his own time and foresaw for the future was the increasing extension of the franchise to those who least understood the inherent norms of liberal culture.

We know that the will of the people, even of the numerical majority, must be supreme. . . . [B]ut in spite of that the test of what is right in politics is not the will of the people, but the *good* of the people, and our object is, not to compel but to persuade the people to impose, for the sake of their own good, some restraint on the immediate and unlimited exercise of their own will.[71]

Throughout *On Liberty* and in other writings, Mill called attention to the rising masses who in their present condition represented a serious threat to liberal culture. They represented a threat precisely because they were unaware of the norms that informed liberal practice and because their previous condition had not given them an opportunity to develop an internal sense of autonomy.

Who are the masses, and what is wrong with them? Mill says the following. Precisely because autonomy is a cultural achievement and a moral practice, it is the case that many, if not most, human beings have failed to achieve it. Most human beings fall far short of their potential; "even the men and women who at present inhabit the more civilized parts of the world . . . are but starved specimens of what nature can and will produce."[72] To be underdeveloped is to fail to cultivate one's individual autonomy.[73] To be a member of the masses is equivalent not to a level of income but to a state of mind. Even "in England . . . the middle class. . . . [is] always a mass, that is to say, collective mediocrity."[74] The masses are exploited politically by demagogues. "The mass do not now take their opinions from dignitaries in Church, or State, from ostensible leaders, or from books.

Their thinking is done for them by men much like themselves. . . ."[75] What the masses demand is equality, so that "bad workmen, who form the majority of the operatives in many branches of industry, are decidedly of opinion that bad workmen ought to receive the same wages as good. . . ."[76] Equality stands in opposition to individuality, where individuality is understood both intensionally as a self-disciplined life and extensionally as variety. The demand for equality (homogeneity) is the demand to live a life where one is protected from accepting the consequences of one's choices.

It is the purpose of Mill's *On Liberty* to save liberal culture from self-destruction by retrieving its moral foundations. No political or economic reform could be sufficient without grounding in a moral regeneration. This explains why for Mill the problem of liberty is one not of government control but of social control, control understood as the undue influence of those who have failed to become autonomous individuals.

I had seen and continued to see many of the opinions of my youth obtain general recognition, and many of the reforms in institutions, for which I had through life contended, either effected or in the course of being so. But these changes had been attended with much less benefit to human well-being than I should formerly have anticipated, because they had produced very little improvement in that which all real amelioration in the lot of mankind depends on, their intellectual and moral state. . . . The old opinions in religion, morals, and politics, are so much discredited in the more intellectual minds as to have lost the greater part of their efficacy for good, while they have still life enough in them to be a powerful obstacle to the growing up of better opinions on those objects. When the philosophic minds of the world can no longer believe its religion, or can only believe it with modifications amounting to an essential change of its character, a transitional period commences, of weak convictions, paralysed intellects, and growing laxity of principle, which cannot terminate until a *renovation* [italics mine] has been effected in the basis of their belief leading to the elevation of some faith, whether religious or merely human, which they can really believe. . . .[77]

Mill diagnosed the failures of liberal culture as the result not of its fundamental institutions but of the presence of many individuals who enjoy its benefits, including political power, but who have failed for one reason or another to recognize and to embrace the moral foundations of liberal culture. Mill's prescription for how to deal with the masses also follows from his moral psychology. The great challenge to liberal culture is to acculturate the masses who are emerging from feudalism. Looking at the suggested alternatives, Mill was appalled. The traditional approaches ran from the reactionary to the philanthropic. Typical of the reactionary response was Carlyle, who maintained that it was not "a sin to control, or coerce into better methods, human swine in any way."[78] The philanthropic approach was represented by the Tories under the leadership of Disraeli, as well as by notable conservatives such as Mill's critic Sir James Fitzjames Stephen. On the assumption that society is a hierarchical structure, it is clearly the responsibility of those above to care for those below who are incapable of caring for themselves. This notion of Tory philanthropy had an international analogue in the defense of imperialism. In a modern democratic society, however, the structure of society is not hierarchical but horizontal. As a consequence, the philanthropic attitude is not only ineffective and inappropriate but also serves, paradoxically, to undermine further the notion that there are higher and lower values.[79]

A second approach to the masses is the social-technological approach, the assumption that there are social scientific–technological means of removing the barriers to the pursuit of the higher self. This "Benthamite" approach falsely conceives of human nature as a product of purely external circumstances. It persistently tries to induce the internal state from the external state; it persistently fails; it squanders limited resources (see, for example, Mill's discussion of taxation); it leads to the ever-growing power of the state (see all of Mill's arguments against government control); and it leads eventually to the moral impoverishment of the entire community. Such moral impoverishment is the result of a philanthropic spirit, a spirit that is less and less able to identify any impulse as bad. To this we might add the threat represented by Comtean authoritarianism.

Mill definitely perceived a collectivist tide. He saw it in Tory paternalism, in Stephens's conception of empire, in trade unionism, in the beehive of Comtean positivism, in Christian socialism, in revolutionary socialism, and in the rising technocracy. The alternative approach is Mill's. It focuses on the moral education of the masses coupled with opportunities to learn self-discipline. It also provides for criminal penalties for those who engage in behavior that morally impoverishes the community (e.g., those lacking in autonomy who bring into the world children whom they are incapable of helping to learn autonomy).

The abuse of democracy reflected a failure to understand the moral conditions that sustain the institutions of liberal culture. Mill's moral philosophy consists in the persistent reiteration of the point that there must be a highest good, and that this highest good must be found in individuals in such a way as to provide for social harmony. The highest good is individual autonomy or self-discipline, the pursuit of which by any individual does not conflict with the pursuit of the same end by any other individual. Moreover, the pursuit of that end by individuals enhances the prospects for others to do so. We quote Mill's own references to Humboldt:

["T]he end of man, or that which is prescribed by the eternal or immutable dictates of reason, and not suggested by vague and transient desires, is the highest and most harmonious development of his powers to a complete and consistent whole;" that, therefore, the object "towards which every human being must ceaselessly direct his efforts, and on which especially those who design to influence their fellow-man must ever keep their eyes, is the individuality of power and development;" that for this there are two requisites, "freedom, and variety of situations;" and that from the union of these arise "individual vigour and manifold diversity," which combine themselves in "originality."[80]

What is being argued here (by Kant, by Humboldt, and by Mill) is that the highest good, teleologically conceived, is not some specific activity but the self-discipline (i.e., autonomy) that accompanies an activity. Aristotelian virtue has been replaced by self-discipline, to which it bears a distinct analogy. What is jettisoned is some hierarchical conception of specific virtues. It follows from this, as we shall see, that the only activities that are ruled out are those that undermine the capacity for self-discipline, either in oneself or in others.

Like Kant and Humboldt, Mill recognized the awesome burden this placed upon the autonomous individual. This burden also reflected the Calvinist notion that an autonomous individual does not merely do a good work but creates a life that is a systematically unified good.[81] Again, this explains why Mill refers to Humboldt's statement about "the highest and most harmonious development of his powers to a complete and consistent whole."[82]

What Mill saw himself doing was extending the religious argument that grounded liberal culture to cover every aspect of that culture.

The only case in which the higher ground has been taken on principle . . . is that of religious belief. . . . It is accordingly on this battlefield, almost solely, that the rights of the individual against society have been asserted on broad grounds of principle. . . . The great writers [Milton and Locke] to whom the world owes what religious liberty it possesses, have mostly asserted freedom of conscience as an indefeasible right, and denied absolutely that a human being is accountable to others for his religious belief.[83]

Locke's argument for religious toleration is that we should tolerate other Christian sects because they subscribe to the view that religious conviction must be voluntary and internal if one is to achieve salvation. Whatever other disagreements they had, all Christian sects shared the fundamental belief about the need for individuals to subscribe voluntarily to any religious doctrine. Salvation was not possible unless the cosmic order was embraced voluntarily. This is the universal truth that allowed them to agree on how to disagree. What Mill proposed was that this argument and this universal truth about human nature applied to more than just religious diversity.

Mill's argument is a broadening of some principles of Calvinism.

But if it be any part of religion to believe that man was made by a good Being, it is more consistent with that faith to believe that this Being gave all human faculties that they might be cultivated and unfolded . . . that he takes delight in every nearer approach made by his creatures to the ideal conception embodied in them, every increase in any of their capabilities of comprehension, of action, or of enjoyment. There is a different type of human excellence from the Calvinistic: a conception of humanity as having its nature bestowed on it for other purposes than merely to be abnegated. "Pagan self-assertion" [words borrowed from John Sterling] is one of the elements of human worth, as well as "Christian self-denial" [reference to Carlyle].[84] There is a Greek ideal of self-development, which the Platonic and Christian ideal of self-government blends with, but does not supersede. It may be better to be a John Knox than an Alcibiades, but it is better to be a Pericles than either; nor would a Pericles, if we had one in these days, be without anything good which belonged to John Knox.[85]

Mill's general critique of Christianity is that it promotes "abstinence from Evil, rather than energetic Pursuit of Good." Mill's specific critique of Calvinism (*On Liberty*, pp. 265–72) is that it narrowly constricts that transformation to the economic realm. "There is now scarcely any outlet for energy in this country except business."[86] This bears an interesting parallel to Matthew Arnold.

In proposing the substitution of poetry for religion, Arnold and Mill believed that they were substituting the cultural ideal of a human nature fully developed on all sides for the religious ideal of a human nature perfect on its moral side. They attributed the narrowness of the religious ideal of their own country to the alliance between the spirit of religion and the spirit of business, and to English parochialism.[87]

This is why Mill believed "that other ethics than any which can be evolved from exclusively Christian sources, must exist side by side with Christian ethics to produce the moral regeneration of mankind."[88] Keep in mind that Mill's other source is the classical pre-Christian world, for "what little recognition the idea of obligation to the public obtains in modern morality is derived from Greek and Roman sources, not from Christian."[89] The issue here is not whether Mill is being fair to Christianity, for Mill explicitly says that Christianity is completely reconcilable with "a complete moral doctrine."[90] What is important to see is that Mill is trying to renovate or reconstruct morality from classical and Christian sources, not to provide a novel morality without roots.

Mill's vision of Christianity can be summarized as follows. He accepts the notion of a cosmic order that is reached as a spiritual realm independent of the temporal realm. This is the root of Western individualism, and Mill clearly subscribes to the de-divinization of the state. In a sense, his vision is Protestant, because he rejects the notion that the cosmic order or spiritual realm is reached through the institution of a church, and because he insists that the individual reaches the spiritual realm on his own. Mill rejects the medieval Catholic and Anglican view that external nature is guided by divine law and that we as human beings are meant to conform to that natural order. Instead, Mill believes that we must transform external physical nature to conform to our internally accessed vision of the cosmic order. In this respect, Mill is close to Calvinism. "The duty of man is the same in respect to his own nature as in respect to the nature of all other things, namely not to follow but to amend it."[91] Unlike the Calvinists, Mill does not believe that we first apprehend the cosmic order internally and then transform it in terms of the internally supplied blueprint. It is not a simple matter of first gaining self-control and then gaining control of the environment. Rather, *it is through the experimental process of gaining external mastery that we come to master ourselves*. At the risk of sounding paradoxical, it would be fair to say that success in external mastery is both a means to and therefore a reflection of internal mastery.

Unlike secular modernists, Mill is not advocating mastery as an act of will or self-expression or as a means of maximizing pleasure and comfort. Recall Mill's contention that a stationary economic state is a good thing if it gives people the time and opportunity to engage in self-reflection. External mastery is a means to self-discovery and internal mastery or autonomy. Since internal mastery is the ultimate goal, there is no prescribed form of external mastery – no utopian scheme. Any disciplined and noncoercive activity that works is acceptable, and this will clearly vary with each individual.

But different persons also require different conditions for their spiritual development; and can no more exist healthily in the same moral, than all the variety of plants can in the same physical, atmosphere and climate. The same things which are helps to one person towards the cultivation of higher nature are hindrances to another.[92]

Understanding the distinction between freedom and liberty and their relationship to each other enables us to understand Mill's answer to the problem of liberty and to clarify what he meant by *harm*. There is a principled basis for deciding the limits of social authority and therefore the resulting sphere of individual liberty. "The only purpose for which power can be rightfully exercised over any member of a civilised community, against his will, is to prevent harm to others."[93] What does it mean to harm someone? The answer is, assuming we have distinguished freedom from liberty, that to harm someone is to deny his freedom. We deny someone his or her freedom when we (a) prevent him or her from becoming an autonomous being or (b) treat him or her as a means rather than as an end. As stated in *Utilitarianism*:

The moral rules which forbid mankind to hurt one another (in which one must never forget to include wrongful interference with each other's freedom) are more vital to human well-being than any maxims, however important, which only point out the best mode of managing some department of human affairs.[94]

Harming someone has nothing to do with preventing someone from reaching a desired end or from maximizing self-interest. It is a matter of preventing someone from living according to self-imposed rules, from being an autonomous and responsible human being. It clearly follows from this that paternalism is self-contradictory and that individuals are not at liberty to abnegate their freedom. Seen in that sense, Mill's principle is a simple one. However, unpacking that principle is not a simple matter.

Misunderstandings about Mill's conception of harm go hand in hand with the traditional criticisms of Mill. One such criticism is that the harm principle does not enable us to make comparative judgments, especially of aggregate welfare. That is, it does not tell us how to tally the net score of harm. This is true as far as it goes, but the criticism misses the point or function of the harm principle. The whole point or function of the zone of autonomy is that it remains under all sets of circumstances inviolable. It establishes or presupposes that all autonomous agents are on an equal footing (each has veto power, so to speak – a point also captured in Kant's categorical imperative). Mill rejected the notion of a central management agency that tallied up harm scores. There are no such scores. The point of the harm principle is not to maximize good but to prevent evil.

A second, and related, traditional criticism is that all actions have social consequences; in that sense, there are no self-regarding actions.[95] This criticism was made against Mill by Sir James Fitzjames Stephen, the brother of Leslie Stephen, in a work entitled *Liberty, Equality, Fraternity*. In a letter to Bain, Mill was to remark of this book that Stephen "does not know what he is arguing against."[96]

To begin with, this is an objection that Mill explicitly recognizes in Chapter 1 (p. 225) of *On Liberty* and answers at length in Chapter 4 (pp. 280–91). Keep in mind that *the point of Mill's treatment is not to rule out external control but to provide a principled basis for deciding when and how to exercise it*. The gist of Mill's answer is that even if every action influenced every other person all the time, we would still have to decide if we should, and how we should, exercise external control. Concerning the "if" question, we have two choices: Either the onus is on the actor to justify the innocence or goodness of his action (the continental view) or the onus is on those who seek to curb the action (the Anglo-Saxon view). If the onus is on the actor, that presupposes some infallibly clear and correct hierarchical conception of the good and leads in practice to complete despotism. Since Mill is unalterably opposed to these implications, his response is to opt to place the onus on those who seek to curb an action. This move captures the Anglo-Saxon notion that a man is innocent until proven guilty. By capturing the traditional norm, Mill shows himself to be much more in touch with the customs of his civilization than his detractors.

Once the onus is placed on the advocates of curbing an action, then what the advocates of curbing must establish is (a) that the action in question *ultimately* violates the autonomy of others ("interests" are legitimate only if treated as means to autonomy) and (b) that the act of suppression is not "more" harmful (in its unintended consequences) than the action in question (where "more" is to be understood qualitatively and with respect to autonomy). The question is not whether Mill faces a formidable practical task but whether his principle helps us to frame that task.

What Mill's harm principle enables us to do is to identify the realm of autonomy and then to focus on the interests that are alleged means to that autonomy. Since autonomy is not causally induced from the outside, the onus is on those who maintain that curbing one person's interest is integrally related to preserving another person's autonomy. There is no notion in Mill, for example, of sequestering someone's resources because others can make better use of them or need them to make them feel good. The advocate of redistribution must establish that a violation of one person's interest promotes another person's autonomy. How many policies of economic redistribution begin by establishing even the remotest connection?

A primary example for Mill concerns individuals who do not lead autonomous lives and who bring children into the world when there is no realistic prospect that those children will become autonomous, largely because those who are to care for the children do not know how to be autonomous. Further, the consequences of bringing into the world more individuals who are not likely to be autonomous is a threat to the safety and livelihood of those who remain autonomous. Here, according to Mill, there are grounds to seek to discourage individuals who are not autonomous from having children. Certainly, Mill did not believe that all forms of sexual expression were integral parts of human autonomy. Moreover, this is not a Millian argument for abortion, nor an argument about what to do with children who are already here, but rather an argument for discouraging marriage and procreation, or at least for postponing it. We are not discussing the "how" of such suppression. Nor is the issue here whether on intuitive or other (perhaps religious) grounds we disapprove of such suppression. The issue is whether Mill's advocacy of suppression is consistent with his position. I suggest that it is consistent. It is important to see here that Mill's position is not merely Malthusian but invokes the moral primacy of autonomy and ties in with his concern about the masses.

Mill provides an authoritative grounding for liberal culture, and it is a grounding that appeals to a conception of human nature with a moral content. It will probably strike some readers as odd to say that Mill has a fundamental conception of the human good, especially given his advocacy of various experiments in living. To say that Mill has a fundamental conception of the human good is not to say that Mill has a theory of human nature according to which all legitimate ends are hierarchically ordered and spelled out in a timeless fashion. There is only one intrinsic end for Mill, and that is autonomy understood in the classical Greek–Christian–Protestant–Kantian–Humboldtian tradition that we have already discussed.[97] It is this fundamental good that permits, encourages, and circumscribes a host of specific alternative life projects. The analogue to Mill's principle is, as we have said, Locke's notion that all Christians can agree that salvation through inner conviction is the ultimate good, however much they may differ about other things. Therefore, Mill has not only a fundamental conception of the human good but also a conception that is compatible with a certain reading of different kinds of experiments in living. That is why Mill can say that his position is not one of indifference. In dealing with another's experiment in living, there are "good reasons for remonstrating with him, or reasoning with him, or persuading him, or entreating him, but not for compelling him."[98]

No political arrangement will function unless there are independent moral considerations that make us take that political arrangement seriously.[99] If the political arrangement is a mere extrinsic good instead of being based on an intrinsic good, its status could change at any time.

There is an important philosophical reason why most "liberal" social philosophy, from Hobbes to the present, cannot provide what Mill provides. The reason is that Mill subscribes to a version of inner freedom, and a good deal of "liberal" social philosophy does not. "Liberal" social philosophers have come to deny natural law, understood as a strictly teleological view of human nature and nature as a whole. What they have come to embrace is a compatibilist position that accepts determinism in some form or other, inexplicably[100] correlated with the pursuit, on the conscious level, of certain ends. These ends have no ontological grounding, since only the deterministic level remains ultimately real. One consequence of this is the inability to designate any form of behavior as abnormal; a second consequence is the legitimization of every end without any formal way of ranking ends; a third consequence is their coming to categorize almost everyone as a victim requiring liberation by some outside agency.

Mill does not confuse self-respect with self-esteem, for the former depends in a way that the latter does not upon a strong inner sense of self capable of resisting how others see us. It is because Mill believes that our will is free, in the sense that we can mould our own characters, that he can make a distinction between freedom and liberty. There is, as well, an important moral reason why Mill can provide a fundamental and contentful conception of the good life. It depends upon his view of how the individual discovers freedom when he enjoys the liberty to do so. We now turn to this notion.

For Mill, the only real sense of fulfillment that a human being can achieve comes when he or she disciplines himself or herself in the service of some inner intuitive conception of an ideal that gives shape and meaning to the projects of his or her life. There need be nothing unconventional or grandiose about the ideal. What is necessary is that we grasp it voluntarily instead of having it imposed from the outside. However, the recognition of this truth is only possible for those who engage in the task of self-discipline. We cannot learn this truth in any other way. Therefore, only those who enjoy the external liberty to pursue inner freedom can come to understand, cherish, and defend this truth. Granting or promoting such external liberty is not a sufficient condition, and therefore there are always risks and costs to social, economic, and political liberty. While all defenders of liberal culture strive to promote the external conditions, only those who, like Mill, subscribe to the belief in inner freedom are able to realize the limits of what can be done externally, to see the importance of dissuading people from thinking of themselves as victims, and to recognize the psychic costs of realizing inner freedom.

It is this notion of fulfillment that explains Mill's complex attitude toward *custom*. To begin with, Mill does not conceive of or define individuals independent of their cultural context. "A person whose desires and impulses are his own – are the expression of his own nature, as it has been developed and modified by his own culture – is said to have a character."[101] All practices originate in some customary context, so that "it would be absurd to pretend that people ought to live as if nothing whatever had been known in the world before they came into it. . . . The traditions and customs . . . are . . . presumptive evidence, and as such, have a claim to his deference."[102] What Mill objects to are people (a) engaged in the customary practice without ever learning the norms that inform that practice and thereby (b) engaged in a practice while violating the spirit of that practice. The first is instanced when custom has degenerated into feeling or mere prejudice, when people believe that "their feelings, on subjects of this nature, are better than reasons, and render reasons unnecessary."[103] The second is instanced by the Christian who pays lip service to the maxims of the New Testament but whose actual practice reflects the unthinking "custom of his nation, his class, or his religious profession."[104] As Mill pleaded, "to conform to custom, merely *as* custom, does not educate or develop . . . any of the qualities which are the distinctive endowment of a human being."[105] We *reflect upon custom in order to recapture the inherent norms that guide that custom so that we can decide how that practice is to be continued and / or modified in the present and future.* Mill said "it is important to give the freest scope possible to uncustomary things, in order that it may in time appear which of these are fit to be converted into customs."[106] Finally, originality has come to mean something quite specific for Mill:

[O]riginality, in any high sense of the word, is now scarcely ever attained but by minds which have undergone elaborate discipline, and are deeply versed in the results of previous thinking. It is Mr. Maurice, I think, who has remarked on the present age, that its most original thinkers are those who have known most thoroughly what had been thought by their predecessors: and this will always henceforth be the case.[107]

What Mill advocated instead was that my individuality necessarily arises not only out of my appropriation of a cultural inheritance but also out of my developing and expanding that inheritance in my own unique way.

To understand the content of Mill's conception of the good life, we shall have to provide some historical background. The classical worldview can be characterized as subscribing to the belief in an external cosmic order that we must first apprehend and to which we are then to conform. The modern worldview subscribes to the belief in an internal cosmic order that we must first apprehend and to which we are then to conform. Mill is clearly a modern. He subscribes to the belief in an internal cosmic order that we must first apprehend and to which we are then to conform. Therefore, Mill's belief in inner freedom is not merely a belief in the formal existence of choice, nor is it the belief in the existence of choice without a framework (as in Sartre). Freedom, for both ancients and moderns, is an internal matter of self-discipline, of conforming the will to some standard. One thing that differentiates the modern from the classical viewpoint is the modern insistence that the standard is not instantiated in some external structure, either philosophical or institutional, but rather in the individual.

One thing that differentiates one modern from another is the manner in which that inner standard is apprehended. Some moderns continued to employ the classic notion that reason discovers the structure, only now the discovery is an internal one. Other moderns, including Mill, insisted that the discovery could take place only in action and not as a mere intellectual or observational state of affairs. To be more specific, for Mill and some other moderns, it is only in action that I come to understand who and what I am and add to what I am; it is only in action that I can come to recognize that the greatest sense of fulfillment comes with self-discipline. Those classicists and moderns who follow Aristotle can appreciate why habit and practice are a necessary supplement to intellectual apprehension. When Mill insists that individuals be given the liberty to experiment, it is because this is the only way in which we can come to recognize this substantive universal truth about ourselves. It is not an argument for allowing people to do whatever they want; instead, it is an argument for allowing people to discover in the only way possible what will truly fulfill them.[108] It is the activity, it is the trying, it is the rehearsing that leads to insight, and not intellectual brilliance. This is an insight about human nature, therefore, that is not confined to an intellectual elite but can potentially be shared by all. This explains why Mill has faith in a liberal culture. It is, finally, an insight that has always been contained within the Western tradition, and that is why Mill is engaged in a moral *renovation*, not a moral revolution or demolition. It is an insight that can be gained only from participation in and reflection upon ongoing practice, and not from theorizing about a structure.

It is in the light of this conception of how we learn – that is, by reflection upon previous practice – that we can begin to appreciate the importance of autobiography in Mill's political thought.[109] One's autobiography is a history of one's moral progress. In autobiographical reflection, we discover, first, an understanding of the norms embedded in previous cultural practice; second, we discover our power to embrace consciously what we did previously in an unreflective manner; third, we discover the responsibility of applying the embedded norms to novel circumstances coherently. There are, in an important sense, two story lines: the cultural (social and historical) development of embedded norms, and the development of the individual from spontaneous action to deliberate choice. This is Mill's individualistic counterpart to Hegel's phenomenology. It is the persistence of the developing norm through changing contexts that gives this process its lawlike character, but it is not the notion of a mechanical law, but rather of an organic and historical law. Its closest counterpart can be found in natural history.

Individuality for Mill is a deeply moral notion embedded within the Western tradition. It is not an accident that Mill's hero is Socrates, understood as someone who systematically encourages us to retrieve the inherent norms of our practice. It is not merely perfunctory on Mill's part that he appeals to traditional Christian notions of self-discipline. What has to be kept in mind, however, is that Mill's Christianity is modern in the sense that conformity means self-discipline imposed in the interest of transforming the world in order to retrieve our inner grasp of the cosmic order.

Mill's quarrel with some religious leaders had to do with predestination. Like many others, he believed it would make a mockery of human freedom to think that what we did made no appreciable difference to the universe. If it is our duty and our greatest fulfillment to externalize the richness of the cosmic order, then that externalization must be a real ontological achievement. For Mill, the external world, including the social world, is not merely a backdrop for an inner drama. The transformation of that external world is the necessary venue for the inner drama if it is to take place at all. There is an important parallel here between Milton and Mill, and a great influence of the former on the latter. Notice the following parallel between the two:

Mill: "Whatever power such a being may have over me, there is one thing which he shall not do: he shall not compel me to worship him. I will call no being good, who is not what I mean when I apply that epithet to my fellow creatures: and if such a being can sentence me to hell for not so calling him, to hell I will go."[110]

Milton: "Though I be sent to Hell for it, such a God [who predestines everything] will never command my respect."[111]

There is a sense in which Mill's understanding of individuality creates an important conceptual link with the social world. Mill does not subscribe to the view that the individual achieves fulfillment by doing good works, externally defined; that is, the individual is not simply to conform to the larger, external, social good. Nor does Mill believe that an inner state of grace leads to an external social good through good works defined by reference to that inner state. Rather, in order to achieve the inner state understood as autonomy, we must discipline ourselves by doing something in the larger social world that reflects some intuitive ideal. Instead of a simple cause-and-effect sequence, there is an integral relationship between self-fulfillment and social fulfillment. That integral relationship works as follows. Mill believes it to be a matter of empirical historical fact that all of the great advances of civilization have come about as the result of individuals who had the courage to pursue an inner intuitive ideal (e.g., Socrates, Jesus). In addition, by creating the external conditions for achieving inner freedom or autonomy (i.e., liberty), we are creating those conditions not only for ourselves but for others as well. What we see here is the combination of the Kantian ideal of autonomy and the Protestant notion of doing God's work in the world (now given a secular twist). Mill unites these notions through a progressive view of history. The parallels to Hegel are striking, but they should not be surprising.

Several important objections are likely to greet such a view. First, how are we to know which of the many intuitive visions of the ideal is the correct one? Answer: There is no way to prejudge, short of a belief in infallibility, predestination, or determinism – all of which are identical doctrines that Mill rejects. What serves as a sign that one's vision is correct is that it incorporates the implicit norms of past historical practice. Second, could one not argue that all the great evil in the world has been caused by individuals with a perverse intuitive sense of the ideal? Answer: What makes any expression of the intuitive sense of the ideal a perverse one is that it is by its nature coercive. Mill's principled account of the individual realm provides a formal criterion for identifying perversity without pretending to identify definitively what forms a correct vision of the ideal. It is part of Mill's sensitivity that he recognized that to be free is to articulate oneself, and to the extent that my articulation involves the coercion of others (i.e., victims) I am not free. "The power of compelling others into it [freedom] is not only inconsistent with the freedom and development of all the rest, but corrupting to the strong man himself."[112] Third, what theoretical justification could one give for a morally progressive reading of history? Answer: Coherent human thought is not achieved through a theory that steps outside to judge what is inside; coherence is achieved only by a historical reflection on past practice that strives to discern the inherent norm in that practice so that we can "renovate" it for application to newly emerging contexts. That is why Mill said he wrote *On Liberty*.

Returning to *On Liberty*, we can now identify the two arguments that Mill gives for individuality and their interconnection. One argument – the genius argument – is that all the great accomplishments of civilization are the products of individuals who have cultivated their individuality. As good as this argument is, it is not the sort of argument that will appeal to more mundane human beings or to those who cannot appreciate the importance of the long-range consequences of "an *atmosphere* of freedom." Another, more subtle argument is that everyone needs to be an individual because no human being can be truly fulfilled unless he has taken responsibility for his own life.

[N]or is it only persons of decided mental superiority who have a just claim to carry on their lives in their own way. There is no reason that all human existence should be constructed on some one or some small number of patterns. If a person possesses any tolerable amount of common sense and experience, his own mode of laying out his existence is the best, not because it is the best in itself, but because it is his own mode.[113]

This second argument is designed to persuade the masses to become the individuals that they are capable of becoming. They should do this not because they are textbook geniuses, and not for the sake of making the world safe for intellectuals, but because individuality (i.e., autonomy) is the *summum bonum*. Mill's *On Liberty* is not a plea for elitism. What he is pleading for is the recognition that liberal culture promotes the highest good, and that certain conditions must be recognized in order for that culture to be sustained.[114] It is worth noting that in a diary entry made during the time of the composition of *On Liberty*, Mill specifically criticized Carlyle's conception of hero worship as incompatible with the need for a universal striving toward autonomy.

Hero worship, as Carlyle calls it, is doubtless a fine thing, but then it must be worship not of a hero but of heroes. Whoever gives himself up to the guidance of *one* man, because that one is the best and ablest whom he happens to know, will in nine cases out of ten make himself the slave of that most misleading thing, a clever man's twits and prejudices. How many are there of the most deservedly great names in history whom their contemporaries would have done well and wisely in implicitly following? One hero and sage is necessary to correct another.[115]

In one important sense, Mill does direct his argument to the power elite of his time (and ours), many of whom were autonomous individuals. Since *it is through the process of gaining external mastery that we come to master ourselves*, the elite can use the argument for the practical benefits of maximizing liberty in the hope that it will also lead to internal mastery. In pursuing external mastery (i.e., the creation of wealth and leisure), we also create the opportunity for more of the masses to achieve internal autonomy.[116] Otherwise, what Mill foresaw was the gradual erosion of the power of the autonomous elite as the untransformed masses gained political ascendancy. If the morally untransformed masses were to obtain power, that would mark the end of liberal culture and its replacement by tyranny.[117]

This helps to clarify Mill's attitude toward a market economy. Although Mill is an unequivocal defender of a market economy, he asserts in *On Liberty* that "Free Trade . . . rests on grounds different from . . . the principle of individual liberty asserted in this Essay."[118] What he meant by this is that a market economy has social consequences that make the question of government responsibility always a relevant question. On the other hand, Mill espouses a market economy because it provides the means for prosperity through the transformation of nature, and that transformation helps in the achievement of autonomy. Mill's fundamental critique of government control of the economy, or of anything else, is that it subverts autonomy. This is another case of where the distinction between liberty and freedom (autonomy) is helpful.

The other function of Mill's argument is to answer the objection that liberal culture promotes indifference to the common good and provides no basis for civic virtue.[119] For Mill, the common good (ontologically speaking) is not something beyond the good of the individuals who make up a community. The only public business worthy of the name is the business of providing the context within which individuals can have greater and greater control over their own lives. It is a contradiction in terms to think that giving greater and greater control to public agencies increases individual freedom. Finally, as we have already seen, in order to sustain one's own autonomy it is necessary to promote it in others. It is a misunderstanding of individuality to see it as opposed to the notion of a cultural whole. One cannot be an autonomous individual on one's own, for individuality requires the support of a liberal culture. In seeking this context for myself, I necessarily seek it for others. To the extent that others do not share it, my own autonomy is less secure.

There is yet another reason. A truly autonomous individual is one who articulates himself. The perception that we have of ourselves as self-articulating cannot be sustained if we are constantly dealing with those whom we think of as, or have to treat as, inferiors. The double standards that prevail in many institutions, standards that demand less of some than of others, invariably reconfirm the perception that we are dealing with inferiors. It takes an enormous act of bad faith to ignore this. Moreover, to adopt a paternalistic attitude toward others is a corrupting experience, not unlike that of the strong man who coerces others for "their" own good.

A true individual can maintain his autonomy only by interacting with other autonomous beings, that is, by interacting with equals. This is the spirit in which we must understand Mill's discussion of the relationship between men and women.

The equality of married persons before the law is not only the sole mode in which that particular relation can be made consistent with justice to both sides, and conducive to the happiness of both, but it is the only means of rendering the daily life of mankind, in any high sense, a school of moral cultivation. Though the truth may not be felt or generally acknowledged for generations to come, the only school of genuine moral sentiment is society between equals.[120]

It follows from this that *civic virtue in a liberal culture requires us to help others, and we can only help others by helping them to achieve autonomy. Equality has to be understood as the moral capacity for being autonomous*, not as an equal division of the spoils or the redistribution of social badges of prestige. "To be helped to help themselves . . . is the only charity which proves to be charity in the end."[121] Mill's conception of individuality necessarily involves social preconditions and has social consequences. It is not, in any sense of the term, atomistic. On the contrary, it is an attempt to preserve the inner spiritual domain and to extend the freedom that is integral to that inner domain to an entire world community.

Mill's conception of individuality provides an integral link between the individual and the social realm. The best example of this in *On Liberty* is the whole of Chapter 2, "Of the Liberty of Thought and Discussion." The purpose of *On Liberty* is to retrieve the fundamental norms of liberal culture. Individual autonomy is the fundamental norm. By arguing against censorship in Chapter 2, Mill is giving a clear example of how the practice of open discussion, so essential to many institutions, really serves to promote individuality.[122] It is important to see that the defense of the liberty of thought and discussion is not designed to encourage a counterculture; it is not designed to advance a particular political agenda; and it is not designed to provide a formal mechanism to achieve truth about an external structure. The liberty of thought and discussion is designed primarily to build character.[123]

Liberty of thought and discussion is not designed to reach objective truths about the external world that can be translated into formulas that automatically lead to internal liberation. Thought is for the sake of clarifying action rather than reaching definitive truths. What justifies our acting is not that we have consulted the elite but that we have engaged in ruthless self-examination. What justifies a representative or parliamentary body in acting is not that all have been instructed by the wise but that all have, through their representatives, had an opportunity to engage in self-examination. It is precisely because Mill's emphasis is upon internal moral transformation that he eschews all utopian schemes and rejects dangerous schemes of external tyranny, such as Comte's. Recall that Comte had argued that the right of free inquiry – or what he considered the dogma of unbounded liberty of conscience – leads to anarchy, and that since it was no longer necessary in sciences such as astronomy, it would soon not be necessary anywhere.

Mill ended the first chapter of *On Liberty* by disclaiming any originality for his arguments. Mill, in fact, borrowed his arguments for the critique of censorship from Milton's *Areopagitica*.

First Argument:

Milton: "[I]f learned men be the first receivers out of books and dispreaders both of vice and error, how shall the licensers themselves be confided in, unless we can confer upon them, or they assume to themselves above all others in the land, the grace of *infallibility* [italics mine] and uncorruptedness?"[124]

Mill: "All silencing of discussion is an assumption of infallibility."[125]

Second Argument:

Milton: "They are the troublers, they are the dividers of unity, who neglect and permit not others to unite those dissevered pieces which are yet wanting to the body of truth."[126]

Mill: "[T]hough the silenced opinion be an error, it may, and very commonly does, contain a portion of truth; and since the general or prevailing opinion on any subject is rarely or never the whole truth, it is only by the collision of adverse opinions that the remainder of the truth has any chance of being supplied."[127]

Third Argument:

Milton: "A man may be a heretic in the truth; and if he believe things only because his Pastor says so, or the Assembly so determines, without knowing other reason, though his belief be true, yet the very truth he holds becomes his heresy."[128]

Mill: "... beliefs not grounded on conviction.... This is not knowing the truth. Truth, thus held, is but one superstition the more...",[74] "... if it [an opinion] is not fully, frequently, and fearlessly discussed, it will be held as a dead dogma, not a living truth."[129]

Fourth Argument:

Milton: "I fear yet this iron yoke of outward conformity hath left a slavish print upon our necks.... We do not see that, while we still affect by all means a rigid external formality, we may as soon fall again into a gross conforming stupidity, a stark and dead congealment ... forced and frozen together, which is more to the sudden degenerating of a Church than many subdichotomies of petty schisms."[130]

Mill: "[T]he meaning of the doctrine itself will be in danger of being lost, or enfeebled, and deprived of its vital effect on the character and conduct; the dogma becoming a mere formal profession, inefficacious for good, but cumbering the ground, and preventing the growth of any real and heartfelt conviction...."[131]

The parallels with Milton are designed to support the following conclusions. First, the point of liberty of thought and discussion is to bring about an internal moral transformation, not to promote skepticism. Mill is no more sowing the seeds of the destruction of Western civilization than Socrates was destroying Athens. Both were trying to rescue their respective communities by reminding them of their inherent norms. The three most recent and important periods of European intellectual history were the Reformation, the Enlightenment ("the speculative movement of the latter half of the eighteenth century"), and German Romanticism ("the intellectual fermentation of Germany during the Goethian and Fichtean period"):

[D]uring all three, the yoke of authority was broken. In each, an old mental despotism had been thrown off, and no new one had yet taken its place. The impulse given at these three periods had made Europe what it now is. Every single improvement which has taken place either in the human mind or in institutions, may be traced distinctly to one or other of them. But the influence of these movements "are well nigh spent."

Mill's task was to attain a "fresh start" by again asserting "our mental freedom."[132] Second, Mill is renovating what he takes to be the inherent norms of liberal culture, norms that stretch back to classical antiquity.[133] In this, Mill was following Milton's lead. Third, Mill's own choice of venue – reconsideration of Milton's arguments – supports the claim that Mill was engaged in historical retrieval, not in radical deconstruction. Fourth, Mill's genius lies not in novelty for the sake of novelty but in recapturing and making his own the insights of his predecessors. Everything that we noted earlier about the influence of Humboldt on Mill reinforces these conclusions.

There is one final point about Mill's advocacy of open discussion. It concerns the conundrum that since Mill believed actions cannot be as free as thought, and since the expression of a thought is an action, some expression cannot be free. To begin with, Mill would agree that some expression of thought is subject to social control. On the other hand, what justifies that social control is a prior debate on the harmful consequences of that form of expression (e.g., inciting to riot). The prior debate about suppression is a meta-debate, and all meta-debate must be free and open. Therefore, one cannot use the conundrum to close off debate about any topic without engaging in a prior discussion of the dangers of that topic. Such free and open prior discussion involves the airing of that topic. What becomes relevant is the venue of the discussion, but what is never in question is whether there should be an open discussion somewhere. Finally, this conundrum merely helps to reinforce Mill's main point that we need frequent reminder-discussions, because it is the reminder-discussion that reviews the meta-debate.

As was to be expected, the publication of this book in 1859 met with some opposition. Carlyle denounced it to his assistant as "the crowing, God-denying, death-stricken spirit, now making such great signs with our fashionable sciences and life-philosophies, – and all the world wondering after it."[134] To his brother, Carlyle would write, "As if it were a sin to control, or coerce into better methods, human swine in any way."[135]

A number of individuals understood the points Mill was making. Walt Whitman, in *Democratic Vistas*, begins with a tribute to Mill's *On Liberty*. Matthew Arnold commented that the work was "one of the few books that inculcate tolerance in an unalarming and inoffensive way."[136] Charles Kingsley, in his inaugural address as Regius Professor of History at Cambridge, saw in it a plea "unequaled" in modern times "for the self-determining power of the individual, and for his right to use that power."[137]

The whole of liberal culture depends upon personal autonomy. Democracy is a great threat to liberal culture, although not the only one. But democracy is also inescapable – in part, curiously, because of a market economy. The only way of dealing with this threat is to allow people the opportunity to discover the importance of autonomy. Liberty as the absence of arbitrary external constraints is a necessary means for the discovery and cultivation of autonomy. What renders a constraint arbitrary is its irrelevance or hostility to autonomy. Mill's defense of liberty, therefore, is not a defense of mindless self-indulgence or of license. An autonomous person is one who is self-governing. Participation in government as a form of self-governance is the cure for the misuse of democracy. But such participation is not just within the political realm; an autonomous person must participate in self-governance within the economy (hence the importance of cooperatives in which workers are part-owners), within the family (hence the importance of legal and moral equality for women), and within education. Self-governing individuals are those who think for themselves. This requires toleration and experiments in living, both to discover new truths and to rediscover old truths in a meaningful way. Finally, the importance of competition, both in the economy and in education, needs to be stressed because it is in the clash of competition that the truth emerges and individuals grow.

What few have seen is the sense in which *On Liberty* is a tribute to Harriet's insights about autonomy. It is no accident that *On Liberty* is a memorial to her. It was the essay that best captured the sense of autonomy that Harriet had helped Mill to grasp at the beginning of their relationship.

Considerations on Representative Government

The Philosophic Radicals had supported democracy as a way of ensuring that the government was responsive to the common good. The social circumstances under which they did so were in transition. For example, the Reform Bill of 1832 gave the right to vote to perhaps at best one in five Englishmen (and to no women). Largely members of the middle class, the philosophic radicals saw themselves as the natural leaders and spokespersons for the working class as well. Between 1830 and 1870, all of these circumstances changed. But the policy of government by means of the middle class, for the working class was about to come to an end.

In 1838, the London Working Men's Association had issued a charter – which earned them the name of Chartists – in which they laid down six demands: (1) universal adult male suffrage, (2) annual parliaments, (3) the secret ballot, (4) equal electoral districts, (5) abolition of property qualification for candidates, and (6) payment for MPs. Chartism failed. It is clear that at least through 1886 they did allow themselves to be led in politics by middle-class and aristocratic elites, but there were early signs that this would not last forever. Many positions taken by working-class organizations showed little inclination to embrace the moral vision that comprised Mill's understanding of liberal culture. Under these circumstances, it is no surprise that Tocqueville's warnings about the tyranny of the majority found a sympathetic response in Mill.[138] Mill would remain a supporter of the first two Chartist demands – and in fact argued for complete universal suffrage, including women – but he would eventually dissent from the other four demands.

Mill addressed the issue of the threat of democracy in 1859 in *Thoughts on Parliamentary Reform*, an essay that reflects both his and Harriet's concerns about potential abuse. In that essay, he specifically suggests that there should be a plurality of votes based upon education. Some have seen in this a sinister elitism, but Mill's sole aim was to guarantee that some educated people, and not just wealthy people, be elected, so that the voice of reason instead of mere interest could be heard. Shortly after the publication of the essay, Thomas Hare, a barrister, published a work suggesting that all candidates run nationally and that there be a transferable ballot. Mill immediately embraced this scheme and dropped his own idea of a plurality of votes. Along with women's suffrage, this became one of the two most important issues for Mill during the latter part of his life.

One other issue in the aforementioned essay is worth noting. Mill, like his Philosophic Radical predecessors, had always been in favor of the secret ballot. It was thought that secrecy would protect the vulnerable from reprisals. Harriet, however, convinced Mill to switch his position. She argued that it was more important than ever for autonomous individuals to stand up and be counted, and that meant accepting public responsibility for one's vote. It is a powerful example of her stress on autonomy. It was much easier for the irresponsible masses to hide behind a secret ballot.

Mill's most comprehensive statement of his political philosophy is contained in *Considerations on Representative Government* (1861).[139] The first thing to notice is the title. Mill is writing a treatise not on democracy but on representative government. He is not a fan of direct democracy except in very small communities. He is an advocate of representative government, where the presumption is that representatives are ultimately concerned with the common good.

In his opening discussion, Mill steers a middle course between what he takes to be two competing views of government. One view is that government is a tool or a means to an end. The end is somehow capable of being formulated as an abstract principle, independently premeditated, and political activity is merely the implementing of that principle or set of principles. What is to be done is somehow independent of how it is to be done. This is all wrong, according to Mill. In the first place, government is an historical entity, so that practice always precedes theory. Any proposed theory is always abstracted and generalized from some previous practice. In the case of the Philosophic Radicals, the previous practice that served as the model of politics was economics. The practice was irrelevant and misleading with regard to politics. The Philosophic Radicals began with "economic man," or the rational maximizer, and proceeded from there to argue that voters would all be rational maximizers and think in terms of their long-term enlightened self-interest, the common good being the product of such behavior. Economics was the wrong model, for two reasons. First, the rational maximizer was a theoretical construct and not an accurate description of all of human action. Second, governments were not constructed de novo but evolved, so that voters always reflected myriad historical circumstances.

The second view is that governments are organic entities with a life of their own. The most a statesman can do is to conserve the ongoing process. This view is better than the first view because it recognizes that governments are not mere mechanical structures to be manipulated to some desired end. But Mill rejected this view as well. Governments, like the societies they reflect, are not merely natural teleological entities.

Governments are historical and therefore evolving entities. It is in this work that Mill disavows the Coleridgean (permanence and progression) and Saint Simonian (order and progress) categories, because both sets of categories believe that societies and governments are objective structures that can be definitively identified and formulated.

What Mill offers is a third approach, a conception of how to understand a practice. It is the approach he found in Guizot and Tocqueville and that he articulated in the *Logic*. We understand a practice by explicating the norms inherent in that practice. The norms cannot be accessed as a permanent substructure (hence the organic theorists are wrong); the norms can never be definitively explicated, but are fertile sources of adaptation. No political tradition entails its own future development.[140] Rather, a political practice is immanent, it involves adjusting existing arrangements by exploring and pursuing what is intimated in them. Everything he says from this point on, then, reflects (a) what he thinks the inherent norms of liberal culture are, (b) what he thinks the given circumstances are in which those norms operate, and (c) what reasonable changes can be made in "existing" practices to better reflect the inherent norms.

The basic value of liberal culture is autonomy. Given that value, the "ideally best" form of government is representative government.

There is no difficulty in showing that the ideally best form of government is that in which the sovereignty, or supreme controlling power in the last resort, is vested in the entire aggregate of the community; every citizen not only having a voice in the exercise of that ultimate sovereignty, but being, at least occasionally, called on to take an actual part in the government, by the personal discharge of some public function, local or general. . . . A completely popular government . . . [i]s both more favourable to present good government, and promotes a better and higher form of national character, than any other polity whatsoever. . . . human beings are only secure from evil at the hands of others, in proportion as they have the power of being, and are, self-protecting; and they only achieve a high degree of success in their struggle with Nature, in proportion as they are self-dependent. . . .[141]

There is no doubt in Mill's mind that this form of government is best realized in Britain and the United States. Mill acknowledges that his understanding of the United States is still largely taken from his reading of Tocqueville.

Among other things, one of the most important functions of a representative or parliamentary body is to provide a forum where the fundamental norms are explicated, where a community lays bare its soul, where every perception and point of view finds a voice. It is not a matter of legitimating every perceived interest or perceived grievance, but of identifying where the nation stands. Like Rousseau and Hegel, Mill wants some public forum where debate about the general will and the common good are formalized.

Parliament has an office . . . to be at once the nation's Committee of Grievances and its Congress of Opinions; an arena in which not only the general opinion of the nation, but that of every section of it, and, as far as possible, of every eminent individual whom it contains, can produce itself in full light and challenge discussion; where every person in the country may count upon finding somebody who speaks his mind as well or better than he could . . . in the face of opponents, to be tested by adverse controversy . . . where every party or opinion in the country can muster its strength, and be cured of any illusion concerning the number of its adherents. . . . A place where every interest and shade of opinion in the country can have its cause even passionately pleaded, in the face of the government and of all other interest and opinions, can compel them to listen, and either comply, or state clearly why they do not, is in itself, if it answered no other purpose, one of the most important political institutions that can exist any where, and one of the foremost benefits of free government.[142]

Mill identified the dangers or infirmities of representative government. Representative government is liable to encourage place hunters, bureaucratization,[143] and, worst of all, class legislation. The great danger, as Mill saw it, was the tendency of the uneducated members of the working class to become a tyrannical majority supporting legislation that encouraged mediocrity, legislation in their immediate short-term interest but to the long-term detriment of all.

Looking at democracy in the way in which it is commonly conceived as the rule of the numerical majority, it is surely possible that the ruling power may be under the dominion of sectional or class interests, pointing to conduct different from that which would be dictated by impartial regard for the interest of all. [Here Mill cites whites versus Negroes, Catholics versus Protestants, the English versus the Irish.] . . . the experience of Trade Unions, unless they are greatly calumniated, justifies the apprehension that equality of earnings might be imposed as an obligation, and that piecework, and all practices which enable superior industry or abilities to gain a superior reward, might be put down. . . . A person who cares for other people, for his country, or for mankind, is a happier man than one who does not; but . . . [i]t is like preaching to the worm who crawls on the ground how much better it would be for him if he were an Eagle. . . . We all know what specious fallacies may be urged in defense of every act of injustice yet proposed for the imaginary benefit of the mass. We know how many, not otherwise fools or bad men, have thought it justifiable to repudiate the national debt [or] think it fair to throw the whole burden of taxation upon savings, under the name of realized property. . . . One of the greatest dangers, therefore, of democracy, as of all other forms of government, lies in the sinister interests of the holders of power: it is the danger of class legislation.[144]

Aristotle could not have said it better. On the other hand, there is something important and different about Mill's concerns. Mill is a modern. He believes in the value and importance of market economies and commerce. Aristotle did not. Aristotle believed in a specific human telos that could be realized by some, but not by the many. Mill did not believe in a specific human telos. He believed in autonomy, something within the reach of all – and it is this that separates Mill from Nietzsche. It is also the market economy, in part, that creates the possibility of near-universal autonomy – something Aristotle could not have imagined. But liberal culture must be and inevitably will be democratic. Liberal culture will not survive unless the democracy (and the market economy) is informed by autonomy. The virtues that Aristotle thought were achievable by only a minority must be achieved by the many in order for democracy to function properly and for liberal culture to survive. Mill understood that institutional design alone will not solve the problem, that moral regeneration was necessary. However, that does not mean that institutions cannot be refurbished to provide opportunities for the development of autonomy. This is the program that animated Mill's proposed reforms.

Given the inherent norms of liberal culture, and given the dangers of representative government in his own time, what remedies did Mill propose? Although Mill supports universal suffrage and thinks that it should include women, he excludes those who are functionally politically illiterate or receiving welfare. These categories of exclusion are, of course, temporary in the sense that those who find themselves in one of the categories can extricate themselves from it.[145] He also proposes a scheme of plural voting – that is, giving more votes to those who meet an education qualification. But, keeping in mind that there was no free public education at the time, he insists that "universal teaching must precede universal enfranchisement."[146] Mill adds other qualifications to this proposal.

The time is not come for giving to such plans a practical shape, nor should I wish to be bound by the particular proposals which I have made. . . . The plurality of votes must on no account be carried so far that those who are privileged by it, or the class (if any) to which they mainly belong, shall outweigh by means of it all the rest of the community. . . . In the mean time, though the suggestion for the present, may not be a practical one, it will serve to mark what is best in principle. . . .[147]

These qualifications should be kept in mind when reading *On Liberty*. Mill's goal is to raise everyone to the level of an autonomous being and not to impose an authoritarian elite.

Following a suggestion first put forward by Thomas Hare in a pamphlet published in 1859 entitled "Treatise on the Election of Representatives," and expanded upon by Mill's friend Henry Fawcett in 1860 in a publication entitled "Mr. Hare's Reform Bill Simplified and Explained,"[148] Mill proposed a system of proportional representation designed to safeguard minorities.[149] Essentially what it amounted to was that any group could be formed and if large enough, regardless of residence, could bullet vote to guarantee the election of someone who represented their point of view. Mill thus tried to do what Hegel tried to do, that is, to come up with some scheme to represent the real interests within a society. However, instead of defining those interests geographically or simply in economic terms, Mill's scheme provides, without gerrymandering, an infinitely flexible definition of what constitutes a legitimate interest. The interests are defined and re-defined by the voters and not by inflexible legal mandate. His suggestions about proportional representation and the education requirement were both intended to guarantee the presence of formidable advocates and to raise the level of debate.

Mill was opposed to a secret ballot. A person who will not make his or her political views public, for whatever reason, is not an autonomous person. This is an issue on which Mill is critical of John Bright, a Quaker and original member of the anti–corn law league as well as a Manchester School advocate of free trade, a liberal MP, and a sometime ally.

Mr. Bright and his school of democrats think themselves greatly concerned in maintaining that the franchise is what they term a right, not a trust. Now this one idea, taking root in the general mind, does a moral mischief. . . . The suffrage is indeed due to him, among other reasons, as a means to his own protection, but only against treatment from which he is equally bound, so far as depends on his vote, to protect every one of his fellow citizens. His vote is not a thing in which he has an option; it has no more to do with his personal wishes than the verdict of a juryman. It is strictly a matter of duty; he is bound to give it accordingly to his best and most conscientious opinion of the public good.[150]

Mill was skeptical about schemes for redistribution. He always insisted that takings be accompanied by compensation and that most social programs consist of loans to be repaid. Consistent with that view, he recommended that only those who pay taxes be allowed to vote on issues of taxation. Remember as well that Mill favored a flat tax and not a graduated rate.

It is also important that the assembly which votes the taxes, either general or local, should be elected exclusively by those who pay something toward the tax imposed. Those who pay no taxes, disposing by their votes of other people's money, have every motive to be lavish and none to economize. . . . It amounts to allowing them to put their hands into other people's pockets for any purpose which they think fit to call a public one, which, in the great towns of the United States, is known to have produced a scale of local taxation onerous beyond example, and wholly borne by the wealthier classes.[151]

Mill made a number of suggestions about the membership of Parliament. He opposed pay for MPs, on the ground that being a representative should not become a career path; rather, it should be a form of public service designed to attract those with a better education and sense of the common good. He opposed the notion that representatives should be required to pledge in advance how they would vote on certain issues. He also suggested what today would be called campaign finance reform as a way to limit the possibility of elections' turning on the basis of the monetary support of special interests. Mill also suggested a division between professional bureaucracies, which were to do most of the technical work of the government, and Parliament, which was to oversee that work rather than engage in it itself. This not only raised the professional level of administration – so necessary in a democracy, where mediocrity was the rule – but also served as a check on bureaucratic power.

With regard to the larger structural features of representative government, Mill made the following observations. He favored more frequent elections and opposed "lame ducks" on the ground that Parliament should reflect "a periodic general muster of opposing forces to gauge the state of the national mind, and ascertain, beyond dispute, the relative strength of different parties and opinions."[152] He was sympathetic to the notion of two houses, but thought that the House of Lords as then constituted was an anachronism at best. "I cannot believe that, in a really democratic state of society, the House of Lords would be of any practical value as a moderator of democracy."[153] He preferred, instead, a second chamber composed of dignitaries who had distinguished themselves in public service, but specifically excluding intellectuals.

> The functions conferring the senatorial dignity should be limited to those of a legal, political, or military or naval character. Scientific and literary eminence are too indefinite and disputable: they imply a power of selection, whereas the other qualifications speak for themselves.[154]

He is not enamored of indirect election, except in the case of the United States Senate. In the nineteenth century, U.S. senators were still selected by the state legislatures rather than directly elected. Mill believed that this permitted more eminent personages to become senators than would have been the case with direct election. The same sort of argument is behind his preference for the British system in which the prime minister is selected by and from within the majority party of representatives instead of being directly elected, as in the case of the president of the United States.

> The eminent men of a party, in an election extending to the whole country, are never its most available candidates. All eminent men have made personal enemies, or have done something or, at the lowest, professed some opinion obnoxious to some local or other considerable division of the community, and likely to tell with fatal effect upon the number of votes. . . . When the highest dignity in the state is to be conferred by popular election once in every few years, the whole intervening time is spent in what is virtually a canvas. President, ministers, chiefs of parties, and their followers, are all electioneers: the whole community is kept intent on the mere personalities of politics, and every public question is discussed and decided with less reference to its merits than to its expected bearing on the presidential election.[155]

Following Tocqueville again, Mill sees merit in a federal system but recognizes that where power is divided between a central authority and member states, a Supreme Court is needed to adjudicate jurisdictions.

Mill's most enduring remarks concern the very nature of government itself. Government performs two great functions. It conducts the public business, and is in itself a "great influence acting on the human mind." Political participation is a form of civic education. Thus, on the one hand, Mill insists upon limiting the sphere of the government so as to prevent abuse and to protect the private sphere. These limits on state action he had made clear in *On Liberty* and in the concluding chapter of the *Principles of Political Economy*. However, to the extent that government does attend to the public business, it should see this as an opportunity to promote civic virtue.

Among the foremost benefits of free government is that education of the intelligence and of the sentiments which is carried down to the very lowest ranks of the people when they are called to take part in acts which directly affect the great interests of their country.[156]

Toward this end, Mill favored as much localism[157] and decentralization as possible, so as to maximize political participation and political education. Consistent with the perceived need for the political education of the masses, Mill arranged for the publications of several of his more famous works in "people's editions," – that is, less expensive editions – and he agreed to forgo his royalties in those editions. Moreover, he made available to workingmen's clubs copies of those of his works not available in the people's editions.

The foregoing summary of Mill's political philosophy shows how difficult it would be to put him into the usual categories. Was Mill a democrat? One insightful way of putting it is to say, as Stafford does, that Mill approved of democratic institutions but objected to democratic society. In this respect, Mill followed Tocqueville, and this is what gives strength to Kahan's thesis of aristocratic liberalism. Democracy was not part of the essence of liberal culture, but it was an unavoidable feature of modern life. As such, the proper response is to tame it in the service of liberal culture. As he put it in a letter to Henry Fawcett about the Hare plan, "[I]t is an uphill race, and a race against time for if the American form of democracy overtakes us first, the majority will no more relax their despotism than a single despot would. But our only chance is to come forward as Liberals, carrying out the democratic idea, not as Conservatives, resisting it."[158]

Was Mill in favor of limited government or of government activism? Again, this is the wrong question to ask. Mill was not an ideologue. If something can be done by private agencies, then the government ought not to do it. What can and cannot be done will vary with circumstance. Was Mill a civic humanist? He certainly believed in promoting civic virtue, but he realized that this was a far more complex issue in a liberal culture that denied the existence of a collective good. Mill's political philosophy has to be seen in its own terms, and in those terms, the primacy of autonomy and the necessity of promoting autonomy for everyone is the key to the coherence of his political vision.

One last item of contrast is worth mentioning. In constructing the federal system of the United States, the founders – specifically, the authors of the *Federalist Papers*, and more specifically, Madison, following the suggestions of Hume – suggested institutions that were focused on limiting the abuse of power and on recognizing the shortcomings of human beings. That was a widely held view in the eighteenth century, as can be seen even in the writings of Kant. In the nineteenth century, and with the presumed benefit of hindsight, Tocqueville and Mill saw something else. There were no institutional structures that could not be altered and corrupted in a democracy. The institutions of liberal culture, including representative government, needed to plumb and retrieve their moral depths if that culture were to continue to survive. It is not a question of whether Britain or the United States survived or even achieved world hegemony. The question would remain, on what terms had it achieved survival or preeminence?

In the wake of 1989 and the collapse of the Soviet Union, a striking thesis was revived by Francis Fukuyama in an article and a subsequent book, *The End of History and the Last Man*. Fukuyama reminded us that it was Hegel who had suggested that history came to an end with the American and French Revolutions, because it was out of these revolutions that there emerged the insight that "what truly satisfies human beings is not so much material prosperity as recognition of their status and dignity,"[159] what we have called autonomy. But as Fukuyama goes on to say, the issue is not who won the cold war but "the goodness of liberal democracy itself" and whether it will fall "prey to serious internal contradictions."[160] It is no accident that Fukuyama cited Hegel. What is remarkable is that this is precisely the state of discussion of the status of liberal culture to be found in Mill's work of 1861!

10

Public Intellectual (1859–1869)

Fashioning a New Life

FOLLOWING Harriet's death and during that part of the year that Mill and Helen had spent at the house in Blackheath Park, Mill began to cultivate a new social life with some old friends, including Grote. Mill had praised Grote's *History of Greece* in the *Edinburgh Review* in 1853, and this had paved the way to reviving their friendship; they had been estranged because of Mrs. Grote's opposition to the marriage with Harriet. Mill made some new friends as well. He organized Saturday dinners at Blackheath Park and dutifully arranged to meet his guests at 5:00 P.M. as they alighted from the train from Charing Cross. Those guests included Bain, the Amberleys (Lord Amberley was the eldest son of Lord John Russell and subsequently the father of Bertrand Russell, to whom Mill would become godfather in 1872), Fawcett, John Elliot Cairnes (a young man Mill had met at the Political Economy Club in 1859), Moncure Conway (an American who had succeeded Fox at South Place Chapel), Herbert Spencer, Louis Blanc (the exiled French socialist), Gomperz (Mill's German translator), Mill's ex-colleague Thornton, Thomas Hare (who had proposed the system of proportional representation), and John Morley.

Thornton had once expostulated to Gomperz on the rare privilege of being one of Mill's friends: "Few enjoyed it, but those who did, knew how to value it. Of the immeasurable goodness of this man he could not as yet have any idea. He himself [Thornton] had many friends, but he rated Mill higher than all of them taken together. The three weeks which he had spent with him at Avignon the previous autumn had been the happiest in his life."[1]

Morley was a young journalist who had caught Mill's attention by writing the "New Ideas" column in the *Saturday Review* and who in 1867 became editor of the *Fortnightly Review*; he was to become one of Mill's outspoken secular defenders. With Mill as his patron saint,[2] Morley turned the *Fortnightly* away from being a sectarian organ of Comte's followers into precisely the kind of periodical that Mill had always wished the *Westminster* to be. Among its illustrious contributors were Bagehot, George Eliot, Harrison, Huxley, Henry Sidgwick, Spencer, Leslie Stephen, and Trollope. In fact, as Bain tells us, "for many years, he [Mill] was wont to encourage young men to send him their productions for criticism and advice. He took a great deal of trouble in recommending such articles to editors; and thus helped to start not a few men in a literary career."[3]

Another of Mill's new friends was the former engineer and self-taught philosopher Herbert Spencer (1820–1903). In 1848, Spencer had become one of the editors of the *Economist*, and this had led to his meeting such figures as Chapman, Lewes, George Eliot, T. H. Huxley, Carlyle, and Mill. Spencer had endeared himself to Mill by constructively challenging the theory of knowledge in the *Logic* in a way that led Mill to revise his views and eventually to address some unresolved issues in *Hamilton*. Spencer became an immensely influential figure not only by championing evolution as a biological theory but also by applying it as a general metaphysical principle, interpreted in a teleological or progressive fashion. In ethics, Spencer adopted a form of utilitarianism that sought to make egoism compatible with altruism; in politics, his social Darwinism was reflected in an extreme defense of laissez-faire. An episode from Spencer's own autobiography reveals Mill's sense of humor. When Spencer invited Mill to go fishing, Mill declined by referring to his own hobby of botany, replying that "my murderous propensities are confined to the vegetable world."[4]

Spencer was for a long time in financial difficulties. Among other things, Mill had subsidized a failed periodical for him called the *Reader*. After trying to talk Grote into getting Spencer a position on the senate of London University, Mill had even tried to help Spencer obtain a position in the new India House. Spencer was overwhelmed by what he could only describe as a "generosity that might almost be called romantic." On Mill's death, Spencer would write an account in the *Examiner* of the nobility of Mill's respect for intellectual disagreement.

In upholding Realism, I had opposed in decided ways those metaphysical systems to which his own Idealism was closely allied; and we had long carried on a controversy respecting the test of truth, in which I had similarly attacked Mr. Mill's position in an outspoken manner. That, under such circumstances, he should have volunteered his aid, and urged it upon me, as he did, on the ground that it would not imply any personal obligation, proved in him a very exceptional generosity.[5]

Henry Fawcett was a blind economist who taught at Cambridge. He was also an admirer of Mill and a man of whom it was said that he had memorized the *Principles of Political Economy*. His wife was Millicent Garrett, a major figure in the British suffragette movement. Fawcett was later to serve in Parliament as an ally of Mill and eventually to become postmaster general under Gladstone, whereupon he introduced the parcel post and post office savings stamps.

Mill began once more to take an interest in public affairs. In the December 1859 issue of *Fraser's Magazine*, he wrote an article entitled "A Few Words on Non-Intervention." He took the opportunity to excoriate Palmerston for his opposition to the Suez Canal project. It was also an opportunity to recognize Britain's unique position on the world stage, which he was later to reiterate, about both Great Britain and the United States, in *Representative Government*. It was Britain that was to bear the torch for the defense of liberal culture, and any criticism Mill had of British culture was to be understood as a constructive attempt to keep it from faltering.

There is a country in Europe... whose foreign policy is, to let other nations alone.... Any attempt it makes to exert influence over them, even by persuasion, is rather in the service of others, than itself: to mediate in the quarrels which break out between foreign States, to arrest obstinate civil wars, to reconcile belligerents, to intercede for mild treatment of the vanquished, or finally, to procure the abandonment of some national crime and scandal to humanity such as the slave-trade.... If the aggression of barbarians force it to a successful war, and its victorious arms put it in a position to command liberty of trade, whatever it demands for itself it demands for all mankind. The cost of the war is its own; the fruits it shares in fraternal equality with the whole human race. Its own ports and commerce are free as the air and the sky: all its neighbors have full liberty to resort to it.... A nation adopting this policy is a novelty in the world; so much so, it would appear, that many are unable to believe it when they see it.[6]

In 1861, Civil War broke out in the United States. Many in Britain, especially in the upper classes, supported the Confederacy. Not so Mill:

I knew that it was in all its stages an aggressive enterprise of the slave-owners to extend the territory of slavery; under the combined influences of pecuniary interest, domineering temper, and the fanaticism of a class for its privileges.... Their success [Confederacy]... would be a victory of the powers of evil and would give courage to the enemies of progress and damp the spirits of its friends all over the civilized world, while it would create a formidable military power, grounded on the worst and most anti-social form of the tyranny of men over men, and ... destroying for a long time the prestige of the great democratic republic.... On the other hand, if the spirit of the North was sufficiently roused to carry the war to a successful termination ... I foresaw ... that the bulk of the Northern population, whose conscience had as yet been awakened only to the point of resisting the further extension of slavery, but whose fidelity to the Constitution of the United States made them disapprove of any attempt by the Federal Government to interfere with slavery in the States where it already existed ... would join their banner with that of the noble body of Abolitionists of whom Garrison was the courageous and single-minded apostle, Wendell Phillips the eloquent orator, and John Brown the voluntary martyr [compared by Mill to Sir Thomas More].... These hopes, so far as related to Slavery, have been completely, and in other respects are in course of being progressively realized.[7]

Mill felt very strongly about support for the North. The antislavery movement struck him as just the sort of defense of liberty that voluntary associations could promote. He was also annoyed and disappointed with his former assistant Thornton for supporting the South. On the other hand, he was delighted to hear that his old adversary Dr. Whewell supported the North to such an extent that Whewell would not allow the *Times*, which was pro-South, to be in his home. Writing to John Elliot Cairnes, whose book *The Slave Power* was dedicated to Mill, Mill compared Lincoln to Socrates: "[T]he death of Lincoln, like that of Socrates, is a worthy end to a noble life, and puts the seal of universal remembrance upon his worth. He has now a place among the great names of history...."[8]

In 1862, Mill visited Greece for a period of two months. He had hoped to be joined by Grote, but Grote's health precluded his taking the trip. Mill later spent Christmas of 1862 at Grote's country residence, Barrow Green – Bentham's old house, where Mill had spent part of his childhood. Grote recalled this visit as one in which Mill was "violent against the South in this American struggle; embracing heartily the extreme Abolitionist views, and thinking about little else in regard to the general question."[9] Although those with a deeper knowledge of United States history may consider Mill's attitude a bit simplistic, it is interesting to note the extent to which Mill projected onto America the British division between Tory landholders on the one side, and the alliance of antislavery and utilitarian advocates on the other.

Theodor Gomperz visited Mill in London during 1863, and his notes give us some indication of what Mill's life was like at that time. Mill took him to a meeting of the Political Economy Club, at which Thornton, Fawcett, and Leslie Stephen were also present. The topic under discussion was whether cab fares should be set by law. Gomperz also accompanied Mill to a meeting of the trade unionists at St. James Hall to hear Bright speak in support of the Northern states in the American Civil War. Gomperz described this meeting as a remarkable spectacle.

I shall never forget the venerable man [Mill], as he sat there like a youth, deeply agitated, applauding the speeches not only of John Bright and Professor Beesley, but also the simple words of an Irish workman. This had been, for some time at least, Mill's first appearance in a public meeting, and by those who knew him, he was warmly greeted.[10]

Mill dealt with emotional pain in the same way throughout his life, that is, by working hard. One of the things he wrote in 1861 was *The Subjection of Women*, but it was not published until 1869. From 1863 to 1865, he wrote *An Examination of Sir William Hamilton*. Mill had a polemical agenda in *Hamilton*,[11] but he also had a serious philosophical one: "I mean in this book to do what the nature and scope of the Logic forbade me to do there, to face the ultimate metaphysical difficulties of every question on which I touch."[12] It is important to note that in several ways Mill had pulled his punches in the *Logic*. Views that are often attributed to Mill as products of his later thinking – or, in less flattering terms, as late fantasying – were views that he had expressed at a much earlier period, but not in print. Mill, whose favorite philosopher was Berkeley, was a philosophical Idealist – that is, he held the metaphysical view that all of reality consists of the contents of the mind or is in some way related to the contents of the mind. Consider the following early statement of Idealism:

What we call our bodily sensations are all in the mind, and would not necessarily or probably cease because the body perishes. As the eye is but the window *through* which, not the power *by* which, the mind sees, so probably the understanding is the bodily eye of the human spirit, which looks through that window, or rather, which sees (as in Plato's cave) the camera obscura images of things in this life, while in another it may or might be capable of seeing the things themselves.[13] Consider as well an early expression in the belief of a free will: "It is necessary, that is, it was inevitable from the beginning of things, that I should freely will whatever things I do will."[14]

Before quoting that agenda, it is interesting to note that in *Hamilton* the adversary is not identified with the German a priori school but specifically with the British context of philosophical intuitionism. Partly, this reflects Mill's focus on domestic political issues (Scottish commonsense realists, starting way back with Dugald Stewart, had been generally in favor of strong government intervention as opposed to laissez-faire); partly, it re-flects his increased respect for Kant, whom he had by now read carefully, and the concessions he will make to idealist metaphysics.

[T]he difference between these two schools of philosophy, that of Intuition, and that of Experience and Association, is not a mere matter of abstract speculation; it is full of practical consequences, and lies at the foundation of all the greatest differences of practical opinion in an age of progress. The practical reformer has continually to demand that changes be made in things which are supported by powerful and widely spread feelings, or to question the apparent necessity and indefeasibleness of established facts; and it is often an indispensable part of his argument to shew, how those powerful feelings had their origin, and how those facts came to seem necessary and indefeasible. There is therefore a natural hostility between him and a philosophy which discourages the explanation of feelings and moral facts by circumstances and association, and prefers to treat them as ultimate elements of human nature; a philosophy which is addicted to holding up favorite doctrines as intuitive truths, and deems intuition to be the voice of Nature and of God, speaking with an authority higher than that of our reason. In particular, I have long felt that the prevailing tendency to regard all the marked distinctions of human character as innate, and in the main indelible, and to ignore the irresistible proofs that by far the greater part of those differences, whether between individuals, races, or sexes, are as not only might but naturally would be produced by differences in circumstances, is one of the chief hindrances to the rational treatment of great social questions and one of the greatest stumbling blocks to human improvement. This tendency has its source in the intuitional metaphysics which characterized the reaction of the nineteenth century against the eighteenth, and it is a tendency so agreeable to human indolence, as well as to conservative interests generally, that unless attacked at the very root, it is sure to be carried to even a greater length than is really justified by the more moderate forms of the intuitional philosophy. That philosophy, not always in its moderate forms, had ruled the thought of Europe for the greater part of a century. My father's *Analysis of the Mind*, my own *Logic*, and Professor Bain's great treatise, had attempted to reintroduce a better mode of philosophizing, latterly with quite as much success as could be expected; but I had for some time felt that the mere contrast of the two philosophies was not enough, that there ought to be a hand-to-hand fight between them, that controversial as well as expository writings were needed, and that the time was come when such controversy would be useful. Considering then the writings and fame of Sir W. Hamilton as the great fortress of the intuitional philosophy in this country, a fortress the more formidable from the imposing character, and the in many respects great personal merits and mental endowments, of the man, I thought it might be a real service to philosophy to attempt a thorough examination of all his most important doctrines, and an estimate of his general claims to eminence as a philosopher.[15]

We are less concerned here with Mill's critique of Hamilton and more with his own positive metaphysical position. The overall argument of *An Examination of Sir William Hamilton's Philosophy* (1865) may be summarized as follows. Sir William Hamilton's philosophy was an attempt to combine Thomas Reid with Kant. In both Mill and Hamilton, metaphysics begins with the analysis of consciousness; but Hamilton used an introspective method, whereas Mill used a psychological one. According to Hamilton, consciousness gives us immediate knowledge of the external physical world (Reid's Scottish realism) and of the mind itself. Mill will argue, in opposition to Hamilton, that consciousness gives us only mental phenomena. Hamilton, moreover, maintained that introspective intuition presented us with (Kant's view) a set of necessary principles and a set of irreducible laws of thought. Mill, on the contrary, will argue for the reduction of these principles and laws to phenomena and the laws of association. Mill's argument is that introspection can show only that we are conscious of certain beliefs, not that these beliefs are original. Instead, Mill maintained that these beliefs were acquired by the process he described as association. Hamilton argued, further, that the intuitive beliefs were immediate, necessary, and indubitable, because we assent to them so readily. Mill countered with the Humean argument that indubitability and necessity reflected habitual association. Moreover, inconceivability often reflects lack of knowledge and the limitations of the imagination, as instanced by the example of our once believing that people could not live at the antipodes because they would fall off the Earth.

There are two main metaphysical issues generated by Mill's phenom-
enalistic epistemology – the status of matter (or the existence of the external world) and the status of mind. Mill challenged the Hamiltonian
contention that the existence of an external world is immediately revealed in consciousness. Using Berkeley's argument from the latter's *New
Theory of Vision*, Mill pointed out that the belief in an external world
could have been acquired or learned in the same way that we learn how to
perceive distance. The belief in the existence of matter (external world)
is explained by means of the "Psychological Theory of the Belief in an
External World."[16] The two elements of this theory are the postulated
existence of a mind and the psychological laws of association.[17] The mind
is able to organize perceptions into "objects" and, through repetition, to
project or anticipate that those "objects" or groupings of perceptions will
reappear. This leads us to ascribe a permanency to those "objects," even
when they are not part of our current experience. In fact, an external object is defined as something that we believe to exist even when we are not
perceiving or thinking about it; we believe that external objects persevere
even when the associated perceptions change within a given range, so long
as others report the same range of change. Matter is thus defined as "a
Permanent Possibility of Sensation,"[18] and bodies are groups of simultaneous possibilities of sensation.

The mind that is postulated in explaining matter cannot itself be accounted for in exactly the same way. Although mind is "nothing but a
series of *our* sensations (to which must now be added *our internal* feelings),
as they actually occur, with the addition of infinite possibilities of feeling"
[italics added],[19] it also encompasses expectation and memory. Expectation and memory go beyond mental phenomena because they presuppose
a continuous subject who has had, continues to have, and will have sensations and feelings to which no one else can have direct access. In short,
the entire series of the past, present, and future states of consciousness
seem to belong to "the self-same series of states."[20] The series seems to
be a whole that has an identity over and beyond the parts that make it up.

"I do not profess to have adequately accounted for the belief in Mind,"
said Mill.[21] We do not experience the mind directly (Hume and Kant had
already made this point). Rather, what we are dealing with phenomenalis-
tically is a series of feelings. What is peculiar about this series of feelings is
that it is aware of itself as having a past and a future. The series thus relies
upon memory and expectation, now understood to be primitive notions

not reducible to sensations: "[I]n so far as reference to an ego is implied in expectation I do postulate an ego."[22] The existence of mind, then, is a necessary presupposition for which we can offer no further account.[23]

There seems to be no ground for believing, with Sir W. Hamilton and Mr. Mansel, that the Ego is an original presentation of consciousness. . . . The fact of recognizing a sensation, of being reminded of it, and, as we say, remembering that it has been felt before, is the simplest and most elementary fact of memory; and the inexplicable tie, or law, the organic union . . . which connects the present consciousness with the past one, of which it reminds me, is as near as I think we can get to a positive conception of self. That there is something real in this tie, real as the sensations themselves, and not a mere product of the laws of thought without any fact corresponding to it, I hold to be indubitable. The precise nature of the process by which we cognize it, is open to much dispute. Whether we are directly conscious of it in the act of remembrance, as we are of succession in the fact of having successive sensations [Hume's view], or whether according to the opinion of Kant, we are not conscious of a self at all, but are compelled to assume it as a necessary condition of memory, I do not undertake to decide.[24]

To sum up, nature or the so-called external physical world is a construct of consciousness. The mind, however, is not a construct of consciousness, because it is the mind that does the constructing.

Although we cannot prove the existence of our own mind, we must assume it. However, we can, according to Mill, prove the existence of other minds.

I am aware, by experience, of a group of permanent possibilities of sensation which I call my body, and which my experience shows to be an universal condition of every part of my thread of consciousness. I am also aware of a great number of other groups, resembling the one that I call my body, but which have no connection, such as that has, with the remainder of my thread of consciousness. This disposes me to draw an inductive inference, that those other groups are connected with other threads of consciousness, as mine is with my own. If the evidence stopped here, the inference would be but an hypothesis; reaching only to the inferior degree of inductive evidence called analogy. The evidence, however, does not stop here. . . . I find that my subsequent consciousness presents those very sensations of speech heard, of movements and other outward demeanor seen, and so forth, which, being the effects or consequents of actual feelings in my own case, I should expect to follow upon those other hypothetical feelings if they really exist; and thus the hypothesis is verified.[25]

The Scottish school of common sense and its leading figure, Thomas Reid, had maintained that sensations are accompanied by an automatic belief in an external cause. This automatic belief in the real world is not, according to Reid, an inference or construct. For Reid, we perceive not the contents of our mind but the objective qualities of physical things. Sir William Hamilton took a somewhat intermediary position, holding that while we cannot know objects in themselves we can know the primary qualities of objects. God guarantees, for Hamilton, the connection between the primary qualities and the objects. Mill agreed that we cannot validly infer the existence of objects from our perceptions. (Berkeley, Hume, Kant, and even Reid agree on this.) He also agreed with Hamilton that we cannot know objects in themselves, a consequence of modern scientific theories. Hence any extreme realist version of Reid's position that insists that we directly perceive objects is sheer dogmatism. Where Mill did score against Hamilton is by pointing out that as soon as Hamilton distinguished between perceptions and objects he would be forced either to infer the one from the other – something he recognized could not be done – or to reopen the gap between sensations and things. The only way to close the gap, thinks Mill, is to recognize that sensations "are all that we have ground for believing to exist."[26] Any further explanation of exactly how the mind "constructs" an object must refer to the laws of association.

It is no longer fashionable to state this problem or the various responses to it in terms of sensations. In the contemporary philosophical context, it would be more apt to say that we are forced to recognize or distinguish between the preconceptual basis of our thinking – that is, common sense (or however we choose to characterize) it – and our technical conceptualizations. The great divide in philosophy is between those who continue to espouse the possibility of conceptualizing the preconceptual and those who deny it. The Enlightenment Project and its positivist heirs, who espouse a totally scientific worldview, still opt for total conceptualization, even if they have not been able to produce it. Mill, like the later Wittgenstein, did not believe it was possible to give such a conceptualization. This explains both why he is thought by some to be an "inferior" philosopher and why, in the end, Mill, like other philosophical idealists, needed to supplement his philosophy with a big picture drawn from religion.

Basic to Mill's metaphysics is the contention that how we understand ourselves is fundamental, and how we understand the world is derivative. It is not possible to understand ourselves as physical entities or to explain our mental contents in terms of physical events. Hence, even though science is an extension of common sense, the extension, or the way in which we use physical science to understand the world, is not the way in which we understand ourselves. In discussing the limits of explanation, Mill remarked that there can be no explanation of "how or why a motion, or a chemical action can produce a sensation of coluor."[27] To be sure, there is continuity between common sense and science, but what this amounts to is the contention that science is an extension of common sense and cannot overrule it.

There can never be a perspective wholly external to humanity such that from that perspective we could give a wholly external, and in that sense objective, validation of our understanding of ourselves and the world. "For in the present state of the discussion on these topics, it is almost universally allowed that the existence of matter or of spirit, of space or of time, is in its nature unsusceptible of being proved; and that if anything is known of them, it must be by immediate intuition."[28] Whatever account we give is going to be internal to the human community.

My able American critic, Dr. H. B. Smith, contends ... that these facts afford no proofs that objects *are* external to us. I never pretended that they do. I am accounting for our conceiving, or representing to ourselves, the permanent possibilities as real objects external to us. I do not believe that the real externality to us of anything, except other minds, is capable of proof. ... He has somehow imagined that I am defending, instead of attacking, the belief in matter as an entity per se. ... I assume only the tendency, but not the legitimacy of the tendency, to extend all the laws of our own experience to a sphere beyond experience.[29]

This will disappoint and frustrate many philosophers, especially those imbued with the spirit of the Enlightenment Project, who had hoped to establish physical science as that objective and externally validating framework.[30]

There is another important consequence. The whole point of the induction discussion in Mill is Wittgensteinian – namely, that there can be no conceptualization of the preconceptual domain. One of the consequences of this doctrine for political philosophy is that there can be no notion of a rigid structure to social institutions. All thinking moves from particular to particular and is always subject to revision pending new experience. There is nothing in the world or in our thinking of the world that is impervious to change. This is the real impetus behind Mill's metaphysical speculation.

It follows as well that there is ultimately something circular about any philosophical account that takes common sense as its starting point. We can never escape the human perspective. In the end, the only logical test of a philosophical system would be its coherence. To reiterate this point, we note[31] that there are three ontological conceptions: either (a) reality is a mechanism, or (b) reality is an organic entity, or (c) reality is personal (consciousness). In addition to these three ontological conceptions, there are three perspectives from which these three conceptions can be viewed: the perspective of (1) an egocentric outside observer, (2) an embodied agent, or (3) a socially engaged agent (common sense). Mill can be characterized as someone who subscribes to the personal conception of reality (c) but who studies it from the perspective of common sense (3).[32] Of all the possible combinations, only this combination, the one found in Mill, is mutually inclusive. All of the other approaches run into irresolvable philosophical problems. Coherence may not be the only intellectual virtue, but it seems to be a virtue exclusive to absolute idealism. Nature, or the so-called external physical world, is a construct of the mind. We cannot explain ourselves in the way in which we explain Nature. Hence, Mill cannot give an account of the mind as a construct from the elements of consciousness. He recognized this and made no such attempt. Bain recognized Mill's "uncompromising Idealism, and . . . his varied and forcible exposition of it."[33] It is important to recognize that British Idealism in the late nineteenth century was not an aberration but the legitimate heir to Mill's own idealism.

Mill's metaphysical discussion, such as it is, did accomplish his negative goal of discrediting Hamilton's position, or the position of intuitionism. Moreover, Mill offers an alternative and plausible account of our thinking without the use of fixed a priori thinking.[34] He does this by transcending it (in a manner analogous to the way in which Hegel goes beyond Kant). Essentially, his negative program succeeds by showing that he shares the same starting point and does not have to arrive at the same terminus. The accomplishment of Mill's negative goal does not lead to the positive goal (in *Hamilton*) of spelling out what the total big picture of Mill's metaphysics would be. The only coherent line of development open to him is the movement toward Hegelian absolute idealism. This was recognized by his acute successor F. H. Bradley.[35] To the extent that Mill did speculate on the big picture in his philosophy of religion, his views moved him even closer to Hegel.

How, then, are we to understand ourselves? Mill's answer is given in part by his abstract discussion of the freedom of the will and in part by his specific explanations in the areas of social science, morality, politics, economics, religion, art, and so on. In keeping with the Romantic and idealist orientation of his thinking, his answers are always given phenomenologically, historically, and causally. Ultimately, this means that we must give an historical account of the growth of our awareness of our autonomy. This historical account applies both to ourselves as individuals and to the larger community. In fact, the growth within the individual mirrors that of the community. History is the history of autonomy. Causal accounts are ultimately historical accounts, and historical accounts are self-constructing accounts. This underscores the importance for social science and social philosophy of a philosophy of history. Consciousness becomes identical with self-consciousness. In the end, explanation must be a narrative.

We come now to the difficult issue of the so-called freedom of the will. There are three questions concerning the issue of free will in Mill's writings. First, did Mill believe that we can form our own characters? The answer to this question is unequivocally yes. It was a central part of his position and of his advocacy of *Bildung*. The second question is, did this commitment to the view that we have the power to form our own characters require the existence of a self with the practical freedom to make unconstrained choices? That is, does the doctrine of autonomy require something like free will? The answer to this question is that in Mill's case there is need of something like free will in order to make sense of autonomy. The third question is whether there are resources in Mill's philosophy for making sense of something like the freedom of the will. On this question there is much scholarly debate, and the consensus is that Mill failed to offer an adequate account. If his critics are right and he failed to provide an adequate account, this does not invalidate or obviate the claims that (a) we can form our own character and that (b) autonomy does presuppose freedom of the will. However, we shall maintain that our previous discussion of Mill's philosophical idealism does provide him with some of the resources to make sense of the conception of the freedom of the will.

Before launching into a discussion of the aforementioned three questions, let us examine the intellectual context in which Mill wrestled with
these problems. The problem of free will goes back to the Old Testament. If God is all-powerful and all-knowing, then everything is pre-
destined and human beings are without free will. Some have responded
that God has the power to give human beings free will. It was much
more difficult to hold this position in the mechanical and deterministic world of early modern physics. For that reason, among others, early
Protestant reformers such as Luther and Calvin embraced some form of
predestination.

There are two other ways of avoiding this problem. One could maintain that God is not all-powerful, as Mill eventually did; but then one
is still faced with the existence of the deterministic world of Newtonian
physics. The other escape was proposed by Kant, who maintained both
that causality was part of the mental apparatus with which we cognize
the world and that God is apprehended transcendentally and not as the
transcendent cause of a mechanical universe. Neither of these solutions
appealed to the religious community.

When Mill returned to the discussion of the philosophical issue of free
will in *Hamilton*, he did three things. First, he repeated the arguments
from the *Logic*.[36] Second, as we saw in our discussion of his philosophic
idealism, he assented to the existence of a self or ego as an additional
metaphysical postulate beyond the existence of phenomenal data. A self
or ego beyond the data provided the opening for a deeper conception of
the freedom of the will. Mill read this doctrine back into the *Logic* by
referring, in later editions of the *Logic*, to the discussion in *Hamilton*. As
one of his archcritics, Jevons, pointed out, Mill explained "[necessity]
away so ingeniously, that he unintentionally converts it into Free
Will."[37]

The third thing that Mill provided was an argument from Kant that
enabled him to answer critics such as Mansel who had pointed out the
weaknesses of Mill's earlier argument. Mansel was a professor at Oxford,
a follower of Hamilton, and later dean of St. Paul's. Among the many
things Mill objected to in Mansel was the latter's assertion, in *The Limits of
Religious Thought*, that the acceptance of God's goodness and omnipotence
were matters of faith and that evil therefore did not really exist. This
sort of argument also lent itself to a defense of the social and economic
status quo.

Mill's Kantian argument is that the predictability needed for social science was compatible with a much stronger sense of freedom. Predictability is compatible with freedom because causality operates between character and action; character formation is where we are free. You may safely predict my actions based upon insight into my character, but this in no way requires that my character be the result of forces beyond my control. By accepting the possibility of a transcendental self,[38] Mill can acknowledge that not only our conduct but also our character is, in part, amenable to our will. As Bain put it, Mill wrote as "a transcendentalist . . . differing only in degree."[39]

So far we have made a case for how the evolution of Mill's thinking on the issue of freedom of the will moved toward the notion of a transcendental self, thereby rendering his position on autonomy more compatible with the need for a robust sense of freedom. We have not yet spelled out the details of that compatibility. Moreover, we have to this point analogized Mill with Kant. Mill's more robust position actually has more in common with Hegel than with Kant. We turn now to that elaboration. As a monist (like Hegel), Mill rejected all forms of dualism. We, as selves, are in the world and influenced by it and by other selves. The explanation we give of our ability to mold the world and to mold ourselves has to be the same kind of explanation. There are causal chains in the world. We learn that we have the power to manipulate these chains. There are causal chains involving ourselves, our beliefs, and our feelings. That is, there is the growing awareness that feelings are constructs from prior social contexts that have been forgotten. We learn that we can overcome these chains as well. That is, we have the power to forge our own characters.

The danger with the process as so far described is that it seems to presuppose that there are prior conditions such that others can (a) manipulate us and (b) undo our best efforts to form our own characters. This danger can be obviated if there are beliefs or forms of knowledge that are inherently emancipatory and irreversible. That is, if there are states of knowledge that, once obtained, cannot be overridden, then there is no longer any danger (beyond a certain threshold) of outside manipulation.[40] Mill recognized such emancipatory beliefs both in individuals and in historical periods. Providing support for this position is Mill's purely historical conception of causality. By making causality simply constant succession, he collapses the distinction between a cause and a prior condition. He also collapses the distinction between a motive and a reason for an action. Emancipatory beliefs are reasons for action that cannot be overridden.

How, then, does choice function? There is no choice in a vacuum. All choices are constrained by context as the prior condition. Choice is a mental event that is clearly influenced by information (another condition). One item of information available to some of us is that we have the capacity to be autonomous. This is an example of an emancipatory belief. This capacity is potentially unconstrained. It is potentially unconstrained because of the existence of a self or ego (a quasi-transcendental self). Will is not an impulse or contextless choice; rather, it is a concatenation of thought and desire. What is true is that there is a self that is supervenient on the concatenation. It is this that makes possible the emancipation of will from desire. This is why it was important to recognize not only Mill's assertion of an ego but also his belief in our historical relationship to God. My belief about myself leads to certain actions, and these actions lead to a transformation of who I am. Irreversible ideas are not possible in a purely mechanical or purely organic universe, but they are possible in an historically evolving universe.

Are we free to choose any course of action? The answer is yes and no. We are "absolutely" free in the sense that there are no purely external conditions that dictate a choice. In reality, however, we are only "relatively" free, in the sense that our belief about or understanding of a situation and of ourselves is a condition that influences choice. There are implicit norms in the historical contexts in which we find ourselves. Responsible action involves the apprehension and pursuit of those implicit norms. The apprehension of those norms is not a matter of the grasping of an external structure but rather of the imaginative identification of the evolving meaning of a practice. Moreover, our capacity for autonomy is precisely what permits us to impose that order upon ourselves. This is how Mill stated this position in his essay *Nature*:

Man necessarily obeys the laws of nature, or in other words, the properties of things, but he does not necessarily *guide* himself by them. Though all conduct is in conformity to laws of nature, all conduct is not grounded on knowledge of them and intelligently directed to the attainment of purposes by means of them. Though we cannot emancipate ourselves from the laws of nature as a whole, we can escape from any particular law of nature if we are able to withdraw ourselves from the circumstances in which it acts. Though we can do nothing except through laws of nature we can use one law to counteract another.[41]

Technically speaking, we are at liberty to disregard those inherent norms. But the decision to disregard those norms, if known, would presuppose a desire to act in opposition to them. Such a desire could only be conditioned by the false belief that freedom consists in self-assertion. Not only is this a false belief, but, as some of us have learned from bitter experience, there is no sense of fulfillment in self-assertion.

We have to learn that we can control ourselves. This is a matter both of information and of practice, hence the importance in the latter case of liberty. With regard to information, we must overcome misinformation. Misinformation includes, for Mill, false theories about fatalism and religious predestination, notions of sexual and racial inferiority, the rhetoric of victimization, and the false message of Tory philanthropy. Once we recognize this capacity for self-control, what do we do? We are not constrained by individual teleology, nor are we constrained by a transcendent social teleology. We are constrained by context. What is interesting for Mill is that the present context, as historically diagnosed by him, is one in which the prevalent conditions promote individuality. Thus our self-discovery is also a discovery about our age.

The foregoing explanation of Mill's conception of freedom is a coherent and consistent one if understood within the context of the metaphysics of absolute idealism. We have insisted throughout this discussion that Mill was not a mechanist and that his philosophical idealism guided most of the discussion. As further support for these views, we offer the following observations. In his discussion of the relationship between art and science in the *Logic*, Book VI, Mill insisted that there could not be a scientific account or reduction of goals. If there could, then he would have had to face the prospect of complete determinism and fatalism, things he obviously rejected. Second, the universality of causation is something that remained an open question for him. The laws of association can only order the data, not generate the data. Among the items of data is the recognition of an ego and that our deepest satisfaction comes from the exercise of autonomy. This is a law made possible by, and compatible with, a transcendental self. Moreover, there cannot be a causal law for discovering the primacy of autonomy. If there were such a causal law, then we would have a scientific reduction of goals (the province of art). We might even be able to reverse the process and thereby undermine the notion of irreversible emancipatory beliefs. Since there are no causal processes for inducing the recognition of the primacy of autonomy, we must permit as much as possible the conditions that promote (but do not cause) this discovery. That is, we must protect liberty and diversity of circumstances and oppose paternalism as incompatible with being human. All we can give is an historical account of the growth of this awareness.

Although insisting upon the importance of a philosophy of history, Mill never provided a full-blown account of progress.[42] It is easy to see why. To begin with, Mill did not think that any kind of future progress was certain. He did not believe that there was or could be a causal law of historical progress, because he was not a mechanist. History would always remain, as it must for any Romantic, a work of art. Rather than explaining history, we use history to explain. History exemplifies certain universal truths about humanity, but only in context and over time. The growing awareness of those truths itself becomes a factor that leads to the evolution of social institutions. Any account we give of an institution must reflect the evolving dialectic of practice and theory. This also explains why all suggested public policy is provisional and time-sensitive.

Mill's *Hamilton* was greeted enthusiastically by Dr. Whewell, whose views on mathematics had been attacked by Hamilton, and by the logician Augustus de Morgan, who charged that Hamilton had plagiarized the principle of quantification. Mill revised *Hamilton* several times to take account of critical responses and, along with Bain, revised his father's *Analysis of the Human Mind* in order to strengthen the case for association.

Not all the responses to *Hamilton* were enthusiastic. Carlyle, who had recently been elected rector of the University of Edinburgh, took advantage of the resentment felt by Scots at an attack on Hamilton to attack Mill at a banquet given in Carlyle's honor. The attack took the form of chanting a refrain from a malicious ballad composed by another guest, Lord Neaves, which ends with "Stuart Mill exerts his skill, To make an end of Mind and Matter." Mill's response was to send the following note to Carlyle: "Please thank Mrs. Carlyle for her remembrance of me. I have been sorry to hear a rather poor account of her health, and to see by your Edinb. Address that your own is not quite satisfactory."[43] Despite disagreements, Mill had sent inscribed copies of the *Principles of Political Economy* and later of *On Liberty* to Carlyle as late as 1859. But by 1864, Mill had remarked to Conway that "Carlyle turned against all his friends."[44]

After completing *Hamilton*, Mill decided to address the issue of Comte and his influence. In his *Autobiography*, Mill took credit for introducing Comte to the English reading public and bringing to their attention the importance of Comte's thinking, especially on certain questions of methodology that had greatly influenced his *Logic*. Comtean positivism was now well established in Britain and its authoritarian character in full view. The later writings of Comte were, however, another matter. Mill castigated Comte's writing of the 1850s as "the completest system of spiritual and temporal despotism which ever yet emanated from a human brain."[45] In addition to having made the unpardonable error of supporting Louis Napoleon, Comte remained an Enlightenment Project authoritarian:[46] Comte envisaged a totalitarian society with complete state supervision of the economy, one that lacked a middle class, one that had no independent source of thought; he even restricted reading to a list of one hundred books. Mill first published his estimate of Comte in two articles in the *Westminster Review* for April and July of 1865. They were published together as a book by Trübner in 1866, entitled *Auguste Comte and Positivism*. In subsequent revisions of the *Logic*, Mill edited out some of the laudatory comments about Comte.

Member of Parliament

During the 1850s, Mill acquired, despite his critics, a great reputation as an *eminence grise*, largely as a result of the publications of the *Logic* and the *Principles of Political Economy*. Several times he had been approached to run for Parliament, but he had declined because of his position at the East India Company. Retirement from that position now made a political life possible.

In 1865, he was approached once again and asked to run as a representative from Westminster. Mill's campaign and his conduct after the election reflect precisely what one would have expected from the author of *Considerations on Representative Government*. He agreed to be a candidate on the following terms: He would not contribute financially to his campaign; he would severely restrict the financial contributions of others; he would not canvas or electioneer; he would give no pledges; he would not be a spokesperson for local interests; and he intended to use his position not only to serve as the conscience of his society but also to support women's suffrage. Remarkably, the leaders of the constituency agreed. "A well-known public figure was heard to say that God Almighty would have no chance of being elected on such a programme."[47] Still, Mill insisted that the electors be given a choice by adding the names of Sir J. Romilly and

Edwin Chadwick. Mill's opponent was W. H. Smith, son of the founder of the famous chain of stores.

The full story of Mill's conditions for running was published in the *Daily News* on March 23, 1865. Mill immediately became the center of attention. The first edition of *Hamilton* sold out in two months; all of his other publications saw a remarkable increase in sales. The students at St. Andrews University elected him rector, a fitting rebuff to Carlyle's election at Edinburgh. Despite his refusal to campaign, Mill's friends – including G. H. Lewes, George Eliot, Chadwick, Holyoake, and even the Amberleys – did much to support him. Subscriptions were given by Fortnum and Mason, Debenham's, Hedges and Butler, and the publisher Longman's.

Why did Mill agree to run and to serve? Part of the reason was his desire to use Parliament as a pulpit from which to preach his vision of liberal culture. At the same time, Mill had not totally lost all hope of forming a liberal party that reflected his vision of liberal culture. He wrote to Gomperz about it.

One ought to be very sure of being able to do something in politics that cannot be as well done by others, to justify one for the sacrifice of time and energies that might be employed on higher work. Time will show whether it was worth while to make this sacrifice for the sake of anything I am capable of doing towards forming a really advanced liberal party; which, I have long been convinced, cannot be done except in the House of Commons.[48]

After spending most of the campaign at Avignon, writing, Mill did agree to attend two mass meetings in order to respond to questions from members of his constituency. At the first meeting, which was attended by those who could actually vote in the election, Mill expressed his views on specific policies: He opposed religious disabilities, the purchase of army commissions, and flogging; he favored death duties on landed estates, votes for workers, votes for women, and Irish home rule; he did not think that the government should interfere with strikes, but he insisted that owners could engage in lockouts. A poignant account of this first meeting, which took place in Covent Garden, is given by the novelist Thomas Hardy:

It was a day in 1865, about three in the afternoon, during Mill's candidature for Westminster. The hustings had been erected in Covent Garden, . . . and when I – a young man living in London – drew near the spot, Mill was speaking. The appearance of the author of the treatise *On Liberty* (which we students of that date knew almost by heart) was so different from the look of persons who usually address crowds in the open air that it held the attention of people for whom such a gathering in itself had little interest. Yet it was, primarily, that of a man out of place. The religious sincerity of his speech was jarred on by his environment – a group on the hustings who, with few exceptions, did not care to understand him fully, and a crowd below who could not. He stood bareheaded, and his vast pale brow, so thin-skinned as to show the blue veins, sloped back like a stretching upland. . . . The picture of him as personified earnestness surrounded for the most part by careless curiosity derived an added piquancy – if it can be called such – from the fact that the cameo clearness of his face chanced to be in relief against the blue shadow of a church which, on its transcendental side, his doctrines antagonized. But it would not be right to say that the throng was absolutely unimpressed by his words; it felt that they were weighty, though it did not quite know why.[49]

At the second meeting, where Mill insisted upon addressing those constituents who did not have the right to vote, several demonstrators carried placards with some of Mill's more controversial published statements. Two are notable; the first comes from *Hamilton*:

"I WILL CALL NO BEING GOOD WHO IS NOT WHAT I MEAN WHEN I APPLY THAT EPITHET TO MY FELLOW CREATURES; AND IF SUCH A CREATURE CAN SENTENCE ME TO HELL FOR NOT SO CALLING HIM, TO HELL I WILL GO."[50]

The second comes from *Thoughts on Parliamentary Reform*:

"The lower classes are habitual liars."

The original read: "[T]he higher classes do not lie, and *the lower*, though mostly *habitual liars*, are ashamed of lying."[51] I have italicized what appeared on the placards.

Standing under a column in Trafalgar Square crowned by a statue of Lord Nelson, and in front of this large gathering, Mill was asked if he had written those words. Mill owned up to them immediately. At that point, one of the leaders of the working class, and someone who would later become Mill's friend, George Ogder, publicly endorsed Mill by saying that "my class has no desire not to be told its faults; we want friends, not flatterers." This supportive gesture was greeted with loud and sustained applause.[52]

Mill's beginning in Parliament was inauspicious. On first seeing him, Disraeli is alleged to have exclaimed, "Ah, I see the finishing governess." Mill's first speech was on February 14, 1866, in support of Bright's opposition to compensating owners of slaughtered diseased cattle. He argued that the bill compensated "a class for the results of a calamity which is bourne by the whole community." He went on to taunt the Tories by pointing out that the aristocracy "ought to be willing to bear the first brunt of the inconveniences and evils which fall on the country generally. This is the ideal character of aristocracy: it is the character with which all privileged classes are accustomed to credit themselves; though I am not aware of any aristocracy in history that has fulfilled those requirements. (Laughter)"[53]

His first few speeches were not generally well delivered. Roebuck, former friend and fellow member of the House – still under a ban of direct contact because he had tried to persuade Mill to break off with Harriet many years before – was moved to offer advice through an intermediary on how to deliver a speech. Mill changed tack, tried to be more supportive of the Liberal Party, and improved his delivery.

Mill's estimate of his role in Parliament,[54] as expressed in the *Autobiography*, is that he was a spokesperson for advanced causes that would otherwise not have had a hearing. There is some truth in that. It is also true, as Bagehot noted, that Mill differed in important respects from the other liberals in Parliament: Mill opposed the secret ballot, wanted indirect as well as direct taxation, supported foreign intervention, and favored a strong military.[55] But what Mill really hoped for was a revived and more radical Liberal Party under Gladstone's leadership that would incorporate the support of the workers. Mill had thus not surrendered his youthful dream of playing a significant parliamentary role in reforming Britain. That is why Mill supported Gladstone's Reform Bill of 1866, a bill that would have reduced the franchise qualification from £10 to £7, even though redistricting was not part of the bill. Gladstone's bill failed. While in Parliament, Mill generally supported Gladstone, who often invited him to dinner meetings, though Mill declined to attend many of the more social ones. Mill admired Gladstone, and even after Mill left Parliament Gladstone's ministry successfully carried through much of Mill's agenda, including the Married Women's Property Act. It was Gladstone who would later describe Mill as "the Saint of Rationalism."[56]

The Tories on a number of occasions took umbrage at Mill's remarks. On one occasion, they drew attention to Mill's statement in *Considerations on Representative Government* that the Conservative Party was, by the law of its composition, the stupidest party.[57] Mill replied[58] to Sir John Parkington as follows: "I did not mean that Conservatives are generally stupid; I meant, that stupid persons are generally Conservative." Nevertheless, as Mill noted in his *Autobiography*, the soubriquet "the stupid party" henceforth stuck to the Conservatives.

After a few false starts, Mill was generally regarded as a strong advocate and successful speaker. A consistent opponent of what he considered the English oppression of the Irish, Mill opposed the suspension of habeas corpus in Ireland and later successfully opposed the hanging of Fenian rebels (Irishmen who had served in the Northern army of the U.S. and then returned to Ireland). He supported environmental proposals such as the enclosure of Hainault Forest. In later years, he was responsible for the preservation both of Epping Forest and the elm trees in Piccadilly.

Mill supported capital punishment. To begin with, in earlier correspondence with Florence Nightingale, Mill had expressed his views on punishment (something he had been persuaded of by Harriet) as follows:

I do not agree ... when you say that there ought to be no punishment (only reformatory discipline) and even no blame. . . . With many minds, punishment is the only one of the natural consequences of guilt, which is capable of making any impression on them. In such cases, punishment is the sole means available for beginning the reformation of the criminal; and the fear of similar punishment is the only inducement which deters many really no better than himself. . . . a strong indignation against wrong is so inseparable from any strong personal feeling on the subject of wrong and right, that it does not seem to me possible, even if desirable, to get rid of the one, without, to a great degree, losing the other.[59]

In Parliamentary debate, Mill asserted with regard to capital punishment:

Much has been said of the sanctity of human life, and the absurdity of supposing that we can teach respect for life by ourselves destroying it. But I am surprised at the employment of this argument. . . . It is not human life only, not human life as such, that ought to be sacred to us, but human feelings. . . . We show, on the contrary, most emphatically our regard to it [human life], by the adoption of a rule that he who violates that right in another forfeits it for himself. . . .[60]

In addition, Mill vigorously opposed smoking in the nonsmoking sections of railway carriages, castigating it as an example of the majority oppression of the minority. He supported a strong national defense (deplored the weakening of the British navy), universal suffrage, and Irish peasant proprietorships. Mill supported an interventionist foreign policy (e.g., during the Crimean War, he advocated the right to seize enemy goods in neutral ships; he supported intervention to help where people were ready to adopt liberal culture)[61] as opposed to liberals such as Cobden and Bright, who favored isolation.[62] Unlike the aforementioned exponents of the Manchester School of laissez faire, Mill always saw a market economy as part of the larger context of liberal culture, not as an abstract principle.

There were three dramatic events during Mill's tenure in Parliament: his participation on the Jamaica Committee (1866),[63] the protest meeting in Hyde Park (1866), and Mill's attempt to gain for women the right to vote.

As a result of competition from the United States, the sugar plantations in Jamaica experienced a serious decline that led to the idling of many black workers. In an uprising by blacks during October of 1865, twenty whites were killed. Governor Eyre imposed martial law, flogged black women, burned the homes of suspected participants in the uprising, conducted trials that violated due process, and executed 439 blacks. Mill chaired the Jamaica Committee that tried to prosecute Eyre for his overzealous repression; he was joined in this move by such allies as Dicey, T. H. Green, Huxley, Lyle, and Spencer. In support of Eyre were Kingsley, Ruskin, Tennyson, Dickens, and, of course, Carlyle. Eyre's case raised questions about race. We recall here the exchange between Carlyle and Mill on race in 1849. Huxley and Spencer joined in, maintaining that there were no biological differences between blacks and whites. As a consequence of his condemnation of Eyre, Mill was even threatened with assassination. A royal commission agreed that Eyre had maintained martial law well beyond the period when it was necessary. However, despite repeated attempts to have him condemned, Eyre was exonerated and even given his pension.

Following the defeat of Gladstone's reform bill in July of 1866, the Reform League planned and organized a mass protest to be held in Hyde Park. The leaders of the League included Edmond Beales, Colonel Dickson, Charles Bradlaugh, and George Jacob Holyoake, a friend of Mill's. In response to the League, Home Secretary Spencer Walpole ordered the gates of the park to be closed two hours before the planned protest. When the protesters arrived at Marble Arch, they were turned away. Most went to Trafalgar Square, but some of Bradlaugh's followers tore down a few of the railings and entered the park, where they caused some minor damage. Some of the protesters went so far as to throw rocks at homes in Belgravia. Damage was relatively minor. The troops were called out, but by the time they arrived, the protesters had departed. Thomas Carlyle's response to this disturbance was an essay entitled "Shooting Niagara," in which he maintained that the advent of democracy was comparable to a descent into the deluge of Niagara Falls.

A second protest was planned. Walpole prepared to order out the troops. At this point, Mill stepped in and used his hard-won influence with the leaders of the working class. He dissuaded them from carrying out their plans by challenging them to consider whether if their condition really demanded a revolution and whether a revolution would be successful. He followed this with a speech at a public meeting held in the Agricultural Hall in Islington. It is there that he argued that "countries where the people are allowed to show their strength are those in which they are not obliged to use it."[64]

Mill, who was still a member of Parliament, then proceeded to help make this a positive event. The government soon realized that it had no legal right to close the park, so legislation was proposed to make this possible. In response, Mill invited the leaders of the Reform League to have tea in the tearoom of the House of Commons. This proved enough of a distraction to allow the proposed legislation to die. From that day, the speakers' corner in Hyde Park has remained a symbol of liberty.

Mill advocated that women be given the right to vote and be allowed full political participation, most significantly during the debate of the 1867 Reform Bill, introduced by Disraeli but bearing the clear influence of Gladstone. Mill did this by moving the substitution of the word "person" for "man" in the original Disraeli bill that extended the vote to all municipal householders He was supported by seventy-three MPs, including Bright, Disraeli, and Salisbury.[65] Mill considered this amendment "by far the most important, perhaps the only really important public service [he had] performed in the capacity of a Member of Parliament."[66] According to Millicent Garrett Fawcett, only someone with Mill's stature would have dared to make such a motion. Moreover, "the most sanguine estimate, previous to the division, of the number of his supporters had been thirty."[67] On the other hand, many of the votes for Mill's women's suffrage amendment were from die-hard Tories who thought that by passing such an amendment, or showing it had strong support, they could scuttle the whole thing. Such tactical voting is not to be confused with support. Mill wrote to the editor of a U.S. publication, the *Anti-Slavery Standard*, that "the disabilities of women are now the only remaining national violation of the principles of your immortal Declaration of Independence."[68]

In 1866, Mill had been elected by the students to become lord rector of St. Andrews University in Scotland. A tribute to Mill's eminence, the election was also special because Mill himself, although recognized as the greatest British philosopher of the nineteenth century and one of the great intellects of his time, had never attended or graduated from any university. As Fawcett put it,

Anyone who resided during the last twenty years [1853–73] at either of our universities must have noticed that Mr. Mill is the author who has most powerfully influenced nearly all the young men of the greatest promise. . . . When I was an undergraduate, I well remembered that most of my friends who were likely to take high mathematical honors were already so intimately acquainted with Mr. Mill's writings, and were so much imbued with their spirit, that they might have been regarded as his disciples. Many looked up to him as their teacher; many have since felt that he then instilled into them principles, which, to a great extent, have guided their conduct in after life.[69]

In his inaugural address, delivered on February 1, 1867, Mill spoke for three hours.[70] His address amounted to a concise summary of all of his philosophical and policy positions. For our purposes, it will be useful to focus on those parts of his address that reinforce important themes in his other writings. From the point of view of issues in higher education, Mill insisted upon distancing higher education from both secondary education and graduate professional training. His address is a plea on behalf of the liberal arts, especially the classical languages, and for educating the whole person.

First, although Mill spent an inordinate amount of time calling attention to the value of a classical education, he underscored the extent to which he remained a modern. He called attention to the battle between the ancients and the moderns as represented by Swift and Fontenelle, only to come down on the side of modernity.

I consider modern poetry to be superior to ancient, in the same manner, though in a less degree, as modern science: it enters deeper into nature. The feelings of the modern mind are more various, more complex and manifold, than those of the ancients ever were. The modern mind is, what the ancient mind was not, brooding and self-conscious; and its meditative self-consciousness has discovered depths in the human soul which the Greeks and Romans did not dream of, and would not have understood.[71]

More specifically, Mill's conception of higher education is directly related to his Romantic conception of *Bildung*.

Whatever helps to shape the human being – to make the individual what he is . . . is part of his education. . . . Their [the university's] object [is] . . . capable and cultivated human beings. . . . All conspire to the common end, the strengthening, exalting, purifying, and beautifying of our common nature. . . . There is, besides, a natural affinity between goodness and the cultivation of the Beautiful. . . . He who has learned what beauty is, if he be of a virtuous character, will desire to realize it in his own life – will keep before himself a type of perfect beauty in human character, to light his attempts at self-culture. There is a true meaning in the saying of Goethe, though liable to be misunderstood and perverted, that the Beautiful is greater than the Good; for it includes the Good, and adds something to it: it is the Good made perfect, and fitted with all the collateral perfections which make it a finished and completed thing.[72]

As part of *Bildung*, higher education is meant to promote autonomy.

It is quite possible to cultivate the conscience and the sentiments too. Nothing hinders us from so training a man that he will not, even for a disinterested purpose, violate the moral law, and also feeding and encouraging those high feelings, on which we mainly rely for lifting men above low and sordid objects, and giving them a higher conception of what constitutes success in life. If we wish men to practice virtue, it is worth while trying to make them love virtue, and feel it an object in itself, and not a tax paid for leave to pursue other objects. It is worth training them to feel not only actual wrong or actual meanness, but the absence of noble aims and endeavor . . . , the poorness and insignificance of human life if it is to be all spent in making things comfortable for ourselves and our kin, and raising ourselves and them a step or two on the social ladder.[73]

Rather than indoctrination, what the university should instill is a capacity for critical judgment. It is in this respect that the university can perform a Socratic function.

To question all things; never to turn away from any difficulty; to accept no doctrine either from ourselves or other people without a rigid scrutiny by negative criticism, letting no fallacy, or incoherence, or confusion of thought, slip by unperceived; above all, to insist upon having the meaning of a word clearly understood before using it, and the meaning of a proposition before assenting to it; these are the lessons we learn from the ancient dialecticians. With all this vigorous management of the negative element, they inspire no scepticism about the reality of truth, or indifference to its pursuit . . . laying an admirable foundation for ethical and philosophical culture.[74]

Finally, Mill reminded the students of what was his religious vision, namely, that life was a constant and unending moral struggle.

Bad men need nothing more to compass their ends, than that good men should look on and do nothing. . . . we learn to respect ourselves only so far as we feel capable of nobler object: and if unfortunately those by whom we are surrounded do not share our aspirations, perhaps disapprove the conduct to which we are prompted by them – to sustain ourselves by the ideal sympathy of the great characters in history, or even in fiction, and by the contemplation of an idealized posterity: shall I add, of ideal perfection embodied in a Divine Being? . . . you have fixed your eyes upon the ultimate end from which those studies take their chief value – that of making you more effective combatants in the great fight which never ceases to rage between Good and Evil, and more equal to coping with the ever new problems which the changing course of human nature and human society present to be resolved.[75]

Matthew Arnold, whose philosophical, political, and religious views were very different from Mill's, nevertheless praised Mill's St. Andrews address and asserted that it identified Mill as one of those contributing to "the best educational opinion of the country."[76]

Mill was defeated for reelection in 1868. So were Chadwick, Roebuck, Amberley, and Morley. As demographic records indicate, the nature of the constituency of Westminster was changing. In fact, the change in the constituency brought about by the 1867 reform included more earnest religious types. During the reelection campaign Mill had personally contributed to another campaign, that of Charles Bradlaugh, a militant atheist spokesman for workers, and this had alienated a number of liberal churchmen who had previously supported Mill. Millicent Garrett Fawcett attributed the defeat to Mill's campaign against Governor Eyre. In any case, Mill was offered another safe seat but declined. Reflecting on his defeat, which came as no surprise, Mill noted that the Tories had been much more opposed to him this time than during his first compaign. Mill's reflections on this serve to reinforce his understanding of his position on democracy.

As I had shewn in my political writings [*Considerations on Representative Government*] that I was aware of the weak point in democratic opinions, some Conservatives, it seems, had not been without hopes of finding me an opponent of democracy: as I was able to see the Conservative side of the question, they presumed that, like them, I could not see any other side. Yet if they had really read my writings they would have known that after giving full weight to all that appeared to me well grounded in the arguments against democracy, I unhesitatingly decided in its favour, while recommending that it should be accompanied by such institutions as were consistent with its principle and calculated to ward off its inconveniences. . . . Some Tory expectations appear to have been founded on the approbation I had expressed of plural voting . . . it was forgotten that I had made it an express condition that the privilege of a plurality of votes should be annexed to education, not to property, and even so, had approved of it only on the supposition of universal suffrage.[77]

During his time in Parliament, Mill had taken a flat in 10 Albert Mansions, Victoria Street, Westminster. After his defeat, the troublesome house in Blackheath Park was sold, and the little time that Mill now spent in London was spent at the flat. Electoral defeat also brought to Mill a sense of relief. As he wrote to Cairnes, "I really have much difficulty in feeling as I ought to do about what is a real defeat to advanced Liberal opinions, so great and fresh is the pleasure of the feeling of freedom, and the return to the only occupations which agree with my tastes and habits. I hope to be quite as active for my opinions out of the House as I was in it."[78]

Last Years (1869–1873)

FREED from public service, Mill turned to completing his life's work as an author: He brought out a revised edition of his father's *Analysis of the Human Mind*, which he had edited with the help of Bain and Grote back in 1867, partly as homage to his father and partly to shore up his case against Hamilton; put the finishing touches on his *Autobiography*; edited the final editions of the *Logic* and the *Principles of Political Economy;* and prepared *The Subjection of Women* for publication in 1869.

What is remarkable about Mill's edition of his father's work is a series of footnotes in which Mill continued to distance himself from his father and to work out his aesthetic theory. Specifically, Mill criticized his father's account of associationism, for while it might be "a sufficient theory of what we may call the mental, or intellectual element of feelings . . . [it] does not furnish, nor does the author anywhere furnish, any theory of what may be called the animal element in them."[1] Moreover, Mill appealed to ideas he had found in the work of Ruskin to supplement his father's views. Mill had read John Ruskin's famous work *Modern Painters*, whose five volumes appeared between 1843 and 1860. Although he rejected Ruskin's political and religious conservatism, Mill found appealing the notion that art reflected both personal and national moral integrity. In good Platonic and Kantian fashion, Mill borrowed from Ruskin the identification of the beautiful and the good (something he had also found in Goethe, and to which he had alluded in his St. Andrews address): "The . . . ideas in Mr. Ruskin's list . . . all represent to us some valuable and delightful attribute, in a completeness and perfection of which our experience presents us with no example, and which therefore stimulates the active power of the imagination to rise above known reality, into a more attractive or a more majestic world."[2]

So great had his reputation become that Mill was more in demand while in retirement. His correspondence was so voluminous that he had Helen respond to much of it under his supervision. It is to her that we owe the preservation of both sides of so much of his correspondence. A look at his later correspondence reveals a number of interesting things about Mill's later opinions. Mill had always disapproved of peace societies and had exclaimed that he "regarded war as infinitely less evil than systematic submission to injustice."[3] Lately, he had come to favor a citizen army based upon conscription: "I do not think it safe to trust entirely to voluntary enlistment for the large defensive force which this and every other country now requires."[4]

The role that Helen Taylor[5] played in Mill's life has lent support in the eyes of some to the thesis that Mill always needed to have his life directed by someone else: his father, then Harriet, and finally Helen. Nothing could be further from the truth. Mill liked nothing better than turning over the practical details to someone else so that he could concentrate on what he felt was most important. He repaid this valuable freeing of his time with elaborate praise. It would be ludicrous to think that someone like Mill, who had carved out a career at India House for thirty-seven years, who had served courageously and defiantly in Parliament, and who had engaged in public policy disputes, including preventing a riot, needed to have his life directed by someone else. Once more, this seems to be an elaborate hypothesis devised to explain Mill's devotion to Harriet on the part of those who fail to see the positive influence that Harriet had wielded in his life.

An example of this misperception of Mill's relationship to Helen can be found in a letter of Charles Eliot Norton,[6] writing to the American philosopher Chauncey Wright:

I doubt whether Mill's interest in the cause of woman is serviceable to him as a thinker. It has a tendency to develop the sentimental part of his intelligence, which is of immense force, and has only been kept in due subjection by his respect for his own reason. This respect diminishes under the powerful influence of his daughter, Miss Taylor, who is an admirable personage doubtless, but is what, were she of the sex that she regards as inferior, would be called decidedly priggish. Her self-confidence, which embraces her confidence in Mill, is tremendous, and Mill is overpowered by it. Her words have an oracular value for him, – something more than their just weight; and her unconscious flattery, joined with the very direct flattery of many other prominent leaders of the great female army, have a not unnatural effect on his tender, susceptible and sympathetic nature. In putting the case so strongly I perhaps define it with too great a force, but you can make the needful allowance for the over-distinctness of words.

Helen may have been a prig, like her mother. Mill was not. Mill was susceptible to female flattery/reinforcement, but this was not the source of his pro-women ideas.

More and more time was now being spent in Avignon. Among his friends in Avignon were a M. Chauffard, a doctor who had once attended to Harriet; the Protestant minister Louis Rey; and J. H. Fabre, who shared his interest in botany. Fabre was another outspoken person to whose financial aid Mill was to come.

At this time the Amberleys were to make a special request. When their third child was born in 1872, the Amberleys wrote to Helen to seek Mill's permission to have him be godfather to the child: "We hesitated to ask such a favour of Mr. Mill . . . for there is no one in whose steps I wd. rather see a boy of mine following in ever such a humble way, than in Mr. Mill's."[7] Mill, of course, agreed and became the godfather of Bertrand Russell.

Women's Liberation

At the time Mill was serving in Parliament, the status of women in the most advanced and civilized country in the world was as follows. Women could not own property or have any right to the proceeds of their labor. Married women had no right to property, including property they had inherited from their fathers, had no protection from marital rape, did not have a voice in the education of their children, and could not obtain the custody of their children in case of divorce. Divorce itself required an act of Parliament. Unmarried women who paid taxes were not allowed to vote. Nor could women serve on juries.

Even Mill's conservative critics (including Sir James Fitzjames Stephen) agreed that this was an unacceptable anomaly. It is easy to see why. Not only did it violate the notion that an autonomous person is entitled to the fruits of her labor (Locke's argument), but fathers were rightly disturbed to see inheritances given to daughters passing into the hands of other men. As a member of Parliament, Mill supported the Married Women's Property Bill.[8] Such bills had been introduced since 1857, but the Married Women's Property Bill did not finally gain passage until

1870,[9] shortly after the publication of *The Subjection of Women*. Mill had also advocated the opening of higher education and the professions to women. Women should be permitted, if not encouraged, to achieve financial autonomy. There was one respect in which Mill remained a traditional Victorian: While he wanted every opportunity made available to women, he anticipated that most women would, if given a choice, choose to be homemakers.

In the first chapter of *The Subjection of Women*,[10] Mill argued that the current subordinate status of women is not based in nature but in historical accident. Mill did not maintain in any dogmatic or a priori fashion that all human beings are totally products of their environment. Recognition that environment is a major factor never escalates into full-scale egalitarianism In fact, it is important to his thesis about individuality in *On Liberty*, as buttressed by arguments in the *Logic*,[11] that human beings are capable of molding their own characters. Differences there may be, but whatever differences may exist, either between the sexes or among individuals, are (a) a matter for empirical determination and (b) irrelevant to each individual's capacity for personal autonomy.

With regard to the issue of natural endowment, Mill presented evidence of the accomplishments of women as an indication of what they are capable of achieving. In his correspondence, he cited the achievements of Elizabeth I, thereby challenging the notion that women lack the capacity for politics (and, indirectly, lack the judgment to exercise the franchise).[12] In one of his speeches, Mill took some delight in reminding the current members of Parliament that Britain was in fact ruled by a woman! With regard to the autonomy issue, Mill insisted that women are as fully capable as men of achieving autonomy. Mill extended to women the same consideration that any autonomous man demands for himself: "Human beings are no longer born to their place in life ... but are free to employ their faculties ... to achieve the lot which may appear to them most desirable."[13]

Mill insisted that women should have equality before the law and thereby gain the protection of the rule of law. "The purpose of that book [*The Subjection of Women*] was to maintain the claim of women, whether in marriage or out of it, to perfect equality in all rights with the male sex."[14] This means, among other things, that women should have a right to control their own resources; that women should share the guardianship of their children, as opposed to the exclusive guardianship of the husband; that women should be protected from domestic violence and have the right to refuse "the last familiarity"; and that divorce should be permitted. As Mill pointed out, "marriage is the only actual bondage known to our law. There remain no legal slaves, except the mistress of every house."[15]

One aspect of this notion of equality before the law deserves special mention. Between 1864 and 1869, Parliament passed the Contagious Diseases acts. The acts permitted compulsory medical inspection of women suspected of being prostitutes in military garrison towns. Mill objected to the acts on the ground that they applied police powers to women but not to the men.[16] In 1869, the same year as the publication of *The Subjection of Women*, W. E. H. Lecky published *A History of European Morals*. In that work, Lecky described prostitution as necessary for maintaining social stability; Mill denied this, arguing that prostitution reduced women to the status of a thing and undermined honesty between marriage partners.[17]

One historical and sociological claim lurked in the background. It had long been maintained that a prosperous country is one in which there is a growth in population. Mill, following Malthus, had come to believe that population growth beyond a certain point was detrimental economically, especially to the laboring classes. Placing a positive value on abstinence, encouraging female autonomy, and protecting women from marital rape were now deemed essential to a civilized and fulfilling life. Curiously, Mill's views on population, on the potential for a stationary state, on sexual relations, and on autonomy all converge at this point.

Not content to confine himself to writing about this issue, Mill engaged in active leadership, along with Helen Taylor, in the establishment of the National Society for Women's Suffrage. Among the members Mill enlisted were Mrs. Fawcett, Lord Romilly, Francis Newman (the brother of the cardinal), and Charles Kingsley. Helen managed to persuade and then enroll Florence Nightingale.

The most significant feature of the argument in *The Subjection of Women* is the claim that the autonomy of men was being corrupted by the then-current conception of the relationship between men and women. In a now-classic restatement of the Hegelian master-slave thesis,[18] Mill emphasized the extent to which "the relation of superiors to dependents is the nursery of" such male vices as "willfulness, over-bearingness, unbounded self-indulgence, and a double-dyed and idealized selfishness."[19] In the end, anyone who tyrannizes over another cannot achieve or retain personal autonomy. For "the love of power and the love of liberty are in eternal antagonism. . . . The desire of power over others [is a] depraving agency among mankind."²⁰ The future of liberal culture requires overcoming this obstacle. "The moral regeneration of mankind will only really commence, when the most fundamental of the social relations is placed under the rule of equal justice, and when human beings learn to cultivate their strongest sympathy with an equal in rights and in cultivation."²¹ This echoes the autonomy thesis that Harriet had expressed in her 1851 essay on the enfranchisement of women:

"[T]hose who are associated in their lives, tend to become assimilated in their character. In the present closeness of association between the sexes, men cannot retain manliness unless women acquire it. There is hardly any situation more unfavourable to the maintenance of elevation of character or force of intellect, than to live in the society, and seek by preference the sympathy, of inferiors in mental endowments.²²

Mill recognized the centrality of the nuclear family. He understood that parents were responsible for initiating children into autonomous adulthood (even reminding us that one should not remain a parent or teacher of the same individuals indefinitely because of the corrupting influence on the mentor).²³ His concern for children extended much further. Mill was concerned with the corrupting effect of inherited wealth; in the *Principles of Political Economy*, he distinguished between the right of disposing of one's own wealth (rather than government confiscation of wealth) and limiting the amount that could be inherited by a single individual.²⁴

Finally, Mill explained what divorce meant in a community of autonomous individuals. In November 1855, his "opinion on Divorce [wa]s that though any relaxation of the irrevocability of marriage would be an improvement, nothing ought to be ultimately rested in, short of entire freedom on both sides to dissolve this like any other partnership."²⁵ But in *On Liberty*, he rejected Humboldt's view that marriage is a contract that could be terminated by "the declared will of either party to dissolve it." Marriage "created a new series of moral obligations . . . which may possibly be overruled, but cannot be ignored."²⁶ In 1870, he reiterated that there could be no proper divorce law "until women have an equal voice in making it"; he went on to deny having advocated dissolution "at the will of either party."²⁷ Personal autonomy can never mean the overriding of someone else's autonomy and always carries some degree of responsibility.

Mill's promotion of the rights of women was not a view that he adopted from Harriet, although it was certainly a view that he shared with her.

What is true is that she made him understand the connection between the rights of women and autonomy, the basic notion in Mill's social philosophy. Defending the rights of women is crucial to Mill's understanding of liberal culture. Liberal culture, as a form of modernity, superseded the classical and medieval worldview – specifically, the notion of a collective (teleological) good over and above, and inclusive and constitutive of, the individual good. What liberal culture substitutes for a collective good is a common good. This raises the basic problem with which modern political theorists have had to grapple: What is the common good, and how are we to understand the relationship between the individual good of autonomous individuals and a common good? The common good consists of the conditions (procedural norms) that promote individual flourishing. Here arises the potential conflict: What guarantees are there that some individuals will not perceive their own flourishing in terms of the domination of others and/or in terms of practices that undermine the conditions for universal flourishing? Hegel answered this best when he asserted that the supreme form of flourishing requires interaction with and recognition of other autonomous individuals. No society, no institution (e.g., the family), and no relationship (male/female, parent/child, etc.) can promote individual flourishing if it is based on a permanent relationship of domination or subjection. Autonomous individuals cannot sympathize with perceived inferiors; they can, at best, only pity them. Even sympathy is transformed in a society of autonomous beings.

Mill carries the point further:

[T]he desire to be in unity with our fellow creatures, which is already a powerful principle in human nature, and happily one of those which tend to become stronger, even without express inculcation, from the influences of advancing civilization. The social state is at once so natural, so necessary, and so habitual to man, that, except in some unusual circumstances or by an effort of voluntary abstraction, he never conceives himself otherwise than as a member of a body. . . . In this way people grow up unable to conceive as possible to them a state of total disregard of other people's interests. . . . He comes, as though instinctively, to be conscious of himself as a being who *of course* pays regard to others. The good of others becomes to him a thing naturally and necessarily to be attended to.[28]

In the culmination and achievement of autonomy in family relationships, in the true friendship of husband and wife,[29] we have the model of the solution to liberal culture's greatest challenge.

The equality of married persons before the law is not only the sole mode in which that particular relation can be made consistent with justice to both sides, and conducive to the happiness of both, but it is the only means of rendering the daily life of mankind, in any high sense, a school of moral cultivation. Though the truth may not be felt or generally acknowledged for generations to come, the only school of genuine moral sentiment is society between equals. . . . We have had the morality of submission, and the morality of chivalry and generosity; the time is now come for the morality of justice. . . . The family, justly constituted, would be the real school of freedom. . . . The moral training of mankind will never be adapted to the conditions of the life for which all other human progress is a preparation, until they practise in the family the same moral rule which is adapted to the normal constitution of human society.[30]

It is only in a marriage of equals that the moral and civic virtues of liberal culture can best be actualized.[31]

Mill was not advocating a collective good, nor was he advocating that the whole of a society be understood as a family. What he advocated was a sense of the common good that was coherent with the individual good, understood as personal autonomy.[32] Mill's *Subjection of Women* is not just about women but about the fundamental issue in liberal culture. Collini was right to point out that this work "offers the whole of Mill's characteristic political and moral arguments in microcosm: themes whose best known *loci* are in the *Principles*, *On Liberty*, or *Representative Government* are here drawn together and focused on a single issue."[33] It is a fitting memorial that Mill's private library is now part of the library at Somerville College, Oxford, a college founded for women.

Religion of Humanity

Mill had waited until 1869 to publish *The Subjection of Women* because he well knew the unpopularity of the case he was about to make. He was, therefore, not surprised by the outcry of his critics. His nemesis, James Fitzjames Stephens, called the subject "the strangest . . . and by far the most ignoble and mischievous of all the popular feelings of the age. . . . [I] dissent from nearly every word he says."[34] His friends Bain and Spencer also distanced themselves from his views on women. Having publicized his views on women, Mill turned to two other areas where he thought it was still necessary to develop his views, and these had to do with religion and with socialism.

The religious scene in nineteenth-century Britain was a complicated one. The vast majority of those with serious religious commitments fell into one of three broad categories: Anglicans, Nonconformist Protestants, and Catholics. The Anglican Church was bitterly divided between High Church types (traditional and close to Catholicism, feudal, hierarchical, and Tory in their politics) and Low Church types (who were Lutheran in theology and defiantly Protestant in self-description, although equally tied to the landed gentry). In general, the Low Church types dominated the hierarchy, although the Newmanite-Puseyites made the most noise. Anglicans tended to see themselves as leaders of their society and of their government and, hence, felt comfortable with statist policies – that is, policies that empowered the government. The Protestant Nonconformists and some Catholics (e.g., Newman and Acton), as political outsiders, were concerned to defend religious freedom, especially from state interference. Newman and Acton would eventually both lose out in English Catholic politics to Cardinal Manning's Ultramontanism. They were, however, not sympathetic to policies that empowered a government controlled by Anglicans. Mention should also be made of the Evangelical movement, under such leaders as Wilberforce, who proposed to reform Anglicanism by moving it more in the direction of Protestantism.

The Industrial Revolution and the development of the middle class added a new dimension to religious affiliation. Anglicanism tended to identify with the landed aristocracy. Nonconformist Protestantism therefore became the venue for the rising middle class and those associated with the promotion of liberal culture. What made this possible was, in part, the spiritual origins of liberal culture in Calvinism and in the Protestant Reformation (Puritans, Independents, Baptists, Quakers, and Methodists). De Ruggiero[35] has summed up this case as follows. "Liberty is consciousness of oneself, of one's own infinite spiritual value; and the same recognition in the case of other people follows naturally from this immediate revelation. Only one who is conscious of himself as free is capable of recognizing the freedom of others."[36] There was a special "respect for the intimacy of man's consciousness."[37] Freedom is "the fruit of one's own activity or the object of one's own choice."[38] Freedom was not merely a mental category but had an outward manifestation in the rejection of external authoritarian imposition. "It is this liberal attitude of the modern man, this sense of the inviolability of his person and his freedom, which will provide the material for the Kantian and post-Kantian conception of liberty, by far the greatest contribution made by philosophy to the history of liberalism."[39] Mill had recognized and argued for the Protestant origins of the liberty of thought and discussion in *On Liberty*, repeating in secular terms the case that Milton had made in *Areopagitica*.

Protestant Nonconformism was more than a set of religious beliefs with political consequences. It was a way of life. Nonconformists, often members of minority communities, defended their rights and promoted autonomy, although in some regions they were often enough in the majority, or at least equal in number to Anglicans. They were legendary for constructing self-help communities; they encouraged egalitarianism in discussion and criticism; and from this openness they expected the emergence of the best talents. That is why they valued competition. Each autonomous individual was to create her or his own prestige ex nihilo. Remembering James Mill's background (in Scotland, Nonconformism was the established church), we should not be surprised that he imbued Mill with precisely these values long after he abandoned the theology. Nonconformism was the backbone of British liberalism.[40] It was Calvinistic in its emphasis on individual initiative, prized competition, organized itself as a series of autonomous congregations, and was located in industrial centers. No wonder it became the religious context of the new middle class. Methodism as a form of Nonconformism was said to be Calvinism without predestination.

These religious correlates to political positions help to explain the peculiar religious–political alliances of nineteenth-century Britain. First, Anglicanism was always the voice of feudalism. That meant it subscribed to the notion that charity was still the duty of a responsible aristocracy. This explains the ease and the brilliance of Disraeli's introduction of a conservative welfare state, as well as the prevalence of Tory philanthropy. It explains as well the origins of Christian socialism as an Anglican movement (e.g., Charles Kingsley), for Anglicans had always been in opposition to the Industrial Revolution. Christian Socialism saw itself as a defender of workers: promoting solidarity, collaboration, and mutual help in opposition to the laissez-faire of the Manchester School. Workers' movements also had their secular and antireligious proponents, but politically these two groups could work together.

Second, there was an alliance between Nonconformist sects and Philosophic Radicalism. Nonconformists and Philosophical Radicals shared the same worldview, one with and one without the theology. One of the great issues on which Nonconformists could join with Philosophic Radicals was the elimination of slavery (in opposition to slaveholders, who frequently were Anglicans engaged in feudal agrarian enterprises).

Mill was a critic of all extant organized religions. To his mind, they were all inadequate in one way or another. For example, Mill believed that Catholicism, which had once been the liberating and organizing principle of Western civilization, had become reactionary with Pius XI, who had overreacted to the events of 1848 and condemned liberalism *tout court*. The Anglican Church fared no better in his estimation, since he perceived it to be a defender of the status quo, which meant Tory aristocracy and feudalism. Anglicans had grievously erred as well, in his estimation, by supporting the slaveholding South in the American Civil War and later coming to the support of Governor Eyre in his brutal repression of blacks in Jamaica. Mill objected most strenuously to Calvinism, because of its emphasis on predestination and repression and its refusal to promote the awareness of autonomy. Part of the motivation for writing his *Examination of the Philosophy of Sir William Hamilton* was to attack Henry Mansel, who was a follower of Hamilton but also an apologist for the status quo. Mansel had maintained in his book *The Limits of Religious Thought* that the problem of evil could be overcome only by faith. That is, Mansel had defended both the omniscience and omnipotence of God, thereby implying that God had His reasons for creating the evil we see in the world. Mill was appalled at this. The attack on Mansel via *Hamilton* earned Mill the sympathetic support of the Christian socialists, because they did not want the status quo of worker poverty rationalized away.

What was Mill's attitude toward Nonconformism? Mill was perhaps closest to the Unitarians, and especially to James Martineau. Mill accepted in some sense the existence of a deity,[41] denied the divinity of Jesus, opposed ritualism, despised biblical fundamentalism or what Coleridge had called "bibliolatry," shared their belief in the freedom of the will, and embraced the notion of a non-omnipotent God with whom we were allies in the struggle against evil. Mill also shared the advanced ideas about women and other social issues that he had found in the Unitarian sect where he had met Harriet Taylor. Beyond this, he found Nonconformism morally vacuous, sentimental, and sometimes incapable of dealing with the fact that to become a decent human being was a serious achievement.

Some indication of this is given in his essay *Nature*:

> The doctrines of Christianity have in every age been largely accommodated to
> the philosophy which happened to be prevalent, and the Christianity of our day
> has borrowed a considerable part of its color and flavor from sentimental deism
> [Rousseau]. ... The people of this generation ... live in a kind of confusion of
> many standards – a condition not propitious to the formation of steady moral
> convictions but convenient enough to those whose moral opinions sit lightly on
> them, since it gives them a much wider range of arguments for defending the
> doctrine of the moment.[42]

In addition to this, Mill despised the fact that so much of traditional religion encouraged selfishness by promoting the idea that good behavior
would be rewarded with immortality. This was, in his estimation, the
wrong motive for the right action. It was consequently also largely inefficacious in promoting concern for the common interest.

At the same time, Mill was aware of the "crisis of faith"[43] that gripped
England during the nineteenth century. The crisis of faith was a crisis
within Nonconformist Protestantism.[44] Nonconformists seemed trapped
between a return to Rome and ritualism and the "bibliotary" of discredited
proofs. To these intelligent and high-minded members of the middle class,
Mill offered a different vision. What he offered was the view that the great
moral insights of Western civilization had been expressed and reexpressed
in different theological languages throughout the last two millennia. His
philosophy of history articulated precisely this view. A responsible reap-
propriation and reaffirmation of those insights required a new religion,
but it would be a religion of humanity. The Religion of Humanity was a
substitute for Christianity. The Religion of Humanity was Hegel's conception of the state made international – the higher social good in which
we were all fulfilled.

If we suppose cultivated to the highest point the sentiments of fraternity with
all our fellow beings, past, present, and to come, of veneration for those past
and present who have deserved it, and devotion to the good of those to come;
universal moral education making the happiness and dignity of this collective
body the central point to which all things are to tend and by which all are to
be estimated, instead of the pleasure of an unseen and merely imaginary Power;
the imagination at the same time being fed from youth with representations of all
noble things felt and acted heretofore, and with ideal conceptions of still greater

to come: there is no worthy office of a religion which this system of cultivation does not seem adequate to fulfil."[45]

In a letter dated February 14 and 15, 1854, Harriet advised Mill to present this view.

About the Essays, dear, would not religion, the Utility of Religion, be one of the subjects you would have most to say on – there is no account for the existence nearly universal of some religion (superstition) by the instinct of fear, hope and mystery etc., and throwing over all doctrines and theories, called religion, and devices for power, to show how religion and poetry fill the same want, the craving after higher objects, the consolation of suffering, the hope of heaven for the selfish, love of God for the tender and grateful – how all this must be superseded by morality deriving its power from sympathies and benevolence and its reward from the approbation of those we respect.[46]

Like Hegel, Mill would go on to say that art, religion, and philosophy were all expressions of the fundamental truths, but that philosophy was the highest such expression.

Is this conception of religion a pious hope on Mill's part, a mere ad hoc addition to his philosophy, or is there a deeper connection with his thought? It will be useful to recall here Mill's conception of poetry, in which the feelings associated with an idea themselves become an important fact about human emotional life and subsequent human action. If that is the case, then one can understand the affirmative answer that Mill gave to the great question faced by the Victorian men and women of letters: "whether the idealization of our earthly life, the cultivation of a high conception of what *it* may be made, is not capable of supplying a poetry and, in the best sense of the word, a religion equally fitted to exalt the feelings and (with the same aid from education) still better calculated to enable the conduct than any belief respecting the unseen powers."[47]

The expression and the concept of a religion of humanity were borrowed from Comte.

[H]is [Comte's] religion is without a God. In saying this, we have done enough to induce nine-tenths of all readers ... to avert their faces and close their ears. ... What, in truth, are the conditions necessary to constitute a religion? There must be a creed, or conviction, claiming authority over the whole of human life; a belief, or set of beliefs, deliberately adopted, respecting human destiny and duty, to which the believer inwardly acknowledges that all his actions ought to be subordinate. ... M. Comte believes in what is meant by the infinite nature of duty

[Carlyle's phrase from *Sartor Resartus*], but he refers the obligations of duty, as well as all sentiments of devotion, to a concrete object, at once ideal and real; the Human Race, conceived as a continuous whole, including the past, the present, and the future.... the feelings it can excite are necessarily very different from those which direct themselves towards an ideally perfect Being ... [for] it really needs our services, which Omnipotence cannot.... [48]

Both in his critique of Comte and in the later essay *The Utility of Religion*, Mill stressed that the Religion of Humanity need not have a supernatural dimension and might be better for it.[49] What is interesting is that in the last religious essay, *Theism*, Mill, as we have previously shown, does go on to subscribe to a belief in a God who lacks omnipotence.

Despite his critique of Comte, Mill praised Comte's contentions that God was immanent, that religion should relate the individual to the rest of humanity, and that religion should provide us with a larger narrative of human meaning. Having praised Comte for formulating the Religion of Humanity, Mill then proceeded to show how Comte's elaboration of that religion was itself alien to the spirit in which religion should operate.[50] In a prescient remark, Mill pointed out how a "secularized" religion carried out under the auspices of positivist social science might become the worst form of despotism. What Comte lacked, of course, was a conception of autonomy.[51]

I agreed with him that the moral and intellectual ascendancy, once exercised by priests, must in time pass into the hands of philosophers, and will naturally do so when they become sufficiently unanimous, and in other respects worthy to possess it. But when he exaggerated this line of thought into a practical system, in which philosophers were to be organized into a kind of corporate hierarchy, invested with almost the same spiritual supremacy (though without any secular power) once possessed by the Catholic church; when I found him relying on this spiritual authority as the only security for good government ... we could travel together no further. M. Comte lived to carry out these doctrines to their extremest consequences by planning, in his last work, the *Système de Politique Positive*, the completest system of spiritual and temporal despotism, which ever yet emanated from a human brain ... by which the yoke of general opinion, wielded by an organized body of spiritual teachers and rulers, would be made supreme over every action, and as far as is in human possibility, every thought, of every member of the community, as well in the things which regard only himself, as in those which concern the interests of others.... *The book stands a monumental warning to thinkers on society and politics, of what happens when once men lose sight, in their speculations, of the value of Liberty and of Individuality.*[52] [italics added]

To what extent do Mill's religious writings throw some light on his metaphysics?[53] We begin by pointing out that John Stuart Mill did not consider himself antireligious. In an 1861 letter to Arthur Weguelin Greene, Mill reiterated that "neither in the Logic nor in any other of my publications had I any purpose of undermining Theism. . . . That the world was made, in whole or in part, by a Powerful Being who cared for man, appears to me, though not proved, yet a very probable hypothesis."[54] To be sure, Mill did not recognize the divinity of Jesus, but he praised him as a great prophet. What we do know from Mill's *Autobiography* is that he was never initiated into the practice of any formal religion. In fact, he never even knew until after his father's death that James Mill had had a career in the Scottish church.[55] Mill read widely in ecclesiastical history; he was concerned about the negative as well as the positive moral impact of religion;[56] he had much to say about the history and sociology of religion; and he considered himself involved in a project for the moral regeneration of religion.

Mill wrote three essays on religion – *Nature, The Utility of Religion,* and *Theism.* The first two were written with Harriet's participation and the third after her death.[57] The first two essays were written during the period 1854–56, at the time that Mill was preparing the early draft of the *Autobiography.*

Much of the writing of the two earlier essays was expressed in terms of arguments for God's existence. This focus in the eighteenth and especially the nineteenth century was a continuing reflection of the transition from a medieval world, in which Aristotelian teleology had explained everything, to a modern world, in which Newtonian physics denied the existence of final causes in nature. Religious writers eventually conceded the absence of final causes in the inorganic world but continued to maintain the existence of purpose in the organic world. This was the form that natural theology took in the nineteenth century – along with a great religiously inspired interest in amateur biology – and it is precisely this form of natural theology that was deeply shaken by the publication in 1859 of Darwin's *Origin of Species.* Darwin offered a hypothesis that went a long way toward explaining biological phenomena without invoking teleology. To many, it seemed as if the last vestige of the rational affirmation of God's existence and benevolence was threatened with extinction.

Curiously, none of this seemed to bother Mill. He read Darwin and remarked that "though he cannot be said to have proved the truth of his doctrine, he does seem to have proved that it *may* be true."[58] Why did this not concern Mill? To begin with, Mill was not obsessed, as some critics seem to think, with discrediting religion. He was not looking for allies in a project of delegitimation. Mill had never subscribed to the belief in teleology at any level, so any argument that raised doubts about teleology in nature would have meant nothing to him. This is a point he made in the *Logic*.

The doctrine that the theological explanation of phenomena belongs only to the infancy of our knowledge of them, ought not to be construed as if it was the equivalent to the assertion that mankind, as their knowledge advances, will necessarily cease to believe in any kind of theology. This was M. Comte's opinion; but it is by no means implied in his fundamental theorem. All that is implied is, that in an advanced state of human knowledge, no other Ruler of the World will be acknowledged than one who rules by universal laws, and does not at all, or does not unless in very peculiar circumstances, produce events by special interpositions. Originally all natural events were ascribed to such interpositions.[59]

What Mill did object to was the claim that nature was teleological and that the teleology of nature was evidence of a benevolent creator who had established a natural order to which we were to conform. This was the classical and medieval perspective that Mill rejected. In his essay on *Nature*, he went out of his way to insist that Nature often contained unmitigated horrors and inexcusable tragedies that it was our moral duty to reverse. In this respect, Mill shared that aspect of the modern Protestant perspective in which internally apprehended standards lead us to transform the world by imposing a divinely inspired order upon it.

[T]he order of nature, in so far as unmodified by man, is such as no Being whose attributes are justice and benevolence would have made with the intention that his rational creatures should follow as an example. If made wholly by such a Being . . . it could only be as a designedly imperfect work which man, in his limited sphere, is to exercise justice and benevolence in amending. . . . No one, either religious or irreligious, believes that the hurtful agencies of nature, considered as a whole, promote good purposes in any other way than by inciting human rational creatures to rise up and struggle against them.[60]

On the other hand, what the evidence of the world did seem to reveal, or to partially support, was the existence of some limited amount of design[61] along with the horrors. Mill's argument for a finite God was an alternative to Darwin's hypothesis.[62] This evidence was enough to justify the idea that if there were a God, then that God was benevolent but not omnipotent. As early as 1860, Mill had written in response to Florence Nightingale that he could not see how to reconcile the world with the idea of a Perfect Being but that he was sympathetic to Manicheanism. In fact, he went on to assert, in what may very well be a personal reference, that

the world is a battlefield between a good and a bad power or powers, and ... mankind may be capable by sufficiently strenuous cooperation with the good power, of deciding, or at least accelerating, its final victory. I know one man, of great intelligence & high moral principle, who finds satisfaction to his devotional feelings, and support under the evils of life, in the belief of this creed.[63]

In his posthumously published essay *Theism* (written in 1869), Mill maintained that (a) God probably existed and that (b) God was beneficent, perhaps omniscient, but not omnipotent.[64] There was evil in the world that could not be rationalized away as part of some mysterious plan in God's mind. God was not a source of evil. This was in part Mill's answer to Mansel's book, which Mill described as a "detestable to me absolutely loathsome book."[65] Further, Mill maintained (c) that since the physical body is a condition, and not the cause, of mental life, some form of immortality was possible.[66] Both Morley and Bain were shocked and disappointed by this avowal. Bain went so far as to ask Helen Taylor, after Mill's death, if he could "edit" those essays in order to preserve Mill's reputation!

It is important to stress the continuity of this argument with Mill's epistemological phenomenalism and metaphysical idealism. It is important to see how crucial was the recognition in *Hamilton* of a self or ego that is not established through inference but is a presupposition of consciousness itself. Some of Mill's supporters were shocked by the posthumous publication of these beliefs,[67] but we see them as completely consistent implications of Mill's metaphysics.[68]

Crucial to Mill's understanding of God was a version of Manicheanism. His father had always found Manicheanism a plausible hypothesis. Mill himself was to express a similar idea with a historical dimension.

One only form of belief in the supernatural – one only theory respecting the origin and government of the universe – stands wholly clear both of intellectual contradiction and of moral obliquity. It is that which, resigning irrevocably the idea of an omnipotent creator, regards Nature and Life not as the expression throughout of the moral character and purpose of the Deity, but as the product of a struggle between contriving goodness and an intractable material, as was believed by Plato, or a Principle of Evil, as was the doctrine of the Manicheans. A creed like this, which I have known to be devoutly held by at least one cultivated and conscientious person of our own day, allows it to be believed that all the mass of evil which exists was undesigned by, and exists not by the appointment of, but in spite of the Being whom we are called upon to worship. A virtuous human being assumes in this theory the exalter character of a fellow laborer with the Highest, a fellow combatant in the great strife. . . . The evidence for it, indeed, if evidence it can be called, is too shadowy and unsubstantial, and the promises it holds out too distant and uncertain, to admit its being a permanent substitute for the religion of humanity; but the two may be held in conjunction; and he to whom ideal good and the progress of the world toward it are really a religion, even though the other creed may seem to him a belief not grounded on evidence, is at liberty to indulge the pleasing and encouraging thought that its truth is possible.[69]

God's plan is not revealed in revelation, or in nature, or by reason; God's plan is revealed in history.[70] This is the kind of God with whom we could be in communion.[71]

What is the logical status of Mill's argument? How we understand ourselves is basic. How we understand the world is derivative. We understand ourselves, thinks Mill, as minds who act to transform the world so as to make it better and in so doing to achieve greater insight into ourselves. What ontological picture would make sense of this? Any metaphysical hypothesis – and it could be only a hypothesis – must take account of the facts of human history as well as the history of the world as we know it. Moreover, the ultimate explanatory principle must be a form of mind or consciousness. Mill's philosophy of history sees history as a dynamic, dialectical, evolving process whose implicit norm is the striving for autonomy. Mill's conception of God is not the mere expression of hope but an imaginative analogical hypothesis that renders meaningful the relation of human beings to the universe as a whole.

The parallels with Hegel are worth drawing. Like Hegel, Mill was a monist for whom God could not be outside the world.[72] If there is an infinite mind, it cannot be wholly distinct from the finite mind. Like Hegel, Mill thought these beliefs were compatible, and his critics, like Hegel's, took this to be a denial of theism. If God cannot be outside of Nature, then this means that there cannot be God's goodness without real evil. Negation and contradiction are not mere logical abstractions but realities in the world. It also means there cannot be truth without error; hence the need for dialectic. Finally, there is an interesting parallel to be drawn with regard to freedom. The awareness of freedom, as discussed in *Nature*, is a product of struggle, self-mastery, and self-consciousness.

> Though we cannot emancipate ourselves from the laws of nature as a whole, we can escape from any particular law of nature if we are able to withdraw ourselves from the circumstances in which it acts. Though we can do nothing except through laws of nature, we can use one law to counteract another. . . . By every choice which we make, either of ends or means, we place ourselves to a greater or less extent under one set of laws of nature instead of another.[73]

The inheritor, so to speak, of Mill's Religion of Humanity was liberal Protestantism.[74] As Eldon Eisenach has called to our attention, Mill's *Logic*, when published in 1843, was almost immediately received into the curriculum at Oxford. Clerical tutors, prominent among them Mark Pattison,[75] found in the discussion of the moral sciences in Book VI a philosophy of history that allowed them to argue for the evolution of Christian doctrine. One of the chief contributors to Pattison's anthology entitled *Essays and Reviews* (1860) was Baden Powell, the founder of the Boy Scouts. Powell reflected the current problems in Christianity. He argued that the Bible was not meant to teach us truths about the physical world and that the truths of revelation are known through moral experience.[76] Recalling the origin of Mill's philosophy of history in Coleridge, and recalling that Coleridge had transformed the way in which Protestantism understood itself, it is easy to see how "these Churchmen could start from Mill's 'Moral Sciences,' add their own liberal Protestant gloss, and end by anticipating much of *On Liberty*."[77]

Mill and the Working Class

It can be said that as his life drew to a close, Mill focused on two major issues: the emancipation of women and the promotion of autonomy within the working class. Given Mill's concern about the democratization of late nineteenth-century British life, this should come as no surprise. "The emancipation of women, and co-operative production, are . . . the two great changes that will regenerate society."[78] Mill, in fact, never lost interest in the economic problems of the Industrial Revolution. When the great American jurist Oliver Wendell Holmes visited Mill in 1866, they attended a meeting of the Political Economy Club. The topic under discussion was "whether the financial policy of England should be governed by the prospective exhaustion of coal in H years as predicted by Jevons."[79]

As we have already seen, Mill had always been actively involved with associations of working men and their leadership. He welcomed the formation in 1864 of the International Workingmen's Association but demurred at the use of the expression "revolution" in their literature. Mill praised Proudhon, whose supporters opposed Marx and proposed cooperative associations. Mill advised workers against the strike as a tactic. He subsequently praised the English labor leaders George Odger, William Randal Cremer, and Applegarth for opposing the proposals of Marx and Bakunin at the congresses of Geneva (1866) and Basle (1869). The English trade unionists would eventually dissociate themselves from the International.[80]

In 1865, Mill wrote to George Howell that successful strikes lead only to a rise in prices that eventually is harmful to the laboring classes.[81] It was Howell who, as secretary of the Parliamentary Committee of the Trades Union Congress, had advised workers to "get Mill on Liberty and Political Economy. There are many other works but go to the fountain head at once."[82] In March of 1867, Mill tried to dissuade Cremer from resorting to calls for force by the Reform League to secure enactment of the enfranchisement bill.[83] In 1869, Mill subscribed to the Labor Representation League, led by Howell. Mill supported Odger's candidacy for Parliament, consoled him in defeat, and in 1871 even introduced him to d'Eichtal. Despite his busy schedule of writing and correspondence, Mill, always on the alert against a lack of toleration, also helped E. S. Beesly, a professor of classics who had been dismissed for speaking in defense of trade unions.[84] Only two months before he died, Mill's name was removed from the membership list of the Cobden Club because of his support of the Land Tenure Reform Association, which advocated "principles radically opposed to those" of the club.[85]

During this period, Mill once again took up the topic of socialism and proposed to write a systematic treatise on it. It was never finished, but what we have is significant. It was published posthumously in 1879 by Helen Taylor with the title *Chapters on Socialism* (the first four completed chapters) in the *Fortnightly*, now edited by Morley, who with Mill's help had turned the periodical into the most advanced organ of liberal thought. Mill gave a specific definition of socialism in *Chapters on Socialism*:

Among those who call themselves Socialists, two kinds of persons may be distinguished. There are, in the first place, those whose plans for a new order of society, in which private property and individual competition are to be superseded and other motives to action substituted, are on the scale of a village community or township, and would be applied to an entire country by the multiplication of such self-acting units; of this character are the systems of Owen, of Fourier, and the more thoughtful and philosophic Socialists generally. The other class, who are more a product of the Continent than of Great Britain and may be called the revolutionary Socialists, propose to themselves a much bolder stroke. Their scheme is the management of the whole productive resources of the country by one central authority, the general government. And with this view some of them avow as their purpose that the working classes, or somebody in their behalf, should take possession of all the property of the country, and administer it for the general benefit.[86]

Mill rejected central planning, nationalization of all property, and the achievement of reform through violent revolutionary acts. He discerned that the animating principle of revolutionary socialism was "hate." Although he did not live to complete the *Chapters on Socialism*, it appears from the portions that he did complete that he was stiffening his opposition to certain aspects of socialism. Mill never wavered on the primacy of promoting autonomy among the working class and on the value of workers' cooperatives. He never wavered on the point that the ultimate test of any reform was its promotion of liberty and autonomy. In the 1850s, he had softened his concern about the success of cooperatives, at Harriet's instigation. But it should be recalled that Mill was never as optimistic as Harriet about the prospect of promoting the common good as a motive. It was not so much that the loss of Harriet had led to a reversion to an earlier view, but rather that Mill's later experience with trade unionists had led to a further evolution of his thinking.

Mill's last chapters on socialism must be regarded as essentially an evaluation founded on the added experience of the English trade unionists with the International. . . . The too generous hopes of Mill in 1848 for the principle of association [i.e., cooperatives] were now basically amended in the light of this new phenomenon of the revolutionary ideologists – this permeation of socialism with a ferocity and hatred which Mill had not previously foreseen.[87]

There is reason to believe that Mill was less enthusiastic about socialist experiments at the end of his life than he had been earlier. Part of this may have been in response to what he took to be the despotic and authoritarian implications of thinkers such as Comte. In his publication *Auguste Comte and Positivism* (1865), he identified Comte as a socialist and described the system as follows:

The owner of capital is by no means to consider himself its absolute proprietor. Legally he is not to be controlled in his dealings with it, for power should be in proportion to responsibility: but it does not belong to him for his own use; he is merely entrusted by society with a portion of the accumulations made by the past providence of mankind, to be administered for the benefit of the present generation and of posterity, under the obligation of preserving them unimpaired, and handing them down, more or less augmented, to those who are to come. . . . Small landed proprietors and capitalists, and the middle class altogether, he regards as a parasitic growth, destined to disappear, the best of the body becoming large capitalists, and the remainder proletaires. . . . One is appalled at the picture of entire subjugation and slavery, which is recommended to us as the last and highest result of the evolution of Humanity.[88]

Mill was concerned that cooperative communities can undermine individual initiative: "[P]rivate life would be brought in a most unexampled degree within the dominion of public authority, and there would be less scope for the development of individual character and individual preferences than has hitherto existed among the full citizens of any state belonging to the progressive branches of the human family."[89] Helen Taylor remarked that "he himself was of the opinion that if his life were prolonged to complete it, his work on Socialism would rank as, at the least, on a level with that of Representative Government."[90] The parallel is important, for in *Representative Government* Mill was concerned with reining in democracy because it threatened autonomy. There is reason to believe that his experience with workers' organizations had left him less than optimistic about the future.[91] What *Chapters on Socialism* adds is strong reason to be wary of even limited cooperatives, a strengthening of the case for capitalism – the lot of workers was improving – and a harsher critique of revolutionary socialism.

Mill had, at first, accepted the wage fund theory – namely, that there was a limit to what the workers could get and that it was already achieved and could not be helped by strikes and collective bargaining. He changed his mind after W. T. Thornton's *On Labour* appeared in the *Fortnightly Review* (May to December 1867). Mill reviewed it in the same publication in May of 1869. However, in the last edition of the *Principles of Political Economy* he greatly qualified his recantation. He once more recognized the importance of supply and demand: higher wages could only be accomplished in the long run by increasing unemployment.

If they [the workers] could do so [combine effectively], they might doubtless succeed in diminishing the hours of labour, and obtaining the same wages for less work. They would also have a limited power of obtaining, by combination, an increase of general wages at the expense of profits. But the limits of this power are narrow; and were they to attempt to strain it beyond those limits, this could only be accomplished by keeping a part of their number permanently out of employment.[92]

For Mill, the best solution lay in profit sharing and in the euthanasia of trade unionism:

[The] growing inconvenience to them [employers] from the opposition of interest between themselves and the workmen should stimulate the conversion of existing business into Industrial Partnerships, in which the whole body of workpeople have a direct interest in the profits of the enterprise; such a transformation would be the true euthanasia of Trades' Unionism, while it would train and prepare at least the superior portion of the working classes for a form of co-operation still more equal and complete.[93]

One recurrent issue that needs to be raised here is Mill's relationship to the forms of socialism that emerged after his death.[94] One such version, and one that claimed Mill as its predecessor, was Fabian socialism, a movement that was first organized during the 1880s. It was so named after the Roman general who finally defeated Hannibal by playing a waiting game. Its most prominent members were Beatrice and Sidney Webb, Graham Wallas, and George Bernard Shaw, all of whom believed that socialism was inevitable and should be brought about gradually. The Fabians asserted the existence of a collective good that could best be achieved through the collective organization of society by the state. The state they hoped to see would be run by technical experts, the kind that were increasingly emerging and being recognized in Britain in the post-1870 period. The society was thus to be a kind of meritocracy. Politically, what the Fabians envisioned was a democratically accountable elite.[95]

What this resonates with in Mill is the suggestion made in *Representative Government* that the government be run by experts, with Parliament being the democratically elected body to oversee the operations of the technocrats. What it more nearly resembles is Comte's version of the future of society. This alone should cause us to be cautious in drawing a parallel with Mill. The differences, however, between Fabian socialism and Mill's view are striking. Mill's suggestion concerned a government civil service, but Mill did not believe that there should be centralized control of the economy. In fact, he denied that it would be possible for experts to have the knowledge that would make it possible (an anticipation of Hayek's argument). More important, Mill denied that there was a collective good of the kind that the Fabians asserted. For Mill, economic freedom was a means to, or necessary condition of, autonomy. Given what Mill said at the beginning of the chapter "On the Probable Futurity of the Labouring Classes" in the *Principles of Political Economy*, he would probably have looked contemptuously upon the Fabians as establishing a feudalism run by intellectuals. Fabian socialism was philanthropy managed by the intellectual sons and daughters of the Tories.

Another British variant of socialism, one that developed after World War I, was guild socialism, an obvious reference to medieval guilds.[96] Like the syndicalists, the guild socialists distrusted state control. Instead, they envisioned a society divided into distinct and autonomous groups of industrial organizations, trade unions, cooperative societies, and local municipalities. Instead of state control, they hoped to see cooperation between the functional units. They advocated that individuals have a say in each and every autonomous unit to which they belonged, an anticipation of the current conception of the stakeholder replacing the stockholder. What remained ambiguous was the exact nature and structure of the cooperation between the functional units.

While this resonates with Mill's suggestion about workers' cooperatives, it differs considerably in three significant ways from Mill's views. First, Mill understood democracy to be the inevitable wave of the future, so that, for Mill, the complex models of associational cooperation worked out by various guild socialists would seem like theoretical constructs having no relation to the perceived ongoing evolution of actual political institutions in liberal culture. In fact, guild socialism was always an academic movement. Second, Mill did not believe that the economy had the kind of structure that permitted the identification of more or less permanent functional units; in fact, this smacks of the notion, rejected by Mill, of a collective organic good with readily identifiable parts. Third, Mill would have insisted, in a way that guild socialists rejected and denied, on the importance of the autonomous individual in the political, economic, and social process. The third point obviously follows from, and is directly related to, the second point. All of this has to do not with Mill's alleged atomism or individualism but with his commitment to individuality as autonomy and as *Bildung*. Among his last letters is one to J. R. Ware written from Avignon on September 13, 1868:

[T]he various forms of Cooperation . . . are the real and only thorough means of healing the feud between capitalists and labourers; and, while tending eventually to supersede trade unions, are meanwhile a natural and gradually increasing corrective of their operation [that] will dispose . . . [the more advanced workpeople] more and more to look for the just improvement of their condition rather in becoming their own capitalists, or allying themselves on fair conditions with the owners of capital, than in their present uncomfortable, and often disastrous, relations with them.[97]

ða.

In June of 1871, George Grote, Mill's last link with his past, died and was buried with full pomp and circumstance in Westminster Abbey. Mill reluctantly agreed to serve as one of the pallbearers. On exiting the ceremony, he remarked to Bain: "In no very long time, I shall be laid in the ground with a very different ceremonial from that."[98] Two years later, having sat for a portrait by G. F. Watts in March, Mill died in Avignon on May 7, 1873, of a local endemic fever known as erysipelas, contracted on one of his beloved long country walks. His last words to Helen were "You know I have done my work." On the tenth of May, "he was buried in the grave to which he had, through fourteen years, looked as a pleasant resting-place, because during fourteen years there had been in it a vacant place beside the remains of the wife whom he so fondly loved."[99] Half of Mill's estate was given to a variety of charitable causes. Even in death, Mill managed, at least inadvertently, to arouse controversy. A Protestant minister from Avignon, Louis Rey, whom Mill had befriended and who continued to champion Mill's cause after his death, delivered a prayer at the interment. Later, Rey had to write an apologetic essay to his own congregation in the local paper for having offered a prayer on behalf of a known religious skeptic.

Mill's posthumous publications, overseen by Helen, included the *Autobiography* in 1873, the *Three Essays on Religion* in 1874, and the *Chapters on Socialism* in 1879. Mill is buried at Avignon with Harriet. One cannot help recalling here Carlyle's advice in *Sartor Resartus*:

Produce! Produce! Were it but the pitifullest infinitesimal fraction of a product, produce it, in God's name! 'Tis the utmost thou hast in thee: out with it, then. Up, up. Whatsoever thy hand findeth to do, do it with thy whole might. Work while it is called Today, for the Night commeth, wherein no man can work.[100]

Mill's Public

Stefan Collini[101] has formulated a useful and illuminating expression to describe a group of writers in Britain. He calls them "public moralists" and classifies Mill among them. They had careers in the civil service (Mill and Arnold), the higher journalism (Stephen, Morley), the universities (Fawcett), or the law. They wrote for a particular group of homogeneous elite middle-class readers, and they wrote in popular periodicals. Rather than seeing themselves as a distinct interest group, they saw their role as reminding "their more self-interested contemporaries of the strenuous commitments entailed by the moral values embedded in the public discourse of their society."[102] Concerned about the conflict between individual interest and the common interest, and about the loss of the moral consensus represented by Christianity that had previously served to resolve that conflict, they sought a replacement in some form of altruism and an emphasis upon work as the domain in which moral worth was developed. There are important changes in the role of intellectuals after roughly the 1870s, but they relate to the change from a liberal to a democratic politics.

In many ways, Mill was an enigma to his contemporaries, and this enigma has remained down to the present. The main reason for this is that Mill expressed a total vision of liberal culture that was shared by almost no one and had in Britain no natural constituency. We may well ask how a writer without a constituency and whose vision was not shared could have had such an enormous impact, both on his own time and on ours. Part of the answer to this question is that what Mill tried to achieve was a synthesis of views, and to the extent that Mill reflected one or another of these viewpoints, he had allies and admirers.

To begin with, Mill was, however qualified, an advocate of those aspects of modern liberal culture that were transforming the world, namely, market economies and democracy. As such, he was opposed to the feudalism of the Tory aristocracy. No matter how much Mill defended the centrality of private property for a market economy, the Tories knew that Mill was their enemy. One would think that this made Mill the natural voice of the rising middle-class industrialists. But as much as he would like to have been, Mill could not be an apologist for the new industrialists, because their conception of liberal culture got no further than an appreciation of the market economy and the accumulation of wealth.

... the two chief influences which have chiefly shaped the British character since the days of the Stuarts: commercial money-getting business, and religious Puritanism. Business, demanding the whole of the faculties, and whether pursued from duty or love of gain, regarding as a loss of time whatever does not conduce directly to the end; Puritanism, which, looking upon every feeling of human nature, except fear and reverence for God, as a snare, if not as partaking of sin, looked coldly, if not disapprovingly, on the cultivation of the sentiments.[103]

What Mill advocated was the Germanic notion of an alliance between property and education (or culture). But the middle classes were not interested in *Bildung*, and the educated voices of culture were largely opposed to the Industrial Revolution that had made liberal culture possible in the first place.[104] Typical of this failure was the comment of Ruskin, who thought Mill "deserves honour among economists by inadvertently disclaiming the principles which he states, and tacitly introducing the moral considerations with which he declares his science has no connection."[105] The cultural-intellectual community was happy to share Mill's critique of the Philistines, but it turned a deaf ear to his attempts to transcend the conflict by creating a new synthesis. As Nancy Rosenblum expressed it:

In adopting this connection between artistic creation and privatization, Mill suggests the possibility of an even more generous openness to romanticism if the benefits of detachment can be enjoyed by everyone, not just artists. But Mill has no patience with romantic sensibilities turning their desire for self-expression into wholesale opposition to commercial society or looking for opportunities for self-assertion in war.[106]

Mill could be accepted as a moralist, or he could be accepted as an explicator of the market economy, but what he could not get was acceptance as both. This is a reflection less upon Mill than upon his contemporaries.

The middle-class business community did not ultimately emerge as the progressive class in Britain, and that failure had a lot to do with the demise of liberalism as a political movement. The entrepreneurial ideal, with its emphasis on autonomy, did not triumph. Individuals apart, Britain did not develop a class that expressed or instantiated that ideal until relatively recently.[107] The successful industrialists were co-opted and absorbed by the Tories. As Martin Wiener put it,

> What Britain never had was a straightforwardly bourgeois or industrial elite.... The capitalism of the aristocracy, although varying in individual cases, was basically rentier, not entrepreneurial or productive. Thus the accommodation between aristocracy and bourgeoisie meant an adaptation by the new middle classes to a comparatively aloof and passive economic role. The rentier aristocracy succeeded to a large extent in maintaining a cultural hegemony, and consequently ... in reshaping the industrial bourgeoisie in its own image.[108]

The intellectual classes, for a variety of reasons and employing somewhat different arguments, identified with labor. The very split in British life that Mill feared and tried to heal became an increasingly unbridgeable gulf.

Dicey was wrong to blame Mill, or even to suggest that Mill in some sense reflected the alleged drift from individualism to collectivism. A misconception similar to Dicey's can be seen in the remarks of J. George Eccarius, a supporter of Marx, who wrote: "As a member of Parliament Mill conducted himself in exemplary fashion, and showed he had the courage to come forward in the interest of the working class.... His political behaviour is in contradiction with his economic philosophy."[109] What Mill advocated was not individualism but individuality, an individuality designed to transcend a society divided between employers and employees. What Mill represented and tried to build between 1830 and 1870 failed to materialize. That failure can be seen in the decline of Gladstone's liberal coalition, which saw the defection of upper-working-class supporters to Labor and of Manchester manufacturers to the Tories.[110]

Mill was in favor of a market economy and private property, but he found the rationale of the Philosophic Radicals inadequate. That rationale could not address the problems of the working class or the status of women or the threat of mass democracy. Others, such as his nemesis Fitzjames Stephen, were only interested in the defense and uninterested in the problems. So Stephen found himself "falling foul . . . of John Mill in his modern and more humane mood . . . which always makes me feel that he is a deserter from the proper principles of rigidity and ferocity in which he was brought up."[111] There were those, such as Eccarius, who sympathized with Mill's attempt to deal with the social problems of industrialization but disagreed with his understanding of liberal culture.

The technical-intellectual elite was another of Mill's potential natural constituencies. The success of the *Logic* and its rapid adoption by the universities could easily have projected Mill into the position of the *eminence grise* of the technological elite. But Mill knew the limitations of science, and he had tried to indicate in the last part of the *Logic* how science needed to be supplemented by art or poetic vision. Unfortunately, the community of intellectuals seemed to be composed of individuals who had either a right-brain dominance or a left-brain dominance. In either case, they did not hear the other half of Mill's argument.[112] Mill's friend, biographer, and protégé, Bain, the man who ultimately founded the British journal of philosophy *Mind*, could only bemoan the fact that Mill "seemed to look upon Poetry as a Religion, or rather as Religion and Philosophy in one."[113] C. P. Snow's later identification of the two cultures, however inadequately explained, is an example of this ongoing problem.[114] The intellectual conflict between the eighteenth-century Enlightenment Project and the nineteenth-century Romantic reaction is still with us, in one form or another. The image of Mill as someone who tried unsuccessfully to combine their virtues is a thesis put forth by partisans who neither understand the other side nor have tried to transcend that conflict. The lack of success may be in the audience and not in the author.

What is frequently missed is the deep sense in which Mill was a philosopher. By that I mean that he was more than someone who took positions on public policy issues, more than someone who tried to understand the way in which major institutions functioned. John Stuart Mill understood that how human beings understood themselves and their place in the universe – the big picture, so to speak – was primary. If the social world was to be more than a truce among contending interests, if the function of argument was more than to create an impregnable position in polite conversation, then fundamental issues in metaphysics, epistemology, and axiology would have to be addressed. Mill thought he had done so, and the primary value to emerge from that achievement was autonomy.

Autonomy is the key to understanding Mill's public policy positions. It is a concept that his contemporaries largely failed to grasp, because it was an insight he had imported into the British context from continental and Romantic sources. Autonomy has a religious origin and even a religious counterpart, but the organized religions of Mill's time were unable, in his opinion, to instantiate it because they could see only the negative dimension of repression and self-denial. That autonomy could have a positive dimension such as *Bildung*, or that the creation of wealth and resources could itself be an expression of *Bildung* or a means to *Bildung*, is something his contemporaries could not see.

What look like confusions or contradictions or inconsistencies on Mill's part are almost always the result of the failure to understand the central role of autonomy. For example, Mill supported liberty in public policies because it allowed for the discovery, exercise, and development of autonomy. Liberty was not an end in itself. Mill critiqued those situations in which he thought that liberty, as the absence of external constraints, was inimical to autonomy. Market economies, private property, individual rights, and representative government with a universal franchise were advocated and defended because they promoted autonomy. Mill was also an advocate of economic reform to help the working class, but the object of his policies was not the mere redistribution of resources but the promotion of autonomy in the form of entrepreneurship. Those who see the world as an inevitable struggle between the "haves" and the "have-nots," those who do not believe in the efficacy of the institutions of liberal culture under any set of circumstances, and those who reject the modern world cannot possibly make sense of Mill's program. Since Mill was an advocate of the fundamental importance of autonomy, he tried to protect it in all of its existing forms. Hence, he favored policies that inhibited the tyranny of the majority. Some readers will be puzzled. Was Mill for or against democracy? That is the wrong question. What Mill favored was autonomy. To the extent that democratic institutions protected and promoted autonomy, he defended them. To the extent that those institutional arrangements discouraged free and responsible behavior, he opposed them. Critics often fail to see which dimension of the issue Mill was addressing, and they thereby miss it, because they do not see autonomy.

For example, Mill can easily defend minority or individual diversity if it is based on *Bildung* but oppose it if it is based on blind custom. He can defend cultural diversity if it is an expression of *Bildung* but oppose it if the culture is not a liberal culture. It is only within liberal culture, Mill thought, that *Bildung* had a chance.

Nobody can suppose that it is not more beneficial to a Breton or a Basque . . . to be brought into the current of the ideas and feelings of a highly civilized and cultivated people – to be a member of the French nationality . . . – than to skulk on his own rocks, the half savage relic of past times, revolving in his own little mental orbit. . . . The same remark applies to the Welshman or the Scottish Highlander as members of the British Nation.[115]

It has been suggested that we might distinguish between organic intellectuals who "teach the doctrines and values around which a society coheres" (Coleridge and the clerisy) and the "intelligentsia" who adopt a critical stance.[116] Mill is neither. On the one hand, he thought that he had correctly identified the implicit norms of liberal culture, and in that sense he was an organic intellectual. On the other hand, changes in the historical context called dialectically for a rearticulation of those norms. Where Mill is critical, it is of those who fail to see the new context. In no sense is this a critique of the fundamental values. It is because of Mill's understanding of the philosophy of history that he saw himself as an explicator and not merely an alienated critic. He always saw himself as playing the Socratic role.

Obituary

It fell to one of Mill's contemporaries, Hayward, to write Mill's obituary in the London *Times*. Abraham Hayward had debated Mill in the London Debating Society during the 1820s and later had protested an article that appeared in the *Westminster Review* (while Mill was editor) accusing Hayward of being a lackey for the aristocracy. In 1873, Hayward got his revenge by publishing a polemical obituary in the *Times* and in *Fraser's Magazine*.[117] He not only excoriated Mill for his views on the rights of women and land reform, but also insinuated that Mill and Harriet had committed adultery, as well as retelling the story of Mill's arrest as a teenager for distributing pamphlets advocating birth control. The obituary was an exercise in character assassination. A memorial had been proposed for Westminster Abbey, but after the obituary even Gladstone withdrew his support for it. This is the same Gladstone who in 1889 would refer to

Mill as "the Saint of Rationalism." The subsequent publication of the *Autobiography* became an excuse for his critics to be even more vituperative than was seemly in an obituary.

There were others, of course, who spoke more positively. Mill's nemesis, Fitzjames Stephen, said of him that "[o]ne who knew Mill only through his writings knew but half of him, and that not the best half."[118] T. H. Green, on his deathbed, said of Mill that he "was such a good man."[119] Sidgwick called Mill "the best philosophical writer – if not the best philosopher – England has produced since Hume."[120] The labor leader George Jacob Holyoake wrote of Mill that "of all the public men whom I can recall, there have been none, certainly no philosophers, who personally cared for the people as he did, and aided those in their ranks who showed individuality or capacity of self-help."[121] Gomperz, writing an obituary for a Vienna newspaper, put it as follows: "What Mill has been to his friends, how inexhaustible his goodness and tolerance, how complete his self-effacement, how he never claimed the slightest privilege for himself, and how he placed himself on a level of complete equality with the youngest and most untried...."[122] Writing to Helen about the account of his relationship with Mill in the *Autobiography*, and having been reassured of Mill's warmth, Roebuck wrote: "The last letter I received from him, was in a tone of tenderness, that spoke of old times and old feelings.... Indeed the contents moved me so much that I tried to find his apartments in Victoria Street but was unsuccessful.... I am indeed glad to hear that he felt respecting me as in his youth he was accustomed to feel."[123]

Reputation[124]

As British intellectuals moved more and more into a university setting, it became fashionable to make one's reputation by attacking Mill's. Leslie Stephen recalled his time at Cambridge as one in which "hour after hour was given to discussing points raised by Mill as keenly as medieval commentators used to discuss the doctrines of Aristotle."[125] It began with Bradley's critique of Mill, caricatured as an individualist; it continued through Jevons's detractions; aimed at promoting Jevons's own reputation as leader of the "marginalist" revolution in economics; it was furthered by Sidgwick; and it reached its apotheosis in G. E. Moore. The works that earned Mill his reputation as a great thinker and for which he was famous in his lifetime, the *Logic* and the *Principles of Political Economy*, were later deprecated by his godson, Bertrand Russell.[126] Russell was particularly vexed by the fact that Mill refused to see the human race as "one among animals."[127]

It was also during the last two decades of the nineteenth century that the standard caricature of John Stuart Mill emerged. During those decades, the debate between individualism and collectivism, as reflected in Dicey's comments, found Mill being identified as the author of *On Liberty* and that text being identified as a defense of individualism. The idealist critics of individualism claimed that individualism was a product of utilitarianism and that utilitarianism was the philosophical foundation of the Philosophic Radicals and political economy. Between his unhappy associates, such as Dicey and Leslie Stephen, and his idealist enemies, the myth of Mill was born. Because he had authored books entitled *On Liberty, Utilitarianism*, and *Principles of Political Economy*, it was easy for his idealist critics to caricature his views. Frederick Harrison, a follower of Comte and a leading positivist, contributed to the myth by identifying Mill only with the tradition of "Locke, Hume, Adam Smith, Bentham, Malthus, James Mill, Austin, Grote, Bowring, Roebuck, [and] the philosophic Radicals,"[128] ignoring completely the Romantic Mill. This misrepresentation of Mill by his critics and the partisan account of history by Dicey had by 1900 "become the dominant interpretation of recent English political and intellectual history."[129] As Collini points out, by the 1920s *On Liberty* was invoked only as an expression of negative liberty. "Its pervasive strenuousness and commitment to altruism passed largely unnoticed."[130]

The Significance of John Stuart Mill

John Stuart Mill's message or messages are remarkable in their breadth as well as their depth. From a cultural point of view and with the advantage of hindsight, he is a symbol of Victorian integrity, with its emphasis on character and delayed gratification. One hopes that he will also be seen as the great expositor of autonomy, the writer who tried to synthesize the Enlightenment and Romanticism. Philosophically, he explicated liberal culture in its most comprehensive sense. No one else has done it better in terms of breadth and depth, identifying its strengths and weaknesses. He synthesized ethics and moral philosophy and united them by making autonomy our goal. Politically, the concept of autonomy seems the only available solution to the problem of relating the individual good to the common good. Economically, his goals of making entrepreneurship universal, of transcending the distinction between employer and employee, and of intrepidly opposing centralization have, at the beginning of the twenty-first century, become the new and accepted foundation of public policy. In public policy generally, he taught us to ask the right questions: What actions promote and which inhibit autonomy? Of the ones that inhibit autonomy, is there a cure that is not itself a greater inhibitor? Of policies intended to promote autonomy, we must always ask: Do they work? Are they the only possibilities? Do they conflict with other legitimate policies?

What makes Mill relevant today? The simple answer is that the practical and intellectual conflicts he tried to resolve are still with us. The humanistic critique of the technological project and the moral-theological critique of the modern corruption of the soul are still with us and just as relevant. The technological project has not faltered but grown with increasing vigor. Humanists have not explained what could meaningfully and practically replace it, nor have they tried to construct a transcending synthesis. As long as this remains the case, Mill's attempted synthesis remains not only relevant but the logical starting point. Mill was the greatest of the English Romantics.

Notes

Preface

1. Hicks (1982), p. 325n.
2. *Autobiography*, CW I, p. 1.
3. Packe (1954), p. 11.

Chapter 1. Childhood and Early Education: The Great Experiment
(1806–1820)

1. See William Thomas, *The Philosophic Radicals* (Oxford: Clarendon Press, 1979).
2. See Leslie Stephen, *The English Utilitarians* (London, 1900), Vol. I, pp. 12–136.
3. According to Bain, A *Biography of James Mill* (London: Routledge/Thoemmes Press, 1995) (1882a), p. 11, John Stuart Mill did not know his own father's early history.
4. I am indebted to L. S. Feuer for this information: "John Stuart Mill as Sociologist" (1976). Feuer quotes from Graham Wallas, *The Life of Francis Place: 1771–1854* (4th ed., London, 1925), pp. 70–1. Feuer also contends that "James Mill could never forget that his wife was not the one he loved. His utilitarianism was as much an outcome of a personal quarrel with society as his son's *On Liberty*" (p. 103).
5. John Stuart Mill was the eldest and born in 1806. The others were Wilhelmina (1808–1861); Clara (1810–1886); Harriet (1812–1897); James Bentham (1814–1862), named after Bentham and who served in the civil service in India; Jane (1816–1883), named after Lady Jane Stuart; Henry (1820–1840), known as Derry; Mary (1822–1913); and George Grote (1825–1853), named after Grote and who also served in India House. None of the other sons, all of whom died relatively young, had heirs. Four of the daughters were married, and three had children.
6. Bain (1882a), p. 334.
7. Ibid., p. 415.
8. James Mill became chief examiner. The Strachey family alleged, in a review of Bain's biography of James Mill, that James Mill had deliberately undermined Strachey's chances to become chief examiner. See Moir's introduction to CW XXX, pp. xiii–xiv.

9. "Had I foreseen that the labour would have been one half, or one third, of what it had been, never should I have been the author of a History of India." Bain (1882a), p. 62.
10. Quoted in Bain (1882a), pp. 180–1.
11. *Autobiography*, p. 612. All references to the *Autobiography* are to CW I.
12. However, other visitors to the Mill household, such as Crompton, report that "John was devotedly attached to his mother and exuberant in his playful tokens of affection." Notes of a conversation between the Rev. J. Crompton and A. S. West at Norwich in 1875 (Library of King's College, Cambridge). This raises the possibility that the *Autobiography*, written in the 1850s, reflected in part Mill's resentment toward what he perceived to be his mother's mistreatment of his wife, Harriet.
13. Graham Wallas, *Life of Francis Place* (London, 1898), p. 75.
14. Letter to Rev. J. Crompton, October 26, 1873. Quoted in Michael St. John Packe, *The Life of John Stuart Mill* (London: Secker and Warburg, 1954), p. 33n.
15. Bertrand and Patricia Russell (eds.), *The Amberley Papers* (London: Hogarth, 1937), Vol. I, p. 421.
16. Henry Solly (friend of James Bentham Mill), *These Eighty Years* (London: Simpkin Marshall, 1893), Vol. I, p. 147.
17. *Autobiography*, p. 52 (early draft).
18. Ibid., p. 53.
19. Bain (1882), p. 4.
20. *Autobiography*, pp. 33–4.
21. "Grant's Arithmetic for Young Children and Exercises for the Improvement of the Senses," *Globe and Traveler* (October 23, 1835), CW XXVII, pp. 786–7.
22. *Autobiography*, p. 17.
23. Ibid., p. 39.
24. Wallas (1898), p. 76.
25. Ibid.
26. Bain (1882a), p. 333.
27. *Autobiography*, p. 17.
28. Bain (1882a), pp. 334–5.
29. Crompton, op. cit.
30. *Autobiography*, pp. 35–7.
31. Ibid., p. 33.
32. Ibid., pp. 251–3.
33. Quoted in Bain (1882a), p. 205.
34. While all Mill's sisters were educated at home, the brothers were permitted to go to school. Both James Bentham Mill and Henry Mill attended University College, London. In Henry's case there was even some talk of sending him to Cambridge. University College, London had itself been founded by dissenters, partly under the leadership of James Mill.
35. See T. W. Heyck, The *Transformation of Intellectual Life in Victorian England*. (New York: St. Martin's Press, 1982).

36. *Autobiography*, p. 21.

37. Ibid., p. 31.

38. Ibid.

39. *Autobiography*, p. 29.

40. Ibid., p. 87. See also his statement on p. 205, where he concedes that radicalism could have prevailed only if he had been "one who, being himself in Parliament, could have mixed with the radical members in daily consultation, could himself have taken the initiative, and instead of urging others to lead, could have summoned them to follow." On this issue consult Janice Carlisle's insightful treatment in *John Stuart Mill and the Writing of Character* (Athens: University of Georgia Press, 1991), pp. 43–63.

41. *Autobiography*, p. 19.

42. Ibid., p. 57.

43. Wallas (1898), pp. 75–6.

44. Mary Taylor, Introduction to *The Letters of Mill*, ed. Hugh S. R. Elliot (London: Longmans, Green, 1910), Vol. I, p. xvi. The letter from Bentham to James Mill was dated July 25, 1812. Bentham's eccentricity and style can be seen in the content of this letter. He was, of course, joking about the use of the whip.

45. Bain (1882a), p. 119.

46. F. A. Cavenaugh (ed.), *James Mill on Education* (Cambridge: Cambridge University Press, 1931), p. 1.

47. Ibid., p. 72.

48. Ibid., p. 71.

49. Joseph Lancaster was a Quaker who achieved notoriety for starting a nondenominational school in London.

50. Cavenaugh, op. cit., p. 24.

51. *Autobiography*, p. 41.

52. Ibid., p. 43.

53. Ibid., pp. 49–51.

54. Mill describes it in his *Autobiography*, p. 44: "I am thus one of the very few examples, in this country, of one who has, not thrown off religious belief, but never had it." Packe (1954), p. 25, contends that James Mill was still a churchgoer when he met Bentham and did not become an agnostic until Mill was ten. Packe also contends that there was more formal religious observance than Mill admits.

55. Bentham, *The Works of Jeremy Bentham*, ed. J. Bowring (London, 1838), Vol. II, p. 253.

56. Ibid., Vol. X, p. 442.

57. Alexander Bain, *John Stuart Mill. A Criticism: With Personal Recollections* (London: Longmans, Green, 1882) (1882b), pp. 23–5.

58. Ibid., p. 38.

59. Wallas (1898), p. 76.

60. *Autobiography*, p. 253.

61. Bain (1882b), pp. 25–6: ". . . doubtless his mind was cast for Logic from the first."

62. *Autobiography*, p. 613 ("Early Draft Rejected Leaves").
63. Ibid., p. 37.
64. Quoted in Bain (1882a), p. 181.
65. Bruce Mazlish, *James and John Stuart Mill: Father and Son in the Nineteenth Century* (New York: Basic Books, [1975] 1988), p. xvi.
66. W. L. Courtney, *Life of Mill* (London, 1889), p. 16.
67. *Autobiography*, pp. 51–3.
68. Ibid., p. 613.
69. Ibid., p. 11.
70. Ibid., p. 59.
71. Mill contributed to the field by publishing short notes in the *Phytologist* between 1841 and 1863.
72. *Autobiography*, p. 59.
73. Letter dated September 14, 1820. Quoted in Bain (1882b), p. 22.
74. Letter to Comte dated August 12, 1842. CW XIII, p. 540. For an English translation of the correspondence, see Oscar A. Haac, *The Correspondence of John Stuart Mill and Auguste Comte* (New Brunswick, NJ: Transaction, 1995), p. 93.
75. *Autobiography*, pp. 59–61.
76. Ibid., p. 63.
77. Christopher Dawson, *The Dividing of Christendom* (New York: Doubleday, 1967), p. 22: "This failure of Protestantism to assimilate the Christian Humanist tradition completely caused a certain impoverishment and aridity in English and American cultures and led ultimately to those defects which Matthew Arnold criticized so vigorously in the 19th century."
78. Mill to Harriet (December 30, 1854), CW XIV, pp. 269–70.
79. *Autobiography*, p. 5.
80. *Autobiography*, p. 35.

Chapter 2. Company Man and Youthful Propagandist (1821–1826)

1. See Martin Moir's introduction to volume XXX of CW, *Writings on India*.
2. *Autobiography*, p. 67.
3. Austin had made a special study of the German legal school of Pandectists, the Pandects being Justinian's codification of Roman Law.
4. We mention this point not only as a way of getting beyond the textbook caricature of Austin but as a way of reminding the reader of two things. First, the Mills socialized with individuals who shared the "Protestant Ethic." This tells us a great deal about Victorian morals. Second, the issue of slavery was one that brought the dissenting religious community and the utilitarians together.
5. *Autobiography*, p. 67.
6. Mill's extremely close relationship with Sarah Austin began to wane in the early 1840s when he discovered her gossip about his relationship with Harriet Taylor. Mill and the Austins finally parted ways in the late 1840s over political disagreements. Reference to her, like reference to his mother, in the *Autobiography* was

deleted. He had originally written in the early draft that she had "known me from a boy, she made great profession of a kind of maternal interest in me. But I never for an instant supposed that she cared for me [hard to believe, given Mill's correspondence with her]; nor perhaps for anybody beyond the surface; I mean as to real feeling, not that she was not quite ready to be friendly or serviceable. She professed Benthamic opinions when Mr. Austin professed the same, and German opinions when he turned in that direction; but in truth, though she had considerable reading and acquirements, she never appeared to me to have anything deserving the name of opinions"; further, Mill noted, she had "a very mischievous tongue. . . . " CW I, p. 186.

7. *Autobiography*, p. 72.

8. CW, XII, p. 14.

9. In 1828, "he was put over the heads of all the clerks, and made an Assistant, at £600 a year; being sixth in rank. In 1830, he stood fifth; his father being at the top. Early in 1836, he gained a step, and on his father's death, the same year, another: he was then third, but David Hill was made second over his head; Peacock was chief. His salary was now £1200 a year; to which, in 1854, a special and personal addition was made of £200 a year. On 28th March, 1856, Peacock and Hill retiring together, he was made Examiner, salary £2000 a year. At Christmas, 1858, on the transfer of the Company's government to the crown, he was superannuated on a pension of £1500 a year." Bain (1882b), p. 31n. By 1836, Mill was a relatively wealthy man by contemporary standards, with an income in the top 10 percent.

10. W. T. Thornton, "His Career in the India House," in Spencer et al. (1873), p. 31. Moir, op. cit., p. xiii, points out that Mill's unusual ability was formally recognized right from the beginning of his employment.

11. *Autobiography*, p. 85.

12. Ibid., p. 84n.

13. Ibid., pp. 31–2.

14. Bain (1882b), pp. 64–5.

15. *Autobiography*, p. 87.

16. Ibid., p. 69.

17. Quoted in John Robson, *The Improvement of Mankind: The Social and Political Thought of John Stuart Mill* (London: University of Toronto Press and Routledge and Kegan Paul, 1968), p. 14.

18. According to Packe (1954), the term "utilitarian" appeared as far back as an 1802 letter from Bentham to Dumont.

19. *Autobiography*, p. 81.

20. Ibid.

21. Bain (1882b), p. 39; Packe (1954), p. 66.

22. R. E. Leader (ed.), *Life and Letters of John Arthur Roebuck: With Chapter of Autobiography* (London, 1897), p. 28.

23. H. R. Fox Bourne, "A Sketch of His Life," in Spencer et al. (1873), p. 12.

24. Randall (1962), p. 924.

25. *Autobiography*, p. 129.

26. Jack Lively and John Rees (eds.), *Utilitarian Logic and Politics: James Mill's 'Essay on Government,' Macaulay's 'Critique' and the Ensuing Debate* (Oxford: Oxford University Press, 1978).
27. Ibid., p. 8.
28. Ibid., pp. 48–9.
29. Ibid., p. 53.
30. Ibid., p. 65.
31. Ibid., p. 67.
32. Ibid., p. 88.
33. Ibid., p. 90.
34. Keep in mind that Mill was writing about these events several decades later. The term "liberal" did not come into use until at least a decade later. Stefan Collini, in *Public Moralists: Political Thought and Intellectual Life in Britain* (Oxford: Oxford University Press, 1991), p. 181, writes: "Liberalism as a set of coherent political principles which found expression not only in actions of the party formed at Willis's Rooms in 1859 but also in the reforming legislation of the 1830s and 1840s was itself essentially a retrospective creation . . . that only became current in the last three decades of the century. In the more fragmented world of the 1850s, a world still very much dominated by Whig peers and Tory squires, Fawcett and his associates naturally and unhesitatingly classified themselves as 'Radicals'."
35. *Autobiography*, pp. 101–3.
36. CW I, p. 538, "Letter to the Editor of the Edinburgh Review on James Mill" (January 1844), in response to a review of Bowring's "Memoirs of Bentham."
37. *Autobiography*, p. 135.
38. Bentham, *Anarchical Fallacies*, in *Works*, ed. Bowring, Vol. II, p. 501.
39. *Autobiography*, p. 107.
40. Ibid., pp. 107–8.
41. Ibid., pp. 109–11.
42. See Nicholas Capaldi, *The Enlightenment Project in the Analytic Conversation* (1998), Chapter 1. Hereinafter we shall use the term "Benthamism" to mean that specific version of the Enlightenment Project that Mill inherited.
43. *Autobiography*, p. 111.
44. Ibid., p. 105.
45. Ibid., pp. 115–17.
46. Ibid., p. 133.
47. Ibid., p. 119.
48. As Bain (1882b) points out, p. 33, there are passages in Mill's 1824 piece on the Carlile Prosecutions that anticipate *On Liberty*: "Christians . . . having gained the power to which so long they were victims . . . employ it in the self-same way, and strive to crush the opposition of opinion. . . ."
49. CW VI, pp. 3–4.
50. *Autobiography*, p. 119.
51. Ibid., p. 133.
52. Hamilton, CW IX, p. 103.

53. *Autobiography*, p. 121.
54. Ibid., pp. 121–3.
55. Ibid., p. 127.
56. Packe (1954), p. 74.

Chapter 3. Crisis (1826–1830)

1. *Autobiography*, p. 137.
2. Ibid., pp. 137–9.
3. Carlyle (1896–99), Vol. I, p. 133.
4. *Autobiography*, p. 149.
5. Ibid., pp. 139–41.
6. Peter L. Berger, *The Capitalist Revolution* (New York: Basic Books, 1986), p. 103. The whole of Chapter 5 is illuminating. Berger follows Weber in locating the immediate source of capitalism in the Protestant Reformation.
7. ". . . in the course of the nineteenth and early twentieth centuries, the Western imagination became almost compulsively concerned with the conflict of fathers and sons[:]. . . . Turgenev's *Fathers and Sons* (1861), or Edmund Gosse's *Father and Son* (1907). . . . When Sigmund Freud took up the subject, then, he was hardly the first to notice the phenomenon." Mazlish (1988), p. 15. Mazlish cites Howard R. Wolf's "British Fathers and Sons, 1773–1913: From Filial Submissiveness to Creativity," *The Psychoanalytic Study of Society*, 3 (1964), pp. 278–328. Wolf cites Marmontel, in whose *Les Incas* the son returns to and submits to his father.
8. *Autobiography*, p. 111.
9. As Mill tells the story in his *Autobiography*, the issues of associationism were resolved prior to the discovery of Wordsworth and the influence of Carlyle. I have chosen to portray the order differently because the issue of associationism is part of the larger issue of a more profound conception of the human predicament.
10. Bain (1882a), p. 414.
11. *Autobiography*, p. 113.
12. Ibid., p. 115.
13. Ibid., p. 127.
14. Ibid., pp. 145–7. See Carlyle, *Sartor Resartus*, 2nd ed. (Boston: Munroe, 1837), pp. 86ff. and 189ff. (BK II, Chapters 1 and 9).
15. The origin of this doctrine is in the Christian (Augustinian) conception of the freedom of the will. Although Stoics and Epicureans espoused the notion of independence from bodily desire, it is the notion of a radically free will and what it means to act consistently with that freedom that is peculiar to Christianity. A secular version is to be found in Rousseau and Kant.
16. *Autobiography*, pp. 175–7. Mill refers here to Book VI, Chapter 2 of the *Logic*.
17. Letter to Tocqueville (November 3, 1843), XIII, p. 612: "I had found peace in these ideas. . . . they alone had entirely satisfied my need to put intellect and conscience into harmony." That this is a temporary psychological solution and not a strictly philosophical one can be seen in the next remark: "Je ne désire pas imposer ma

propre solution à ceux qui sont satisfaits de la leur, mais je crois qu'il y a beaucoup d'hommes pour qui elle sera, come elle a été pour moi, une véritable ancre de salut."

18. The presumption that the common good is guaranteed by representative government, and therefore that government need not be viewed with suspicion, is precisely what Mill identifies as the cardinal error of liberalism in Chapter 1 of *On Liberty*.

19. Thomas Babington Macaulay, "Utilitarian Logic and Politics," *Edinburgh Review*, 49 (March 1829), pp. 159–89.

20. Mary Wollstonecraft (1759–1797) had already published the influential *A Vindication of the Rights of Women* (1792). It was Wollstonecraft who first argued that the relationship between men and women was a key to a just social order as a whole, a theme that is central to Mill's treatment. William Thompson, an Irish philosopher and friend of Bentham, also attacked James Mill's position in *The Appeal of Women* (London: Longmans, 1825).

21. Quoted in Bain (1882a), p. 369. Macaulay was making a speech in Parliament on the second reading of the India Bill.

22. Quoted in Bain (1882a), p. 370.

23. *Autobiography*, p. 165.

24. Ibid., p. 107. Collini, in his introduction to CW XXI, p. xxx, emphasizes that Mill was an advocate of feminine equality before he met Harriet Taylor.

25. A. W. Levi, in "The 'Mental Crisis' of Mill," *Psychoanalysis and Psychoanalytic Review* 32 (January 1945), p. 100, claims that Mill's crisis was the result of a suppressed death wish with respect to his father: ". . . by an act of empathy [Mill] identified himself with the bereaved Marmontel. . . . In experiencing his father's death and the freedom which this would mean to his own ego, but under the literary and imaginative circumstances which would absolve him of the guilty wishes themselves, Mill brought to the surface what had hitherto been laboriously repressed. . . ."

26. *Autobiography*, p. 145. Jean François Marmontel, *Mémoires d'un père*, 4 vols. (London: Peltier, 1805), Vol. I, pp. 87–8.

27. Mill met Wordsworth at the home of Henry Taylor, and in July 1831 he visited Wordsworth at Grasmere.

28. Ibid., p. 147.

29. Robson (1968), p. 26.

30. Mazlish (1988), pp. xxii–xxiii. Rosenblum (1987), p. 136: "The internal culture he [Mill] speaks of is not purely intellectual. It is more than taking stock of wants and choices, or calling up the moral capacity to choose. Inner culture refers to emotional resources."

31. Wordsworth, Preface to *Lyrical Ballads*, added in the 1802 edition. See R. L. Brett and A. R. Jones (eds.), *Lyrical Ballads* (London: Methuen, 1963), p. 253.

32. James Mill, *Analysis of the Phenomena of the Human Mind*, ed. John Stuart Mill (London, 1869), Vol. II, p. 247.

33. *Autobiography*, p. 143.

34. Ibid., pp. 111–17, 137–45.

35. Mill to Sterling (April 15, 1829), XII, p. 30.

36. July 5, 1833, XII, p. 163. Intuition is not to be confused here with innate ideas.

37. Ibid.

38. Wordsworth, *Poetical Works* (1827), Vol. IV, pp. 346–55.

39. Anna Jean Mill, "Mill's Visit to Wordsworth," *Modern Language Review*, 44 (July 1949), pp. 341–50.

40. Letter to Sterling (October 20, 1831), XII, p. 81.

41. "This failure of Protestantism to assimilate the Christian Humanist tradition completely caused a certain impoverishment and aridity in English and American cultures and led ultimately to those defects which Matthew Arnold was to criticize so vigorously in the 19th century." Christopher Dawson, *The Dividing of Christendom* (Garden City, NY: Image, 1967), p. 22.

42. See Packe (1954), p. 375.

43. *Bentham*, X, p. 108; see also Semmel (1984), p. 158.

44. Letter to Carlyle (October 22, 1832), XII, p. 128.

45. *Autobiography*, p. 133.

46. *Autobiography*, pp. 159–61.

47. Ibid., p. 161. Sterling made the following comment on Mill: "How the sweet, ingenuous nature of the man has lived and thriven out of his father's cold and stringent atheism is wonderful to think, and most so to me, who during fifteen years have seen his gradual growth and ripening." October 7, 1843, Sterling to R. W. Emerson, *A Correspondence between John Sterling and Ralph Waldo Emerson*, ed. by E. W. Emerson (Boston: Houghton Mifflin, 1897). Mill to Sterling (August 16, 1844): "I have never so much wished for another life as I do for the sake of meeting you in it. . . . I shall never think of you but as one of the noblest, and quite the most lovable of all men I have known or ever look to know." XIII, p. 635.

48. Quoted in Anne Kimball Tuell, *John Sterling* (New York: Macmillan, 1941), p. 69.

49. *Autobiography*, p. 161.

50. Eugène d'Eichthal (ed.), *Mill, Correspondence Inédite avec Gustave d'Eichthal* (Paris, 1898), p. vi.

51. The articles were signed A.B. Previously, Mill had used the pen name "A" or Antiquus.

52. *Autobiography*, p. 181.

53. Gertrude Himmelfarb, introduction to *Essays on Politics and Culture: John Stuart Mill* (Garden City, NY: Anchor, 1963), pp. viii–ix.

54. In his *Autobiography*, p. 171, Mill notes that what he took at the time to be St. Simonian ideas were better expressed by Fichte in "the Characteristics of the Present Age." The connection between romanticism and conservatism in German thought is evidenced in this work of Fichte.

55. Letter to Sterling (October 20–22, 1831), XII, p. 84.

56. *Autobiography*, pp. 173–5.

57. Mill to d'Eichthal (May 15, 1829), XII, p. 31.

58. Mill to d'Eichthal (October 8, 1829), XII, p. 36.

59. *Autobiography*, p. 169.

60. Mill to Carlyle (September 17, 1832), XII, p. 120.

61. Mill described John Taylor as "a most upright, brave, and honourable man, of liberal opinions and good education, but without the intellectual or artistic tastes which would have made him a companion for her. . . ." *Autobiography*, p. 193.

62. Thomas Carlyle, *Reminiscences*, ed. J. A. Froude (London, 1881), Vol. I, p. 110.

63. "Unitarians might be described as Utilitarians in their Sunday Best" – Packe (1954), p. 127.

64. Quoted by Richard Garnett, *The Life of W. J. Fox* (London, 1910), p. 98. The source of the quote is one of Fox's daughters, Mrs. E. F. Bridell Fox.

65. There was a romantic entanglement of the married Fox with Eliza Flower, his ward and Harriet's closest friend.

66. F. A. Hayek, *Mill and Harriet Taylor* (Chicago: University of Chicago Press, 1951), pp. 275–6.

67. CW I, p. 623 (Appendix G: "Early Draft Rejected Leaves").

68. Iris Mueller, *Mill and French Thought* (Urbana: University of Illinois Press, 1956). According to Bain (1882b), p. 42, "I heard him long afterwards say he detested Thiers." Tocqueville shared the dislike of Thiers.

69. Bain (1882a), p. 357.

70. *Autobiography*, pp. 177–9.

Chapter 4. The Discovery of Romance and Romanticism (1830–1840)

1. Henry Taylor, *Autobiography* (London, 1885), Vol. I, p. 78.

2. She is described in Mill's *Autobiography* as "a person of genius, or of capacities of feeling or intellect kindred with [Harriet Taylor]" (p. 195).

3. J. A. Froude, *Thomas Carlyle, a History of His Life in London, 1834–1881* (London: Longmans, Green, 1891), Vol. I, p. 79.

4. *Autobiography*, p. 169.

5. J. A. Froude, *Thomas Carlyle, the First Forty Years* (London: Longmans, Green, 1882), Vol. II, p. 190.

6. Mill apparently had some difficulty in learning German and certainly never felt as comfortable with it as he did with French. See Mill, letter to Comte (March 13, 1843), XIII, p. 576.

7. At about the same time, Crabb Robinson wrote a now classic series of articles on Goethe for the *Monthly Repository*.

8. *Autobiography*, p. 185.

9. A good guide that integrates both the philosophical and literary aspect is Bruce Wilshire, ed., *Romanticism and Evolution* (New York: G. P. Putnam's Sons, 1968). Others who have noted the importance of Romanticism in Mill include Knut Hagberg, *Personalities and Powers* (London: John Land, 1930), p. 196; Rosenblum (1987); Semmel (1984); and Robson (1968).

10. ". . . 'think John Mill,' Place wrote in 1838, 'has made great progress in becoming a German meta-'physical [sic] mystic,'" Dicey ([1905] 1948), p. 423.

11. Dicey ([1905] 1948), pp. 423–4.

12. F. Parvin Sharpless, in *The Literary Criticism of John Stuart Mill* (The Hague: Mouton, 1967), p. 138n, tells us that Coleridge was the first to praise many-sidedness. See also Houghton (1957), pp. 176–80.

13. "Humboldt, like Hegel ... is trying to derive a coherent intellectual position from an inheritance and *milieu* which contain heavy doses both of the Enlightenment and of the Romanticism which is generally set in opposition to it. ... J. S. Mill ... was able ... to present his two archetypal figures, Bentham and Coleridge, representing the characteristic intellectual virtues of the eighteenth and nineteenth centuries respectively, as two sides of a dialectic, needing, in fact, to be *aufgehoben* in the Hegelian sense." Burrow (1993), p. xxii.

14. For further discussion of Mill's understanding of poetry, see Sharpless (1967); and John M. Robson, "J. S. Mill's Theory of Poetry," *University of Toronto Quarterly*, 29 (1960), pp. 420–38.

15. CW I, p. 346.

16. Ibid., p. 357.

17. Ibid., p. 362.

18. Ibid., pp. 363–4.

19. "Mill's ideal is, on analysis, neither Greek, nor Goethian – nor Arnoldian: it is Romantic." Houghton (1957), p. 290.

20. Mill to Comte (March 13, 1843), quoted in Haac (1995), p. 140; CW XIII, p. 576.

21. Packe (1954) offers an especially detailed and insightful discussion of Mill's relationship with Carlyle. He is justifiably critical of the extent to which Carlyle both exploited Mill's friendship and was never grateful for all that Mill had done for him.

22. Froude, *Thomas Carlyle, the First Forty Years*, Vol. II, p. 190.

23. *Autobiography*, p. 181.

24. Mill to Sterling (October 20–22, 1831), XII, p. 85.

25. Mill to Carlyle (July 17, 1832), XII, p. 113.

26. Mill to Carlyle (March 2, 1834), XII, p. 219.

27. Ralph Waldo Emerson was introduced to Mill and Carlyle through a d'Eichthal letter.

28. XX, p. 118.

29. Packe (1954), p. 168: "The main point of his [Carlyle's] philosophy of clothes is that the vestments of society, the Church, State, Aristocracy, and Body of Learning, were all worn out and rotten, and no longer bore resemblance to the pure ideals of which they were the outward manifestations."

30. Thomas Carlyle, *Sartor Resartus*, Chapter 10.

31. Mill to Carlyle (September 3, 1833): "our Utilitarian Radicals ... will no longer rely upon the infallibility of Constitution-mongering. ..." XII, pp. 145–6.

32. For a sampling of this view, see: P. P. Alexander, *Mill and Carlyle* (Edinburgh, 1866); Emery Neff, *Carlyle and Mill: An Introduction to Victorian Thought* (New York: Columbia University Press, 1926).

33. Semmel (1984), p. 12.

34. I am indebted to Christopher Turk's *Coleridge and Mill* (Aldershot: Gower, 1988). Note as well: "Mill's attempt to absorb, and by discrimination and discarding to unify, the truths alike of the utilitarian and the idealist positions is, after all, a prologue to a very large part of the subsequent history of English thinking." Raymond Williams, *Culture and Society, 1780–1950* (London: Chatto and Windus, 1958), p. 49.

35. Thomas Carlyle, *Life of John Sterling* (London, 1851).

36. *On the Constitution of Church and State* (London, 1830), pp. 76–7.

37. This was a new kind of political and social consciousness. See John Colmer, *Coleridge, Critic of Society* (Oxford: Clarendon Press, 1959).

38. Caroline Fox, *Memories of Old Friends, Being Extracts from the Journals and Letters of Caroline Fox, 1835–1871*, ed. H. N. Pym, 2 vols. (London: Smith, Elder, 1882), Vol. I, p. 147.

39. XII, p. 221.

40. *Coleridge*, X, p. 146.

41. CW IV, p. 213.

42. Ibid., pp. 213–14.

43. See Abraham L. Harris, "Mill: Servant of the East India Company," *Canadian Journal of Economics and Political Science*, 30 (1964), pp. 185–202.

44. Bain (1882b), p. 46. Bain complains that only someone ignorant of real universities could hold such a view.

45. Mill to Carlyle (January 12, 1834), XII, p. 206.

46. Ibid., p. 207.

47. Although Mill rejects the notion of a divine plan in the mind of an omnipotent God, what he does come to advocate in his later theological writings is the notion of a finite God who asks for our help in the struggle against evil.

48. An account of this group may be found in Leigh Hunt, *Bluestocking Revels*, first published in the *Monthly Repository* (July 1837).

49. Fox had been made ward of the Flower sisters by their father, a prominent Unitarian.

50. Sarah married William Bridges Adams in 1834. Adams had previously been married to a daughter of Francis Place, the radical. Adams published a book, *The Producing Man's Companion*, under the pseudonym Junius Redivivus, to which Mill gave some prominence.

51. The source of this information was Carlyle. See Sir Charles Gavan Duffy, *Reminiscences and Conversations with Carlyle* (London: Sampson Low, 1892), p. 168.

52. R. E. Leader, *Life and Letters of J. A. Roebuck* (London, 1897), p. 38.

53. This story comes from Moncure Conway, Fox's American successor at South Place Chapel. See Moncure Daniel Conway, *Centenary History of the South Place Society* (London: Williams & Norgate, 1894), p. 89.

54. *Autobiography*, pp. 193–5.

55. Bertrand and Patricia Russell (eds.), *The Amberley Papers* (London: Hogarth, 1937), Vol. II, p. 375.

56. *Genius*, I, p. 330. The "dwarf" metaphor occurs again in *On Liberty*, a work in which Mill, among other things, tries to synthesize elitism and universal autonomy.

57. William C. DeVane, *A Browning Handbook* (New York: F. S. Crofts, 1935), p. 44.

58. Mill and Harriet use the term "sensualist" in the pejorative sense of someone whose personality is ruled by physical drives.

59. Hayek (1951), pp. 60–8.

60. Ibid., p. 75.

61. Ibid., pp. 46–7.

62. Ibid., p. 38.

63. *Letters*, CW XII, p. 149.

64. Hayek (1951), p. 47.

65. Alexander Carlyle (ed.), *Letters of Thomas Carlyle to Mill, John Sterling, and Robert Browning* (London: Haskell House, 1923), pp. 225–6.

66. XII, p. 229.

67. Hayek (1951), p. 82.

68. Ibid., p. 99.

69. Ibid., p. 78.

70. Ibid., p. 100.

71. Leader, *Life and Letters of J. A. Roebuck*, p. 38.

72. A few years before his death, Mill did send Roebuck a book accompanied by a letter with reminiscences about the past.

73. Bain (1882b), p. 43.

74. Ibid., p. 163.

75. *Autobiography*, pp. 612–13 (rejected leaves).

76. Mill to Sterling (April 15, 1829), XII, p. 30.

77. Quoted in Frank E. Manuel, *The Prophets of Paris* (New York: Harper, 1965), p. 126. See also his *The New World of Henri Saint-Simon* (Cambridge, MA: Harvard University Press, 1956).

78. In response to Carlyle's misgivings and gossip, Mill's friend Sterling wrote as follows: "I think it is a good sign of a man that he feels strongly that kind of temptation, but a far better one that he both feels it and conquers it, which I trust that Mill has done and will do." Anne Kimball Tuell, *John Sterling* (New York: Macmillan, 1941), p. 71.

79. The romantic (in the cultural sense) dimension of Mill's relationship to Harriet Taylor has been noted by Hayek (1951), who claims that "[f]ar from it having been the sentimental it was the rationalist element in Mill's thought which was mainly strengthened by her influence" (p. 17). Hayek then quotes Hagberg, *Personalities and Powers*, p. 196: "[I]t was this woman who made him into a Radical rationalist. She has given the impress of her personality to all his greater works; to all her opinions Mill has given the form of philosophic maxims. But even in his most arid reflexions on woman's similarity with man and on the nature of Logic, *Mill is in reality a romantic*." [italics added]

80. Mill admired autonomous women, including George Sand and George Eliot (to whom he sent a copy of the *Principles of Political Economy*).

81. Mill to Lord Amberley (February 2, 1870), XVII, pp. 1692–3. Those who accuse Mill of fostering licentiousness have failed to understand this most crucial aspect of his personal and professional life.

82. Richard Garnett, *The Life of W. J. Fox* (London: Walter Scott, 1887), pp. 166–7.

83. Quoted in W. Minto, "His Place as a Critic," in Spencer et al. (1873), p. 52.

84. Carlyle to John Sterling, October 3, 1836. Alexander Carlyle, *Letters of Thomas Carlyle to Mill, John Sterling and Robert Browning* (London, 1910), pp. 197–8.

85. Carlyle to John Sterling, January 17, 1837. Alexander Carlyle (ed.), *New Letters of Thomas Carlyle* (London and New York: J. Lane, 1904), Vol. I, p. 53.

86. Letter to Dr. John Carlyle dated July 22, 1834. Froude, op. cit., Vol. II, p. 441.

87. This incident is described by Emery Neff, *Carlyle and Mill: An Introduction to Victorian Thought* (New York: Columbia University Press, 1926), pp. 27–30; see also Packe (1954), pp. 185–7.

88. Mill's sister Harriet Isabella Mill, in a letter to *The Times*, February 17, 1881, attests to this.

89. *Examiner* (December 2, 1832), XXIII, p. 531.

90. Bain, for one, has suggested that Mill had a weak sex drive. It is difficult to see how Bain was in a position to know this other than from conversational contact. Mill always treated Bain as a professional protégé and not an intimate friend.

91. *Diary*, March 26, 1854, XXVII, p. 664.

92. Letter to Harriet Taylor (February 17, 1857), XV, pp. 523–4. This letter is discussed in Semmel (1984), Chapter 2.

93. A longer version appears in his essay *Bentham*, published in 1838, about which we shall have more to say in the next chapter.

94. Mill to Sterling (October 20–22, 1831), XII, p. 81; Lady Amberley reports Mill as saying in 1865 that "the great thing was to consider one's opponents as one's allies; as people climbing the hill on the other side." Russell and Russell, *The Amberley Papers*, Vol. I, p. 373.

95. Darwin borrowed the conception of evolution from social and historical theorists and applied it to biological nature.

96. See Mill's letter to Comte (March 22, 1842), XIII, p. 509.

97. Mill to Sterling (October 20–22, 1831), XII, p. 84.

98. The exception was "Definition of Political Economy," which was published in 1836 in the *Westminster Review*.

99. Mill continued to judge institutions in their historical context. In his review of Guizot's essays (1845), he praised feudalism as a stage that permitted its own transcendence. CW XX, pp. 257–94. In his review of Grote's *History of Greece* (1853), he saw slavery as "a temporary fact, in an early and rude state of the arts of life, it may have been, nevertheless, a great accelerator of progress." XI, p. 315. Mill never argued the fatalistic position that every practice was justified in its context.

100. I mention this date because it has become customary since Bain, and then more recently since Mazlish, to attribute Mill's twitching to psychosomatic problems

surrounding his father's death. The eye problem is mentioned in a letter to Victor Cousin (November 30, 1833), XII, p. 199.

101. *Autobiography*, p. 209.
102. Ibid., pp. 209–11.
103. Froude (1891), pp. 79–80.
104. Quoted in Bain (1882a), p. 326.
105. Leslie Stephen called Bowring's biography of Bentham the worst biography ever written in the English language.
106. *Autobiography*, pp. 211–13.
107. Bain (1882b), p. 1.
108. Mill to Bulwer (November 23, 1836), XII, p. 312.
109. Mill to Nichol (January 29, 1837), XII, p. 322.
110. Mill to Nichol (July 10, 1833), XII, p. 166.
111. *Autobiography*, pp. 203–5.
112. Ibid., p. 209.
113. Sarah Austin to Mill (March 3, 1837): "Mr. Lewis and my husband [Austin] are clamorous against poor Carlyle's article and say that you will ruin the review if you admit anymore. I am afraid this is a very general opinion, though I grieve it should be so." Mill-Taylor Collection, British Library of Political and Economic Science.
114. *London and Westminster Review*, July 1837.
115. Tocqueville to Mill (December 3, 1835), quoted in the introduction to *Democracy in America*, ed. Philip Bradley (New York: Knopf, 1945), Vol. I.
116. Tocqueville to Mill (December 18, 1840) in *Memoir, Letters, and Remains of Alexis de Tocqueville*, 2 vols. (Cambridge, 1861), Vol. II, p. 114.
117. "Armand Carrell" (1837), XX, pp. 183–4.
118. Bain (1882b), p. 57n.
119. Letter to Fonblanque (January 30, 1838), XIII, p. 370.
120. This is a Harriet whom Mill did not like. There were many Harriets, a popular name, during this period.
121. Mill married Harriet Taylor in 1851. In the same year, John Chapman assumed ownership of the *Westminster Review*. Harriet Martineau offered to contribute a history of Mill's relationship with Mrs. Taylor. Gordon S. Haight, *George Eliot and John Chapman* (New Haven, CT: Yale University Press, 1940), p. 213.
122. XII, p. 152.
123. The inspiration for the Rossini opera is Tasso's poem *Gerusalemme Liberata* (1575).
124. It is interesting that both radicals and ultraconservatives like Carlyle complained of Harriet's alleged influence or interference. Either this showed that Harriet had no such great influence or that she encouraged Mill to adopt a more centrist and mildly conservative position. The one thing it surely does not show is that Harriet pushed Mill toward radicalism. The reason this is important is that it contravenes Himmelfarb's (1974) interpretation of Mill, one that makes him a conservative only before and after Harriet. Of course, one could always argue

that Harriet went through phases, but then there would have to be an early and a later or even a middle "Harriet," and this sounds increasingly implausible.

125. Letter to an unknown correspondent, quoted in Bain (1882b), p. 45; the original has not been located.

126. Mill to Robertson (April 6, 1839), XIII, pp. 396–7.

127. Mill to Fonblanque (February 13?, 1837), XII, p. 327.

128. Mill sold the *Review* to John Hickson, who in turn sold it in 1851 to John Chapman. Chapman was assisted by George Eliot (née Marian Evans).

129. *Autobiography*, pp. 221–3.

130. Bain (1882b), p. 60, makes the following comment on this suggestion: "That his father would have made an able minister or party-leader, we must cheerfully allow; but his sentiments and views would have required a thick covering of disguise to allow even his being elected to Parliament. . . ."

131. Wilson Harris, *Caroline Fox* (London: Constable, 1944), p. 159.

132. Caroline Fox, *Memories of Old Friends* (London, 1882), journal entry for March 21, 1840.

133. David Alec Wilson, *The Life of Carlyle* (London: K. Paul, Trench, Trubner, 1923–34), Vol. III, p. 85.

Chapter 5. The Transitional Essays

1. This essay appeared in five parts spread over seven issues of the *Political Examiner* from the ninth of January to the twenty-ninth of May, 1831. The title may have been borrowed from William Hazlitt's *The Spirit of the Age; or Contemporary Portraits* (1825). Hazlittt, who also wrote for the *Examiner*, had referred in an 1816 article to Ernst Mortiz Arndt's *Der Geist der Zeit* (1805). One of Hazlitt's "portraits" was of Bentham.

2. *Spirit of the Age*, XXII, p. 230.

3. Ibid., p. 252.

4. Ibid., p. 290.

5. Ibid., p. 233.

6. Ibid., p. 244.

7. Ibid., p. 245.

8. Ibid., p. 316.

9. For further insight into Mill's political sociology, see "State of Parties in France" (1831), XXIII, pp. 336–41.

10. *Spirit of the Age*, XXII, p. 293.

11. Ibid., pp. 257–8.

12. I know of no satisfactory alternative to this resolution. Hence it is important to see that Mill's theism plays an important intellectual role in his mature thought. The attentive reader will no doubt notice that this is Hegel's resolution as well. Jacques Maritain, in *Man and State* (Chicago: University of Chicago Press, 1951), pp. 90–2, makes a similar case for natural law.

13. *Civilization* appeared originally in the *London and Westminster Review*, April 1836.

14. *Civilization*, XVIII, p. 120. Mill's discussion very much reflects the influence of Scottish Enlightenment writers he had read as a youth.

15. Ibid., p. 127.

16. Ibid., p. 125.

17. Ibid., p. 124.

18. Ibid., p. 126.

19. Ibid., pp. 131, 129–30.

20. Ibid., p. 132.

21. Ibid., p. 127.

22. Ibid., p. 136.

23. As he puts it in the essay on Bentham: "There must, we know, be some paramount power in society; and that the majority should be that power, is on the whole right, not as being just in itself, but as being less unjust than any other footing on which the matter can be placed. But it is necessary that the institutions of society should make provision for keeping up, in some form or other, as a corrective to partial views, and a shelter for freedom of thought and individuality of character, a perpetual and standing Opposition to the will of the majority." X, p. 108.

24. *Civilization*, XVIII, p. 119.

25. This essay appeared in the *London and Westminster Review* in August 1838.

26. Carlyle (1896–99), Vol. 28, pp. 133–5.

27. *Bentham*, X, p. 77.

28. Ibid., p. 90.

29. Ibid., p. 91.

30. Ibid., p. 93.

31. Ibid., p. 95.

32. See the discussion of autonomy in Chapter 9.

33. *Bentham*, X, p. 92.

34. The expression "ordeal of consciousness" is borrowed from Michael Oakeshott, whose discussion of learning seems to reflect exactly what Mill is saying here about the imagination. See *The Voice of Liberal Learning: Michael Oakeshott on Education*, ed. Timothy Fuller (New Haven, CT: Yale University Press, 1989). Oakeshott's views were probably derived more directly from Coleridge.

35. *Bentham*, X, p. 98. The expression "great duty" replaced "grand duty of man" in the original manuscript. At the very least, this seems to be laying the groundwork for *On Liberty*. More intriguing is the similarity to the epigraph for that work, taken from Humboldt's work originally translated into English only in 1852 as *The Sphere and Duties of Government*. It is intriguing to speculate on whether Mill was familiar with the earlier German version that appeared in 1791–92. See the introduction by J. W. Burrow to Wilhelm von Humboldt, *The Limits of State Action* (Indianapolis: Liberty Fund, 1993).

36. *Bentham*, X, p. 112.

37. Ibid., p. 92.

38. Ibid.

39. Ibid., p. 99.
40. Ibid., p. 105.
41. Mill saw "as his political and philosophical mission: to transform features of his father's creed that were part of the inheritance of the 18th century by the introduction of certain central conceptions of German transcendental philosophy." Semmel (1984), p. 17.
42. *Coleridge* first appeared in the *London and Westminster Review*, March 1840.
43. *Coleridge*, X, p. 123.
44. Ibid.
45. Since Mill is frequently accused of being a careless philosopher, we note that he understands quite correctly that the doctrine of a priori knowledge is not the doctrine of innate ideas, since the a priori could not "have been awakened in us without experience" (ibid., p. 126).
46. Ibid., p. 128. By the time Mill wrote *An Examination of Sir William Hamilton's Philosophy* (1865), he had conceded the existence of a self that was known only transcendentally. We shall maintain in a later discussion that this actually made Mill's position on free will and personal autonomy more consistent, as well as bringing him into the camp of the philosophical idealists.
47. Letter to Bain (November 4, 1867), XVI, p. 1324.
48. In 1840, Mill read some German logicians at the suggestion of Sterling but found it "a rather tiring business." Caroline Fox, *Memories of Old Friends* (London, 1882), Vol. II, pp. 320–2.
49. In a letter to Sterling (September 28, 1839), Mill said, "I have often had moods in which I would most gladly postulate like Kant, a different ultimate foundation, 'subjectiver bedürfnisses willen' if I could." XIII, p. 407.
50. *Coleridge*, X, p. 138.
51. Ibid., p. 139. It is obvious from these essays that the historians who most impressed Mill were Guizot and Tocqueville.
52. Graham Wallas, *Francis Place* (London, 1898), p. 91.
53. *Coleridge*, X, p. 147.
54. Ibid., p. 140.
55. Ibid., pp. 139–40.
56. Ibid., p. 163.
57. Ibid.
58. Ibid., p. 136.
59. Ibid., p. 133.
60. Ibid., p. 140.
61. Ibid.
62. We must not forget that the Augustinian notion of self-discipline was transmitted to Mill via Protestantism and his early upbringing. Mill would also have imbibed this notion from his early reading of Cicero and especially Seneca.
63. For an enlightening discussion of the different strands of individualism and their weaving together in various forms during the nineteenth century, see Steven Lukes, *Individualism* (Oxford: Blackwell, 1973) and his article "Types of Individualism,"

in *Dictionary of the History of Ideas*, ed. Philip P. Wiener (New York: Scribners, 1973), Vol. II, pp. 594a–604a.

64. "For Mill and the German theorists of *Bildung*, excellence can allow for variety." William Stafford, *Mill* (London: Macmillan, 1998), p. 92.

65. We shall discuss this conception of individuality more fully when we turn our attention to *On Liberty*. For now, it is important to note that it is a fundamental idea in Mill already present in explicit form in 1840.

66. *Coleridge*, X, p. 134.

67. Ibid., p. 123.

68. Ibid., p. 135.

69. Ibid., p. 156. The obvious rebuttal to Mill's point is that the government's resources come from taxation on economic activity, and this is a kind of interference. However, keep in mind that at the time Mill wrote this and throughout his lifetime there was no income tax and that the government's share of the gross domestic product was minuscule compared to contemporary times.

70. Tocqueville's *Democracy in America*, Part I, was first published in French in 1835 and translated into English in 1835. Mill's review of it appeared in the *London Review*, 1 (October 1835). Part II of *Democracy in America* appeared in 1840. Mill's review of Part II appeared in the *Edinburgh Review* (October 1840). Tocqueville's concern about the tyranny of the majority caused Part I to be greeted by British conservatives as an endorsement of Tory policies.

71. Note that the essays *Civilization*, *Bentham*, and *Coleridge* were all published between the two reviews.

72. Tocqueville [I], XVIII, p. 56. Mill reviewed Tocqueville twice, that is, each volume as it appeared. Tocqueville [I] will refer to the first review (1835), and Tocqueville [II] will refer to the second review (1840).

73. Ibid., p. 51.

74. Ibid., p. 54.

75. Ibid., p. 86.

76. Tocqueville [II], XVIII, p. 159.

77. "That such has been the actual course of events in modern history, nobody can doubt, and as truly in England as in France." Ibid., p. 162.

78. Ibid., p. 197.

79. Ibid., pp. 197–8.

80. Ibid., pp. 191–2.

81. Ibid., p. 198.

82. Ibid., p. 187.

83. Ibid., p. 193.

84. Ibid., p. 195.

85. Ibid., p. 167.

86. Ibid., p. 200.

87. Ibid., p. 198.

88. Thomas (1979), pp. 439–53.

89. Tocqueville [II], XVIII, p. 178.

90. Ibid., p. 179.
91. Alan Kahan (2001), pp. 147–9, makes a strong case that this "should throw doubt on the idea that all representatives of education were in firm support of the aspirations of the middle class. . . . many English liberals found the commercial spirit problematic. . . . One must be wary of simple equations of ideology, that is, liberalism and class interests. . . . all European liberalism of 1830–1870 presumed the present and future hegemony of the middle class in some form. But not all liberalism regarded middle-class hegemony as an unmixed blessing."
92. Tocqueville [II], XVIII, p. 156.
93. Ibid., p. 157.
94. Tocqueville was rather dubious about the whole notion of "national character"; although he used it, he wrote notes to himself saying it was only a concession to public taste. The aspects of *Democracy in America* that Mill most uses are those that relate to democracy as an international phenomenon, not an American phenomenon.
95. Ibid.
96. It should be noted (1) that many thinkers of the period 1789–1914 liked to proclaim that they lived in a transitional age and (2) that what Mill was unable to notice, because it hadn't lasted very long, was that the characteristics of his transition were in fact the permanent characteristics of what Constant called modern freedom.

Chapter 6. Intellectual Success (1840–1845)

1. *Autobiography*, p. 229.
2. Whewell's views are very close to those of Karl Popper and to some extent to those of Thomas Kuhn.
3. It should be noted that Mill's firsthand acquaintance with science extended only to his hobby of botany. Henry Trimen pointed out that "the chapters on classification in the 'Logic' would not have taken the form they have, had not the writer been a naturalist as well as a logician. The views expressed so clearly in these chapters are chiefly founded on the actual needs experienced by the systematic botanist; and the argument is largely sustained by references to botanical systems and arrangements." "His Botanical Studies," in Spencer et al. (1873), p. 47.
4. *Autobiography*, pp. 233–5.
5. Kant would have called this a synthetic a priori truth.
6. T. Babington Macaulay, "Mill's Essay on Government," in his *Critical and Miscellaneous Essays* (Philadelphia, 1852), p. 270.
7. *Autobiography*, p. 165.
8. Ibid., pp. 229–31.
9. This work was translated into English in 1853 by Harriet Martineau.
10. Mill to Nichol (December 21, 1837), XII, p. 363. Comte's *Cours de philosophie positive* was published between 1830 and 1842.
11. With an eye on its relevance to Mill, see the very helpful discussion in the *Encyclopedia of Philosophy* (1968) by Bruce Mazlish, Vol. I, pp. 173b–177b.

12. Comte's *Système de politique positive* (1851–54).

13. In his *Système de politique positive* (1851–54), Comte replaced sociology with "sociolatry." His *Appeal to the Conservatives* (1855) embraced oligarchic dictatorship (and Louis Napoleon).

14. *Autobiography*, p. 219.

15. Mill to John Pringle Nichol (September 30, 1848), XIII, p. 739.

16. *Logic*, VIII, p. 902. Here Mill quotes from his earlier work "Essays on Some Unsettled Questions in Political Economy," IV, pp. 321–3.

17. The Mill-Comte correspondence is now available in English translation in Haac (1995).

18. Packe (1954), p. 276.

19. Comte to Mill (August 8, 1845), in Haac (1995), p. 332.

20. Mill to Comte (June 9, 1842), ibid., p. 75.

21. Harriet to Mill (1844), Hayek (1951), p. 114.

22. Ibid., p. 115.

23. Mill to Nichol (September 30, 1848), XIII, p. 739.

24. Mueller (1956), p. 129.

25. See H. Gouhier, *La vie de Auguste Comte*, 2nd ed. (Paris: J Vrin, 1965).

26. Mill to Comte (May 12, 1847), in Haac (1995), pp. 382–4.

27. *Logic*, VIII, p. 879.

28. Mill to d'Eichthal (August 10, 1829), XII, p. 36. See also Mill to Comte (June 9, 1842), in Haac (1995), p. 75. Mill rejects, to use Oakeshott's terminology, the notion that society is an enterprise association.

29. *Auguste Comte and Positivism*, X, p. 304.

30. Bain (1882b) claims that Grote saw the despotism in Comte before Mill did (p. 75).

31. "I have felt the same difficulty which you feel about the *axiomata media*. I suspect there are none which do not vary with time, place, & circumstance. I doubt if much more can be done in a scientific treatment of the question than to point out a certain number of *pro's* and *con's* of a more or less general application, & with some attempt at an estimation of the comparative importance of each, leaving the balance to be struck in each particular case as it arises." Mill to Austin (April 13, 1847), XIII, p. 712.

32. *Logic*, VIII, pp. 861–2.

33. N. Capaldi, "Mill's Forgotten Science of Ethology," *Social Theory and Practice* 2 (1973), pp. 409–20. See also Alan Ryan, *The Philosophy of Mill*, 2nd ed. (Atlantic Highlands, NJ: Humanities Press, 1990), Chapters 8, 9, and 10.

34. *Logic*, VIII, p. 864.

35. Skorupski (1989), pp. 249–50: "Psychology may be the irreducible base-level of the moral sciences, but historical sociology is the jewel in their crown. . . . Associationist psychology fortifies Mill's belief in the mutability of human nature. . . . the bridge between historical sociology and the constant laws of associationist psychology can be provided . . . by . . . a science he [Mill] calls 'ethology', which will study the different forms of human character in different social formations." Skorupski interprets Mill as trying to combine a naturalistic and deductive conception of the

social sciences (what we have called the Enlightenment Project) with a recognition of "an interpretive or hermeneutic paradigm, the historico-anthropological tradition of Schleiermacher, and of Dilthey on the *Geisteswissenschaften*" (p. 276). Skorupski admits that Mill never produced the ethology which was to make possible that combination, and Skorupski refers to Feuer's (1976) discussion of the failure. In opposition to Skorupski, I maintain that Mill's mature social science is much more hermeneutic. Skorupski insists upon seeing Mill as committed to naturalism. I see Mill coming to the idealist and transcendental position, especially in his later work, such as *Hamilton*. Mill was a phenomenalist, an adherent of British common sense, and never a dogmatic naturalist. Having stated this disagreement with Skorupski, I hasten to add that Skorupski is one of the few even to have seen that there was an issue here.

36. *Logic*, VIII, p. 869.
37. Ibid., p. 872.
38. Ibid., pp. 877–8.
39. L. S. Feuer, "Mill as a Sociologist: The Unwritten Ethology," in Laine and Robson (1976), p. 86: "... the most enduring essay on the method of the social sciences which has ever been written."
40. Bain (1882b), pp. 78–9, 84.
41. Feuer, op. cit., is one of the few to have seen the importance of this. According to Feuer (p. 97), Mill subscribed to a "Manichean theology" in *Theism* as a "meta-sociological postulate."
42. *On Liberty*, XVIII, pp. 244–5.
43. See James Mill's *Fragment on Macintosh* (privately circulated in 1830 and publicly available in 1835), a defense of utilitarian ethics against Macintosh's critique in the *Encyclopaedia Britannica*.
44. See especially VIII, pp. 839–42.
45. Letter to R. B. Fox (February 14, 1843), XIII, p. 569; see also letter to James Martineau (May 21, 1841), XII, pp. 476–7; and letter to Tocqueville (November 3, 1843), XIII, p. 612.
46. Tocqueville [II], XVIII, pp. 197–8.
47. See Ryan (1990), Chapter 7.
48. Bain (1882b), p. 52, strongly disagrees with this position of Mill's.
49. Two qualifications need to be added. First, some goals may be subsidiary and in that sense can be made the object of scientific scrutiny, but then other goals would have to remain primary and not so subsumable. Second, we can scientifically study the goals of the past, but such studies would always conclude that "given" certain goals that cannot be explained scientifically, we can explain the less primary goals.
50. *Logic*, VIII, p. 944.
51. Ibid., pp. 911–12.
52. By 1854, Mill was no longer happy with calling this function the function of the artist. "The Germans and Carlyle have perverted both thought and phraseology when they made Artist the term for expressing the highest order of moral and intellectual greatness.... Philosophy is the proper name for that exercise of the

intellect which enucleates the truth to be expressed. The Artist is not the Seer; not he who can detect truth, but he who can clothe a given truth in the most expressive and impressive symbols." Diary (April 11, 1854), XXVII, p. 667.

53. Consider the following statements from Herbert Butterfield's *Christianity and History* (New York: Scribners, 1949): "When we have reconstructed the whole of mundane history it does not form a self-explanatory system, and our attitude to it, our whole relationship to the human drama, is a larger affair altogether – it is a matter not of scholarship but of religion" (p. 22). "Ultimately our interpretation of the whole human drama depends on an intimately personal decision concerning the part we mean to play in it" (p. 86).

54. Letter dated October 7, 1843. *A Correspondence between John Sterling and Ralph Waldo Emerson*, ed. E. W. Emerson (Boston: Houghton Mifflin, 1897).

55. Edward Bouverie Pusey (1800–1882) was one of the founders of the Oxford Movement, the group also known as the Anglo-Catholics (Newman) and as the High Church Party as opposed to the Low Church or Evangelical Party.

56. Bain (1882b), p. 69.

57. *Autobiography*, pp. 235–7.

58. Ibid., p. 197.

59. In *On Liberty*, in his espousal of the importance of constantly critiquing and rehashing the arguments pro and con regarding any issue, Mill insisted that anyone could benefit from this process, both intellectually and morally, without having the genius of being the first to formulate the specific insights.

60. Fanny Sterling to Helen in 1859, Mill-Taylor Collection 54/32, ms.

61. In the nineteenth century, people still wrote letters with the expectation that they would be saved and reread, perhaps by others than those to whom they were addressed. Correspondence thus had a quasi-public character.

62. Diary (January 21, 1854), XXVII, p. 645.

Chapter 7. Worldly Success (1846–1850)

1. *Civilization*, XVIII, p. 120.

2. Ibid., p. 122.

3. *Representative Government*, XIX, p. 394.

4. *Guizot*, XX, pp. 270–1.

5. Mill to Austin (February 22, 1848), XIII, p. 731.

6. Especially useful here is Kahan's (2001) notion of Mill as an aristocratic liberal and Rosenblum's (1987) notion of Mill as a romantic liberal.

7. Mill to d'Eichthal (May 15 and October 8, 1829), XII, p. 31.

8. Mueller (1956).

9. *Civilization*, XVIII, pp. 130–1.

10. *Coleridge*, X, pp. 123–5.

11. Tocqueville (1840), XVIII, p. 200.

12. Ibid., pp. 184–5.

13. Mill to John Austin (April 13, 1847), XIII, p. 713.

14. Mill to d'Eichthal (October 8, 1929), XII, pp. 36–7.
15. *Principles of Political Economy* (hereinafter PPE), III, p. 754.
16. *Coleridge*, X, p. 156.
17. Mill to Carlyle (April 11 and 12, 1833), XII, pp. 151–2.
18. CW, IV, p. 225. "A Review of Miss Martineau's Summary of Political Economy" originally appeared in the *Monthly Repository* for May 1834.
19. Ibid., pp. 225–7.
20. *Autobiography*, p. 239.
21. Ibid., p. 175.
22. Ibid., p. 179.
23. Ibid., pp. 239–41.
24. C. L. Ten, "Democracy, Socialism, and the Working Classes," in Skorupski (1998), p. 372.
25. Ibid., p. 197 ("region of ultimate aims").
26. See Chapter 3.
27. *Autobiography*, p. 197 ("the immediately useful and practically attainable").
28. CW, XXVI, p. 972.
29. Mill to Comte (May 17, 1847), in Haac (1995), pp. 382–3.
30. *Coleridge*, X, p. 157.
31. Kinzer, Robson, and Robson (1992), pp. 174–7.
32. *Autobiography*, pp. 255–7.
33. Hayek (1951), pp. 120–1.
34. *PPE*, II, p. xci.
35. Mill to William Conner (September 26, 1849), XIV, p. 37.
36. *PPE*, III, p. 759.
37. Ibid., pp. 643–4.
38. For the historical background on the larger debate concerning the poor, see Gertrude Himmelfarb, *The Idea of Poverty* (New York: Knopf, 1984).
39. Mill to Chapman (November 8, 1844), XIII, pp. 640–1.
40. Mill to Comte (May 17, 1847), in Haac (1995), pp. 382–3.
41. *PPE*, III, pp. 763–5.
42. An estate tax involves the government taking a percentage of the deceased person's resources. An inheritance tax need not involve a government taking, because the tax only comes into play when someone inherits money over a certain limit. One could specify in one's will that the estate be divided among enough inheritors that no one paid a tax.
43. See *Principles of Political Economy*, II, p. 225: Book II, Chapter II, section 4, note appended to the 1865 edition. However, in an industrial economy of modern financial capitalism, it is now an extremely rare occurrence for any person or family to own totally a large corporation. Precisely the kind of wide distribution that Mill wanted to see has largely taken place. One thinks of, among other things, the huge blocks of stock owned by the pension funds of unions and other collective professional organizations. Nevertheless, Mill's point still applies to the taxation of a large and presumably successful enterprise.

44. Ibid., p. 199.
45. *Doctrine Saint-Simonienne* (Paris: Exposition, 1854), pp. 123–7.
46. J. E. Carines, "His Work in Political Economy," in Spencer et. al. (1873), p. 69.
47. *PPE*, first edition (1848), II, p. 200.
48. *Coleridge*, X, p. 158.
49. *PPE*, III, p. 766.
50. *Autobiography*, p. 237.
51. Property owned by a voluntary cooperative in a noncentralized economy is private but not individual.
52. Mill is referring to the Lockean argument about labor, an argument accepted by Adam Smith but not by David Hume.
53. Mill makes clear that he is not in favor of any kind of rectification principle, Nozickean or otherwise.
54. Mill makes clear that he would be in opposition to anything like affirmative action understood in terms of quotas or holding any position outside the competitive system.
55. *PPE*, II, pp. 207–8.
56. Ibid., p. 203.
57. See Mill to H. S. Chapman (May 28, 1849), XIV, p. 34
58. Considérant tried to establish such a community or colony in Texas with the help of Horace Greeley.
59. Preface to the English edition of 1888. "Communist Manifesto," in Lewis S. Feuer (ed.), *Marx and Engels: Basic Writings on Politics and Philosophy* (Garden City, NY: Anchor, 1959), pp. 3–4.
60. Mill had favored producers and consumers cooperatives as early as 1834. See CW VI, p. 190.
61. *PPE*, III, p. 775
62. "[T]he chief difference [from the Saint-Simonians] was that Mill avoided as much as possible the direct regulation of economic life by the state. He would use legislation to remove obstacles from the way of economic improvement of the people ... but he would not propose wholesale reorganization and direction of industry and agriculture by a group of functionaries in the name of the people." Mueller (1956), pp. 84–5.
63. *PPE*, II, p. 274.
64. *PPE*, III, p. 775.
65. CW, IV, p. 385.
66. *PPE*, III, pp. 794–5.
67. Ibid., p. 795.
68. Schwartz (1972), p. 226.
69. *PPE*, III, pp. 944–5.
70. *August Comte and Positivism*, X, p. 303.
71. *PPE*, III, p. 804.
72. Ibid., pp. 937–8.

73. Mill to Villari (May 19, 1872), XVIII, p. 1899.
74. Mazlish (1988), p. 354.
75. *PPE*, III, p. 955.
76. *PPE*, III, pp. 810–11.
77. CW XVIII, p. 1848.
78. *PPE*, II, p. 225.
79. CW III, p. 956.
80. *PPE*, II, p. 225.
81. *Autobiography*, p. 241.
82. *PPE*, III, p. 982.
83. Mill to John Jay (November 1848), XIII, pp. 740–1.
84. Mill to Dr. Adolf Soetbeer (March 18, 1852), XIV, p. 84.
85. Hayek's misrepresentation of Mill is remarkable. In his outstanding biography *Friedrich Hayek* (New York: Palgrave, 2001), Alan Ebenstein says the following: "One of the most prominent examples of Hayek's later negative view toward Mill occurred in . . . *Law, Legislation and Liberty*. . . . 'The tragic illusion was that the adoption of democratic procedures made it possible to dispense with all other limitations on governmental power. . . . He then footnoted [that] . . . J. S. Mill argues in *On Liberty* that '*the nation did not need to be protected against its own will* [emphasis added].' This interpretation of a relatively well known passage by John Stuart Mill was surprising because it was so inaccurate. . . . What makes this misinterpretation all the more surprising is that . . . in the *Constitution of Liberty* Hayek accurately made the interpretation of Mill that he later inaccurately made in *Law, Legislation, and Liberty*. . . . The socialism he [Mill] foresaw was workers' cooperatives within a competitive economy, not all-encompassing state control – Hayek's definition of socialism" (pp. 188–9). Ebenstein reminds us that Packe was much influenced by Hayek in this regard.
86. *PPE*, III, p. 767.
87. Mill to Harriet Taylor (March 21, 1849), XIV, p. 19.
88. *Autobiography*, p. 241.
89. *Nature*, X, p. 395. This essay was largely written between 1850 and 1858.
90. Himmelfarb (1974); see also Packe (1954), pp. 306–15; Hayek, *Mill and Harriet Taylor* (London: Routledge and Kegan Paul, 1951), especially pp. 134–9, 299–300. Harriet also accepted the first draft of the *Autobiography* (see CW I, pp. 173–5, for the critique of the practicability of socialism).
91. *PPE*, II, p. 214.
92. *PPE*, III, p. 977.
93. Mill to Austin (April 13, 1847), XIII, p. 713.
94. By the time Mill wrote "Recent Writers on Reform" in 1859, he had concluded that the gradualism inherent in the British and American systems was superior to the wished-for radical change in France.
95. Some of these letters (see below) may have been unavailable to Hayek, but in any case, given his focus and thesis, it is easy to see how they would be ignored.
96. Mill to Chapman (May 28, 1849), XIV, p. 33.

97. *Recollections of Alexis de Tocqueville*, ed. J. P. Mayer (New York: Columbia University Press, 1949), p. 11.

98. Mill to Sarah Austin (March 7, 1848), XIII, p. 734.

99. Mill to H. S. Chapman (May 28, 1849), XIV, p. 32.

100. Mill to J. P. Nichol (September 30, 1848), XIII, p. 739.

101. "England and Ireland," *Examiner* (May 13, 1848), pp. 307–8; CW XXV, p. 1100.

102. *PPE*, II, pp. 211–12 (Book II, Chapter 1, §4). Mill probably had in mind the work of Considérant, who was both the editor of Fourier's work *Destinée sociale* (1847–49) and the author of his own *Principes du socialisme* (1847).

103. *PPE*, III, p. 1006 (Book IV, Chapter 7, §5); this passage was edited out of the third edition.

104. CW XIX, p. 255. Iris Mueller (1956) notes that "[w]ithin the capitalist economy, Mill saw, through the application of voluntary Fourierism, the possible means of achieving many of the socialist goals without imposing the restrictions of Saint-Simonism or of Comptism" (p. 204).

105. The review appeared in the *Westminster Review*, 56, October 1851. The review of Newman further indicates that there was no substantive change in Mill's views about the problems of socialism. There he argued that "[s]ocialism as long as it attacks the existing individualism, is easily triumphant; its weakness hitherto is in what it proposes to substitute." CW V, p. 444.

106. *PPE*, II, p. 213 (Book II, Chapter 1, §4).

107. See letter (February 21, 1849), XIV, p. 11.

108. Samuel Hollander, *The Economics of John Stuart Mill* (Oxford: Basil Blackwell, 1985), Vol. II, p. 791.

109. Lionel Robbins, *Theory of Economic Policy in English Classical Political Economy* (London: Macmillan, 1953), p. 167.

110. Schwartz (1972), p. 106.

111. Collini (1991), p. 110.

112. Harriet to Mill on July 16, 1849. Quoted in Hayek, op. cit., p. 161.

113. I owe this point to David Levy, *How the Dismal Science Got Its Name: Classical Economics and the Ur Text of Radical Politics* (Ann Arbor: University of Michigan Press, 2001).

114. J. S. Mill, "On the Negro Question," CW XXI, p. 93.

115. Ibid., p. 95.

Chapter 8. Private Years (1850–1859)

1. Mill to Harriet (March 20, 1854), XIV, p. 190.

2. Document dated March 6, 1851. CW XXI, pp. 97–9.

3. *Autobiography*, p. 247.

4. Algernon Taylor, *Memoirs of a Student* (London, 1895), p. 11n.

5. Quoted in Adelaide Weinberg, *Theodor Gomperz and John Stuart Mill* (Geneva: Librairie Droz, 1963), p. 16.

6. Mary Mill to Mill (April 3, 1854), quoted in Packe (1954), p. 355. Mill/Taylor Collection, 47/26.
7. Mill to Mrs. James Mill (April 5, 1854), XIV, p. 197.
8. Diary, March 31, 1854, XXVII, p. 665.
9. Ibid., March 30, 1854.
10. Ibid., January 12, 1854, p. 642.
11. Ibid., February 7, 1854, p. 652.
12. Ibid., April 14, 1854, p. 668.
13. Mill to Harriet (August 30, 1853), XIV, p. 112.
14. Mill to Harriet (February 7, 1854), XIV, p. 152.
15. The first is his discussion of the "self" and "freedom" of the will in *Hamilton*, and the second is his final essay on religion.
16. *Principles of Political Economy*, Book 5, Chapter 11, III, p. 938.
17. "Mill narrates his life in such a way as to imbue it with complex meaning, inscribing it within a wider history. It is described as a journey from the chilly house of his father to the radiant home of his wife. This journey is also a process of *Bildung*, of self-development both emotional and intellectual. It is the story of how a man, with pain and travail of the soul, created his own character. It has a Saint-Simonian pattern, from narrow certainty through doubt to an enriched certainty. It gains added significance by being described as going hand-in-hand with, and helping along, the evolution of European thought and culture. Mill's revolt against Benthamism is not narrated as a mere private affair; it purports to symbolize and give voice to the protest of a whole generation against the aridities of the Enlightenment. If we buy Mill's story, then we accept him as a cultural leader, a bellwether, one who lived and experienced the travails of the European soul as it took the next step forward; a representative man who articulated the issues of the age with peculiar insight and incisiveness." Stafford (1998), p. 44.
18. Cumming (1964), pp. 235–56, claims that Mill reinterpreted his crisis in terms of the later evolution of his ideas. Carlisle (1991) has also expressed reservations.
19. Eisenach (1988), p. 2349.
20. The genre of intellectual biography might be said to have begun with Carlyle. Among Mill's associates and friends who wrote in a similar vein we find Lewes's *Goethe* (1855) and Morley's *Burke* (1867) as well as the work of Leslie Stephen. As Eisenach (1988), p. 2357, reminds us, "the 'English Men of Letters' and the 'English Statesmen' series became important texts in liberal education."
21. *On Genius*, I, p. 332.
22. *Dissertations and Discussions*, Preface, p. iv, reprint of the 1859 edition by Haskel House Publishers, New York, 1973.
23. Mill to Harriet (February 17, 1855), XIV, p. 332.
24. Some critics, including Williams (1963), pp. 81–3, claim he never integrated the two as successfully as Coleridge did.
25. Mill to Harriet (January 15, 1855), XIV, p. 294.
26. Mill to Harriet (February 17, 1855), XIV, p. 332.

27. W. T. Thornton, "His Career in the India House," in *John Stuart Mill*, ed. Fox Bourne (Boston, 1873), p. 32.
28. Quoted in Weinberg (1963), p. 17.
29. Quoted in Thornton, op. cit., p. 32. See "The Petition of the East India Company," CW XXX, p. 75.
30. Mill to William Napier (January 5, 1838), XVIII, p. 1983.
31. Mill to David Urquhart (October 4, 1866), XVI, p. 1205.
32. CW XXX, pp. 81–2.
33. Zastoupil (1994), pp. 87, 204–5.
34. *Considerations on Representative Government*, XIX, pp. 562–3.
35. Ibid., p. 565.
36. Aside from Moir, see Joseph Hamburger, "The Writings of John Stuart Mill and His Father James Mill in the Archives of the India Office," *American Philosophical Society Yearbook*, 1957, pp. 324–6; Eric Stokes, *The English Utilitarians and India* (Oxford: Clarendon Press, 1959); R. J. Moore, "John Stuart Mill at East India House," *Historical Studies* 20 (1983), pp. 497–519; Zastoupil (1994).
37. *Considerations on Representative Government*, Chapter 18, CW XIX, pp. 562–77.
38. W. T. Thornton, "His Career in India House," in H. R. Fox Bourne (ed.), *John Stuart Mill – Notices of His Life and Works* (London, 1873).
39. Mill to Guerney (October 28, 1858), XV, pp. 571–2.
40. Bain (1882b), p. 102.
41. Mill-Taylor Collection, 24/708.
42. *Autobiography*, pp. 264–5.

Chapter 9. The Memorial Essays

1. Diary, January 19, 1854, XXVII, p. 644.
2. There can be no such thing as an "unfree" will, but custom dictates the use of the expression "free will" to reinforce the claim that the will is not determined.
3. See Nicholas Capaldi, *The Enlightenment Project in the Analytic Conversation* (Dordrecht: Kluwer, 1998), for a rebuttal of all extant versions of the claim that meaningful human action can be explained naturalistically.
4. Presumably, one of the things that would distinguish a modern from a classical Christian is that whereas a classical Christian would subordinate himself or herself to God, the modern Christian freely loves God. It is not a question of whether to take the implied obligations seriously but the spirit in which one does it.
5. "[T]he standard by which he [Mill] tried to justify personal freedom itself was its tendency to foster self-development." Mueller (1956), p. 229.
6. Diary, March 29, 1854, XXVII, p. 664. "All systems of morals agree in prescribing to do that, and only that, which accords with self-respect . . . that with which their self-respect is associated . . . [i]n the best, with the sympathy of those they respect and a just regard for the good of all." Ibid., April 9, 1854, p. 667.

7. We must distinguish between 'ethics' and 'morals.' Ethics applies, strictly speaking, only to teleological systems; moral philosophy (deontology, the concern for duty) denies the existence of teleology. From Kant onward, however, a number of theorists, including Hegel and Mill, combine the two by making autonomy our ultimate "end."

8. Michael Oakeshott (1996) describes the situation as follows: "[T]his conclusion may be greeted with various mixtures of revulsion, anxiety, and confidence; it is both gratifying and burdensome, the sort of fulfillment it promises is partnered by a notorious risk of self-estrangement or self-destruction.... this disposition [self-determination or personal autonomy]... is not to be understood as a surrender to so-called 'subjective will', or a relapse into the effortless indulgence of inclination, or as the canonization of 'conscience'; it is a difficult achievement. The self here is a substantive personality, the outcome of an education, whose resources are collected in a self-understanding [that] both acquires and confirms its autonomy. Nor does the experience of this disposition imply the worship of non-conformity, a devotion to arbitrary so-called 'self-expression', or a resolution to be different at all costs. The conduct it prompts is not composed of unconditional choices, and it does not require indifference to moral or prudential practices or aversion from any but self-made rules. It is composed of actions and utterances which reflect contingent sentiments, affections, and beliefs this particular self has made its own, performed in its own subscriptions to practices whose resources it has made its own. The autonomy of such a self and the independence or originality of such conduct lies not at all in an unconcern for the conditions which specify the arts of agency. Nor, again, does this disposition forbid association in a co-operative undertaking to pursue with others a common purpose; what it requires is that such association shall be in terms of continuous choices to be associated which reflect the self-understanding of the person concerned. In short, what is postulated and emphasized here is a collected personality, autonomous on account of its self-understanding and its command of resources it has made its own. And the half of this self-understanding is knowing its own limits" (pp. 236–7).

9. The concept of autonomy has a rather long and complicated history that derives, in part, from Christianity. It is obvious why modern Christians, specifically Protestants, would be among the first to emphasize their capacity for personal autonomy. There is a direct line of influence from Augustine to Luther and Calvin, from Luther to Rousseau, from Rousseau to Kant, and finally from Kant to Mill via Humboldt. The secular sources are many and varied, starting with Renaissance writers such as Pico della Mirandola and continuing to early modern philosophers such as Montaigne and Spinoza.

10. According to Anschutz (1953), p. 5, Mill was "thoroughly representative of his age" because "somewhere or other in his writings you can discern traces of every wind that blew in the early nineteenth century." In the Introduction to *The Spirit of the Age* (Chicago: University of Chicago Press, 1942), Hayek points out that Mill was "representative of his age only because of his rare capacity of absorbing

new ideas made him a kind of focus in which most of the significant changes of thought of his time combined" (p. vii).

11. F. A. Hayek, *The Counter-Revolution of Science* (Indianapolis: Liberty Fund, 1979), pp. 371–2.

12. "The preoccupation with *Bildung* was in some respects a secular version of German Pietism. . . ." J. W. Burrow (ed.), Wilhelm von Humboldt, *The Limits of State Action* (Indianapolis: Liberty Fund, 1993), editor's introduction, p. xxxi.

13. For a comparison between Humboldt's work and Mill's *On Liberty*, see the comparative table of subjects prepared by Stuart Warner as an addendum (pp. 158–61) to the Burrow's Liberty Fund version of Humboldt (1993), cited in note 12.

14. Stafford (1993) recognizes the prominence of *bildung* in Mill but fails to see its connection with autonomy. Lukes (1973) is a useful corrective because he details the many strands of individualism and how they come together.

15. Burrow (1993), pp. xxxi–xxxii.

16. Walter Houghton, in *The Victorian Frame of Mind: 1830–1870* (New Haven, CT: Yale University Press, 1957), distinguishes between Goethe's classical ideal, with its emphasis on harmony, and the Romantic ideal of uniqueness. Houghton argues that "Mill's interpretation of this ideal is neither Greek nor Goethean – nor Arnoldian; it is Romantic" (pp. 284, 287–91).

17. Richard Wollheim, "Mill and Isaiah Berlin: The Ends of Life and the Preliminaries of Morality," in *The Idea of Freedom: Essays in Honor of Isaiah Berlin*, ed. Alan Ryan (Oxford: Oxford University Press, 1979), pp. 254–5; Mill avoids appeal to abstract rights and is a kind of utilitarian (contra Berlin).

18. "Moral regenerators in this age mostly aim at setting up a new form either of Stoicism or of Puritanism. . . . [this] must be a failure now when an earthly life both pleasant and innocent can be had by many and might be had by all. What is now wanted is the creed of Epicurus warmed by the additional element of an enthusiastic love of the general good." Diary, April 8, 1854, XXVII, p. 666.

19. Dicey (1908), p. 308n2.

20. See Steven Lukes, *Individualism* (Oxford: Blackwell, 1973).

21. *On Liberty*, CW XVIII, p. 224.

22. Rosenblum (1987), p. 125: "For Humboldt, Mill, and Constant, who share this vision, public and private life are mutually compensatory. Each sphere provides a corrective for the excesses or deficiencies of the other." Rosenblum (1987), p. 139: "Privatism is a corrective, not a world to itself. The world it serves, and the necessary setting for full self-development, is pluralist liberal society."

23. Burrow (1993), p. lvii.

24. This kind of criticism about fragmentation had been enunciated by Adam Smith, Adam Ferguson, and Benjamin Constant.

25. *Autobiography*, p. 21.

26. Mill to Robert Barclay Fox (December 19, 1842), XIII, pp. 563–4.

27. Misguided critiques of Mill's *Utilitarianism* have been an industry since the time of Sidgwick's *Methods of Ethics* (1874) and G. E. Moore's *Principia Ethica* (1903). Some of this egregious misrepresentation is summarized in Skorupski (1989),

Chapter 9. However, as we pointed out, Skorupski does not share our view of the central role of autonomy. Especially egregious is the charge that Mill committed any number of logical howlers. If the critics had taken the time to read the *Logic*, they would have noticed, among other things, Mill's understanding of what the suffix "able" adds to the meaning of a word (I, iii, 14); Mill's claim that some words cannot be defined because they cannot be analyzed into parts, especially colors (I, vii and viii, and IV, iv, 5); and his discussion of the relation of quality and quantity of feelings (II, iv, 7). In 1953, Urmson (1969) pointed out that "[i]nstead of Mill's own doctrines a travesty is discussed, so that the most common criticisms of him are simply irrelevant" (p. 180).

28. *Utilitarianism*, CW X, p. 210.

29. Ibid. Although Hegel made the master-slave metaphor famous, the metaphor goes back to ancient times. In the modern period, it is also to be found in the writings of Rousseau and Fichte, both of whom Mill had read, and in Nietzsche.

30. "[H]e [Mill] has obtained a very wide acceptance of the utilitarian doctrines; they were presented by Bentham in a form so harsh and unattractive as to produce an almost repelling effect. Mr. Mill, on the contrary, showed that the utilitarian philosophy might inspire the most active benevolence and the most generous enthusiasm." Henry Fawcett, "His Influence on the Universities," in Spencer et al. (1873), p. 78. Frank Knight, in *Freedom and Reform* (Indianapolis: Liberty Fund, 1982), maintains that something like freedom was always implicit in Bentham's views: "When we ask in what respect each is to count for one or what is the content of the good, Bentham – especially in his economic writings – interprets pleasure to mean freedom" (p. 135n).

31. Bain (1882b), pp. 83–4.

32. Heyck (1982), pp. 190–1: "[P]erhaps the strongest theme in nineteenth century English literature was criticism of industrial society and the utilitarian and *laissez-faire* philosophies that went with it."

33. Mill "found that Bentham's ethics needed correction by the addition of a private morality founded on personal development." Robson (1968), p. 35.

34. "Remarks on Bentham's Philosophy," CW X, p. 15.

35. Ibid., pp. 5–6.

36. *Autobiography*, CW I, p. 209.

37. "Whewell," CW X, p. 194.

38. *Autobiography*, p. 49.

39. *Utilitarianism*, X, p. 207.

40. Hastings Rashdall (1858–1924) is a later exemplar of this ideal utilitarianism, a position inspired in Rashdall by T. H. Green and expressed in Rashdall's book *The Theory of Good and Evil*. More recently, Robert Nozick has tried to formulate a deontological position of this kind.

41. *Utilitarianism*, X, p. 249.

42. Ibid., p. 210.

43. Ibid., p. 212.

44. Ibid., pp. 213–14.

45. Ibid., pp. 235–6.
46. Ryan (1970), p. 255.
47. W. S. Jevons, "Mill's Philosophy Tested," in his *Pure Logic and Other Minor Works* (London: Macmillan, 1890), pp. 200–1.
48. *A System of Logic*, CW XVIII, p. 223.
49. "Grote's Plato" (1866), CW XI, pp. 391–2, 416, 419.
50. *Utilitarianism*, X, p. 236.
51. Ibid., p. 238.
52. Ibid., p. 231.
53. Ibid., p. 220.
54. Ibid., p. 232.
55. This also allows Mill to reply to Herbert Spencer that "everybody has an equal right to happiness [read: autonomy]. . . . This, however, is not a presupposition; not a premise needful to support the principle of utility, but the very principle itself." Ibid., p. 258n.
56. Ibid., p. 234.
57. Ibid., pp. 255–6.
58. *Autobiography*, I, p. 259.
59. Mill to Emile Acollas (September 20, 1871), XVIII, pp. 1831–2. See also Fred R. Berger, *Happiness, Justice, and Freedom: The Moral and Political Philosophy of Mill* (Berkeley: University of California Press, 1984), Chapter 5.
60. Semmel (1984), p. 14.
61. Ibid., p. 165: "The support German philosophy gave to liberty was the principal theme of Mill's best-known tract." See also letters to Arnold Ruge (March 2, 1859), XV, p. 598; to Theodore Gomperz (October 5, 1857), XV, p. 539; and to Pasquale Villari (March 9, 1858), XV, p. 550. "The essay was also, primarily, a plea for positive liberty, for the sense of participation and self-realization in the idea of freedom associated with the German thinkers. . . . Mill hoped to place the ultimate spiritual power in neither a positivist priesthood nor a utilitarian bureaucracy, but in line with the intuitive morality of the German idealists, in the conscience of the individual." Semmel (1984), pp. 166–7.
62. *Liberty*, XVIII, p. 243. Skorupski (1989), Chapter 1, recognizes the Kantian sense of autonomy in Mill but thinks it is incompatible with Mill's naturalism. I shall argue that by the time Mill wrote *Hamilton*, he had abandoned his naturalism.
63. Wilhelm von Humboldt, *The Limits of State Action*, ed. J. W. Burrow (Cambridge: Cambridge University Press, 1969), p. 86.
64. Ibid., p. 81. Rosenblum (1987), p. 55: ". . . J. S. Mill's observation that individualism was triumphant at the same time that individuality was in danger of becoming extinct."
65. Ibid., p. 79.
66. *Autobiography*, p. 260. There is a mention of Fichte in the same paragraph. Goethe and Fichte are also explicitly mentioned and linked in *On Liberty*, XVIII, p. 243.
67. Mill calls attention in *On Liberty* to Tocqueville's "last important work" (*The Old Regime and the French Revolution*) and notes that Tocqueville there quotes

Humboldt on "freedom and variety of situations" (*On Liberty*, XVIII, p. 274). This double reference should make clear the extent to which Mill's *On Liberty* is a rewriting of Humboldt in the light of the danger underscored by Tocqueville.

68. See Tocqueville, *Democracy in America*, Vol. I, Chapter 15; *Autobiography*, CW I, pp. 199–201.

69. *On Liberty*, XVIII, p. 227.

70. *On Liberty*, p. 223.

71. *Examiner*, July 15, 1832, XXIII, p. 503.

72. *On Liberty*, XVIII, p. 263.

73. Ibid., p. 267.

74. Ibid., p. 268. Cf. Bagehot (1958) [1865]: "The middle classes – the ordinary majority of educated men – are in the present day the despotic power in England" (p. 235).

75. *On Liberty*, XVIII, pp. 268–9.

76. Ibid., p. 287.

77. *Autobiography*, pp. 245–7. Mill is describing his state of mind right before he began to work on *On Liberty*.

78. Alexander Carlyle (ed.), *New Letters of Thomas Carlyle* (London: J. Lane), Vol. II, p. 196.

79. A more thoughtful conservative response was represented by Matthew Arnold. "Both men [Mill and Matthew Arnold] favored democracy for England, but feared that, unless it were prepared for properly, it would become the enemy of culture instead of its ally. Both believed the essence of democracy to be equality rather than liberty, but whereas for Mill this meant that liberty had to be jealously protected to prevent democracy from becoming tyrannical, for Arnold it meant liberty had to be carefully circumscribed in order to make democracy successful. Mill, unlike Arnold, thought liberty an essential element of culture." Alexander (1965), p. 232.

80. *On Liberty*, XVIII, p. 261; Wilhelm von Humboldt, *The Limits of State Action* (Indianapolis: Liberty Fund, 1993), pp. 11–13.

81. "The God of Calvinism demanded of his believers not single good works, but a life of good works combined into a unified system." Max Weber, *The Protestant Ethic and the Spirit of Capitalism* (Gloucester, MA: Peter Smith, 1988), p. 117.

82. *On Liberty*, XVIII, p. 261.

83. Ibid., p. 222.

84. A. J. Campbell, *Two Centuries of the Church of Scotland 1707–1929* (London: Paisley, A. Gardner, 1930), p. 28: "During the seventeenth century Scottish religion had fallen greatly under the influence of English Puritanism; and when to this we add the memory of the bitter strife of sixty years, and the economic misery of the moment, we can perhaps understand why at the Union and for many years after, religion was seen in its grimmest form. . . . [It] depicted God as an implacable despot, swift to wrath. . . . It held by the doctrines of election and reprobation in all their severity. . . . Both in church and in home the most relentless discipline was maintained. . . . The observance of the Sabbath was enforced with penalties."

85. *On Liberty*, XVIII, p. 265–6.

86. Ibid., p. 272. The critique of Calvinism on this point must be related to Mill's notion of a stationary state and seen in the light of his claim that "the most serious danger to the future prospects of mankind is the unbalanced influence of the commercial spirit" (CW, XVIII, p. 198 – review of Tocqueville).

87. Alexander (1965), p. 192.

88. *On Liberty*, XVIII, pp. 256–7.

89. Ibid., p. 256.

90. Ibid.

91. *Nature*, X, p. 397.

92. *On Liberty*, XVIII, p. 270.

93. Ibid., p. 223. "[I]t is not enough to justify such restrictions, that an action should imply damage to another person; it must, at the same time, encroach upon his rights. But this second position requires explanation. Right, then, is never infringed except when some one is deprived of a part of what properly belongs to him, *or of his personal freedom* [italics mine], without his consent or against his will." Humboldt, op. cit., pp. 86–7.

94. *Utilitarianism*, CW X, p. 55. "Even in those portions of conduct which do affect the interest of others, the onus of making out a case always lies on the defenders of legal prohibition." *Principles of Political Economy*, Book V, Chapter 11, section 2, CW III, p. 938.

95. This criticism was originally made by Bosanquet (1923), pp. 60–3. Mill was defended by Rees (1960). Rosenblum (1987), p. 81: "Arendt tends to ignore the manifoldness of private life. For her, civil society and membership in partial publics are privatizing so long as they are based on narrow self-interest and not on exchanges of opinion about the shared ends of the community. In her political vision the possessive individualist's interest in property is just as detached from the genuine public life of democratic participation as Christian otherworldliness; romantic self-absorption is as privatized as stoic detachment. For Arendt, Mill is indistinguishable from Epictetus."

96. Bain (1882b), p. 111.

97. "There is no pursuit whatever that may not be ennobling and give to human nature some worthy and determinate form. The manner of its performance is the only thing to be considered; and we may here lay down the general rule, that a man's pursuits react beneficially on his culture, so long as these, and the energies allied with them, succeed in filling and satisfying the wants of his soul." Humboldt, op. cit., pp. 28–9.

98. *On Liberty*, XVIII, p. 224.

99. N. Capaldi, "Censorship and Social Stability in J. S. Mill," *Mill Newsletter*, 9 (1973), pp. 12–16.

100. In the absence of a belief in God, miracles, providence, etc., it is not clear why there should be any correlation at all.

101. *On Liberty*, XVIII, p. 264.

102. Ibid., p. 262.

103. Ibid., p. 221.

104. Ibid., p. 248.
105. Ibid., p. 262.
106. Ibid., p. 269.
107. *Subjection of Women*, CW XXI, p. 315.
108. Did Mill advocate liberal neutrality, or did he have a substantive conception of the human good? Berlin (1969, pp. 173–206) and Gray (Gray and Smith 1991, pp. 193, 201, 205) claim Mill as an advocate of diversity; Duncan (1973, p. 268) disagrees with Berlin. Cowling (1990) and Letwin (1965) claim that Mill had a substantive conception but that it was elitist and intolerant. Capaldi (1995) argues that Mill had a substantive view but that it was not intolerant and not incompatible with diversity, properly understood, once autonomy is seen as its foundation.
109. I am deeply indebted to my astute colleague Eldon Eisenach for this insight. See his "Mill's Autobiography as Political Theory," *History of Political Thought*, 8:1 (Spring 1987), pp. 111–29. "What Mill gave us instead was a *magnum opus* in miniature, a personal ethology demonstrating the ways in which the laws of social progress and the consciousness of moral freedom become manifest in one person's life and character" (p. 128).
110. *An Examination of Sir William Hamilton's Philosophy*, IX, p. 103.
111. Cited in Weber, op. cit., p. 101.
112. *On Liberty*, XVIII, p. 269.
113. Ibid., p. 270.
114. In his review of Tocqueville, Mill enumerates his objectives as "to sustain the higher pursuits of philosophy and art; to vindicate and protect the unfettered exercise of reason, and the *moral freedom of the individual* [italics mine]." CW XVIII, p. 189.
115. Diary, April 7, 1854, XXVII, p. 666.
116. "Mill accepts the Scottish account of the growth of civil society as the economically-led diffusion of a new set of urbane manners, values and practices, linked also to the rise of a middle class, a popular press, and their concomitants: a public opinion." Iain Hampsher-Monk, "Mill," in *A History of Modern Political Thought* (Oxford: Blackwell, 1992), p. 349.
117. *On Liberty*, XVIII, p. 270.
118. Ibid., p. 293.
119. Rosenblum (1987), p. 125: "For Humboldt, Mill, and Constant, who share this vision, public and private life are mutually compensatory. Each sphere provides a corrective for the excesses or deficiencies of the other." See also p. 139: "Privatism is a corrective, not a world to itself. The world it serves, and the necessary setting for full self-development, is pluralist liberal society."
120. *Subjection of Women*, CW XXI, p. 293.
121. Ibid., p. 331.
122. Mill to Rev. Stephen Hawtrey (August 10, 1867), XVI, p. 1304: "I have long thought that while French schoolboys are better taught and learn more than English boys, the freer system of the English schools has much to do with

the superiority of England in the love and practice of personal and political freedom."

123. "Doubt is torture only to the believer, and not to the man who follows the results of his own inquiries; for, to him results are generally far less important. During this inquiry, he is conscious of his soul's activity and strength; he feels that his perfection, his happiness, depend upon this power; and instead of being oppressed by his doubts about the propositions he formerly took to be true, he congratulates himself that his increasing mental powers enable him to see clearly through errors that he had not till now perceived." Humboldt, *op. cit.*, p. 67.

124. John Milton, *Areopagitica* (New York: Library of Liberty, 1992), pp. 66–7.

125. *On Liberty*, XVIII, p. 229; also p. 258.

126. Milton, op. cit., p. 142.

127. *On Liberty*, XVIII, p. 258.

128. Milton, op. cit., p. 124.

129. *On Liberty*, XVIII, p. 244.

130. Milton, op. cit., pp. 171–2.

131. *On Liberty*, XVIII, p. 258.

132. Ibid., p. 243.

133. "To question all things; – never to turn away from any difficulty; to accept no doctrine either from ourselves or from other people without a rigid scrutiny by negative criticism; letting no fallacy, or incoherence, or confusion of thought, step by unperceived; above all, to insist upon having the meaning of a word clearly understood before using it, and the meaning of a proposition before assenting to it; – these are the lessons we learn from ancient dialecticians." J. S. Mill, inaugural address as rector, University of St. Andrews, February 1, 1867, CW XXI, pp. 229–30. Mill also referred in *On Liberty* to the practice of "devil's advocate" within the Catholic Church.

134. Henry Larkin, "Carlyle and Mrs. Carlyle: A Ten Years' Reminiscence," *British Quarterly Review* (July 1881).

135. Alexander Carlyle (ed.), *New Letters of Thomas Carlyle*, Vol. II, p. 196.

136. *Letters of Matthew Arnold*, ed. G. W. E. Russell (New York, 1900), Vol. I, p. 111.

137. Charles Kingsley, *The Limits of Exact Science as Applied to History* (London: Macmillan, 1860), p. 40.

138. *Autobiography*, I, pp. 199–201.

139. The classic discussion of the evolution of Mill's political thinking is J. H. Burns, "Mill and Democracy, 1829–61," *Political Studies*, 5 (1957), reprinted Schneewind (1969).

140. As Wittgenstein would put it, a rule does not come with instructions for the application of itself.

141. *Representative Government*, CW XIX, p. 404.

142. Ibid., pp. 432–3.

143. Mill thinks this is an even greater problem for the continent than it is for England. One wonders what he would have thought about the bureaucracy of the EU.

144. *Representative Government*, CW XIX, pp. 442–6.

145. Ibid., pp. 471–2.
146. Ibid., p. 470.
147. Ibid., pp. 475–6.
148. Mill had already proposed the same idea in a slightly earlier publication, *Thoughts on Parliamentary Reform* (1859), CW XIX, p. 325.
149. This stratagem eliminated the necessity for remedy previously suggested by Mill, namely, plural voting by those with an educational qualification.
150. Ibid., pp. 488–9.
151. Ibid., p. 471.
152. Ibid., p. 502.
153. Ibid., p. 514.
154. Ibid., p. 517.
155. Ibid., p. 525.
156. Ibid., pp. 467–8.
157. Ibid., p. 554.
158. Mill to Henry Fawcett (February 5, 1860), XV, p. 672.
159. Fukuyama (1992), p. xviii.
160. Ibid., p. xxi.

Chapter 10. Public Intellectual (1859–1869)

1. Quoted in Weinberg (1963), pp. 32–3.
2. E. M. Everett, *The Party of Humanity – The Fortnightly Review, 1865–1874* (Chapel Hill: University of North Carolina Press, 1939).
3. Bain (1882b), pp. 162–3.
4. Herbert Spencer, *Autobiography* (London: Williams and Norgate, 1904), Vol. II, p. 213.
5. Herbert Spencer, "His Moral Character," in Spencer et al. (1873), p. 41.
6. "A Few Words on Non-Intervention," CW XXI, p. 111.
7. *Autobiography*, I, p. 266.
8. Mill to Cairnes (May 28, 1865), XVI, p. 1057.
9. Letter from Grote to G. C. Lewis, quoted in Fox Bourne (1873), p. 20.
10. Quoted in Weinberg (1963), p. 34.
11. Writing to Bain in 1861, Mill said: "The great recommendation of this project is, that it will enable me to supply what was prudently left deficient in the Logic, and to do the kind of service which I am capable of to rational psychology, namely, to its *Polemik*" (XV, p. 752). "I mean in this book to do what the nature and scope of the Logic forbade me to do there, to face the ultimate metaphysical difficulties of every question on which I touch" (XV, p. 816).
12. Letter to Bain (December 1863), XV, p. 816.
13. Mill to Robert Barclay Fox (May 10, 1842), XIII, p. 520. Mill's expression of belief in immortality in his posthumously published essay *Theism* is often attributed to the sentimental hope of seeing Harriet in the next life. Perhaps it was, but it was also a view Mill held on philosophical grounds from a much earlier period.

14. Diary, February 27, 1854, CW XXVII, p. 657.

15. *Autobiography*, CW I, pp. 269–70.

16. *Hamilton*, CW IX, Chapter 11; the distinction between this Lockean approach and what Mill calls Cousin's introspective approach is discussed in Chapter 9.

17. "I have postulated, first, sensations; secondly, succession and simultaneousness of sensations; thirdly, a uniform order in their succession and simultaneousness. . . ." *Hamilton*, CW IX, p. 201.

18. Ibid., p. 184.

19. Ibid., p. 189. To identify them as "ours" is already to presuppose a self.

20. Ibid., p. 194.

21. Ibid., p. 196.

22. Ibid., p. 203.

23. It is precisely here that philosophical idealists argue we must recognize an absolute self uniting all the parts in the mental series; William James, and even Bertrand Russell for a while, will opt for identifying the self totally with the stream of consciousness.

24. *Hamilton*, IX, p. 207.

25. Ibid., p. 205.

26. Ibid., p. 7.

27. *Logic*, CW VII, p. 485.

28. Ibid., pp. 8–9.

29. *Hamilton*, CW IX, p. 187n.

30. This is in the end the basis of Skorupski's (1989) disappointment with Mill. Capaldi (1998) argues that even the program to construct such a perspective is incoherent.

31. These distinctions are emendations of a view originally presented by Shotter (1975), pp. 124–5.

32. It looks, at times, as if Mill, like Descartes, is using the perspective of the egocentric outside observer. This is what Reid had criticized as the way of ideas. However, even Mill's discussions of how the mind constructs a coherent view are indicative of a commonsense viewpoint, something his critics have been quick to point out. However, this cannot be a fault unless Mill proposed to reduce the commonsense view to a mechanistic or wholly organic ontology, something he did not propose. It is a consistent and coherent approach – perhaps the only one.

33. Bain (1882b), p. 120.

34. Like Hegel, Mill did not deny that the mind "constructed" or interpreted experience, but he insisted that the categories in terms of which it did so were historically evolving ones.

35. "We see how Mill must have infuriated his absolute-idealist critics: just because in one way – in accepting the standpoint of consciousness – he was so close to them." Skorupski (1989), p. 245.

36. See Chapter 6, pp. 180–2.

37. Jevons, "Mill's Philosophy Tested," in his *Pure Logic and Other Minor Works* (London: Macmillan, 1890), p. 203.

38. Skorupski (1989), p. 254, denies that Mill has a transcendental conception of the self. Our discussion of philosophic idealism reveals that Mill was willing to countenance such a possibility.

39. Bain (1882b), p. 121.

40. There is an interesting parallel to Mill's notion of emancipatory beliefs in Freud's notion of psychoanalysis. Freud claimed that Mill was "perhaps the man of the century who best managed to free himself from the domination of customary prejudices." Ernest Jones, *The Life and Work of Sigmund Freud* (New York: Hogarth Press, 1953), pp. 1, 55, 176.

41. *Nature*, CW X, p. 379.

42. Feuer (1976), p. 86: "Among the great social thinkers of the nineteenth century, Mill was the only one who failed to write a system encompassing the evolution of humanity. Hegel, Comte, Marx, and Spencer felt they could enunciate and derive the law of social progress."

43. Mill to Carlyle (April 11, 1866), XVI, p. 1157.

44. Moncure D. Conway, *Thomas Carlyle* (New York, 1881), p. 90.

45. *Autobiography*, I, p. 221.

46. Bain (1882b) claims that Grote saw the despotism in Comte before Mill (p. 75).

47. Packe (1954), p. 449.

48. Mill to Gomperz (August 22, 1866), XVI, pp. 1196–7. Mill had defined "advanced liberalism" in a speech to the electors of Westminster (July 5, 1865; CW XXVIII, p. 23): "There are truths which the time has now arrived for proclaiming, though the time may not yet have arrived for carrying them into effect. This is what I mean by advanced Liberalism."

49. Thomas Hardy. Letter to the *London Times*, May 21, 1906.

50. *Hamilton*, IX, p. 103.

51. *Thoughts on Parliamentary Reform*, CW XIX, p. 338.

52. Writing in support of Mill's candidacy, W. D. Christie wrote in "Mr. John Stuart Mill for Westminster," *MacMillan's Magazine*, 12, (May–October 1865), p. 96: "...one whose eminent philosophy embraces all letters, art, and imagination, combines the ancient and the new, reform and tradition, the principle of permanence and the principle of progression, the practical spirit of Bentham and the reverent ideal politics of Coleridge...." This is an important recognition of the Romantic dimension of Mill's thought.

53. "Cattle Disease Bill," in *Public and Parliamentary Speeches*, CW XXVIII, pp. 48–9.

54. See Bruce Kinzer's introduction to CW XXVIII.

55. Walter Bagehot, "Mr. Mill's Address to the Electors of Westminster," *Economist*, April 29, 1865.

56. W. L. Courtney, *Life of Mill* (London, 1889), p. 147.

57. *Considerations on Representative Government*, CW XIX, p. 452n.

58. *Public and Parliamentary Speeches*, CW XXVIII, p. 85 (May 31, 1866).

59. Mill to Nightingale (September 23, 1960), XV, pp. 709–10.

60. *Public and Parliamentary Speeches*, CW XXVIII, p. 270 (April 21, 1868).

61. "A Few Words on Non Intervention" (1859), CW XXI, p. 123. In an August 5, 1867 speech in Parliament, he argued that England's might was both "the freedom of the world" and "the greatest and most permanent interests of every civilized people." XXVIII, p. 223.

62. Semmel (1984) claims Mill was Palmerstonian rather than an advanced liberal (p. 107).

63. The best discussion of this is to be found in Bernard Semmel, *Jamaican Blood and Victorian Conscience: The Governor Eyre Controversy* (Boston, 1963).

64. *Public and Parliamentary Speeches*, CW XXVIII, p. 104 (July 31, 1866).

65. Gladstone and Queen Victoria opposed women's suffrage.

66. *Autobiography*, CW I, 285.

67. Millicent Garrett Fawcett, "His Influence as a Practical Politician," in Spencer et al. (1873), p. 85.

68. Mill to Parker Pillsbury (July 4, 1867), XVI, p. 1289.

69. Henry Fawcett, "His Influence at the Universities," in Spencer et al. (1873), pp. 74–5.

70. Bain (1882b) is largely critical of Mill's address (pp. 126–8).

71. *Inaugural Address*, CW XXI, p. 230. Mill, although admiring him, had criticized Goethe for advocating balance and symmetry but never achieving it in his own works. For Mill, this was evidence of "the utter impossibility for a modern with all the good will in the world, to tight-lace himself into the dimensions of an ancient." Hayek (ed.), *John Stuart Mill and Harriet Taylor* (London: Routledge and Kegan Paul, 1951), p. 225. In this respect, Mill had recorded in his diary (February 6, 1854) his disagreement with Goethe: "As well might he [Goethe] attempt to cut down Shakespeare or a Gothic cathedral to the Greek model, as to give a rounded completeness to any considerable modern life. Not symmetry, but bold, free expansion in all directions is demanded by the needs of modern life and the instincts of the modern mind. Great and strong and varied faculties are more wanted than faculties well proportioned to one another; a Hercules or a Briareus more than an Apollo." CW XXVII, p. 651.

72. *Inaugural Address*, XXI, pp. 217, 218, 220, 255.

73. Ibid., pp. 253–4.

74. Ibid., pp. 229–30. "It is somewhat rare to find that those who profess themselves undoubted liberals are prepared to accept a consistent application of their principles. . . . No one was ever more free from this kind of bigotry, than Mr. Mill, and probably constitutes one of the main causes of his influence." Fawcett, op. cit., p. 79.

75. *Inaugural Address*, XXI, pp. 247, 254, 256.

76. Edward Alexander, *Matthew Arnold and Mill* (London: Routledge and Kegan Paul, 1965), p. 31. Alexander's book is an important contribution to showing how very different Victorian figures were responding to the same great issues of the age. Mill, by the way, in his address, had praised Matthew Arnold's famous and influential father, Dr. Arnold of Rugby, for his educational innovations. Alexander makes a very strong case for the similarities between Mill and Arnold.

77. *Autobiography*, CW I, pp. 288–9. See *Thoughts on Parliamentary Reform*, CW XIX, pp. 324–5; "Recent Writers on Reform," ibid., pp. 353–7; and *Considerations on Representative Government*, ibid., pp. 474–9.

78. Mill to Cairnes (Dec. 4, 1868), XVI, p. 1506.

Chapter 11. Later Years (1869–1873)

1. James Mill, *Analysis of the Phenomena of the Human Mind*, ed. J. S. Mill (London, 1869), Vol. II, p. 234n.

2. Ibid., pp. 254–5n.

3. Mill to J. F. Mollett (December 30, 1847), XIII, pp. 728–9.

4. Mill to Edwin Chadwick (January 2, 1871), XVII, p. 1792.

5. For a balanced assessment, see Ann Robson, "Mill's Second Prize in the Lottery of Life," in Laine (1991).

6. September 13, 1870. Sarah Norton (ed.), *The Letters of Charles Eliot Norton* (Boston: Houghton Mifflin, 1913), Vol. I, p. 400.

7. Mill/Taylor Collection 19/45, Kate Amberley to Helen Taylor, June 16, 1872.

8. *Public and Parliamentary Speeches*, CW XXVIII, pp. 283–6 (June 10, 1868).

9. See Lee Holcombe, *Wives and Property: Reform of the Married Women's Property Law in Nineteenth Century England* (Oxford: Martin Robinson, 1983).

10. This work was published in 1869 but had been written during the 1850s.

11. J. S. Mill, *System of Logic*, Book VI, Chapter 2, section 3, CW VIII, pp. 839–42.

12. Mill to John Nichol (August 18, 1869), XVII, p. 1633.

13. *The Subjection of Women*, CW XXI, pp. 272–3.

14. Mill to Henry Keylock Rusden (July 22, 1870), XVII, p. 1751.

15. *The Subjection of Women*, CW XXI, p. 323; see also pp. 284–6.

16. An even more fundamental reason given by Mill is that "I do not think it is part of the business of the Government to provide securities beforehand against the consequences of immoralities of any kind." CW XXI, p. 353.

17. Mill to Lord Amberley (February 2, 1870), XVII, pp. 1692–3.

18. Stefan Collini notes this in his introduction to CW XXI, p. xxxiv.

19. CW XXI, pp. 288–9.

20. Ibid., p. 338.

21. Ibid., p. 336.

22. Harriet Taylor Mill, "Enfranchisement of Women," CW XXI, p. 408.

23. In connection with this, it is important to note that Mill was largely educated by his father and that, despite criticisms of that education, John Stuart Mill took for granted a world in which parents, including fathers, were personally involved and invested a great deal of time in their children's education. This should be kept in mind by those critics who point out that Mill still expected the traditional division of labor between men (work in the economic world) and women (responsibilities at home). Like Hegel, Mill was also very critical of education that pandered to children and made no demands on them, thereby "training up a race of men who

will be incapable of doing anything which is disagreeable to them." *Autobiography*, CW I, p. 55.

24. CW II, p. 225.
25. CW XIV, p. 500 (unidentified correspondent).
26. *On Liberty*, XVIII, p. 300.
27. Letter to Henry Rusden (July 22, 1870), XVII, p. 1751.
28. *Utilitarianism*, CW X, pp. 231–2. Both Hegel and Mill recognize what we now call a social epistemology. That is, individuals are socialized in their learning right from the beginning. However, the recognition that individuals require a social context in order to become autonomous does not entail a social or historical determinism. Once autonomous, the individual is free to critique his or her society to become more consistent and coherent.
29. Ruth Abbey, "Odd Bedfellows: Nietzsche and Mill on Marriage," *History of European Ideas*, 23 (1997), p. 92: "The ideal marriage is one modeled on friendship; it unites equals, it is freely chosen, it is constantly freely renewed, it forms character and has a pedagogic function and it is a relationship whose partners can spur one another on to ever greater heights."
30. *The Subjection of Women*, CW XXI, pp. 293–5. Mill also anticipated that the emancipation of women and their rise to personal autonomy would alleviate the problems of overpopulation and poverty. Autonomous women would, presumably, neither need to nor permit themselves to be treated as objects of sexual pleasure.
31. This view is also to be found in the writings of Mill's friend Millicent Garrett Fawcett, wife of the blind Cambridge economist Henry Fawcett: "The Electoral Disabilities of Women," *The Fortnightly Review*, 13 (May 1870), pp. 622–32.
32. Mill's so-called socialism was of the same sort. There was no collective economic good to be planned. What he advocated was a world of autonomous individuals who chose to cooperate at many levels instead of a world permanently divided into employers and employees.
33. Stefan Collini, p. xxxiii of the introduction to CW XXI.
34. Fitzjames Stephen, *Liberty, Equality, Fraternity*, ed. Stuart Warner (Indianapolis: Liberty Classics, 1993), pp. 133, 135.
35. De Ruggiero's (1959) argument is similar to Weber's thesis about the relationship between capitalism and Protestantism.
36. De Ruggiero (1959), p. 13.
37. Ibid., p. 17.
38. Ibid., p. 23.
39. Ibid.
40. Gladstone, *Gleanings of Past Years, 1843–76* (London, 1879), Vol. I, p. 158.
41. In a letter to Carlyle on January 12, 1834, Mill spoke of a "probable God." XII, p. 206.
42. *Nature*, CW X, p. 376.
43. See Lightman (1990).
44. My discussion is indebted to Eldon Eisenach, "Mill and Liberal Christianity," in Eisenach (1999).

45. Diary, January 24, 1854, CW XXVII, p. 646.
46. F. A. Hayek, *John Stuart Mill and Harriet Taylor* (London: Routledge and Kegan Paul, 1951), pp. 195–6.
47. *Utility of Religion*, CW X, p. 420.
48. *Auguste Comte and Positivism*, CW X, pp. 332–3.
49. *Utility of Religion*, CW X, pp. 420–8.
50. *Auguste Comte and Positivism*, CW X, pp. 341–68.
51. Joseph Hamburger, in *John Stuart Mill on Liberty and Control* (Princeton, NJ: Princeton University Press, 1999), runs together two theses. First, he maintains that Mill was some kind of authoritarian (a similar view to those of Letwin and Cowling). Second, he maintains that Mill was an anti-Christian thinker who sought to impose a quasi-Comtean and authoritarian religion of humanity. The first thesis is mistaken and reflects Hamburger's completely ignoring the concept of autonomy in Mill. The second thesis has to be modified: Since Mill was no authoritarian, and since no one denies that Mill tried to replace Christianity with the Religion of Humanity, the latter becomes a lot less threatening and interesting. The only connection Hamburger draws between these theses is the claim that Mill concealed his religious views, thereby implying that Mill was up to no good. This so-called evidence is presented in a chapter entitled "Candor or Concealment." Questions of prudence aside, we have suggested that Mill's views evolved along philosophical idealist lines, that *Theism* is much closer to traditional views than the first two essays on religion, and that some of the people who were scandalized by Mill's later religious views were not just traditional believers but scientifically inclined followers such as Bain.
    Note as well a letter written by Mill to Bain on August 6, 1859: "The 'Liberty' has produced an effect on you which it was never intended to produce if it has made you think that we ought not to attempt to convert the world. I mean nothing of the kind, & hold that we ought to convert all we can. We *must* be satisfied with keeping alive the sacred fire in a few minds when we are unable to do more – but the notion of an intellectual aristocracy of *lumières* while the rest of the world remains in darkness fulfills none of my aspirations – & the effect I aim at by the book is, on the contrary, to make the many more accessible to all truth by making them more open minded. But perhaps you were only thinking of the question of religion. On that, certainly I am not anxious to bring over any but really superior intellects & characters to the whole of my own opinions – in the case of all others I would much rather, as things now are, try to improve their religion than to destroy it." CW XV, p. 746.
52. *Autobiography*, CW I, pp. 220–1.
53. "[W]e are asking whether the idea of God, manifestly itself a religious notion, can be incorporated into scientific knowledge and actually fill some of the logical gaps in that knowledge. Mill thinks it can (and so, after all, did David Hume)." Britton (1976), p. 24.
54. Mill to Arthur Greene (December 16, 1861), XV, p. 754.
55. A. Bain, *James Mill: A Biography* (London, 1882), p. 11n.

56. "...John Sterling, Coleridge, Wordsworth, and Maurice. No doubt all these men shared some religious belief – whether Christian or near-Christian. What they all had for Mill was a certain grace in their lives that was for him a new experience – they had something now. It is easy to see that this notion of religion as something now connects with Mill's well-known introspective account of the effect of Wordsworth's poetry on him during his recovery from his mental crisis." Britton (1976), p. 22.

57. The argument of *Theism* is not appreciably different from that of the first two essays but summarizes the other two. It is, however, more explicit about immortality. Britton (1976) maintains that the two earlier essays were attempts to show how religion could exist without transcendental beliefs, but that *Theism* does deal with transcendental beliefs through hope (pp. 22–3). *Theism* was written after *Hamilton* and possibly reflects the need to come to terms with the big picture. Its posthumous publication was not an attempt to avoid the attacks of the zealots or the orthodox. Nor was it an attempt to settle scores without fear of rebuttal. In fact, it is conciliatory in tone. The only people to be shocked by *Theism* were those of Mill's followers who adhered more rigidly to the Enlightenment Project or to Benthamism (e.g., Bain) and who were less than sympathetic to the Romantic and idealistic strains in Mill's thinking.

58. Mill to Bain (April 11, 1860), XV, p. 695.

59. *Logic*, CW VIII, pp. 928–9n.

60. *Nature*, CW X, pp. 383, 386.

61. Mill's argument for design goes contrary to Darwin's theory. Curiously, Mill exemplifies his claim for design by reference to the human eye, a case that caused Darwin much perplexity. It is also the example of the eye that forms the basis of Michael J. Behe's microbiological argument against Darwin in *Darwin's Black Box* (New York: Simon and Schuster, 1996). Rational design as a hypothesis has recently taken on new life.

62. See Mill's comment on Darwin added to the *Logic* in 1862, CW VII, pp. 498–9n, namely, that it is a "legitimate hypothesis," as well as a letter to H. C. Watson (February 24, 1869), XVII, p. 1567.

63. Mill to Nightingale (September 23, 1860), XV, p. 709.

64. *Theism*, CW X, pp. 451, 453, 459.

65. Mill to Bain (January 7, 1863), XV, p. 817.

66. "All matter apart from the feelings of sentient beings has but an hypothetical existence: it is a mere assumption to account for our sensations; itself we do not perceive, we are not conscious of it, but only of the sensations, which we are said to receive from it: in reality it is a mere name for our expectation of sensations, or for our belief that we can have certain sensations when certain other sensations give indication of them. Because these contingent possibilities of sensation sooner or later come to an end and give place to others, is it implied in this, that the series of our feelings must itself be broken off? This would not be to reason from one kind of substantive reality to another, but to draw from something which has no reality except in reference to something else, conclusions applicable to that

which is the only substantive reality. Mind (or whatever name we give to what is implied in consciousness of a constituted series of feelings) is in a philosophical point of view the only reality of which we have any evidence; and no analogy can be recognized or comparison made between it and other realities because there are no other known realities to compare it with." *Theism*, CW X, p. 463.

67. Bain (1882b), pp. 158, 134–6, 139, was shocked; John Morley worried about a revival of supernaturalism and the seeming incongruity in John Stuart Mill's appeal to a mystic sentiment. John Morley, "Mr. Mill's Three Essays on Religion," *Fortnightly Review*, 22 (November 1, 1874), p. 637; 23 (January 1, 1875), pp. 103–31.

68. It is interesting to note that the John Stuart Mill who is routinely dismissed for not recognizing the important role of hypotheses in science – a charge against which we have defended him – makes a case for the importance of imagination and grand imaginative hypotheses at the end of *Theism*, CW X, pp. 483–9. He also discusses the moral consequences of believing this hypothesis, anticipating a similar line of argument made famous shortly thereafter by William James.

69. *Utility of Religion*, CW X, pp. 425–6. Consider the following statements from Herbert Butterfield's *Christianity and History* (New York: Scribners, 1949): "When we have reconstructed the whole of mundane history it does not form a self-explanatory system, and our attitude to it, our whole relationship to the human drama, is a larger affair altogether – it is a matter not of scholarship but of religion" (p. 22). "Ultimately our interpretation of the whole human drama depends on an intimately personal decision concerning the part we mean to play in it" (p. 86).

70. "[T]he science of human nature and history, is considered to show that the creeds of the past are natural growths of the human mind, in particular stages of its career, destined to disappear and give place to other convictions in a more advanced stage. In the progress of discussion this last class of considerations [historical] seems even to be superseding those which address themselves directly to the question of truth." *Theism*, CW X, p. 430.

71. Letter to Henry Jones (June 13, 1868), CW XVI, p. 1414.

72. ". . . indicate that origin to be Design but do not point to any commencement, still less creation. . . ." *Theism*, CW X, p. 452.

73. *Nature*, CW X, p. 379.

74. Eisenach (1999).

75. Pattison edited an anthology entitled *Essays and Reviews* in 1860. The other contributors included Benjamin Jowett, Rowland Williams, Henry Bristow Wilson, Frederick Temple, C. W. Goodwin, and Baden Powell. The book became a cause célèbre.

76. Owen Chadwick, *Victorian Church* (London: Trinity Press International, 1966), Vol. II, p. 31, points out that theology in the late Victorian period became "immanentist."

77. Ibid., p. 192.

78. Mill to Parke Godwin (January 1, 1869), XVII, p. 1535.

79. Mark De Wolfe Howe, *Justice Oliver Wendell Holmes: The Shaping Years* (Cambridge, MA: Harvard University Press, 1957), pp. 226–7.

80. In 1872, Henry Fawcett, Mill's disciple and professor of political economy at Cambridge, wrote in opposition to the International because its program would lead to a "weakening and lessening of individual responsibility." "The Nationalization of the Land," *Fortnightly Review*, 73, p. 637.

81. *Letters*, CW XVI, p. 1102.

82. Quoted in Feuer (1976), p. 105n.

83. *Letters*, CW XVI, pp. 1247–8.

84. Ibid., p. 1297.

85. Clive Dewey, "The Rehabilitation of the Peasant Proprietor in Nineteenth-Century Economic Thought," *History of Political Economy*, 6 (1974), p. 38.

86. *Chapters on Socialism*, V, p. 737.

87. Feuer (1976), p. 107.

88. *Auguste Comte and Positivism*, CW X, pp. 348–51.

89. *Chapters on Socialism*, V, p. 746.

90. CW I, p. 625.

91. According to Feuer (1976), p. 94, "Mill's views on the hatred-vector in revolutionary socialism clearly became the basis for Freud's analysis of communism." Freud had translated Mill's *Chapters on Socialism* along with the *Enfranchisement of Women, Plato*, and Thornton's *On Labour and Its Claims*. See Ernest Jones, *Sigmund Freud: Life and Works* (London: Hogarth 1957), Vol. III, p. 368. Freud's translations are also mentioned in Weinberg (1963), p. 60.

92. *PPE*, III, p. 930.

93. "Thornton," CW V, p. 666.

94. There was a manuscript found among Mill's papers after his death entitled "On Social Freedom." The thesis of the manuscript was the advancement of something like democratic socialism. For some years, it was assumed that Mill was the author. Recent scholarship has shown otherwise. See J. C. Rees, *Mill and His Early Critics* (Leicester: Leicester University Press, 1956).

95. Julius West, *John Stuart Mill*, Fabian Tract 168 (London: Fabian Society Pamphlets, 1913), p. 21, "[H]ad he lived another ten years he would almost certainly have been amongst the founders of the Fabian Society." See M. A. Hamilton, *John Stuart Mill* (London: Hamilton, 1933), especially pp. 76–8. See also Willard Wolfe, *From Radicalism to Socialism: Men and Ideas in the Formation of Fabian Socialist Doctrines, 1881–1889* (New Haven, CT: Yale University Press, 1975).

96. The most important author of this movement was G. D. H. Cole, author of *Self-Government in Industry* (1917) as well as of a multivolume *History of Socialist Thought*.

97. *Later Letters*, CW XVI, letter 1288, pp. 1439–40.

98. Bain (1882b), p. 133.

99. Fox Bourne, op.cit., pp. 28–9.

100. Carlyle, *Works*, I, p. 157.

101. Stefan Collini, *Public Moralists: Political Thought and Intellectual Life in Britain 1850–1930* (Oxford: Clarendon Press, 1991). I shall combine Collini's expression "public moralist" with Kahan's (2001) expression "aristocratic liberal." Kahan cites as his three representative figures Mill, Burckhardt, and Tocqueville, and he identifies the heyday of "aristocratic liberalism" with the period 1830–1870. Heyck (1982) usefully documents the changes that occurred after 1870 that make it possible to isolate the special nature of Mill as public moralist in the period before 1870.

102. Collini (1991), p. 58.

103. *Inaugural Address at Saint Andrews*, XXI, p. 253.

104. T. W. Heyck, *The Transformation of Intellectual Life in Victorian England* (London: Croom-Helm, 1982).

105. John Ruskin, *The Works of John Ruskin*, ed. E. T. Cook and Alexander Wedderburn (London: Longmans, Green, 1905), Vol. XVII, p. 79.

106. Rosenblum (1987), pp. 24–5.

107. Martin Wiener, *English Culture and the Decline of the Industrial Spirit* (Cambridge: Cambridge University Press, 1981).

108. Ibid., p. 8.

109. *Eines Arbeiters Widerlegung der National-okonomischen Lehren John Stuart Mill's* (Berlin, 1869), p. iv.

110. Kahan (2000), Conclusion.

111. Leslie Stephen, *The Life of Sir James Fitzjames Stephen* (London, 1895), p. 308.

112. "The representative quality of Arnold and Mill in the Victorian period . . . their recognition that the great problem of modern life is the preservation of the ancient humanistic ideal of culture in democratic society . . . inspired their attempts to establish a liaison between the tradition of humane letters and the modern scientific movement." Alexander (1965), p. 12.

113. Bain (1882b), p. 154.

114. F. R. Leavis, noted critic and opponent of Snow, was a great admirer of Mill's sensitivity to and attempt to bridge the gap. See his Introduction to the edition of Mill's essays *Mill on Bentham and Coleridge* (London: Chatto and Windus, 1959), pp. 5–6, 12–15, 36–7.

115. *Considerations on Representative Government*, CW XIX, p. 549.

116. Kent (1978), p. 4; Stafford (1998), pp. 41–2.

117. Mill was defended against these and other charges by Thomas Hare in a piece in the *Westminster Review*, n.s. 45 (1874), pp. 122–59, entitled "John Stuart Mill."

118. *The Letters of Charles Eliot Norton*, Vol. I, p. 331.

119. Harvie (1976), pp. 38, 151.

120. Henry Sidgwick, "John Stuart Mill," *Academy* (May 15, 1873), p. 193.

121. George Jacob Holyoake, *John Stuart Mill, as Some of the Working Classes Knew Him* (London, 1873), p. 5.

122. Quoted in Weinberg (1963), p. 56.

123. Quoted in Packe (1954), p. 454n.

124. The most thorough discussion of this is to be found in Stefan Collini's magisterial account, "From Sectarian Radical to National Possession: John Stuart Mill in English Culture, 1873–1945," in Laine (1991), pp. 242–72.

125. Leslie Stephen, "Some Early Impressions," *The National Review*, 42 (October 1903), p. 217.

126. Russell (1969), pp. 1, 2, 4, 9. Russell was especially critical of Mill's alleged lack of mathematical sophistication.

127. B. Russell, "John Stuart Mill," *Proceedings of the British Academy*, 41 (1955), p. 46.

128. Frederick Harrison, "John Stuart Mill," *Nineteenth Century*, 40 (1896), pp. 487–508.

129. Collini (1991), p. 253.

130. Ibid., p. 261.

Bibliography

A bibliography of works on Mill in English can be found in Michael Laine, *Bibliography of Works on John Stuart Mill* (Toronto and London: University of Toronto Press, 1982), in *The Mill Newsletter*, 1965–8, and in *Utilitas*, 1989–.

The Mill–Taylor Collection, British Library of Political and Economic Science, is a collection of letters between Mill and Harriet Taylor; some of these letters are from Harriet and therefore are not included in Mill's collected works.

Works by Mill

All references to Mill are made to the complete edition, *Collected Works of John Stuart Mill*, ed. J. M. Robson and others, 33 volumes (Toronto and London: University of Toronto Press). The form of referencing is as follows: (CW XXVIII, p. 358) and (XXI, p. 505).
These are the volumes:

I (1980) *Autobiography and Literary Essays*
II, III (1965) *Principles of Political Economy*
IV, V (1967) *Essays on Economics and Society*
VI (1982) *Essays on England, Ireland and the Empire*
VII, VIII (1973) *System of Logic: Ratiocinative and Inductive*
IX (1979) *An Examination of Sir William Hamilton's Philosophy*
X (1969) *Essays on Ethics, Religion and Society*
XI (1978) *Essays on Philosophy and the Classics*
XII, XIII (1962) *Earlier Letters, 1812–1848*
XIV. XV, XVI, XVII (1972) *Later Letters, 1848–1873*
XVIII, XIX (1977) *Essays on Politics and Society*
XX (1985) *Essays on French History and Historians*
XXI (1984) *Essays on Equality, Law and Education*
XXII, XXIII, XXIV, XXV (1986) *Newspaper Writings*
XXVI, XXVII (1988) *Journals and Debating Speeches*
XXVIII, XXIX (1988) *Public and Parliamentary Speeches*
XXX (1990) *Writings on India*

XXXI (1989) *Miscellaneous Writings*
XXXII (1991) *Additional Letters*
XXXIII (1991) *Indexes*

Dissertations and Discussions (New York: Haskel House, 1973; originally published in 1859) is a collection that Mill published during his lifetime; it contains previously published articles (included in the collected works) and an Introduction. It is referred to in the text as D&D.

Other Works

Abbey, R. (1997) "Odd Bedfellows: Nietzsche and Mill on Marriage." *History of European Ideas*, 23, pp. 81–104.
Alexander, E. (1965) *Matthew Arnold and John Stuart Mill*. New York: Columbia University Press.
Annan, N. (1969) "John Stuart Mill." In *Mill: A Collection of Critical Essays*, ed. J. B. Schneewind. London: Macmillan, pp. 22–45.
Annas, J. (1977) "Mill and the Subjection of Women." *Philosophy*, 52, pp. 179–94.
Anschutz, R. P. (1953) *The Philosophy of J. S. Mill*. Oxford: Oxford University Press.
Arblaster, A. (1984) *The Rise and Decline of Western Liberalism*. Oxford: Blackwell.
Arnold, M. (1971) [1867] *Culture and Anarchy*. New York: Bobbs-Merrill.
Ashcraft, R. (1998) "John Stuart Mill and the Theoretical Foundations of Democratic Socialism." In *Mill and the Moral Character of Liberalism*, ed. E. Eisenach. University Park: Pennsylvania State University Press, pp. 169–90.
Ashton, R. (1980) *The German Idea: Four English Writers and the Reception of German Thought 1800–1860*. Cambridge: Cambridge University Press.
Bagehot, W. (1865) "Mr. Mill's Address to the Electors of Westminster." *Economist*, April 29, 1865.
Bagehot, W. (1958) [1865] *The English Constitution*. Oxford: Oxford University Press.
Bain, A. (1882a) *James Mill: A Biography*. London: Routledge/Thoemmes Press, 1995.
Bain, A. (1882b) *John Stuart Mill. A Criticism: With Personal Recollections*. London: Longmans, Green.
Bentham, J. (1838) *The Works of Jeremy Bentham*, ed. J. Bowring. London: Longman.
Bentham, J. (1967) *A Fragment on Government and An Introduction to the Principles of Morals and Legislation*. Oxford: Blackwell.
Berger, F. R. (1984) *Happiness, Justice and Freedom: The Moral and Political Philosophy of John Stuart Mill*. Berkeley: University of California Press.
Berger, P. L. (1986) *The Capitalist Revolution*. New York: Basic Books.
Berlin, I. (1969) "John Stuart Mill and the Ends of Life." In his *Four Essays on Liberty*. Oxford: Oxford University Press, pp. 173–206.
Bosanquet, B. (1923) *The Philosophical Theory of the State*. London: Macmillan.
Bradley, F. H. (1876) *Ethical Studies*. Oxford: Oxford University Press.
Britton, K. (1976) "John Stuart Mill on Christianity." In *James and John Stuart Mill: Papers of the Centenary Conference*, ed. J. M. Robson and M. Laine. Toronto: University of Toronto Press, pp. 21–34.

Bruford, W. F. (1975) *The German Tradition of Self-Cultivation: Bildung from Humboldt to Thomas Mann*. Cambridge: Cambridge University Press.

Burns, J. H. (1969) "J. S. Mill and Democracy, 1829–1861." In *Mill: A Collection of Critical Essays*, ed. J. B. Schneewind. London: Macmillan, pp. 280–328.

Burrow, J. (1988) *Whigs and Liberals: Continuity and Change in English Political Thought*. Oxford: Oxford University Press.

Butterfield, H. (1949) *Christianity and History*. New York: Scribners.

Caine, B. (1978) "John Stuart Mill and the English Women's Movement." *Historical Studies*, 18, pp. 52–67.

Campbell, A. J. (1930) *Two Centuries of the Church of Scotland 1707–1929*. London: Paisley, A. Gardner.

Canovan, M. (1987) "The Eloquence of John Stuart Mill." *History of Political Thought*, 8, pp. 505–20.

Capaldi, N. (1973a) "Censorship and Social Stability in J. S. Mill." *John Stuart Mill Newsletter*, 9, pp. 12–16.

Capaldi, N. (1973b) "Mill's Forgotten Science of Ethology." *Social Theory and Practice*, 2, pp. 409–20.

Capaldi, N. (1983) "The Libertarian Philosophy of John Stuart Mill." *Reason Papers*, no. 9, pp. 3–19.

Capaldi, N. (1998) *The Enlightenment Project in the Analytic Conversation*. Dordrecht: Kluwer.

Carlisle, J. (1991) *John Stuart Mill and the Writing of Character*. Athens: University of Georgia Press.

Carlyle, A. (ed.) (1904) *New Letters of Thomas Carlyle*. London and New York: J. Lane.

Carlyle, A. (ed.) (1923) *Letters of Thomas Carlyle to Mill, John Sterling, and Robert Browning*. New York: Haskell House.

Carlyle, T. (1837) *Sartor Resartus*, 2nd ed. Boston: Munroe.

Carlyle, T. (1851) *Life of John Sterling*. London.

Carlyle, T. (1881) *Reminiscences*, ed. J. A. Froude. 2 vols. London.

Carlyle, T. (1886) *The Correspondence of Thomas Carlyle and Ralph Waldo Emerson*. ed. C. E. Norton. Boston.

Carlyle, T. (1896–99) *The Works of Thomas Carlyle*, ed. H. D. Traill. London.

Cavenaugh, F. A. (ed.) (1931) *James Mill on Education*. Cambridge: Cambridge University Press.

Chadwick, O. (1966) *Victorian Church*. London: Trinity Press International.

Christie, W. D. (1865) "Mr. John Stuart Mill for Westminster." *MacMillan's Magazine*, 12, pp. 92–104.

Claeys, G. (1987) "Justice, Independence, and Industrial Democracy: The Development of John Stuart Mill's Views on Socialism." *Journal of Politics*, 49, pp. 122–47.

Coats, A. W. (1987) "Samuel Hollander's Mill: A Review Article." *The Manchester School of Economic and Social Studies*, 55, pp. 310–16.

Coleman, J. (1983) "John Stuart Mill on the French Revolution." *History of Political Thought*, 4, pp. 94–114.

Coleridge, S. T. (1830) *On the Constitution of Church and State*. London.

Collini, S. (1991a) "From Sectarian Radical to National Possession: John Stuart Mill in English Culture, 1873–1945." In *A Cultivated Mind: Essays in J. S. Mill Presented to John M. Robson*, ed. M. Laine. Toronto: University of Toronto Press, pp. 242–72.

Collini, S. (1991b) *Public Moralists: Political Thought and Intellectual Life in Britain*, Oxford: Oxford University Press.

Collini, S., Winch, D., and Burrow, J. (1983) *That Noble Science of Politics: A Study in Nineteenth-Century Intellectual History*. Cambridge: Cambridge University Press.

Colmer J. (1959) *Coleridge, Critic of Society*. Oxford: Clarendon Press.

Conway, M. D. (1881) *Thomas Carlyle*. New York.

Conway, M. D. (1894) *Centenary History of the South Place Society*. London: Williams and Norgate.

Courtney, W. L. (1889) *Life of Mill*. London.

Cowling, M. (1990) [1963] *Mill and Liberalism*. Cambridge: Cambridge University Press.

Cumming, R. D. (1964) "Mill's History of His Ideas." *Journal of the History of Ideas*, 25, pp. 235–56.

Dawson, C. (1967) *The Dividing of Christendom*. New York: Doubleday.

d'Eichthal, E. (ed.) (1898) *Mill, Correspondence Inédite avec Gustave d'Eichthal*. Paris.

De Ruggiero, G. (1959) [1927] *The History of European Liberalism*, trans. R. G. Collingwood. Boston: Beacon Press.

DeVane, W. C. (1935) *A Browning Handbook*. New York: F. S. Crofts.

Devlin, P. (1965) *The Enforcement of Morals*. Oxford: Oxford University Press.

Dewey, C. (1974) "The Rehabilitation of the Peasant Proprietor in Nineteenth-Century Economic Thought." *History of Political Economy*, 6, pp. 17–47.

Dicey, A. V. (1908) *Lectures on the Relation between Law and Public Opinion in England during the Nineteenth Century*. London: Macmillan.

Donner, W. (1991) *The Liberal Self: John Stuart Mill's Moral and Political Philosophy*. Ithaca, NY: Cornell University Press.

Donner, W. (1993) "John Stuart Mill's Liberal Feminism." *Philosophical Studies*, 69, pp. 155–66.

Duffy, C. G. (1892) *Reminiscences and Conversations with Carlyle*. London: Sampson Low.

Duncan, G. (1973) *Marx and Mill: Two Views of Social Conflict and Social Harmony*. Cambridge: Cambridge University Press.

Ebenstein, A. (2001) *Friedrich Hayek*. New York: Palgrave.

Eisenach, E. (1987) "Mill's Autobiography as Political Theory." *History of Political Thought*, 8, pp. 2347–62.

Eisenach, E. (ed.) (1998) *Mill and the Moral Character of Liberalism*. University Park: Pennsylvania State University Press.

Elliot, Hugh S. R. (ed.) (1910) *The Letters of John Stuart Mill*. London: Longmans, Green.

Emerson, R. W. (ed.) (1897) *A Correspondence between John Sterling and Ralph Waldo Emerson*. Boston: Houghton Mifflin.

Everett, E. M. (1939) *The Party of Humanity – The Fortnightly Review, 1865–1874*. Chapel Hill: University of North Carolina Press.

Fawcett, M. G. (1870) "The Electoral Disabilities of Women." *The Fortnightly Review*, 13, 622–32.

Fawcett, M. G. (1873) "His Influence as a Practical Politician." In *John Stuart Mill: His Life and Work, Twelve Sketches*, ed. H. Spencer et al. Boston: James R. Osgood and Co., pp. 81–7.

Feuer, L. S. (ed.) (1959) *Marx and Engels: Basic Writings on Politics and Philosophy*. Garden City, NY: Anchor.

Feuer, L. S. (1976) "John Stuart Mill as a Sociologist: The Unwritten Ethology." In *James and John Stuart Mill: Papers of the Centenary Conference*, ed. J. M. Robson and M. Laine. Toronto: University of Toronto Press, pp. 86–110.

Fitzjames Stephen, J. (1993) *Liberty, Equality, Fraternity*, ed. Stuart Warner. Indianapolis: Liberty Classics.

Fox, C. (1882) *Memories of Old Friends*, 2nd ed. 2 vols. London: Smith Elder.

Fox Bourne, H. R. (ed.) (1873) *John Stuart Mill: Notices of His Life and Works*. London.

Francis, M., and Morrow, J. (1994) *A History of English Political Thought in the Nineteenth Century*. London: Duckworth.

Freeden, M. (1978) *The New Liberalism: An Ideology of Social Reform*. Oxford: Oxford University Press.

Friedman, R. B. (1966) "A New Exploration of Mill's Essay on Liberty." *Political Studies*, 14, pp. 281–304. Reprinted in Eisenach (1998).

Friedman, R. B. (1969) "An Introduction to Mill's Theory of Authority." In *Mill: A Collection of Critical Essays*, ed. J. B. Schneewind. London: Macmillan, pp. 379–425.

Froude, J. A. (1882) *Carlyle, the First Forty Years*. 2 vols. London.

Froude, J. A. (1891) *Thomas Carlyle, a History of His Life in London, 1834–1881*. 2 vols. London: Longmans, Green.

Garnett, R. (1887) *The Life of W. J. Fox*. London: Walter Scott.

Gilligan, C. (1982) *In a Different Voice*. Cambridge, MA: Harvard University Press.

Gladstone, W. E. (1879) *Gleanings of Past Years, 1843–76*. London.

Glassman, P. J. (1985) *J. S. Mill: The Evolution of a Genius*. Gainesville: University of Florida Press.

Gouhier, H. (1965) *La Vie de Auguste Comte*, 2nd ed. Paris: J. Vrin.

Gray, J. (1983) *Mill on Liberty: A Defence*. London: Routledge and Kegan Paul.

Gray, J., and Smith, G. W. (1991) *J. S. Mill On Liberty in Focus*. London: Routledge.

Haac, O. A. (1995) *The Correspondence of John Stuart Mill and Auguste Comte*. New Brunswick, NJ: Transaction.

Hagberg, K. (1930) *Personalities and Powers*. London: John Land.

Haight, G. S. (1940) *George Eliot and John Chapman*. New Haven, CT: Yale University Press.

Halévy, E. (1955) *The Growth of Philosophic Radicalism*. Boston: Beacon.

Halévy, E. (1961) *The History of the English People in the Nineteenth Century*. 6 vols. New York: Barnes and Noble.

Halliday, R. J. (1976) *John Stuart Mill*. London: George Allen and Unwin.

Hamburger, J. (1957) "The Writings of John Stuart Mill and His Father James Mill in the Archives of the India Office." *American Philosophical Society Yearbook*, pp. 324–6.

Hamburger, J. (1965) *Intellectuals in Politics: John Stuart Mill and the Philosophic Radicals*. New Haven, CT: Yale University Press, 1965.

Hamburger, J. (1976) "Mill and Tocqueville on Liberty." In *James and John Stuart Mill: Papers of the Centenary Conference*, ed. J. M. Robson and M. Laine. Toronto: University of Toronto Press, pp. 111–25.

Hamburger, J. (1989) Review of Burrow, *Whigs and Liberals*. *Utilitas*, 1:2 (November), pp. 300–5.

Hamburger, J. (1999) *John Stuart Mill on Liberty and Control*. Princeton, NJ: Princeton University Press.

Hamilton, M. A. (1933) *John Stuart Mill*. London: Hamish Hamilton.

Hampsher-Monk, Ian. (1992) *A History of Modern Political Thought*. Oxford: Blackwell.

Harris, A. L. (1964) "Mill: Servant of the East India Company." *Canadian Journal of Economics and Political Science*, 30, pp. 185–202.

Harris, W. (1944) *Caroline Fox*. London: Constable.

Harrison, F. (1896) "John Stuart Mill." *Nineteenth Century*, 40, pp. 487–508.

Harrison, F. (1911) *Autobiographical Memoirs*. 2 vols. London: Macmillan.

Harvie, C. (1976) *The Lights of Liberalism: University Liberals and the Challenge of Democracy 1860–86*. London: Allen Lane.

Hayek, F. A. (1942) *The Spirit of the Age*. Chicago: University of Chicago Press.

Hayek, F. A. (1951) *John Stuart Mill and Harriet Taylor*. London: Routledge and Kegan Paul.

Hayek, F. A. (1979) *The Counter-Revolution of Science*. Indianapolis: Liberty Fund.

Hayward, A. (1873a) "John Stuart Mill." *The Times*, May 10, p. 5.

Hayward, A. (1873b) "John Stuart Mill." *Fraser's Magazine*, n.s. 8, pp. 663–81.

Helmstadter, R. J., and Lightman, B. (eds.) (1990.) *Victorian Faith in Crisis: Essays on Continuity and Change in Nineteenth-Century Religious Belief*. Stanford, CA: Stanford University Press.

Heyck, T. W. (1982) *The Transformation of Intellectual Life in Victorian England*. New York: St. Martin's Press.

Himmelfarb, G. (ed.) (1963) *John Stuart Mill, Essays on Politics and Culture*. New York: Doubleday.

Himmelfarb, G. (1968) *Victorian Minds*. New York: Knopf.

Himmelfarb, G. (1974) *On Liberty and Liberalism: The Case of John Stuart Mill*. New York: Knopf.

Himmelfarb, G. (1984) *The Idea of Poverty*. New York: Knopf.

Hoag, R. W. (1992) "J. S. Mill's Language of Pleasures." *Utilitas*, 4:2, pp. 247–78.

Holcombe, L. (1983) *Wives and Property: Reform of the Married Women's Property Law in Nineteenth Century England*. Oxford: Martin Robinson.

Hollander, S. (1985) *The Economics of John Stuart Mill*. Oxford: Blackwell.

Holyoake, G. J. (1873) *John Stuart Mill, as Some of the Working Classes Knew Him*. London.

Houghton, W. E. (1957) *The Victorian Frame of Mind, 1830–1870*. New Haven, CT: Yale University Press.

Howe, M. W. (1957) *Justice Oliver Wendell Holmes: The Shaping Years*. Cambridge, MA: Harvard University Press.

Humboldt, W. von (1993) *The Limits of State Action*. Introduction by J. W. Burrow. Indianapolis: Liberty Fund.

Jacobs, Jo Ellen (2002) *The Voice of Harriet Taylor Mill*. Bloomington: Indiana University Press.

Jevons, W. S. (1871) *Theory of Political Economy*. London: Macmillan.

Jevons, W. S. (1890) *Pure Logic and Other Minor Works*. London: Macmillan.

Jones, E. (1953) *Sigmund Freud: Life and Works*. 2 vols. London: Hogarth Press.

Kahan. A. (2001) *Aristocratic Liberalism: The Social and Political Thought of Jacob Burckhardt, John Stuart Mill, and Alexis de Tocqueville*. New Brunswick, NJ: Transaction.

Kent, C. (1978) *Brains and Numbers: Elitism, Comtism and Democracy in MidVictorian Britain*. Toronto: University of Toronto Press.

Kingsley, C. (1860) *The Limits of Exact Science as Applied to History*. London: Macmillan.

Kinzer, B. L., Robson, A. T., and Robson, J. M. (1992) *A Moralist in and out of Parliament: John Stuart Mill at Westminster 1865–1868*. Toronto: University of Toronto Press.

Knight, F. (1982) *Freedom and Reform*. Indianapolis: Liberty Fund.

Knights, B. (1978) *The Idea of the Clerisy in the Nineteenth Century*. Cambridge: Cambridge University Press.

Kurer, O. (1991a) *John Stuart Mill: The Politics of Progress*. New York and London: Garland.

Kurer, O. (1991b) "John Stuart Mill and the Welfare State." *History of Political Economy*, 23:4, pp. 713–30.

Kurer, O. (1992) "J. S. Mill and Utopian Socialism." *The Economic Record*, 68, pp. 222–32.

Laine, M. (ed.) (1991) *A Cultivated Mind: Essays in J. S. Mill Presented to John M. Robson*. Toronto: University of Toronto Press.

Larkin, H. (1881) "Carlyle and Mrs. Carlyle: A Ten Years' Reminiscence." *British Quarterly Review*, 74, pp. 28–85.

Leader, R. E. (ed.) (1897) *Life and Letters of John Arthur Roebuck: With Chapter of Autobiography*. London.

Leavis, F. R. (1959) *Mill on Bentham and Coleridge*. London: Chatto and Windus.

Letwin, S. R. (1965) *The Pursuit of Certainty: David Hume, Jeremy Bentham, John Stuart Mill, Beatrice Webb*. Cambridge: Cambridge University Press.

Levi, A. W. (1945) "The 'Mental Crisis' of Mill." *Psychoanalysis and Psychoanalytic Review*, 32, pp. 86–101.

Levy, D. (2001) *How the Dismal Science Got Its Name: Classical Economics and the Ur Text of Radical Politics*. Ann Arbor: University of Michigan Press.

Lively, J., and Rees, J. (1978) *Utilitarian Logic and Politics*. Oxford: Oxford University Press.

Lukes, S. (1973) *Individualism*. Oxford: Blackwell.

Lyons, D. (1994) *Rights, Welfare and Mill's Moral Theory*. Oxford: Oxford University Press.

Macaulay, T. B. (1829) "Utilitarian Logic and Politics." *Edinburgh Review*, 49, pp. 159–89.

Macaulay, T. B. (1852) "Mill's Essay on Government." In his *Critical and Miscellaneous Essays*. Philadelphia, pp. 388–419.

Macpherson, C. B. (1977) *The Life and Times of Liberal Democracy*, Oxford: Oxford University Press.

Majeed, J. (1996) Review of Zastoupil, *John Stuart Mill and India*. *Utilitas*, 8, pp. 258–60.

Manuel, F. E. (1956) *The New World of Henri Saint Simon*. Cambridge, MA: Harvard University Press.

Manuel, F. E. (1965) *The Prophets of Paris*. New York: Harper.

Marmontel, J. F. (1805) *Mémoires d'un père*. 4 vols. London: Peltier.

Mazlish, B. (1988) *James and John Stuart Mill: Father and Son in the Nineteenth Century*. New York: Basic Books.

McCloskey, H. J. (1971) *John Stuart Mill: A Critical Study*. London: Macmillan.

Mendus, S. (1989) "The Marriage of True Minds: The Ideal of Marriage in the Philosophy of John Stuart Mill." In *Sexuality and Subordination: Interdisciplinary Studies of Gender in the Nineteenth Century*, ed. S. Mendus and J. Rendall. London: Routledge, pp. 171–91.

Mendus, S. (1994) "John Stuart Mill and Harriet Taylor on Women and Marriage." *Utilitas*, 6:2, pp. 287–99.

Mill, A. J. (1949) "Mill's Visit to Wordsworth." *Modern Language Review*, 44, pp. 341–50.

Mill, James (1869) *Analysis of the Phenomena of the Human Mind*, ed. J. S. Mill. London.

Milton, J. (1992) [1644] *Areopagitica*. New York: Library of Liberty.

Moore, G. E. (1903) *Principia Ethica*, Cambridge: Cambridge University Press.

Moore, R. J. (1983) "John Stuart Mill at East India House." *Historical Studies*, 20, pp. 497–519.

Morley, J. (1874–75) "Mr. Mill's Three Essays on Religion." *Fortnightly Review*, 22 (November 1, 1874), pp. 634–51; 23 (January 1, 1875), pp. 103–31.

Morris, J. N. (1966) *Versions of the Self: English Autobiography from John Bunyan to John Stuart Mill*. New York: Basic Books.

Mueller, I. (1956) *John Stuart Mill and French Thought*. Urbana: University of Illinois Press.

Neff, E. (1926) *Carlyle and Mill: An Introduction to Victorian Thought*. New York: Columbia University Press.

Norton, Sarah (ed.) (1913) *The Letters of Charles Eliot Norton*. 2 vols. Boston: Houghton Mifflin.

Oakeshott, M. (1989) *The Voice of Liberal Learning: Michael Oakeshott on Education*, ed. Timothy Fuller. New Haven, CT: Yale University Press.

Oakeshott, M. (1996) *On Human Conduct*. Oxford: Clarendon.

O'Brien, D. P. (1975) *The Classical Economists*. Oxford: Oxford University Press.

Offen, K. (1988) "Defining Feminism: A Comparative Historical Approach." *Signs: Journal of Women in Culture and Society*, 14:1, pp. 119–57.

O'Grady, J. (1991) "'Congenial Vocation': J. M. Robson and the Mill Project." In *A Cultivated Mind: Essays on J. S. Mill Presented to John M. Robson*, ed. M. Lame. Toronto: University of Toronto Press, pp. 3–18.

Okin, S. M. (1979) *Women in Western Political Thought*. Princeton, NJ: Princeton University Press.

Packe, M. St. John. (1954) *The Life of John Stuart Mill*. London: Secker and Warburg.

Pankhurst, R. K. P. (1957) *The Saint Simonians, Mill and Carlyle*. London: Sidgwick and Jackson.

Pappe, H. O. (1960) *John Stuart Mill and the Harriet Taylor Myth*. Cambridge: Cambridge University Press.

Peterson, L. (1986) *Victorian Autobiography: The Tradition of Self-Interpretation*. New Haven, CT: Yale University Press.

Plamenatz, J. P. (1958) *The English Utilitarians*. Oxford: Blackwell.

Pyle, A. (ed.) (1994) *Liberty: Contemporary Responses to John Stuart Mill*. Bristol: Thoemmes Press.

Pyle, A. (ed.) (1995) *The Subjection of Women: Contemporary Responses to John Stuart Mill*. Bristol: Thoemmes Press.

Qualter, T. H. (1960) "John Stuart Mill, Disciple of Tocqueville." *Western Political Quarterly*, 13, pp. 880–9.

Randall, J. H., Jr. (1962) *The Career of Philosophy*. New York: Columbia University Press.

Rees, J. C. (1956) *Mill and His Early Critics*. Leicester: University of Leicester Press.

Rees, J. C. (1960) "A Re-reading of Mill on Liberty." *Political Studies*, 8, pp. 113–29.

Rees, J. C. (1985) *John Stuart Mill's On Liberty: Constructed from Published and Unpublished Sources by G. L. Williams*. Oxford: Clarendon Press.

Riley, J. (1996) "J. S. Mill's Liberal Utilitarian Assessment of Capitalism versus Socialism." *Utilitas*, 8:1, pp. 39–71.

Riley, J. (1998) "Mill's Political Economy: Ricardian Science and Liberal Utilitarian Art." In *The Cambridge Companion to Mill*, ed. J. Skorupski. New York: Cambridge University Press, pp. 293–337.

Robbins, L. (1953) *The Theory of Economic Policy in English Classical Political Economy*. London: Macmillan.

Robson, A. (1991) "Mill's Second Prize in the Lottery of Life." In *A Cultivated Mind: Essays in J. S. Mill Presented to John M. Robson*, ed. M. Laine. Toronto: University of Toronto Press, pp. 215–41.

Robson, J. M. (1960) "J. S. Mill's Theory of Poetry." *University of Toronto Quarterly*, 29, pp. 420–38.

Robson, J. M. (1968) *The Improvement of Mankind: The Social and Political Thought of John Stuart Mill*. London: Routledge and Kegan Paul.

Robson, J. M. (1976) "Rational Animals and Others." In *James and John Stuart Mill: Papers of the Centenary Conference*, ed. J. M. Robson and M. Laine. Toronto: University of Toronto Press, pp. 143–60.

Rosenblum, N. L. (1987) *Liberalism: Romanticism and the Reconstruction of Liberal Thought*. Cambridge, MA.: Harvard University Press.

Rossi, A. S. (ed.) (1970) J. S. *Mill, Essays on Sex Equality*. Chicago: University of Chicago Press.

Ruskin, J. (1905) *The Works of John Ruskin*, ed. E. T. Cook and Alexander Wedderburn. London: Longmans, Green.

Russell, B. (1969) [1955] "John Stuart Mill." In *Mill: A Collection of Critical Essays*, ed. J. B. Schneewind. London: Macmillan, pp. 1–21.

Russell, Bertrand and Patricia (eds.) (1937) *The Amberley Papers*. London: Hogarth.

Russell, G. W. E. (ed.) (1900) *Letters of Matthew Arnold*. New York: Macmillan.

Ryan, A. (1970) *The Philosophy of John Stuart Mill*. London: Macmillan. See also 2nd ed.: Atlantic Highlands, NJ: Humanities Press, 1990.

Ryan, A. (1974) *J. S. Mill*, London: Routledge.

Ryan, A. (1991a) "Sense and Sensibility in Mill's Political Thought." In *A Cultivated Mind: Essays on J. S. Mill Presented to John M. Robson*, ed. M. Laine. Toronto: University of Toronto Press, pp. 121–38.

Ryan, A. (1991b) "John Stuart Mill's Art of Living." In *J. S. Mill On Liberty in Focus*, ed. J. Gray and G. W. Smith. London: Routledge, pp. 162–8.

Saint-Simon, H. (1854) *Doctrine Saint-Simonienne*. Paris: Exposition.

Sarvasy, W. (1984) "John Stuart Mill's Theory of Democracy for a Period of Transition between Capitalism and Socialism." *Polity*, 16, pp. 567–87.

Sarvasy, W. (1985) "A Reconsideration of the Development and Structure of John Stuart Mill's Socialism." *Western Political Quarterly*, 38, pp. 312–33.

Schneewind, J. B. (1976) "Concerning Some Criticisms of Mill's Utilitarianism, 1861–76." In *James and John Stuart Mill: Papers of the Centenary Conference*, ed. J. M. Robson and M. Laine. Toronto: University of Toronto Press, pp. 35–54.

Schwarz, R. (1968) *The New Political Economy of J. S. Mill*. London: Weidenfeld and Nicholson.

Semmel, B. (1962) *The Governor Eyre Controversy*. London: MacGibbon and Kee.

Semmel, B. (1984) *John Stuart Mill and the Pursuit of Virtue*. New Haven, CT: Yale University Press.

Shanley, M. L. (1981) "Marital Slavery and Friendship: John Stuart Mill's *The Subjection of Women*." *Political Theory*, 9, pp. 229–47.

Sharpless, F. P. (1967) *The Literary Criticism of John Stuart Mill*. The Hague: Mouton.

Shotter, J. (1975) *Images of Man in Psychological Research*. London: Methuen.

Sidgwick, H. (1873) "John Stuart Mill." *Academy*, May 15.

Skorupski, J. (1989) *John Stuart Mill*. London: Routledge.

Skorupski, J. (ed.) (1998) *The Cambridge Companion to Mill*. New York: Cambridge University Press.

Smith, G. W. (1992) "Enlightenment Psychology and Individuality: The Roots of J. S. Mill's Conception of Self." *Enlightenment and Dissent*, 11, pp. 70–86.

Solly, H. (1893) *These Eighty Years*. London: Simpkin Marshall.

Soper, K. (ed.) (1983) *Harriet Taylor Mill, Enfranchisement of Women and John Stuart Mill, The Subjection of Women*. London: Virago.

Spencer, H. (1904) *Autobiography*. London: Williams and Norgate.

Spencer, H., et al. (ed.) (1873) *John Stuart Mill: His Life and Work, Twelve Sketches*. Boston: James R. Osgod and Co. Reprinted in 1977 by Folcraft Library Editions.

Stafford, W. (1998) *Mill*. London: Macmillan.

Stephen, J. E. (1967) *Liberty, Equality, Fraternity*. Cambridge: Cambridge University Press.

Stephen, L. (1895) *The Life of Sir James Fitzjames Stephen*. London.

Stephen, L. (1900) *The English Utilitarians*. London: Duckworth.

Stephen, L. (1903) "Some Early Impressions." *The National Review*, 42, pp. 130–63.

Sterling, J. (1897) *A Correspondence between John Sterling and Ralph Waldo Emerson*, ed. E. W. Emerson. Boston.

Stillinger, J. (ed.) (1961) *The Early Draft of John Stuart Mill's Autobiography*. Urbana: University of Illinois Press.

Stillinger, J. (1991) "John Mill's Education: Fact, Fiction, and Myth." In *A Cultivated Mind: Essays on J. S. Mill Presented to John M. Robson*, ed. M. Laine. Toronto: University of Toronto Press, pp. 19–43.

Stokes, E. (1959) *The English Utilitarians and India*. Oxford: Clarendon Press.

Stove, D. (1993) "The Subjection of John Stuart Mill." *Philosophy*, 68, pp. 5–13.

Sullivan, E. T. (1983) "Liberalism and Imperialism: J. S. Mill's Defense of the British Empire." *Journal of the History of Ideas*, 44:4, pp. 599–617.

Taylor, A. (1895) *Memoirs of a Student*. London.

Taylor, C. (1989) *Sources of the Self: The Making of the Modern Identity*. Cambridge: Harvard University Press.

Taylor, H. (1885) *Autobiography*. 2 vols. London.

Ten, C. L. (1980) *Mill on Liberty*. Oxford: Oxford University Press.

Ten, C. L. (1998) "Democracy, Socialism, and the Working Classes." In *The Cambridge Companion to Mill*, ed. J. Skorupski. New York: Cambridge University Press, pp. 372–95.

Thomas, W. (1979) *The Philosophic Radicals: Nine Studies in Theory and Practice 1817–1841*. Oxford: Oxford University Press.

Thomas, W. (1985) *Mill*. Oxford: Oxford University Press.

Tocqueville, A. de (1861) *Memoir, Letters, and Remains of Alexis de Tocqueville*. 2 vols. London: Macmillan.

Tocqueville, A. de (1949) *Recollections of Alexis de Tocqueville*, ed. J. P. Mayer. New York: Columbia University Press.

Tuell, A. K. (1941) *John Sterling*. New York: Macmillan.

Tulloch, G. (1989) *Mill and Sexual Equality*. Hemel Hempstead: Harvester Wheatsheaf.

Turk, C. (1988) *Coleridge and Mill*. Aldershot: Gower.

Urbinati, N. (1991) "John Stuart Mill on Androgyny and Ideal Marriage." *Political Theory*, 19:4, pp. 626–48.

Urmson, J. O. (1969) [1953] "The Interpretation of the Moral Philosophy of J. S. Mill." In *Mill: A Collection of Critical Essays*, ed. J. B. Schneewind. London: Macmillan, pp 179–89.

Vincent, J. (1966) *The Formation of the British Liberal Party*. New York: Scribner's.

Wallas, G. (1898) *Life of Francis Place*. London.

Warnock, M. (1969) "On Moore's Criticisms of Mill's 'Proof.'" In *Mill: A Collection of Critical Essays*, ed. J. B. Schneewind. London: Macmillan, pp. 199–203.

Weber, M. (1988) *The Protestant Ethic and the Spirit of Capitalism*. Gloucester, MA: Peter Smith.

Weinberg, A. (1963) *Theodor Gomperz and John Stuart Mill*. Geneva: Librairie Droz.

West, J. (1913) *John Stuart Mill*. (Fabian Tract 168). London: Fabian Society Pamphlets.

White, H. (1973) *Metahistory: The Historical Imagination in Nineteenth-Century Europe*. Baltimore: Johns Hopkins University Press.

Wiener, M. J. (1981) *English Culture and the Decline of the Industrial Spirit, 1850–1980*. Cambridge: Cambridge University Press.

Williams, R. (1963) *Culture and Society 1780–1950*. Harmondsworth: Penguin.

Wilshire, B. (ed.) (1968) *Romanticism and Evolution*. New York: G. P. Putnam's Sons.

Wilson, D. A. (1923–34) *The Life of Carlyle*. 6 vols. London: K. Paul, Trench, Trubner.

Wilson, F. (1990) *Psychological Analysis and the Philosophy of John Stuart Mill*. Toronto: University of Toronto Press.

Winch, P. (1963) *The Idea of a Social Science and Its Relation to Philosophy*. London: Routledge and Kegan Paul.

Wolfe, W. (1975) *From Radicalism to Socialism: Men and Ideas in the Formation of Fabian Socialist Doctrines, 1881–1889*. London and New Haven: Yale University Press.

Wollheim, R. (1979) "Mill and Isaiah Berlin: The Ends of Life and the Preliminaries of Morality." In *The Idea of Freedom: Essays in Honor of Isaiah Berlin*, ed. Alan Ryan. Oxford: Oxford University Press, pp. 254–5.

Wordsworth, W. (1827) *Poetical Works*. 4 vols. London.

Wordsworth, W. (1963) [1798, 1800] *Lyrical Ballads*, ed. R. L. Brett and A. R. Jones. London: Methuen.

Wright, T. R. (1986) *The Religion of Humanity: The Impact of Comtean Positivism on Victorian Britain*. Cambridge: Cambridge University Press.

Zastoupil, L. (1994) *John Stuart Mill and India*. Stanford, CA: Stanford University Press.

Index